How to Use a Handbook Page

P9-BHY-006

1. Main heading introduces the writing topic to be discussed in the section.

Section number identifies the chapter and section.

Running head identifies the topic treated on the page.

If you need to delete a comma, an editor may draw a slash through the mark and write "no comma" (*no,*) in the margin.

The car that I sold had declined in value. *no,*

2. Troubleshooting paragraph explains problems with the topic that you should anticipate as you write, revise, edit, or proofread your papers.

26a   DO YOU UNDERSTAND COMMAS THAT SEPARATE?

Troubleshooting

Commas are frequently used to keep words and phrases from running into each other and confusing readers, so use one at any juncture where your readers might get lost if a comma is left out. Often, however, you may have to depend on your judgment as well as a rule. If you use too many commas, your writing can seem fussy and old-fashioned, but if you omit one where it's needed, your readers may be puzzled. So where inserting a comma is a judgment call, try reading your draft out loud. Are there places where the reader should pause? Put in a comma if it is compatible with the guidelines in this chapter. Is a comma needed to make the sentence clearer or easier to read? If so, insert one.

26a
^
,

Tab includes the section number and an abbreviation for the topic under discussion.

To handle commas effectively . . .

26a–1 **Use commas after introductory phrases of more than three or four words.** Pauses at these points can make a sentence easier to read.

To appreciate the pleasures of driving in snow, you have to live in Michigan or Wisconsin.

Over the loud objections of all the occupants of the Jeep, I turned off the main road.

An introductory comma isn't necessary when an introductory phrase is only three or four words long and the sentence is clear without the punctuation.

On glare ice the Jeep just spun its wheels.

On Tuesday we'll be in New Mexico.

3. Action headings explain what to do to solve the problem described in the "Troubleshooting" paragraph. Action heads are numbered for easy reference: 26a–1, 26a–2, and so on.

CAUTION

26a–2 **Use commas after introductory subordinate clauses.** **Subordinate clauses** are signaled by words like *although, if, when, because, as, after, before, since, unless, while,* and so on. (See Section 9a–2.)

Although the roads were crowded, we drove on to Detroit.

Symbol indicates the difficulty of a rhetorical or grammatical issue. (See the symbols and their descriptions on the opposite page.)

Where to Find Useful Information in Boxes

The
SCOTT, FORESMAN
HANDBOOK *for*
WRITERS

Fourth Edition

Maxine Hairston
University of Texas at Austin

John J. Ruszkiewicz
University of Texas at Austin

HarperCollins*College*Publishers

Executive Editor: Anne Elizabeth Smith
Developmental Editor: Leslie Taggart
Project Editorial Manager: Robert Ginsberg
Design Manager and Cover Designer: Wendy Ann Fredericks
Cover Photograph: Jess Koppe/Tony Stone Worldwide; back cover photo
    manipulation: Wendy Ann Fredericks
Art Studio: Academy ArtWorks, Inc.
Electronic Production Manager: Valerie A. Sawyer
Electronic Page Makeup: Carole Desnoes
Manufacturing Manager: Helene G. Landers
Printer and Binder: RR Donnelley & Sons Company
Cover Printer: Phoenix Color Corp.
Insert Printer: The Lehigh Press, Inc.

For permission to use copyrighted material, grateful acknowledgment is made to
the copyright holders on pp. 809–810, which are hereby made part of this copyright page.

The Scott, Foresman Handbook for Writers, Fourth Edition
Copyright © 1996 by HarperCollins College Publishers

HarperCollins® and ▟® are registered trademarks of HarperCollins Publishers Inc.

Library of Congress Cataloging-in-Publication Data

Hairston, Maxine.
    The Scott, Foresman handbook for writers/Maxine Hairston, John J.
Ruszkiewicz.—4th ed.
        p.   cm.
    Includes index.
    ISBN 0-673-99728-6 (student edition)
    ISBN 0-673-98197-5 (instructor's edition)
    1. English language—Rhetoric—Handbooks, manuals, etc.
    2. English language—Grammar—Handbooks, manuals, etc.
    I. Ruszkiewicz, John J., II. Title.
PE1408.H2968 1996
808'.042—dc20   95–22311
                                                                        CIP

95 96 97 98   9 8 7 6 5 4 3 2 1

Contents

Note: A complete list of Checklists, Charts, Highlights, and Summary boxes will be found on the front endpapers. See "Where to Find Useful Information in Boxes."

Part IV *Research and Writing* — 515

Part V *Tools for Writers* 737

Preface

Why another edition of a handbook? It's a fair question posed often enough by people who prefer that language and communication not change much. They would like to regard correct writing as one of life's constants. Unfortunately, it isn't.

Evidence of change is everywhere. Readers and listeners are more impatient and more visually oriented today than ever before. They expect clear presentations professionally illustrated on the job, at school, and in their clubs and organizations. In just the last five years, *multimedia* has gone from being a buzzword to a practical reality in school and business, and even home computers now come equipped with programs that conveniently integrate sound, video, and the written word. As a result, most professional writers admit that many of their cherished assumptions about knowledge and communication need recasting. They may still find themselves behind a desk in Kansas, but their color monitors can take them off to Oz—or the Vatican library, a White House briefing room, or the Reuters news service.

Not every writer is plugged into these new technologies, but as the authors of *The Scott, Foresman Handbook for Writers*, we believe we have an obligation to anticipate change as well as to mark it. We want our readers to feel knowledgeable about electronic sources. Even writers who don't anticipate using the Internet today should know what it promises them tomorrow.

Novices to desktop publishing, on-line research, and net surfing ourselves, we have felt the excitement and challenge of applying new technology in the work we do. We realize that not every writing class will design complex documents or establish news groups connected to other writers across the country. But such innovations are part of the world we live in now, and they will shape the composing we do tomorrow. We want writers who use *The Scott, Foresman Handbook* to be ready for the realities of the world ahead.

WHAT'S NEW?

Classical rhetoricians, who appreciated that how a message was conveyed was as important as the message itself, stressed the importance of delivery—the way a message is presented. In this fourth edition of *The Scott, Foresman Handbook for Writers,* we give delivery a fresh emphasis with a new section on document design (pp. 89–104) that will help writers shape their documents for maximum appeal. Its guiding principle is simple: *If you're writing something you want people to read, you need to gain and hold their attention.* The new strategies for desktop publishing make that task easier than it has ever been.

Since even basic word-processing programs now typically come with design and drawing programs, anyone who can type can also draw borders and boxes, vary typefaces and fonts, and create or import illustrations. Writers are doing exactly that in schools and offices everywhere, preparing fliers, brochures, newsletters, and posters that formerly required the services of a print shop. Our aim in the new document design section is to offer practical advice for producing handsome and persuasive documents.

Computers and electronic technologies have similarly reshaped the way writers find and share information. We explain those changes to writers, anticipating a time when *The Scott, Foresman Handbook for Writers* and books like it may become on-line documents themselves. We have revised our entire discussion of research to incorporate technology into the full research process. A new section—32c How Do you Navigate Electronic Sources?—covers techniques for searching on-line indexes and describes Internet features such as World Wide Web sites, Usenet groups, and Gopher search tools. Realizing that electronic sources sometimes provide more books and articles than writers can possibly use, we wrote a new section on assessing sources. We even reframed our discussion of scholastic honesty to consider issues of intellectual property raised by the new relationships between writers and their materials.

Recognizing that most people will use traditional resources and materials for years to come, we have been careful to insure that the research sections of *The Scott, Foresman Handbook* still speak clearly to writers using hard-copy books and articles. The three basic forms of scholarly citation used in the United States—MLA, APA, and CBE— have changed since our last edition, and we have updated our directories of citation forms to reflect these modifications, both major and minor. For the convenience of writers, we continue to separate MLA, APA, and CBE citations and have expanded the number of entries to cover more of the puzzling situations researchers routinely encounter—for example, citing works within other works as well as on-line and electronic sources. Dozens of smaller changes now make the guides to documentation easier to use and more thorough. We have added a new MLA-style paper on mountain biking on public trails.

To supplement our coverage of traditional documentation systems, we have added citation forms recently approved by the Alliance for

Computers and Writing (ACW). The ACW documentation system provides clear directions to writers who need to know how to acknowledge electronic sources not fully covered by MLA, APA, or CBE—including e-mail, Telnet and World Wide Web sites, and MUDs and MOOs.

Unique to the new edition of *The Scott, Foresman Handbook* is a software ancillary we call *Rhetoric On-Line*. Available in both Windows and Macintosh formats, *Rhetoric On-Line* is a complete rhetoric covering six writing assignments common in undergraduate courses: a personal narrative, a cause-and-effect analysis, an exploratory essay, an evaluation, a paper proving a thesis, and a persuasive essay. Used in tandem with the handbook, *Rhetoric On-Line* provides a coherent framework for a complete writing course.

WHAT'S IMPROVED?

Good writers treat all people with respect, but sometimes the guidelines for appropriate language for writing about an ethnic, religious, or minority group can be puzzling. In the fourth edition of *The Scott, Foresman Handbook for Writers*, we offer a heavily revised and expanded section on avoiding biased language that addresses this timely subject with clarity and common sense. We hope this new section helps careful writers make wise choices.

We've completely reorganized Chapter 25 ("Problems with Modifiers?") to make our discussion of adjectives and adverbs easier to follow. Here, as elsewhere throughout the volume, we've revised many examples and illustrations to keep references up-to-date and lively.

New material ranges from better illustrations of sentence fragments in Chapter 24 to an expanded discussion of essential modifiers in Chapter 26. Throughout, we have reworked many exercises to tighten and focus them. Our discussion of essay examinations now also includes advice about impromptu essays students may have to compose as part of state-mandated competency exams.

We've tightened our chapters on college writing and argumentation to make them livelier and more pragmatic. We took a hard look at the sections on spelling and vocabulary, cutting to insure that readers can find essential material more quickly. We hope most readers will find the new edition tight, clean, and readable.

WHAT REMAINS THE SAME?

In the fourth edition of *The Scott, Foresman Handbook for Writers*, we have retained all the features that have proved so popular with instructors and students over the previous three editions: a pragmatic approach, an accessible format, and a cordial tone.

Approach

We have designed *The Scott, Foresman Handbook for Writers* as a *tool* for writers, a do-it-yourself manual to help writers get started, to assist them in developing and revising their writing, and to give them practical, easy-to-understand guidelines by which to spot problems and to solve them. A system of distinctive marginal icons labeled **Stop, Caution,** and **Tricky** helps writers learn which errors our research has shown to be most serious for readers.

Format

The Scott, Foresman Handbook is divided into five parts: *The Writing Process, Style, Grammar and Usage, Research and Writing,* and *Tools for Writers. The Writing Process* introduces students to college-level writing projects, both individual and collaborative, and includes two chapters on critical thinking and argument. *Style* consists of nine chapters on making paragraphs, sentences, and words clear and effective. *Grammar and Usage* is a concise, comprehensive reference to solving problems of agreement, pronouns, sentence boundaries, modifiers, and punctuation. It ends with a chapter devoted to the special problems ESL writers encounter as they write in college. Research and Writing provides a complete guide to the process of researching and writing a paper with sources, with sections on MLA, ACW, APA, and CBE citation styles. Full-length student papers illustrate the MLA and APA styles. A chapter on writing résumés, job application letters, and business letters ends the section. Finally, *Tools for Writers* offers brief help in improving spelling and vocabulary and in using a dictionary to best advantage.

HOW DOES *THE SCOTT, FORESMAN HANDBOOK FOR WRITERS* ANCILLARY PROGRAM AID YOU IN TEACHING COMPOSITION?

The *Scott, Foresman* ancillary package offers a full range of printed and software supplements to support instructors teaching composition and students needing extra assistance.

Book-Specific Supplements

Instructor's Resource Manual: Creating a Community of Writers. This succinct yet comprehensive guide to teaching writing was prepared by Christy Friend of the University of Texas at Austin, with Maxine Hairston and John Ruszkiewicz. The *Instructor's Resource Manual* offers guidance to new and experienced writing teachers in using the handbook and the ancillary package to best advantage—according to your goals for the course. Chapters include

- how to establish a positive attitude toward writing in your class-room
- how to manage the psychological and ethical components of teaching writing
- how to handle controversial issues in the writing class
- how to get your writing class off to a good start
- how to plan and run successful class periods
- how to encourage collaborative learning in your writing class
- how to create stimulating, well-structured writing assignments
- how to incorporate document design into your classroom
- options for responding to student papers
- options for grading efficiently and productively
- how to handle issues of appropriate language
- how to teach the research paper

The *Instructor's Resource Manual* includes an introduction to *Rhetoric On-Line* and the answer key to all handbook exercises. The printed version comes in a three-hole-punched format to allow you to transfer pages to your class teaching notes. The *Resource Manual* is available on disk in DOS and Mac formats.

Teaching On-Line: Internet Research, Conversation, and Composition.
An introduction to Internet resources for teaching writing, prepared by Daniel Anderson, Bret Benjamin, Chris Busiel, and Bill Paredes-Holt, all of the University of Texas at Austin, *Teaching On-Line* is accessible to instructors who have never surfed the net, offering in each chapter basic definitions, numerous examples, and detailed information about finding and using Internet resources. *Teaching On-Line* shows you how and why to

- use the Internet in your classroom
- use e-mail and Listservs
- use Usenet newsgroups to emphasize critical reading
- use MOO and IRC to link conversation and composition
- browse with Gopher and the World Wide Web to begin a research project and learn how to evaluate sources
- use HTML to expand audience, publish Web pages, and use graphics and imagemaps

Chapter-end case studies and a sample research paper show numerous applications of on-line composition, conversation, and research. *Teaching On-Line* is available in both printed and DOS and Mac disk formats.

Writing and Designing Documents. Written by Margaret Batschelet of the University of Texas at San Antonio and Maxine Hairston, this collection of sample designs for documents includes academic, extracurricular, business, and personal applications. Chapters on planning documents, working with print, and working with visual elements precede 28 specific projects you can tear out and share with your students. Projects include

- reports, process descriptions, and in-class presentations
- informational charts and graphs
- brochures, newsletters, and computer presentations
- résumés, memos, fax cover sheets, and letterheads
- posters, flyers, announcements, and press releases
- invitations and programs
- personal World Wide Web pages

Reading Critically: Text, Charts, and Graphs, **2nd Edition.** Prepared by reading specialist Judith Olson-Fallon of Case Western Reserve University, *Reading Critically* introduces students to college-level critical reading skills. Newly revised to augment the coverage of critical reading in the handbook, this ancillary text

- helps students develop critical reading questions
- shows students how to read, understand, and question information presented visually in charts and graphs
- presents reading as an interactive, flexible process
- gives detailed information on preparing reading notes, study summaries, and graphic organizers
- gives sample essays, charts, and graphs for students to practice their critical reading skills

Teaching Writing to the Non-Native Speaker. Developed by Jocelyn Steer, an ESL specialist, this supplement examines issues that arise when nonnative speakers enter the first-year composition classroom. It includes

- profiles of international and ESL students
- factors influencing second-language acquisition
- how to teach writing to ESL students
- how to respond to ESL writing
- how to manage a multicultural classroom

Each chapter includes questions about your teaching methods and summaries of key information.

Model Research Papers from Across the Disciplines, **4th Edition.** Edited by Charlotte Smith of Virginia Polytechnic Institute and State

University and Albert C. DeCiccio of Merrimack College, this collection of student-written research papers illustrates discipline-specific variations in format and documentation styles for the humanities and sciences. The collection has been completely updated to reflect the most recent revisions to the major documentation styles.

Documentation Guide. The *Documentation Guide* is a fast, easy reference for students writing research papers in the humanities and sciences. Adapted from the research writing chapters in *The Scott, Foresman Handbook for Writers*, the guide provides up-to-the-minute coverage of MLA, APA, and CBE styles, as well as the newly developed Alliance for Computers and Writing documentation style, in a pocket-sized format. It includes two full-length sample research papers in MLA and APA styles.

ESL Worksheets. Prepared by Jocelyn Steer, the *ESL Worksheets* provide ESL students with extra practice in areas they find troublesome. They are keyed to the fourth edition of *The Scott, Foresman Handbook for Writers*. A diagnostic test and post-test are provided to gauge students' skill levels and to measure their progress. Suggested topics for writing and an answer key to the exercises are included.

Transparency Masters. This collection of over 100 reproductions of helpful charts and checklists from the handbook is available to enhance classroom presentations.

Answer Key. The *Answer Key* provides answers to all the exercises in the handbook.

Software

The Scott, Foresman Handbook Rhetoric On-Line. Developed by Dan Seward of IconElastic, *Rhetoric On-Line* offers detailed instruction in six types of writing common in college courses: personal narrative, cause and effect, evaluations and reviews, exploratory essays, thesis and support, and persuasion. Each chapter contains five sections covering the entire writing process: understanding the aim; examining a sample paper; choosing a topic; preparing and planning; drafting and revising.

The program features quick-reference section icons and context-sensitive cues, and it allows students to record observations they make while reading the guide. It provides suggestions for topics, helpful tips, sample papers, a glossary, and numerous illustrations and checklists to guide students through the writing process. Available in Windows and Mac versions.

The Writer's Workshop. Prepared by the Daedalus Group, this interactive program "pops up" over any existing commercial word-processing program (IBM or Mac) to provide writing prompts—invention heuristics, revision strategies, and writing techniques—for students while they compose their papers. It includes the *Documentor* program to help students put their reference citations into correct MLA or APA format, and reference material from *The Scott, Foresman Handbook for Writers* to provide grammar help on-line.

HarperCollins Resources for Instructors Ancillary Program

Teaching Composition in the 90's: Sites of Contention. Edited by Christina G. Russell of Texas Christian University and Robert L. McDonald of the Virginia Military Institute, this intriguing collection of papers, inspired by the Second Annual Symposium on the Teaching of Composition held at Texas Christian University, explores the current debates on teaching composition that are raging among today's leading rhetoricians. Participants in these lively and informative discussions include Gwen Gong, Jim Corder, and James L. Kinneavy.

Teaching Writing: Theories and Practices, **4th Edition.** Designed for beginning instructors, this practical guide offers advice in designing a course, selecting a text, managing a classroom, and evaluating student writing. Josephine Koster Tarvers of Winthrop College discusses current ideas about grammar, standard English, sexist language, and plagiarism.

Video: Writing, Teaching, and Learning: Incorporating Writing Throughout the Curriculum. Produced by David A. Jolliffe of DePaul University, this 24-minute color video demonstrates techniques that help students produce good writing in any field and shows instructors how to critique student writing. Classroom examples are drawn from political science, sociology, and advanced math.

Video: Writing Across the Curriculum: Making It Work. Produced by Robert Morris College and the Public Broadcasting System, *Writing Across the Curriculum* is a video of the 1992 WAC Video Conference, which features faculty presenters from science, business, and math sharing their experiences in analyzing their course objectives and developing writing activities to meet the needs of students in their disciplines.

HarperCollins Resources for Writers Ancillary Program

Learning Together: An Introduction to Collaborative Learning. Written by Tori Haring-Smith of Brown University, this manual teaches students how to work effectively in groups, how to revise with peer response, and how to co-author a paper or report. It includes numerous exercises and suggested paper topics.

Student Manual for Peer Evaluation. Prepared by Tori Haring-Smith of Brown University, this book offers students forms for peer critiques, including general guidelines and specific forms for different stages in the writing process and for various class emphases.

Using WordPerfect in Composition and *Using Microsoft Word in Composition.* Prepared by Marcia Peoples and Karen G. Druliner of the University of Delaware, these two brief guides assume no prior knowledge of WordPerfect or Microsoft Word. Each guide begins with word processing basics and gradually leads students through more sophisticated functions. From logging onto a network to using a spelling checker, these user-friendly manuals introduce students to various word-processing capabilities, all in the context of the writing process. The WordPerfect guide covers both DOS and Macintosh versions of this program; the Microsoft Word guide addresses Macintosh and IBM-Windows versions.

Eighty Readings. Compiled by the HarperCollins editors, this collection of professional and student-written essays—written to inform, persuade, or inspire—is arranged thematically, with an alternate rhetorical table of contents.

Eighty Practices. Compiled by the HarperCollins editors, *Eighty Practices* is a collection of photo-reproducible, 10-item exercises that provide additional practice for specific grammatical usage problems such as comma splices, capitalization, and pronouns. It includes an answer key.

Testing Programs

TestMaster and *QuizMaster.* HarperCollins' computerized testing program *TestMaster* allows instructors to customize any of the questions contained in the HarperCollins Testing Program: TASP, CLAST, Diagnostic, and Competency Profile tests. *QuizMaster*, an extension of *TestMaster*, allows instructors the opportunity to offer their *TestMaster* tests on-line to their students. It will also generate test scores.

Diagnostic and Editing Tests. Prepared by Sarah Harrold of Southwestern Oregon Community College, and John Feaster and Edward M. Ueling of Valparaiso University, this collection of diagnostic tests helps instructors assess students' competence in standard written English for purposes of placement or to gauge progress. The *Diagnostic Tests* are keyed to *The Scott, Foresman Handbook for Writers*, Fourth Edition. Available in reproducible sheets or on disk.

Competency Profile Test Bank. Prepared by Judith Olson-Fallon of Case Western Reserve University, this series of objective tests and the accompanying answer key covers ten general areas of English competency. Each test is available in remedial, standard, and advanced versions. Available in reproducible sheets or on disk.

CLAST Test Package, 3rd Edition. Developed by Helen Gilbart of St. Petersburg Junior College, these two 40-item objective tests evaluate students' readiness for the CLAST exams. Strategies for teaching CLAST preparedness are included. Available in reproducible sheets or on disk.

TASP Test Package, 2nd Edition. Prepared by Judith Olson-Fallon of Case Western Reserve University and Carolyn Comeaux of Lamar University, these twelve practice pre-tests and post-tests assess the same reading and writing skills covered in the TASP examination. Available in reproducible sheets or on disk.

Dictionaries and Thesauruses

The following reference works are available with *The Scott, Foresman Handbook for Writers* at a discounted price.

The Collins Gem Thesaurus and *Webster's Dictionary*, handy, pocket-sized references. The thesaurus includes over 120,000 synonyms, and the dictionary over 45,000 entries.

Funk and Wagnalls Standard Dictionary, a paperback reference with more than 75,000 entries, with sample phrases to ensure correct usage.

Roget's Thesaurus, a desktop-sized version of the best-selling thesaurus, contains a detailed index to the entries.

ACKNOWLEDGMENTS

For helping us to improve the fourth edition of *The Scott, Foresman Handbook for Writers*, we are grateful to the following reviewers. Bret Benjamin, University of Texas at Austin; Susan-Marie Birkenstock, University of Florida at Gainesville; Ed Block, Marquette University; Adam Collins, Grambling State University; Joanne E. Gates, Jacksonville State University; G. Kenneth Guthrie, Jacksonville State University; Jan Hall, Louisiana Technical University; Regan Hicks-Goldstein, Delaware Technical and Community College; Michael Hogan, Southeast Missouri State University; Michael Keller, South Dakota State University; Judith Kohl, Dutchess Community College; Douglas Krienke, Sam Houston State University; Sarah Liggett, Louisiana State University; Alan Merickel, Tallahassee Community College; Jane Peterson, Richland College; Ed Reynolds, Spokane Falls Community College; William B. Testerman, Castleton State College; Mark Withrow, Columbia College; and Janet Wingeroth, Spokane Falls Community College Library.

For assistance with details of documentation, we'd like to thank Janice Walker of the University of South Florida and Donald J. Foss of Florida State. Finally, we are grateful to a remarkably talented group of people at the University of Texas at Austin: Daniel Anderson, Bret Benjamin, Tonya Browning, Chris Busiel, Joi Chevalier, Christy Friend, Bill Paredes-Holt, Dan Seward, and John Slatin.

MAXINE HAIRSTON
JOHN J. RUSZKIEWICZ

To the Writer

A handbook is a reference book for writers who need advice about composing or guidance about a point of grammar or usage. It is one of a writer's basic tools, just as a word processor or a dictionary is a tool. In three distinctive ways, we have tried to make this handbook a practical manual, easy to understand and easy to use.

First, we have tried to write in a friendly, reassuring tone to reduce any fears you may have about composition, particularly about mechanics and usage. Writing isn't easy, but it's nothing to be afraid of either. We want this handbook to encourage, even cajole you, into doing your best. We have heard too many stories about students bullied so much about their prose that they have stopped writing entirely and even arranged their course schedules to avoid classes requiring papers. That's unfortunate because writing about a subject is among the best ways of learning it.

Second, we have applied a problem-solving approach to most aspects of writing covered in the book. Our intention is to help you realize that most writing problems are manageable; you aren't the first to face them. Most sections of the handbook open with discussions labeled **Troubleshooting** that identify the questions or problems most writers have with a particular issue, whether it is using the library efficiently or figuring out the semicolon. Then we list strategies for handling these problems, beginning with the basics and narrowing down to more technical matters, which we label **Fine Tuning**.

Third, we have developed three symbols for marking rhetorical and grammatical issues in the handbook according to their difficulty. When you see one of these symbols in the margin, you'll know that a certain error is very serious or is especially troublesome. We have done this because handbooks typically contain hundreds of guidelines and injunctions and users need a way of telling which issues are minor, even trivial, and which are really serious. We have not attempted to assign symbols to every item in the book; rather we have put them by only those items we think warrant unusual attention. We consulted a panel of experts in deciding which problems deserved which symbols. Here is what the three symbols mean.

Stop! This is a serious blunder that could be very damaging

 Caution. This is a key point or issue that deserves your special attention.

 Tricky. This point confuses many writers.

We hope these symbols and the problem-solving arrangement of the text will encourage you to use *The Scott, Foresman Handbook for Writers* as a fix-it manual. But you should know that writing involves much more than correcting mistakes and avoiding problems. For that reason, the opening part of the book (Chapters 1–6) discusses the entire writing process—finding a topic, developing ideas, analyzing your audience, constructing and evaluating an argument, and producing a draft.

WHEN SHOULD YOU USE A HANDBOOK?

We advise you not to use the style and usage parts of the handbook (Parts II and III) in the early stages of the writing process. Many people who write professionally find that they work best if they don't worry about grammar, spelling, or usage while composing a first draft. If they do, their best ideas often float away while they tinker with details. Similarly, student writers who worry too early about getting everything perfect often abandon their writing projects when they bog down in a minefield of potential errors: they are puzzling over the placement of commas when they should be chasing ideas. Writing that could have been fun thus becomes a chore. So a "write first and fix it later" attitude makes fine sense for most writers—both professionals and novices.

For this reason, in Part I of the handbook we emphasize the importance of producing a draft of any paper you are writing. Using whatever strategies work best for you, set down your ideas in some form early—even if your thoughts are not yet well organized or fully developed. The important thing is to produce a first draft that you can polish into a more finished project by revising, editing, and proofreading.

We also suggest that you wait to look up specific problems of grammar and usage until you have completed your revisions of style—which are covered thoroughly in Part II. You'll use your time most efficiently if you don't waste it polishing sentences that you eventually decide to cut.

But when you are ready to make sure everything is right, consult Part III of *The Scott, Foresman Handbook for Writers*.

WHAT OTHER FEATURES DOES THE HANDBOOK HAVE?

In addition to the features explained above, *The Scott, Foresman Handbook for Writers* employs a series of special headings and boxes to emphasize specific kinds of information.

Special Headings

- *Tip*. Look here for practical advice and commonsense observations about writing. Tips are marked by ●.
- *Point of Difference*. These sections focus on aspects of composition, mechanics, and usage where authorities don't agree. Points of difference are marked by ◆.
- *Window on Writing*. Look here for samples of student writing that illustrate principles discussed in the book. Windows on Writing are highlighted by a green bar.

Boxes

- *Checklist*. Checklists tell you what you need to do to manage some aspect of writing. These checklists are especially helpful and numerous in the chapters on revising and research.
- *Chart*. Charts explain a grammatical point or list items such as irregular verbs or conjunctive adverbs.
- *Summary*. Summaries wrap up a complicated section or issue, providing you with a quick list of major points to remember.
- *Highlight*. Highlights provide interesting bits of information about language and various reference works.

MAXINE HAIRSTON
JOHN J. RUSZKIEWICZ

A Visual Guide To:

THE SCOTT, FORESMAN HANDBOOK FOR WRITERS

Fourth Edition

Maxine Hairston
The University of Texas at Austin

John J. Ruszkiewicz
The University of Texas at Austin

ISBN 0-673-99728-6

The fourth edition of *The Scott, Foresman Handbook for Writers* reaffirms the principles evident since the first edition: that a handbook should encourage students to write; that it should speak to writers cordially and with respect; that it should treat writing as a lively and creative process; and that it should recognize not all errors are created equal. In this edition, the authors retain all the innovations that have supported these concepts, from the troubleshooting structure of the chapters themselves to the marginal symbols that guide writers through difficult and tricky issues of rhetoric, mechanics, and usage.

8a
¶

How Should You Manage Opening and Closing Paragraphs?

A Opening Paragraphs
B Closing Paragraphs

8a WHAT MAKES AN OPENING PARAGRAPH EFFECTIVE?

Troubleshooting

CAUTION

Opening paragraphs warrant special attention because they introduce you and your paper to your readers, and that first impression is important. Newspaper editors talk about the **lead** for a news story, the opening that has to catch the readers' attention and give them a strong signal about what to expect. The opening paragraph for whatever you write is your lead, the part of your paper that gets you off to a good or bad start with readers. Remember, then, that a first paragraph should do the following things.

- Get your readers' attention and interest them in reading more.
- Announce or suggest your main idea without delay.
- Give your readers a signal about the direction you intend to take.
- Set the tone of your essay.

These are important functions, and that's why first paragraphs can be challenging, but it is also why they are worth your time and attention.

● **Tip**

Just because first paragraphs are so important in the final versions of papers, don't let yourself get stalled at the draft stage by trying to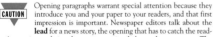

NOT ALL ERRORS ARE CREATED EQUAL

The authors take a problem-solving approach to grammar and usage. Troubleshooting sections identify the difficulties or questions most writers have. Icons throughout the book tell you how damaging a certain error may be, or how troublesome an element of writing is likely to prove.

2e HOW DO YOU ORGANIZE A PAPER?

2e HOW DO YOU ORGANIZE A PAPER?

PROCESS MENU
PREPARING
PLANNING
DRAFTING
INCUBATING
REVISING
EDITING
PROOFREADING

Troubleshooting

No matter how good your ideas are,
most readers will not have the patience to
read your paper unless it is well organized. If
you don't make the effort to organize a paper,
your readers will get lost and blame you for
the confusion. So don't think that good organization is optional; rather, it is the foundation of a college paper.

You're likely to need a specific plan
when you are doing explanatory writing to
get your material under control and to arrange
it clearly for readers. But you also need at least
a tentative plan when you start doing ex-
ploratory writing. A plan gives reflective or personal pieces a sense of direction.

It is true that many good writers never consciously select a design
before writing a paper. They know intuitively what events they want a
story to contain or what order the information in a report should follow.
Still, understanding the options available when you organize a paper

Foreign Aid: Should We Keep It At Home?

We are a group of first year English composition students instructed by Tonya Browning at The
University of Texas at Austin. Our project concerns the United States and its involvement in
providing foreign assistance to underprivileged nations. This presentation examines both sides of
the debate regarding foreign aid to other countries.

The Drawbacks of U.S. Foreign Assistance

The United States sends billions of
dollars in supplies, labor, and actual
funds to other countries each year. Even
though we are experiencing record
unemployment, increased racial tension,
skyrocketing infant mortality rates,
woeful underfunding of education,
crumbling infrastructure and a record
budget deficit that will probably mortgage
our grandchildren's grandchildren, we are
still sending the taxpayer's hard earned
money to countries thousands of miles away. The question remains: if the government has
billions of dollars to spend on these other countries, then why are Americans suffering at home?
These funds need to stay in our own country to help fight these domestic problems. Not only
should we keep this money at home, but United States officials need to consider reallocation of
current funds.

The Advantages of U.S. Foreign Assistance

There are a number of reasons why
foreign assistance programs are a
sound investment for the future of the
United States. First and foremost, they
help the US economically while
insuring global stability. In addition,
trading partners are gained, strategic
allies are secured, and democracies are
fostered around the world.
Humanitarian acts also play a
substantial role in the intervention of
the US because the welfare of the underdeveloped is advanced. Hence, the advantages to solid
foreign aid programs benefit not only the US, but the impoverished countries as well. Most
importantly, it is sh[...] foreign aid and the compassion of the Americ[...] le that peace and
[...] the globe.

CRITICAL READING

The Scott Foresman Handbook shows students how to examine ten factors to determine whether a printed or electronic source is reputable, thorough, and up-to-date.

5b–3 Look closely at a writer's or speaker's claims to see if they go beyond what the evidence actually supports. Here are two cases in which critical thinkers have recently challenged the results of long-accepted research.

Many psychologists now question the long-standing practice of researchers in psychology who gather their data solely from college students and from that data make claims about psychological characteristics of the general population. The critics point out that college students are chosen because they're available (often they *have* to participate) and cost very little, but they certainly don't constitute a random sample of the general population.

Women's groups have begun to challenge some major research projects in medicine because they included no women. Take some studies done on heart disease, for example, that included only men. Given the differences in the physiology, body chemistry, diet, and living habits of men and women, is it valid to base treatment for women heart patients on the data from such studies? Probably not.

In the first example, the writer points out that psychological researchers are drawing conclusions that go well beyond what their data warrant. In the second, the writer points out that medical researchers have failed to get important data that would affect their conclusions.

10d HOW DO YOU CONTROL FOR BIAS IN YOUR LANGUAGE?

CRITICAL WRITING

Students learn to assess their writing for unproven claims, unstated assumptions, inconsistencies, bias, stereotypes, and black-and-white thinking in order to create effective college papers.

Troubleshooting

Biased language isn't always bad. Slanted but colorful writing regularly enlivens articles in popular books and magazines and the editorial pages of any newspaper. Consider the following sentences.

As brokers upstairs sorted through the shambles [of the 1987 stock market crash], hollow-cheeked models with crosses around their necks drifted down through the courtyard's runway, their clothes-hanger bodies swaying under the weight of twenty pounds of crinoline and taffeta.
—Susan Faludi, *Backlash*.

He hasn't been home in decades, but [Aaron] Spelling has a true Texan's passion for busty blondes and big deals.
—Mimi Swartz, *Texas Monthly*, September 1994.

These writers make no pretense to objectivity—they're writing to entertain audiences they feel comfortable with, and they're quite sure that people who choose to read their work won't take offense at the exaggerated images they're presenting.

When you write in college or in business, however, you face a different kind of audience. Usually you'll be writing to inform or to persuade readers you don't know well, and you can't afford to offend them by using language that suggests that you don't respect certain people or groups or that you think in stereotypes. Because of ingrained habits, however, writers or speakers sometimes unthinkingly lapse into such language; by doing so, they damage their credibility and alienate many readers or listeners. When that happens, they fail to get what they want.

This section suggests ways you can work toward eliminating offensive bias when you speak or write. Some of the strategies mirror those we discussed in the sections on critical thinking in Chapter 5.

Using the View Window

When you open the View Window of the *SFH Rhetoric Online*, you will find that the text contains images and symbols. You will also note that there are buttons above the text and a menu at the top of the window. This section of the User's Manual explains how to use these images, symbols, buttons, and menus to navigate the *SFH Rhetoric Online*. The View Window contains the following elements:

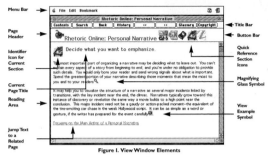

Figure I. View Window Elements

You'll need to learn these elements to get the most out of the *SFH Rhetoric Online*.

INTERACTIVE WRITING GUIDE

This software, available in both Windows and Macintosh formats, provides students with a complete rhetoric covering six key writing assignments: a personal narrative, a cause and effect analysis, an exploratory essay, an evaluation, a paper proving a thesis, and a persuasive essay. This software enables students to work their way through the entire writing process for each assignment, from invention to revision, choosing their own pace and direction.

SFH Apple

 Click on the *SFH Apple* to see a key to the symbols described in "The Reading Area" section of this manual.

Quick Reference Section Icons

 Click on the current chapter icon to see a key to images used throughout the chapter. These images help you to understand the particular style of writing being discussed. From the key, you can go to the "Understanding the Aim" section which opens each chapter. (Note that the icon for the "Understanding the Aim" section changes for each assignment.)

 Click on the *Example* image to display the "Examining a Sample Paper" section of the current chapter. The Sample Paper represents a successful application of the concepts introduced in the current chapter.

 Click on the *Topic* image to display the "Choosing a Topic" section of the current chapter. These topics suggest assignments designed to use concepts in the current chapter.

 Click on the *Preparing and Planning* image to display the "Preparing and Planning" section of the current chapter.

 Click on the *Drafting and Revising* image to display the "Drafting and Revising" section of the current chapter.

INTERNET SOURCES

The fourth edition introduces students to Listserv, USENET newsgroups, Gopher, and the World Wide Web, including their major characteristics, uses, and search techniques.

CHECKLIST

Internet Resources

There are different layers to Internet resources, but here are some that can enliven and enhance your thinking and writing.

GOPHER

A client/server program that uses menus in a hierarchical fashion. A top menu can be divided into submenus, those submenus into sub-submenus, and so forth.

Major characteristics: Allows users to move forward and backward quickly through a large amount of textual information.

Use for: Structured navigation through Internet resources. The menus help you develop a mental map of the Internet. May provide subject access to electronic journals, documents, and indexes.

Searching: Keyword searches are supported when appropriate. A *bookmark* feature enables you to keep a record of key addresses and to facilitate subsequent searches.

WORLD WIDE WEB (WWW)

A type of client/server program (examples are *Mosaic, Netscape, Cello, Lynx*) that supports hypertext. Users may effortlessly follow connections or "links" from document to document by simply clicking or choosing the connection.

Major characteristics: Weaves together Internet functions to form a smooth work surface for users, who can concentrate on subject matter instead of computer commands. Formats can be images, sounds, video, or text.

Use for: Easiest interface with information in cyberspace.

Searching: A variety of search methods are available now and others are being developed. Results will vary, so try different search starting points, or search engines. Save locations of sources to a *hot list* so you can return to them later.

Internet Resources *(continued)*

LISTSERV

A type of mail program that maintains lists of subscribers interested in discussing a specific topic. Users must subscribe in order to read or post messages.

Major characteristics: Lists are run on large computers; subscribers tend to be active experts working in fields related to the list topic.

32c
on-line

(continued)

Lists are often moderated, thereby screening out nonrelevant material or 'noise.' Old text may be archived.

Use for: Excellent window on current issues. Good for listening in on the practitioners' conversations, discovering opinions, noting solutions to common problems.

Searching: When you subscribe, check the welcome message for instructions for searching the archives.

USENET NEWS GROUPS

Interest groups publicly accessible in a conference format.

Major characteristics: Thousands of groups focus on topics ranging from *A* to *Z*. Wide variation in expertise of contributors. Anyone may read or post messages. Just browsing the list of Usenet groups can suggest topic ideas.

Use for: Conversations about popular topics and about little-known, obscure subjects. Almost every political group, social interest, religion, activity, hobby, and fantasy has a Usenet group.

Searching: Check the welcome messages and the FAQs (frequently asked questions) for information on how to search. Many lists have archives of older discussions.

ELECTRONIC SOURCES

The fourth edition covers on-line techniques for searching electronic indexes, provides descriptions of Internet resources, and explains how to document on-line materials. Also, included now is an entirely new section on evaluating sources.

44. **On-line Database, Journal, or Conference—MLA** On-line sources come to you via an electronic hookup—a modem, for example, or a direct link to the Internet. Because of this electronic connection, on-line information can grow and change rapidly, complicating the task of documentation. To cite a book, poem, article, Web page, or other source located on-line, begin with the elements used to document conventional printed sources: author, title, publication information, date of publication or posting, and page numbers. Then provide the following additional information: the publication medium (*Online*); the name of the computer service or computer network that provides the source (for example, *Dialog, CompuServe, Internet*); and the date you accessed the material. An optional but useful addition is the electronic address of the source, beginning with the word *Available*. (*Note carefully:* the period that ends the citation is not a part of this electronic address.)

Works Cited

Austin, Mary. "The Little Coyote." <u>Atlantic</u>

<u>Monthly</u> 89 (1902): 249-54. Online.

U of Virginia Electronic Text Center.

Internet. 3 May 1995. Available WWW:

http://etext.lib.virginia.edu/english.html.

Parenthetical note: (Austin 250)

Cite an article from an on-line electronic journal or magazine (that is, one not available in a printed version) by giving the con-
 ...ed source—author, name of jour-
 ...lso give the number of pages or
 ... *pag.* to indicate *no pagination*.
 ...edium (*Online*); the name of the
 ...etwork that provided the source;
 ...material. If page numbers aren't
 ...avoid in-text parenthetical cita-
 ...your paper: "Nachman and Jenk-

 ...Cited

 ...nkins. "What's Wrong
 ...rica?" <u>Trincoll</u>
 ... pag. Online.

34b
MLA

Bessemer 4

bike bums in California, Colorado, and other places

were pounding local hills and inventing mountain bike

racing (Schwartz 77). These first mountain bikes were

custom jobs, but in 1981 a Californian named Michael

Sinyard produced the first commercial mountain bike,

the Stumpjumper, a copy of which is now in the

Smithsonian museum (Castro 42). It quickly sold out

and spawned a vigorous new industry--served eagerly

now by manufacturers in Taiwan, Japan, Italy, and the

United States. By 1993, 30 million mountain bikes had

been manufactured (Schwartz 80).

¶5   What distinguishes mountain bikes from touring

or racing bikes are flat handlebars for upright

34c
MLA

Sales of Trek brand bikes   Percentage of bike sales

1981   1991   1981   1991

50,000 units sold

Touring bikes

Mountain bikes & Hybrids

Fig. 1. U.S. sales of mountain bikes

These conventions are likely to evolve over the next few years.

34g-2 **(Step 2) On a separate page at the end of your paper, list every source cited in a parenthetical note.** The alphabetical list of sources is labeled Works Cited. For the general arrangement of a Works Cited page, see Section 34a–2. For individual ACW Works Cited entries, use the following formula.

```
Author's Last Name, First Name. "Title of Work."

    Title of Complete Work. [protocol and address]

    [path] [date of access, visit, or message].
```

The formula varies slightly, depending on the type of electronic source you need to document: FTP (File Transfer Protocol) sites; WWW (World Wide Web) sites; Telnet sites; synchronous communications (MUDs, MOOs, IRC); Gopher sites; Listserv and Newslist items; and e-mail.

A typical **ACW Works Cited entry for an FTP site** (where files can be downloaded) includes the following basic information.

- Name of author(s), if known, last name first, followed by a period and a space.
- Title of work, followed by a period and between quotation marks.
- Address of the FTP site and the full path needed to access the information. This address is followed by a space but no period.
- Date of access in parentheses, followed by a period.

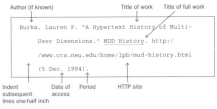

Author (if known)   Title

- Title of work, followed by a period and between quotation marks. This might be an individual Web page within a larger Web site.
- Title of the full work (if applicable), underlined or in italics.
- Full HTTP address. This address is followed by a space but no period.
- Date of access in parentheses, followed by a period.

Author (if known)   Title of work   Title of full work

```
Burka, Lauren P. "A Hypertext History of Multi-

    User Dimensions." MUD History. http:/

    /www.ccs.neu.edu/home/lpb/mud-history.html

    (5 Dec. 1994).
```

Indent   Date of   Period   HTTP site
subsequent   access
lines one-half inch

A typical **ACW Works Cited entry for a Telnet site** includes the following basic information.

- Name of author(s), if known, last name first, followed by a period and a space.
- Title of work, followed by a period and between quotation marks.
- Title of the full work (if applicable), underlined or in italics.
- Complete Telnet address, as well as any directions for accessing the source. This address is followed by a space but no period.
- Date of access in parentheses, followed by a period.

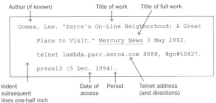

Author (if known)   Title of work   Title of full work

```
Gomes, Lee. "Xerox's On-Line Neighborhood: A Great

    Place to Visit." Mercury News 3 May 1992.

    telnet lambda.parc.xerox.com 8888, @go#50827,

    press13 (5 Dec. 1994).
```

Indent   Date of   Period   Telnet address
subsequent   access   (and directions)
lines one-half inch

A typical **ACW Works Cited entry for Synchronous Communications (MOOs, MUDs, IRC)** includes the following basic information.

DOCUMENTATION FOR COMPUTER REFERENCES

The Scott Foresman Handbook is the first handbook to introduce documentation style specifically designed for electronic sources and adopted by the Alliance for Computers and Writing.

34g
ACW

34g
ACW

I

The Writing Process

We *write* in order to produce *writing*. That makes writing both a process and a product. In this first section of the handbook, we examine processes that generate various kinds of writing and suggest ways to make composing more efficient and, we hope, more enjoyable.

1a WHAT MYTHS DISCOURAGE WRITERS?

Troubleshooting

Writing is not a mysterious activity at which only a few people can succeed; rather it is a craft that can be learned by almost anyone willing to invest the necessary time and energy. Contrary to what many people believe, the main qualities you need to succeed as a writer are not inspiration and talent but confidence and determination—confidence that you are an intelligent person with something to say and determination to work at your writing until you grow competent. If you feel insecure about your writing ability, remember this: In our information-dependent world, millions of people have to write on their jobs every day, and they do so successfully. If they can, so can you.

Unfortunately many people underestimate their potential as writers because they've bought into myths that discourage them whenever they start to compose. We aren't sure where these myths came from, but they are pervasive and persistent. Don't be victimized by any of them.

Recognize these myths about writing . . .

- **Myth:** *Good writers are born, not made.* **Fact:** People become good writers by working at writing. It's as simple as that. If you want to write well, you can if you'll invest the time.

- **Myth:** *Good writers work alone.* **Fact:** Good writers often rely on colleagues for suggestions and help. They collaborate to generate ideas and work out their writing problems.

- **Myth:** *Good writers know what they are going to say before they start writing.* **Fact:** Good writers often begin with only a general idea of what they are going to say. Frequently they expect to find their ideas as they write. They know that writing is a way of generating new ideas or rediscovering what they already know.

- **Myth:** *Good writers plan carefully before they write and always prepare full outlines.* **Fact:** Many good writers make only sketchy plans and outlines. As they develop a paper, their initial strategies change to reflect what they learn about a subject or about their readers.

- **Myth:** *Good writers get it right the first time.* **Fact:** Although experienced writers can sometimes produce polished work in the first draft, for important jobs professional writers usually write several drafts. They expect to revise extensively.

- **Myth:** *Good writing comes from knowing all the rules of grammar.* **Fact:** Success as a writer does not depend on being able to recite grammatical rules, and learning rules alone won't make anyone a good writer. Mastering the conventions of grammar, however, makes most people more confident when they write.

- **Myth:** *All writers compose in the same way.* **Fact:** Writers work differently, and the same person will write differently in various situations. The craft of writing cannot be reduced to a single "correct" method.

■ **Exercise 1.1** Discuss the myths above with your colleagues. Pick out one you have encountered before (or describe a myth not covered here) and, in a few paragraphs, explain how it affected you.

■ **Exercise 1.2** When you think of the term *writer*, what kind of person comes to mind? Many people reserve the term for the relatively few authors and journalists who make their living solely by writing. But can you think of other people who write frequently even though writing might not be the major focus of their professions? Discuss the issue with classmates.

1b   HOW DOES THE WRITING PROCESS WORK?

PROCESS MENU
PREPARING
PLANNING
DRAFTING
INCUBATING
REVISING
EDITING
PROOFREADING

Troubleshooting

It's tempting to believe that there's a secret formula for writing papers and that if you could just discover it, your life would be much easier. We assure you that no such formula exists, and you're not a failure because you haven't discovered one. Nevertheless, researchers who have studied the process of composing agree that writers do seem to follow particular patterns of behavior comparable to those that occur in other creative activities.

To understand writing . . .

1b–1 View writing as a process. When you are given an assignment, don't begin by visualizing the final product—five or ten pages, typed, corrected, paginated, and clipped together. You'll just feel intimidated by all the work required to produce so slick a package. Instead think about more immediate goals and the smaller steps you can take to pull off that finished paper. Writing, you see, is a process that moves through stages almost anyone can manage. Any schematic view of the writing process merely hints at what writers really do: a chart can't express the nuances of the process or the differences between individual writers. Still, you'll probably find the pattern of writing offered on page 6 helpful when you're faced with a college assignment.

1b–2 View the writing process as cycling through the stages. Many successful authors say they shift freely between the preparing, planning, and revising stages as they work on a writing project. Some writers delay all their major revisions until they have a first draft; others revise as they work, preferring to compose a paper sentence by sentence. For complex assignments writers may repeat steps in the process several times before they produce a finished piece. They also adjust their composing processes to the job they are doing. Writing a term paper may require much planning and revising; writing a summary may take very little. So writing should not be thought of as a lockstep march from outlining to editing. Instead it's a dynamic, free-flowing process that writers adapt to their needs.

CHART

Stages of Writing

• **PREPARING**

In this stage you read, brainstorm, and talk to people in order to decide what you want to write about and generate ideas about it.

• **PLANNING**

In this stage you develop your ideas and organize your materials. To do that you may prepare working lists, outlines, summaries, and charts.

• **DRAFTING**

In this stage you start to put words down on a page or screen. You may compose one or more drafts, rethinking and reshaping your materials as necessary.

• **INCUBATING**

In this stage you give yourself time off to let your ideas simmer. Solutions or ideas may develop in the unconscious before taking conscious shape.

• **REVISING, EDITING, AND PROOFREADING**

In this stage you review what you have written, *revising* to make large-scale changes in topic, organization, or audience adaptation; *editing* to make smaller-scale changes in style and readability; and *proofreading* to rid your paper of mechanical problems such as spelling and punctuation errors.

1b-3 **View the writing process as something you can manage.** Almost everything in your life prepares you for writing: things that have happened in your family or on your job, your hobbies, your experiences in sports or with your car, your relationships with friends or lovers, your days and nights in college, your experiences as a citizen in a complex society. You have ideas to explore, opinions to examine, and beliefs to explain and defend. In other words, your memory is crammed with material that you can draw on to develop papers.

All this adds up to such a rich stock of resources that you should not run yourself down by saying, "I have nothing to write about." Of course you do! You have an abundance of experience that will interest other people. And the more alert you become to the world around you,

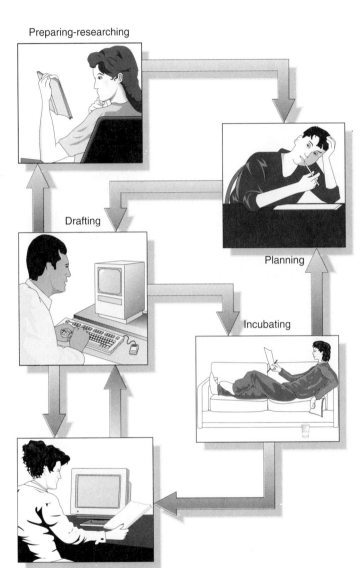

Preparing-researching

Planning

Drafting

Incubating

Revising, editing, proofreading

the more material you'll have to work with. So approach the writing process with confidence. Even if you haven't written much before, you can communicate with others. You do so every day.

■ **Exercise 1.3** If you have done a piece of writing you were proud of—perhaps an article in the student newspaper, a letter to the editor that was published, a song or story, or a personal statement that won you a scholarship—write a paragraph describing the preparation you put into it, how many times you revised it, and why you think it was successful.

■ **Exercise 1.4** Write a paragraph or two candidly describing your most hectic writing experience, when you were most pressed to get an assignment done. What did you have to do to finish the paper? Was it successful?

1c WHAT KINDS OF WRITING DO YOU DO?

Troubleshooting

People do many different kinds of writing, but most of the writing students do in college, aside from note taking and lab reports, falls into two general categories: explanatory writing and exploratory writing. We think you will write more effectively if you learn to distinguish them. Explanatory writing explains or presents ideas, theories, or data; it usually focuses on facts or events. The writer usually begins an explanatory piece with a specific goal in mind. Exploratory writing, on the other hand, reflects on or speculates about ideas, concepts, or experiences. The writer often discovers a subject while composing and may not even have a specific goal in mind when he or she begins.

For instance, if a writing assignment requires that you gather information, classify it, and draw conclusions—say, for a paper reporting on an experiment in a sociology class—you're probably doing explanatory writing. It's best to start out with a goal in mind and a plan.

But if an assignment requires that you examine how a crisis in your childhood affected your behavior and thinking—a paper you might prepare for a psychology class—you're probably doing exploratory writing. Although you need to do some planning, you shouldn't try to plot out the whole paper ahead of time since you don't know what you're likely to say. You need to start with ideas and impressions but develop your content and refine your organization as you write.

To manage your writing process . . .

1c-1 **Recognize when your writing will be explanatory.** If you know what a paper is going to be about and what you want to accomplish in it, you will likely be doing explanatory writing. For example, suppose for a nutrition class you were asked to report on current medical theory about the relation between diet and cancer. The content for such a paper already exists. You just have to look it up, organize it, and present it. Your goal—in addition to learning about the topic—is to educate readers and hold their interest.

H I G H L I G H T

Some Explanatory Paper Topics

- The development of rhetoric in Greece (for a classics course)
- The mechanics of a scramjet (for an engineering course)
- The poetry of Phillis Wheatley (for an American literature course)
- The classic symptoms of schizophrenia (for a psychology course)
- Understanding Jewish dietary laws (for a religious studies course)

Many of your college assignments will require explanatory papers. If you typically outline your ideas, analyze your audience, and collect your sources before you compose, you're probably comfortable doing explanatory writing. It's the kind of writing for which a systematic, problem-solving approach works well. If that's not your style, however, you can still do a good job with explanatory assignments. In Section 1d and other parts of the book we present strategies for gathering, organizing, supporting, and presenting material for explanatory papers. The techniques are not difficult to learn.

1c-2 **Recognize when your writing will be exploratory.** When you have a general notion of what you hope to accomplish in a paper but haven't figured out its specific content or organization, you will likely be doing exploratory writing. A writer often begins an exploratory piece with no more than a feeling or an intuition—he or she has an idea to discuss, a problem that demands attention, a topic that won't go away until it's been more fully explored. Obviously the exploratory essay will evolve from an open-ended process of discovery; you are counting on generating fresh ideas and insights as you write. So don't be reluctant to express your views in an exploratory piece. Your instructor probably made the assignment to encourage venturesome thinking.

Typically, writers reflect on their own experiences in exploratory papers, or they may speculate about interesting cultural phenomena—those issues that shape our social and political worlds. Quite often your exploratory writing will be about ethics and values. Most of the essays in an anthology for a college composition course are likely to be examples of exploratory writing.

HIGHLIGHT

Some Exploratory Paper Topics

- Experiences of recent immigrants to the United States (for an ethnography course)
- Returning to college as a single parent (for a women's studies course)
- Impact of car ownership on high school students (for a sociology course)
- Rock lyrics as poetry (for an English course)
- A comparison of Jesus and Muhammad (for a religious studies course)

You'll find that the first version of an exploratory paper often serves as a "discovery draft." That is, while not yet good enough to meet the assignment, it furnishes the idea that propels and energizes the next draft. Although composing an exploratory piece will be a less predictable process than writing an explanatory paper from an outline, readers will ultimately expect an exploratory essay to be as coherent as an explanatory one. So exploratory writing nearly always requires heavy revision and editing.

1c–3 **Recognize when to combine explanatory and exploratory strategies.** We have divided writing into these two categories mainly to help you understand that there is no one best way to write a paper. Sometimes you'll do better by planning extensively; at other times, you need to explore ideas by writing about them. However, when you do see the differences between these writing processes, you may appreciate why certain assignments appeal to you more than others. Some feel congenial, even easy; others are formidable and challenging. You'll probably like best those assignments suited to your temperament, but that doesn't mean you can't master other kinds just as completely.

In fact, you'll often need to combine the two processes of writing. You can use explanatory writing to organize information and then switch to exploratory writing to reflect on what you've learned. For instance, you might start a paper by documenting the specific differences between American and Japanese schools—number of school days, length of days, required subjects, kinds of examinations, and so on. Then you ponder the implications of these differences: What do they say about the attitudes of Americans toward their children? You have moved from explanation to exploration.

C H A R T

Types of Writing

EXPLANATORY	EXPLANATORY AND EXPLORATORY	EXPLORATORY
Report on laboratory experiment	Comparison of child-care programs in Sweden and the United States	Article about coming to the United States as an immigrant
Environmental impact study	Account of the decline of communism in Poland	Paper in a literature course interpreting a short story
Case study of pregnancy-induced diabetes	Commentary on the economics of professional basketball	Speculative article on the psychological attractions of dangerous sports
Term paper on superconductivity and its applications	Argument paper on how to combat homelessness in one city	Article about Americans' fascination with celebrities

---

■ **Exercise 1.5** Think about writing you have done in the past several months—perhaps an editorial for the student paper, a paper for a course, a personal essay for your college application, a report on a trip you made, or some writing you did on your job. Which pieces of writing would you call explanatory writing? Which exploratory? Which ones would you say were mixed? Why?

■ **Exercise 1.6** Working with other students in a group, look over several issues of the student newspaper published on your campus and pick out three or four items: editorials, news stories, feature stories, and so on. Discuss which pieces seem to be mainly explanatory writing, which exploratory. On what do you base your judgment?

1d HOW DO YOU DEFINE A WRITING SITUATION?

Troubleshooting

CAUTION

Writing is a *social activity*, a way of interacting with other people; thus, every time you write, you enter a *writing situation* in which you try to

- Say *something*
- To *somebody*
- For *some purpose*

Unless a piece of college writing meets these three goals, it doesn't really exist as writing. It's just an exercise.

Since we have found that people write better when they think in these terms—*what* do I want to say to *whom* and *why*—you should start thinking about *meaning, audience,* and *purpose* every time you write. Probably no other single habit will do more to help you become an effective writer.

To begin your project . . .

Decide whether your topic deserves attention. Do you have an idea you want to write about and someone else wants to read about? Will your paper tell your readers something they want or need to know? We don't mean that every time you write, you should come up with a fresh idea or that you always have to write about serious and complex topics. But you should try to tell your readers something informative, interesting, or surprising.

Perhaps you can furnish your readers with useful information, give them fresh insights on a familiar topic, or just amuse them. If you were writing an exam for a professor, "informative" might mean writing an essay that demonstrates your understanding of a basic concept—for instance, pulsar stars in an astronomy class. In an essay written for an English composition class, "interesting" could mean a paper that vividly narrates a personal experience.

Don't underestimate your ability to write something other people will enjoy reading. Anyone who has traveled, held a job, or pursued a hobby or who simply enjoys talking with people has gathered experiences that can be developed into intriguing papers. If you write about something you know well or are curious about—even something as simple as observations about students you see on campus every day—other people are likely to find your paper worth reading. However, if you rely on clichés and canned ideas to recycle what most people already know, you'll produce boring work that readers will ignore. It's that simple.

■ **Exercise 1.7** In a small group, debate the merits of the following topic ideas. Which do you think might lead to successful explanatory or exploratory papers directed at an audience of college students? Discuss your conclusions and how you might narrow and develop one of these subjects.

> The metric system
> Heterosexuals and AIDS
> What are family values?
> The role music plays in our culture
> Suicide among teenagers
> Multimillion-dollar contracts in professional sports
> New trends in American cars
> Getting up in the morning
> Campus politics
> The best thing about college
> Space flights to Mars

■ **Exercise 1.8** Write a paragraph or two about some aspect of one of your hobbies that would interest your classmates. You might choose, for instance, new techniques in skiing, the latest developments in virtual reality, or the most recent CD of your favorite singer.

1e HOW DO YOU WRITE FOR AN AUDIENCE?

Troubleshooting

Suppose that you have written for your college classmates an informative paper about the geysers in Yellowstone National Park. Now imagine being asked to modify that piece for an audience of third graders. How would you change the first paper to reach the second audience?

CHECKLIST

Know Your Readers

- What are their values and attitudes?
- What reasons might they have for reading your work?
- How much do they already know about your subject?
- What do they believe about your subject?
- What questions are they likely to have about your subject?
- How best can you inform, persuade, or otherwise appeal to them?

Revise to simplify the structure? Reduce the degree of technical sophistication? Use different examples? Change the vocabulary? Define more terms? Shorten the paper? All of these changes would represent *audience adaptations*.

As the example suggests, you almost always have to adjust your writing to your audience. But first you have to understand who that reading audience will be. Perhaps highlighting the differences between third-grade and college-level readers makes audience recognition and adaptation seem simple. It's not. Even sophisticated writers sometimes misjudge their readers, offering them material they cannot or will not digest. And sometimes writers have to deal with multiple and possibly conflicting audiences: men and women; young, middle-aged, old; fundamentalists and atheists; Democrats and Republicans. Even the typical college paper may be written for two quite different kinds of readers—your classmates and your instructor. So you need to analyze your audience almost every time you write.

To reach your audience . . .

1e-1 **Visualize the people to whom you are writing.** Draw a mental picture of your readers as a group, or perhaps choose one individual who you think typifies that audience. (It may be someone you know.) Keep that group picture or that individual portrait in mind as you write. In this way you'll learn to direct your work to somebody. "Somebody," of course, can be a readership of one person (an instructor), a small group of people (perhaps your classmates), a larger group of people (members of a professional organization to which you belong), or a comprehensive general audience of educated readers such as that reached by a major newsmagazine (*Time* or *Newsweek*).

Occasionally you may want to defer thinking about audience until you get to a second draft. This may be the case with an exploratory es-

A U D I E N C E   W O R K S H E E T

1. Describe the audience specified by the assignment (if any).

2. Whom do I visualize as readers for this paper?	**a.** What is their interest in the topic?
	b. Will they be receptive, neutral, or hostile?
	c. What interests or beliefs do we have in common?
	d. What is important to these readers?
	e. What kind of appeal is likely to move them?
3. What do my readers already know about this topic?	**f.** How familiar are they with the issues and facts?
	g. What new information do they need?
	h. What kinds of details will hold their interest?
	i. How do they probably feel about the issue now?
4. How can I reach my readers?	**j.** What values and concerns should I appeal to?
	k. What kind of opening is likely to appeal to them?
	l. What questions do they hope to have answered?
	m. What tone should I take? How can I be credible?

Strategy: Don't think of this as a fill-in-the-blanks worksheet. Instead, use the questions as prompts for brainstorming and write as much as you can in response to each one. When you do, you'll generate a wealth of material that will help you get started.

say when you need to take some risks with your subject before worrying about what readers may think. For instance, if you are furious about a proposal to raise the tuition at your school, you might blow off steam in the first draft of a guest editorial you're writing for the school paper.

Such angry explosions can get your ideas flowing and make you feel better. Then, in a second version, consider how you can more effectively reach those with the power to prevent the tuition increase. Revise the essay with this audience firmly in mind.

1e–2 **Analyze the characteristics of your readers.** You needn't rely on intuition alone to "psych out" your readers. The required information is fairly straightforward. Obviously, learning to analyze an audience effectively takes time and practice, but mastering the skill is critical to any writer.

To help you think about your readers, we've developed an audience worksheet (see p. 15) that you can apply to many writing situations. All you have to do is answer the questions it poses and record your answers. When you're done, review your responses; you'll find a fairly sharp profile of the readers you must address. If within a single paper you must reach several different audiences, you may have to run through the worksheet more than once to define each audience. Then you'll need to reconcile the differences among those groups as you write the paper—admittedly not an easy task. But at least you'll have a clearer idea of the challenge.

■ **Exercise 1.9** Very briefly analyze what you think your readers would want to know if you were writing

1. A personal statement for a college admissions board
2. A description for the Division of Motor Vehicles of an accident you had
3. A letter disputing a charge on your Visa account
4. An application for financial aid
5. A description of an experiment you carried out in psychology class

---

■ **Exercise 1.10** Write a paragraph describing a time when you had to be unusually sensitive in writing for a particular audience. Why was it so important for you to understand that audience?

■ **Exercise 1.11** Working with another student in your class, select a magazine—some possibilities are *Sports Illustrated, Rolling Stone, Vanity Fair, Harper's, Newsweek, Esquire, Money*—and study the advertisements and the kind of articles it carries. Then draft a description of the kind of people you think the editor and publisher of the magazine assume their readers to be. Use the audience worksheet to guide your work.

1f HOW DO YOU DEFINE YOUR PURPOSE IN WRITING?

Troubleshooting

When you think in large-scale terms about why you're doing a particular piece of writing, it helps to identify a general goal: *to inform, to explain, to entertain,* or *to persuade.* Such focusing helps you set your tone and think about the kinds of support you'll need. But for every writing task, you also need to think in advance about your specific goals. This section helps you to do that.

To determine your purpose in writing . . .

1f-1 State what you hope to accomplish. You will usually write more effectively if you think about your purpose ahead of time and use it to guide your draft. In college courses, for example, a term paper assignment may be designed both to teach you something and to gauge what you've already learned. Those are two subtly different aims, and you'll have to appreciate both of them if your paper is to be a success. Out of school you may be asked to prepare a report or evaluate another employee. In these cases you may need to ponder how the report will be used or why the employee is being judged. These aren't abstract considerations but down-to-earth matters that affect your credibility, job, and colleagues. In short, you need to know why you are writing. And that means being able to state your goals. If you can't, you probably need a clearer explanation of your assignment or task.

Sometimes, of course, especially in exploratory projects, you may not be able to define a purpose until you've explored the topic by writing a draft. That open-endedness is, after all, the whole point of exploring. You ramble a bit in the first draft to find out what you know. But eventually even an exploratory essay must be revised to achieve a purpose satisfactory to both writer and readers.

1f-2 Consider how readers shape your goals. Although we discussed the concept of audience separately in Section 1e, we know from experience that it's difficult to consider either audience or purpose in isolation.

To a great extent, the purpose you have in writing will help define your audience. For example, if you are angry about a proposal to double student parking fees and want to stop it, you have a choice of audiences. If you want direct action, you need to write to the person in charge of such matters, perhaps the university vice president for business affairs. For such a reader your specific purpose in writing would be to make a calm but convincing cause-and-effect argument demonstrating the

PURPOSE WORKSHEET

1. **List any description of purpose in the assignment itself: focus on words such as** *narrate, explain, compare, evaluate,* **or** *argue.*

2. **What type of paper are you writing?**

    a. My paper will **explain, explore,** or **both.**
    b. I will **inform, persuade,** or **entertain** readers, or I will **write expressively.**
    c. My paper will **narrate, describe, define, classify, compare, contrast, evaluate,** etc.

3. **What specific goals do you have for this paper?**

    d. I expect to **report what I already know** or **learn new things.**
    e. I want readers **somewhat interested, seriously concerned,** or **deeply involved.**
    f. I want readers to **respond intellectually, emotionally,** or **both.**
    g. My paper should **affirm, question,** or **alter** the status quo.
    h. I want readers to **agree with, listen to,** or **question** me.

4. **What form do you see this paper taking?**

    i. This paper would work best as a **journal entry, report, research article, news article, essay, editorial, letter, note, memo** (or other suitable form).
    j. Ideally I'd publish this piece in . . .

Use these questions as brainstorming cues to help you generate material.

harmful results of the increased fees: hardships for commuting students, reduced enrollment, and so on. If, however, you want to get other students to join you in a protest and try to get the fee reduced that way, you could write an editorial for the student paper.

1f–3 **Consider the various purposes of your paper.** The purpose worksheet on page 18 can remind you of some goals at which a paper might aim. Respond to the questions in the first column by selecting choices from the second column or by generating choices of your own. (Not every question applies to every potential situation; skip any items that don't fit.)

■ **Exercise 1.12** What purpose might you have in each of the following writing situations? Think about the impression you want to make as well as the immediate goal for the writing.

1. An autobiographical sketch to accompany an application for admission to college
2. An ad to sell your car, motorcycle, or stereo
3. A letter to your college president to protest poor security on campus at night
4. A report for the supervisor at your job
5. A note to a former teacher asking for a letter of recommendation

■ **Exercise 1.13** Write a sentence or two about the audience and purpose of each of the following writing situations. (Use the audience and purpose worksheets to stimulate your thinking.)

1. You write a fund-raising letter to local businesspeople, asking them to give money to a charitable project you're interested in—for example, Recordings for the Blind, adult literacy, Big Brothers and Sisters, or a center for battered women.
2. You write a letter to one of your college instructors, asking for an interview to discuss the *D* you received from that person in summer school.
3. You write to an agency that grants funds for overseas study to students, asking that it finance a year abroad for you.
4. You write to a vacationing roommate to explain how his or her almost-new Miata (the one you borrowed) wound up at the bottom of a lake.

WINDOW ON WRITING: Audience and Purpose

Occasionally an instructor may ask you to write a brief statement explaining the audience and purpose of a paper you are writing. Two such statements follow. The first statement—by Hoang Nguyen—describes the audience and purpose of the paper shown in draft and final versions in Chapters 3 and 4.

Hoang Nguyen, Little Dragon in the

Land of the Free

I especially want my paper to reach young adults from Vietnam who have recently arrived in America. I am assuming that they have learned enough English to read and write. However, they are having difficulties making a psychological adjustment to American schools. I want to let them know that they are not alone. I also want to tell them that at first things may be rough, but if they are willing to examine the cultural differences and appreciate them for what they are, they will be enriched by the knowledge they will gain. I do not know of any publication that caters to such students. I do know that the Vietnamese Students Association here on campus publishes an annual magazine. The magazine is distributed throughout the state wherever there is a large Vietnamese community. Perhaps my article can find a home in that magazine.

Brandy Parsons, Vegetarianism:

Healthy or Limiting?

My purpose is to explore the pros and cons of vegetarianism, emphasizing the pros and citing the harmful consequences of eating meat. I will argue that vegetarianism, if practiced properly, is a healthy way of life. In discussing the vegetarian life-style, I will classify three types of vegetarians.

My audience will be the readers of a monthly health and fitness magazine called <u>American Health</u>. This magazine targets many groups in our society, including fitness-minded professionals, intellectuals, and health-conscious senior citizens. It is likely that my readers will have preconceived notions of vegetarianism. But the readers of <u>American Health</u> are also likely to be interested in learning about the advantages of vegetarianism. Questions my readers are likely to have: What do vegetarians eat? Can vegetarians be as well nourished or better nourished than meat-eaters? Why would a person be a vegetarian?

2

How Do You Prepare and Plan to Write?

A Finding a Topic

B Focusing a Topic

C Constructing a Thesis Statement

D Exploring a Thesis

E Organizing a Paper

F Outlining a Paper

G Choosing a Title

2a HOW DO YOU FIND A TOPIC?

PROCESS MENU

PREPARING
PLANNING
DRAFTING
INCUBATING
REVISING
EDITING
PROOFREADING

Troubleshooting

Sometimes an instructor may give you a specific topic, define its limits, and explain clearly what you need to do. In such instances you don't have to find your topic, so you can begin immediately to generate material, plan your paper, and draft it.

Often, however, instructors encourage students to choose their own topics, believing that most people work better when writing on topics that interest them. "Being able to choose is fine," you may say, "but how do I find a good topic, one that will interest both me and my readers?"

To find a stimulating topic . . .

2a–1 **Brainstorm the possibilities.** When you have to invest as much energy in a task as you do in writing a paper, be good to yourself. Choose a topic you'll enjoy, one that won't bore you. If possible, select one on which you already have some ideas and information. Begin by listing some broad possibilities that sound interesting. Here's a sample list.

College basketball scandals	Teenage pregnancy
Campus politics	Drinking among first-year
TV programs for children	college students
Cowboy folklore	Computers in music
Rhythm and blues	Professional athletics
Programs for the homeless	Special effects in movies
Credit card theft	Women marathon runners
Images of women in advertising	Fraud in welfare programs

After you've made such a list, run through it quickly to reject topics that seem too broad or on which material might be scarce. For instance, "teenage pregnancy" and "professional athletics" are much too broad for a three- to five-page paper. "Computers in music" might be too technical or require more research than you have time for. Focus instead on two or three that can be narrowed and seem manageable. At this point, it's often helpful to talk with other students; they may see possible angles that haven't occurred to you or point out some problems you don't anticipate.

2a–2 **Assess your interests and strengths.** Too often students think that they should be writing about what Janis Joplin called "subjects of great social and political import." Does this list of topics look familiar?

Capital punishment	Abortion
Legalizing drugs	Criminal justice system
Mercy killing	Child abuse

If you are passionate about one of these subjects and willing to do the research that will enable you to write something fresh and informative about the issues, you may, with help, be able to produce a good paper, but you risk getting bogged down in generalities and clichés almost immediately. You're not likely to impress your instructors by your show of social conscience—in fact, they've probably had their fill of inauthentic topics. Instead write about a subject that will allow you to show your strengths and your special interests. Here are three prompts to lead you toward more honest subjects when you're given the liberty to choose.

CHECKLIST

To Find a Topic, Ask Yourself . . .

- **What three subjects do I enjoy reading about most?** What magazines do you pick up? In what kinds of books do you browse? What sections of the newspaper do you read first?
- **What three subjects do I know the most about?** What subjects could you lecture on for half an hour without notes? About what subjects or problems do people seek your advice or expertise? What could you teach someone else to do?
- **What three subjects do I enjoy arguing about most?** On what subjects can you hold your own with just about anyone? What subjects do friends connect you with? For what causes would you volunteer your time?

2a-3 **Freewrite about the assignment.** Even when you are free to choose the topic for a paper, an instructor will often suggest a subject area. Perhaps you are expected to write a paper about the French Revolution or the American judiciary. In such a case you might try freewriting, that is, writing nonstop on a subject area for ten or fifteen minutes, exploring what you know or would like to learn about it. Just putting words down on the page in this way may remind you of things you have heard or ideas you have always associated with the subject.

Freewriting on that assignment on the French Revolution might provoke you to recall stories about the "Reign of Terror." Or maybe your paragraph leads you to wonder what—if anything—Napoleon Bonaparte was doing during the early stages of the revolution. The point of the freewriting is to unshackle your thinking, so continue to write as long as ideas come, and don't cross out or reject anything prematurely. But be alert for the stimulating concept that can move you from topic area to specific topic.

2a-4 **Browse in the library.** If you have a general topic area to explore, you can find all sorts of suggestions in the library. Look up the subject on the Internet, in the card catalog, in the on-line catalog, or in the directory of the Library of Congress (better known as the *Subject List*). Just the way a broad subject is broken down into headings and subheadings should suggest many possibilities for topics. Consult encyclopedias too. A general article on civil rights, Greece, or the ocean may contain hundreds of subject possibilities.

Even when you don't have a general subject area to direct your library search, you could do worse than to browse in the periodicals room or new book section to find topics.

2a–5 **Use a computer to find ideas.** A computer makes freewriting for a topic especially easy, even for the less-than-expert typist. If you already have a topic, begin the freewriting by placing that topic idea at the top of the screen, boldfacing or underlining it for emphasis. If you are freewriting to find a topic, just start typing words onto the screen. Hammer away nonstop at the keyboard for a predetermined length of time. Don't worry about misspellings, missed letters, or faulty grammar. The freewriting is between you and the computer.

Some people find that they freewrite with less inhibition if they turn down the screen brightness until the text becomes invisible. Turning up the screen at the end of the time limit may thus reveal surprising ideas, interesting themes, or significant repetition. Print out your freewriting and underline any such discoveries.

Many campus writing centers or writing labs also have software programs designed to help you brainstorm a subject for a paper. Some programs ask a series of probing questions. Others help you to outline or free-associate. All can be valuable.

■ **Exercise 2.1** Let each member of a small writing group answer these three questions.

1. What three subjects do I enjoy reading about most?
2. What three subjects do I know the most about?
3. What three subjects do I enjoy arguing about most?

Then trade your answers and discuss the range of interests and expertise in your group. What subjects might members of the group write about with authority?

2b HOW DO YOU FOCUS A TOPIC?

Troubleshooting

Once you have found a topic to write on, you usually have to narrow it down. If you don't focus your efforts, you may wind up writing a superficial paper of little interest to anyone, no matter how promising your initial subject seems to be. You may even have read professional articles that seem out of focus. Their titles promise exciting information ("New Discoveries in Astronomy"; "How to Win a Scholarship"), but the pieces themselves deliver few new facts or ideas. The problem of focus is common in college papers, in which students often try to do too much be-cause they are afraid of having too little to say. The result can be papers long on platitudes but short on lively details.

To focus your topic . . .

2b–1 **Don't try to tell everything you know.** You may dearly love your subject and look forward to learning much more about it. But remember that your time to develop a paper is usually going to be limited. You won't have the chance to discover all there is to know, for example, about Civil War military tactics. Better narrow your research to some-thing more manageable, perhaps naval strategy in the war. Better yet, fo-cus on tactics in the battle between the first ironclad ships, the *Monitor* and the *Merrimac*.

Does that kind of topic reduction seem too severe? It's probably not, especially when you consider that any paper you write should con-tain only a portion of what you have learned about the subject treated in it. To write an authoritative piece, you have to select your materials carefully, not just include everything you've read. So for obvious reasons it makes better sense to commit yourself to a smaller project. In other words, learn to write more about less.

2b–2 **Highlight a single portion of your topic.** Think about narrow-ing your topic in the same way that you think about focusing a flashlight. If you adjust the beam to its broadest range, you will throw diffused light over a large territory but will not be able to see details. If you want to see the details, you will have to narrow the focus of your light and concen-trate its beam on a small area. You can reduce a writing topic in the same way. For example:

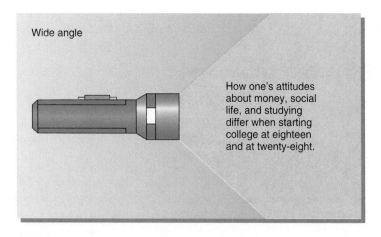

Wide angle

How one's attitudes about money, social life, and studying differ when starting college at eighteen and at twenty-eight.

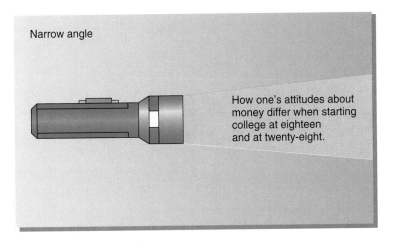

Narrow angle

How one's attitudes about money differ when starting college at eighteen and at twenty-eight.

2b-3 **Tree down your topic.** Another way to narrow a topic to manageable size is to draw diagrams that "tree it down." To do this make a chart on which you divide and subdivide the topic into smaller and smaller parts, each of which branches out like an inverted tree. The upside-down tree helps you see how many ideas you can generate under each division and what the relationships between different aspects of a topic are. You can choose to develop the branch that seems to offer the most promising material. For example:

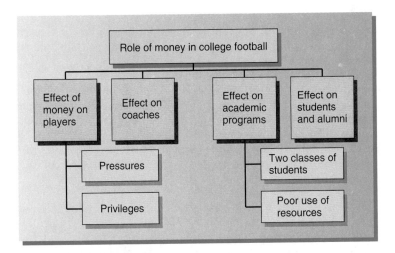

After you select the most promising branch from your first diagram, you tree it down a second time to refine your thinking. For example:

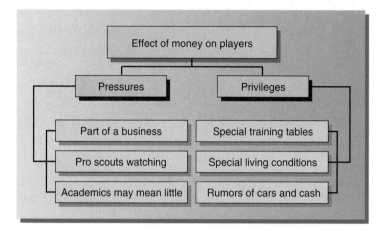

2b-4 **Cluster.** Another way to narrow a topic is to look within the subject for patterns that might represent ideas worth exploring. Clustering is easy and even fun. In the middle of a blank sheet of paper write down a word or a phrase that represents your general subject. Circle that word—say, *football*—and then, for about ten minutes, attach every word you can think of either to that original term or to any that you attach to it. Circle all those additional words as you write them and draw lines connecting them to the words that triggered them. It's important not to think much about the words you are putting down. Clustering is an exercise in free association: you want to see what your mind comes up with. Your finished cluster might look something like the one on page 29, though it will probably be fuller and more complex if you work for the entire ten minutes.

When you're done, examine the sheet to see whether any clusters of words suggest topics you might develop. For example, one of our football clusters (fans-cold-blankets-beer) suggests a paper about what goes on in the grandstands during a game. A second cluster (college-players-money) might lead into a paper on National Collegiate Athletic Association recruiting violations. What you can do with any idea you spy in a first clustering is to make that concept the focal point of a second exercise, focusing on the narrowed subject to develop more ideas.

2b-5 **Talk to your friends about your topic.** You'll be surprised at how productive a simple conversation about your topic can be. Tell classmates what you are interested in and let them ask questions and make suggestions. Be sure to keep notes. If you can't find someone to talk to about your paper, talk into a tape recorder, explaining your ideas as you would to a friend. You'll find the very act of talking out loud, even to

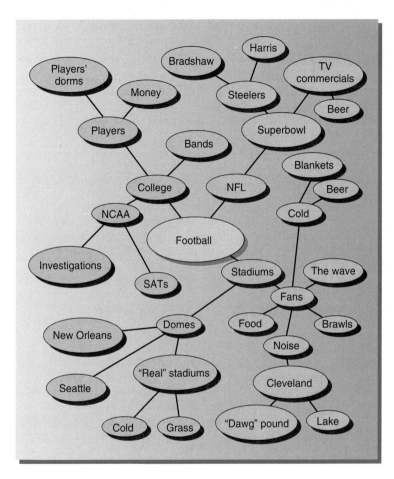

yourself, will help you appreciate the need to find a focal point for your paper.

■ **Exercise 2.2** Working in a group, everyone write down several subtopics that might be extracted from one of these broad topics.

Gun control
College basketball
Cable television
Multiculturalism
Religion in America

Then compare your subtopics and decide which are still too broad and which are narrow enough to be turned into effective papers.

■ **Exercise 2.3** Working with two or three other classmates, draw tree diagrams for two broad topics, such as public education or contemporary films. Look back at the examples on pages 27 and 28 to help you get started. In discussion decide which branches of each topic look like good possibilities for writing.

● **Tip**

After writing a first draft, especially of an exploratory paper, you may find that your topic is still broader than you thought it would be. You see a need to narrow and focus it even more. Fine. Do it. You can re-focus a paper at any point in the writing process. ●

2c HOW DO YOU CONSTRUCT A THESIS STATEMENT?

Troubleshooting

A thesis in an essay is a sentence that explicitly identifies the point of the paper or previews its main ideas. Many writers like to construct thesis statements early in the composing process and then use them as one of their major organizational tools. That's because a thesis commits writers to specific ideas and shifts developing papers from soft to hard focus. By keeping a tentative thesis statement in mind as a paper progresses, you can be sure of covering all the important points. In explanatory papers, thesis statements are especially evident because they provide clear directions to readers. A thesis statement can also be useful when you are planning an exploratory paper because it helps you hold key points in mind, even when you aren't sure how they'll evolve.

To produce an effective thesis . . .

2c–1 **Make a strong point.** A thesis statement is more than just an observation; it is a statement that might be questioned or challenged.

> **Observation**   Lawns in many suburbs are green all year.
>
> **Thesis**   People are poisoning the environment with chemicals just to keep their lawns green.

Examine any thesis you compose and ask: Does this thesis provoke reactions? Could someone legitimately disagree with it? If not, change it to say something that sparks interest or raises expectations. Take a stand.

Not A youngster who has a computer at home has many educational advantages.
That's obvious but too vague to be helpful.

But Increasingly, elementary school teachers are concerned about the growing gap between youngsters who have computers at home and can enjoy math games and reading programs and those whose parents cannot afford such advantages for their children.

2c-2 **Preview the direction your paper will take.** Write a complete sentence (not a phrase, not a fragment) that explains in some detail what you expect to write about. While writing a paper, you'll probably revise a thesis several times to make it more precise. The final version should be *succinct* but *comprehensive*—that is, it should indicate the major points you want to make in your paper. Here is a thesis sentence with both of these qualities.

Sixteen-year-olds seeking that first part-time or summer job need to think beyond hourly wages and congenial working companions and look for jobs where they could learn something about a profession—for instance, as a runner at a law firm, a clerk in a hospital, or a gofer on a construction job.

The thesis could use some polishing, but a writer who built a paper on it would have a tight and easy-to-follow piece. Here are two examples of weak thesis statements revised into stronger ones.

Not Today's college students look different from those of twenty-five years ago.
Probably true, but what's the point?

But When I look at a snapshot of my parents and their friends when they were in college twenty-five years ago, I think that the difference in their clothes and ours today reflects more than a difference in taste; it also reflects how students' values have changed since that time.

Not In many small towns, everyone is obsessed with football.
Interesting observation, but what are the implications?

But In many small towns such as my own, students, parents, and townspeople are obsessed with football to the point that students interested in other school activities, such as debate, the school paper, science fairs, and sports like tennis, are made to feel like cultural dropouts.

Notice that both of the stronger thesis statements are more specific than their originals.

2c–3 **Be sure your point is worth making.** Ask yourself whether an intelligent member of your audience might respond to your thesis with a hostile "So what's your point?" or a disappointed "Big deal!" If he or she might, look for a more significant idea or sharpen the point you intend to make.

Not Phillis Wheatley was an African-American poet of the eighteenth century.
What's your point?

But Brought to Boston as a slave in 1761, Phillis Wheatley would become the first black woman in America recognized for her poetry.

Not Today's professional athletes have set new records.
A well-known fact—what's interesting about it?

But To understand why the peak performance of today's professional athletes is so superior to that of athletes fifty years ago, one has to consider multiple factors: training, nutrition, coaching, and the huge salaries earned by today's stars.

2c–4 **Place your thesis sensibly.** Don't assume that your thesis must be the first sentence of your paper, although it can be. Often you need to guide readers to your thesis idea, explaining why the assertion you intend to make is important. Or sometimes you must provide a context for your thesis, defining key terms or giving background information. That's why thesis statements often appear at the end of introductory paragraphs.

WINDOW ON WRITING: A Thesis in Context

Sometimes a thesis statement pulled out of context can sound rather dull. Consider this one: *There are many good reasons for adopting a vegetarian life-style*. Standing alone, the assertion is as bland as broccoli. Fortunately, in practice a thesis isn't solely responsible for shaping a reader's initial response to a paper. The sentences that precede it in an introductory paragraph (or section) can play an important part. Here's the opening paragraph that introduces the thesis above. Notice how it sets the relatively bland statement into a bolder context.

```
The word "vegetarian" evokes certain images from

most people. Some folks view vegetarians as fanatical

animal rights activists who hang out at health food
```

```
stores and distribute leaflets promoting fruit-

worshiping religions. Or they imagine Gandhi-like

characters who live to be one hundred by sipping

carrot juice and eating turnip greens every day.

Despite its eccentric image, vegetarianism is

becoming increasingly praised by nutritionists and

more widely accepted by mainstream society. After

all, there are many good reasons for adopting a

vegetarian life-style.
```

■ **Exercise 2.4** Review the guidelines for an effective thesis sentence; then rank the following thesis statements as "good," "not too bad," and "hopeless."

1. In trying to promote meaningful campaign finance reform, organizations like Common Cause run into formidable opposition from lobbyists, major companies, television and newspapers, and, most of all, the candidates themselves.
2. Sneakers are often a major status symbol among youth gangs.
3. The Disney film *The Lion King* was hugely profitable.
4. When students in their thirties return to the college classroom after having been in the work force several years, they sometimes feel inadequate, but they actually enrich the classroom with their wealth of experience.
5. Many drivers seem to think of traffic rules as guidelines.

2d HOW DO YOU EXPLORE AND DEVELOP A THESIS?

Troubleshooting

When you finally have your topic and thesis, what's the next step? It's finding supporting ideas and details. Since classical times rhetoricians have looked for ways to stimulate thinking, even coming up with the term *invention* to describe methods for generating subject matter. This section describes a number of invention techniques.

Remember that you can use any of the invention techniques at any time in the writing process. Although it's logical to review them before starting a draft, you may want to return to them while writing or even when revising—in short, anytime you need to expand your essay.

To explore and develop a topic . . .

2d–1 **Brainstorm your topic either in a group or by yourself.** Write your thesis at the top of the paper or on the screen and then jot down any words, phrases, or ideas that come immediately to mind. Don't stop to evaluate these points or worry that you're repeating yourself—just get them down. Accept all possibilities and let one suggestion trigger another. In this exercise you aren't looking for complete concepts or orderly sequences of ideas. You simply want to examine your subject from as many perspectives as you can.

When the ideas have stopped flowing, you can begin sorting them. Group the ideas into appropriate categories. Look for major points and minor ones. When you see logical divisions and headings, underline them. Fill out any incomplete sequences you detect. Look especially for ideas that are opposites or that might be grouped in some other way.

2d–2 **Use the journalist's questions.** Beginning journalists are taught to keep six questions in mind when writing a news story.

Who?	What?	Where?
When?	Why?	How?

Simple as they may seem, these questions can help you be sure you have covered all the bases, especially when you are writing an informative paper. Obviously not every question will apply to every topic.

2d–3 **Write a zero draft.** You may find that your best device for generating material is just to start writing. The very act of writing, of seeing words on paper or the screen, will often get the creative juices flowing and help you to come up with ideas and make connections that you hadn't thought of before. Think of this first try as a "zero draft," a trial run that doesn't really count. Zero drafts are easy to write, yet they can suggest all sorts of possibilities.

2d–4 **Look at your subject from different perspectives.** One way of doing that is to consider the patterns people traditionally use to organize ideas. Among the most familiar are description, narration, process, classification, definition, cause and effect, comparison and contrast, and testimony. Each of these patterns represents a way of looking at a subject. Each suggests questions that can help you generate ideas.

Here, for example, are ways a writer might use these patterns to find material for a paper on some aspect of the modern American family.

- **Description:** Describe three generations of the same family and show how their living patterns have changed through those generations.

- **Narration:** Tell stories to illustrate certain points about modern American families. (A dramatic anecdote can be a good attention-getting opening for a paper.)

- **Process:** Show some process that seems to typify a modern American family—for instance, the pandemonium of everyone leaving for work and school in the morning.

- **Classification:** Create a system for classifying some typical kinds of modern American families: stepfamilies, two-working-parent families, traditional one-working-parent families, single-parent families, and so on.

- **Definition:** List important traits that characterize the modern American family—more educated, more family members working, more dependent on day care, fewer children, fewer live-in relatives, and so on.

- **Cause and Effect:** Speculate about forces that have created the modern American family or changed it from the typical family of fifty years ago.

- **Comparison and Contrast:** Compare two categories of modern American families—rural versus urban, single-parent versus two-parent, employed mother versus homemaker, poor versus affluent. You could also compare families from different American cultures: Asian-American, Italian-American, African-American, and so on.

- **Testimony:** Use case studies of the type of modern American family you are most familiar with to illustrate your points.

2d-5 **Try reading.** No one said you have to come up with ideas on your own. Get to the library, look up your subject, and read. (You'll find detailed instructions for finding information on any academic topic in Section 32b.) But reading isn't just to find facts. You can examine books and magazines to discover how other writers have treated subjects like yours. Perhaps you want to write about a railroad trip you took across the American Southwest. Look in the library (or the bookstore) for travel literature. Your eyes may be opened by the sheer variety of approaches available to record your adventures, everything from a serious day-by-day journal to a rollicking narrative. The same might be true if you are asked to review a book or a movie. Seeing how others have reviewed works will suggest possibilities for your own review.

2d–6 **Talk with colleagues about your topic.** In many writing classes the instructor arranges for groups of students to meet before they start work on a writing assignment so they can help each other to generate ideas. If so, take advantage of the opportunity. You'll find that as you start to explain your topic to others, more and more ideas will come to you. You'll quickly see aspects you hadn't considered, particularly any weaknesses if you are developing an argument. You'll also think of new examples and sources.

2d–7 **Return to the computer.** Many college writing labs are equipped with fairly sophisticated invention programs that walk you through a topic by asking numerous questions about it, recording your replies, and then presenting them to you as stimuli for composing. These programs may be open-ended or tailored to support a specific kind of writing. Depending on the program, you may be asked to list a series of events, to supply information, or to find arguments in support of an idea. When you exit an invention program, it's often with a printout full of good ideas for a paper, usually arranged in some logical order. The moral is simple: If you have access to invention software, give it a try.

If commercial invention software isn't available, make your own. A helpful prompt can be no more complicated than the list of journalist's questions discussed in Section 2d–2: *Who? What? Where? When? Why? How?* To use them as an invention program, simply create a file named *Journ?* (or something similar) containing just these questions. Then, whenever you are writing an explanatory paper (the kind most appropriately controlled by these questions), copy the brief contents of the file into the document at its beginning. If you have a split-screen feature, keep the questions visible at the top of the monitor while you compose on the remainder of the screen. The journalist's questions will remind you to supply all the needed facts.

A slightly different list of questions may help you keep ideas on track.

- What is my purpose in writing?
- For whom am I writing this?
- What is my key point or assertion?
- What is my evidence? (This is particularly important.)

Again, you can create a simple file to store these questions and then transfer them into whatever document you are creating.

■ **Exercise 2.5** Examine an article from the front section of your local paper to see how many of the journalist's questions it satisfies (see Section 2d–2). Then apply the same questions to a different kind of short piece, perhaps a feature story in the same paper or an article in a periodical. Do both articles show the same interest in recording facts and information?

■ **Exercise 2.6** The journalist's questions *why* and *how* work particularly well with exploratory assignments that are reflective and loosely structured. Think of some serious problem in your college or in your community—perhaps drug use or an unusually high high school dropout rate—and draft an introductory paragraph on *why* the problem exists and a concluding paragraph on *how* it might be handled.

■ **Exercise 2.7** Choose three of the thought patterns described in Section 2d–4 and write three short paragraphs in which you apply them to one of your hobbies or sports interests: skiing, sports cars, soap operas, hockey, dancing, stamp collecting, photography, and so on.

2e HOW DO YOU ORGANIZE A PAPER?

PROCESS MENU

PREPARING
PLANNING
DRAFTING
INCUBATING
REVISING
EDITING
PROOFREADING

Troubleshooting

No matter how good your ideas are, most readers will not have the patience to read your paper unless it is well organized. If you don't make the effort to organize a paper, your readers will get lost and blame you for the confusion. So don't think that good organization is optional; rather, it is the foundation of a college paper.

You're likely to need a specific plan when you are doing explanatory writing to get your material under control and to arrange it clearly for readers. But you also need at least a tentative plan when you start doing exploratory writing. A plan gives reflective or personal pieces a sense of direction.

It is true that many good writers never consciously select a design before writing a paper. They know intuitively what events they want a story to contain or what order the information in a report should follow. Still, understanding the options available when you organize a paper can help you. Some of the basic patterns in college writing are discussed below, arranged from the simpler ones to the more complex.

To organize a paper . . .

2e-1   **Consider an introduction/body/conclusion structure.** You begin by telling your readers clearly and simply what topics a paper will cover. You follow with examples and explanations that support and develop your claim. You finish with a section that ties your points together and leaves your readers with a sense of closure. Lawyers, scientists, and writers in many academic fields especially favor this design because it suggests a logical movement from statement to proof. Many professors will expect to find this pattern in your responses to essay examination questions and in your college papers.

Yet another way of describing this basic structure is to call it a commitment and response pattern. That's because in the first section of the paper a writer promises to cover certain issues or address particular questions. The opening commitment can be direct or indirect. In a *direct commitment*, the writer addresses an issue squarely, almost as if making an announcement.

> While it is possible that syphilis was brought to Europe by Christopher Columbus on his return from the Americas, it is just as likely that the disease had infected the Old World as early as biblical or Roman times.

Such an opening obliges the writer, then, to cover every point mentioned. Another kind of direct commitment can take the form of a provocative question.

> Why are students once again facing a registration period when all required courses are full, all interesting courses have impossible prerequisites, and most advisers seem unable to answer even the most elementary of questions?

A commitment can also be made *indirectly*, by narrating an anecdote or an incident.

> Did you leave fall registration today with a rearranged schedule because two of the courses you planned to take had been canceled? Did you find that all the courses you wanted had prerequisites that you can't meet because all the prerequisite courses are filled? When you got to your first class, did you find standing room only? If so, welcome to the biggest club on campus.

Through this indirect commitment, the writer has clearly indicated without ever actually saying so that the subject of his paper will be registration problems.

Papers that result from a variation of the introduction/body/conclusion pattern will usually take a simple shape.

| Introduction: Thesis |
| Argument 1 + |
| examples/ |
| illustrations |
| Argument 2 + |
| examples/ |
| illustrations |
| Conclusion |

But even such papers can include significant digressions and variations. When you make a point or support an argument, you must usually deal with the opposing arguments; if you don't address them, the paper will seem to evade key questions. Counterarguments inevitably make the structure of the paper more complex. They can be addressed immediately, near the beginning of the paper, or they can be dealt with as they arise in the body of the piece. But don't end with a counterargument. Here's what the "basic model" might look like when counterarguments are added to the mix.

| Introduction: Thesis |
| Argument 1 + |
| examples/ |
| illustrations |
| Counterargument 1 |
| Argument 2 + |
| examples/ |
| illustrations |
| Counterargument 2 |
| Argument 3 + |
| examples/ |
| illustrations |
| Conclusion |

This pattern—or any of its numerous variations—works especially well for essay exams, advanced placement exams, or any other impromptu writing when you have to organize your ideas quickly. It's easy to outline and readily expandable.

2e-2 **Consider a narrative or a process design.** When you narrate a story, you usually describe events in the order they occurred. The structure can be quite straightforward.

| Introduction |
| Event 1 |
| Event 2 |
| Event 3 |
| Event 4 . . . |

For instance, for an astronomy course you might want to narrate the discovery of pulsar stars, beginning with the scientists at Bell Laboratories who thought that they were receiving messages from extraterrestrial beings when they first intercepted radio signals from pulsars. A narrative can also be more complicated—for instance, moving back in time as a movie does with flashbacks.

A process pattern is essentially the same as a narrative one, only instead of telling a story, you are explaining how something works. You list and describe each step in the process.

| Introduction |
| Step 1 |
| Step 2 |
| Step 3 |
| Step 4 . . . |

Be careful to include all the necessary steps in the proper order. You can find good examples of process patterns in instructional and technical manuals.

2e-3 **Consider a comparison and contrast structure.** In many kinds of papers you will have to examine different objects or ideas in relation to each other, especially when evaluating or arguing. In organizing such papers you can use one of two basic plans, either describing the things you are comparing one at a time (subject by subject) or describing them in an alternating sequence (feature by feature). These models and some sample outlines follow.

SUBJECT BY SUBJECT

| Introduction: Thesis |
| Subject #1 examined |
| Feature A |
| Feature B |
| Feature C . . . |
| Subject #2 examined |
| Feature A |
| Feature B |
| Feature C . . . |
| Conclusion |

SUBJECT BY SUBJECT

   I. Viewing wildlife in Africa differs from observing it in India.
  II. Subject 1. Viewing Wildlife in Africa
  A. *Feature A (Quantity)* Game in Africa is abundant and easy to spot.
  B. *Feature B (Variety)* Africa offers a greater variety of wildlife: zebras, lions, baboons.
  C. *Feature C (Mode of Viewing)* Wildlife in Africa is best viewed from Land Rovers with the help of expert guides.
 III. Subject 2. Viewing Wildlife in India
  A. *Feature A (Quantity)* Wildlife in India is sometimes difficult to see.
  B. *Feature B (Variety)* India offers some distinctive animals, notably the tiger and the Indian rhino.
  C. *Feature C (Mode of Viewing)* Wildlife in India is best viewed from the backs of elephants or from behind blinds.
  IV. Expect different rewards when viewing wildlife in Africa and India.

FEATURE BY FEATURE

| Introduction: Thesis |
| Feature A |
| In subject 1 |
| In subject 2 |

| Feature B |
| In subject 1 |
| In subject 2 |
| Feature C |
| In subject 1 |
| In subject 2 |
| Conclusion |

FEATURE BY FEATURE

I. Viewing wildlife in Africa differs from observing animals in India.

II. *Feature A (Quantity)* Africa and India differ in quantity of wildlife.
   A. *Subject A (Africa)* The abundant wildlife in Africa is easy to spot.
   B. *Subject B (India)* The scarcer wildlife in India is sometimes difficult to see.

III. *Feature B (Variety)* Africa and India differ in the variety of animals that can be viewed.
   A. *Subject A (Africa)* Africa offers a greater variety of game: zebras, lions, baboons.
   B. *Subject B (India)* India offers some distinctive animals, notably the tiger and the Indian rhino.

IV. *Feature C (Mode of Viewing)* Africa and India differ in the best method for seeing wildlife.
   A. *Subject A (Africa)* Wildlife in Africa is best viewed from Land Rovers with the help of expert guides.
   B. *Subject B (India)* Wildlife in India is best viewed from the backs of elephants or from behind blinds.

V. Expect different rewards when viewing wildlife in Africa and India.

The subject-by-subject plan probably works best in short papers involving only a few comparisons; in such pieces readers don't have to recall a large quantity of information to make the necessary comparisons. When you're doing a longer paper, however, use the feature-by-feature pattern; otherwise your readers have to keep too much information in mind. They'll lose track of the features being compared.

2e-4 **Consider a division or classification structure.** These two ways of organizing a paper are quite different, though both involve creating categories to make material more manageable. A paper organized according to the principle of division simply breaks a topic into its various components—its separate parts. A paper on the solar system might devote a paragraph to each planet; a paper on sports cars might describe their various major aspects in an order that seems appropriate.

Introduction: Sports cars
Feature 1 Engines and drivetrains
Feature 2 Suspensions
Feature 3 Interior accommodations
Feature 4 Exterior styling
Conclusion

Organizing a paper by division is a simple matter.

Classification involves breaking a large item into categories according to some consistent and useful principle of division. Classification must follow rules that don't apply to division. First, classifications must be *exhaustive*: every member of the class must fit into a category. A classification of the planets might divide those that have significant moons from those that do not; obviously all of the nine planets fall into one of these classes.

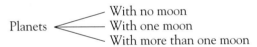

Any principle of division you use must also be consistent. You can't classify by more than one principle at a time. You are listing, not classifying, if you decide to divide planets this way.

Finally, classes must not overlap. That means you should be able to place an object in only one category.

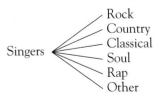

Yet most systems of classification break down at one point or another, like the one above. What do you do with singers—such as Linda Ronstadt or Johnny Cash—who sing more than one kind of song? Well, you can create yet another class (country-rock) or classify by the singer's major body of work. But you probably won't be able to eliminate all objections to your classification.

2e-5 **Consider a cause-and-effect design.** Such a design is appropriate when you write a paper explaining why something has happened. The typical cause-and-effect paper moves from an explanation of some existing condition to an examination of its particular causes. In other words, you see what has happened and want to know why.

Effects →	**Causes?**
Acid rain	Burning fossil fuels
Good grades	Studying, reading

Typically you'll look for more than one explanation for any given event, so the structure of a cause-and-effect paper may include an examination of various causes, from the most distant to the most immediate or from the least likely to the most plausible.

Effects(s)
↓
Cause 1: Most obvious
Cause 2:
Cause 3:
Cause 4: Least obvious, deepest

You can start your essay by identifying an effect and then go on to hypothesize about the causes, or you can start by listing a number of events or facts and then show how they cause a certain effect.

Here's what the cause-and-effect pattern might look like applied to a particular topic.

Effect: In the fourth century B.C., the art of rhetoric established itself as a major subject for study in Greece.

Cause 1: The rise of democracy in Greece made public speaking and persuasion important.

Cause 2: Political power depended on being a good speaker.

Cause 3: Legal disputes were settled in public forums where citizens had to serve as their own lawyers.

2e-6 **Consider a problem-and-solution pattern.** You can use this pattern effectively for papers in which you argue for change or propose an idea to settle a problem.

The problem—need for a solution

Possible solutions (rejected)

Alternative 1

Advantages/

Disadvantages

Alternative 2

Advantages/

Disadvantages

The proposed solution

Feasibility of solution

Disadvantages

Advantages

Implementation

The first part of the pattern says, "We've got a problem and we've got to solve it—now." Here's how one student began a problem-and-solution essay.

In *The Atlantic Monthly* for May 1994, a prominent black sociologist says that a combination of forces in the inner city promotes an "etiquette of violence" in which self-respect too often comes from being willing to kill or be killed over seemingly minor incidents.

The nature of the problem is evident from just this single sentence.

The second part of the exploratory pattern steers the reader through various proposals for solving the problem. Since most of these ideas will be rejected (or furnish only part of the recommended solution), the advantages and limitations of each one are examined carefully. This section of the exploratory essay assures readers that no plausible approach to the problem has been ignored.

In the third part of this pattern you propose some solution to the problem. You may then want to discuss the disadvantages and advantages of this proposal, highlighting the advantages. Readers need to feel that nothing is under wraps and that no hidden agendas guide your proposal. The paper can then conclude by explaining how the change can be put into place.

■ **Exercise 2.8** Working with two or three other students, consider what patterns you might use for writing about two of the topics given below. Give reasons why you think those patterns would work well in each case.

Choosing a stereo system   The future of cable TV
   for your car   Choosing your college major
The popularity of violent movies   Life as a single-parent
Movie stars of the 1990s   student

2f   HOW DO YOU OUTLINE A PAPER?

Troubleshooting

No question about it, an outline can help you keep a paper on track, whether you are following one of the patterns examined in Section 2e or one of your own. But a blueprint for your essay doesn't have to be a full-sentence outline. You can choose from among a number of simpler but equally effective organizational devices, including the working list and the scratch outline. Be sure, however, to follow any instructions on outlining given by your instructors.

You should also be aware that powerful outlining programs are now often available on personal computers. Such programs enable you to write, revise, expand, contract, and rearrange your ideas in outline form quickly and easily. Some programs even work directly within word-processing programs, thus enabling you to plan, write, and revise all on the same screen. Computerized outlining programs combine the organizational power of the traditional outline with the flexibility of less rigid planning strategies.

To outline a paper . . .

2f–1   **Try a working list.** The working list is the most open-ended and flexible of all organizational devices. You start one simply by jotting down the key points you want to make, leaving plenty of room under each major idea. Here are major headings you might use for an exploratory paper titled "What's Happening to Family Dinner?"

- Eating patterns today
- Effects of changed eating patterns on parents
- Effects of changed eating patterns on children

Working from a brainstorming list or perhaps notes from freewriting on the subject, you select subpoints to fit under these major headings.

- **Eating patterns today**
  - Fewer meals together
  - More people work
  - People work longer hours
  - Different schedules
  - Fast food—eat on the run
  - People eat out more
  - People choose different foods
  - School activities clash with mealtimes

- **Effects of changed eating patterns on parents**
  - Harder to spend time with children
  - Feel contrast with own childhood
  - May feel frustrated, guilty
  - Spend less time shopping and cooking
  - Don't have to listen to children fight at table

- **Effects of changed eating patterns on children**
  - Some miss contact with parents
  - May fight less among themselves
  - Spend more time with others their age
  - Might not eat well
  - Don't have to eat stuff they don't like

You might also want to jot down some "cue notes" in the margin of the working list to remind yourself of examples or anecdotes that illustrate specific points. A typical cue note might say "Check article in Jan. *Good Housekeeping*" or "Use story about Uncle Henry's bouillabaisse here."

When you think you have enough material, look over your list to decide which points you want to treat first and how you can arrange the others. Then start writing and, as you work, refer to your list to check that you are staying on track and not forgetting important items. Add and delete items from the list as you need to. Nothing in a working list is untouchable.

2f-2 **Make an informal (scratch) outline.** Many writers like working from careful plans but dislike the formality and restrictions of formal outlines. For them informal or scratch outlines provide a happy medium between a bare-bones working list and an elaborate sentence outline. Scratch outlines, which arrange points in categories and subcategories, are easy to make and flexible.

A scratch outline should begin with a thesis that states your topic. Then you decide what major points you'll use to support that thesis. For each major point you'll need subpoints that support, explain, or illustrate the main points. However, your statement of these points and subpoints can be quite loose since the scratch outline is for your eyes only. The conventions of the full-sentence outline need not be followed. Here's a sample scratch outline on the topic of family meals again, following a cause-and-effect pattern of the sort described in Section 2e–5. Notice that the scratch outline is considerably fuller than the working list; thus it provides somewhat more guidance.

Thesis: Pressures from outside the home are changing the tradition of the family meal.

1. The traditional practice of families having meals together seems to be changing.
   - Most families used to eat breakfast and dinner together—now both children and parents may be working shifts and hardly see each other.
   - Everyone got caught up on family news at the dinner table and had a chance to tell about their triumphs and exasperations of the day.
   - But often the worst family fights also took place at mealtimes.
2. What's caused these changes to the family meal?
   - In many modern families everyone works, sometimes on shifts or at odd hours. Makes more hectic schedules.
   - Today's teenagers are apt to be involved in lots of activities that cut into family mealtimes.
     – School activities
     – Clubs and sports
     – Cruising the malls
     – Jobs
   - Working moms have less time to arrange family meals. More families now eat out regularly.
3. What are the consequences?
   - Many of the consequences are bad.
     – Less family time together
     – Not as much communication or bonding
     – Families don't eat as well or as regularly
     – Outside activities overwhelm parents and children

– Harder to pass on family traditions
- Some of the consequences are good.
    – Fewer opportunities for mealtime conflicts
    – More opportunities for peaceful meals for parents
    – Children learn to fend for themselves

2f-3 **Make a sentence outline.** A formal outline is a fairly complex structure that compels you to think rigorously. That's why teachers often require them. If your major points really aren't compatible or parallel, a formal outline will expose the problems. If your supporting evidence is thin or inconsistent, those flaws may show up too.

In a formal sentence outline you state every point in a complete sentence, and you make sentences within each grouping parallel. You pay attention to the formalities of arrangement, aligning points carefully according to the following scheme.

C H A R T

Setting Up a Formal Outline

I. —
  A. —
  B. —
     —
    1. —
    2. —
    3. —
      a. — — — — — — — — — — — — — — — — — — —
      b. — — — — — — — — — — — — — — — — — — —
  C. —
II. —

THE MEALS, THEY ARE A-CHANGIN'

Thesis: Pressures from outside the home are changing the tradition of the family meal.

I. Pressures from outside the home are changing the traditional American family meal.
  A. Families rarely gather for meals today the way they did routinely thirty or forty years ago.

        B. Families used to share news and problems at the table.
        C. Families sometimes squabbled over problems brought to light at meals.
  II. Changes in American life-styles and habits have made family meals inconvenient.
        A. More family members work today than before, sometimes on shifts or at odd hours.
            1. More mothers work than ever before.
            2. Teenagers often have afterschool jobs.
        B. Family members are involved in more nonfamily activities than before.
            1. Parents belong to clubs or community organizations.
            2. Teenagers are involved in sports or other extracurricular activities at school.
                a. Many teens have more money to spend.
                b. Many teens also have cars, making them more independent.
        C. Eating out has become a reasonable alternative to the family meal.
            1. Eating out is quicker than cooking and relatively inexpensive.
            2. Eating out relieves working parents of worries about menus or food preparation.
            3. Eating out allows parents and children to order what they want.
 III. The waning of the family meal has changed the American home.
        A. The American family may be less healthy than before, mentally and physically.
            1. Families communicate less because they get together less often.
            2. Families have fewer traditions.
            3. Families eat more randomly and consume more junk food.
        B. The American family may be less authoritarian than before.
            1. Families probably fight less now than they did when meals were routine.
            2. Children may learn to fend for themselves earlier.
            3. Many men share in shopping and cooking.

2f-4 **Use an outlining program on a computer.** What makes outlining on a computer preferable to doing the job on paper is the ease with which an on-screen outline can be expanded, contracted, rearranged, and otherwise altered. Rather than constraining ideas, a computer outline encourages a writer to be flexible because there's no drudgery in experimentation. Adding new ideas is as easy as moving the cursor and typing; moving an idea from heading to subheading involves no more than marking a line and hitting a few keys. Whole categories within the outline structure can be cut, renumbered, or rearranged.

◆ Point of Difference

Outlining works well for some writers. They claim that they can compose a piece more easily and quickly because they invest so much time in an outline. John McPhee, who writes for *The New Yorker,* organizes his work in this way. But Jacques Barzun, also a famous author and philosopher, finds outlines "useless and fettering." He favors lists. One author of this handbook almost always outlines; the other rarely does. Neither is necessarily doing the right thing. ◆

■ **Exercise 2.9** If you have had a job, make an informal outline for an explanatory paper on that topic. Let someone interested in similar employment know what qualifications he or she needs, what kind of work is required, and what benefits and drawbacks you find in the job. When you are done, describe the changes you would have to make in your scratch outline to turn it into a full-sentence outline.

■ **Exercise 2.10** Make a working list for an exploratory paper you might write describing the single most important improvement you would like to see on your campus. Imagine that the editor of the campus paper has asked you to write this article. When you are done, describe the changes you would have to make in your working list to turn it into a full-sentence outline.

2g HOW DO YOU CHOOSE A TITLE?

Troubleshooting

It may seem odd to choose a title while you are still planning and organizing a paper. But a working title (one you can change as the work progresses) will keep you on track as you move from planning to drafting stages. Titles are surprisingly important. Readers want and expect them; in fact, readers will be annoyed if they don't find one that helps them anticipate what they will be reading. So don't make your title an afterthought, something you scrawl in pencil on the typed final version of your paper.

To find a good title . . .

2g-1   Experiment with a working title. To keep your writing focused, choose a preliminary title early in your drafting. For instance, if you are going to write an article about a computer business that a friend of yours has started, you might begin with the title "Student Entrepreneur Makes Software Sell." The title contains several cues to help you organize your writing and keep you on target: *student* focuses the paper on one person, *entrepreneur* suggests you will be stressing his success and ambition, and *makes software sell* provides you with a possible structure for organizing the paper. You have promised to explain to readers how your friend does his work, so a process design (see Section 2e–2) seems logical.

2g-2   Revise the working title to reflect your finished product. When you've completed an essay, you need to check the title again to be sure it still fits the paper. For instance, as you worked on your paper you might have learned that your friend doesn't really care as much about selling software as developing it. He doesn't much like being called an entrepreneur either, especially since he's not making any money. In fact, he doesn't want to talk about himself at all. So you shift the focus of the paper from your friend to his software designs for elementary school children. Naturally the title of your piece must change too. The final version might be "Developing Friendly Software for Kids."

2g-3   Keep your readers in mind. Be sure your title accurately reflects the content of your paper. No cute titles, please. People doing computer searches work by looking for what are called "descriptors" in titles—that is, key words that help to identify the content of a book or an article and direct the researcher to the place where he or she can find it. If an essay on Napoleon is titled "Short Guy, Big Ego," it will be hard to find. So it's essential that your title let readers know what your paper is really about.

■ **Exercise 2.11** Suggest titles for papers on the following subjects.

1. A complaint about the way your campus bookstore is run
2. An exposé of a drug-selling operation on campus
3. A satire on the kind of clothes or music currently fashionable
4. A review of a band playing at your favorite music spot
5. A feature story about student fathers at your college

■ **Exercise 2.12** Which of these titles seem as if they would be good predictors of content in a paper? Why?

1. Cruising the Universe with Physicist Stephen Hawking
2. Beautiful Daydreams
3. Choosing the Best Car Stereo for You
4. Tricking Your Body into Losing Weight
5. What's in a Name?
6. Drugs
7. My Father, My Mentor
8. An American Problem
9. Keeping the Faith: Fundamentalism in the 1990s
10. Insurance Costs Keep Rising

3

How Do You Write a Draft?

A Getting Started

B Keeping on Track

C Taking a Break

D Knowing When You Have a Draft

E Working Collaboratively

3a HOW DO YOU GET STARTED ON A PAPER?

PROCESS MENU
PREPARING
PLANNING
DRAFTING
INCUBATING
REVISING
EDITING
PROOFREADING

Troubleshooting

Most writers agree that getting the first words down on paper may be the hardest part of writing. Professional authors have described the paralyzing anxiety they sometimes feel as they sit before a typewriter and stare at a blank sheet of paper. Columnist Russell Baker tells of pulling one empty sheet out of the typewriter and rolling in another that might be "friendlier." Today, instead of staring at the typewriter or gnawing on a pencil, many of us gaze in frustration at the blinking cursor on our computer screens. The problem remains the same, though: How do you get started on a project and then keep moving?

Well, recognize that beginnings *are* hard. If you have trouble getting those first few sentences down, don't assume it's because you're a bad writer with nothing to say. It just usually seems easier to procrastinate than to write, so most of us procrastinate. In this section we offer suggestions for overcoming this form of delay so common it has a name: writer's block.

To get started on a paper . . .

3a–1 **Find a place to write and gather your equipment.** If you can, pick a spot away from friends, family, and stereos where you won't be distracted. Collect the materials you need—computer disks, notes, paper, pencils—and lay them out where you can see them. Be sure you have a copy of the assignment and a dictionary nearby. If you're using a computer, turn it on and let it hum. In making preparations like these, you aren't fussing or procrastinating. You're creating an environment for writing.

3a–2 **Don't take beginnings too seriously.** Some people agonize over their first paragraphs, tinkering endlessly until they get them exactly right. Unfortunately such writers may not progress much beyond that opening. First paragraphs *are* difficult. But they shouldn't become excuses for avoiding writing.

Just remember that you don't have to get an opening right the first time. What appears in a draft won't necessarily become a permanent part of an essay. So treat the first paragraph in your early versions of a paper as a device to get you rolling—as a starting block or runway. Write three or four sentences nonstop to build momentum, no matter how bad you think they may be. You may be surprised how quickly and naturally words begin to flow once you've warmed up to your theme. Remember, too, that you don't have to write the opening paragraph first. You can begin with the body of the essay and then come back to the introduction.

3a–3 **Don't criticize yourself as you write.** When you are working on a first draft, cut yourself some slack. Don't moan, "Oh, this is awful" or "I hate my writing." You wouldn't say that to a friend who was struggling to write a first draft, so don't say it to yourself. Remember that writing can be a slow and challenging business; you should congratulate yourself when you're getting any work done at all. Most pieces of good writing develop over a period of time; you can't expect something to be polished and satisfactory when you first start working on it.

3a–4 **Don't edit your writing prematurely.** In early drafts don't fiddle with problems of mechanics and style. You can go back and fix difficulties with spelling, punctuation, sentence fragments, parallelism, and the like after you've captured your ideas in writing. If you bog down in details of form too early in the writing process, you may lose your momentum for composing, letting your brightest ideas fade while you hunt for the spelling of *nitpicker*. Worse, you may find yourself always playing it safe, writing only the kinds of sentences you can compose easily, never pushing yourself to a more precise or polished style. Finally, the time you spend looking for errors might become yet another form of procrastination.

3a–5 **Set your own pace.** If you are not sure what speed of composing suits you best, try writing quickly at first. If you hit a snag or can't turn up the precise phrase you want or the specific example you need, skip the troublesome part and move on. Above all, keep writing. A draft in hand, even a quick one, will give you a sense of accomplishment. You'll have material to develop and refine.

◆ Point of Difference

If you're the kind of writer who just isn't comfortable composing quickly, don't feel that you must change your behavior. Many competent writers do work slowly. They may take several hours to turn out a page or two, but their first drafts often are quite polished. In the long run, slow writers may not spend any more time completing a paper than writers who seem to produce material faster. ◆

3a–6 **Create incentives for keeping the work moving.** Commit yourself to writing for one hour or to producing a full page before getting up from your desk. Promise yourself a small reward when you meet that goal—a bag of popcorn, a cold drink, a brief interlude of music. Then go back for another session and treat yourself again. Plan a bigger reward when you finish the first draft—perhaps a computer game or a movie.

3a–7 **Get ideas from other writers.** One of the best ways to be sure writing gets done is to work with other people. In college and in the work force, members of writing groups routinely brainstorm for ideas, compare research findings, evaluate organizational strategies, and test out arguments. They serve as important first audiences for drafts and provide motivation for finishing work. After all, no one wants to let colleagues down.

This sort of collaborative work can create a community of writers interested in each other's work. It also reinforces the social character of writing. Because most of us do much of our writing alone, it's easy to forget that writing is an activity we engage in to communicate with other people. Working in groups helps us to remember that.

● Tip

In Section 3e you will find guidelines for working with others on writing projects. A checklist explains how to respond to your classmates' writing and how to make suggestions for revision. ●

3a–8 **Draft on a computer.** Working on a word processor makes it easy to try new ways of drafting papers. For example, you can write quick, short versions of essays that you gradually expand and refine. There's no need to begin at the beginning, to end at the end, or to worry about material that seems weak when you write it, because readers will see only the version you print out.

This flexibility should encourage you to start on a paper early, especially when a deadline remains days or weeks away. In a file, record your initial impressions on a topic the day an assignment is made and then, in the same file, gradually accumulate notes from your reading, quotations from sources, remarks from discussions, and any tentative conclusions. Type in phrases, statistics, and complete sentences or paragraphs as you see fit. Over time you'll accumulate a surprising amount of prose—already keyboarded—that you can shape into a final text. If you are comfortable composing in this way, you'll be surprised at how easy the process of assembling an essay can become. And you'll be taking full advantage of the freedom your word processor offers.

With a computer it's also easy to take risks with drafts. Just duplicate an existing file containing a draft you want to rework and give it a new version number. For example, if the first draft of a paper on hypochondria is named *Hypo*, the second experimental version could be *Hypo2*, the third *Hypo3*, and so on. You can then experiment with new versions while preserving all the work you've already done—should you prefer to go back to an earlier version. (After all, revising a text doesn't automatically improve it.)

If your computer can display multiple windows, open all files related to any paper you're developing—that is, all preliminary versions, any files that contain notes, any related papers you have written. Then you can move between versions as necessary, borrowing lines you liked from earlier drafts and transferring statistics you've gathered in note files. You can even compare versions of a paper by sizing the separate files so that you can look at two papers at the same time. When working in this way, don't forget occasionally to save the window that contains the latest version of your paper. You don't want to lose it.

Finally, many computers now make it easy to create illustrations. If your computer has this capacity, take advantage of it. See the section on document design (pp. 89–104) for more information about how you can enhance your writing with graphics.

3b HOW DO YOU KEEP A DRAFT ON TRACK?

Troubleshooting

When you start a draft, you should have a focus for the paper and a plan of organization. You know that a narrative paper will usually follow chronological order and that an argument will state a thesis and then defend it. You probably have worked out the thesis and sketched an outline. But the real work of organization doesn't start until you begin putting words on the page. Only then do you see precisely how your organizational blueprint may have to be altered to fit a particular writing situation—in the same way an architect might move a window in a house to improve the view. As a writer you have to be both organized and flexible: organized enough to guide readers sensibly through a piece and flexible enough to shift strategies as your subject develops.

To keep a draft on track . . .

3b-1 **Put your main ideas up front in most college papers.** In the first paragraphs of explanatory essays, give readers a clear notion of what to expect. Then follow with supporting ideas that build toward conclusions, the kinds of conclusions that leave readers with a clear sense of your purpose. For example, here is an opening paragraph that tells readers what the rest of the paper will be about.

> At the end of the 1980s one-third of the doctors graduating from medical schools were women. Women doctors will soon be in the majority in specialities such as obstetrics-gynecology, pediatrics, and psychiatry, and they are rapidly making inroads into traditionally male territories such as surgery and orthopedics. This shifting balance in what up to now has been a male-dominated profession is changing American medicine in a number of ways. One can already see changes in medical education as the number of women professors in medical school increases.

For exploratory essays you may want to ease your readers into the subject, perhaps catching their attention with a memorable fact or an intriguing anecdote in the first paragraph. Then you will lead them gradually to your main idea—an idea that may be still evolving in your own mind. For example, if the paragraph above about women in medicine had been from an exploratory rather than an explanatory essay, it might look like this.

> A slight woman with long blond hair tied back in an Alice-in-Wonderland coiffure, Vera Gaines is accustomed to having her patients in the Dallas Veterans Hospital refuse at first to take her seriously in spite of her stethoscope, white coat, and a name badge that says V. Gaines, M.D. One crusty veteran complains bluntly, "I don't want a female doctor." Another repeatedly asks Dr. Gaines to fluff his pillows or rub his back. But veterans who have been at the hospital several months see in her a new kind of doctor and welcome the change.

3b–2 **Highlight key ideas with phrases that underscore their signif-icance.** The right phrase ought to snap a reader to attention.

> The points we must consider are . . .
> The chief issue, however, is . . .
> Now we come to the crucial question . . .
> It is essential that . . .

You can keep readers on track too with constructions that express the doubts, concessions, and feelings you think are appropriate.

> I want to stress that . . .
> While it may be true that . . .
> We must concede that . . .
> Although I appreciate why . . .
> Still, we should not allow that . . .

Even signals as simple as *first*, *second*, and *third* can help readers follow the structure of a paper.

3b–3 **Keep the amount you write on each point roughly proportion-ate to the importance of that idea.** Be careful not to write a lopsided draft that misleads readers. If what you intend as an introduction takes up half the paper, it's no longer an introduction. If you conclude a lengthy argument (or a paper) with a weak one-sentence summary, you may not convince your reader. If you expend too much time on an interesting but minor example, readers may mistake that minor point for a major one.

3b–4 **Keep the ideas coming.** While respecting the principle of pro-portion just discussed, be generous with words and ideas in your draft. You'll discover in editing that it is easier to prune material you don't like than it is to fill gaps where your ideas are skimpy. Obviously you don't want to wander too far from your thesis. But do capture any fresh thoughts that emerge as you write. If they don't work, you can cut them later. The same is true of examples, illustrations, facts, figures, and details. Too many is better than too few.

3b–5 **Allow enough time to write a strong conclusion.** Because con-clusions are important, be sure to leave time to draft a good one. If you have only a limited amount of time to invest in a paper, don't put so much energy into the introduction and body of your essay that you skimp on the conclusion. You can weaken your paper badly if you do. If you have time, work up several endings. Conclusions are what readers are likely to remember best.

■ **Exercise 3.1** What point might you emphasize in papers on the following topics?

1. For an American history course, the role of black soldiers in the Civil War
2. For a newspaper editorial, a claim that your city's schools are not giving enough attention to Asian-American students
3. For freshman English, a report on America's love affair with celebrities

3c WHEN SHOULD YOU TAKE A BREAK?

PROCESS MENU
PREPARING
PLANNING
DRAFTING
INCUBATING
REVISING
EDITING
PROOFREADING

Troubleshooting

In the midst of a writing project you may suddenly find yourself stumped. You gaze at the computer screen or listen to your typewriter hum, but nothing happens. No ideas come; no words flow. Such a lull can be scary, especially when a deadline nears, but you just may need to kick back and let your thoughts *incubate*. In writing, incubation is an interval during which a writer stops composing for a time to let ideas cook or germinate in the subconscious. When you feel you've reached such an interval, put your writing task aside for a while and do something else.

No one really knows what happens during these incubation periods. The creative or problem-solving part of the mind seems to retreat into the subconscious. It sorts through what it finds there, discovers fresh ideas, and makes unexpected connections. You can't force or rush incubation; you can only be ready to grab an idea when it surfaces.

To help ideas develop . . .

3c-1 **Expect both long and short incubation periods.** Incubation periods may occur several times during a writing project. For authors who work consistently, such periods of rest are absolutely necessary. When they've written themselves out for the day, they know it's fruitless to stare at the computer or the typewriter any longer.

The periods that lapse between writing the first, second, and even third draft of a paper can be similarly productive. But shorter incubation periods help too. When you are stuck for a word or can't think of the example you need to illustrate a point, get away from the desk long enough to do an errand or to chat with someone. Even such a brief pause can trigger an insight that breaks barriers to writing. So you don't have to keep yourself glued to the chair all the time in order to write—minor interruptions can actually be productive.

`3c-2` **Don't use incubation as an excuse for procrastination.** You should relax occasionally and take time out while writing, but you can't afford to wait indefinitely for inspiration. If you're still having problems composing after a few hours (or a weekend) of rest, get back to work anyway. Review your notes or outlines; reread what you've already written; talk to a friend about the assignment. Most important, just write!

■ **Exercise 3.2** Recall a time when you solved what seemed an insoluble problem after taking a break from worrying about it. (The problem does not have to be connected with writing a paper.) Describe that experience in a short narrative. Was the solution you arrived at obvious? If so, why do you think you didn't discover it earlier?

`3d` **WHEN DO YOU HAVE A DRAFT?**

PROCESS MENU
PREPARING
PLANNING
DRAFTING
INCUBATING
REVISING
EDITING
PROOFREADING

Troubleshooting

As the deadline approaches to turn in that first draft, relax. Although a paper you are laboring over may not be as good as you'd like, it *is* a draft that you will have the chance to work on again. Other people's first drafts probably aren't in great shape either; if writers in your class exchange papers and comment on drafts, you'll see evidence of that quickly. But how do you know when you have a rough draft that's worthy of the name, one that your instructor is going to accept as a legitimate effort?

When you can say yes to the following three questions, you probably have a draft that will satisfy you, your instructor, and your classmates reasonably well.

To determine whether you have a draft, ask . . .

3d–1 **Does the draft represent a good-faith effort?** Have you made an honest effort to produce something worth reading and discussing? A decent first draft shows that you have invested time and thought in your paper. If, however, you write a sloppy, superficial first draft because it's not going to be graded, you're working in bad faith. You shouldn't expect anyone else, including your instructor, to spend time responding to your writing. You're also passing up an opportunity you may not get again— the chance to get substantial and useful criticism on your paper *before* it is graded.

3d–2 **Is the draft reasonably complete?** Have you stated a thesis, de- veloped it with supporting arguments and examples, and finished with a defensible conclusion? If so, you can legitimately claim to have a work- ing draft that represents a starting point for revision. An outline or a few paragraphs don't qualify as a working draft. Neither does a carefully writ- ten opening followed by descriptions of what the rest of the paper will cover. If you want helpful feedback from others, you shouldn't give them a fragmentary paper.

3d–3 **Is the draft legible?** You can't expect instructors and classmates to respond carefully to a paper that's almost unreadable. Legibility is particularly important when you are working in a group and need to photocopy your draft. So give your readers a break. Be sure to double- space a typed or printed paper, leaving ample margins all around the text for comments. Check too that your typewriter or printer has a ribbon fresh enough to make dark, readable copies. If you must handwrite a draft, *print* in ink on every other line. Always write on one side of a page only. And number those pages.

■ **Exercise 3.3** Evaluate a draft you have written against the three cri- teria discussed above. Does your paper meet the standards? Or should you go back to the drafting table?

3e **HOW DO YOU WORK ON A DRAFT COLLABORATIVELY?**

Troubleshooting

It's common these days for students in writing classes to work to- gether on their papers. Meeting in small groups, writers read photocopies of each other's drafts and respond to them. The instructor also comments on drafts and makes suggestions. In this way each writer in the class can receive comments on a draft from several different readers.

This method of responding to drafts (sometimes called *peer editing*) gives writers the benefit of real audiences. Colleagues, acting as friendly editors, provide the kind of feedback that helps writers make sensible revisions. With an explanatory paper, peer editors can tell you whether you have included all the information you need and whether your paper is clear; for an exploratory paper they may be able to suggest approaches you haven't considered or rein in ideas that have galloped too far. So you can obviously profit by getting other people's reactions to your work *before* the writing is submitted for a grade—the same way an author profits from an editor's comments before a book gets into print.

But it takes skill to be an honest and critical reader of another person's writing. Remember that you aren't taking the place of that student's writing instructor: you're an editor, not a grader. You can help a fellow writer most by showing an interest in what he or she has written, asking questions, giving encouragement, and making constructive suggestions for future drafts.

When editing a colleague's paper . . .

3e-1 **Read the draft straight through once.** Read it as a real piece of writing intended to inform, persuade, or entertain. Get a feel for the big issues before worrying about details of mechanics and usage. Do you understand what the writer was trying to achieve? Could you summarize the point of the paper? Did you find it informative, persuasive, or pleasurable reading? First impressions are important. If you don't think the draft works, try to explain why in words the writer will understand.

3e-2 **Read the paper a second time.** Use the guideline questions in the checklist on page 65 to help you formulate responses to particular features of the paper. It's important that you say more than "I really like your paper" or "Well, you could maybe add some examples." Explain *what* you like about it, such as well-researched facts, colorful turns of phrase, or memorable examples. Show where you believe the paper needs more development. At this stage keep your critical focus on large-scale issues, not on misspellings or errors that are really editing problems to be dealt with later.

3e-3 **Make marginal comments.** If you are working with a photocopy of the draft, jot comments in the margins as you read it the second time. Editorial comments should be genuine queries or pointed observations, not stinging criticisms. A question can sometimes be the most helpful remark.

Can you say more about this?
Have you left something out here?
Would your opening be stronger if you cut this sentence?

Be as specific as you can about your reaction to the paper. Show precisely where you got lost if the organization is faulty. And let the writer know where something is working well.

3e-4 **Write out your responses to the paper.** After you have read the paper carefully and annotated the margins, you still want to give the writer a general comment—something to ponder. That comment should come in a paragraph at the end of the paper and be a thoughtful piece summarizing your reaction to the draft. It often helps a writer if you begin by saying what you think the paper has accomplished.

Your paper explains how you reacted to seeing so much wealth and poverty side by side in New York. You try to understand why these contrasts are more evident in New York than in other parts of the country.

That way the writer knows whether the paper has achieved at least part of what he or she hoped. Then you can say something about how well the paper works.

I saw the two worlds of New York very vividly in the essay. You do a particularly good job illustrating the prosperity of theatergoers and the poverty of street people. I like the way your description of different streets and blocks leads to your conclusion that New York puts two different worlds on a collision course, though I was not certain really why the conflict occurs more in New York than, say, San Francisco or Minneapolis.

Conclude your comment with some suggestions for revision, stressing what you believe the writer's priorities might be.

You might make it clearer in your first paragraph where the whole paper is headed. And use more transitional phrases between the first three paragraphs to highlight the contrasts between wealth and poverty. The topic sentences in your paragraphs tend to be wordy and vague and that makes the middle of the paper bog down a bit and blurs your details.

A nice touch is to open this paragraph of commentary with your colleague's name and to conclude it with your signature.

3e-5 **Use a limited number of proofreading symbols.** When reading a first draft, you don't want to waste time editing minor points of mechanics and usage the writer can deal with in later versions. On the other hand, you may occasionally be asked to read a late draft of a paper, or you may know that the writer wants special help with a weakness such as spelling or punctuation. In such cases give the draft one last careful reading and look for mechanical problems only. At this time circle misspelled words (but don't correct them). Place words you think might be omitted in parentheses (but don't cross them out). Put a wavy line under words or phrases you don't think represent the writer's best choice.

> The subway station smells of (stinking) urine and rats flutter across the tracks in search of food. The train arrives. As soon as we sit down, the car lurches and a (women) begins singing loudly in (Spannish.) No one notices.

To mark other items, consult the endpapers in this book for proofreading symbols.

CHECKLIST

Responding to a Draft

- What do you like most about the paper? What particularly impressed you when you read it?
- Does the paper achieve its purpose—that is, does it meet the goals of the assignment? Where does the purpose come through clearly?
- Do you think the writer has a good sense of his or her audience? What suggestions might you make for better adapting the paper for its intended readers?
- What suggestions can you make about focusing the topic? Should the focus be narrower? Does the paper need a sharper thesis?
- What suggestions can you make about additional readings or sources that might add greater authority or strength to the paper?
- What questions does the paper raise? What additional information, discussion, or examples would you like to have? Can you suggest some details that the writer might mention?
- What general comments do you have for the writer?

WINDOW ON WRITING: First Draft

Here is the first draft of a paper by undergraduate student Hoang Nguyen. It's a fine draft in many respects—serious, thoughtful, and exploratory. Its dramatic and memorable details catch a reader's attention, making him or her eager to complete the piece. Untitled at this stage, the paper is quite readable, with no pretentious language and few tangled sentences. Hoang's native language is Vietnamese, but his command of English is formidable.

The draft does have significant weaknesses. To get at them we've included the marginal comments an instructor made on Hoang's draft and a concluding comment of the sort you might prepare in responding to a colleague's draft. Notice that these early comments largely ignore the various mechanical problems.

Notice too the questions Hoang himself poses about his own draft at the end of the text: "Where can I go from here? What is my purpose?" They are just the sort of questions you might face when writing an exploratory paper, knowing the ideas you want to explore but unsure of what form to give them or what conclusions to draw. Hoang's final version of this paper appears in Chapter 4.

In 1975, the democratic South Vietnam *Will readers find this* was defeated by the Communists. Fearing for *opening abrupt?* our lives, my family fled to the United States. I was eight years old then. *Do we need to know more about your family?*

I don't remember much about the trip except that I was in the huge belly of a military airplane sitting on its flat metallic floor surrounded by women and children. Everyone looked solemn. Some people were crying. My mom had tears flooding her eyes. *This is quite moving.*

I remember feeling sad and confused. I didn't understand the reason why we left and why people were crying. I wanted to be in my neighborhood playing soccer with my friends. I wanted to know where my father was and why he wasn't with us. I wished that I could comfort my mother and stop her from crying. But all I managed to do was sit there with my chin on her knees and my arms wrapped around her legs.

Your story is interesting, but do you want to make a point?

The plane landed, and I found myself in Guam, a small island in the Pacific Ocean. The military base there was hastily converted into a refugee camp. We were assigned to a tent and given blankets and water. To get food, we had to wait in a line that stretched literally for half a football field. We stayed on that barren hot island for a month. We waited for any news of the whereabouts of our father. We waited for someone to tell us about our future. We waited.

Finally, we were flown (in a commercial airplane this time) to Fort Chaffee, Arkansas. Again we stayed at a military base. We were assigned a room in one of the barracks. Conditions at the fort were better than at the refugee camp. We had running water and air-conditioned room. The food lines were only 20-30 people long. Although people were grieving for their loss homeland, there was hope on their faces. News of family members reunited changed a solemn atmosphere to a hopeful one.

Sentences seem choppy; do too many begin with <u>we</u>?

I was surprised when I woke up one morning and heard my father's voice. I almost fell off the bunkbed in my eagerness to run to him. He had arrived late at night. I hugged him tightly to feel his presence and to give my senses time to process the fact that my father was here, in America, in Fort Chaffee, with us. The months of waiting, of loneliness, of fear vanished at that instant. I was reunited with my father. It no longer frightened me that I was in a foreign land and unable to speak the language. I was not upset for not having any friends to play soccer with. I felt happy. My family was whole again.

A bit repetitious?

We stayed in that Fort for three months before an American family sponsored us. They were farmers and lived in the Texas Panhandle. They had one daughter, Shannon, who was younger than I was, but she was much bigger. My brothers and I used to form a human chain by holding each other hands. Shannon would come charging at us and knocked us down. We could not stop her wild charge no matter how tightly we held our hands.

Why include Shannon in this paper? Does you playing with he make some point?

After the brief Summer, I was enrolled in the fourth grade. School was my first introduction to American culture. I was shocked when I walked into the classroom and saw rows of desk. I had expected to see long tables and benches like the classroom in Vietnam. My next surprise came when our teacher introduced herself and wrote her name on the

The details her are fascinating I'm not sure where you are heading. Maybe you can focus paper more sharply on your introduction to education in America?

chalkboard. I did not know why she would write her name for us. When my classmates called her by her name instead of just "teacher," I was in dismay. "How can they be so disrespectful?" I asked myself. In Vietnam, you never call your teacher by his or her name. To do so would be disrespectful. You address your teacher as "teacher."

Another difference between Vietnam and America that I delightly noticed concerned books. Vietnam is a poor country. We could not afford books. The teacher would read a lesson to us from a book and we would copy it down and later memorized it. Thus when my fourth grade teacher called me up and then gave me a book, I did not know what to do. I stood there petrified that I had to read a lesson from it for the other kids to copy down. My teacher did not notice at first that I had not returned to my seat because she was busy checking the books out to each student. When she finally noticed that I was standing there staring at her, she asked what was wrong with my book. I didn't answer because I didn't know English. She took the book back and examined it. I sighed a relief and turned to walk back to my desk thinking that she must have realized I couldn't read English. I took one step before I heard her called my name. I turned around and saw her offering me

3e
collab

The book incident is interesting, but it seems like just another event. I think you might look for a way to link the experiences in this draft more closely.

the book. Confused I accepted the book and again waited for her to tell me to read. She pointed to my desk. I didn't understand so I stood there staring at her. One of my classmates grap my arm and led me to my desk. He then pointed to my chair indicating that I should sit down, so I did. It took me the rest of the class period to figure out that I can keep the book for the rest of the year.

Where can I go from here? What is my purpose?

Hoang,

Readers are going to pay attention to this paper just because the subject is so interesting and your memory of events is so strong and clear. (The metallic floor of the military plane is a believable detail.) Your first five or six paragraphs were quite strong, but the paper started to go off track after your father returned. Each incident you wrote about was interesting, but the paper didn't seem to be heading anywhere. You might ask yourself what you want the paper to accomplish and then revise it with that aim in mind. Don't lose the good stuff here, but give the essay more direction. I didn't mark any of the mechanical problems, but there are some you'll need to take care of eventually.

Allie

4

How Do You Revise, Edit, and Proofread?

A   Revising
B   Editing
C   Proofreading

Why make a fuss distinguishing among terms as similar as *revising, editing*, and *proofreading?* It's because revising, editing, and proofreading are different phases of the writing process. Think of them sequentially and you'll train yourself to move efficiently from early time-intensive aspects of writing to narrower but still significant details.

CHART
Revising, Editing, Proofreading

Revision
(first draft)

Editing
(later draft)

Proofreading
(final draft)

Purpose, audience, organization

Style, emphasis

Mechanics

When you start *revising* your draft, don't think in terms of *fixing* or *correcting* your writing—that's not really what you are doing. Rather you are *shaping a work in progress*, reviewing what you have written and looking for ways to improve it. You may get new ideas and shift the focus of the paper entirely; you may decide to cut, expand, and reorganize. At this point you are making large-scale changes.

When you *edit* a paper, you are less concerned with the thrust of your argument or the substance of your paper. Instead you turn your attention to matters of style that affect clarity and emphasis. You may rewrite sentences you find awkward or correct problems with parallelism and repetition. Your goal is to create sentences and paragraphs that present your ideas effectively. These are small-scale changes.

When you *proofread* a paper, you go back over it line by line, reading carefully to correct typographical errors, to check for words that may have been omitted, to verify details, to eliminate inconsistencies, and to remove embarrassing gaffes. This is the fix-it stage, when you're finally preparing the paper to appear in public. However, it's a good idea to postpone proofreading until the end of a project. If you start correcting errors while you are composing or revising, you're liable to waste time repairing sentences that later might be deleted.

4a WHAT DOES REVISING INVOLVE?

PROCESS MENU
PREPARING
PLANNING
DRAFTING
INCUBATING
REVISING
EDITING
PROOFREADING

Troubleshooting

When you revise a draft, don't try to work through it paragraph by paragraph, making changes as you go. The problems of a first draft are likely to involve large-scale issues of content and rhetorical strategy—serious concerns you need to address before you start polishing individual sentences. A major change in audience or focus, for example, is likely to affect every paragraph in the paper. But that's the point of serious revision—to reconsider everything you have already written. At this point THINK BIG. Don't tinker.

Large-scale changes include revising for focus, purpose, proportion, commitment, adaptation to audience, organization, and content. Begin by reading your first draft from start to finish, thinking about these major elements. If you are working with a computer, you need to print out a copy and revise from that (see Section 4a–9).

● **Tip**

Don't turn to the grammar and usage section of this handbook yet. Wait until you have finished your first revision to start checking specific problems. ●

To revise your paper . . .

4a–1 **Read your draft thoughtfully.** At this point you might want to review the original assignment and any general comments your instructor and classmates have made on the draft. Ask yourself frankly how you feel about the paper. What's good that you definitely want to keep? Where does it seem weak?

Ideally you should appraise your draft several days (or at a minimum several hours) after you have completed it. Put some distance between you and the text so that you can read it more objectively. Obviously you can enjoy the advantages of setting a draft aside only if you start on an assignment early.

One bold option you should consider at this point is writing a second, entirely new draft. Take this radical path when you really dislike what you've written, when editors have found little to praise in your first effort, or when you'd just like to start fresh on a subject. Creating a new draft may seem discouraging, but it's a form of revision all serious writers occasionally select. In the long run, starting a second time from scratch may be easier than repairing a draft that just won't work. Even then, your first draft need not be a waste of effort. Quite often an unsuccessful version points a writer toward what he or she really wanted to write about. So don't mourn a discarded first draft; it can lead to a stronger new version.

4a–2 **Refine the focus of the paper.** If your draft is workable, be sure that it makes and develops a point. You have a problem with focus if the draft is largely generalities. Check your examples and supporting material. Have you relied mostly on common knowledge? If so, your draft may lack the credibility that comes from specific information. To check for focus, ask yourself these questions.

Revising for Focus
- Have you taken on a larger topic than you can handle adequately?
- Have you generated more material than you can deal with?
- Are you generalizing about your topic instead of stating specific positions supported by verifiable facts and details?

4a–3 **Consider your purpose.** Ask yourself whether someone reading your draft would immediately understand what you're trying to achieve. Here are some additional questions to ask yourself.

Revising for Purpose
- In the first paragraph or two of an explanatory paper, did you state clearly what you intend to do?
- In an exploratory paper, were you able to express the ideas important to you?

- Does the draft develop all the main points you intended to make?
- After reading the draft, were most readers able to summarize your main idea?

If you lacked a sense of purpose when you began drafting the paper, you now need to decide exactly what you want to accomplish. Be sure that your intentions are evident to yourself and to your readers. You can't seriously revise the paper further unless you know what its goals are.

4a–4 **Examine the proportions of your paper.** *Proportion* means the distribution and balance of ideas in a piece. You should develop your ideas in relation to their importance. Ask yourself these questions.

Revising for Proportion
- Are the parts of the paper out of proportion? For example, have you gone into too much detail at the beginning and then skimped on the rest of the paper?
- Can your readers tell what points are most important by the amount of attention you've given to them?
- Does the paper build toward the most important point?
- Does the conclusion do justice to the ideas it summarizes?

4a–5 **Check that you have kept your promises to readers.** The introduction and thesis of your paper create certain expectations in your readers. When you revise, check your response to any commitments you've made to them. Now is the time to tie up loose ends, so ask these questions.

Revising for Commitment
- What exactly did you promise your readers at the beginning of the paper? Did you fulfill those promises?
- Did you support all claims made in your thesis?
- Did you finish what you started? Have you inadvertently raised questions you can't or don't intend to answer?
- Does your conclusion agree with your opening?

4a–6 **Check for adaptation to audience.** Have you adjusted a paper to the needs and interests of your readers? Consider these questions as well.

Revising for Audience
- Have you identified your readers? What do you think they want from your paper?
- Have you considered what they already know about the topic? Have you covered material that most of your readers will find too familiar?
- Have you answered all the questions that readers might have about your topic?

- Have you left important concepts unexplained?
- Have you failed to define terms that your readers need to know?
- Have you used language your readers will understand?

Sometimes a first draft is what we call *writer-centered;* that is, the writer has concentrated mostly on expressing his or her ideas, without thinking much about the audience. Such an approach can be productive in a first draft, but a major goal of revising should be to change *writer-centered* writing to *reader-centered* writing. You do that by trying to put yourself in the place of your readers. Going back over the audience worksheet on page 16 can help.

4a-7 **Check the organization.** A well-organized paper has a plan and clear direction. Readers can move from the beginning to the end of a paper without getting lost. To check your organization, ask these questions.

Revising for Organization

- Does your paper state a thesis, or focus on a point? Does it then develop the point significantly?
- Does the development of your point follow a pattern readers will recognize?
- Do the transitions move readers sensibly from point to point?
- Would the paper work better if you moved some paragraphs around and thus changed your emphasis?

To revise the structure of a draft, you usually need a typed or printed copy because organizational problems can be hard to detect in a handwritten paper or on a computer screen. You need a sense of the whole to feel how the parts are meshing.

4a-8 **Check that information in the paper is sufficient.** When you revise, you may need to add information to give a paper more substance. That is especially true if you decide to focus on only one of your original points. Ask yourself these questions.

Revising for Content

- Have you answered the questions *who, what, where, when, how,* and *why?*
- Can you add specific information and concrete examples that will make your case stronger?
- Do you need more details to satisfy your readers' curiosity?

Return to the library or other sources if necessary. A college paper needs the "weight of facts" to advance its argument.

4a-9 **Revise from hard copy if you are working on a computer.** Whether revising, editing, or proofreading, you'll probably work better from a hard copy of your paper than from an on-screen text. Problems that seem all but invisible on the screen (weak organization, sprawling paragraphs, poor transitions, repeated words, transposed letters) seem to show up more readily on a printed page.

Many printers have draft modes to produce quick hard-copy texts suitable for revision. So don't avoid hard-copy revision just because it may take a little time. After you've marked a draft, be sure that you transfer any corrections made on the printed version to the computer file. And don't inadvertently introduce new mechanical errors, especially typos or misspellings.

S U M M A R Y

When Revising . . .

- Concentrate on large-scale issues.
- Refine your focus if necessary.
- Reassess your reason for writing—your purpose.
- Check the distribution and balance of your ideas.
- Judge whether you've met your commitments.
- Assess how well your paper works for its intended readers.
- Analyze the effectiveness of your organization.
- Fill any gaps in information.

■ **Exercise 4.1** Apply the criteria for large-scale revision summarized in the box above to a draft you have written.

WINDOW ON WRITING: Revising

Carl Jackson wanted to write a paper for general readers exploring the corrupt practices used by some colleges to recruit high school basketball players. Here's the opening paragraph of his first draft exactly as he wrote it.

```
Basketball is one of the most exciting games to

watch because of the nonstop action at every minite

of the game. Unlike football where time is taken to

huddle and the average play last only about five

seconds, or even worse, baseball which is America's
```

```
sport, seems to drag on forever until something

exciting happens. My opinion of basketball being the

most exciting sport to watch is arguable but what is

not arguable is the amount of unethical practices

found in the sport. It seems that every year another

team has been placed on probation or a school has had

to suspend its program for various reasons. Among

these are recruiting violations and payments to

recruits and active players by alumni. These are the

areas in which I would like to focus on and possibly

give a few suggestions on how to clean up college

basketball.
```

If Carl began editing and proofreading this paragraph before undertaking larger-scale revisions, he'd probably make such corrections as the following: (1) change *minite* to *minute*; (2) change *average play last* to *average play lasts*; (3) simplify the sentence that begins *Unlike football*; (4) change *amount* to *number*.

But Carl's classmates who reviewed the paper thought that the paragraph had bigger problems. For one thing, they were confused about Carl's focus. If he was interested in basketball, why the comments on football and baseball? The first few sentences seem unrelated to the conclusion of the paragraph, and that conclusion isn't very intriguing. They doubted that this opener would keep readers interested. Clearly Carl needed to overhaul his paragraph, not just tinker with spelling and grammar problems.

Here's the heavily revised paragraph that opened his second draft. The new version cuts the distracting allusions to football and baseball, gets to the point more quickly, and teases the reader with the possibility of a solution to the recruitment problem. Though open to additional revision, the paragraph nonetheless demonstrates what we mean by large-scale revision.

```
    Basketball is one of the most exciting games to

watch, mainly due to its fast-paced, nonstop action,

but even avid fans might be hard pressed these days

to keep up with NCAA investigations of the sport. It
```

```
seems that every year another college basketball

program has been placed on probation by the NCAA for

recruiting violations. This widespread problem has

generated much debate on what should be done to clean

up the sport of basketball. The suggestions range

from cutting athletic scholarships to paying the

athletes to play. Although both of these are extreme

measures, a case can be made for each one. However, I

believe that there is a better way to bring back the

integrity of basketball without such measures.
```

Notice that none of the mechanical and grammatical items that needed to be corrected in the first version are present in the second draft. To have spent time fixing them *before* making the needed revisions would have been a waste of energy.

4b WHAT DOES EDITING INVOLVE?

PROCESS MENU
PREPARING
PLANNING
DRAFTING
INCUBATING
REVISING
EDITING
PROOFREADING

Troubleshooting

Revision should give you a better-focused, better-organized, more interesting draft. If you're reasonably satisfied with your revised paper, go over it again and begin to *edit*, that is, to make the small-scale changes that you put on hold while you were adding, cutting, and rearranging material. Now you are ready to edit for concrete and specific language, word choice, wordiness, transitions, and a better introduction and conclusion.

● **Tip**

Now is the time to use the handbook to check on details of style, mechanics, or usage. ●

To edit your draft . . .

4b–1 Make the language more concrete and specific. Language is *concrete* when it describes things so that they can be perceived through the senses: colors, textures, sizes, sounds, smells, actions. Language is *specific* when it names particular people, places, or things.

Early drafts of a paper often turn out to be too abstract because a writer developing ideas may not be thinking about the examples, anecdotes, or vivid expressions that bring concepts to life. When you start editing, however, look for ways to add people to your discussions, to illustrate generalizations with examples, and to supply your readers with more facts and images. Give your writing texture.

4b–2 Test your language. Look at your word choices to see where they can be improved. Is your style formal, "noun heavy," or laden with jargon (see Chapter 12)? Are your subjects specific and do your verbs express powerful actions? Examine your modifiers to determine whether they are vivid and accurate. Careful use of a thesaurus is appropriate at this stage.

Check any words you're not sure of in a dictionary to be certain the meaning you intend is appropriate and contemporary. (Avoid slang or archaic expressions.) Resolve any questions your editors have raised about word choice; revise any expressions they have described as awkward or confusing.

4b–3 Cut wordiness. Many writers produce wordy first drafts, especially when they are generating ideas. In subsequent drafts, however, it's time to cut. In particular, go after sprawling verb phrases ("make the evaluation" → "evaluate"), redundancies ("initial start-up" → "start-up"), and boring strings of prepositional phrases ("in the bottle on the shelf in the refrigerator" → "in the bottle on the refrigerator shelf"). Be ruthless. You can usually cut as much as 25 percent of your prose without losing anything but verbiage (see Chapter 12).

4b–4 Test your transitions. Transitions are words and phrases that connect sentences, paragraphs, and whole passages of writing. When transitions are faulty, a paper will seem choppy and disconnected. To decide whether that's the case, read your draft aloud. If you pause, stumble, and detect gaps, you should improve the connections between ideas. Quite often you'll just need to add words or phrases to the beginnings of sentences and paragraphs—expressions such as "on the other hand," "however," and "nonetheless." In some cases you'll have to edit more deeply, rearranging whole sections of the piece to put ideas in a more coherent order (see Chapter 9 for additional suggestions).

4b–5 **Polish the introduction and the conclusion.** Most of us know intuitively that the introduction of a draft is important enough to merit special attention. It makes sense, however, not to edit the first paragraph until you know precisely how your paper is going to come out. That way you can be sure that the introduction is both accurate and interesting. The first paragraph might well be the last one you bring to its final form.

Conclusions also warrant special care, but they may be even harder to write than introductions. So don't fuss too much with the conclusion until you have the main part of the paper under control. Then try to work out a strong ending that pulls the paper together and leaves your readers satisfied.

For more specific suggestions on how to improve introductory and concluding paragraphs, see Sections 8a and 8b.

4b–6 **Use a computer style checker.** Style or editing programs have various functions: they may calculate the readability level of sentences in a paper, locate expletive constructions (*it is; there is*), spot clichés, detect repetitions, highlight racist or sexist terms, and so on. For all their cleverness such programs deal with stylistic problems chiefly by locating and counting items. They can't assess context. And it is usually context that determines, for example, whether expletives or repetitions are appropriate. If you have access to a style checker, try it, but don't let it intimidate you.

If you don't have access to a commercial style checker, create a simple version on your own. You can use the search/change command in your word-processing program to look for specific weaknesses in your writing. If you use *to be* verbs too frequently, direct the computer to find all uses of *be, is, are, was,* and *were* and replace them, when possible, with more action-oriented expressions. If expletive expressions such as *there is, there were,* and *it was* are your weakness, ask the computer to locate these constructions in your paper. If punctuation around the word *however* baffles you, double-check each occurrence of the word. Do you often

---

S U M M A R Y

When Editing . . .

- Sharpen your language.
- Check your word choice.
- Lop out wordiness.
- Test your transitions.
- Polish your opening and closing.
- Use a style checker if available.

misuse semicolons? Order the computer to find each one, and then be sure you can explain its function well enough to justify its use in the paper. Obviously the longer the paper, the more helpful the search/change command can be.

WINDOW ON WRITING: Editing

Here are some sentences from student papers that have been improved by judicious small-scale revision. Notice that the editing does not greatly alter the meaning of the selections. Examine these selections and discuss the changes the writers have made.

ORIGINAL

wordy, passive opening

It has been maintained throughout history by

hyphen needed   *wrong connotation*

some of the most well trained and (notorious)

redundant?

nutritionists and (specialists) that a vegetarian diet

is superior to a nonvegetarian diet.

REVISED

Over the years, many well-trained and respected

nutritionists have maintained that a vegetarian diet

is superior to a nonvegetarian diet.

ORIGINAL

Be specific. Which border?

The immigrants cross the border believing that

where?

they will not be here forever. They come to make more

"to" repeated too often

money to take home to Mexico to build a better life.

REVISED

The immigrants cross the Texas-Mexico border

believing that they will not be in the United States

forever. They hope to make enough money in the United

States to return to Mexico and build better lives.

■ **Exercise 4.2** Apply the criteria for editing to a draft you are working on. Give your paper all the attention to detail it deserves. And don't back away from more complicated revisions when they are necessary.

4c WHAT DOES PROOFREADING INVOLVE?

PROCESS MENU
PREPARING
PLANNING
DRAFTING
INCUBATING
REVISING
EDITING
PROOFREADING

Troubleshooting

When you are reasonably satisfied with the content, organization, and style of your paper, you're ready to put it in final form. You probably know that readers will be influenced by the surface appearance of the paper, the professional gloss you give it. So spend time *proofreading*. Like checking your appearance in the mirror before an important date, proofreading provides a final measure of quality control. The more you care about the impression a paper makes, the more important it is *not* to neglect this last step.

● **Tip**

Use the handbook again to check punctuation, correct usage, or the conventions of edited American English. ●

To proofread thoroughly . . .

4c–1 **Check your weakest areas.** If you are a poor speller, pick out words that might be misspelled and look them up in a dictionary. If you're prone to write sentence fragments, review all your sentences to be sure they have both subjects and verbs. If you are inclined to put commas where they're not needed, check to be sure commas don't interrupt the flow of ideas. And check that you have used the correct forms of these troublesome words: *its/it's; your/you're; there/their/they're*.

4c–2 **Check for inconsistencies.** Have you switched your point of view in ways that might be confusing—for example, addressing readers initially as "you" but later referring to them as "we" or "they"? Do you use contractions in some parts of the paper but avoid them in others? Make certain the tone of the paper is consistent throughout, not light in some places and stiff in others.

4c–3 **Check punctuation.** Look for comma splices—that is, where you might have mistakenly joined a pair of independent clauses with a comma instead of a semicolon. Take a moment to review all semicolons while you're at it. See that proper nouns and adjectives (England, African) and "I" are capitalized. And check that you have used quotation marks and parentheses in pairs.

4c–4 **Use a computer spelling checker.** If you are using a word-processing program that includes a spelling checker, run your text through it. However, a spelling checker won't catch many serious misspellings, such as writing *where* for *were* or *no* for *know*.

4c–5 **Proofread for typographical errors.** Look especially for transposed letters, dropped endings, faulty word division, and omitted apostrophes.

4c–6 **Check the format of your paper.** Be sure to number your pages, to keep accurate and consistent margins, to underline titles that need to be underlined, to put other titles between quotation marks (see Section 28e–3), and to clip your pages together.

A step important to anyone writing on a computer is to be sure you've instructed the computer to paginate the paper in the right spot and to add a running head (often a last name) when required:

Balarbar 2

Set the margins correctly and review the page breaks. You don't want the computer to leave a heading at the bottom of a page or to separate an illustration from its caption.

4c–7 **Get help from your friends.** Exchange papers with another student or get your roommate to read yours for mistakes and lapses.

S U M M A R Y

When Proofreading . . .

- Check spelling, grammar, and usage.
- Eliminate inconsistencies.
- Get the punctuation right.
- Double-check spelling.
- Eliminate typographical errors.
- Check the format of your paper.

■ **Exercise 4.3** For practice, proofread Hoang Nguyen's first draft (pp. 66–70) as if it were a final draft, taking care of the mechanical problems you see in it. For this exercise do not concern yourself with matters of content or aspects of style. Proofread only for the problems discussed in this section.

WINDOW ON WRITING: Final draft of paper by Hoang Nguyen

On the next few pages you can read the final draft of the paper we looked at in first draft form at the end of Chapter 3. In the first draft Hoang Nguyen told of his experience as a young Vietnamese who had fled the Communists and begun his education in the United States. His editors found the first draft interesting but unfocused. As you'll see, Hoang's final draft is an almost entirely new piece. He used the first draft as a "discovery draft," then worked through a second draft that helped him to retain the drama of his memories of leaving Vietnam, but finally to shift his focus to his experiences in American schools and his adapting to a new culture. Compare this final version to his original. In what ways do you think it is stronger? Are there any elements of the first draft you think he should have kept? Why?

FINAL DRAFT

Hoang Nguyen

Rhetoric and Composition

Professor Hairston

Little Dragon in the Land of the Free

In southeast Asia, there is a little country called Vietnam. Legend has it that its people came from a Dragon Lord and a Fairy Queen. The Dragon Lord and the Fairy Queen had 100 sons and daughters who hatched from 100 eggs. Since the Fairy Queen belonged to the mountains and the Dragon Lord lived in the sea, they could not stay together. So, the Dragon Lord and the Fairy Queen divided their 100 sons and daughters. The Dragon Lord took 50 sons and daughters and went into the sea, while the remaining 50 followed the Fairy Queen into the mountains. If the legend is true, I am a descendent of the Dragon Lord and the Fairy Queen.

Regretfully, when I was only eight years old, I had to leave the magical land of my birth because Communists had taken control of the government. Under the Communists, my family would have been spied upon constantly. Our freedom to travel would have been limited: we would have had to explain to the government our reason for any trip. If my family had stayed in Vietnam, the Communists likely would have killed my father and sent me to a reeducation camp. The function of a reeducation camp was to make persons more susceptible to Communist ideas by using brainwashing techniques to diminish the human spirit. Fortunately, my family managed to escape the Communist onslaught in 1975, fleeing first to Guam in a military transport and then finally taking refuge in America.

America was like a dream, strange but peaceful. Instead of the noise of military jets flying over my head, I heard the birds singing for the first time in my life. Instead of seeing soldiers and their guns, I found myself in a flat and vast land planted with rows and rows of cotton crops. The cotton grew on farms near a town called New Deal, deep in the panhandle of Texas, where I had my first real contact with American culture.

I was only eight years old. My parents had enrolled me in the fourth grade. At that time, I did not know a single English word, and I was going to a school where no one spoke Vietnamese.

Looking around, I felt tiny and insignificant among much bigger and taller classmates. Since Vietnamese are small people compared to Americans, I found myself suddenly in a land of giants. I had no friends and no understanding of how the American educational system worked. I was frightened, yet I could not communicate my fear. I searched desperately for something familiar, something that I had known from my schooling in Vietnam. However, the two schools were so different that I could find nothing to comfort me.

I remember that the first time I got off a school bus in America, I feared the driver had dropped me off at the wrong place. I had expected to see a courtyard enclosed by a brick wall and protected by a metal gate. My image of a school building came from what I had experienced in Vietnam, where most schools are surrounded by a seven-foot wall to protect their students from stray bullets. Of course American schools do not have brick walls around their perimeters or gates on their entrance, but I did not know that then. I did not realize that the United States had not had a war on its land since 1865, when the Civil War ended, and that there was no reason for a school to protect its students from stray bullets. Vietnamese schools also needed their walls to keep people out who could not pay the tuition because school was not free, as it is in the United States. Yet somehow the walls of my Vietnamese school made me feel secure. By contrast, my American school left me feeling vulnerable and naked. I tried to explain my insecurity to my classmates, but the language barrier made communication impossible. I felt truly alone and abandoned.

However, I quickly learned to cope with my insecurity by focusing on specific tasks such as memorizing spelling words and doing math homework. I learned to use gestures and the few English words I knew to communicate my needs. As time passed, some of my classmates became friends. The daily routine of classes comforted me as well. My outlook on school and on living in America in general changed from gloomy to optimistic.

Now, after living in the United States for sixteen years, I no longer find it the strange place it appeared to be. It is truly a great

```
country. Most of my original misconceptions about

American schools have changed too. My experiences,

however, have made me realize how easy it is to

take one's culture for granted, to believe that

what happens in one's life is normal, even when

bullets are flying. Appreciating the differences

between the two cultures has enriched my life. In

fact, I think the Dragon Lord and the Fairy Queen

might be surprised to learn that one of their

descendents is now living in the Land of the Free

and the Home of the Brave.
```

■ **Exercise 4.4** No paper is ever absolutely done. Even a final version can be rethought and revised. After reading the second version of Hoang Nguyen's "Little Dragon in the Land of the Free," apply the revising guidelines on page 76 to it as if it were, once again, a first draft. What new suggestions might you have for the paper? Do you think Hoang might have used more material from his original first draft (pp. 66–70) in this final paper? Write a paragraph summarizing the suggestions you'd make to Hoang were he to think about yet one more version of this paper.

Document Design

If you are writing something you want people to read, you need to gain and hold their attention.

Although the writing you are currently doing in college may not call for special layouts or graphics, all writers today need to know how they can add visual elements to their writing to make it more appealing and accessible to their readers. In our visually oriented culture, how a document *looks* sends a message that is as important as what it *says*. That's why it's crucial for you to think about strategies you can use to present your messages attractively. Fortunately, most writers can now draw on two sources for help: computer programs and the principles of document design.

WHAT YOU CAN DO

At the most basic level, even simple word-processing programs give you a wide selection of fonts (type styles), let you choose type in varied sizes, and let you put boxes around some sections. You can also make lists and put symbols (bullets) before items.

With a simple graphics program, you can insert charts and graphs in a document, add drawings, and use symbols and figures to create special effects that would have required a professional print shop a few years ago. With a clip art program or certain CD-ROM encyclopedias, you can add pictures and maps. If your computer and printer support color, you can produce documents like the examples we show in this section, but you can also turn out good-looking work in black and white if you know a little about document design.

● **Tip**

"Graphic design should provide a road map that steers your readers from point to point."

"Effective graphic design favorably predisposes people to accept your...point of view."

—Roger Parker, *Looking Good in Print* ●

WHY YOU SHOULD DESIGN YOUR DOCUMENTS

When you plan the layout of your writing and add graphics to it, you help your readers in several ways.

- You help them follow the flow of ideas by using layout to guide their reading and by presenting key information in lists or boxes.
- You make abstract information easier to grasp by reinforcing it with charts, graphs, and illustrations.
- You break up large blocks of continuous type with headings and subheadings, illustrations, and pull-quotes* and by arranging the type so that it doesn't look crowded or dense.
- You show your readers you value them when you make your writing accessible and visually attractive.

WHAT TO EXPECT FROM THIS SECTION

This section, though necessarily brief, will get you started on creating attractive documents. It covers

Fonts/print styles
Academic papers
Overhead slides
Charts and graphs
Web pages for World Wide Web
Brochures
Newsletters

We also include general tips about document design that may be helpful. The topic is rich and complex, and we can only skim the surface here. You can learn more from a number of books on graphic design and desktop publishing that are available in the computer section of bookstores and libraries. Among the best is *Looking Good in Print* by Roger Parker.

TYPEFACES AND STYLES

It's fun to play around with sizes and styles of type that can make your documents look better and work better for your readers. For in-

---

*A *pull-quote* is a key sentence taken from an article and enlarged and highlighted to give the reader an idea of the article's content. Pull-quotes are especially common in newspapers and popular magazines.

stance, here are some of the typefaces (usually called *fonts*) likely to be available through your computer and printer.

Helvetica
Bookman
Courier
Geneva
Delphian
Times
Zapf Chancery
New Century Schoolbook
Chicago
𝔒𝔩𝔡 𝔈𝔫𝔤𝔩𝔦𝔰𝔥

The newer your computer, printer, and word-processing program, the more fonts you're likely to have. We suggest that you check out the fonts available through your word-processing program or computer. Then print a sample of each one so you'll have them to refer to. Some fonts give you symbols rather than letters; they're useful if you're doing writing that requires symbols for math, science, or foreign languages. Also look at "key caps" options.

The font *Zapf Dingbats* is useful mainly for ornament and emphasis. Here are some of the symbols available in that font.

❀ ❄ ◯ ▲ ↗ ♥ ❧ ✚ ✖ ⬥ ❖

Different dingbats give different effects. For example, ▲'s can highlight items in a list; a row of ❄'s can give a decorative effect; or you could use ❧'s to set off a quotation. To find out what you have available, select Zapf Dingbats from your menu and print out the symbols for both the regular and optional keyboards. Other useful symbol and icon fonts available in some programs are Wingdings and Monotype Sorts.

You can change type size from <small>very small</small> to larger or even larger. Or you can use *italics*, **boldface,** <u>underline</u>, **shadow**, outline, or SMALL CAPS. You can also expand or condense a word—for example, HOLIDAY or HOLIDAY—to fit your space.

We've barely skimmed the surface of the subject of fonts here—it's fascinating in its own right. If you're interested in learning more, check out texts in the computer section of your bookstore or library or look at books on printing.

Discussion of Model 1:
First Page Only of an Academic Paper

Creating an Academic Paper Special effects and attention-getting strategies aren't suitable in most academic papers; you don't want to give the impression that you're paying more attention to appearance than to content. Nevertheless, it makes sense to have the papers you turn in be as attractive as possible as long as they conform to the style your instructor recommends. (See Chapters 34 and 35.) If he or she accepts an informal style, in many papers you can use the strategies we talk about in this section. Illustrations or pictures are particularly useful, and graphs and charts can reinforce statistics.

What You Can Do First, double-space; even medium-length paragraphs are hard to read when they're single spaced. Be sure to leave ample margins—wide enough so the instructor can write comments—and enough white space so the paper doesn't look crowded. Set off paragraphs clearly, either by indenting or by leaving extra space between them, and break the paper into sections if it runs more than three pages.

Student Paper on B. B. King The writer uses a sharp, easily read font with subheadings to mark off sections and preview what's coming. The photo of King and his guitar, labeled "Fig. 1," also breaks up the text and adds interest. The image came from Microsoft's CD-ROM *Encarta Encyclopedia*; it was copied from the computer screen to the Macintosh clipboard, then "pasted" directly into the paper. For noncommercial use of an image, writers don't have to get permission. (This photo is copyrighted by Encarta.)

● **Tip**

When you're in the planning stage for any paper, start thinking about how you can use pictures, diagrams, or sketches to add interest to your document and break up long blocks of type. You'll find sources in clip art programs and encyclopedias. If you can use a scanner, you can copy other documents. And, of course, there's always good old cut and paste. Be sure to give credit for whatever you use. ●

Jason Miller
American Culture 363
March 16, 1995

A GIANT OF THE BLUES: B. B. KING

Fig. 1. B. B. King and "Lucille"

Blues, sometimes called the heart of jazz, has its roots in African-American folk music. Its rhythms and patterns resonate of Africa itself, and its lyrics still reflect the pleasures and pains of its originators, telling of love and sex, poverty and death. Working without written music—often with only the most basic of instruments, the banjo and the harmonica—blues and jazz musicians made improvisation into an art unique to jazz.

One of the most talented, and a crossover musician, is B. B. King, born Riley B. King in Indianola, Mississippi, in 1925. Known as the "Blues Boy of Beale Street," when he was a disc jockey in Memphis, King was one of the pioneers with the acoustic guitar. Although it had been a featured instrument with earlier players—T-Bone Walker and Louis Jordan—King brought new sounds to the stage and initiated the style that later became known as rhythm and blues.

King's style revealed a fresh approach. Using his own acoustic guitar, "Lucille," he developed a style that moved toward economy and combined traditional blues rhythms with a touch of jazz. This innovation

Discussion of Model 2:
First Slide for Overhead Projection or Computer Presentation

Creating an Overhead Slide In some of your classes, you may already be making oral or computer multimedia presentations. If so, you're getting excellent practice for giving such presentations at future business and professional meetings, where your audience would have no patience with your reading a paper. Slides that preview your main points and reinforce them for your audience are essential.

Keep your slides simple, and use a plain, boxy font that's easy to read. Develop only one idea per slide. Use bullets to set off points, and make your format consistent through all the slides.

What You Can Do First rule for an overhead or computer projection: **The audience has to be able to see what it says!** Nothing is so annoying as sitting in a dark room peering at a slide with print too small to read. So make your print highly visible, and test each overhead or screen ahead of time. Remember too that what you put on your slides or screen serves only as cues for you to expand on. You're talking to the people in your audience, not reading to them. But keep the slide on the screen as long as you're talking about that idea.

Overhead on *Understanding Exercise* The topic is announced immediately in the largest type, followed by a provocative slogan to stimulate interest. In this first slide, your four points preview your talk and let your listeners know what to expect. The next slide might list main points about the benefits of exercise: REDUCES STRESS, STRENGTHENS THE IMMUNE SYSTEM, HELPS CONTROL WEIGHT, and so on. In your talk, you illustrate each point with examples to keep your listeners on track.

● **Tip**

For a document like this, in which you want to present a few points to the best effect, sketch your layout ahead of time using pencil and paper. It's a good idea to do such preliminary layout for newsletters and brochures, too, because careful advance planning is essential to creating effective documents. ●

UNDERSTANDING EXERCISE

**Exercise is like money:
it's good for almost everything.**

Overview

◆ **What are the benefits of exercise?**

◆ **Who should participate?**

◆ **What types of exercise are best?**

◆ **What does current research say?**

Discussion of Model 3:
A Page of a Paper Using Charts and Graphs

Creating a Paper with Charts and Graphs You can incorporate charts and graphs into a paper, or you can use them separately in overhead or computer presentations to emphasize points and act as visual cues and reinforcers. When you use them in computerized or overhead presentations, be sure they're large enough to read from a distance. (See the discussion of Model 2.) However you use them, charts and graphs are important additions to any presentation that involves statistics because they put abstract information into visual form and make it more accessible to viewers. See the chart on page 641 of the research paper in Chapter 34, pages 630 through 652.

What You Can Do If you are working from spreadsheet programs such as *Lotus*, *QuatroPro*, or *Excel*, you can create your graphs and charts within those increasingly sophisticated programs. You provide the numbers, and the program will offer you several options for displaying your data in pie charts, line graphs, or bar graphs. Create your graphs, then copy them and paste them into the paper you're writing. You can also use graphics presentations programs such as *PowerPoint* or *Claris Impact*—feed in the numbers and the graphs magically appear. Some word-processing programs—for instance, *Microsoft Word 6* — also have the capacity to do charts. If none of these programs is available or if you don't yet have the expertise to use them, do your graphs by hand and paste them in.

Model Paper on Ice Cream This is a page of a model paper created to illustrate graphs. Even the most basic charts and graphs make the material more interesting by giving the statistics a visual dimension, breaking up the text, and enlivening the paper with color.

● **Tip**

Keep in mind the "body language" of your document. It should look inviting and easy to read. One good way to achieve that look is to leave plenty of white space, especially around titles and illustrations. Cut the number of words rather than put too much on a page. Use graphics to support your message in a way that makes your document say "Read me!" ●

Ice Cream Consumption at Center College

Despite recent innovations in the dessert business that have brought frozen yogurt, exotic sherbets, and the decadent and expensive chocolate truffles, students at Center College still favor that all-American favorite, ice cream. George Wilcox, head of Student Food Services, says that ice cream outsells all other desserts. Asked whether he had seen student tastes in ice cream change over the years, he said, "Not much. In spite of the fancy new concoctions that come along all the time, they like pretty much what they've always liked." The chart in Fig. 1 shows those tastes.

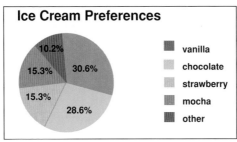

Fig. 1

Dr. Leona Martin, director of nutrition at the college, says she's not surprised. "Ice cream is part of everyone's childhood, and it's what most of us think of when we want a treat." She worries, however, about the high fat and cholesterol of ice cream. "It's just loaded," she says.

Students, however, seem to care mostly about the high cost of their favorite dessert. When one looks at the price increase per gallon for good ice cream from 1990 to 1994, one can understand their concern. Fig. 2 shows more than a 100% increase in those years.

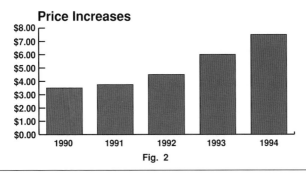

Fig. 2

Discussion of Model 4:
World Wide Web Home Page

Creating a World Wide Web (WWW) Page Students who regularly cruise the Internet know about the WWW, a resource that connects sites on the information superhighway by using documents called "pages." These pages furnish information and provide links to related sources on the Internet. Tens of thousands of Net users—from corporations and the U.S. Congress to students in writing classes—have already established home pages and Web sites designed to attract and serve readers. Web pages can be creative, playful, and highly personalized.

What You Can Do If you or your group would like to create your own Web page, you can learn the rapidly evolving conventions of Web home pages by browsing the Net and noting those pages that work well. Some are organized by graphic "maps"; others use print only. Some contain interactive forms that a user can fill in to get more information.

To design your page, decide what you want to feature and how you want to organize your page. Sketch out a design, opening with a heading that clearly identifies you, your group, or your project. Place your images and graphic designs in a way that highlights your message and catches the browser's eye. Then write your text, keeping it succinct and clear. Establish those key points or links that, when clicked on, will take readers to other Web sites that you identified as related to your topic. Those links could be phrases in your text or graphics on the page.

You can even use film clips and sound in your home page, but remember that every element on the page must support the information—don't distract your reader with what design expert Edward Tufte calls "chartjunk," design elements that convey little information. When you're done, review the page and ask yourself: Will this page invite readers in and provide the data and links they seek? If not, redo it.

Model WWW Home Page This home page, done by first-year writing students at the University of Texas, announces its topic with a graphic, then shows two groups of students who will argue on different sides of the issue, "Foreign Aid: Should We Keep It at Home?" Their text lays out their main points and guides readers to subtopics of possible interest.

Foreign Aid: Should We Keep It At Home?

We are a group of first year English composition students instructed by <u>Tonya Browning</u> at The <u>University of Texas at Austin</u>. Our project concerns the United States and its involvement in providing foreign assistance to underprivileged nations. This presentation examines both sides of the debate regarding <u>foreign aid</u> to other countries.

The Drawbacks of U.S. Foreign Assistance

The United States sends billions of dollars in supplies, labor, and actual funds to other countries each year. Even though we are experiencing <u>record unemployment</u>, increased racial tension, skyrocketing infant mortality rates, woeful <u>underfunding of education</u>, crumbling <u>infrastructure</u> and a record budget deficit that will probably mortgage our grandchildren's grandchildren, we are still sending the <u>taxpayer's hard earned money</u> to countries thousands of miles away. The question remains: if the government has billions of dollars to spend on these other countries, then why are Americans suffering at home? These funds need to stay in our own country to help fight these domestic problems. Not only should we keep this money at home, but United States officials need to consider reallocation of current funds.

The Advantages of U.S. Foreign Assistance

There are a number of reasons why foreign assistance programs are a sound investment for the future of the United States. First and foremost, they help the US <u>economically</u> while insuring global stability. In addition, <u>trading partners</u> are gained, strategic allies are secured, and democracies are fostered around the world. <u>Humanitarian acts</u> also play a substantial role in the intervention of the US because the welfare of the underdeveloped is advanced. Hence, the advantages to solid foreign aid programs benefit not only the US, but the impoverished countries as well. Most importantly, it is through foreign aid and the compassion of the American people, that peace and prosperity are allowed to advance around the globe.

Discussion of Model 5:
Brochure

Creating a Brochure In today's information-saturated culture, brochures have become one of the major means of delivering information to people. They combine pictures, graphic design, and print into an inexpensive and efficient package of information. They can be plain or fancy, succinct or crammed with information. The simpler ones, those that use only print and perhaps a few borders and some symbols, are relatively easy to produce and can be quite attractive. Things get more complicated when you incorporate sketches or pictures, but with a desktop publishing program such as Pagemaker or Quark and some clip art, they're manageable too.

What You Can Do The keys to a good brochure are (1) Keep the message simple, (2) Leave plenty of open space, and (3) Use graphics when you can. You want your brochure to be eye-catching so people will pick it up, so find a logo or sketch that captures the spirit of your message. Then you want to entice your readers to read it and remember the important points. To accomplish that, use lists, set items off with colors or borders, and divide the text into chunks with pictures or graphics. Avoid giving too many details, but tell the reader how to get more information. Phone numbers can do that.

Model 5 shows both pages of a brochure that could be done with a desktop publishing program. You could also do a brochure on a word-processing program that lets you divide a horizontal page into three columns, but you might do better to create the panels separately, then add graphics. Photographs can be scanned in with a computer or pasted in. You can then photocopy the completed brochure. Using black and white or only two colors keeps costs down.

Tourism Brochure This colorful brochure was done by Lorne Foss, a first-year student at the University of Texas at San Antonio. Eye-catching headings divide the brief but informative text, and the author has used photographs to set off the blocks and engage the readers' interest in specific attractions. Bright colors catch the fiesta atmosphere the student wants to convey. A border unifies the page.

Welcome to San Antonio!

Whether you're here for a day or a week, San Antonio has something for everyone to enjoy! If your stay is a short one, visit the River Walk (it's a must!) and SA's newest attraction, Fiesta Texas. But if your stay is a long one, why not visit everything! We hope you enjoy your stay in our beautiful city. Come back anytime!

Tower of the Americas

The Tower is the nation's tallest free-standing tower. Built for the 1968 HemisFare, it stands 750 ft and has an observation deck, lounge, and revolving restaurant.

Open Daily 8 am - 11pm   299-8615

Alamo

The Alamo, the most famous mission among several in San Antonio, became part of history when 189 men defended the site from 4,000 Mexican troops for 13 days. The Alamo now contains 2 museums, a shrine, and a research library.

Open Mon - Sat 9 am -5:30 pm   225-1391
Sun 10 am - 5:30 pm

River Walk

The Paseo del Rio (River Walk in English) is a 2.5 mile walkway along the San Antonio

River. The walk is lined with shops, nightclubs, and restaurants. River Center Mall is also accessible from the River Walk.

Sea World of Texas

The world's largest marine life park. More than 25 aquatic shows, water rides, the 16-acre Cypress Gardens, and several marine exhibits. Celebrity entertainers

perform throughout the season.

Open Daily 10 am - 8 pm   523-3611
10 am - 10 pm starting June 11

Fiesta Texas

Fiesta Texas is a theme park created around 4 towns - a German village, a Mexican town, a 1920's boom town, and Rockville of the 1950's. Live shows, food, rides, and crafts carry out the themes.

Open Daily -
10 am - 10 pm.

697-5050

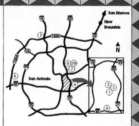

1. Tower of the Americas
2. Alamo
3. River Walk
4. Alamo Dome
5. Fiesta Texas
6. Sea World of Texas

Other attractions

7. Witte Musem ~ 829-7262
8. Splash Town ~ 227-1100
9. San Antonio Zoo ~ 734-7183
10. San Antonio
   Botanical Gardens ~ 821-5115

Tower picture - SA Chamber of Commerce Membership Directory '94
Shamo - Sea World picture - Luby's Brochure

Viva San Antonio

Tower of the Americas

Discussion of Model 6:
Newsletter

Creating a Newsletter Almost every organization publishes a newsletter because it's a good tool for getting out information and for networking. Newsletters are generally informal; they're designed to attract readers and let them know what's going on. Often they're excellent examples of clever ways to use headlines, dingbats, pull quotes, borders, and different styles of type. Be careful, however, not to clutter the page with too many devices—the effect can be like mixing stripes, plaids, flowers, and polka dots in one garment.

What You Can Do Newsletters take considerable planning in order to fit all the elements into an attractive presentation. Generally they have a consistent format for the heading and sometimes a logo for the organization. The body of the letter is usually in two columns for easy reading, and boxes or borders are used to unify and highlight individual articles. It's useful to sketch your layout before you actually begin working on the computer.

A good desktop publishing program will give you the tools you need to do newsletters, but they can also be done in regular word-processing programs once you learn to set up columns.

The SOTA Newsletter This one-page letter is set up to give maximum information in little space. Paragraphs are short, subtitles are used to separate items, and the picture for the most important story takes the prominent upper right-hand corner. For this illustration the author chose a picture of an early Montessori school that was available from the CD-ROM *Encarta Encyclopedia*. Another major announcement is boxed for emphasis.

● **Tip**

Working in document design takes patience, particularly if you're using more than one graphics program. Unless you're a computer expert, you'll take many a false turn, and fine-tuning the last details is time consuming. But the payoff is handsome in writing that makes you look good. ●

STUDENTS OLDER THAN AVERAGE

The Newsletter for Students Older Than Average
at Center College, March 1995

SCHOLARSHIPS FOR RETURNING WOMEN

What? $2500 a year
How many? 5 each year
When? Beginning Fall 1995
Who? Women over 30 returning to college as undergraduates
Why? To prepare older women for professions
Where? Any Ohio four-year college
How? Apply at Room 10, Bost Hall, by May 5

Sponsored by the Geneva Holt Foundation, Toledo, Ohio

Berlin

SOTA EARLY CHILDHOOD CENTER TO OPEN IN APRIL

At last it's happening. With the support and cooperation of Center University Parents Organization, we will open our SOTA Day Care Center on campus on April 1 with room for 60 children, age one through five years. It will feature

→ Professionally trained staff
→ Meals prepared on site
→ Specialists in childhood learning
→ Fully equipped playground

For those who have not yet reserved a place, call Joy at **774-8080.**

SOTA SPRING PICNIC

The annual spring SOTA picnic will happen at Pease Park on Saturday, April 21, starting at 10 a.m. with horseshoes, swimming, Frisbee contests, and general celebration. Plan to bring the kids—there'll be lots for them to do. SOTA will furnish barbecue. Bring your own drinks.

If you're coming, call Barbara at 782-9038—we need to let the park people know about numbers. Hope to see you—

"The most important part of your child's education happens before she goes to school."

—*Ann Oatken*

Fine Points

Academic Papers Your instructor may have specific guidelines he or she wants you to follow; if so, check them out (see Chapters 34 and 35) and follow them carefully. If you're free to experiment a little, however, by all means do so. Use lists or charts, or insert illustrations or graphics to break up text. You can use italics rather than underlining for titles and add color occasionally. You may use boldface for emphasis, but do so sparingly. Sometimes titles and subtitles look good in small caps, and you can capitalize words in subheadings.

For most papers stick with plain type fonts. Courier, Times, or New Century are good choices; they're clean and not too heavy. Chicago is so heavy it makes the page look crowded, and italic fonts like Zapf Chancery are too fancy. Choose either 10- or 12-point size, and use only two or at most three different fonts in a paper.

Posters, Brochures, Announcements, and Other Documents For writing outside of class, try more interesting fonts and styles. For posters or overheads, try a square, heavy font such as Chicago for the most important information. For personal announcements or invitations, try one of the italic fonts, such as Zapf Chancery. Here are examples that use appropriate fonts.

Toastmasters presents **Stephen Carter** author of THE CULTURE OF DISBELIEF	*Come to the* *Grand Opening of the* *Mercury Art Gallery* *on June 20* *twelve noon*

Other Possibilities Even if you don't have access to a commercial desktop publishing program or a graphics program, with most computers you can still enhance your written presentations by putting boxes around text, shadowing titles, or using your option keys to create bullets for a list. Some word-processing programs also include a few drawing tools so you can draw and insert figures. Remember too that what you see on your screen doesn't always show exactly how the printer copy will look, so print out a trial copy to make a final check of your work. The bottom line is, *ENGAGE YOUR READER.*

5

How Do You Write Critically in College?

A   Writing in College
B   Critical Thinking

5a   HOW DO YOU WRITE PAPERS IN COLLEGE?

Troubleshooting

As a college student, you can count on having to write papers. That's a fact of life, regardless of your major. But if you wrote only a few papers in high school or if you have been out of school for several years and written almost nothing during that time, you may come close to panic when you think about starting to write again, not only in English classes but in history, philosophy, or even science courses. Understandably, you wonder what college writing is like. What do professors expect?

The answer is that college writing is not necessarily difficult, but it is different from high school writing because college instructors and professors have special requirements in mind when they read student papers. Once you understand what they expect, you should do well in your work.

For writing in college you need to . . .

5a–1 **Support any claim you make with reasons and evidence.** If one word could be used to describe college instructors and professors, it would be *skeptical*, especially when they read an explanation or argument. For them it's not enough that someone claims on the basis of opinion or feelings that something is true or recommends that something should be done. Their immediate response to any claim they see in writing is likely to be "Why?

105

Show me." In the margins of papers they put comments and questions such as "What's your source?"; "Who says so?"; "I'd like to see more evidence"; "Do you *know* this is true?"; "You're claiming too much here."

Professors act like this because they want students to get in the habit of examining their ideas and thinking about where those ideas came from and whether they're justified. They also want them to realize that academic writing requires that all claims be supported. So if you want your instructors to value what you write, you need to anticipate such questions and comments as you draft a paper and be sure they're answered in your final version.

5a-2 **Remember not to take on too much in your paper.** When you're writing an academic paper, make it a golden rule not to take on too much. When you make a claim in a paper, think of yourself as having staked out a piece of territory; you've asserted what you believe and drawn lines around it, and now you have to defend it. You don't want to find out when you're halfway through that you've taken on more than you can handle, that your boundaries are so overextended you don't have the resources to back up the commitments you've made. You'll do better to stake out a smaller territory that you can defend and one you can explore thoroughly. Then you'll have a chance to explore and write about your topic in detail.

So don't begin with a thesis as big as Texas: "Rock and roll is the crowning achievement of American popular music." Instead remember the adage "Write more about less" and explore something more manageable—for instance, an explanatory paper about how Bruce Springsteen got his start at The Stone Pony, a New Jersey nightclub.

5a-3 **Make the scope of your paper proportionate to its length.** When instructors ask students to write papers, they often specify a certain length: four to six pages, ten pages, fifteen pages, and so on. In one sense that's helpful—you do want to know whether you're being asked to write a short paper or a long one. But in another sense, such limits are not helpful at all. How much can you do in five or six pages? How big a topic should you take for a ten-page paper? What does a twenty-page paper imply? These are hard questions to answer out of context, but there is one useful rule of thumb: Make the scope of your paper proportionate to its length. Sounds simple enough, but it's not always easy to keep in mind. As a result, some of the worst papers instructors receive are those in which the writer takes on too large a topic, tries to cover it in a short paper, and bogs down in generalities.

When you're writing a short paper, keep your topic small enough so you'll be able to use facts and other supporting material. On the other hand, if you're asked to write a twenty-page paper for a history course and you choose a very narrow topic, you may not find enough to say on it without padding your writing. So think ahead about what you can realistically accomplish in an assigned paper and focus it accordingly.

5a–4 **Understand what constitutes evidence and good reasons in academic writing.** Most of us are used to voicing our opinions freely even when we haven't thought about them carefully. Thus it's not unusual to hear a student saying, "Well, that's *my* opinion. Isn't it just as good as the next person's?" Most professors would reply, "Outside the classroom, yes. But not here, not unless you can give me good reasons and back them with evidence."

In academic writing that evidence should be rational and factual: historical documents, eyewitness accounts, expert testimony, research data, case studies, statements from authorities, and other kinds of arguments designed to appeal to readers' intelligence. Good arguments are the sort lawyers use in court: analogies, predictions about cause and effect, examples of similar cases, and so on. Sometimes you can include personal experiences in your argument, but you need to be sure they are relevant. A single personal incident or anecdote isn't sufficient.

When you're arguing in an academic paper, remember that seldom can you prove something is absolutely, irrefutably true. Thus it's better not to overstate a claim. Instead settle for making a forceful, well-supported, carefully reasoned case with high probability. And do remember that reasoning means just that—appealing to your readers' intellect and rational faculties. Most professors find strictly emotional appeals out of place in college papers although they'll grant they have their place in other kinds of writing.

You'll find more on writing arguments in college papers in the next chapter.

SUMMARY

Evidence for College Papers

Some appropriate evidence for college papers includes

- Historical documents
- Articles from respected newspapers and magazines
- Eyewitness accounts
- Expert testimony
- Statistics
- Case studies
- Interviews with and quotes from authorities
- Analogies
- Data from government reports and documents

5a–5 **Remember to document your sources and give credit to others when appropriate.** College instructors expect writers in their classes always to cite their sources and to give credit for any quotations or ideas that have come from someone else. If you write, "It is generally believed that . . . ," your instructor is likely to ask, "By whom? Where?" If you cite statistics or research, your professor wants to know where you got your data. If you quote a television program or a magazine article, college instructors want the title and date. And if you use *any* material that someone else thought of or wrote first, you're obligated to give that source credit. If you don't, you're plagiarizing, and that's a serious offense.

Documenting sources takes time, but it's a very important part of writing in college. It's not difficult to do once you know where to look for guidelines (see Chapters 33 and 34), and good documentation will win you points with your instructors.

5a–6 **Learn to assess the constraints on your writing.** Remember the practical constraints you face when you're writing college papers: How much time do you have? Will a computer be available? Where is the material you need? What other commitments do you have?

Before you get too far into a topic, consider how much research you may have to do. How long will it take? Some books may not be available, particularly if you wait until the last minute. Are you planning interviews for your paper? When can you do them? If you need files of recent newspapers, does the library have them? Do you need to check important facts?

In other words, think ahead just as you would for any other project—getting to the airport on time or getting your income tax mailed by the deadline—so you can avoid last-minute snags that will put you in a crisis.

5a–7 **Remember that college instructors expect the papers you turn in to look good.** Even if your instructors have been lenient about usage or punctuation errors when they read your drafts or haven't given special warnings about using standard English when they assigned papers, they care about those details on the final product. Proofread for faulty punctuation, agreement errors, and spelling. If you know you're a poor speller, get help from a friend who can spell. Run your paper through the spelling checker on your computer if it has that feature.

If you can, write the paper on a computer or type it, double spaced. Be sure your printer or typewriter has a good ribbon; if you have to write the paper in longhand, make sure it's highly legible. Professors hate getting papers they can barely read. Use decent-quality paper, not stuff so thin you can see through it, and tear off the perforated edges on computer paper. Separate the pages. *Never* turn in pages torn out of a spiral notebook with the ragged edges still attached.

CHECKLIST

Writing College Papers

When you write a college paper, remember to . . .

- Support your claims with evidence and reasons.
- Limit your claim to one you can adequately support.
- Keep your topic narrow enough to be developed within the specified length.
- Keep in mind what constitutes good evidence in college writing.
- Document your sources.
- Assess the limitations under which you must work, and plan accordingly.
- Hand in only neat, carefully edited, and proofread papers.

■ **Exercise 5.1** Below are several claims you might make in writing a college paper. For each claim, suggest specific kinds of supporting evidence you think a college instructor would find satisfactory.

1. The western states are compromising future generations by becoming dumping grounds for toxic waste from the more industrialized eastern part of the country.
2. On the whole, the claims made for artificial intelligence a decade ago do not seem to be justified.
3. The most expensive crimes of the 1980s were not those connected with drugs; they were the frauds practiced by the savings and loan industry.
4. The movie industry cannot escape its share of responsibility for the increasing violence in our society.
5. The long-awaited day of the electronic book seems to be dawning at last.

■ **Exercise 5.2** Working with other students in a group, analyze the titles below that students proposed for the short papers—three to five double-spaced pages—they planned to write in a composition class. What does each title suggest about the breadth of the topic for the proposed paper? Do you think such a paper could be adequately developed and supported within the space limits?

1. Alexander the Great: The Building of an Empire
2. How One Drug Abuse Program Succeeded
3. Chemical Dependency Among the Upper Middle Class
4. Subtle Forms of Sexism in Magazine Advertising
5. Illiteracy in America: Who's Contributing?

5b   HOW CAN YOU BECOME A CRITICAL THINKER?

Troubleshooting

One of the main reasons you are going to college is to sharpen your intellectual skills and become a *critical thinker,* a person who explores ideas, asks questions, challenges statements, and looks for new solutions to old problems. Although reading and discussion will play an important part in the process, writing is one of your best tools for developing the ability to think critically. Through writing you can inquire, test, analyze, compare, and evaluate the ideas and information you will encounter both in and out of the classroom as you go through college, and through writing you will cultivate the higher-order thinking skills you need to succeed in college.

Much of the *information* you absorb in college today will be obsolete ten or twenty years from now, but if you acquire the *knowledge* of how to think critically, you will develop analytical and problem-solving abilities that will serve you the rest of your life.

In college, a crucial element in your critical thinking is learning *to read critically* because much of what you write in college will be in response to what you read. Although we cannot take time here to guide you through the steps of the reading process, we will be stressing several ways in which you need to bring your critical faculties to bear on what you read and hear.

To develop your abilities for critical thinking . . .

CAUTION

5b–1 Remember that learning to think critically means cultivating an attitude of inquiry rather than developing a set of skills. Critical thinking is only an extended and focused version of the kind of thinking we all do every day when we set out to solve problems: we gather evidence, we examine options, we look at advantages and disadvantages, and we examine testimony and opinions for possible bias. We *inquire* and *reflect* in order to get the best information possible before we judge or decide.

A person shopping for groceries thinks critically when he or she juggles concerns about budget, nutrition, time, and family likes and dislikes before buying food. So does the person who reads *Consumer Reports* and does some comparative shopping before she buys a cordless phone or a CD player. So do you when you consider all the factors you need to balance when you decide whether a part-time job that pays $11 an hour is really a better job than one that pays $9.50.

The critical thinking you have to do in college differs from the critical thinking of everyday life primarily because you're often working with larger, more abstract issues, and the process takes longer and involves more research. You may be asked to read about an issue or a problem, analyze what you've read, and write about your conclusions. Or you may be asked to do an experiment in which you gather evidence, examine it, and make a judgment. In either case you're looking at data and reflecting about it: that's what critical thinking involves.

5b-2 **Start any inquiry by looking at the evidence presented.** For example:

- How much evidence does the writer or speaker present? Does the sample seem large enough for the claims being made?
- Where did the evidence come from? Does it seem trustworthy? Is the writer scrupulous about separating fact from opinion?
- If the writer cites authorities, what are their credentials?
- What are the writer's credentials—experience, education? Who does the writer work for?
- What biases or vested interests may be concealed behind an organization's name?
- Is the evidence fairly and fully presented? Do you suspect something has been omitted?

Critical thinkers also watch for bias in their own thinking and guard against the tendency we all have to select evidence that confirms our beliefs. When you're researching a case, consult articles that reflect different perspectives—for example, *Rolling Stone* as well as *The New York Times*, *Ms.* as well as *Esquire*. And be sure your sources include both women and men.

5b-3 **Look closely at a writer's or speaker's claims to see if they go beyond what the evidence actually supports.** Here are two cases in which critical thinkers have recently challenged the results of long-accepted research.

Many psychologists now question the long-standing practice of researchers in psychology who gather their data solely from college students and from that data make claims about psychological characteristics of the general population. The critics point out that college students are chosen because they're available (often they *have* to participate) and cost very little, but they certainly don't constitute a random sample of the general population.

Women's groups have begun to challenge some major research projects in medicine because they included no women. Take some studies done on heart disease, for example, that included only men. Given the differences in the physiology, body chemistry, diet, and living habits of men and women, is it valid to base treatment for women heart patients on the data from such studies? Probably not.

In the first example, the writer points out that psychological researchers are drawing conclusions that go well beyond what their data warrant. In the second, the writer points out that medical researchers have failed to get important data that would affect their conclusions.

5b–4 **Learn to look for what's *not* there: the unstated assumptions or premises that underlie a person's claims or arguments.** Does someone making an argument take it for granted that he or she and the audience share certain knowledge or beliefs when in fact they don't? If what someone takes for granted can reasonably be disputed, then his or her claims should be challenged.

For example, for years traditional politicians assumed that women were not likely to be a significant source of money for political campaigns. The politicians assumed that women weren't very interested in politics and that men did nearly all the big giving. In fact, one anecdote tells of a major figure in one of the parties going up to a wealthy woman at a political fund-raiser and asking, "And whose little woman are you?" They also assumed that women candidates would be at a disadvantage in elections because they would have trouble raising money.

One well-to-do woman, Ellen Malcolm, was thinking critically when she challenged that assumption. She knew that millions of women were indeed interested in politics and wanted more women in office, and she believed they were willing to contribute money to help elect women candidates. On the basis of that hunch, in 1985 she founded Emily's List, a political action committee committed to electing pro-choice Democratic women candidates. The organization solicits money almost entirely from women; in the 1992 elections Emily's List contributed over $6 million to women candidates and was a major factor in the victories of four women senators.

That's how critical thinking can bring about change.

5b–5 **Learn to look for anomalies, those spots in an argument or discussion where inconsistencies creep in.** One of the marks of critical thinkers is that they are continually alert for contradictions or something that doesn't fit.

For example, the rhetorician Richard Weaver claimed that arguments from definition are superior to those of cause and effect because the former appeal to our sense of what's naturally true and the latter are simply practical. Weaver didn't seem to realize, however, that people don't agree on what is naturally true, and that some of history's worst practices have been based on arguments from definition. Witness the Nazis' persecution of the Jews, whom they defined as inferior, and nineteenth-century laws that prohibited women from voting because they were deemed less rational than men. The facts about such arguments don't fit with Weaver's claim.

Discoveries also emerge when people think critically about anomalies. Galileo revolutionized astronomy when he observed that the orbits of the planets didn't fit the patterns described by the classical astronomer Ptolemy, who believed that planets and stars circled the earth. The chaos theory of modern physics was developed by Edward Lorenz when he got an unexpected answer from working out a mathematical equation.

5b-6 **Learn to look critically at the language a writer or speaker is using and check for possible bias.** As you read articles or books in which writers are laying out arguments and drawing conclusions, learn to run a "bias check" in the process.

For instance, here's a sentence from an *Atlantic Monthly* article (August 1994, p. 34) on underground construction: "It offers an altogether new kind of development medium: quiet, earthquake resistant, weatherproof, secure, and energy efficient, with virtually no constraints of geometry, scale, or location, and perfectly compatible with conservationist and preservationist values, no matter how strictly construed."

Now that's the kind of sentence that should make your bias detector buzz—all good words and positive connotations. Sure enough, checking back in the article reveals that the person who made the statement, Gary Brierly, is president of the American Underground Space Association. His claims may well be true, but given his built-in bias, a critical thinker will withhold judgment until he or she gets more information. Get in the habit of checking out the source any time you encounter language that seems either overly enthusiastic or overly negative. Mystery writers often ask, *"Cui bono?"* which roughly translated means "Who benefits?" That's a good question.

Being a critical thinker doesn't mean you have to distrust everything you read—it's understandable that people who want to convince others might use language that favors their point of view. But we should be alert when writers or speakers overload their prose with what rhetoricians call "god terms"—words such as *democratic, progressive,* or *natural*—or with "devil terms"—words like *destructive, vicious,* or *irresponsible.*

5b-7 **Pay attention to a writer's metaphors and analogies and be aware of their underlying implications.** Although metaphors and analogies are an integral and important part of our language, you need to recognize the extra meanings they often carry. For instance, if you read an article that says, "The battle against AIDS has put new stresses on all the reserve forces of the city's hospitals," recognize that the author is using a war metaphor to dramatize and draw attention to his point. When you encounter sports metaphors in political writing or speaking, phrases such as "We need a full court press" or "We're going for a touchdown," recognize that the writer may be trying to appeal to what he or she believes is a predominantly male audience and is using a common language to win its approval. Such metaphors can backfire, of course, if some in the audience resent such assumptions.

5b-8 **Avoid stereotypes.** Most of us are occasionally too quick to classify people and groups and put labels on them without thinking about how accurate or descriptive those labels really are. It's easy to do, but it's also irresponsible, and, at times, even vicious. Here are some typical stereotypes that one is likely to encounter.

> Professors are disorganized, forgetful people who can't find their keys or remember appointments.
>
> Men are sloppier than women and care less about how they look.
>
> Women are always late.
>
> People of Nordic origin are more melancholy than people who come from Mediterranean stock.

You may know individuals from any of these groups who have characteristics that fit these generalizations, but you probably also know professors who are extremely well organized, men who dress meticulously, women who are always on time, and Spaniards and Italians who are melancholy.

Stereotypes such as these are more annoying than damaging, but be alert for any stereotyping that attributes certain qualities to people of different races, groups, or gender—for instance, that people of African origin are more musical or more athletic than Caucasians; that women are more intuitive and emotional than men; that writers and musicians are more temperamental and less stable than people of other occupations; that women have low aptitude for science and math. Such generalizations reflect clichéd thinking, and they can lead to prejudice and discrimination. Critical thinkers refuse to take such judgments at face value without substantial support and documentation because they recognize the harm these stereotypes can do.

5b–9 **Be suspicious of simple solutions to complex problems and resist polarized, black-and-white thinking.** Critical thinkers are wary of arguments or explanations that offer quick, easy answers to difficult problems. They realize that most serious problems in our society are so complex that anyone who hopes to write about them intelligently must resist casting those involved as "good guys" and "bad guys" or suggesting that the problem could be solved quickly if someone would just do the right thing. There is seldom one "right thing."

For instance, consider the complex issue of welfare reform and the promises of many candidates to drastically reduce the amount of money spent on welfare. Here are just a few of the questions such an issue raises.

1. Just what qualifies as welfare? Does welfare mean all government payments to people who didn't earn them? Farm subsidies, for instance? Aid to military dependents?
2. Should there be a time limit on welfare payments to indigent families? How long should it be? What happens to those families after the time limit runs out?
3. Does the government have an obligation to provide the safety net of welfare for all its citizens? If so, where do the funds come from? If not, what is the long-range effect of letting all people fend for themselves?
4. If Congress were to pass a law requiring every able-bodied person to work in return for welfare, what kind of jobs would they work at? Are such jobs available? Would the recipients need training to hold those jobs? How would it be paid for?
5. How would mothers on welfare find adequate child care? Should such child care be provided on site for workers? Who would fund it?
6. What are the characteristics of the typical welfare recipient? How long does the average recipient stay on the rolls?
7. What does welfare to families cost the U.S. government? How does that cost compare with other government expenditures?
8. What is the states' obligation to families on welfare? How much does it vary from state to state?

Critical thinkers also know that any solution to a problem, however good it may seem, always has consequences, and they are willing to look at long-term implications. If you raise the minimum wage, some employers will hire fewer people. If you close the center of a city to reduce traffic congestion, some businesses will suffer. If the board of regents decides to strengthen the faculty at a college, student tuition may have to rise.

Finally, to become a critical thinker is to learn to observe, reflect, ask questions, test answers, and refuse to settle for easy explanations. If you become adept at critical thinking and learn to incorporate it into the writing you do for your college courses, you'll get more out of those courses and improve your grades. But even more important, you will lay the foundation for dealing intelligently with the quantities of information and persuasive language that will surround you for the rest of your life.

SUMMARY

Elements of Critical Thinking

To become a critical thinker . . .

- Ask questions about what you read and hear.
- Scrutinize the claims you make and the claims a writer or speaker makes to see if they are warranted.
- Check out the sources of a writer's evidence. Are they biased? Too few? Are you yourself using biased sources?
- Look for the unstated assumptions underlying an argument.
- Check for anomalies or inconsistencies in a writer's argument.
- Be alert for biased language or persuasive metaphors in an argument.
- Watch for stereotyped thinking in your writing and that of others.
- Be suspicious of simplistic solutions and black-white arguments.

WINDOW ON WRITING: Thinking Critically in Writing

In his paper for an English composition course, James Skaggs demonstrated an attitude of inquiry about television news and encouraged his readers to think critically. Here are some excerpts from that paper.

James Skaggs

Rhetoric and Composition

Professor Hairston

TV News: Uniquely Unqualified

to Bring You the World

Are things really the way we see them on the

network news? Not always. Television news has

serious inadequacies that should keep it from being

the sole news source for viewers. Let's look at some of them.

To start off with, television news doesn't have the time or facilities to show you much of what happened in the world today. Although news agencies like Associated Press report over five million words a day, with most news broadcasts limited to thirty minutes a day, minus commercials, only a fraction of that news reaches your screen. Only 5 percent of what TV camera crews film is shown.

Another big problem is the pressure to turn a profit. The way to do that is to be as entertaining as possible, to keep a large audience so that the viewers will stay tuned and watch the commercials. That's tough since the American public has a short attention span and a game show like Wheel of Fortune can steal a large chunk of the network news audience. As a result, the networks focus on action stories where their cameras can have the most impact. News people even make a conscious effort to add drama to their stories, one executive saying that he wanted their news stories "to display the attributes of fiction and drama."

In 1986 when Len Bias, a college basketball star, died of an overdose of cocaine, television viewers were treated to summer-long reports on the drug crisis in America. Viewers saw a series of reports informing them what a potent high "crack" produces, how highly addictive it is, where to buy it, and how cheap it is. The series was a virtual "how to" for potential crack addicts. Networks saw what a profit could be garnered by hyping "crises" after CBS broadcast its documentary "48 Hours on Crack Street" and earned the highest audience, almost fifteen million, for a television documentary in the past five and a half years.

Was there a good reason for all this hubbub over drugs all of a sudden? No. Statistics released by the National Institute on Drug Abuse show the rate of cocaine use among high school seniors to have stayed the same for the past seven years. The real drug problem remains alcohol abuse, with 1,131 teenage deaths directly accounted for by it and 100,000 more indirectly related. However, alcohol abuse is not as interesting as drug abuse. And what about other social problems like poverty, unemployment, illiteracy, malnutrition, and murder? The drug "crisis" was a good example of how television has the power to set our agenda of social issues in America.

■ **Exercise 5.3** Write out an unstated assumption that underlies each of these claims.

1. Until we can have a bipartisan dialogue about controlling immigration, we're unlikely to come to a lasting solution.
2. The outrageous salaries our society pays to entertainers—athletes,

movie stars, and rock musicians—reveal a great deal about the value system of our time.

3. It's an intelligent parent who manages to stay calm when her son comes home sporting a ponytail, three earrings, and jeans that show more skin than they cover.

4. If major universities really think they need a football team, they should just go ahead and hire professional players and do the thing right.

5. The savvy college student of the 1990s will head toward a career in the information business.

■ **Exercise 5.4** Working with several other students in a group, critically analyze the metaphors in these quotations from professional writers and consider what the author's purpose might be for using them. A spokesperson from each group can then report your conclusions for class discussion.

1. The French Alps offered a holiday weekend from hell just a few days before Christmas. For 24 miserable hours, cars backed up—and piled up—in sclerotic masses clogging the narrow mountain valleys.
   —Christopher Dickey, "Remodeling the Slopes."

2. In the halls of the [Texas] capitol, a train wreck refers to something more than a difficult problem. It means a head-on collision between opposing forces that can explode in a spectacular burst of ill feeling, ruining relationships and even careers—the political equivalent of the staged Waco crash of 1896, when the Katy Railroad aimed two speeding locomotives at each other before 50,000 spectators.
   —Paul Burka, "Perils of Politics."

3. The Taking Clause of the Fifth Amendment ("nor shall private property be taken for public use, without just compensation") is not one of your more fashionable constitutional freedoms. But it has a cult following among conservatives, who see it as a vehicle for a revival of so-called economic rights. "Economic rights" in this context does not mean anything so bleeding-heart as a right to food, shelter, or a job. It means the right to conduct your business unmolested by the government.
   —Michael Kinsley, "Taking Exception."

6

How Do You Write Arguments and Detect Fallacies?

A Inductive Arguments
B Claims and Warrants Arguments
C Logical Fallacies

6a HOW DO YOU WRITE INDUCTIVE ARGUMENTS?

Troubleshooting

College writing assignments often involve constructing an argument. A pattern of argument that works especially well for academic papers is *induction*, or *inductive reasoning*, the process of gathering evidence, analyzing it, and then drawing a conclusion from it. This pattern is sometimes called the "scientific method" because it is the basic process by which scientists work.

Inductive arguments are particularly appropriate when you are doing a research paper or a major project that involves making surveys or doing interviews. You might start out with little more than a broad topic—for example, an assignment to research some economic issue that is of direct concern to college students. When you start to explore the possibilities, you remember that at the beginning of the semester you noticed that several banks had set up solicitation tables on the campus mall, trying to persuade students to apply for credit cards and even offering bonus prizes.

That observation could trigger research that would uncover data you could use in an inductive argument. For instance:

- College and sometimes even high school students are prime targets for credit card promotions because these young people represent the last unsaturated segment of the credit card market.
- *Credit Card News* estimates that college student customers spent $3.5 billion in 1990.
- National student associations often get into the credit card business themselves because it's so profitable.
- Counseling centers at many colleges report increasing numbers of students seeking help because they're in serious trouble with overcharges on their cards.

Using this and other data, you could put together a factual, well-documented paper that's interesting to write and interesting to read, making the argument, if you chose, that credit card companies ought to be banned from soliciting business on university property. Or you could write an equally forceful argument that banks' solicitations on campus are simply healthy signs of free enterprise, and although some people might condemn the banks, students are adults and should have the right to make their choices rather than be protected by the university.

For at least two reasons inductive arguments are likely to work well when you're doing academic writing. First, professors are often partial to the kind of argument in which you gather information about a topic, analyze it, and then draw your conclusions. That's the dominant method in scholarly writing, so it's natural they would favor it. Second, inductive argument emphasizes the weight of facts in making a case for a claim or point of view, and to faculty, that approach usually seems more substantial than emotional appeals.

The writer who wants to use this method, however, must be careful because it's easy for inductive reasoning to go wrong. There are definite criteria for valid inductive arguments, and you must observe them if you want your arguments to work, particularly for academic readers. In this section we outline and explain those criteria.

To write good inductive arguments you must . . .

6a-1 **Formulate a hypothesis and test it.** Most people writing an inductive argument start with a tentative thesis and then consider how they can get evidence to prove it either true or false; they don't get their data first and then decide what they want to do with it. For instance, a television and film student might get an idea for a paper on the portrayal of Hispanics on TV by seeing what she considered patronizing portrayals of Hispanics on television and formulating her thesis. Then by watching more programs, she could either confirm or disprove her original hypothesis. She would have to be careful, however, not to choose mainly programs that she felt in advance would confirm her thesis.

Such possible bias is always a hazard of inductive argument (see Section 6a–3).

 6a–2 **Base your conclusions on sufficient evidence.** The larger the group about which you are generalizing, the larger the sample you need. If you attend a college of twelve thousand students and you want to generalize about their patterns of credit card use, it won't do just to take a survey of a dozen people you happen to know. You would need to query from fifty to one hundred students, carefully chosen to represent a cross section.

In another bit of informal induction, you might notice two Jaguars, a Lexus, and two Mercedes in a faculty parking lot and raise an eyebrow about recent claims you've heard that faculty on your campus are poorly paid. You're hardly warranted, however, in concluding that such complaints are unjustified solely on the evidence of one parking lot. Only if you noticed a substantial percentage on most lots would your conclusion be justified. Even then you couldn't be sure you were right because your data may not be relevant (see Section 6a–5). Several faculty may have inherited money or may make money from consulting.

The professional poll takers who do surveys for large newspapers or marketing agencies use sophisticated methods that tell them how many samples they need from a large group to be able to make reasonably accurate generalizations about that group. Students can scarcely use such methods, nor does anyone expect them to. As an amateur pollster you have to use common sense to decide how large your sample should be. Be sure to give your readers a clear idea of the size of your sample so they can judge for themselves whether it's sufficient.

 6a–3 **Base your conclusions on a random sample.** The amount of your evidence is often less crucial than how you choose it. Your sample must be randomly chosen and represent the various categories within the group about which you are generalizing. You can avoid skewing your sample in two ways: you can choose your data totally by chance, or you can get your data by taking samples from a representative cross section of the group you're sampling.

If you wanted to choose your data about student credit card use strictly by chance, you could make a phone survey by going through the student directory and choosing every fiftieth or hundredth name to call. If you were doing a survey on what kind of transportation students use to get to campus, you could station yourself at a main crossroads on campus and question as many students as you need for an adequate sample.

The other way to ensure a random sample would be to set up categories that you think would represent a cross section of the student population. For instance, if you were researching the modes of transportation students use, you might establish categories based on where students live: those living in married students' housing, students who live at home, students who commute from out of town, students living in university dorms, and students living in off-campus condominiums. This method is more complicated to set up and takes more time, but it would be more scientific if you did it well.

Always keep in mind how easily any of us can fall into the trap of drawing conclusions from biased evidence. It's so easy to go to people we know or to familiar neighborhoods or groups when we're looking for evidence, but by doing so, we can badly warp our sample. Be conscious of that danger in your own work and always be alert for it when you read someone else's arguments. When you read reports based on surveys or inductive investigations, make it a habit to ask yourself if the sample seems random.

6a–4 **Base your conclusions on accurate evidence.** When you're making an inductive argument, you should verify your evidence. Are you sure you're using facts that can be checked, not reports that may be only opinion? Do you know the source of your facts? Is it reliable? For example, if you are looking for evidence about whether your community is recovering from a period of recession, your local newspaper should not be your only source. A newspaper has a vested interest in the prosperity of its own community and is likely to emphasize positive economic indicators and downplay negative ones. If you want accurate data on the effects of cholesterol, look for information from medical journals or columns; don't unquestioningly accept data put out by the food industry. When you use statistics, check to see whose statistics they are.

6a–5 **Base your conclusions on relevant evidence.** When you're working with induction, take care that you can show a legitimate connection between your data and the inferences you draw. For instance, if you're not a television watcher but suddenly start to see MTV programs on the television at your new health club when you're working out on the treadmill, you might be struck by the sexuality that permeates both the lyrics and the performances on such programs and speculate about the effects on the young people who are the prime target of these programs. If the topic interests you, you could do a survey of music videos and put together a series of film clips for a class project. But if you moved from that survey to the claim that the popularity of MTV contributes directly to the high teenage pregnancy rate in this country, you'd have trouble substantiating such a conclusion. There may be some relation, but you can't prove that the two phenomena are directly connected.

If, however, you collected evidence on the states that have motorcycle helmet laws, researched the data on when they passed those laws, and correlated the rate of motorcycle fatalities with the dates the laws were passed, such data might be relevant to a claim that there are fewer fatal accidents among riders who wear safety-approved helmets.

CHECKLIST

Criteria for an Effective Inductive Argument

- It should state a hypothesis and support it with data.
- It should be based on sufficient evidence to warrant the conclusion.
- It should be based on evidence that is representative and randomly chosen.
- It should be based on accurate evidence.
- The conclusion drawn should be relevant to the evidence used.

WINDOW ON WRITING: Inductive Argument

Here is the inductive opening paragraph of Ann Oetken's paper on the problem of defining whether Olympic athletes are amateurs or professionals.

Ann Oetken

Rhetoric and Composition

Professor Hairston

Amateurs on Track

Carl Lewis, one of the fastest men in the world today, earned well over $780,000 in 1984. Mary Decker Slaney earned almost $150,000 a year during her reign as the world's fastest woman miler. From 1976 to 1982 Dwight Stones, the best high jumper at this time, estimated he earned over $200,000. Although these three track athletes received tremendous bonuses, appearance fees, and endorsements, they were still

```
considered amateurs by the Amateur Athletic

Association of the United States and allowed to

compete in the Olympic games. Decisions like this

have led to many problems within the amateur world

and rekindled the question, What is wrong with

allowing professionals to compete in the Olympics?
```

■ **Exercise 6.1** The following paragraphs illustrate some patterns of inductive reasoning. Given the evidence in the paragraphs, how do you think they measure up to the criteria for inductive reasoning outlined above? Are you convinced by the arguments?

1. Most Vietnamese refugees who came to the United States in the 1980s have done fairly well. A survey of five thousand recent Vietnamese immigrants by the International Refugee Committee showed that over one-third have gone into business for themselves, another 20 percent have jobs earning substantially more than the minimum wage, more than 20 percent are in school or college, a small but growing number own their homes, and fewer than 5 percent are receiving public assistance.

2. Obviously influence counts for more than qualifications when the Postal Service hires new employees. Joe Carter just got word that he hadn't been accepted for a postal job, while Constanza Warren, niece of Congressman Hatfield, was hired although her score on the Civil Service exam was two points lower than Joe's.

3. A recent survey on housing in our city revealed some distressing patterns of discrimination. In the survey, twenty-five couples called the same three rental agencies in response to classified ads for rental houses in the northeast part of the city. When they told the rental agents they had no children, twenty-two couples were invited to look at the houses; of those who said they had young children, more than half were told that those same houses had already been rented.

4. According to the New York newspapers, city hospitals in at least three boroughs are in serious trouble. Because of budget cuts, most are 20 percent below strength in their nursing staff, their pharmacies are closed for several hours each day, their emergency rooms are so overcrowded that critically ill patients must often wait hours to be seen, and fewer residents are applying for positions every year.

6b HOW DO YOU WRITE CLAIMS AND WARRANTS ARGUMENTS?

Troubleshooting

Suppose you want to begin a paper with a claim or generalization and then build a case for it. For instance, you might argue in a paper that many college students who move away from home to go to a large university benefit from getting a job their first year even though it limits their study time. That's a claim that would be difficult to prove by marshaling inductive evidence, so you need to find another pattern. One that works particularly well for academic papers is the *claims and warrants argument*, a pattern we all use frequently without thinking about it.

For this discussion, we begin by defining certain terms that are necessary for discussing claims and warrants arguments. They are:

C H A R T

Claims and Warrants Terms*

- **Deduction:** Arguing from the general principle to the specific example.
- **Claim:** An assertion; the conclusion being drawn.
- **Data:** The evidence given to support the claim.
- **Warrant:** The statement that links the claim and the evidence given to support it. For instance, we say a conclusion is "warranted" or "unwarranted," depending on whether we accept the connection between evidence and claim that an arguer tries to establish. A warrant can be stated directly or simply implied.
- **Support:** Material added to strengthen any part of the argument.
- **Qualifier:** A phrase or statement that limits the claim; often expressed as "probably," "in most cases," or "usually."
- **Reservation:** A statement giving an exception to the claim; usually expressed by "except" or "unless."

*Terms adapted from Richard D. Reike and Malcolm Sillar, *Argumentation and the Decision-Making Process*.

Such arguments follow a pattern similar to patterns lawyers use in court. The arguer starts out with a *claim*, that first-year students at large colleges and universities benefit academically from a job. She then introduces *supporting data* to show that new students at large schools feel less isolated and more confident on campus if they work. She then presents a *warrant* that links her claim and data: that students who feel comfortable and confident on campus are likely to succeed academically. She might add a *qualifier*, in this case that such a job must be on campus and involve working with other students.

Another name for this type of argument is *deduction*, but we prefer "claims and warrants" because in the formal deduction process one can get bogged down in too many rules. (Claims and warrants argument is also called *Toulmin argument*, after Stephen Toulmin, the legal philosopher who analyzed the process and established the terminology.)

The only term that may be troublesome here is *warrant*. The warrant is the link, the connector that ties the evidence to the claim. Sometimes the warrant is so obvious that if the arguer makes the claim and presents the supporting data, readers will supply the warrant (usually a noncontroversial one) themselves. At other times, readers may need to be shown the warrant and persuaded to accept it. Here, for example, is an argument in which a professional writer provides an elaborate warrant.

> Marxism has no promise for America. Since 1917, it has failed after three-quarters of a century of tests in every society where it was applied. It has produced nothing but misery, tyranny, and mediocrity. The fact that it often replaced other systems which were also tyrannous, mediocre and miserable does not mitigate its failure. The historian learns never to say "never" but all the same **it is highly improbable that large numbers of people, in the imaginable future, will submit themselves to the yoke of a political ideology that assumes that mankind is capable of objectively discerning, judging, and controlling everything that exists in terms of a "rational," "scientific" program, a single model propagated by central planning.** Marxism set itself against nationalism, spread by adapting to it, and in the end was laid low by it.
>
> —Robert Hughes, *The Culture of Complaint.*

In this paragraph, Hughes supports his opening claim with facts about the failure of Marxism as an economic philosophy. He then explicitly states the connection between his claim and supporting data in a warrant that states an overriding principle: people won't submit to a failed ideology.

You can use this pattern to good effect when you begin to map out the argument you are thinking of using in a paper. Start by asking yourself, "What's my claim going to be?" That's an important question right at the beginning. You may not need to start with your claim fully spelled out, but you do need to know the position you're going to take. If you can't state it clearly, you may not be ready to try to convince someone else.

After you have your claim, ask yourself, "What evidence can I use to support my claim? Do I have it? Can I get it? Is it solid?" Whether or not you can develop a sound argument may depend on those answers. Then ask, "What is the warrant that will tie the evidence to the claim?" and "Do I need to qualify the claim in some way?" Once you've roughed out answers to these preliminary questions, you'll find you have a good start on putting together an effective argument.

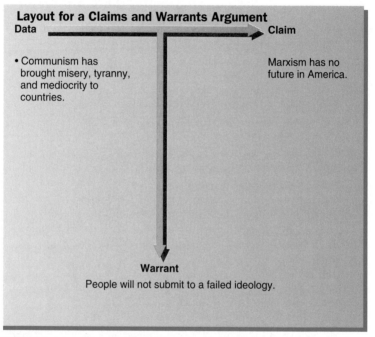

Layout for a Claims and Warrants Argument

Data ➝ Claim

• Communism has brought misery, tyranny, and mediocrity to countries.

Marxism has no future in America.

Warrant
People will not submit to a failed ideology.

To develop a claims and warrants argument . . .

6b–1 Decide on your claim. Begin by figuring out what is the main point you want to make; that is your claim. Suppose that after discussion in a child development course about the influence of movies on children, you decide to write a paper arguing that parents should be discouraged from buying many of the films sold as children's classics because they are not, in fact, suitable for children. That assertion is your claim, the one set forth in the diagram on the following page.

6b–2 Consider what data you can use to support your claim. What material can you find to expand on and strengthen your claim? In this kind of argument, your data can be theories and anecdotes as well as factual evidence. Your interest in writing an argument about films for children stems from your memories of being very frightened at certain so-called children's classics. You want to use that experience but need to get firsthand evidence about the films themselves and realize you should probably also bring in some expert opinion. To gather your evidence you rent several films that you remember frightened you when you were a child—*The Wizard of Oz, Fantasia, Peter Pan, 101 Dalmatians,* and *The Black Stallion*—and looking at them again confirms your opinion. Then you go to the *Reader's Guide to Periodical Literature* and find two or three articles about children's response to movies; they confirm your own experience that children's movies often frighten children.

6b-3 **Identify the warrant or link that connects your data and your claim; decide whether it must be stated or can be left unstated.** For the paper on children's movies the link between the data—certain films and your own experience—and your claim that many of the so-called children's classic films may not be at all suitable for very young audiences is a warrant that seems obvious. That is, conscientious parents will not deliberately expose children to things that frighten them. You decide, however, that you should make it explicit since so many parents don't realize the problem.

Now lay out your paper in a rough diagram or outline, something like this.

DATA ⟶ **CLAIM**

The Wizard of Oz	Parents should be discouraged
Fantasia	from buying many of the films
Peter Pan	sold as children's classics
101 Dalmations	because they are not, in fact,
The Black Stallion	suitable for children.
(specific frightening scenes	
taken from these movies)	

WARRANT

Children should not be deliberately
exposed to films that frighten them or
make them feel insecure

SUPPORT

Your own reactions as a child

Quotation from your three-year-old nephew after
he saw *101 Dalmatians*

Testimony of child psychologist

The diagram sets out the elements you will want to organize into your argument; you could expand on any part as you write.

Here is another example of a claims and warrants argument you could use for an academic paper in sociology or business management. You want to argue that women will continue to be handicapped as professionals until most corporations and firms recognize that providing good and convenient child care for their employees is as necessary a benefit as adequate health insurance. You could diagram the elements of your argument like this.

DATA ——————————————→ **CLAIM**

In our culture women still have the major responsibility for child rearing.

Women who take leaves of absence to have children lose out on promotions

Few offices or corporations provide good child care.

Women professionals with children are at a disavantage in corporations or firms because usually they do not have the flexibility in hours that on-site child care would provide.

QUALIFICATION

Unless they can afford a nanny.

WARRANT

Employees who can't work long hours or overtime often don't get promoted.

6b-4 **Decide which element of your argument you want to emphasize.** The claims and warrants pattern allows a writer to choose what he or she wants to emphasize in an argument. For instance, in the argument diagrammed above, after analyzing your audience you could decide which part of your argument you needed to develop. If the audience you were writing for needed to be convinced that women don't advance as fast as men in the corporate world, you could expand on your claim, backing it with statistics about the proportion of men to women executives of the same age in the major five hundred corporations or the percentages of men and women partners in selected major law firms. If, however, you wanted to emphasize some element of your evidence, you could quote articles showing how frequently fathers take off work to care for children compared to how frequently mothers take off. If you felt you needed to explain your warrant, you could cite authorities and studies to show that employees who tend to be promoted are able to work long hours on flexible schedules.

In other words, you can lay out the elements of your argument, analyze them, and decide which need the most expansion and support or which ones you have the most information on. You can consider your audience and decide which points are most likely to appeal to them. Sketching out the argument as we have done in the sample diagrams also lets you see which parts of it might be weak and perhaps should be discarded or rethought.

S U M M A R Y

Procedure for Laying Out a Claims and Warrants Argument

1. Identify your claim and state it.
2. Look for data to support your claim.
3. Establish the warrant between your data and your claim; decide whether it should be stated or unstated.
4. Decide which part of your argument you should emphasize and focus on developing it.

WINDOW ON WRITING: Claims and Warrants Argument

Student Reggie Rice uses several claims and warrants arguments in the following excerpt from a paper titled "The Wild West Hero: America's Oldest Cover-up." Here is an excerpt.

```
Reggie Rice

Rhetoric and Composition

Professor Hairston

     Legend builds up many champions of the West

as brave, rugged, and noble. In fact, many heroes

appear pathetic when you contrast what they were

supposed to be with what they really were.

     The legendary Belle Starr epitomized the

frontier woman, gracious but with a will of iron,

and always loyal to her man. According to legend,
```

Belle was also handy with a six-gun and a rifle; however, the manner of her death seems to contradict that. She was shot down from behind by her son, who used a charge of buckshot to throw her off her horse. Robert Sherill, in The Saturday Night Special, also tells us that the real Belle Starr was a prostitute who had two illegitimate children--a boy who grew up to be her murderer and a girl who followed in her mother's footsteps.

Belle Starr's son was not the only back shooter in the West. A young man named Billy the Kid, about whom Hollywood has made no fewer than twenty-one movies, was also a come-from-behind artist. In Hollywood's movies, the hero is represented by virile, handsome actors such as Paul Newman, who portrayed Billy the Kid in The Left-Handed Gun in 1958. A more accurate description of Billy, according to Peter Lyon in The Wild, Wild West, would be a "slight, short, buck-toothed, narrow-shouldered youth whose slouch added to his unwholesome appearance." Billy usually killed from ambush; his only recorded face-to-face gun murder was of an unarmed man.

Here Reggie makes his claim early: Hollywood's portrayal of the heroes and heroines of the Old West represents more myth than fact. As data for that claim, he gives descriptions and facts about several legends of the time, taken from two contemporary books by writers who have researched the period. The unstated warrant is that people who live disreputable lives should not be idolized.

■ **Exercise 6.2** Work together with a group of other students to analyze these claims and warrants arguments. Identify the statements that come after each number as claim, data, warrant, qualifier, support, or reservation. Some statements may fall into more than one category.

A. (1) Primitive tools and ancient pottery found in recent excavations close to the Tibetan border (2) indicate that a culture may have been there that predated the equestrian culture of the Mongols. (3) Archaeologists have assumed that Mongol culture was the first in the region. (4) Unless carbon-14 dating puts these new finds at a far later date than its discoverers anticipate, (5) much theory will have to be reformulated.

B. (1) Few business executives who have proved themselves to be strong leaders and gifted long-range planners are willing to run for public office. (2) Some are unwilling to subject themselves to the insulting questions and harassments of the press or endure the intrusions into their personal lives. (3) Others are not used to the compromises and group negotiation that being a senator or congressional representative demands. (4) It's hardly surprising that individuals who are already powerful and affluent wish to avoid harassment.

■ **Exercise 6.3** Each example below contains a claim and supporting evidence. Supply the unstated warrant that links each claim to its data. Evaluate the argument that you think is implied in each sentence. Could you make a convincing case for it?

1. When members of the so-called creative community in Hollywood are accused of polluting the cultural environment with violent and sexually explicit movies, they reply that they're only giving the public what it wants. Yet the popularity of films like *Forrest Gump* and *Aladdin* suggests that many moviegoers today prefer more wholesome entertainments.

2. Starting early in the 1990s, the introduction of well designed family vans and sport utility vehicles such as the Ford Windstar and Jeep Grand Cherokee helped put American car manufacturers back into the black. Perhaps those who said that Americans who bought foreign cars helped U.S. makers by forcing them to improve their product were right.

3. Fear of flying is irrational because statistics demonstrate that traveling on an airliner is far safer than taking a train, driving an automobile, or even walking across the street.

4. Once limited largely to Las Vegas and Atlantic City, legalized gambling is quickly spreading across the United States as state after state approves lotteries in order to avoid raising taxes. But when governments go into the gambling business and entice people to gamble through misleading ads, they put themselves in a very dubious moral position.

5. More and more high schools are requiring that students take algebra and trigonometry—no more "consumer math"—and two years of physical sciences in order to graduate. Although such standards may worsen the dropout problem, young people will not be ready to work in the twenty-first century unless they know math and science.

6c HOW CAN YOU RECOGNIZE FALLACIES AND AVOID THEM?

Troubleshooting

Learning to recognize fallacies is an important part of becoming a critical thinker. Fallacies are counterfeits of legitimate arguments, shoddy imitations comparable in quality to the imitation Seiko watches or phony Gucci luggage offered for sale by sidewalk vendors in New York and other cities. At first glance they may look good, but they don't hold up.

Fallacies invite an audience to bypass critical thinking and accept faulty claims, dubious assumptions, and deceptive generalizations. Once you learn to identify the most common fallacies you'll not only be able to spot them in arguments of others but also strengthen your own arguments by avoiding them. Here are ten you're likely to encounter frequently.

To argue logically . . .

6c–1 Avoid argument to the person (in Latin, *ad hominem*): The strategy of focusing on the personality or character of an opponent rather than on the issue that is supposed to be under discussion. Used negatively, *ad hominem* arguments become smear attacks. Speakers and writers abandon rational debate and descend to personal attacks, trying to discredit their opponents by attacking their integrity, their intelligence, or their family connections or even by attributing unproven and often damaging beliefs and attitudes to them. Here are two examples.

A legislator arguing for her bill that would raise taxes on alcohol to provide low-cost housing claims that those who oppose the bill are heartless people concerned more with keeping down the price of their evening cocktails than they are with the welfare of others.

A candidate for city council suggests that anyone who opposes his proposal to establish an agency he claims will help minority women is automatically sexist and racist.

Such attacks are abusive and irresponsible, and you should suspect that the person who resorts to them wants to avoid the real issues, such as whether a proposal is practical and cost-effective.

People also use arguments to the person to play on sentimental associations and distract attention from the real issues. That's what is going on when a candidate calls attention to his war record, poses with children for television ads, or plays up her church activity. Strategies such as these do little to advance genuine argument and debate.

6c-2 **Avoid begging the question:** Assuming that audience members share basic assumptions and beliefs with the arguer when in fact they don't. When you spot someone using certain phrases—"Everyone knows," "We all agree," or "It's obvious that"—or smoothly trying to pass off as a fact a statement that is no more than an opinion, you're encountering a question-begging argument. If you don't quickly challenge the arguer, you may find yourself being hustled along to conclusions you don't want to reach. For example:

A student arguing for an exemption from a foreign language requirement might claim that since all educated people now know English because it is the accepted international language, college students in the United States no longer need to learn another language.

A campus activist might suggest that since grades promote unhealthy competition and damage students' self-esteem, the university should abolish letter grades.

In the first example, the assertion that all educated people now know English is inaccurate. English is indeed the accepted international language for pilots, mariners, and scientists, but most of the people in the world cannot read or speak it. In the second example, the arguer is also trying to pass off a claim as a fact. He or she would need to furnish a wealth of evidence to establish what may, in fact, be the relationship between grades and self-esteem. Thus both arguments beg the question.

If you hope to be an effective writer or speaker yourself, you have to guard constantly against this fallacy. You slip into it if you assume that the people in your audience agree with you on important points when, in fact, they don't. It's one of the most common fallacies all of us commit because it's so natural to take for granted that other people think the way we do. But any argument has to start from premises both parties agree on; otherwise, it literally has no foundation.

Suppose, for instance, that as part of your job with a social agency you are asked to write a brochure for an audience of underachieving high school girls introducing them to a library-sponsored reading program that will help them learn about women's health, family relationships, and new career opportunities for women. If you take your book-oriented values for granted with such an audience, you're begging the question. Some young women may have negative associations about books and also fear that being seen carrying books or going to the library will hurt their social lives.

6c–3 **Avoid hasty generalization:** Drawing conclusions from too little evidence. You cannot legitimately draw broad generalizations from only a few instances. For example:

> It's not safe to travel this summer because terrorists set off a bomb in the Tel Aviv airport and two months later a letter bomb blew up at Heathrow Airport in London.

Terrorist incidents at two airports do not provide sufficient evidence from which to generalize about travel safety all over the world.

Be careful about making claims that use absolute terms such as *always, never, everyone, no one, all,* and *none.* When you're talking about human events, such inclusive adjectives are seldom accurate, so cover yourself by using *some, a substantial number, in many cases,* or similar qualifiers. And as a reader or listener, you should always be skeptical about arguments in which others overstate their claims by using *all* or *never.*

6c–4 **Avoid false cause arguments (in Latin, *post hoc, ergo propter hoc,* or "after this, therefore because of this"):** The faulty assumption that because one event follows another, the first event caused the second. Such reasoning underlies superstitions (walking under a ladder will bring bad luck) and glib political pronouncements (we're in this mess because of our Republican Congress). Setting up false causes is another form of oversimplification that grows out of the desire we all have to believe easy answers rather than wrestle with complex issues about who caused what and why. For example:

> The comparatively low fatality rate on the German autobahn with

its speed limits of eighty miles an hour and more proves that the United States could safely raise its speed limits.

Too many factors enter into such statistics to draw such a conclusion legitimately: Germany has much stricter requirements for a driver's license, traffic regulations on the autobahn are tight and stringently enforced, and there is a higher percentage of fast, well-engineered cars on the road.

Of course, advertising is riddled with false cause reasoning: buying a red convertible will enhance your social life; serving a new brand of coffee will bring domestic bliss at your house; and subscribing to an at-home course in personality improvement will make you the star salesperson in your firm. It's unlikely you're gullible enough to be taken in by such claims; be equally skeptical when you encounter facile solutions for serious problems in the form of political prescriptions and scapegoat formulas.

6c–5 Avoid either/or arguments (also called *false dilemma* or the *fallacy of insufficient options*): Faulty reasoning that states an argument in terms that imply one must choose between only two options—right/wrong, good/bad, moral/immoral, and so forth. This is another form of simplistic reasoning that glosses over complex issues and instead attacks the opposition. For example:

What's your alternative to my proposal? Fascism?

Instead of discussing the merits of her proposal, this arguer resorts to labeling her opponents with the worst term she can think of.

If we allow that factory to come into our town, we are dooming ourselves and our children to a lifetime of breathing filthy air.

Many other options are available between no factory and filthy air; one would be to require the factory to install scrubbers to clean emissions. The loaded rhetorical question that allows for only one acceptable answer is a form of the either/or argument. For instance:

Are we going to increase the number of police officers in this city, or are we going to abandon it to thugs, gangs, and dope dealers?

When an arguer tries to force a false dilemma on you, your best response is to challenge your opponent's polarized thinking immediately and point out other alternatives to his or her oversimplified view of the world. Also be careful to avoid slipping into either/or statements in your own writing: at best, they make you look naive; at worst, they make you seem like a fanatic or a charlatan.

6c–6 **Avoid red herrings:** The tactic of diverting the audience's attention from the main issue by bringing up an irrelevant point. The phrase refers to the practice of dragging a strong-smelling smoked herring across a trail to confuse hunting dogs and send them in the wrong direction. Arguers who fear they have a weak case may employ a red herring by bringing in some emotionally charged but irrelevant point in the hope they can distract their audience and keep them from focusing on the real issue. For example, a mayor might complain:

> While it may be true that my press secretary submitted false expense account vouchers, my administration is just being targeted by a hostile media.

Her charges of press bias might be partially true, but the attitude of the media has no bearing on the official's misbehavior.

6c–7 **Avoid special pleading:** The strategy of presenting a biased viewpoint based on partial truths and implying that it represents the whole truth. The points the arguer makes for or against a position may be accurate and effectively presented, but he or she gives a warped picture that misleads the audience. Here is a paragraph that attacks a type of special pleading.

> Some critics of business write articles that focus entirely on examples that show business in a bad light. They emphasize the savings and loan scandals of the 1980s, stock market manipulations by insider traders, and company executives indulging themselves in grandiose benefits such as the use of ski lodges and private jets while they trim benefits for the employees. They don't mention the jobs business creates, companies' involvement with public schools, their contributions to the arts, or the sacrifices of executives such as David Kearns, who gave up a million-dollar salary as president of Xerox Corporation to become Undersecretary of Education.

If you look only for the negative elements of any institution or system, whether it's higher education, the public schools, city government, or marriage, it's not hard to find enough examples on which to build a totally negative argument. But such special pleading marks the person who does it consistently as blatantly biased or seriously uninformed—perhaps both.

6c–8 **Avoid false analogy:** A comparison between two things that does not hold true or proves misleading. Analogies can be invaluable in helping readers to understand abstract or elusive ideas and concepts; for instance, a writer might clarify how the turbocharger in an automobile works by comparing it to a windmill or a waterwheel. Sometimes, however, in order to make an argument more attractive to readers, writers create a false analogy in which the comparison drawn simply won't hold up. For example:

> A sports writer compares a touchdown drive in a football game to a military campaign and by doing so dramatizes some of the team's strategies—for instance, a flanking operation or a diversionary movement.

So far so good, but the analogy becomes false if the writer carries it further and suggests that casualties on the football field have to be accepted as part of the campaign just as a general would accept casualties in battle.

As a critical thinker, pay attention to the analogies you use and those you encounter in your reading. Ask yourself this: Are the similarities between the things being compared strong enough to warrant the conclusions being drawn? If they're not—for instance, if someone is comparing the responsibilities of the president of the United States to those of a football coach—reject the analogy.

6c-9 Avoid *non sequitur* (Latin for "it doesn't follow"): A statement that suggests a cause-and-effect link between two events or conditions that aren't necessarily connected. Here are some examples.

> She's a physician—I doubt she'll give money to a liberal organization like People for the American Way.

> I'm sure Mark's parents are wealthy since he went to an excellent private school.

> If elected, he'll do something about juvenile crime—after all, he's been a Little League coach, so he knows boys.

Some of these conclusions might be true, but none of the statements shows any direct connection between claims. They reflect clichéd or simplistic thinking rather than reasoning.

In more complex arguments, *non sequitur* fallacies can be harder to identify. For example, in many election campaigns of the early 1990s, candidates claimed the rising cost of welfare was directly tied to an increase in the number of single mothers. It was persuasive campaign talk but simplistic. A 1994 New York City study showed that the main increase in welfare payments had come from spending on medical bills for the disabled and for older people in poverty; three times more welfare money went to them than to single-parent households.

6c–10 **Avoid bandwagon appeal:** The argument that an activity or product must be worthwhile because it is popular. Youngsters who try to persuade their parents that they must have a particular brand of jeans or a new kind of roller skate because "everybody else has them" are using bandwagon tactics. As millions of parents have pointed out, popularity doesn't necessarily determine merit.

That's true of some political polls, too, when questions are posed in ways to make most people agree or disagree. Polls have to be scrutinized carefully to determine what any claimed majority truly believes.

6c–11 **Learn to detect and avoid fallacies.** One of your major concerns should be to avoid fallacies in your own writing. It's especially important to do so when you're writing academic papers because professors and instructors recognize fallacies quickly and penalize them. Remember, however, that you can't expect any argument to be completely free of fallacies or totally logical. The demand for perfection is a sort of fallacy in itself.

S U M M A R Y

Ten Common Fallacies

1. **Argument to the person (*ad hominem*):** Attacking the person making the argument instead of focusing on the issues involved
2. **Begging the question:** Assuming common ground with an audience when there is none; assuming what should be proved
3. **Hasty generalization:** Drawing conclusions from scanty evidence; related to stereotyping
4. **False cause:** Presuming that if B follows A, A caused B
5. **Either/or:** Suggesting that only two choices are possible when in fact there may be several
6. **Red herring:** Bringing in an irrelevant issue to deflect attention from the main point
7. **Special pleading:** Showing only one side of a case and ignoring conflicting evidence
8. **False analogy:** Making a comparison between two things that are too dissimilar for the comparison to be useful
9. **Non *sequitur*:** Drawing a conclusion that is not warranted by the data given
10. **Bandwagon:** Claiming that widespread popularity makes an object or idea valuable

■ **Exercise 6.4** Work in a group with other students to spot the fallacies in these arguments. In some instances, you may find more than one.

1. Two kinds of young women come into corporations at the entry level:
   those who just want to work for a few years before they start a family
   and those who take their work seriously and want to become professionals. A company has to be careful not to hire the first kind.
2. Everyone knows that the 1990s will be a poor time to go into medicine because government regulation is ruining the profession.
3. This candidate for senator deserves your support on the basis of his
   combat record in the Gulf War and because there has never been a
   breath of scandal about him.
4. The great peasant rebellions in the Middle Ages happened because
   the rulers and nobles taxed the peasants to the limit to pay for foreign
   wars and neglected conditions in their own country; the United
   States can expect similar uprisings if it doesn't drastically cut its defense budget and invest in domestic social programs.
5. As a legislator, I can't get too upset about the proposed tuition raise
   when every time I drive by our state university I get caught in a traffic jam of students in their four-wheel-drive vehicles and snazzy con-
   vertibles.

PART

II
Style

Style comes from choice; it is the product of the many decisions about words and sentences that you make as you write. You decide what kind of words you will use, what the length and shape of your sentences should be, how you will begin and end, and how formal or casual you will be. The result is writing with a special voice and tone, writing that reflects you.

This section is a guide to some of the stylistic choices you can make. Because the subject of style is so large and the options for shaping language so numerous, we concentrate on what we regard as the major choices you make to enhance style, those places where your writing will show significant improvement if you invest time and attention.

CHAPTER

7

What Makes Paragraphs Work?

A Achieving Unified Paragraphs

B Using Different Paragraph Patterns

C Finding Ways to Reduce Paragraph Sprawl

D Improving Paragraph Appearance

Conventionally, textbooks define a paragraph as a unit of writing that develops a single idea. A neat definition, but unfortunately when you are the writer, it's not always easy to decide when you have developed an idea and when you need more than one paragraph to do so. Nor is it always easy to decide where to break a paragraph and where to start a new one. Yet the decisions you make about paragraphs can significantly affect how readers respond to your work.

To manage paragraphs well, you need to know how to handle two common paragraph problems. We term them *paragraph sprawl* and *bad paragraph appearance*.

Paragraph sprawl is an *internal* problem because it concerns the way a paragraph *works*. In a sprawling paragraph, the sentences do not fit together tightly or focus on a central point. Paragraph sprawl can occur when the sentences in a paragraph go off in different directions, when a single paragraph seems to include several unconnected ideas, or when sentences in a paragraph seem not to be in a logical order; that is, if they would fit just as well in one place as another.

Bad paragraph appearance is an *external* problem because it concerns the way a paragraph *looks*. Paragraphs may look bad because they are so long that they discourage readers; they may also look bad because the writer has jammed together several points that should be presented in a list. A series of short paragraphs may also look bad because they chop ideas into too many small parts and make it hard for the reader to see connections.

In this chapter we'll suggest ways to address both internal and external paragraph problems.

7a   HOW DO YOU ACHIEVE UNIFIED PARAGRAPHS?

Troubleshooting

Readers will feel your work is out of control if your paragraphs sprawl and fail to present a unified idea. Typically this problem crops up when a writer starts a paragraph by just writing down thoughts as they occur rather than by jotting down ideas in notes or an outline and then developing one thought at a time. The result is a paragraph like the following, filled with ideas but shapeless.

Sprawling

There are thousands of school districts across this country, reflecting widely different social, ethnic, and intellectual mixes. Yet students from all of these districts are admitted to college according to the dictates of two nationwide placement examinations, the SAT and the ACT. Such examinations, which tend to reflect the biases of the people who write them, are economically efficient because they are easy to grade. But many students may not be exposed to the kind of intellectual and cultural material covered on these examinations. Smaller school districts may not be able to prepare students as adequately as larger districts. How can scores from these tests really represent the achievements of four years of high school and the differences between what different students learn in Vermont, New York City, or rural Arkansas? These are problems.

The reader has trouble following the point of the paragraph because its sentences go off in several different directions instead of developing one point. The following revised draft eliminates much of the sprawl, making the paragraph more readable.

Focused

There are thousands of school districts across this country, reflecting widely different social, ethnic, and intellectual mixes. Yet students from all of these districts are admitted to college according to the dictates of two nationwide placement examinations, the SAT and the ACT. Standardized examinations of this kind tend to reflect the biases of the people who write them, not the native abilities of the students who take them. How, then, can scores from one test reflect fairly the knowledge and aptitude of both a Puerto Rican student from a New York City public high school and that of a Vietnamese student from a rural high school in Arkansas?

Paragraphs also sprawl when they contain several sentences on a high level of generality (see Section 11a). Instead of making one general statement and then developing it with specific details or examples, the paragraph strings together a series of generalizations. All of those generalizations may touch on the same main idea, but they still don't develop it. For example:

7a
¶

> Everyone is interested in preserving the quality of our environment and natural habitats. The beauty of nature is something almost everyone responds to. Respect for nature comes from a feeling we all share that the environment is something important to our own well-being today and to that of our children and grandchildren tomorrow. Without a healthy environment, we will all find ourselves ravaged by disease and deprived of the beauties of nature. Unless we do something about the environmental crisis in our society today, we soon won't have a society to worry about.

Any one of these sentences might provide the topic statement for a single paragraph, but the paragraph as a whole probably isn't worth salvaging. It would be better to take one idea from it and start over.

To reshape sprawling paragraphs . . .

7a-1 **Use topic sentences.** One way to avoid paragraph sprawl and keep a paragraph tight is to use a topic sentence that states your main idea clearly and directly. The topic sentence doesn't have to be the first one in the paragraph, although it often is, particularly in academic writing. Wherever it is located, a topic sentence acts like a magnet around which related sentences cluster. Here is an example by a professional writer; the topic sentence is boldfaced.

> **There were three things the children in my family, both immediate and extended, were expected to do: go to church each Sunday; clean our rooms each Saturday; and go to college.** I never really gave a lot of thought to which college. I think I more or less had decided the lot of the toss would make my decision. My parents were graduates of Knoxville College; my grandfather was a graduate of Fisk University; my sister was attending Central State in Ohio. To some degree, like all younger

people, I did not want to attend any school where there had been a previous person. I had spent entirely too much of my life hearing about being so-and-so's sister, so-and-so's daughter, so-and-so's grandbaby. I was rather looking forward to going to places unknown, forging my own path, cutting new ground and all that. I attended Fisk.   —Nikki Giovanni, *Racism 101*.

Giovanni leads into her topic with the opening sentence, going on to develop its most important phrase: *go to college*.

7a
¶

A writer can also lead up to a topic sentence, first giving readers details that build their interest and then summarizing the content in one sentence. Here is an example from a professional writer; the topic sentence is boldfaced.

Felix is in his 20s and gangly. Heinrich is in his 40s, a solid block of a man who has survived three avalanches. He is one of a team of scientists at the University of Bern. With the big drills that he designed and built in the university machine shop, the Bern team brings up cylindrical cores of ice from hundreds of feet below the surface of Swiss glaciers, and from many thousands of feet down in the Antarctic and Greenland ice sheets. The ice holds an abundance of bubbles the size of seltzer fizz. **The bubbles hold a wealth of stories on themes that encompass the planet: the death of the fabled island of Atlantis; the history of the greenhouse effect; the cause of ice ages; scenarios of the Earth's climate in the next hundred years.**
                              —Jonathan Weiner, "Glacier Bubbles."

Not all paragraphs have topic sentences, nor do they need them. Some paragraphs are unified in other ways. We have no evidence that professional writers even think about topic sentences when they are writing paragraphs. Nevertheless, you can use topic sentences to good effect when you want to write clear, well-developed paragraphs. Beginning a paragraph with a sentence that states your main idea will help you to stay focused on that idea. Topic sentences work especially well to control academic writing—analyses, reports, critiques, and so on. They can help you keep your writing organized and readable and give readers a sense that you know your subject well enough to write about it with confidence.

7a-2 **Organize according to a commitment and response pattern.**
The phrase *commitment and response* describes a simple concept: making a promise to your readers and then keeping it. It means raising your readers' expectations and then fulfilling them. Here is an example in which the commitment sentence is boldfaced.

> **During the summer of 1970, the women's movement
> came of age and proved to the media and the nation that
> Americans were going to have to take feminism seriously.**
> First, the *Ladies' Home Journal* appeared on the newsstands with its
> liberated supplement. Then, on August 10, the House passed the
> ERA for the first time. Finally, on August 26, tens of thousands of
> women in cities all over the country took to the streets to demand
> equality—and shocked the nation by their sheer numbers. This
> massive demonstration, known as the Women's Strike for Equality,
> was such a publicity coup that it triggered a further growth spurt in
> the movement.   —Flora Davis, *Moving the Mountain.*

Davis promises to give her readers evidence that the women's movement came of age in 1970 and does so with three examples.

Another form of commitment and response is to begin a paragraph with a question, then use the rest of the paragraph to answer it. In
this paragraph the commitment question is boldfaced.

> **What is it about the cave paintings discovered in the
> south of France late in 1994 that has so excited archaeolo-
> gists?** One extraordinary feature is the variety of animal images.
> Horses, reindeer, bison, yes—these are familiar to European cave
> experts. But elephants, rhinos, owls, and lions? Such paintings are
> unique to this newly discovered cave at Chauvet. These beautifully
> executed figures are also artistically more sophisticated than even
> the drawings of the famous cave at Lascaux, yet tests show that
> they're more than 30,000 years old, twice as old as any previously
> known cave paintings.

The opening question of this paragraph makes a promise to explain
what's special about a newly discovered prehistoric cave, then does so
with specific details.

7a-3 **Downshift to develop your paragraph with specific details.**
Downshifting, a term originated by grammarian Francis Christensen,
means developing a paragraph by starting with a broad, general statement and then moving down through a series of more and more specific
statements that give additional details. Each new statement enriches
and expands on the statement before it. Such paragraphs can move
through several levels, rather like subdividing a topic into smaller and
smaller details. For example, if we designate the opening sentence of a
paragraph as having a level of generality of 5, here is how a writer might
develop that sentence by moving to lower levels of generality.

5. There are signs, however, that girls are finding their way into the world of computing, despite its male bias.

> **4.** A large proportion of the current enrollment in college computing classes is female.
>
>> **3.** For example, at Mount Holyoke, a women's college, 50 percent of this year's graduates have used computers in their courses—up from 15 percent seven years ago.
>>
>>> **2.** According to John Durso, professor of computer studies, the number of terminals available to Mount Holyoke students has increased from one to forty over the same period.
>>>
>>> **2.** The basic course in computing, taught twice a year, has quadrupled in enrollment from 30 students seven years ago to 120 today. —Sara Kiesler, Lee Spoull, and Jacquelynne S. Eccles, "Second-Class Citizens?"

(The two final sentences are at the same level of generality.)

Downshifting is a good cure for those paragraphs made up of several sentences all on the same level of generality. Here is an example of that kind of problem.

> The 1990s may be remembered as the era when millions of people became obsessed with fitness. For many people, this is the decade in which they thought continually about how their bodies functioned. A preoccupation with one's body was a sign of the times. It was very fashionable to talk about how important it is to be fit.

This is a paragraph that doesn't go anywhere; it merely repeats the same generality four different ways, and that's not paragraph development. If, however, the writer starts with the main idea, puts it in a specific context that he or she knows, and develops it by downshifting to lower levels of generality and adding specific details, it can become interesting. For example:

5. The 1990s may be remembered as the era when millions of people became obsessed with fitness.

> **4.** Ambitious young people took up aerobics and weightlifting as a flat belly and sloping shoulders became assets on the career ladder.
>
> **4.** Others took up running, and comparing marathon times became approved cocktail party talk.
>
>> **3.** Even the cocktail parties themselves were affected.
>>
>>> **2.** The boss began drinking Perrier water instead of white wine, and the really strong stuff like martinis brought raised eyebrows from everyone.
>>>
>>>> **1.** Smoking at any party made the offending culprit feel like a pariah, someone polluting the air.

● **Tip**

By now you may have noticed that these three strategies for controlling paragraphs—topic sentences, commitment and response, and downshifting—resemble each other. If you have trouble figuring out which technique you should use, don't worry about it. The label for what you're doing isn't particularly important. The principle behind it is.

This principle is that as you write, you must be sure to keep the contract you make with your readers. Give them signals about what to expect, and follow through. ●

■ **Exercise 7.1** Read the following opening sentences of paragraphs to decide which seem like potentially good topic sentences. Then choose one sentence and write a paragraph that develops it.

1. Americans like to pretend that, unlike the British, they have no class system.
2. Some of the most startling new hairstyles show up on young men.
3. Any good comedian is necessarily a shrewd judge of audience.
4. The first car to come around the curve was a Porsche, followed by a Mercedes, and then a BMW.
5. Many educational critics claim that insipid textbooks smother children's interest in reading.

■ **Exercise 7.2** Working in a group with other students, discuss how you might develop paragraphs that begin with the following commitments. Then each person should write a paragraph based on the same first sentence; compare your paragraphs.

1. Who doesn't recall the first time he or she tried to drive a car?
2. Many of today's best-selling items are things consumers didn't even know they wanted ten years ago.
3. Someone buying athletic shoes faces a bewildering array of choices.
4. Students entering college are often unprepared for learning in the fast lane.
5. When blue denim originated in France in the last century, it was used only as a sturdy material for work clothing.

■ **Exercise 7.3** Working in a group with two or three other students, try to plot the levels of generality in the following paragraph. Mark the first level as 5 and work your way down until all sentences are accounted for. Remember that you may have more than one sentence at any level of generality. After you have diagrammed the paragraph, decide whether it should be revised to eliminate sprawl.

The term *student* doesn't seem to mean the same thing at an urban commuter college and on the wooded campus of a large state university such as Penn State or the University of Washington. At urban campuses the students are all ages. In fact, most of them look closer to thirty or forty than to twenty. Many are even parents dropping off their children at the campus day-care center on their way to class. At Penn State, however, you rarely see a student who looks over twenty-five. To encounter a student walking with or carrying a child is unusual. Clothes are different too. At urban colleges, students are dressed like most of the other working people hurrying by because they too are working people, coming to campus after their jobs or before they go to work. At a state university, the costume is likely to be blue jeans or shorts and a T-shirt adorned with some slogan; shoes are Reeboks or Nikes, and a backpack adorns every shoulder.

■ **Exercise 7.4** Develop a paragraph from one of these opening lines by downshifting through several levels of generality. Pair up with other students who have chosen to develop the same paragraph and compare your results.

1. The huge super bookstores of the 1990s are changing the environment in which people buy books.
2. Music of one kind or another seems to play a major role in the lives of most young people today.
3. Glance over the display of magazines at the checkout counter of any large grocery store, and you'll get a fairly good idea of what kind of reading interests the average shopper.
4. The American automobile industry has made a strong comeback in the past few years by building different kinds of cars.
5. The rise of the radio and television call-in talk shows has brought about important changes in American politics.

7b WHAT OTHER PATTERNS CAN YOU USE FOR PARAGRAPHS?

Troubleshooting

If you sometimes have trouble deciding what kind of paragraph works best in a particular situation, you might find it useful to learn some of the more common paragraph patterns. We don't know how many writers use these patterns consciously—perhaps the patterns just emerge in the process of writing because they so closely resemble typical ways of thinking. Nevertheless, it is worth your time to learn what the patterns are and how you can use them to develop your paragraphs. The patterns parallel the organizational patterns already identified in Chapter 2. Here are those you are likely to find most useful.

7b

¶

S U M M A R Y

Common Paragraph Patterns

Cause and effect	Classification
Comparison and contrast	Narration or process
Definition	Analogy
Illustration	

To try out various paragraph patterns, consider . . .

7b–1 **Cause and effect.** In a paragraph explaining why or how something happened, you can begin with a statement of effect and then enumerate the causes, or you can give your causes first and conclude with the effect. Here is an example of the former pattern.

Effect

Yet another example of competition in the world market that helped consumers occurred in the automobile industry.

Causes

By the mid-1980s, the prices of economy cars had risen substantially, with the smallest Japanese and American sedans bearing sticker prices that approached or exceeded five figures. American car companies claimed that the profit margins on cheap cars were too small to justify producing vehicles under $6,000. Because of import quotas, the Japanese could export only a limited number of vehicles, so they understandably preferred to ship their more profitable luxury and sporty lines to America. As a consequence, a gap opened at the lower end of the automobile market, leaving room for manufacturers from Third World countries, with their reduced labor and production costs, to compete. They introduced to America some of the lowest-priced cars consumers had seen in years.

7b–2 **Comparison and contrast.** Similarly, a paragraph can be built quite naturally upon a comparison and contrast pattern. Here's an easy-to-follow paragraph that sets up a comparison in the first sentence, discusses each item in alternating sentences, and concludes with a sentence that again compares both objects.

7b
¶

> Counselors and psychologists often point out that much of the conflict between men and women stems from the very different ways in which they use language. Linguistics expert Deborah Tannen supports this theory in her book *You Just Don't Understand*. She says men use language for "report talk" while women use it for "rapport talk." She believes that for women, conversation is a way of establishing connections and negotiating relationships; emphasis is on finding similarities and matching experiences. For men, talk is used to show independence and maintain status; this is done by exhibiting knowledge and skill and holding center stage by verbal performance. Thus men are usually more comfortable doing public speaking and can be taciturn at home while many women talk little in public situations but are articulate in small groups.

7b–3 **Definition.** Paragraphs of definition often work in the introductory part of a paper that explains or argues. They're helpful in setting limits or establishing the meaning of a crucial term. For example, the following paragraph would get an article on aerobic exercise off to a clear start.

> Aerobic exercise is exercise involving steady movement performed at a rate sufficient to reach a target heart rate substantially above the normal pulse and to sustain it at that rate for a prescribed period of time, at least twenty but preferably thirty minutes. For beneficial aerobic effect, an individual needs to maintain a target heart rate of approximately twice his or her normal heart rate. Steady rowing, swimming, bicycling, running, or brisk walking are aerobic activities. Golf, tennis, weightlifting, and other activities in which one rests frequently are not. Aerobic exercise benefits the cardiovascular system and helps the body to burn calories.

7b–4 **Illustration.** A paragraph of illustration starts out with a general statement (or question) and develops it by furnishing examples that support or elaborate on the statement. Notice that this pattern is similar to downshifting.

Gold is the universal prize in all countries, in all cultures, in all ages. A representative collection of gold artifacts reads like a chronicle of civilizations. Enameled gold rosary, 16th century, English. Gold serpent brooch, 400 B.C., Greece. Triple gold crown of Abuna, 17th century, Abyssinian. Gold snake bracelet, ancient Roman. Ritual vessels of Achaemenid gold, 6th century B.C., Persian. Drinking bowl of Malik gold, 8th century B.C., Persian. Bulls' heads in gold . . . Ceremonial gold knife, Chimu, pre-Inca, Peruvian, 9th century.   —J. Bronowski, *The Ascent of Man.*

7b-5 **Classification.** A writer develops a classification paragraph by first naming the subject to be classified, then explaining the system by which he or she is going to carry out the classification and giving examples to illustrate the various classes. In the following paragraph the author begins with a question that shows how he is going to divide his topic, gives his authority for making that division, names the first division, and gives examples to illustrate that division.

You did not know that superstition takes four forms? Theologians assure us that it does. First is what they call Vain Observances, such as not walking under a ladder and that sort of thing. Yet I saw a deeply learned professor of anthropology who had spilled some salt throwing a pinch of it over his left shoulder; when I asked him why, he replied, with a wink, that it was "to hit the Devil in the Eye." I did not question him further about his belief in the Devil: But I noticed that he did not smile until I asked him what he was doing.
—Robertson Davies, "A Few Kind Words for Superstition."

7b-6 **Narration or process.** One popular and simple way to control and develop a paragraph is to use a narrative to relate events in chronological order. You would probably use it instinctively in writing personal or historical accounts, but you can also use it effectively when writing reports that tell what happened or even in describing a process. For example, here is the narrative of a naturalist studying wolves.

Quite by accident I had pitched my tent within ten yards of one of the major paths used by the wolves when they were going to, or coming from, their hunting grounds to the westward; and only a few hours after I had taken up residence one of the wolves came back from a trip and discovered me and my tent. He was at the end of a hard night's work and was clearly tired and anxious to go home to bed. He came over a small rise fifty yards from me with his head down, his eyes half-closed, and a preoccupied air about

7b

¶

him. Far from being the preternaturally alert and suspicious beast of fiction, this wolf was so self-engrossed that he came straight on to within fifteen yards of me, and might have gone right past the tent without seeing it at all, had I not banged my elbow against the teakettle, making a resounding clank. The wolf's head came up and his eyes opened wide, but he did not stop or falter in his pace. One brief, sidelong glance was all he vouchsafed to me as he continued on his way. —Farley Mowat, *Never Cry Wolf*.

7b-7 **Analogy.** Writers who are explaining a concept they want to elaborate on or make vivid often turn to analogy to communicate better with their readers. An analogy is an extended comparison. One especially good use of analogy is to help readers understand a concept by showing a resemblance between the known and the unknown, as physicist John Wheeler does in this paragraph on black holes. In the preceding paragraph, he has asked his readers to imagine they are flying over a city and see a domed stadium. Then he writes:

> The domed-over stadium gives no evidence to the traveler of the crowd within. However, he sees the lines of traffic converging from all directions, becoming more and more tightly packed in traffic jams as they approach the center of attraction. A black hole whirling about, and being whirled about in orbit by, a normal star will also be the recipient of clouds of gas from this companion, with all the puffs and swirls that one can imagine from watching a factory chimney belch its clouds of smoke. This gas will not fall straight in. It will orbit the black hole in ever tighter spirals as it works its way inward, making weather on its way. It, like the traffic approaching the stadium, will be squeezed more and more.
> —John Wheeler, "Black Holes and New Physics."

■ **Exercise 7.5** Use two of the paragraph patterns discussed and illustrated in the previous section to write paragraphs for two of the following topics.

1. Define in detail a term you have learned recently—for instance, *CD-ROM*, *credit by examination*, *computer-assisted instruction*, or *tenure*.

2. Explain how to operate a machine you use regularly—for instance, a food processor, a jet ski, an off-road vehicle, or a computerized ticket machine.

3. Set up a classification of your relatives at a family get-together, the students in the lounge of your student union, or the passengers you encounter every day on a bus or subway.

4. Narrate an incident that happened to you recently.

5. Employ an analogy to explain the success or failure of a sports team you follow.

___

■ **Exercise 7.6** Read the following paragraphs and classify them into one of the paragraph development patterns discussed above. Then, working with other students in a small group, compare your answers. If you have differences of opinion about your classification, analyze the examples to find out why you differ.

1. "In the seventeenth century," [Willie] Ruff continued, "when West Africans were captured and brought to America as slaves, they brought their drums with them. But the slave owners were afraid of the drum because it was so potent; it could be used to incite the slaves to revolt. So they outlawed the drum. This very shrewd law had a tremendous effect on the development of black people's music. Our ancestors had to develop a variety of drum substitutes. One of them, for example, was tap dancing—I'm sure you've all heard of that. Now I'd like to show you a drum substitute that you probably don't know about, one that uses the hands and the body to make rhythm. It's called hambone."   —William Zinsser, *Willie and Dwike*.

2. Self-help is a system of medicine addressed not to rare diseases treatable in hospitals but to the aches and pains of everyday life, treatable at home. Its central philosophy grows out of medical research and clinical observation borrowed from mainstream medicine, experience that indicates that many serious diseases can be avoided by treating the minor ones. The belief is that your aches and pains are important messages from your body, telling you to do something, to change something in your life so that you'll be more comfortable.
          —Hal Zina Bennett, *The Doctor Within*.

___

7c   HOW CAN YOU USE TRANSITIONS AND PARALLELISM TO REDUCE PARAGRAPH SPRAWL?

Troubleshooting

If your instructor or another reader says your writing seems choppy and disconnected, you may need to make your paragraphs unified and more coherent by using one or more of the following strategies.

To keep your paragraphs unified . . .

7c–1 **Use pointer words.** Set up a path for your readers to follow by putting in words such as *first, second, next, last,* and so on.

> One student in particular, a nonsmoker, argued eloquently before the committee that there are many reasons to oppose a campuswide ban on smoking. **First,** such a policy unduly penalizes an activity that, though obnoxious, is not, in fact, illegal. **Second,** enforcement of the policy might encourage insidious intrusions upon the privacy of students in their dormitory rooms and faculty in their offices. **Last,** a ban on smoking might set an unfortunate precedent, leading to the elimination of other habits and activities certain groups regard as similarly offensive or harmful: drinking alcohol or coffee, eating fatty foods, dancing, listening to rock music, or even driving a car.

7c–2 **Use relationship words.** Connect sentences by using words such as *consequently, therefore, nevertheless, yet,* and so on.

> Opinion at the hearing had generally favored the proposal to abolish smoking on campus. **However,** the student's arguments made some proponents waver as they considered the wider implications of their actions. What would happen, **for example,** if one group on campus, citing statistics on heart disease, demanded a campuswide ban on fast foods? The ban on smoking would provide grounds for such a restriction.

7c–3 **Use repetition.** Using one or two key words several times through a paragraph can tie it together effectively.

> What makes **smoking** a social problem, not an individual one, an instructor from the medical school argued, is the phenomenon of **passive smoking. Passive smoking** describes the inhalation of combustion by-products by **nonsmokers** living or working in the vicinity of smokers. Scientific studies suggest a **correlation** between certain health problems in **nonsmokers** and **passive smoking.** Because of this **correlation,** institutions must act prudently to protect their employees and residents from a possible health hazard.

7c–4 **Use parallel structure.** Establishing a strong pattern of parallel sentence structure in a paragraph is an excellent way to tie it together.

> **Should smoking be banned** because it imposes a health hazard upon individuals who do not smoke? Then **shouldn't drinking be similarly outlawed,** since alcoholism victimizes mil-

lions of families and drunk driving kills thousands of innocent people every year? **Shouldn't automobiles be banned** because they maim hundreds of pedestrians every day? **Shouldn't the printing of controversial books be halted** because they plant dangerous ideas in the minds of millions of readers every hour?

You will find more on transitions and achieving links *between* paragraphs in Section 9a–6.

7c
¶

■ **Exercise 7.7** Examine the following paragraphs, identifying any transition words the writer has used to achieve unity. Put parentheses around such devices and then try to read the paragraph without them. How is the paragraph hurt by removing the transitional words and phrases?

1. These things are known about Houdini. The same tireless ingenuity, when applied to locks and jails, packing cases and riveted boilers; the same athletic prowess, when applied at the bottom of the East River or while dangling from a rope attached to the cornice of the *Sun* building in Baltimore—these talents account for the vast majority of Houdini's exploits. As we have mentioned, theater historians, notably Raymund Fitzsimons in his *Death and the Magician*, have carefully exposed Houdini's ingenuity, knowing that nothing can tarnish the miracle of the man's existence. Their accounts are technical and we need not dwell on them, except to say they mostly support Houdini's oath that his effects were achieved by natural, or mechanical, means. The Houdini problem arises from certain outrageous effects no one has ever been able to explain, though capable technicians have been trying for more than sixty years.
   —Daniel Mark Epstein, "The Case of Harry Houdini."

2. In the face of nutritional ignorance, myths and downright quackery have gained a strong foothold. People lambaste "chemicals" in our foods and overlook the fact that major nutrients like fat and sugar are actually doing the most damage. Millions search for the elixir of youth in bottles of vitamins and minerals, cakes of yeast, or jars of wheat germ. The current interest in micronutrients—vitamins, minerals, and trace elements—has prompted many to conclude that haphazard eating habits and unbalanced menus can be compensated for by swallowing a pill or potion of concentrated nutrients. This is not true. It's comparable to giving a Lincoln Continental an occasional shot of premium gasoline to make up for the low-octane fuel you fill it with most of the time. Your body is a machine; it will run as well as its fuel allows.　　　　—Jane Brody, *Jane Brody's Nutrition Book.*

7d   CAN YOU IMPROVE PARAGRAPH APPEARANCE?

Troubleshooting

You may not want to worry about paragraph divisions when you are writing your first draft or even the second one. But when you prepare your paper for its public debut, you need to check paragraph appearance. Printed material has a kind of body language that affects the way readers respond to it. In fact, the way an essay or a book or an article looks affects a potential reader's attitude even before he or she reads a word. If the print goes on for long stretches unbroken by headings, spaces, or segments of dialogue, most readers will assume the subject matter is going to be difficult and the style stiff and not "reader friendly." A strong message comes through: **I am hard to read.**

Where do we get that message? From our experience, for one thing. We know that unbroken pages with long sentences and long paragraphs usually deal with fairly difficult topics. But we also respond negatively for another reason that we may not be as aware of. That is, our brains process information in chunks, so we like to have it presented to us in manageable units. If the unit is too long or looks too jammed with information, we react negatively and don't want to read it because we suspect we'll have trouble. Of course, a persistent reader can dig out meaning from long stretches of unbroken print, but it's tough going and most of us would rather avoid that kind of reading.

That's why writers should consider breaking up their paragraphs to help their readers. Your readers are much more likely to take a friendly attitude toward what you write if they see that your paragraphs are fairly short. How short is a "fairly short" paragraph? Probably no more than seven or eight sentences—fewer if possible.

We also have to caution you, however, about writing one- or two-sentence paragraphs. Many writers have a tendency—perhaps picked up from reading newspapers, in which narrow columns can make a paragraph of a few sentences look quite long—to begin a new paragraph every few sentences, without much regard for content or unity. If too many long paragraphs intimidate readers, too many short ones can distract them or make them feel the content of a paper is trivial. Yet short paragraphs have their place, too, for emphasizing ideas.

To improve paragraph appearance . . .

7d-1 **Break up long paragraph blocks that look hard to read.** Of course, you shouldn't just chop up paragraphs arbitrarily to make your paper look more inviting. A paragraph is supposed to develop an idea, and it usually takes several sentences to do that. But often after you write a paragraph and reread it, you can spot places where you can divide it. Here are the kinds of junctures where you can start paragraphs.

CHECKLIST

Points at Which You Can Start Paragraphs

- **Shifts in time.** Look for spots where you have written words such as *at that time*, *then*, or *afterward*, or have given other time signals.
- **Shifts in place.** Look for spots where you have written *another place* or *on the other side* or have used words that point to places.
- **Shifts in direction.** Look for spots where you have written *on the other hand*, *nevertheless*, or *however*, or have indicated contrast.
- **Shifts in emphasis or focus.** Look for spots where you have shifted to a new point, perhaps used words such as *another*, *in addition*, or *not only*.

7d
¶

7d-2 **Reconsider short paragraphs.** Paragraphs can be too short as well as too long. A paragraph is, after all, supposed to develop an idea—that is, to consist of a group of sentences that focus on and explain or illustrate a point. That's hard to do in one sentence. So if you use a series of one- or two-sentence paragraphs in your paper, either you are not developing your ideas sufficiently or you're chopping what should be a coherent unit into segments that are going to confuse your readers.

Sometimes, of course, short paragraphs work well, particularly when the writer wants to make a transition, to emphasize a point, or to introduce a series. Here is an example of a single-sentence paragraph from a professional writer on science and medical issues whose work is often praised.

> Tennis has become more than the national sport; it is a rigorous discipline, a form of collective physiotherapy. Jogging is done by swarms of people, out onto the streets each day in underpants, moving in a stolid sort of rapid trudge, hoping by this to stay alive. Bicycles are cures. Meditation may be good for the soul but it is even better for the blood pressure.
>
> As a people, we have become obsessed with Health.
>
> There is something fundamentally, radically unhealthy about all this. We do not seem to be seeking more exuberance in living as much as staving off failure, putting off dying. We have lost all confidence in the human body.
>
> —Lewis Thomas, "The Health Care System."

Don't be afraid to use one- or two-sentence paragraphs occasionally, but do so sparingly. When you do make that choice, think about how those paragraphs are going to look and the message they will give your readers.

Finally, then, how long should a paragraph be? Of course, there is no simple answer. It depends on who your readers are, what you're trying to accomplish, what kind of writing you're doing, what kind of style you've chosen to write in, and other factors. When you're writing formal reports, term papers, or other kinds of academic papers, you can use some long paragraphs without creating problems. When you're writing an informative narrative, a brochure, or a process paper, short paragraphs work best. So, as with most decisions about writing, you have to consider your purpose and your audience when you edit for paragraph length.

7d
¶

WINDOW ON WRITING: Breaking Up Paragraphs

Here is an example of a long paragraph at the beginning of Robert Irmen's paper that, in revision, was broken into three shorter ones, each of which still develops a point effectively.

ORIGINAL VERSION

Fire Down Below

While I was in high school, I had an unusual summer job working as a chimney sweep's assistant. Even though chimney sweeps have been around for hundreds of years, my partner and I were an odd sight. Clad in black tails and top hat, we would search out jobs in Chicago neighborhoods with lots of chimneys. We always generated an audience as we pulled up in front of someone's house in our old station wagon. In a cloud of soot, we would unload our chimney sweeping equipment and begin preparing for our ascent to the chimney top. At each job we organized our tools to avoid unnecessary climbing, the most dangerous part of our job. I often wondered what I was doing climbing on hot rooftops and risking

my neck for a summer job. My partner tried to
persuade me that chimney sweeps had a special
significance in the world and that I was lucky to be
welcomed into people's homes for their yearly sweep.
In the past, chimney sweeping was an important
industry because people burned considerably more wood
and coal for heating and cooking than they do now.
Ben Franklin wanted chimney sweeps to be public
servants like policemen and firemen. My partner told
me of youngsters in England who, like Oliver Twist,
were kidnapped in the early 1800s and forced to be
"climbing boys." Their job was to squeeze through
large chimneys and scrape the walls clean. As the
story goes, if a boy got stuck in a chimney, a fire
would be lit under his feet to encourage him along.

7d

¶

Revised Paragraphing

　　While I was in high school, I had an unusual
summer job working as a chimney sweep's assistant.
Even though chimney sweeps have been around for
hundreds of years, my partner and I were an odd
sight. Clad in black tails and top hat, we would
search out jobs in Chicago neighborhoods with lots of
chimneys.

　　We always generated an audience as we pulled up
in front of someone's house in our old station wagon.
In a cloud of soot, we would unload our chimney
sweeping equipment and begin preparing for our ascent

to the chimney top. At each job we organized our tools to avoid unnecessary climbing, the most dangerous part of our job. I often wondered what I was doing climbing on hot rooftops and risking my neck for a summer job. My partner tried to persuade me that chimney sweeps had a special significance in the world and that I was lucky to be welcomed into people's homes for their yearly sweep.

In the past, chimney sweeping was an important industry because people burned considerably more wood and coal for heating and cooking than they do now. Ben Franklin wanted chimney sweeps to be public servants like policemen and firemen. My partner told me of youngsters in England who, like Oliver Twist, were kidnapped in the early 1800s and forced to be "climbing boys." Their job was to squeeze through large chimneys and scrape the walls clean. As the story goes, if a boy got stuck in a chimney, a fire would be lit under his feet to encourage him along.

WINDOW ON WRITING: Using Short Paragraphs Well

Tien-huei Tung wanted to give his entertaining paper on the history of zippers a snappy ending (dare we say, "zippy ending?"). This is how he did it.

Today zippers have become a necessity. While the zipper has not fully replaced the button and perhaps never will, just look around you, count the

```
zippers you see, and you'll know they have taken

over the world.
```

■ Exercise 7.8 Read this paragraph by the well-regarded essayist John McPhee and decide how it could be reasonably broken up into shorter paragraphs. Use the symbol for paragraph (¶) to indicate possible breaks. Then, working with a small group of students, compare the new paragraph breaks and discuss any places where members of the group don't agree.

7d
¶

    If a wolf kills a caribou, and a grizzly comes along while the wolf is feeding on the kill, the wolf puts its tail between its legs and hurries away. A black bear will run from a grizzly, too. Grizzlies sometimes kill and eat black bears. The grizzly takes what he happens upon. He is an opportunistic eater. The predominance of the grizzly in his terrain is challenged by nothing but men and ravens. To frustrate ravens from stealing his food, he will lie down and sleep on top of a carcass, occasionally swatting the birds as if they were big black flies. He prefers a vegetable diet. He can pulp a moosehead with one blow, but he is not lusting to kill, and when he moves through his country he can be something munificent, going into copses of willow among the unfleeing moose and their calves, touching nothing, letting it all breathe as before. He may, though, get the head of a cow moose between his legs and rake her flanks with the five-inch knives that protrude from the ends of his paws. Opportunistic. He removes and eats her entrails. He likes porcupines, too, and when one turns and presents to him a bouquet of quills, he will leap into the air, land on the other side, chuck the fretful porcupine beneath the chin, flip it over, and, with a swift ventral incision, neatly remove its body from its skin, leaving something like a sea urchin behind him on the ground. He is nothing if not athletic. Before he dens, or just after he emerges, if his mountains are covered with snow he will climb to the brink of some impossible schluss, sit down on his butt, and shove off. Thirty-two, sixty-four, ninety-six feet per second, he plummets down the mountainside, spray snow flying to either side, as he approaches collision with boulders and trees. Just short of catastrophe, still going at bonecrushing speed, he flips to his feet and walks sedately onward as if the ride had not occurred.

    —John McPhee, *Coming Into the Country.*

CHAPTER

8

*How Should You Manage
Opening and Closing Paragraphs?*

A Opening Paragraphs
B Closing Paragraphs

8a WHAT MAKES AN OPENING PARAGRAPH EFFECTIVE?

Troubleshooting

Opening paragraphs warrant special attention because they introduce you and your paper to your readers, and that first impression is important. Newspaper editors talk about the **lead** for a news story, the opening that has to catch the readers' attention and give them a strong signal about what to expect. The opening paragraph for whatever you write is your lead, the part of your paper that gets you off to a good or bad start with readers. Remember, then, that a first paragraph should do the following things.

- Get your readers' attention and interest them in reading more.
- Announce or suggest your main idea without delay.
- Give your readers a signal about the direction you intend to take.
- Set the tone of your essay.

These are important functions, and that's why first paragraphs can be challenging, but it is also why they are worth your time and attention.

● **Tip**

Just because first paragraphs are so important in the final versions of papers, don't let yourself get stalled at the draft stage by trying to write the perfect introduction. You could waste hours tinkering to get it exactly right only to find that you have to revise it later. If you find your-self bogging down on a first paragraph, just write something obvious and go on. You can come up with a better lead after you finish your first or second draft. ●

To write an effective opening paragraph . . .

`8a–1` **Remember that different kinds of writing call for different opening paragraphs.** For certain kinds of writing—for example, labo-ratory reports, grant proposals, or environmental impact statements—your readers expect specific kinds of opening paragraphs. You may need to start with a statement of the problem to be discussed or a review of what others have written. In such cases, find out what the typical pattern is and use it. In other kinds of writing, such as newspaper articles, re-views, critical analyses, personal experience papers, or opinion pieces, you have more choice and can try different approaches to write interest-ing opening paragraphs. In every case, you need to consider the impres-sion you want to make, what kind of reader you're writing for, and the tone you want to set.

8a
¶

`8a–2` **Make a commitment to your reader.** We mentioned commit-ment and response in Section 7a–2 as an organizational strategy, but commitment can also serve you well in an opening paragraph. It can take several forms—an anecdote, a description of a situation, a statement of a problem, a narrative, even a question. Whatever shape it takes, a com-mitment introduces readers to a topic and promises to give them more information.

Here is an example of an opening paragraph for a newspaper arti-cle about an upcoming sporting event.

> This weekend, a formidable competitor on the bicycle racing circuit will be in town to ride in the annual 25-kilometer obstacle race. Twenty-one-year-old Michael Lombardi captured the atten-tion of the racing world two years ago when he staged a dramatic, last-minute sprint to second place in the grueling Seaboard Tour. The Louisiana-born cyclist went on to rack up an impressive series of victories in regional competitions around the country. Recently, however, he has turned in a string of disappointing performances that have left fans scratching their heads. To find out how much of a challenge he poses to our local riders on Saturday, I interviewed Michael recently during a training break.

Here the writer catches the attention of bicycle enthusiasts among her readers, signals them that she is going to write about an upcoming race, and *commits* herself to giving them more information about what to ex-pect in the competition.

Many professional authors are especially skilled at making their opening commitment with an attention-getting narrative or anecdote that catches their readers and pulls them into the article. Here is an example from *Newsweek* magazine.

> John Collins couldn't believe his eyes. Having been turned down for a Visa card, the Milltown, N.J., accountant fetched a copy of his credit report and found that agencies mixed his data with files on other men named John Collins. He called credit bureaus and recalls one company saying, "We don't make mistakes." I said, "I'm sorry—I didn't know I was talking to God." . . .
> —John Schwartz, "Consumer Enemy No. 1."

Here Schwartz engages the reader's sympathy and clearly signals that he's going to talk about abuses and mix-ups by companies that give out credit ratings.

8a-3 **Make a direct announcement of your intentions.** Sometimes you will do best to open your essay by simply telling your readers exactly what you are going to write about. Such openings work well for many of the papers you write in college courses, for reports that you might have to write on the job, for grant proposals, and for many other kinds of factual, informative prose. Here is an example of a first paragraph from a paper for a business course.

> Despite recent claims in *Business Week* and *The Wall Street Journal* that the travel agency business is overcrowded, two recently opened agencies in Boulder, Colorado, are thriving, thanks in large measure to their innovative package trips to Mexican resort cities during college vacations. Their strategy for success combines three important ingredients: striking deals with dollar-hungry Mexican hotels, negotiating for blocks of cheap seats on airliners, and advertising heavily at low rates. This is how they did it.

The writer has announced the topic directly and forecast the main points the paper will cover.

For a more formal paper, you may want to write a particularly straightforward announcement in your opening paragraph. Here is the first paragraph of a chapter in a book by a professional writer.

> When Enrico Fermi, an Italian immigrant to the United States, and his colleagues triggered the world's first atomic pile in Chicago in 1941, science opened Pandora's box. Out of it came new ways of healing, new tools with which to study the structure of the universe, the potential for virtually free electric power—and the atomic bomb. Of all the developments of atomic physics, two

possibilities affect our future more than any others: electricity produced by the fission process and annihilation by nuclear strike.

—James Burke, *Connections*.

◆ Point of Difference

Most people who have grown up in the United States like to get
straight to the point when they talk or write. They have little patience
with what they see as wasting time on formalities or going through ritu-
als, especially when they are working on a business matter. In other cultures, however—particularly those of Asia or the Arab world—both
readers and listeners would find such directness very rude. For them, it's
an important part of communication to exchange pleasantries and formal
statements before getting down to business.

If you are in a position where you must write to people from these
cultures, particularly on a formal matter such as a letter of inquiry or a request of some kind, try to honor their customs. If possible, talk to someone from your correspondent's culture and ask him or her what the
traditions are for writing, and use those patterns as best you can. Plan to
allow more time to get into your topic and avoid being blunt or straightforward in your first paragraphs. ◆

8a–4 **Ask a question.** A third strategy for an opening paragraph is to
pose a question that highlights a problem or piques readers' curiosity.
Sometimes writers may elaborate on a single question, and sometimes
they may raise several questions in an opening paragraph. Not only can
questions provide a tantalizing lead-in, but they also make commitments.

Here's an example from the opening paragraph of a chapter in a
book on friendship.

> What draws us to one person as opposed to another? Those
> who study behavior seem to agree that friendship thrives on simi-
> larity. Thus, although "opposites attract" (heterophily) some of
> the time, "birds of a feather flock together" (homophily) most of
> the time.   —Letty Cottin Pogrebin, *Among Friends*.

8a–5 **Focus on key facts.** Another good anchor for an opening paragraph is the statement of an important fact that clues the readers in to
what your topic is going to be and gives them the information that
they need to continue with their reading. Such a statement of fact (or
facts) becomes the takeoff point for the essay. For example, the following opening paragraph starts with a remarkable fact that grabs the
reader's attention.

> Every major industrial country in the Western world except
> the United States has an extensive system of subsidized child care

that assures working women their children will be adequately taken care of by qualified people. In Sweden, for example, every city and town has government-sponsored day-care centers; in other countries, factories and corporations provide on-site care that allows women to visit their children during the day. Studies have found that on-site care significantly lowers the rate of absenteeism among both male and female employees. Yet despite these encouraging statistics, most businesses in America are still in the Stone Age when it comes to child care.

Here the writer has focused her opening paragraph on important information about child-care policies in other countries and indicated that she is going to use that information to discuss resistance to child care in the United States.

● **Tip**

Check the introductory paragraphs in a draft you have written to see if you're just stating generalities or telling your readers what they already know. Such "wheel spinning" is like a pilot's circling the field getting ready to land or a driver's racing the motor while waiting to pull away from the stoplight. There's a lot of activity but little real progress. If you think your first paragraph doesn't accomplish much and your readers may start skimming to get to the point, try cutting it and starting the paper with the *second* paragraph. Quite often a paper really begins there.

Remember, though, that you haven't necessarily wasted your time writing a rambling paragraph in the first draft. Such paragraphs can help you break through a writing block and work up the momentum to get started. ●

WINDOW ON WRITING:
Using a Descriptive Narrative to Revise an Opening Paragraph

An ardent football fan, Robert Wills wanted to write an informative paper for young people who were interested in football, perhaps the readers of *Sports Illustrated for Kids*. In it he wanted to explain a play known as the two-minute drill. Just to get started on his first draft, he wrote this paragraph, which even he didn't like.

```
One of the most exciting parts of football is

the perfectly executed two-minute drill. Nothing

thrusts the crowd into the action and keeps them

on the edges of their seats more than the
```

perfectly executed drive ending in a game-winning
touchdown.

After the members of his writing group suggested he try for a more dramatic and visual opening, he came up with this for his final version.

8a
¶

It was a bone-chilling day in Cleveland
Municipal Stadium as thousands of anxious fans
watched the American Football Conference championship
game between the Cleveland Browns and the Denver
Broncos. The score stayed close for the first fifty-
nine minutes. Then with fifty-eight seconds left in
the game, the Broncos took over inside their own ten-
yard line, with virtually no chance of winning. But
then the Bronco offense, led by quarterback John
Elway, began what would later be known as "The
Drive." Using short passes and controlling the clock,
Denver drove down the field and scored on a nine-yard
touchdown pass from Elway to receiver Vance Johnson.
This is just one example of one of the most exciting
plays in football: the two-minute drill.

WINDOW ON WRITING:
Using an Anecdote to Revise an Opening Paragraph

In an article on fraudulent antiques aimed at the readers of *House Beautiful,* Sheila Joy, a part-time antique dealer herself, started her first draft with this routine opening paragraph.

How common is dishonesty in the antique
business? I recently interviewed three antique
dealers who admitted to dishonesty in their business.

8a

¶

> These three dealers have good reputations within the
> business, and they minimized the importance of the
> dishonest practices they admitted to, saying the
> business as a whole is mostly honest.

A useful paragraph for getting started, but Sheila knew she wanted a more vivid opening that involved specific people. Here is her final version.

> American writer Wilson Mizner, along with his
> brother Addison, ran an antiques business in Florida
> in the 1920s. The brothers were later famous for
> designing homes and developing property in the early
> Florida land boom. Wilson invited friends to his
> "antiquing factory" and offered to let them help
> inflict the ravages of time on a new dining room
> suite. "Don't shoot straight at it. Remember a worm
> always charges at a piece of furniture from an
> angle," he instructed.

■ **Exercise 8.1** Draft an opening commitment paragraph that might begin an informal essay with one of these titles. For these topics, an anecdote or question might work particularly well.

1. What Jobs Do for—or to—Teenagers
2. The Best (or Worst) Course You Can Take on This Campus
3. Who Is Going to Teach Today's Children?
4. The Tragedy of Teenage Pregnancy
5. Can You Really Work Your Way Through College?

If your instructor thinks it's a good idea, join with other students who have chosen to write on the same title and read your paragraphs aloud. Discuss which ones seem to work well and why.

■ **Exercise 8.2** Write a "direct statement" opening sentence or paragraph for an article that would develop one of these titles.

1. What It Means to Live Below the Poverty Level: A Case Study
2. My Latest Experience with Computers
3. The Option Racket and Car Prices
4. The Result of No Pass/No Play Rules in High School
5. Some Good Jobs for College Students

■ **Exercise 8.3** Working in a small group, each student should write opening questions that might make a good lead-in for articles or essays on two of the following topics. Then compare and discuss your questions with the group.

1. A board of regents' proposal to ban student cars from the central campus and impose a student fee for shuttle buses
2. The fact that only two of the twelve copying machines in the college library work
3. The effects of television on salaries in professional sports
4. The revelation that assistant professors at your college are paid less than custodians
5. New designs in athletic shoes that have made a difference in the performance of high school students

8b   WHAT MAKES A CONCLUDING PARAGRAPH EFFECTIVE?

Troubleshooting

CAUTION

Concluding paragraphs can be even harder to write than opening paragraphs because it's often difficult to wind up a subject gracefully without lapsing into clichés. The only direct advice we can give is that your concluding paragraph should satisfy your readers that you have left no loose ends or unanswered questions. You don't want your readers asking, "Then what?" or "And so?" when they finish or looking on the back of the page to see if they have missed something.

There are no simple prescriptions for achieving that important goal; however, we can suggest three patterns that make for satisfying endings.

To write an effective concluding paragraph . . .

8b–1 **Make a recommendation when one is appropriate.** Such a recommendation should grow out of the issue you have been discussing. This approach usually gives a paper a positive ending and closes off the topic. For example, here is a conclusion from a paper on nutrition.

But even if you are an athlete who wants quick results, you should not go to extremes in trying to improve your overall nutrition. When you decide to change your eating habits, your motto should be "Eat better," not "Eat perfectly." By increasing carbohydrates and reducing fat in the diet—that is, by eating more fruits, vegetables, and whole grains and less whole milk and meat—you can improve your energy level rather quickly. You will also feel better, play better, and look better than you ever imagined.

8b–2 **Summarize the main points you have made.** Sometimes you can bring your paper to an effective close by reemphasizing your main points, though not in precisely the same words you have used before. You want to be careful, however, not to write an ending that sounds forced, as if you were tying the paper up in red ribbon and sticking on a bow.

Here is the conclusion for a paper in which the writer has argued convincingly that restaurant customers should tip their waiters even if they will never see them again.

Anyone who has ever worked in a restaurant knows that all too often the food isn't hot, the salads are soggy, or customers have to wait thirty minutes for a steak that should take ten minutes. When that happens, it's easy for customers to justify shortchanging the waiter by saying, "The food wasn't good," or "I had to wait too long." But ask yourself, Was it really the waiter's fault? The bottom line is that tips are part of a waiter's pay, and if you don't tip, you've stolen part of his or her labor.

8b–3 **Link the end to the beginning.** Another effective way to end your paper is to tie your conclusion back to your beginning in a way that makes a kind of frame for the paper and unifies it. Notice how the boldfaced words in the example below forge a connection between the opening and closing paragraphs in a student paper on astronomy.

Opening paragraph
In 1931 an event occurred in Holmdel, New Jersey, that was to turn the world of astronomy on its ear. **An electrical engineer named Karl Jansky** was trying to find out what was causing **the static** that was interfering with radiotelephone reception between the United States and Europe. What he found instead was that the heavens were broadcasting! The "static" was caused by radio waves reaching the earth from the center of our **Milky Way** galaxy.

Closing paragraph
If Karl Jansky had not stumbled onto the "static" in the **Milky Way** that led to the development of the radio telescope, we would probably still know nothing about quasars, one of the most

astonishing discoveries of our day. And it is doubtful that **Jansky** himself ever fully realized what a powerful tool he had hit upon for investigating the secrets of our universe.

● **Tip**

Probably the most important thing to remember about closing a paper or essay is this: Stop when you've finished. If you have covered all your points and are reasonably well satisfied with what you've said, quit. Don't bore your reader by tacking on a needless recapitulation or adding a paragraph of platitudes. ●

8b
¶

WINDOW ON WRITING: Improving a Concluding Paragraph

In this paper about the ballerina Maria Tallchief, written for the young readers of *Seventeen* magazine, Jessica Vincent concluded her first draft rather unimaginatively, saying,

> Maria Tallchief went on to be the darling of
> American ballet, dancing all over the country and the
> world. She was the first winner of the Dance
> magazine award, which recognizes achievement and
> accomplishment in the dance world. She was also one
> of the first Americans to be asked to dance as a
> guest with the prestigious Paris Opera ballet. All
> this from a dancer whose first stage performance had
> been twirling and waving a flag to the tune of "The
> Star-Spangled Banner."

For her final draft, which was a longer, more in-depth account of Tallchief's career, Jessica concluded with this smoother and more sub-stantial paragraph in which she incorporates more about the theme of her article, Tallchief's contributions to the great traditions of ballet.

> As the first American-born prima ballerina,
> Maria Tallchief sprang from the parent flame of 300
> years of classical tradition. Brought over to the
> New World and tended by the old guard, this grand

tradition was given to the next generation only when
they had become worthy. In Maria burned a new facet
of that tradition, but it was the same parent flame
that had produced all the European greats, from
Pavlova to Nijinsky. In a hundred years when people
write about ballet, they will remark on the
glimmering fierceness that was Tallchief's special
gift and consider what it gave to the ballet
tradition.

■ **Exercise 8.4** Read the following closing paragraphs from professional articles. What features do you find in them that give the reader a
sense that the author has brought his or her essay to a satisfactory close?

1. No one could wish for a more advantageous heritage than that be-
queathed to the black writer in the South: a compassion for the earth,
a trust in humanity beyond our knowledge of evil, and an abiding love
of justice. We inherit a great responsibility as well, for we must give
voice to centuries not only of silent bitterness and hate but also of
neighborly kindness and sustaining love.
—Alice Walker, "The Black Writer and the Southern Experience."

2. I think it is time for those who seek identity and power through grievance groups to fashion identities apart from grievance, to grant themselves the widest range of freedom, and to assume responsibility for
that freedom. Victimhood lasts only as long as it is accepted, and to
exploit it for an empty sovereignty is to accept it. The New Sovereignty is ultimately about vanity. It is the narcissism of victims, and it
brings only a negligible power at the exorbitant price of continued
victimhood. And all the while integration remains the real work.
—Shelby Steele, *The New Sovereignty.*

■ **Exercise 8.5** Exchange drafts with two or three other students who
are working on the same assignment. Each person should read the closing paragraphs from the other papers. As a group, discuss what features
each writer used to bring his or her writing to a conclusion. Discuss how
those strategies are useful and what others might also be helpful.

CHAPTER

9

How Do You Manage Transitions?

A Overcoming Problems with Transitions
B Strengthening Transitions

9a WHERE DO PROBLEMS WITH TRANSITIONS OCCUR?

Troubleshooting

CAUTION

If your instructor suggests that your drafts are choppy or not well unified, you need to work on your transitions as you revise. Ask yourself if you're showing your readers connections between sentences and paragraphs by putting in the links they need to keep them moving in the direction you want them to go. Remember, though, that the best transitional devices are *organizational* and *internal*; that is, they come from the plan and logic that underlie a piece of writing. Thus the best way to produce the smooth prose that is the mark of a skilled writer is to establish patterns that run through an essay and carry readers along naturally. For example, you might use a cause-and-effect or a comparison and contrast pattern. You could also use repetition, parallelism, and balance in your sentences and paragraphs.

But even with such patterns, you sometimes need to use *external* transitional terms, those words and phrases that act like hooks, links, and directional signals to keep readers moving from point to point. These are the principal transitions we discuss in this section.

To overcome problems with transitions . . .

9a-1 Avoid series of short, unconnected sentences. Do you frequently write paragraphs made up of mostly short, simple sentences with very few commas? Do you avoid complex sentences with clauses or introductory phrases? If so, you may be leaving out the phrases and clauses that would help readers to follow your thinking. You need to show connections, not leave it up to your readers to guess about them.

Here's an example of a paragraph where the sentence structures are too simple to connect ideas significantly. All the sentences are fairly short, with similar patterns and no commas. Although you don't get lost in the paragraph, the style is choppy and graceless.

9a
trans

Weak transitions

> Antonio Diaz is the senior sports columnist for the *Sunday Tribune*. He is an avid amateur painter. He devotes all his spare time to his hobby. Whenever he has a free day, he sets up his easel in the Botanic Garden. His favorite subject there is the water lily pond. His work also furnishes him with subjects. He often brings a sketchbook to the games he covers. He finds his rapid sketches of the athletes useful. They help him reconstruct the excitement of a game for his column.

Here is a revised version, with some sentences combined and others connected (transitional terms are boldfaced).

Revised

> The senior sports columnist for the *Sunday Tribune*, Antonio Diaz, is **also** an avid amateur painter **who** devotes all his spare time to his hobby. Whenever he has a free day, he sets up his easel in the Botanic Garden, **where** his favorite subject is the water lily pond. Mr. Diaz's work also furnishes him with subjects, **and** he often brings a sketchbook to the games he covers. He finds his rapid sketches of the athletes useful **when** reconstructing the excitement of a game for his column.

`9a-2` Check whether you're using subordinate clauses effectively.

Do your sentences have few subordinate clauses, that is, clauses introduced by words such as *although, if, since, because, so,* and *unless?* If so, you may not be clearly showing connections between your ideas.

Weak transitions

> Nuclear fusion may someday provide us with virtually limitless quantities of cheap, clean energy. The technology is still in its infancy. The most successful fusion trials to date use a mixture of tritium and deuterium. These fuse to form helium. The process gives off energy. Tritium and deuterium are both hydrogen derivatives. Plain water could supply all the fuel we need.

You get no sense of the connection of one idea to another in this paragraph. Here is a revised version that hooks ideas together by joining sentences and using terms that show subordination; the transitional terms are boldfaced.

Revised

> **Although** the technology is still in its infancy, nuclear fusion may someday provide us with virtually limitless quantities of cheap, clean energy. The most successful fusion trials to date use a mixture of tritium and deuterium, **which** give off energy **when** they fuse to form helium. **Since** tritium and deuterium are both hydrogen derivatives, plain water could supply all the fuel we need.

9a
trans

9a–3 **Be suspicious of expletive constructions.** Do you write a lot of sentences beginning with the constructions "There is," "It is," and "There are"? If so, you may be putting together sentences that are weakly connected, and you may also be creating a monotonous rhythm in your paper.

Weak transitions

> It is a truism that good manners are like skeleton keys. There are few doors they will not open. Some people think that good manners are pretentious. They are a way of condescending to people. That is a misunderstanding. The real purpose of manners is to make social situations comfortable and to put the people you are with at ease. Manners are also practical to have. There are many companies that insist that their executives have good manners. For this reason, some business schools include a course on manners in their curricula.

Again, you get little sense of the relationship between these sentences, and the repetitive patterns are boring. Here is the paragraph reworked with better sentence openings and stronger connections. Transitional terms are boldfaced.

Revised

> Good manners, like skeleton keys, will open almost any door. **While** some people think that good manners are pretentious and condescending, that's a misunderstanding. **On the contrary,** manners exist to make social situations comfortable by putting everyone at ease. **Moreover,** manners are a practical asset in the job market. Many companies insist on well-mannered executives, **which** has prompted some business schools to include a course on manners in their curricula.

9a–4 **Use frequent markers to show time and sequence.** Move your readers along from one part to another by putting in words such as *once,* *when, ago, formerly, finally,* and *after*; you can also use *first, second, then, last,* and similar words to good effect. Time markers can be important links in your writing.

**9a
trans**

Weak transitions

Traditionally, girls learned to cook from their mothers. Many young women in the 1990s aren't learning to cook. Some women think it's sexist to assume that women should cook. Many young men don't expect their wives to cook. Both partners in a marriage work. Eating out is considered the norm. Supermarket freezers are stacked with frozen dinners. Frozen breakfasts are popular too. It's possible to eat satisfactorily with only a freezer and a microwave. It's not much fun though.

The paragraph is readable but choppy and graceless because the reader gets no help from transitions. Here is a revision with time markers and links boldfaced.

Until recently, most girls learned to cook from their mothers. **Today, however,** many young women aren't learning to cook at all, **and** some claim that it's sexist to assume they should. **Moreover, since** both partners work in most modern marriages, young men don't expect their wives to cook. **Today,** eating out or buying prepared food seems to be the norm. **Now** supermarket freezers are stacked with frozen dinners and breakfasts, so it's possible to eat satisfactorily with only a freezer and a microwave. **But** it's not much fun.

9a–5 **Check your drafts for connecting words of all kinds.** Does your writing lack those crucial words that signal connections between ideas? Some of the more common ones are *and, but, or, too, moreover, consequently, nevertheless, therefore,* and *also*. If they're missing, your writing may seem fragmented.

Weak transitions

Computers, television, and video games are changing the ways people receive information. The impact on education is enormous. Publishers and authors of textbooks are using new strategies to present facts and theories. They have unprecedented technology and resources to work with. The new approaches are visual and interactive. Many educators believe the materials will reach a group of students who don't respond well to the printed page.

Reading this paragraph, you sense a gap at the end of each sentence; the ideas don't seem tied together. Here is a revision with transitional links boldfaced.

Revised

Computers, television, and video games are changing the ways people receive information, **and** the impact on education is enormous. Authors and publishers, **who now** have unprecedented technology and resources to work with, are using new strategies to present facts and theories. **These** new approaches, **which** are visual and interactive, lead many educators to believe they can **now** reach students who don't respond well to the printed page.

9a
trans

● **Tip**

We suspect that for some writers, problems with transitions stem from worrying about how to punctuate sentences. Because they're not sure where to put commas or how to use semicolons, they don't try to compose the more complex sentences they would like to use for fear their writing will become tangled. So they limit themselves to an immature and choppy style that doesn't do justice to their ideas.

If you think this might be your problem, we suggest that, at first, you forget about the punctuation in those complex or involved sentences. Just go ahead and write them. You can figure out how to fix them later, getting help if necessary from a teacher or writing center. With most instructors, you'll get more points for expressing good ideas in interesting sentences than you will for having all your commas in the right places. ●

9a–6 **Check for gaps between paragraphs.** Major transitional problems are most likely to occur as you move from paragraph to paragraph. Unless you have a strong overall pattern that unifies your writing, you may need some device to link your paragraphs. It could be as simple as starting paragraphs with an appropriate transitional word. You could also use a key word at the end of one paragraph, then repeat it at the beginning of the next. Or you might end one paragraph with a question, then answer the question in the paragraph that follows. Whatever device you use, you are giving your readers signals that say, "Come this way."

Here are some examples to illustrate how a paragraph can be tied in with the one that comes before it.

First are some opening paragraphs for an article about suburban tract housing. Notice how after the opening sentence, each subsequent paragraph starts with a connecting term that links it to the previous paragraph. Linking words are boldfaced.

Opening line, first paragraph

In the years following World War II, the United States experienced an unprecedented building boom as veterans came home and started their families.

First line, next paragraph

But perhaps the most characteristic creation of **those optimistic years** was **tract housing**—row upon row of look-alike houses on small, featureless plots.

**9a
trans**

First line, next paragraph

Still, despite their numbing uniformity, **tract houses** made possible an attractive new way of life, and young couples by the thousands moved to **the suburbs** to live the American dream.

First line, following paragraph

Today, the suburban life-style has become an integral part of the American psyche, and **the houses** that started it all are the objects of nostalgic affection.

First line, following paragraph

However, since **tract houses** were designed to be added on to as families grew, very few of them survive in their original form.

First line, last paragraph

Consequently, community groups and historical societies are seeking landmark status for mint-condition **tract houses.**

Now here are some ways you might forge a link between the last line of one paragraph and the first line of the next.

Key word at end of one paragraph

Among the earliest of all suburban tract developments, the one that appears most often in sociology texts is **Levittown,** Long Island.

Word repeated in opening line of next paragraph

Built between 1947 and 1951, **Levittown** was a vast development of 17,447 houses in two basic styles: cape and ranch.

Question at the end of one paragraph

The young newlyweds had only one question after touring the house: **When can we move in?**

Answer at beginning of next paragraph

Two weeks later, they were receiving guests at their housewarming. Thousands of similar parties would be held during the euphoric postwar years as young couples flocked to the newly created suburbs.

● **Tip**

Take special care that any paragraph that ends at the bottom of a page has a clear link to the paragraph at the top of the next page. If it doesn't, readers may get lost and think they've skipped a page. Be sure to check these links in papers you write on a computer. Revise them for transitions after you print them out. ●

■ **Exercise 9.1** Rewrite the following paragraph, reorganizing and changing some sentences or adding signal words to improve transitions.

9a
trans

Washington, D.C., presents a challenge to photographers. It is not that there is a lack of possible subjects. There are actually too many well-known subjects. Any image of them risks looking trite. Do we really need another photograph of the Lincoln Memorial or some other famous sight? We think we know these sights well enough. We really don't know them well enough, however. We can never know them well enough. Tourists may click mindlessly away. A gifted photographer is patient and dedicated. He or she will be able to show us something new.

■ **Exercise 9.2** Working with two or three other students, read over the following two paragraphs, then diagnose the transition problems you find between the paragraphs and within each one. Working together, rewrite the paragraphs in a way that would solve those problems.

The dangers of exercise are not only that one might injure one's back or pull a hamstring. True, people new to exercise need to guard against such injuries. No one wants to be a fallen weekend athlete, crippled on Monday morning from running a ten-kilometer race or biking up a mountain on Sunday. The newcomer to exercise can become a fanatic. In some ways, the atmosphere around a health and fitness club encourages fanaticism. At 6:00 a.m., the hard-core weightlifters and triathlon competitors are there sweating and puffing, but enjoying every minute of it. They look great and exude confidence. They seem to have their priorities straight —workouts come before work.

The fitness craze can take over one's life. What with aerobics, weightlifting, and stretching, it's easy to use up three hours a day before you know it. What happens to earning a living or to studying if one is a student? What happens to one's social life? Not only do exercisers have to go to bed early, but when they start to preach—and they usually do—nonexercising friends can quickly disappear.

9b   HOW CAN YOU STRENGTHEN TRANSITIONS?

Troubleshooting

TRICKY   Once you have learned to diagnose your problems with transitions, you can use various strategies to solve them. The concept that underlies all of them is this: Each sentence should leave a little trace or residue out of which the next sentence can grow. There should always be a reference, a hint, a repetition, a key word that links what you're saying with what's come before and what lies ahead. A plan of organization is the best tactic, of course, but we also offer a few smaller-scale ways to establish connections between ideas.

To improve your transitions . . .

9b–1 **Accumulate a stockpile of the conventional transition words.** When you edit, check to see if you need to insert one or more of the traditional linking terms in order to firm up connections in your writing.

Remember, however, that transitional words and phrases are not neutral. On the contrary, they give strong but diverse signals to readers. They say, "Turn here," "Stop for a qualification," "Notice the cause and effect," "Here's something similar," or "Here's something different." You can't just use a transitional term at random; you have to be sure to give the signal you want.

The most common transitional words and phrases are listed on page 185 according to their function.

9b–2 **Repeat a key idea throughout a paragraph to establish a** *motif,* **or central idea, running through it.** An idea can be a key word plus variations. For example, if you are writing a paper about rockets, then *rockets* becomes a key idea that can be repeated through a variety of potential synonyms and connected terms: *missiles, boosters, launchers, launch vehicles,* and so on. Each word helps to establish a connection to the central topic. In the example below, the key theme of health is repeated through related terms that include *physical condition, vigorous,* and *energetic.*

> **Key words boldfaced**
> On a nasty Monday night in January ten years ago, faced with yet another evening of watching her boring husband putter around with his boring model trains, Keesha left for the **Hillcrest Health and Fitness Club.** She braved the icy streets not only to improve her own **physical** and mental **health,** but also to safeguard her husband's **physical condition:** she was afraid she was

going to kill him. Today, Keesha is a **vigorous, energetic** woman with a new career as a **physical** therapist. She is also divorced.

9b–3 Use the demonstrative pronouns *this, that, these, those,* and *such* within sentences to tie ideas together. Notice how the bold-faced words in the following example hook directly into the previous sentences.

Demonstrative terms boldfaced

Making a movie is a collaborative endeavor, and script-writers point **this** out frequently. Occasionally a screenplay will survive the transfer from paper to film intact, but **that** is the exception rather than the rule. Typically, producers, directors, actors, and agents all have a say in the final product. Coping with **such** high-handed meddling is often difficult for young writers, and **those** who cannot compromise rarely stay in the business for long.

9b–4 Use relative pronouns to show links between sentences. *Who, which, where,* and *that* are powerful words that link a descriptive or

9b

trans

CHART

Common Transitional Words and Phrases

SHOWING SIMILARITY
likewise
similarly
in the same way

SHOWING CONTRAST
however
instead
nevertheless
although
in spite of
on the other hand
not only

SHOWING ACCUMULATION
moreover
in addition to
for example

SHOWING CONSEQUENCE
hence
consequently
therefore
as a result of
thus

SHOWING CAUSATION
because
since
for

SHOWING SEQUENCE
next
subsequently
after
finally
first, second, third

informative statement to something that has preceded it. Notice how the boldfaced words in this paragraph serve as links to other words and ideas.

9b
trans

Relative pronouns boldfaced

Miranda's first few weeks at the conservatory were exhausting but exhilarating. It was a place **that** challenged her, one **where** she could meet talented people **who** shared her passion for dance. The competition among the students was friendly but intense, **which** only increased her determination to practice and learn.

9b–5 **Use parallel structures and downshifting to link ideas within a paragraph.** Putting your ideas into parallel sentences ties them together by a repeated pattern. Ideas that branch off from one another also seem tightly connected.

The following example employs both techniques. The first sentence states the topic of the paragraph: serving in the Peace Corps. The next three parallel sentences downshift to develop that main idea. Finally, the last sentence downshifts again to enlarge on the fourth sentence, providing an illustration of the main point.

Parallel structures and downshifting boldfaced

Young men and women who plan to serve in the Peace Corps **must be prepared** for hard work and perhaps a bit of culture shock. They **must be willing** to put in long hours of physical labor. They **must reconcile** themselves to life without such luxuries as daily showers and private bathrooms. They **must** even **cultivate** a broad-minded attitude about food. Former volunteers have wittily recounted their attempts to share the local enthusiasm for such delicacies as fried locusts and roasted slugs.

9b–6 **Use a semicolon to link two closely related statements.** Although many writers ignore this useful piece of punctuation, the semicolon signals a tight connection that says, "These groups of words go together." Often a semicolon can connect parts of a sentence more effectively than *and* or *also*. For more details about the semicolon, see Section 27a.

Connecting semicolons boldfaced

Sculptor Ilya Karensky no longer has to endure his neighbors' contempt for his work**;** now he has to put up with their insincere and inept praise. Ilya knows perfectly well that what his neighbors admire most about his work is the amount of money for which it now sells**;** they like the sculptures themselves no better than they did before.

In this paper titled "The Ill Effects of Our Obsession with Dieting," Brandy Parsons writes tightly connected, easy-to-follow paragraphs. Here is an example with transition devices highlighted.

One out of every 100 women has anorexia nervosa, an eating disorder characterized by self-starvation, low self-esteem, and a strong desire to achieve perfection or be perfect. Although studies have revealed that the tendency to be anorexic is hereditary, our culture in particular favors it. For most anorexics, rigid dieting provides a feeling of power and control. In most cases, after a young woman reaches her initial weight goal, she sets another, lower goal. As weight loss continues, a woman with anorexia may suffer from malnutrition and weakness, but her psychological need for feeling in control will override her physiological need for nutrients. Losing weight becomes the most important part of the victim's life and takes precedence over friends, family, school, and work.

■ **Exercise 9.3** Underline the transitional words and phrases in the following paragraph.

On that July evening in 1890 when an obscure, deeply disturbed painter named Vincent van Gogh lay dying of self-inflicted gunshot wounds, few people could have predicted that he would someday be considered one of the greatest artists of all time. After all, the man had never sold a single painting in his entire life. Yet today there is no artist more famous among the general public.

Fueled by novels, movies, and even a popular song, van Gogh's fame has spread so far that even people who cannot name a single other artist have heard of him. His works appear routinely on T-shirts, table mats, curtains, and lampshades, and the rare auction of a Van Gogh original always makes the nightly news. No one—least of all the artist himself—could have hoped for so much attention and admiration.

9b
trans

What Kinds of Language Can You Use?

A Levels of Language

B Meaning

C Dialects

D Biased Language

Most people are as unlikely to use the same kind of language every time they write as they would be to wear the same kind of clothes on every occasion. We instinctively, often unconsciously, adapt our language to our audience and situation because we have developed a sense of what is appropriate; we know that what works on one occasion may not work as well on another. And just as the person with good clothes sense knows how to choose the right outfit to make the desired impression, skillful writers know how to choose language that fits their needs. The purpose of this chapter is to explain some of the language choices available to you.

10a HOW DO YOU CHOOSE THE APPROPRIATE LANGUAGE LEVEL?

Troubleshooting

When you start to work on a report or article or even an important letter, one of your first questions will probably be, "How formal or informal should I make this?" Should you use the rather impersonal and conventional diction and tone of formal language or the more casual language and conversational tone of informal language? The answer, of course, is "That depends." It depends on who your audience is and how you want to come across to that audience. To make appropriate choices about how formal you want to be, you should ask yourself

- Who are my readers?
- What do they expect from me?
- What do I want to accomplish with this audience?

**10a
lang**

Only after you have an idea of the answers to these questions can you choose language that will work well for a specific writing situation.

Unfortunately, many writers assume that to impress professors, colleagues, or other demanding readers, they must adopt an excessively formal style. They think writing in an "academic style" means drafting hard-to-read prose stuffed with big words and long, dull sentences—something so impersonal and dry that it reads as if it came from an insurance policy or a badly written textbook (see Section 12c–2 on bureaucratic prose). So they turn out writing like this example from a paper for a psychology course.

Original

Neonate infants are believed to have the ability to relate visual sensory perception with motor function. The neonatal visual system is probably the most prefunctional of the senses at birth. Manifestly, this competence is not correlated with time outside the womb, for in early months infants have the problem-solving ability that comes from linking sensory systems and motor activity. The observation that these subjects manifest visual preference for facial forms upholds the assumption that a connection exists between visual and motor activity.

Although the writer worked hard at composing this paragraph, the writing is dull and difficult. Most readers, and particularly professors, who have to examine a great many papers, want to be able to understand easily what they read. This revision, while still formal, is much clearer.

Revised

Observers now realize that newborn infants can coordinate sight and movement. In fact, vision seems to be the sense that is best developed when babies are born, for it is evident very early that they can solve problems that require linking vision and motor ability. The fact that they can recognize different facial expressions and respond to them supports this theory.

It's true that, broadly speaking, there is something called *academic style*, and it's useful to be able to shift into that style when you need to.

But we think that mastering the conventions of academic writing is not a matter of commanding a formal style and an intimidating vocabulary. Rather it is learning how professors want you to organize and present your ideas and what kind of support they expect for those ideas (see Section 5a). Most care far more about clear thinking and informed writing than they do about an elevated style.

When you write, you'll often find yourself looking for the word, phrase, or expression that seems to fit your writing situation and creates the tone you want. Such choices are tricky because we cannot make a simple, black-and-white classification of formal and informal language. You should think of levels of formality in language as a scale or a continuum (like the one below) that has very formal language, the stiff and intimidating language of legal documents, at one end of the scale and very informal language, slang and colloquialisms, at the other end.

Neither of the extremes on this scale need concern us here. Virtually no academic writing that students do requires them to be very

10a
lang

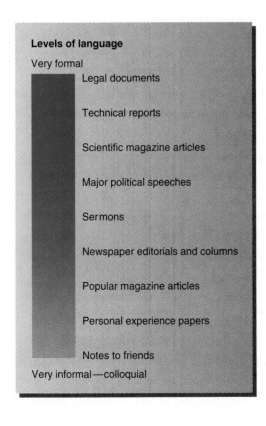

Levels of language

Very formal

Legal documents

Technical reports

Scientific magazine articles

Major political speeches

Sermons

Newspaper editorials and columns

Popular magazine articles

Personal experience papers

Notes to friends

Very informal—colloquial

formal. And for most college writing, with the possible exception of personal journals, a highly colloquial style isn't appropriate. It is, however, useful for you to know something about the general characteristics and uses of at least three of the intermediate levels of language.

To handle language levels appropriately . . .

10a–1 **Recognize formal writing.** Formal writing tends to have these characteristics.

SUMMARY

Characteristics of Formal Style

- Long sentences and long paragraphs
- Abstract language
- Impersonal tone—few personal references; few contractions
- Little action and few strong, active verbs
- Serious tone
- Considerable distance implied between reader and writer

Writers who choose a formal style may do so for several reasons. First, they may be writing on a serious and complex topic, one for which a casual, personal style would not be appropriate. Second, they may be writing for a serious formal occasion, such as a public speech, and don't want their writing to sound too much like everyday speech. Or they may want to sound impersonal and not emotionally involved with their topic, so they adopt a style that distances them from their reader. For example, here is an opening paragraph from a paper for an environmental studies course.

> An inescapable fact of the world energy situation today is that fossil fuel resources are finite and that continued reliance on coal, gas, and oil for generating electricity is not viable. However, meeting future electricity needs requires raising public awareness about finding alternatives. The most important characteristics of these options will be flexibility, cost, and low risk. Two programs currently under investigation are cogeneration and renewable power production.

This is a clear and informative paragraph that gets the reader off to a good start, but it's not much fun to read because of the impersonal, formal language. Nevertheless, much of the writing done in fields such as engineering or social studies sounds like this, and professors may well want their students to cultivate this style. Skilled writers, however, know how to revise writing like this to appeal to a broader audience.

◆ Point of Difference

When choosing an appropriate style for a college paper, you're likely to find that instructors vary greatly in their attitudes toward formal and informal writing. Some want students in their classes to write in a formal style; they don't want to see contractions or colloquialisms, and they prefer an impersonal tone—no first- or second-person pronouns. Others welcome a more informal style and encourage students to write casually, using a personal voice.

Frequently, instructors don't tell students directly what kind of writing they expect, although you may get hints. If you're unsure, it's a good idea to ask for guidelines before you turn in that final draft. ◆

10a **lang**

10a–2 **Recognize moderately informal writing.** Although there are many kinds of moderately informal writing, and it occupies a considerable spread across the continuum of styles, we find that it has these general characteristics.

S U M M A R Y

Characteristics of Informal Style

- Variety of sentence lengths
- Short- to medium-length paragraphs
- Mixture of abstract and concrete language
- Some use of first- and second-person pronouns
- Some use of contractions
- Frequent action verbs
- Variety of topics, from casual to serious
- Little perceived distance between reader and writer

The writing in this book is an example of moderately informal prose; so is the work of newspaper columnists such as Ellen Goodman and William Raspberry and most of the writing you may read in magazines such as *Newsweek, Sports Illustrated,* or *Elle.* Most writing in *The New York Times* would be toward the high end of informal prose; writing in *Reader's Digest* would be at the low end of informal prose.

Writers who choose an informal writing style usually do so because, although their topics may be serious, they don't want to sound solemn. Part of their purpose is to entertain, and they want their readers to feel as if they are talking to them at a close and comfortable distance. An informal style seems relaxed. Here is a moderately informal opening from a paper on computers and education.

> In the last year, interest in preparing America for its high-tech future has exploded. The current scenario predicts that we will be a huge information society, and the current generation of youngsters will need to be perfectly at ease using computers. School districts are now scrambling to meet this need by adding computer courses to their curricula. They're trying to make as many students as possible "computer literate." One of the major problems, however, is that too often the teachers in these schools have little training or experience with computers and certainly do not feel at ease themselves.

Here is another, more informal opening—this time from a descriptive travel article.

> When you think of tourism in Africa, do you think of East Africa, especially big game safaris in Kenya and Tanzania? Most people do. What you and other potential visitors probably don't realize is that West Africa has treasures and wonders to equal, if not surpass, anything else on the African continent. Not only treasures and wonders, but mystery and adventure can be found in one country in particular—Mali, the land that is reached by the road to Timbuktu.

10a-3 **Recognize casual writing.** Casual writing tends to have these characteristics.

S U M M A R Y

Characteristics of Casual Style

- Short- to medium-length sentences, short paragraphs
- High proportion of specific words and vivid language
- Many personal pronouns, references to people
- Frequent use of contractions
- Some slang terms and colloquial language
- Many lively action verbs
- Topics that may be light
- Very little distance between reader and writer

10a
lang

Writers who choose a casual style usually do so when their subject is popular or light, and they want their writing to give a fast-moving, breezy impression. They want to make their readers feel very comfortable. Here as an example is an opening paragraph from an article by a student on drinking and driving.

> You've been hitting the books all weekend. A new guy from your chemistry class calls and wants to cruise out to the lake for a swim. He's kind of cute, so you go, picking up a couple of six-packs along the way. The afternoon passes, and it's been fun. But now it's time to go home, and your date's had one too many. You're feeling kind of buzzed yourself. What d'ya do?

Each of the writers in the preceding examples chose the level of formality for his or her work by thinking about the purpose of the paper and the audience who would read it. The engineering student knew his professor wanted the impersonal and abstract tone of an official report—no personal pronouns, no contractions. The education student knew that her professor wanted a factual but not stuffy article on computers in schools, one that might be printed in a departmental newsletter. The travel writer wanted to be a little less formal in his article on Mali because he was writing for popular magazines and knew that if the article sounded like a research paper, no one would want to read it.

Finally, the author of the drinking and driving article chose an informal and colloquial style for two reasons. First, she was writing for student readers of the college newspaper and felt a light, informal style would appeal to them. Second, she thought a colloquial style would sound less preachy, and she knows students don't like to be lectured to. She also knows, however, that such a style is much too informal for most papers she would write in college.

WINDOW ON WRITING: Making Writing Less Formal for a Broad Audience

James Armstrong's first draft of a proposal to improve programs dealing with child abuse used social studies terminology and thus was too formal for the magazine readers he wanted to reach. Here's a sample paragraph.

> That child abuse produces chronic adversities
>
> in the adult stages of life is supported by the
>
> overwhelming relationship between the history of

```
abuse as a child and subsequent delinquent or

criminal behavior. . . . Thus not only does the

abused child suffer, but society bears the burden

as victims of the criminal acts and delinquency

of adults abused as children. Consequently society

pays for incarceration, parole and probation

efforts, and the massive legal cost of

prosecuting and adjudicating the cases against

the defenders.
```

James's writing group suggested that for his target audience he needed to write more informally and be more specific. Here's his revision.

```
We know that virtually every criminal was

abused as a child--the link is undeniable. Thus not

only does the abused child suffer, but all of us

suffer as we become the victims of those criminals

who were abused as children. We also have to pay

the massive costs for jails and prisons, for the

parole system, and for all the judges and lawyers

necessary to run our courts.
```

■ **Exercise 10.1** Working in a small group, decide how you would classify the levels of formality in these passages from two professional writers. Discuss reasons for any differences.

1. Reading opened up the world. There I was, a skinny bookworm drawing the attention of street kids who, in any other circumstances, would have had me for breakfast. Like an epic tale-teller, I developed the stories as I went along, relying on a flexible plot line and a repository of historical events. I had a great time. I sketched out trajectories with my finger on Frank's dusty truck bed. And I stretched out

each story's climax, creating cliffhangers like the ones I saw in the Saturday serials. These stories created for me a temporary community.

—Mike Rose, *Lives on the Boundary*.

2. The women who assembled as delegates at Seneca Falls had demanded equality of opportunity for men and women in affairs of state, church, and family. Elizabeth Cady Stanton, the organizing force and intelligence behind this historic conclave, was an advanced and innovative thinker on women's issues, who understood the complex sources of sexual subordination and, in addition to the vote for women, advocated domestic reforms including the right of women to affirm their sexuality if they chose to do so, or contrarily, to refuse sexual relations altogether when necessary to avoid pregnancy. Stanton also supported cooperative child rearing, rights of property, child custody, and divorce. Though venerated within her own small circle, she came to be viewed by more traditional supporters as a source of potential controversy and embarrassment.

—Ellen Chesler, *Woman of Valor*.

■ **Exercise 10.2** What level of formality do you think would be appropriate for writing done in each of these situations? In each case, consider what impression the writer wants to make and the distance he or she wants to maintain between reader and writer. Give reasons for your choice.

1. A letter to a representative or senator asking to be considered for a summer internship in his or her office
2. A biographical statement to accompany an application for college
3. A brochure promoting a student-organized ski trip

10b DENOTATION AND CONNOTATION: WHAT'S APPROPRIATE?

Troubleshooting

The more sensitive to language you become, the more you'll notice that sometimes words shift meaning and change on you. You can't count on them to hold still, and it's often hard to determine when a word is *denotative*, objective and purely descriptive, or *connotative*, biased and loaded with associative meanings. It's also often hard to tell whether a certain word is the right one to use in a particular situation.

That's hardly surprising. Language is so vital and dynamic it is

Denotative

Legal documents

Technical reports

Summaries/abstracts

Scientific writing

Scholarly articles

News stories

Magazine articles

Human interest stories in newspapers

Letters of recommendation

Movie reviews

Graduation and inauguration addresses

Speeches to juries

Fund appeals

Advertising

Campaign speeches

Funeral eulogies

Wartime oratory

Propaganda

Connotative

seldom possible to put words into strict categories. Thus rather than try to say, "This word is denotative and this word is connotative," we think it works better to set up a continuum (like the one on p. 198), putting strict denotation at one end and extreme connotation at the other. By doing so, we create a rough yardstick on which we can arrange types of writing.

At the denotative extreme of the yardstick, we would find language so flat, impersonal, and uninteresting that no one would read it unless absolutely necessary—for example, the language of an insurance policy.

10b
lang

> The amount of loss for which the Company may be liable to the Insured under Section I shall be payable 60 days after Proof of Loss, as herein provided, is received by the Company and ascertainment of the loss is made either by agreement between the Insured and the Company expressed in writing or by the filing with the Company of an appraisal award as herein provided.

At the connotative extreme of the yardstick we find language so emotional and inflammatory that most readers would feel insulted at the blatant assault on their senses and emotions. Most propaganda could be put in this category. For instance:

> The bleeding heart do-gooders who are conniving to pass these laws want to grind freedom underfoot and allow despicable and depraved criminals to wander the streets of our cities terrorizing helpless citizens.

In between these two extremes, neither of which you are likely to encounter in your college reading or need to use in your college writing, falls a broad range of language for different kinds of writing. In the following sections, we make suggestions about the *degree* of denotation or connotation that's appropriate in a variety of writing situations.

To use different kinds of language effectively . . .

10b-1 **Know when to choose denotative language.** A contemporary astronomy textbook begins its chapter "Introduction to Astronomical Observations" with this quotation.

> "The comet was so horrible and frightful . . . that some people died of fear and others fell sick. It appeared as a star of excessive length and the color of blood; at its summit was seen the figure of a bent arm holding a great sword in its hand, as if about to strike. On both sides . . . were seen a great number of axes, knives, and spaces colored with blood, among which were a great number of hideous human faces with beards and bristling hair."
>
> —Ambrose Pare, physician, 1528

The authors of the textbook follow with this comment.

> The observation quoted above is clearly lacking in objectivity. Along with such famous observations as the one of Aristotle that women had more teeth than men (he couldn't have looked very hard), we would tend today to label such work as "unscientific." The rapid progress made in the twentieth-century physical sciences stems largely from a method of investigation in which the systematic and objective measurement of the phenomena of nature is the ultimate arbiter of truth. . . . It is only from the interplay between theoretical speculation and careful measurement that new knowledge is attained rapidly and efficiently.
> —William H. Jeffreys and Robert Robbins,
> *Discovering Astronomy*.

**10b
lang**

What the authors are criticizing is, in part, the language of the sixteenth-century observer; it is heavily connotative and inexact, reflecting hysteria and fear. Such language contradicts everything modern science stands for: "systematic and objective measurement" reported in clear, objective language. As scientists, Jeffreys and Robbins insist that to be scientific, knowledge must be communicated by *denotative* language.

Today, professionals in science, technology, law, medicine, and the academic world in general expect writing in those fields to fall heavily at the denotative end of the denotation/connotation scale. They value objective, factual writing that reports accurately and speaks to the intellect, writing that informs but does not make an appeal to the emotions. (Interestingly, however, such writing does, in fact, appeal to *their* feelings, precisely because scientists value rational language over emotional language.)

Here is a good example of objective writing from a book written by an eminent physicist for an audience of nonspecialists.

> In every strategic defense system there are three main components. The first is the tracking and discrimination apparatus, the radars and optical sensors which are supposed to find and identify the targets. The second is the data-handling system, which takes the information from the sensors and feeds it to the computers which launch and steer the interceptors. The third is the interceptor system, the rockets or other more exotic weapons which actually hit and kill targets. The first two jobs, discrimination and data handling, are by far the hardest part of the problem of defense. The third job, sending up an interceptor to kill a target once you know exactly where it is, is comparatively easy.
> —Freeman Dyson, "Star Wars."

Clustered toward the middle of the denotative/connotative scale we find various kinds of writing in which authors seek not only to inform but to persuade. They're still focusing on facts and ideas, but they also want to communicate their attitudes and emotions, so they use connotative language. We give only one representative example from a broad spectrum of writing that fits into the category. It is autobiographical writing in which the author tries to convey his feelings.

> I stand there. I continue thinking about what she [my mother] has asked me [what is psychiatry?]—and what she cannot comprehend. My parents seem to me possessed of great dignity. An aristocratic reserve. Like the very rich who live behind tall walls, my mother and father are always mindful of the line separating public from private life. Watching a celebrity talk show on television, they listen for several minutes as a movie star with bright teeth recounts details of his recent divorce. And I see my parents grow impatient. Finally my mother gets up from her chair. Changing the channel, she says with simple disdain, "Cheap people."
> —Richard Rodriguez, *Hunger of Memory*.

10b
lang

Finally, far toward the connotative end of the scale lies patriotic, religious, or ethical writing designed to move the emotions of people and arouse their fervor and support. You can find stirring examples in the war speeches of Winston Churchill, the inaugural address of John Kennedy, or the presidential speeches of Abraham Lincoln. No one, however, was a greater master of this form than Martin Luther King, Jr. Here is a brief passage from his "I Have a Dream" speech.

> Let us not seek to satisfy our thirst for freedom by drinking from the cup of bitterness and hatred. We must forever conduct our struggle on the high plane of dignity and discipline. We must not allow our creative protest to degenerate into physical violence. Again and again we must rise to the majestic heights of meeting physical force with soul force. The marvelous new militancy which has engulfed the Negro community must not lead us to a distrust of all white people, for many of our white brothers, as evidenced by their presence here today, have come to realize that their destiny is tied up with our destiny and their freedom is inextricably bound to our freedom. We cannot walk alone.
> —Martin Luther King, Jr., "I Have a Dream."

10b–2 **Choose denotative or connotative language according to your writing situation.** The examples given above can't begin to cover the range of denotative and connotative writing you will meet in everything from technical journals at one extreme to political propaganda at the other, but we hope they will suggest how professional writers choose language appropriate to their situations and audiences. You should make your choices in the same way.

When writing papers for academic courses, you should rely chiefly on denotative language and use value words only when you want to make a judgment. In scientific and technical reports, case studies, and write-ups of statistical data, you should be as objective as possible and avoid connotative language. When working in the social studies, humanities, or fine arts, you can use connotative language a little more freely, particularly when you're writing criticism. Nevertheless, you should still show restraint and stay near the denotative end of the scale. Professors expect objectivity, not bias, in papers for most college courses.

When doing other kinds of writing—perhaps business writing, an editorial or a review for a newspaper, a column for the newsletter of a church or social group, or an appeal for funds—you can move toward the center of the scale, mixing denotative and connotative language as seems appropriate for your purpose and your audience. Sometimes you may want to move far toward the connotative end of the denotative/connotative scale if you're writing on an issue about which you feel strongly and for an audience you think would be receptive to such language. But know your audience and use caution.

In the final analysis, you can make intelligent choices about denotative and connotative language only if you are aware of your purpose and your audience. What seems like the right word with one group of readers may prove to be exactly the wrong word with a different group.

● **Tip**

Don't think of denotative and connotative language in either/or terms. Even in academic writing, denotative language isn't always good just because it seems to be objective, and connotative language isn't always bad just because it appeals to the senses and emotions. In order to write effectively in a wide range of situations, you need to use both and to be able to move easily up and down the continuum. ●

10b-3 **Avoid "whoopee" words in public writing.** There is a special group of connotative words called "whoopee" words—terms of exaggeration so overused they're virtually meaningless. Here are some of the more popular ones.

fantastic	unbelievable
sensational	fabulous
incredible	marvelous
terrific	tremendous
wonderful	devastating

These are hardly more than hackneyed buzzwords, and they have little place in college writing except, perhaps, in dialogue.

■ **Exercise 10.3** Copy two advertisements from magazines or newspapers and underline the connotative words. Compare the ads you choose with those chosen by some of your classmates and discuss what you think the ad writers are trying to achieve with connotative language.

10c
lang

■ **Exercise 10.4** Find and clip a syndicated newspaper column such as those written by Ellen Goodman, George Will, Molly Ivins, or William Raspberry. Underline the connotative language. Then clip a news story from the same paper and compare the amount of connotative language with that of the column.

10c WHEN IS DIALECT APPROPRIATE?

Troubleshooting

Dialects are spoken variations of languages. The written version of a language is generally standardized and uniform, but the dialects of different groups of people within the area in which that language is used are often quite different, sometimes radically so. In some places, such as India or parts of Africa, dialects of various groups and tribes vary so much that these groups cannot communicate with each other at all.

In the United States, our dialects cause fewer communication problems. New Yorkers can understand people from California, and someone who was born in Detroit usually has no trouble understanding natives of Alabama, although their accents may sound strange. Moreover, Americans travel and move so frequently that young people often partially lose their early speech patterns and adapt to those of their new regions. But we do have many different dialects in this country—southern dialect, northeastern dialect, midwestern dialect, African-American dialect, Creole dialect, to mention a few—and their marks are quite distinctive, enough so that foreigners whose command of English is good enough to understand the announcers on television can have serious problems understanding southern or Texan dialect.

You may be an American who has a dialect markedly different from varieties considered "standard." Occasionally you may have problems when some of its features appear in your writing. Use this handbook and other resources to edit out those features so that your readers focus on the content of your writing instead of on features of your dialect. But just because you choose to mute those features doesn't mean you should abandon your dialect. Even though it may cause problems at times, it plays an important part in your life. Being bi-dialectal is often as much of an accomplishment as being bilingual. But all educated people also need to be able to use the standard written dialect of the United States, edited American English, so they can communicate easily with the millions of others who command it.

To give dialects their due . . .

10c–1 Recognize their uses and importance. Dialects are important and useful to the groups that speak them. A dialect helps to hold a group together, gives it a sense of community and identity, and provides its members with a sense of being insiders. Those who belong to a dialect group feel comfortable with each other because it's reassuring to be around other people who "talk your language." Thus dialects act as a major source of strength within a group and, as such, should be appreciated and protected for private communication between individuals within a particular dialect community. Usually such communication is spoken.

For example, here is how the writer James Lee Burke represents the Cajun dialect of southern Louisiana in a novel.

> She had put my three-legged raccoon, Tripod, on his chain. . . . She pulled him up in the air by his chain. His body danced and curled as if he were being garroted.
>
> "Clarise, don't do that."
>
> "Ask him what he done, him," she said. "Go look my wash basket. Go look your shirts. They blue yesterday. They brown now. So smell, you."
>
> "I'll take him down to the dock."
>
> "Tell Batiste not to bring him back, no. . . . He come in my house again, you gonna see him cooking with the sweet potato."
>
> —James Lee Burke, *Black Cherry Blues*.

10c–2 Acknowledge their limitations. The problem with some dialects is that when they show up in *public writing*—and that is what most of the writing you do in college and your profession will be—they can be misunderstood and misinterpreted. Items of vocabulary within a dialect may not be understood by those outside it. Certain grammatical forms that are completely natural and logical within a community may be regarded as nonstandard by other users of the language.

For example, in this passage from the novel *The Bluest Eye*, Toni Morrison represents the dialect known as Black English.

The onliest time I be happy seem like was when I was in the picture show. Everytime I got, I went. I'd go early, before the show
started. They'd cut off the lights, and everything be black. Then
the screen would light up, and I'd move right in on them pictures. . . . Them pictures give me a lot of pleasure, but it made
coming home hard, and looking at Cholly hard.
—Toni Morrison, *The Bluest Eye*.

The passage shows the character Pauline's most private kind of communication, inner speech to herself.

Here is another example of private dialect in this personal letter
between two characters in Larry McMurtry's *Lonesome Dove,* a novel
about a cattle drive from Texas to Montana.

Dear Ellie—

We have come a good peace and have been lucky with the
weather, it has been clear.

No sign of Jake Spoon yet but we did cross the Red River
and are now in Texas, Joe likes it. His horse has been behaving all
right and neither of us has been sick.

I hope that you are well and have not been bothered too
much by the skeeters.

Your loving husband,
July
—Larry McMurtry, *Lonesome Dove*.

**10c
lang**

In the letter, we read the disarming words of a man not comfortable
expressing his feelings in words. The salutation and formal closing show
that July knows the form a letter should take, but since this is a private
communication, the vocabulary and rhythms of his day-to-day speech
dominate. We don't expect Ellie will criticize the comma splices July uses
to link his ideas or his spelling of *piece* and *mosquitoes*. But we can easily
imagine situations in which such writing would seem out of place and
colloquial.

Letting your private dialect intrude into your public writing, then,
is not so much "wrong" as it is inappropriate. When your readers find the
marks of your personal language in writing that is directed toward a
group of readers who don't share that dialect, they're going to feel that it
doesn't belong there.

10c–3 **Use dialect when appropriate.** When can you use your dialect without its interfering with communication in standard English?
First, you can use it in your private life among friends or others who share

the dialect, either in conversation or in letters. Second, you might also use it in a first, discovery draft where you are trying to get down ideas and reflections and don't want to make your task more difficult by worrying about the conventions of standard written English. In subsequent drafts you can edit out dialect features. Finally, you might also use dialect in an anecdote you are adding to your paper to illustrate some point, or you could use it in dialogue that plays a necessary part in a paper. Except for these instances, though, spoken dialect generally doesn't fit into the kind of public writing you'll be doing in college or business.

**10d
lang**

10d HOW DO YOU CONTROL FOR BIAS IN YOUR LANGUAGE?

Troubleshooting

Biased language isn't always bad. Slanted but colorful writing regularly enlivens articles in popular books and magazines and the editorial pages of any newspaper. Consider the following sentences.

> As brokers upstairs sorted through the shambles [of the 1987 stock market crash], hollow-cheeked models with crosses around their necks drifted down through the courtyard's runway, their clothes-hanger bodies swaying under the weight of twenty pounds of crinoline and taffeta. —Susan Faludi, *Backlash*.

> He hasn't been home in decades, but [Aaron] Spelling has a true Texan's passion for busty blondes and big deals.
> —Mimi Swartz, *Texas Monthly*, September 1994.

These writers make no pretense to objectivity—they're writing to entertain audiences they feel comfortable with, and they're quite sure that people who choose to read their work won't take offense at the exaggerated images they're presenting.

When you write in college or in business, however, you face a different kind of audience. Usually you'll be writing to inform or to persuade readers you don't know well, and you can't afford to offend them by using language that suggests that you don't respect certain people or groups or that you think in stereotypes. Because of ingrained habits, however, writers or speakers sometimes unthinkingly lapse into such language; by doing so, they damage their credibility and alienate many readers or listeners. When that happens, they fail to get what they want.

This section suggests ways you can work toward eliminating offensive bias when you speak or write. Some of the strategies mirror those we discussed in the sections on critical thinking in Chapter 5.

- Be sure you're not making faulty assumptions about groups or people.
- Check for subtle tinges of bias in your language.
- Be careful that you're not lapsing into stereotypes.

Your most important tool for controlling bias, however, is your imagination. Each of us sees the world though a unique lens, a lens shaped and tinted by our particular culture and specific experiences. If, after you have written something, you can *imagine* how your piece looks when seen through the lens of your audience, you have a good chance to revise it successfully.

10d lang

Try also *imagining* that your readers or listeners are your clients or customers. In an important way, of course, they are. How is your language going to strike them? Would they feel valued and want to engage you as their lawyer or accountant? Would they buy what you're selling? If you reread what you've written and consider it in that light, you may want to rethink some of your word choices.

To reduce offensive bias in your writing . . .

10d–1 **Control your language to eliminate sexist bias.** Activists in the women's movement of the last thirty years have made most of us more aware of how profoundly language shapes attitudes and reinforces traditional gender roles. Twenty-five years ago when the typical writer consistently referred to doctors, scientists, inventors, and artists as "he" and to secretaries, nurses, teachers, and receptionists as "she," youngsters got strong messages about which professions they were expected to choose. Fortunately you seldom see such ingrained bias in today's newspapers, books, or magazines, although occasionally a quotation reveals a person's biased attitudes. For instance, a 1990 article in *The New York Times* quotes a federal appeals judge as saying (emphasis added),

> "Whatever the philosophy of the particular judge, and whether **he** views **his** proper role as broad or narrow, **his** decisions—some of them at least—necessarily resolve issues previously unsettled and thus will declare law."

With their new consciousness, most women—and many men—are going to find his statement sexist and offensive.

If you want to keep such sexist blunders out of your writing, here are some guidelines to keep in mind.

1. **Avoid using *he* and *him* as all-purpose pronouns to refer to people in general.** For example, don't write "Everyone should remember *he* is a student."

WHY WRITE . . .	WHEN YOU COULD WRITE . . .
Every executive expects *his* bonus.	Every executive expects *a* bonus.
	Executives expect *their* bonuses.
	Every executive expects *his or her* bonus.

2. **Guard against using the term *man* as a catchall term to refer to all people or all members of a group.** For example, don't write "All *men* are subject to disappointment" or "The recession threw thousands of *men* out of work." Instead use *people* as a general term, or refer to a specific occupation or role rather than gender: *worker, parent, voter, consumer.*

WHY WRITE . . .	WHEN YOU COULD WRITE . . .
the man who wants to be an astronaut	anyone who wants to be an astronaut
men who do their own auto repairs	car owners who do their own auto repairs

3. **Watch out for assumptions that professions or roles are primarily for men or for women.** For example, don't write "Any senator will improve *his* chances of election by going back home frequently" or "A nurse usually starts in *her* profession when *she* is in *her* twenties." Also be careful not to slip into hidden assumptions by writing "woman doctor" or "woman engineer," thus suggesting one wouldn't expect to find women in those professions.

WHY WRITE . . .	WHEN YOU COULD WRITE . . .
men who hope to become scholarship athletes	young people who hope to become scholarship athletes
housewives who like to cook	anyone who likes to cook
policeman	police officer
mailman	mail carrier
cleaning woman	custodian/janitor
businessmen	business executives
poetess	poet

4. **When possible, find out what name a married woman wants to go by and honor that choice.** Some women are satisfied to be called by their husband's name: for example, Mrs. Robert Collins or Mrs. Wendell Wright. Many others, however, prefer to be referred to by their given name and their husband's last name: Rosita Collins or Pamela Wright. Some want to incorporate their maiden name with their married name: Hillary Rodham Clinton. Others

prefer to have their maiden name hyphenated with their husband's name: Jane Katz-Elson or Joan McNair-Walsh. And some, an increasing number, insist on retaining their original name after they marry. Some traditionalists may find this array of choices complicated and unnecessary; to a great many women, however, the distinctions are important. Many women, single or married, also prefer the title *Ms.* to either *Miss* or *Mrs.* If you're not sure, *Ms.* is probably the best choice.

5. **Watch out for between-the-lines implications that men and women behave in stereotypical ways.** For example, don't suggest that women are generally talkative and love to shop or that most men are sports-minded and sloppy. Also avoid sexist descriptions such as "a showy blonde" or "a dazzling brunette" unless you make the same kinds of comments about men.

10d lang

■ **Exercise 10.5** Rewrite the following sentences to get rid of sexist language or implications. If necessary, refer to Section 23d for strategies.

1. A woman who wants to avoid premature wrinkles should use sunblock and avoid tanning.
2. Today even a high school physics teacher should know his astrophysics, or he'll look out of date to his students.
3. A graduate student can hardly survive financially without his wife working.
4. The program appeals to mothers who are concerned about their children's health.
5. Businesswomen sometimes neglect their personal lives to get ahead.

■ **Exercise 10.6** Working with a group, read and discuss this passage from a forty-year-old classic of literary criticism. In what ways do you find it sexist? How could it be revised? As a group, try drafting a revision.

[Among writers] a fairly common sexual pattern is for the writer to have many affairs in his youth, to marry a woman older than himself, to watch the marriage break up in quarrels resulting from a conflict of standards . . . then to marry a woman his own age and stay married, perhaps with minor infidelities. If the second marriage is a failure, he either makes the best of it or else tries again, for he can't get along without a wife. In a writer's household the wife discharges a whole group of functions besides the simple one of being his mate. She not only acts as housekeeper, nursemaid, chauffeur, and hostess . . . but also serves, on occasion, as secretary, receptionist, office manager, business consultant, first

audience for the writer's work, guardian of his reputation, and partner in what has become a family enterprise.

—Malcolm Cowley, *The Literary Situation*.

10d–2 **Control your language to eliminate ethnic or racial bias.** In
many writing situations, you simply don't need to mention race or national origin—it's not relevant. For example, in writing about general
topics—business or the media or education, for example—the race or nationality of individuals is often unimportant. At other times, however, issues of race or nationality may be central to your discussion. In such
cases, these guidelines may be helpful.

1. **Be as accurate as possible.** For example, the term *Asian* (now
   widely preferred to *Oriental*) is so broad as to be almost useless.
   There are dozens of countries in Asia, and their cultures and the
   physical characteristics of their people vary greatly. You'll do much
   better to use *Filipino, Japanese, Chinese, Korean, Indian, Indonesian*,
   and so on. When you're referring to individuals whose forebears
   came from one of these countries but who are themselves Ameri-
   can-born, combine the term with *American: Japanese American,
   Korean American*, and so on.

   Many people of Spanish descent in the Americas no longer
   like the term *Hispanic*—again, it's extremely broad and suggests
   that all such people share similar traits and cultures. You'll do better to be specific: *Cuban, Puerto Rican, Mexican, Brazilian*, and so
   on. If appropriate, combine the name with *American—Mexican
   American, Cuban American*, and so on.

   American Indian and *Native American* are both acceptable
   when you're writing about the people who originally populated
   North America. In the last decade or so, many of the North American natives whom we have traditionally thought of as *Eskimos*
   have come to prefer the designation *Inuit*, and that term is now official with the Canadian government. *Eskimo* is still appropriate,
   however, in an archaeological or cultural context, such as speaking
   of *Eskimo carvings*.

2. **Use the terminology preferred by the people you're writing
   about, insofar as you know their preferences.** If you're not
   sure, adopt the terminology you see in newspapers and magazines
   or hear on television or radio news shows (not call-in talk shows,
   though). On the whole, the editors of those media are careful
   about their language.

   At this writing, the term favored by individuals whose forebears came from Africa seems to be shifting to *African American*,

although *black* is still widely used. At a Justice and Society seminar one of us attended in the summer of 1994, a judge and a law professor of African descent consistently referred to their race as "African American"; a third professional of the same race preferred "black." *The New York Times*, that bellwether of up-to-date usage, shifts back and forth between the terms. The term *Negro* is seldom used now, nor is *colored people*. The term *people of color*, popular with many writers and speakers concerned about choosing unbiased language, seems too vague to be useful for identifying African Americans and probably should be reserved to broadly designate nonwhite groups.

**10d
lang**

3. **In editing, check to see that you have not allowed hints of ethnic or national stereotypes to seep into your writing.** Might one infer from your language that you think of Jews as rich financiers? Is there a hint that someone with an Italian surname has underworld connections? Or an innuendo suggesting a person of German origin would be skeptical about the Holocaust? Run your bias monitor to check.

■ **Exercise 10.7** Almost everyone has had some experience with the difficult issue of ethnic labels and names. Working together, make a list of all the ethnic groups represented in your composition class, writing on the board the terms preferred by members of each particular group. Discuss those preferences and a writer's responsibility to know and use them.

■ **Exercise 10.8** Consider which of these sentences might be inappropriate in a paper you are submitting for a course. Which seem acceptable? Why? Write a possible alternative for those that aren't appropriate.

1. That proposal doesn't stand a Chinaman's chance of being accepted.
2. Negro baseball players formed their own leagues in the early 1900s.
3. Redskins are now often portrayed sympathetically in the movies.
4. Branson, Missouri, is the popular new center for hillbilly music.
5. The ability to work long hours and to save are typical Asian qualities.

10d-3 **Control your language to eliminate bias toward age, physical condition, or sexual orientation.** If you were born in the United States, part of your heritage is the assertion in the Declaration of Independence that "all men are created equal." We haven't done a good job of living up to it, of course. Slavery, the Chinese Exclusion Act, the disenfranchisement of women and African Americans, and many other instances testify to that. But most of us still want to work toward the ideal of fair and equal treatment, and in language such treatment translates into not demeaning or patronizing people because of qualities or traits over which they have no control. These guidelines may be helpful.

1. **Consider that many persons over sixty don't like being called "elderly," "senior citizens," or "old people."** Most seem to prefer "older people" or, even better, a specific designation, such as "people in their early or late sixties" or "early or late seventies" and so on. And don't slip into patronizing remarks such as "For a seventy-year-old man, he's remarkably astute."

2. **Reserve the terms *boys, girls,* and *kids* for people under eighteen.** Young working adults just out of high school deserve to be called men and women. So do college students, whether they are first-year students or graduate students. The phrase *college kids,* which many people use unthinkingly, is rather patronizing. It's also inaccurate since almost half of all U.S. college students now are over twenty-five, and a great many of them have families and major responsibilities.

3. **When referring to individuals or groups with disabilities or illnesses, be as specific as possible and avoid language that implies pity—for example, *crippled* or *victim*.** The phrases *visually handicapped* or *hearing impaired* are descriptive and objective; so is *a person with multiple sclerosis* or *paraplegic*. In general, it works well to mention the individual first and his or her handicap or disease second—"a woman who is HIV positive" or "my cousin who is autistic." Terms such as *disabled veteran* or *a person with muscular disability* seem generally acceptable. Once again, however, it's useful to know with what terms the individuals themselves feel comfortable.

4. **Mention a person's sexual orientation only when it is relevant to the issue under discussion, and use specific, nonjudgmental terminology.** Many people whose sexual orientation is toward their own gender seem comfortable with the designation *homosexual* to refer to both men and women but less comfortable with the singular, *a homosexual*. They choose the terms *gay* and *lesbian* when they want to be specific about an individual's sexual orientation. Although some groups of gay rights activists use the word *queer* in their literature, that term is clearly offensive coming from someone outside such a group.

■ **Exercise 10.9** Working in a group, decide which of these sentences have hints of offensive bias—some of them are certainly arguable. Which might be acceptable in some circumstances? How could you change those that are not?

1. College kids are at that wonderful period in their lives when they can enjoy learning without thinking about having to earn a living.
2. Barney Frank, who is almost the only open homosexual in the U.S. Congress, represents a district in Massachusetts.
3. Although Betty Friedan is over seventy, she still writes extensively.
4. Barbara Jordan, the victim of a degenerative nerve disease, is confined to a wheelchair.
5. She was the last of the girls who had played bridge together for more than four decades.

10d-4 **Avoid using language that reflects flippant or derisive attitudes about some professions or implies unflattering class distinctions.** When you're writing at a somewhat formal level, it's better to
avoid occupational labels that carry a tinge of contempt. *Shrink* for psychiatrist, is certainly one; so is *cop* for police officer. *Prof* for professor
doesn't go over well either. On the other hand, calling a medical doctor
a *physician* or a lawyer an *attorney* conveys respect for those individuals,
as does the word *journalist* instead of *reporter*.

Be careful, too, about using terms that may have negative class
connotations. For example, the phrases *Junior Leaguer, fraternity man,*
and *country club set* may be literally accurate, but they have accusatory
overtones that suggest frivolity and snobbery. Many social work professionals have come to feel that the label *underclass* is demeaning; they prefer *disadvantaged.* They also believe that the term *inner city* is preferable
to *slum,* which suggests squalor. Some other class markers to avoid are
welfare mother, dropout, redneck, and *hard hat.*

■ **Exercise 10.10** Which of these sentences might alienate a bias-
conscious reader? Should all of them be changed? Why or why not?
What changes would you suggest?

1. The cops used poor judgment about gathering evidence at the crime scene.
2. Welfare mothers and tax cheats have both become the target of bud-
get-conscious legislators.
3. That college is known for attracting sorority girls and future Junior Leaguers.
4. Woody Allen often portrays the kind of person who spends half his life at his shrink's office.
5. A prof who wears a tie on this campus is as rare as a blue heron.

10d-5 **Use your good judgment and keep your sense of humor when you edit for bias.** Don't sanitize your writing to the point that it becomes deadly dull. Every day you read columnists or listen to commentators who use biased language to spoof, satirize, persuade, or praise, and they do it very well. Consider this example from *Harper's* Magazine.

> He [the Frugal Gourmet on TV] wears a dangling talisman, a three-hundred-year-old jade fish, around his neck; he offends the serious cook, the inquiring mind. He has an awful lot of facial hair (a grizzly beard joins forces with a full mustache, some of which must surely find its way into the cock-a-leekie) and a kind of halo of wiry Bride of Frankenstein hair on his underpopulated head. A toothy grin. Hard eyes behind thick glasses. He twitches his eyebrows at lobsters, slaps and tickles tongues (not his own, which would be a mercy), caresses lamb livers, fondles kidneys; he addresses internal organs with the anthropomorphic infatuation of a Jeffrey Dahmer. . . . Rolling his eyes upward in a simulation of ecstasy, he stands in front of the Spanish Steps eating pasta next to Bernini's fountain of a sinking boat, working up the orgasmic facial raptures one sees on the face of the tone deaf when they are confronted with a Beethoven string quartet.
>
> —Barbara Grizzuti Harrison, "P.C. on the Grill."

Exaggerated images? Of course. Insulting about physical traits? Definitely. Biased language? Certainly. But fun? Absolutely. Offensive or insulting to *Harper's* Magazine readers? Almost certainly not. They probably loved it.

So it's unrealistic to say you should never use biased or exaggerated language to convey a mood, create an image, or make sardonic comments. Like a professional writer, however, you should make it your goal to be so attuned to your readers that you can write for them with respect, awareness, and good taste and still have fun with language.

11

Can You Make Your Writing Clearer?

A Being Concrete and Specific
B Making Your Writing Visual
C Using Actor/Action Sentences and Active Verbs
D Making Your Writing More Readable

When you're writing, remember that first prize always goes to clarity; whatever comes second—and probably experts couldn't agree on what that is—comes way down the line. After all, if your readers can't understand what you mean, they're not likely to admire your smooth writing or fresh ideas.

Now, a few talented souls may be naturally clear writers, just as a few lucky people in the world have bodies that are naturally fit. But there aren't many people in either group. If you want to learn to write clearly or to develop a fit body, you have to care about results and be willing to work to get them. There are no quick fixes. But you can attain both goals by developing habits that, over time, virtually guarantee impressive results. This chapter gives you the guidelines for developing such writing habits.

11a CAN YOU BE MORE SPECIFIC?

Troubleshooting

Among the most frequent comments instructors make on student papers are "You're using too many generalizations that don't give enough facts—you need to narrow your focus and give specific details" and "Your language is too vague and abstract—let's have some concrete examples." If you're getting responses like these to your drafts, you can improve your writing by learning more about general/specific language and abstract/concrete language, how each category works, and how to combine them for clearer, more interesting papers.

To make your writing more specific . . .

11a–1   **Learn to combine abstract and concrete language.**   Writers who use a great deal of abstract language are often hard to understand. When their writing is weighed down with nouns such as *accountability, confrontation, realization, ambiguity,* and *misapprehension,* we begin to have trouble because we can't see anything. Such abstractions transmit no images to our brains and give us no examples with which to identify; therefore it takes longer for us to read a passage and remember it. That's why you have so much trouble with some of the material you have to read for your courses and with documents such as insurance policies and legal descriptions.

Of course, we all have to use abstract language; it's impossible to discuss ideas without it. But the writer who wants to communicate with an audience learns to use abstractions and still write clearly. This can be done by combining abstractions with specific language and concrete examples.

Here's a passage that's unnecessarily difficult to read because it's overloaded with abstract nouns. It's from the first draft of a report on some of the political issues about health care for women. The abstract terms are boldfaced.

Original

There is a **paucity** of medical information on women's health worldwide. The isolated **cultural position** of women in many non-Western cultures presents a **hindrance** to accumulating data. This **insufficiency** has serious negative **ramifications** for the **establishment** of **policies** that could bring about improvement in women's health from childhood, where malnutrition has its greatest **prevalence** among females, to the postreproductive years.

Such writing is harder to understand than it needs to be. The revision below says the same thing in clearer, more concrete language.

Revision

We don't know nearly enough about women's health worldwide. In many non-Western countries, women are often isolated from any contact with outsiders, so it's difficult for researchers to get good information. Without that information, health workers have trouble setting up women's health programs that would stretch from childhood, where girls are more often malnourished than boys, to the postmenopausal years, when bone thinning cripples more women than men.

You may have noticed that the writing in textbooks, professional articles, and certain periodicals such as *The Atlantic* or *Scientific American* is often quite abstract—not incomprehensible, but difficult nevertheless. To some degree, that's inevitable since the writers for these publications are writing about complex and sometimes technical issues and must use abstract terms; often they are also writing for readers who know the vocabulary. But those who are especially concerned about getting their ideas across to a broad audience can find ways to clarify their writing with vivid details and personal anecdotes. Here is an example from a Pulitzer Prize–winning historian.

11a
clear

> In background, interests, personality, in everything from the sound of their voices to the kind of company they enjoyed to the patterns of their careers, [Franklin Roosevelt and Harry Truman] could not have been much more dissimilar. Roosevelt was now in his twelfth year in office. He had been president for so long and through such trying times that it seemed to many Americans, including the junior senator from Missouri, that he was virtually the presidency itself. His wealth, education, the social position he had known since boyhood were everything Harry Truman had never had. Life and customs at the Roosevelt family estate on the upper Hudson River were as far removed from Jackson County, Missouri, as some foreign land. Roosevelt fancied himself a farmer. To Truman, Roosevelt was the kind of farmer who had never pulled a weed, never known debt, or crop failure, or a father's call to roll out of bed at 5:30 on a bitter cold morning.
>
> —David McCullough, *Truman.*

You can make your writing clearer if you routinely check your first drafts to see if they go along for several paragraphs without references to people or familiar examples to help readers grasp your ideas. If so, when doing the second draft, look for ways to use everyday examples, analogies, and visual details to bring your writing down to earth and make it clear.

11a–2 **Use specific details and examples to clarify and develop general statements.** As a writer, you have to make general statements; otherwise you would never be able to theorize or summarize, and you'd never rise above the level of the individual facts. But if you make too many generalizations and don't support them with specific details and examples, you may quickly lose your readers.

One way to bring specific details into your writing is to downshift, a strategy explained in Section 7a–3. When you downshift, you move from a high level of generalization to a series of more and more specific statements. For example, here is a level diagram for the opening sentences of a student article on the difficulties of finding a place to live.

Level 5. Anyone who has ever tried to find an affordable apartment in a big city like New York has enough stories to freeze your blood twice over.

>**Level 4.** The experience starts with an optimistic wade through the apartment listings in the newspaper.

>>**Level 3.** But optimism, as is so often the case, proves short-lived, for you quickly discover that most apartments aren't for rent; they're for sale.

>>>**Level 2.** They're all co-ops. Or condos. Or maybe condops.

>>>**Level 1.** The average price seems to hover around $250,000. You do have a trust fund, don't you?

Notice that at each level, the writer gives more concrete details that expand on the first point.

● **Tip**

For additional suggestions about how you can revise your writing to be more readable and less abstract and wordy, read Section 12c on streamlining bureaucratic prose. ●

■ **Exercise 11.1** Classify the words in this list into abstract and concrete, then compare your answers with those of another person in your class. Notice that you may not be able to agree on all the answers; words are not always easy to classify.

responsibility	sunshine	mockery
soldiers	racketeers	antiques
admiration	convenience	antagonism
teenagers	video games	white water
inspiration	militarism	ambivalence

■ **Exercise 11.2** Below is a highly readable paragraph from a medical writer who is known for writing well. Working in a group with other students in your class, analyze the particular words and phrases that help to make the paragraph clear and readable.

The worst thing that has happened to science education is that the great fun has gone out of it. A very large number of good students look at it as slogging work to be got through on the way to medical school. Others look closely at the premedical students themselves, embattled and bleeding for grades and class standing, and are turned off. Very few see science as the high adventure it really is, the wildest of all explorations ever taken by human beings, the chance to catch close views of things never seen before, the shrewdest maneuver for discovering how the world works. Instead, they become baffled early on, and they are misled into thinking that bafflement is simply the result of not having learned all the facts. They are not told, as they should be told, that everyone else—from the professor in his endowed chair down to the platoons of postdoctoral students in the laboratory all night—is baffled as well. Every important scientific advance that has come in looking like an answer has turned, sooner or later—usually sooner—into a question. And the game is just beginning.

> —Lewis Thomas, "Humanities and Science."

11b clear

■ **Exercise 11.3** Working in a group with other students, develop these sentences by downshifting with two or three more sentences that give specific details or examples.

1. If you are a cable television subscriber in the United States, you have an astonishing array of programs available.
2. A come-on ad for a new car may claim the price is $9,995, but what it doesn't give are the costs of those options that are near necessities.

11b CAN YOU HELP YOUR READERS SEE YOUR POINT?

Troubleshooting

Writing is more readable and interesting when it helps us to visualize something. That's always been the case—it's why we all like stories. But today, as we emphasized in the section on document design, more than ever we live in a visually oriented culture in which television is the major means of communication and videos and computer graphics are common tools of instruction. You will communicate with your readers more effectively if you can create pictures for them, make them *see* things. In this section, we suggest several ways to make your writing more visual and thus clearer.

To make your writing more visual . . .

11b–1 **Show something happening.** You can create a scene or drama; you can show action; you can describe a colorful picture or object—there are dozens of ways of showing ideas in action. Here is a visual example in which a writer clarifies a hard-to-grasp, abstract concept by showing something happening.

11b
clear

> The distinction between Newton's and Einstein's ideas about gravitation has sometimes been illustrated by picturing **a little boy playing marbles in a city lot. The ground is very uneven, ridged with bumps and hollows. An observer in an office ten stories above the street would not be able to see those irregularities in the ground. Noticing that the marbles appear to avoid some sections of the ground and move toward other sections,** he might assume that a "force" is operating which repels the marbles from certain spots and attracts them toward others. But another **observer on the ground would instantly perceive that the path of the marbles is simply governed by the curvature of the field.**
> —Lincoln Barnett, *The Universe and Dr. Einstein.*

11b–2 **Add people.** Another way to add a visual element to your writing is to put people in it. Most of the issues and ideas we discuss do involve human beings, after all, and your readers are more likely to understand what you are writing about if you bring those human beings into your work. For example, notice how an abstract discussion of an economic issue becomes clearer when the author puts people into it. Here is the first draft of a student paragraph.

First draft

> Although the federally funded student loan program has made education accessible to low-income populations, the increasing number of that population who are in default on their loans has had significant effects on the future of that program. The problem schools are mainly the so-called proprietary schools, private institutions that are providers of training for such occupations as mortician, technician, or beauty operator. Deceptive advertising and unrealistic promises encourage the application of high-risk students with poor academic backgrounds.

You'd never know that the points the writer makes affect actual people, individuals with real concerns and worries. Notice how this revision brings it to life.

Revision

Although hundreds of thousands of young people have been able to go to college because of the federally funded loan program, those students who have defaulted on their loans may be jeopardizing the entire program for everyone. The schools that have caused the problems are mainly the proprietary, for-profit training schools whose recruiters have used unscrupulous methods and dishonest promises to lure high-risk students who fail and then cannot repay their loans.

Notice that when the author added people to the paragraph, other specific details also emerged.

**11b
clear**

● **Tip**

Remember, however, that abstract phrases and peopleless writing may be appropriate when you are doing technical or scientific writing. ●

11b-3 **Use metaphors and analogies.** You can also make your writing clearer by adding metaphors and analogies that help readers make connections with something they already know. **Metaphors** use figurative language to suggest similarities: "Our child-care system is a dinosaur." **Analogies** compare two things in order to explain: "The Los Angeles freeway system resembles an aging person whose arteries are clogging up."

In the following example, a Nobel Prize–winning astrophysicist reinforces a necessarily abstract explanation with a familiar and concrete analogy. The visual elements are in boldface type.

This technique [measuring the motion of a star] makes use of the familiar property of wave motion, known as the Doppler effect. When we observe a sound or light wave from a source at rest, the time between the arrival of wave crests at our instruments is the same time between the crests as they leave the source. On the other hand, if the source is moving away from us, the time between arrivals of successive wave crests is increased over the time between their departures from the source because each crest has a little farther to go on its journey to us than the crest before. . . . Similarly, if the source is moving toward us, the time between arrivals of wave crests is decreased because each successive crest has a shorter distance to go. . . . **It is just as if a traveling salesman were to send a letter home regularly once a week during his travels: while he is traveling away from home, each successive letter will have a little farther to go than the one before, so his letters will arrive a little more than a week apart. On the homeward leg of his journey, each successive letter will**

have a shorter distance to travel, so they will arrive more frequently than once a week.

—Stephen Weinberg, The First Three Minutes.

WINDOW ON WRITING: Making Your Writing Visual

**11b
clear**

In a paper on the history of the Olympic Games, Ann Oetken made the spectacle come alive for her readers with visual touches.

```
In the sixth century B.C., Milo of Croton won

the wrestling crown at Olympia six times. He was said

to have developed his fabulous strength by carrying

a calf on his shoulders every day of its life until

it was a full-grown bull.

    Milo performed many tricks for his admirers.

He would stand on an oiled and slippery discus and

challenge anyone to push him off it. No one could

ever budge him. He would also tie a cord around his

forehead, then take a deep breath and hold it until

the veins in his head swelled to the point where the

cord burst.
```

■ **Exercise 11.4** Working in a group with other students, discuss what writing strategies one could use to give a visual angle to articles on the following topics.

1. An editorial about the high cost of housing at your college
2. An article comparing various kinds of motorcycles
3. A guide to inexpensive restaurants close to your campus
4. An article about ways to combat racism on your campus
5. An article about pollution from power lawn mowers

■ **Exercise 11.5** Working with other students in a group, try to create metaphors or analogies that would add a visual element to the following sentences. For example, you might compare Coach Rudenko to a triumphant general returning from battle.

1. Coach Rudenko returned in triumph from the women's intercollegiate swimming and diving championships yesterday, feeling justifiably exuberant as she got off the plane.
2. When she and the team left campus last Friday, almost no one would have bet any money that there was a chance they would do very well.
3. In fact, their chances were rated so low that the team had trouble even finding the money for their plane fare, since whoever figured out the budget for the athletic department obviously didn't anticipate any postseason travel.
4. The fund-raising for the trip must have also raised some consciousness, for a surprisingly large group of fans turned out at the airport to help make up for the neglect the team has suffered this season.
5. What the welcoming fans learned to their surprise was that not only had the team brought home a trophy and a national championship, but their coach had also brought home an offer for a new and more profitable contract for herself.

11c
clear

11c **CAN YOU MAKE YOUR WRITING MORE DIRECT AND EASIER TO READ?**

Troubleshooting

If your instructor or fellow students tell you that your writing is adequate but a little dull, think about how to make it more readable. You do want people to enjoy what you write, not just plow through it because they have to. One of the quickest remedies for dull writing is to revise your sentences so that readers get immediate answers to two questions: *What's happening? Who's doing it?* They will get those answers if you use *actor/action sentences* that quickly identify who is doing what and to whom. You'll also make your writing clearer if you use direct, active verbs.

For example, look at these understandable but not very interesting sentences.

Bicycles are the mode of transportation for millions of Chinese. It's a common occurrence to see two or three people on one bike.

When they are revised into actor/action patterns with active verbs, they become more interesting and easier to read.

Millions of Chinese ride bicycles. An astonished visitor often sees two or three people on one bike.

To make your sentences clearer and easier to read . . .

11c-1 **Ask yourself, "Who or what is acting?" and make that person or thing the subject of your sentence.** Then find a direct verb that describes the action. These short examples show how much clearer your writing can be.

First draft   It is not unusual for a successful business enterprise to begin as a small operation on a college campus as a response to a student's need to earn his or her way through school.

Revision   Many a successful business began on a college campus when a student found a new way to work his or her way through school.

First draft   Access to a constant stream of lively and diverse cultural events is one of the advantages of attending college in a big city.

Revision   Students attending college in a big city can enjoy a constant stream of lively and diverse cultural events.

Naturally you wouldn't want to use actor/action patterns for all your sentences since often you need to write about concepts, theories, or processes that require more abstract language. But you can probably use actor/action sentences more often than you realize—after all, even when you're writing about history, philosophy, or economics, you're still writing about people and what they do. You may want to wait until a second draft to adapt some of your sentences to an actor/action pattern, but if you work at it, eventually you can produce such sentences even in a first draft.

11c-2 **Favor active verbs over "to be" verbs, such as *is, are, were,* and so on.** "To be" verbs are crucial to writing, of course; none of us could get along without them. But when you use them too often, they can drain the life out of your writing. For example, look at the improvement in the sample sentences when we replace forms of *is* with livelier verbs.

Original   It **is** because of the way the nature of research **is** understood that the joy of discovery **is** unknown to most students.

Revision Many students miss the joy of discovery because they don't understand the nature of research.

Original Once research **is** thought of as an exercise in reading articles in the encyclopedia instead of as a search for new knowledge, enjoyment for the task **is** unlikely.

Revision Few people will enjoy research if they think of it as reading articles in the encyclopedia rather than searching for new knowledge.

11c
clear

● **Tip**

Watch out for sentences that begin with "It is . . . ," "There is . . . ," "There are . . . ," or "There were. . . ." These phrases, called *expletive constructions*, can make your writing seem strung out and monotonous. If you have several in a paragraph, find ways to rephrase the sentences when you revise. (See Section 12b–5.) ●

■ **Exercise 11.6** Recast these sentences in actor/action patterns that show more clearly who is doing what to whom. You can separate some sentences into shorter ones if you like.

1. Alumni Friends of Undergraduate Drama, a fund-raising organization that has already raised over $30,000 to refurbish the university's dilapidated theater, is the brainchild of Lincoln Barstein, to whom the lack of adequate performance space for the drama students was astonishing when he arrived on campus to take over as president.

2. Helping to convince people that restoring the theater was a worthwhile endeavor was the participation in the fund-raising drive of several noteworthy actors, who are among the school's alumni.

3. Barstein's studies in chemistry were enlivened in his own undergraduate days by his performing in the chorus and appearing in several plays, which is what started his belief in the importance of the arts in a college education.

4. Their possible failure to come up with the $75,000 necessary for the renovation was of major concern to the alumni organization, and they were relieved when an unexpected gift of $50,000 from a family who are prominent patrons of the arts, the Metcalfs, brought the total to more than they needed.

5. A new production of *All's Well That Ends Well*, a play by Shakespeare, opens the newly completed theater tonight, which was named the Metcalf Theater in the family's honor after a unanimous vote by grateful alumni.

■ **Exercise 11.7** Rewrite the following sentences and substitute active verbs for the various *to be* verbs. (*Tip:* Try redoing each sentence with a person or thing as its subject.)

1. The idea of having to write on a trumped-up topic just because the author of some textbook thought it would be good for him was a real pain to Luis Garcia.
2. Luis's belief is that for writing to be good it should be concerned with the writer's real-life interests and experience.
3. It was lucky for Luis that an alternative topic turned up that was interesting to him, and the topic was ocean liners.
4. The topic of ocean liners is one that has been of fascination to Luis since he was fourteen.
5. It is, however, such a huge topic that it was difficult for him to narrow it down to one of manageable size.

11d
clear

11d   **CAN YOU MAKE YOUR WRITING MORE INVITING TO READ?**

Troubleshooting

A piece of writing has its own "body language" that can make readers react to it positively or negatively (see the document design insert and Section 7d on paragraph appearance). If a sentence or paragraph looks too long and complex, your readers' instinctive reaction may be, "Oh, that's too hard to tackle. I'm sure I won't be able to understand it, so I won't even try."

Even if readers are willing to try, you're likely to overload their mental circuits. They may have to go back and reread what you have written—not because your ideas are difficult, but because you have tried to pack too much into one unit. And if their circuits overheat too often, your readers will probably just give up.

To make your writing more readable . . .

11d-1   **"Chunk" your writing; break up sentences and paragraphs into manageable parts.** When you divide up or "chunk" your writing, it becomes much easier to read and to remember. Chunking is the principle behind dividing telephone numbers; instead of ten numbers jammed together in a long sequence that would overload a reader's memory, they are broken up into three units that the brain can process. If they weren't, you'd have to deal with 2140280390 instead of 214-028-0390. And could you ever remember your social security number if it weren't divided? The same principle applies to jamming too many words into one sentence or too many sentences into one paragraph. For example, look at this sentence.

Original

Citing an instance in which a sixteen-year-old student was work-ing forty-eight hours a week at Burger King in order to pay for a new car and simultaneously trying to attend high school full time, and claiming that the fast-food restaurants often pressure young-sters to work overtime on school nights, New York educators have recently proposed legislation that prohibits high school students from working more than three hours on a night before school, limits the total amount of time they can work in one week to twenty hours when school is in session, and sets fines of up to $2,000 a violation on employers who violate these regulations.

11d
clear

Whew! The sentence is overloaded. It would work much better if it were broken up like this.

Revision

Educators in New York recently proposed legislation to limit the number of hours high school students can work during the school year to three hours on school nights and no more than twenty hours during the week. As an example of why such laws are needed, the bill's sponsors cited the case of a sixteen-year-old high school student who was working forty-eight hours a week at Burger King to buy a new car. They also claim that fast-food restaurants frequently pressure employees to work overtime on school nights. Under the new law, employers could be fined up to $2,000 per vi-olation.

The sentences, while not overly simplified, are much easier to follow.

You should also try to chunk long paragraphs by breaking them into two or three smaller units. For examples, review Section 7d on paragraph appearance and the exercise that goes with it.

11d-2 **When you have to present a substantial amount of informa-tion, arrange it in a list.** Instead of writing overpacked sentences or paragraphs in which readers will get lost, organize the information for them by putting it into a list. For example, here is a paragraph from a first-year English paper reacting to the new limitations proposed on working hours for high school students.

Original

Before passing the proposed law, New York legislators need to consider why so many high school students work. Most don't do it to buy new cars. Some other, more important reasons are that their jobs provide meals as well as money, they have to buy their own clothes, they contribute to household expenses, their jobs increase opportunities to meet people, their jobs meet requirements in Distributive Education, their work increases their self-confidence, and they need to save money for college.

11d
clear

After the third or fourth reason, the reader loses track of the argument. Notice how much easier it is to follow when the writer breaks the reasons down into a list.

Revision

Before passing the proposed law, New York legislators need to consider why so many high school students work. They don't all do it to buy new cars. Some other important reasons are these:

- Jobs often provide meals as well as money.
- Jobs help students to buy their own clothes.
- Jobs enable young people to contribute to household expenses.
- Jobs increase opportunities to meet people.
- Jobs meet requirements for Distributive Education.
- Jobs increase young people's self-confidence.
- Jobs help young people save money to go to college.

Breaking information down into a list like this takes more space but pays off handsomely in readability.

● **Tip**

Remember all items in a list should be in parallel form, as the sentences above are (see Sections 7c–4 and 17b for more on this convention). ●

■ **Exercise 11.8** Reorganize the following sentences by breaking them into more manageable chunks.

1. The job a girl has in high school can play an important part in introducing her to new responsibilities, increasing her confidence in herself, and getting her used to the idea that she can earn her own way and doesn't have to spend the rest of her life asking someone else, usually a man, for spending money or always letting someone else make the final decisions about what she can buy.
2. Parents are often ambivalent about having their high school young-

sters work because almost inevitably it causes conflicts about whether their job or their schoolwork is more important, and although ideally one can always say that both are important and students have to learn to balance them, finding that balance often proves to be difficult, particularly when the parents cannot give their children the allowance that would enable them to have the clothes and privileges that their peers have.

3. Other conflicts can also arise, especially for parents and children who think it's important for young people to be involved in extracurricular activities such as sports, music, and debate, but also think that it's important and somehow quintessentially American for young people to "earn their own money" and demonstrate the values of self-discipline, responsibility, and thrift, and, in addition, get good grades so they'll be able to get into the college they want to attend.

11d
clear

■ **Exercise 11.9** Working with a group, rearrange these instructions for setting up a personal computer to make them more readable. Remember parallelism!

> You will find it easy to get started with your new personal computer. Unpack it from its case, saving all the Styrofoam pads in which it is packed so that you can reuse them when moving your machine. Check to see that you have grounded electrical outlets at the location where you plan to plug the machine in. Set up your computer, being sure that you keep it well away from any magnets such as the ones that may be found in telephones. Place the printer near the computer, either on a printer stand to hold paper or on an edge that allows a space through which paper can feed. Plug the keyboard, mouse, and printer into the ports on the back of the computer, using the cables provided and following the icons printed over each port. Finally, attach the power supply cord to the computer and plug it into the grounded outlet. Turn on your machine.

12

Can You Be Less Wordy?

A   Prune Words to Highlight the Main Idea
B   Trim Excess Words and Phrases
C   Streamline and Tighten Bureaucratic Prose

Most readers are impatient with writers who use far more words than they need to express ideas. So if your writing is wordy, work on ways to make it tighter. As you revise to get rid of unnecessary words, your writing will become more forceful and more professional. In this chapter you'll find several strategies for trimming your writing to make it lean and effective. Elsewhere in the book, we suggest more ways to make your writing more concise, especially in the chapters on sentences.

● **Tip**

Wait until you have a first draft before you start trimming your writing. Many writers write rambling prose in their first versions of a paper because they want to establish their ideas before pruning and shaping them. That's fine. If you start to worry about wordiness too soon, you might lose momentum. Be reassured that it's better to have too much than too little to start with—you can always cut. ●

12a   CAN YOU PRUNE WORDS TO GET TO YOUR POINT MORE QUICKLY?

Troubleshooting

Sometimes the point of a sentence gets lost in a thicket of introductory phrases and abstract language—there are just too many words. If your readers complain that your sentences are too long or hard to follow, you need to revise.

To highlight your point . . .

`12a-1` **Look for the central idea of the wordy sentence and feature it.** Often you can do that by making the key idea the subject of the sentence. Then trim out any words or phrases camouflaging the point you want to make.

Here is a sentence with the main idea buried beneath unnecessary words.

12a wordy

> **Original** The encouragement of total reliance on the federally sponsored student loan program for medical students from low-income families to pay their way through school causes many young doctors to leave medical school deeply in debt.

The grammatical subject of the sentence is a twenty-five word phrase filled with abstract nouns that overwhelms the verb "causes"; the real center of the sentence is "young doctors." If we focus on "young doctors" and make them the subject of the sentence, notice how much it improves.

> **Revision** Many young doctors from low-income families leave medical school deeply in debt because they have relied on student loans to pay their way through school.

▼
CAUTION
▼

`12a-2` **Focus on the action.** Strung-out verb phrases such as "give consideration to" and "make acknowledgment of" slow down your writing and add excess words. To get rid of them, read your draft and focus on the action. Ask, "What's happening?" When you find out, try to express that action in a single lively verb. For instance, look at how this sentence, sagging with weak verbs, can be revised to show action. (The action is boldfaced in the revision.)

> **Weak and wordy** Some of the groups who are in opposition to the death penalty feel there is doubt about its morality.
>
> **Revised** Some groups who **oppose** the death penalty **doubt** its morality.

Condense verb phrases that weaken your sentences because they lack the power of direct, active verbs. Consider the following examples.

WHY WRITE . . .	WHEN YOU COULD WRITE . . .
put the emphasis on	emphasize
have an understanding of	understand
make a comparison	compare
is reflective of	reflects
give permission to	allow
in opposition to	oppose

The changes will enliven your style.

● **Tip**

When you cut verb phrases and focus on the action, you'll get an added bonus. You're more likely to match subjects and verbs correctly because you have trimmed out intervening words that camouflage the subject. ●

12a–3 **Use people as the subjects of your sentences when you can.** When you start a sentence off with a person rather than an abstract term, your sentence will move faster and you'll probably use fewer words. Notice what happens when we change the subject of the next sentence from "strong pressures" to "Alex" and make a similar change in the next pair.

> **Dull** **Strong pressures** were felt by Alex about his first research paper.
>
> **Lively** **Alex** felt strong pressures about his first research paper.
>
> **Dull** **The excitement of doing original research** has not been experienced by most new college students.
>
> **Lively** **Most new college students** don't know the excitement of doing original research.

See Section 11b–2 on adding people to your writing and Section 11c–1 on actor/action sentences.

12a–4 **Reduce the number of passive verbs.** Passive verb constructions (clauses in which the subject does not act, but is acted upon) usually take up more space than active verbs, not only because they use more words, but also because they tend to cluster with abstract nouns and prepositional phrases. For example:

> **Passive construction** The process by which nominees **are chosen** for the annual Academy Awards **is viewed** by many veteran movie critics as highly political.

Active   Many veteran movie critics **regard** the Academy
construction   Awards nominating process as highly political.

Notice that the revised version omits no details; it's just tighter.

For a more extensive discussion of passive verbs and their uses and misuses, see Section 17e.

■ **Exercise 12.1** Rewrite the following sentences to pinpoint their centers or real subjects.

1. The fears of many prospective women students over thirty about returning to school are understandable to college counselors, who know how intimidating entrance exams can be.
2. The confidence and self-esteem of such prospective students can be undermined by a combination of myths and lack of information.
3. The demonstrated ability of people over thirty to master new information quickly because of their broader experience is a fact not known to most of these women students.
4. In addition, negative attitudes about opportunities for women in higher education are being rethought by educators as a result of books such as *Women's Ways of Knowing.*
5. It might easily come about in the next decade that the proportion of women students might be more than 50 percent in the prestigious graduate schools in the United States.

■ **Exercise 12.2** Working with other students in a group, discuss how you could rewrite these sentences to highlight the action taking place and to reduce words.

1. Among many people who are unhappy about the violence and sensationalism in the movies and on television, there is cynicism about ever bringing about change.
2. Government censorship is not acceptable to them, and the profit motive of producers seems to be stronger than concerns about good taste or community values.
3. The claim of the so-called creative community in Hollywood has traditionally been that what they are producing is only a reflection of the preferences and interests of the public, and they deny all responsibility for any impact on the behavior of young people.
4. The validity of both claims, however, has been challenged by those who make a study of the electronic media.
5. Critics of the industry's allegations point out that scores of millions of people among the American public hold strong religious beliefs, and

that violent and sexually explicit material on television and in the movies doesn't reflect their preferences. Moreover, these same media producers who allege that their programs have no influence on behavior market this entertainment to advertisers on the basis of its being attractive to young people.

■ **Exercise 12.3** Identify the passive verbs in the following sentences, then rewrite them, changing passive verbs to active verbs where you think it would improve the sentence.

1. The writing of research papers is traditionally dreaded by students everywhere.
2. Unfortunately the way in which the research paper is sometimes taught often accounts for the attitudes felt by students.
3. When topics are assigned with little concern for the students' interests, boredom and apathy can be expected from the students.
4. But if students are allowed to choose their own topics, writing a research paper can be transformed into an adventure.
5. For the lucky ones, it will be discovered that few things are as exciting as original research.

12b **CAN YOU TRIM CLUTTER AND REPETITION?**

Troubleshooting

When your instructor and fellow students suggest that your writing rambles, check to see if you are using words and phrases that take up space but add nothing to your meaning. Writer and editor William Zinsser calls them "clutter": the clichés, extra adjectives and adverbs, and obvious comments that keep your writing from being as trim and crisp as it could be.

Unfortunately for most writers the war against clutter never ends. Even professional writers find that overstuffed phrases and pointless repetitions creep into their writing despite years of fighting them. You can, however, develop strategies to combat clutter.

To reduce clutter, you can . . .

12b–1 **Condense lead-in phrases.** To write clean sentences, get rid of wheel-spinning expressions that pad and don't add. Ask yourself:

WHY WRITE . . .	**WHEN YOU COULD WRITE . . .**
in the event that	if
in light of the fact that	since
on the grounds that	because
regardless of the fact that	although
on the occasion of	when
at this point in time	now
it is obvious that	obviously

We are so accustomed to these wordy phrases that we forget they don't say much; they do, however, clutter your writing. For example:

12b
wordy

Wordy	Regardless of the fact that Miguel graduated from the police academy last year, he still seems more like a cadet than a police officer.
Revised	Although Miguel graduated from the police academy last year, he behaves more like a cadet than a police officer.
Wordy	At this point in time, I have given very little thought to choosing my major subject.
Revised	I haven't yet given much thought to choosing my major.

12b-2 **Eliminate redundant expressions.** When you are trying to streamline your sentences, look for those places where you have repeated yourself or where you have used double constructions or pointless modifiers.

- *Avoid doubling.* We have become so accustomed to using some words in pairs that we forget they mean the same thing—for example, "we **hope** and **trust**," "he shows **insight** and **vision**," "it is **fitting** and **proper**," or "she is **trim** and **slender**." On your final revision, trim out one word from such pairs.
- *Get rid of empty modifiers.* It's easy to pad direct expressions with phrases that inflate your writing but contribute nothing because they repeat the meaning already present in the word they're modifying. For instance:

WHY WRITE . . .	**WHEN YOU COULD WRITE . . .**
trading **activity** was heavy	trading was heavy
the papers were of a **confidential nature**	the papers were confidential
obstetrics is her **area of specialization**	her speciality is obstetrics
the banner was **blue in color**	the banner was blue
the pool was **round in shape**	the pool was round

12b–3 **Eliminate surplus intensifiers.** The function of an intensifying word is to increase power. For instance, in the sentences "That chemical is **extremely** dangerous" and "She is **extraordinarily** talented," the boldfaced intensifiers serve a legitimate purpose because something can be more or less dangerous and someone can be more or less talented. If, however, you add words that can't logically increase the power of the word you've modified, you're loading your writing with excess baggage. For instance:

WHY WRITE . . .	WHEN YOU COULD WRITE . . .
We're **completely** finished	We're finished
It's an **awful** tragedy	It's a tragedy
The **eventual** outcome will be	The outcome will be
The funds are **totally** exhausted	The funds are exhausted
The letter is **absolutely** pointless	The letter is pointless

Such phrases can add emphasis in casual conversation but are out of place in carefully edited writing.

12b–4 **Condense sentences into clauses, clauses into phrases, and phrases into single words.** Often you can tighten your writing by making one forceful adjective or adverb do the work of a whole string of words. For example:

Original   Queen Elizabeth I was a complex and sensuous woman. She seemed to love men, yet she never came close to marrying one of her many suitors.

Revision   Complex and sensuous, Queen Elizabeth I seemed to love men, yet never came close to marrying.

Original   Elizabeth I was like her father Henry VIII in many ways. She especially resembled him in her bad temper, which was legendary.

Revision   Like her father, Henry VIII, Elizabeth I had a legendary bad temper.

See Section 14c for more suggestions about tightening sentences by combining elements.

12b–5 **Cut down on expletives.** Expletives are short expressions such as "it was" and "there are" that function like starting blocks for pushing off into a sentence. For example:

It was a dark and stormy night. **There were** five of us huddled in the room.

There are a great number of gopher holes on the golf course.

It is an unusual opportunity for the students to learn a new language.

Habitually using "there is" and "there are" at the beginning of sentences or clauses can give your writing a tedious, singsong rhythm and make it sound amateurish and flat. Sometimes you cannot avoid using expletives—"It is cold today"—but more often, such expressions just delay getting to your subject. Notice the improvement when the sentences above are condensed.

12b
wordy

The night was dark and stormy. Five of us huddled in the room.

Gopher holes cover the golf course.

The students have an unusual opportunity to learn a new language.

WHY WRITE . . .	WHEN YOU COULD WRITE . . .
there is a desire for	we want
there are several reasons for	for several reasons
there was an expectation of	they expected
it is obvious that	obviously
it is clear that	clearly
it is to be hoped	we hope

12b-6 Get rid of *who, which,* or *that* when you can do so without changing the meaning of your sentence. Sometimes you can cut excess words and also not have to decide between *who* and *whom* or *which* and *that*. For example, look at these puzzlers.

Millie Novak is a woman (*who* or *whom?*) everyone likes.

The classic Studebaker coupe is a car (*which* or *that?*) antique car buffs cherish.

A passion for old cars is an obsession (*which* or *that?*) many former race drivers share.

Now notice how easy it is to solve these problems.

Millie Novak is a woman everyone likes.
Antique car buffs cherish the classic Studebaker coupe.
Many former race drivers share a passion for old cars.

Notice too how much tighter the following paragraph becomes when unnecessary *who*'s, *which*'s, *that*'s, and other fillers are eliminated.

Wordy version

People who are right thinking naturally applaud recycling. Who among us would dare to oppose it? But if one takes into consideration the water that is used to wash out cans and bottles and the fuel that it takes to pick up newspapers which have been discarded, recycling may not be as virtuous as it is made to appear.

Tighter version

Right-thinking people naturally applaud recycling. Who would dare oppose it? But if one considers the water used to wash out cans and bottles and the fuel required to pick up discarded newspapers, recycling may not be so virtuous.

TRICKY

12b-7 **Try to use affirmative expressions.** Your writing will be more economical and easier to understand if, whenever you can, you phrase ideas affirmatively instead of negatively. Try to get rid of words such as *not* and *never* and prefixes such as *un-* and *non-*. Use "do" forms instead of "don't" forms. Phrasing your points positively will also make your writing seem more confident. For example:

Negative   It is not improbable that I will be able to attend the conference.

Affirmative   I can probably attend the conference.

Negative   He is not an inexperienced writer, nor is he unre-sourceful.

Affirmative   He is an experienced and resourceful writer.

■ **Exercise 12.4** Rewrite the following sentences to reduce clutter by substituting single words for wordy phrases. You can rearrange some sentences if you like.

1. In the event that the Antiquarians' Fall Jamboree is open after church, you should not miss the opportunity to see their unique exhibits.
2. It's true that the women who have run the show for twenty years have an uncanny ability to find bargains, and they are quick to take advantage of any chance to add to their stock of memorabilia from the 1920s and 1930s.
3. It is also possible that you may have a chance to see some spectacular, outstanding old vintage clothing—beaded flapper dresses, patent leather pumps with bows, or even a raccoon coat.
4. And there is a certain possibility that Millie and Annie will extend you an invitation to come around back behind the scenes to take a look at their special pride, an old-time Wurlitzer jukebox.
5. There near the vicinity of the rear door also stands a monument to

one of Millie's much-admired heroines from the world of fashion: a mannequin completely dressed in a 1937 Coco Chanel classic suit.

■ **Exercise 12.5** Rewrite these sentences to get rid of *who, whom, that,* or *which* or unnecessary phrases when you can do so without altering meaning. Not all of those words should be deleted.

1. Some of the people who might be happy to see a little less publicity about the environment are parents of children whom environmentalists have turned into Green Police.
2. Third graders who used to read only "Calvin and Hobbes" suddenly can't wait to read "Tips to Save Our Planet" in that same newspaper that includes three pounds of slick, colored, unrecyclable inserts with the Sunday edition.
3. Full of moral superiority, third graders who can barely read are circulating petitions that condemn industries which are polluting the air.
4. We notice that these eight-year-old Green Police who plague their parents about paper napkins have not offered their services to iron the cloth napkins.
5. The shrewd parents are the ones who have outflanked their miniature Green Troops by setting them to reading labels on paper towels and napkins, looking for the ones that say "Made of recycled paper."

**12c
wordy**

12c CAN YOU STREAMLINE BUREAUCRATIC PROSE?

Troubleshooting

If you're a chronically wordy writer, it's going to take more than paring excess words to make your prose economical. You'll have to look at whole sections of your writing to see if you can cut redundant sentences. You may even need to lop off entire paragraphs or get rid of those portions of your draft written in the dull, wordy style known as "bureaucratic prose." Not only does such writing inflict unnecessary pain on your readers, but it confuses them and wastes their time.

To reduce wordiness . . .

12c–1 Prune out obvious generalizations and unnecessary explanations. You may be boring your readers by telling them things they already know or by giving them too many details. For example, here's an overblown opening paragraph in the first draft of a research paper on bicycles in China.

Inflated first draft

Bicycles are a major form of transportation in many Third World countries because they are inexpensive and easy to maintain. Asians in particular seem to depend on them heavily. Nowhere, however, are they more important than in China, where one can see masses of them on the streets of every city. Probably no one knows how many bicycles there are in the country, nor does there seem to be any way of finding out. Virtually everyone seems to ride—well-dressed businessmen with their briefcases strapped to the frame, a husband with his wife riding behind and a child on the handlebars, women of all ages, some even in their narrow long dresses, and college students carrying their books on their backs. The newly arrived American cyclist in Beijing or Shanghai, however, would be astonished not only to see the great numbers of bicycles, but to see what kinds of bicycles the Chinese ride and how many other uses, besides simply riding, the Chinese have been able to figure out for bicycles. They're an amazingly ingenious and resourceful people when it comes to adapting the common bicycle.

When revising this, the writer quickly realized he could get rid of most of the first two sentences—they're tedious generalizations. He can also cut the sentence about no one knowing how many bikes there are—that's not important. The sentence giving examples of different kinds of riders should stay, however, since it illustrates a key point and it's colorful. The last two sentences have too much information and need to be cut and revised, but the idea is important as a lead-in to the rest of the paper.

When the writer finished streamlining his paragraph, it looked like this.

Streamlined

Although bicycles are a major form of transportation in all Asian countries, nowhere are they more important than in China, where one sees masses of them on the streets of every city. Virtually everyone seems to ride—well-dressed businessmen with their briefcases strapped to the frame; a husband with his wife riding behind and a child on the handlebars; women of all ages, some even in their narrow long dresses; and college students carrying their books on their backs. The newly arrived American cyclist, however, would be astonished to see how many other uses besides simple riding the Chinese have been able to devise for bicycles.

12c–2 **Streamline bureaucratic prose by cutting heavy-duty nouns.**
Writers in college or even in business sometimes think their readers ex-

(margin: 12c wordy)

pect them to write stodgy, impersonal prose loaded with nominalizations (called "heavy-duty nouns"). **Nominalizations** are nouns made by
adding endings to verbs and adjectives. There are thousands of them in
English, far too many to list, but this sample will show you what we
mean.

utiliza**tion**	account**ability**
maximiza**tion**	imprecise**ness**
specific**ity**	avoid**ance**
valid**ity**	simplifica**tion**
prioritiza**tion**	expan**sion**
finaliza**tion**	homeless**ness**

12c
wordy

Militant becomes *militancy, accountable* becomes *accountability, specific*
becomes *specificity,* and so on. Often you have to use words like these, but
too many of them will inflate your style and clog up your writing, making it much harder to read.

12c–3 **Cut the number of prepositional phrases in your writing.**
(Check the glossary for a definition.) These are typical.

to the limit	**for** the duration
with the exception	**of** the opinion
by the side	**against** the advice
above the average	**with** the proviso that
over the objections	**under** those conditions
across the board	**until** the next case

Although you must use prepositional phrases, try to keep from stringing
them out in a sentence. Heavy-duty nouns and prepositional phrases
tend to attract each other, and when a writer habitually uses both, too
often the product is wordy and lifeless. Here is a passage made almost unreadable by too many heavy-duty nouns (shown boldfaced) and prepositional phrases (shown italicized).

Original

The **proliferation** *of credit cards among college students* is the
result *of extensive* **marketing** *by banking* **institutions** who see college students *in terms of future* **profitability.** The **manifestation** *of
such* **promotions** *at our college* is the recent **placing** *of credit card*
applications *in prominent view at local restaurants, convenience
stores,* and *video shops.* Such placement does not reflect **generosity**
toward students or **misconceptions** *about their current wealth.*
Rather it shows hopes *of their* **acquiring** the credit card habit *at an
early age.*

Revision

More and more students have credit cards because banks expect to make money from those students in the future. Several banks place card applications prominently at campus restaurants, convenience stores, and video stores not because they think students are going to spend a lot of money, but because they want them to acquire the credit-card habit while they are still young.

■ **Exercise 12.6** Streamline and strengthen this paragraph from a student's first draft by cutting unnecessary generalizations or explanations and trimming at other places that seem wordy.

There are many different views concerning Alexander the Great's goal in relation to his military pursuits. Some historians consider Alexander to have been a power-hungry tyrant whom the world would have been better off without. Others see Alexander as the great unifier of mankind, one who attempted to bring many cultures together in one empire, with one worldview. Others view him as the ultimate pragmatist—not necessarily having any preplanned goals of conquering the world, but merely a king who made the best of his existing circumstances. Some believe that Alexander's accomplishments were not great at all, but that most of what is spoken concerning Alexander is a mixture of legend and myth. Others feel his achievements stand as monuments in human history to the enormous capability of the human spirit and will.

Can You Revise for Clearer Sentences?

A   Revising to Clarify Tangled Sentences
B   Revising to Fix Derailed Sentences
C   Reorganizing Overloaded Sentences
D   Revising to Make Sentences Parallel

When we speak casually, most of us construct sentences just as naturally as we put one foot ahead of the other when we walk. Because we know instinctively how our native language works, we can put words together in understandable sentences—no problem. When we write, however, things get more complicated. Then we need to think more about the various forms sentences take—how the different parts match up and which patterns can be used. That's what this chapter and the next two are about.

We'll deal with sentence issues in the order of their priority. In this chapter, we'll focus on the first concern in revising sentences: how you can make them clear. In the next chapter, we'll focus on how you can rewrite sentences to make them express your ideas more efficiently. In the third sentence chapter, we'll focus on some finer points about revising.

● **Tip**

Notice that throughout the discussion, we talk about how you can *revise* sentences, not about how you write them in the first place. That's important. We think it's seldom practical to start out trying to decide what sentence patterns you're going to use. Just start writing and put down sentences as they come to you. Sometimes you may write yourself into a tangle and start again, but trust your natural sense of language to help you compose sentences that say what you mean. Wait until you have written at least a paragraph or two before you start to revise. As many writers have found, too much early tinkering with sentences will slow you down. ●

13a   CAN YOU REVISE TO CLARIFY TANGLED SENTENCES?

Troubleshooting

Sometimes readers may tell you they get lost trying to follow your sentences. They may complain that you've tried to do too much in one sentence or that your wording is too complicated. In such cases, there's not much point in trying to explain what you meant. You'll do better to reread the sentences that are confusing your readers and rewrite them to make them clearer. This section offers some suggestions.

To clarify tangled sentences . . .

Look first for the subject of your sentence when you start to revise. Then, if possible, make that subject a person or thing, put it close to the front of the sentence, and put an active verb with it. Often the tangles will disappear. If they don't, look for other reasons your sentence has gone astray. Here are three common ways sentences get tangled.

1. The writer begins a sentence with a clause or phrase but fails to connect it to the subject of the sentence.

    Tangled   While waiting in line to buy movie tickets, jugglers and other street performers can be watched enjoyably.

    Readers expect the introductory clause "While waiting in line to buy movie tickets" to give information about "jugglers and other street performers," the subject of the sentence, but it doesn't.

    Possible   (a) While waiting in line to buy tickets, a moviegoer
    revisions   can enjoy watching jugglers and other street performers. (b) Moviegoers waiting in line to buy tickets can enjoy watching jugglers and other street performers.

2. The writer starts with a dependent clause but doesn't connect it to an independent main clause. In effect he or she combines two sentence fragments.

    Tangled   If a person is energetic and bright, expecting to do well at our firm.

    The second part of this combination is a phrase without a subject or a verb; it can't serve as the main clause of the sentence.

Possible (a) Anyone who is energetic and bright can expect to
revisions do well at our firm.

(b) People who are energetic and learn quickly can expect to do well at our firm.

3. The writer doesn't keep track of the main subject of the sentence and forgets to put in a verb to complete the sentence.

Tangled Anyone who reads *The Daily Mirror* regularly, soon realizing that the letters to the editor are the most entertaining feature.

The reader looks for a verb to go with the subject, "Anyone who reads *The Daily Mirror*," but doesn't find it. By themselves, *-ing* words can't act as verbs.

Possible (a) Anyone who reads *The Daily Mirror* regularly soon
revisions realizes that the letters to the editor are the most entertaining feature.

(b) The letters to the editor are the most entertaining feature of *The Daily Mirror*, as anyone who reads it regularly soon realizes.

**13a
sent**

● **Tip**

Usually you can find several good ways to revise a faulty sentence. Don't assume there's just one correct way to write every sentence. ●

■ **Exercise 13.1** Working with a group, consider why these sentences don't work. With the group, work out a complete and effective version of each one.

1. If local college students want to try out their foreign language skills, finding a perfect opportunity at Café Budapest, a restaurant popular with foreign visitors to Boston.
2. While eating at Café Budapest, a special appeal to it for many because the atmosphere is so international.
3. Among the many reasons to frequent Café Budapest, daily newspapers from all over the world and many different kinds of coffee are available.
4. In thinking about good Hungarian cooking, Café Budapest or Magyar Tavern is the choice most local restaurant critics recommend.
5. The restaurant's owner, Georgy Sandor, who was responsible for creating the Bohemian atmosphere which everyone who goes there enjoys.

13b   CAN YOU REDIRECT SENTENCES THAT GO OFF TRACK?

Troubleshooting

 Sometimes writers construct sentences that start off in one direction, then at a connecting place seem to "derail" and take off in a different direction. When this happens, the writer should pinpoint the intersection where the sentence went wrong and set it going back in the right direction.

13b sent

Derailed	What made Lori Wentworth want to be a veterinarian, no one else in her family had ever cared about animals.
	The sentence derails after "veterinarian" because the writer hasn't shown a clear connection between the two ideas. To get it back on track, she needs to rethink her meaning.
Possible revisions	(a) Although no one else in her family had ever cared about animals, Lori Wentworth wanted to be a veterinarian.
	(b) Lori Wentworth wanted to be a veterinarian although no one else in her family had ever cared about animals.
Derailed	Since Cameron is athletic and adventurous, and it's not so surprising for him to be interested in mountain climbing.
	Here the sentence derails at the comma after "adventurous" and goes off in another direction because the writer has given a confusing signal by connecting the two parts of the sentence with "and."
Possible revisions	(a) Since Cameron is athletic and adventurous, his interest in mountain climbing is not surprising.
	(b) Cameron's interest in mountain climbing is not surprising since he is both athletic and adventurous.

■ **Exercise 13.2** Working with other students in a group, decide what has gone wrong with these sentences. Then each person should rewrite the sentences, and, in a group, compare the revisions.

1. Neighborhood teenagers like to work at Diego Mena's health food store, but in most cases it doesn't happen.
2. When Diego sees the truck from Crest Farm Breads pull up outside, and a glass of iced tea is poured for the deliveryman.
3. People in Diego's neighborhood remember when he was the star of the high school basketball team, and when his store opened, an instant hit.

4. Looking like someone without a care in the world, Diego standing behind the cash register in a crisp white shirt, but the hours are long and the work is hard.
5. Sometimes Carmen Mena, Diego's mother helping out at the store, pleased to see her son doing so well but wondering why health food customers never look as happy as people at a steak house.

13c CAN YOU REORGANIZE OVERLOADED SENTENCES?

Troubleshooting

Long sentences aren't necessarily confusing sentences; if they're well organized and written in a lively style, they can work well. You can, however, run into trouble when your sentences get too long, particularly if you've stuffed them with a good deal of information. When revising, look carefully at sentences that run to more than about twenty-five words—about three lines on your computer screen or on a typed page. You may find they're rambling and harder to follow than they need to be.

You can improve overloaded sentences if you . . .

13c–1 Divide the material into two or three shorter sentences.

Too long   The employee training program at the Crow's Nest chain of restaurants, a rapidly growing organization that promises to challenge the acknowledged giant in the franchise seafood business, the Red Lobster chain, may seem raucous and occasionally even juvenile in its manufactured enthusiasms, but employees who have graduated from it seem to know their business.

Possible revision   Though the training program at the Crow's Nest chain of restaurants may seem raucous and juvenile, employees who have graduated from it seem to know their business. The rapidly growing Crow's Nest chain promises to challenge Red Lobster, the acknowledged giant of the franchise seafood business.

13c–2 Keep introductory clauses and phrases brief. They shouldn't overwhelm the main part of the sentence or contain so much information that the reader gets lost. For example, here is an overly long introduction that makes the sentence lopsided.

Overloaded	**Having a family who worked very hard to send her to college and believed that the main reason a woman would spend four years in earning a degree was so that she could get a prestigious professional job,** Emily Chang was nervous when she thought about telling them she might like to open a catering business.

Possible revision	Emily Chang got nervous when she thought about telling her family that she might like to start a catering business. They had worked hard to send her to college, and they believed that the main reason a woman would spend four years earning a degree was to get a prestigious professional job.

13c-3 Avoid sentences in which the subject dwarfs the verb that follows it. When sentence subjects are lengthy groups of abstract terms combined with weak verbs such as *is* or *are*, they can be particularly confusing.

Inflated subject	The assumption, long held by many people in certain cultures, that people who have a college education should never have to work with their hands is often a deterrent to bright young people in those cultures who seek nontraditional careers. The subject is grammatically correct but inflated and leaves the reader scrambling to find the verb to go with it.
Possible revision	Many people in certain cultures assume that educated people should never have to work with their hands. That attitude deters many bright young people in those cultures from going into nontraditional careers.

■ **Exercise 13.3** Revise these overloaded sentences to make them easier to read and understand. You can divide them, reorganize them, and, if you like, trim out words that don't affect meaning.

1. Guides with the Capitol Bus Tour program are expected to have energy, enthusiasm, and a smile for every passenger; be able to speak one foreign language fluently and answer basic questions in three others if the need arises; and memorize information about over one hundred important sites around the city as well as cope calmly and expertly with unexpected emergencies such as a tour member's sudden illness.
2. Considering how little the camp can afford to pay, it is heartening to see that the Nightingale Camp for Disabled Children and other in-

stitutions like it continue to attract bright young men and women who are willing to go through the intensive training program required to work as counselors, and then, if they pass, put in long hours at jobs that are both physically and emotionally exhausting.

13d CAN YOU REVISE TO MAKE SENTENCE ELEMENTS PARALLEL?

Troubleshooting

CAUTION A sentence can mislead your readers if parts of it aren't parallel—that is, if related elements don't follow the same pattern in which they start out. The disrupted pattern jars the flow of the sentence.

The principle behind **parallelism** is similar to one tested on aptitude tests in which you are shown several objects and asked to identify the one that doesn't fit. When you are shown several different fruits and a potato, you know the potato doesn't fit. The pattern isn't consistent; it's not parallel. Thus in a sentence, if you use two adjectives in a series, the third element should also be an adjective; otherwise it doesn't fit—it's not parallel. If you use two noun phrases of one pattern, the third noun phrase should be in the same pattern or it's not parallel.

To correct faulty parallelism . . .

13d-1 Check your sentence patterns for faulty parallelism. Do this routinely if in the past you have had your sentences marked for problems with parallelism. You can also ask people who will be reading your drafts to point out faulty parallelism.

Here are examples of how sentence patterns can go wrong and some suggested ways of fixing them. Both faulty and revised elements are boldfaced.

Faulty When one starts to use a new computer program, it's easy to get lost, frustrated, and **don't know what you're supposed to do.**
Adjectives are used in the first two slots following "to get," but the third slot is filled with a verb phrase.

Parallel When one starts to use a new computer program, it's easy to get lost, frustrated, and **confused about what to do.**
Now the adjectives in all three slots are similar.

Faulty   John was quick to learn which teachers were the most interesting and **figuring out how to get in their classes.**
The first part of the phrase that completes "was quick" is an infinitive (*to learn*), but the second completer (*figuring*) is not; it also needs an infinitive.

Parallel   John was quick to learn which teachers were the most interesting and **to figure out how to get in their classes.**
Now both phrases that complete "was quick" are infinitives.

13d-2 **Learn to identify correlative conjunctions.** *Correlative conjunctions* are those pairs of words that join the parts of a sentence; they must be followed by words or phrases that are parallel in form. The most common pairs are

> Not only . . . but also
> Either . . . or; neither . . . nor
> Both . . . and
> On the one hand . . . on the other hand

For example:

> Janet is *not only* **the most ambitious** of the applicants *but also* **the best prepared.**
>
> A musician's manager sees to it that the performer is *neither* **overscheduled** *nor* **undervalued.**

In both examples each correlative conjunction is followed by phrases or words that are parallel in form.

Here is an example of how such a pattern can go wrong and how it can be corrected.

Faulty   Anyone who learns to drive late in life can either **be exhilarated** at mastering a new skill or **worrying** every time he or she gets behind the wheel.
Here the phrase following "either" is a verb phrase with *be*, so the phrase after "or" also needs to be a verb phrase with *be: be worried*.

Parallel   Anyone who learns to drive late in life can either **be exhilarated** at mastering a new skill or **be worried** every time he or she gets behind the wheel.

● **Tip**

Remember that elements in a list need to be parallel too.

FAULTY	**CORRECT**
Prepare menus	Prepare menus
Assign tasks	Assign tasks
Nametags	**Order nametags**
Choose menu	Choose menu
Rent conference room	Rent conference room
Parking	**Arrange for parking** ●

13d

//

■ **Exercise 13.4** Working in a group, read these sentences and decide which ones have faulty parallel structures. Then work together to revise those in which you find inconsistent or faulty patterns, making all the parts consistent or parallel with each other.

1. On opening night at her new Caribbean restaurant, Martine Duval called together all the waiters and waitresses to be sure that their shirts and pants were pressed, their colorful ties neatly knotted, their shoes shined, and without a spot on their white aprons.
2. Two waiters, Jared and Ian, had a bet on to see which one's customers would spend the most on drinks, order the most expensive items, and, of course, the biggest tip that would be left.
3. By far the most popular waiter of the evening, however, was Raoul, thanks to his beautiful Jamaican accent, his talent for convincing timid customers to try exotic foods such as turtle soup and goat curry, and he could limbo under the bar with an entire trayful of piña coladas.
4. Halfway through the evening, a group of ten exchange students from Denmark sat down at one of Jared's tables and not only began to order endless quantities of shrimp and coconut curry, but also lit up the restaurant with flaming desserts.
5. Martine asked the steel drum band to stay late, and after the last customers had left, she locked the front door, kicked off her shoes, and was dancing with her staff until 3:00 a.m. in celebration.

■ **Exercise 13.5** Write three sentences with good parallel structure, incorporating the elements given below for each one. Here is how one example might work.

> *Subject:* A coach   Three actions during a game.
>
> *Sample sentence:* Holding his temper as best he could, the coach paced the sidelines, gnashed his teeth, and tried not to cry.

1. *Subject:* The grandparent   Three actions in visiting for Christmas
2. *Subject:* The senator   Two actions in giving a speech
3. *Subject:* The teacher   Three actions in calming a class

14

Can You Revise for More Effective Sentences?

A Revising for Better-Coordinated Sentences
B Revising for Better Sentence Subordination
C Revising to Combine and Improve Sentences
D Revising to Correct Faulty Sentence Predication

The traditional terminology we use to talk about organizing sentences—subordination, coordination, compound and complex sentences, and so on—makes it sound as if writing sentences is complicated. It isn't. You use well-coordinated sentences all the time when you talk. Writing them isn't much more complicated. So at first don't worry about how to organize your sentences and don't assume that there are specific rules about when to use a compound sentence or a complex one. However, if you learn more about coordinating and subordinating the parts of a sentence, you'll be able to revise for tighter, more effective sentences.

14a CAN YOU REVISE FOR BETTER-COORDINATED SENTENCES?

Troubleshooting

If you write mostly simple sentences in your first drafts because you want to avoid punctuation problems, your writing may seem choppy and disconnected. Simple sentences are often clear and forceful, but too many linked together can make your style seem immature. For that reason, on second drafts it's useful to look for ways to coordinate some of your simple sentences. You can make them into compound sentences by tying them together with conjunctions or appropriate punctuation.

To write better-coordinated sentences . . .

14a–1 **Join two independent clauses or sentences that are closely related and about equally important.** When you join such units, you tell your reader to consider the separate points as parts of one main idea, even though they could work as sentences by themselves. These are the most common devices used to join coordinate clauses.

14a coord

1. The conjunctions *and, but, yet, or, for,* and *so*

   Example   Captain Starbuck didn't know which galaxy to head for, **so** he asked his crew for advice.

2. The conjunctions *either . . . or, neither . . . nor,* and *not only . . . but also,* or a semicolon used alone

   Example   **Not only** was the captain a pioneer in space travel, **but** he **also** captained the first spaceship.

3. Adverbs such as *but, nevertheless, however,* and *although,* if used with a semicolon

   Example   Everyone defers to Captain Starbuck's judgment when the spaceship is in outer space; **however,** when the spaceship returns to the surface of the earth, his authority evaporates.

14a–2 **Pay attention to coordinating words.** Different joining words give different signals, so be sure to pick the ones that do what you want them to. For example, *and, moreover, also,* and the semicolon show that you're joining ideas of the same kind.

   Example   The crew often suspects that the captain's second-in-command, Commander George Maxey, knows more than the captain; **moreover,** he's a better navigator when the chips are down.

If you write too many sentences in which clauses are joined by *and,* your writing may seem monotonous and amateurish. When you find you have used several *ands* to join sentence parts, combine some of the clauses or subordinate them as modifiers. (See the next section, on subordination.)

But, yet, however, and *nevertheless* signal contrast between the two independent clauses of a coordinate sentence.

> **Example** The statue's hair is carved in the style of early archaic sculpture, **yet** its feet show stylistic traits of late archaic sculpture.

When you use *but, and, yet,* or *or* to join two independent clauses, be sure to put a comma before the joining word. (See Section 26c–1 for punctuation in this kind of sentence.)

The words *for* and *so* usually show cause and effect.

14a
coord

> **Example** Michelangelo's frescoes on the Sistine Chapel ceiling are among the greatest works of the Renaissance, **so** conservators approached the task of cleaning and restoring them with great caution.

Or, either . . . or, and *nor* signal that the clauses being joined are alternatives.

> **Example** Oil paintings should not hang in a room that is too damp or too dry, **nor** should they be exposed to direct sunlight.

■ **Exercise 14.1** Combine the following sentences by joining the independent clauses. Use one of the conjunctions or joining adverbs given in Section 14a–1 in a way that shows a clear relationship between the ideas. Be alert to get the punctuation right!

> **Example** Pencils were invented in the sixteenth century. Erasers were not added to them until 1858.
>
> **Possible** Pencils were invented in the sixteenth century; how-
> **revision** ever, erasers were not added to them until 1858.

1. Today, French Impressionist paintings are favorites with art lovers. When the paintings were first shown in the nineteenth century, the public rejected them.
2. Painters such as Renoir and Monet felt that art should depict modern life. They painted what they saw around them.
3. Many critics of the time were disturbed by the Impressionists' banal subject matter. They thought the paintings looked crude and unfinished.
4. The painters were forced to exhibit independently. The official Salon refused to hang their work.
5. Although wounded by the public's incomprehension, the Impressionists did not abandon their examination of modern life. They did not change their style to please the critics.

14b CAN YOU REVISE FOR BETTER SUBORDINATION?

Troubleshooting

CAUTION

In going over your first draft, you may realize that in some sentences you haven't made your emphasis clear or haven't shown the relationship between the parts of the sentence. When that happens, look for places where you need to change or rewrite the sentence to subordinate one part to another.

To correct problems with sentence subordination . . .

14b–1 **Use signals to show that one clause depends for its meaning on another clause.** The most common way to signal subordinate clauses is to use the words *although, as, after, since, before, until, unless, when, while, if,* and *because.* Words like *who, whoever, that, which,* and so on can also signal dependent clauses. Another common method of subordination is to use the phrases *so that, in spite of, in case of, no matter how, even though,* and *if only.*

Here are two examples.

> **Unless** Rita decides to go for a graduate degree, she must find a job.

> **While** one is in school, it's easy to put off making career decisions.

14b–2 **Choose subordinating signals carefully to convey the meaning you intend.** Subordinating words give such strong messages that you need to be sure you put the right word in the right place. Notice the differences here.

> **Before** professional sports became a major source of revenue for television, no team owner thought of paying players million-dollar salaries.

> **Although** members of Congress often campaign for a balanced budget, each of them jealously tries to protect all projects in his or her district from cuts in federal spending.

One construction shows causation; the other one shows contrast.

Here is another set of examples.

> Jared had never walked a picket line before, **although** he had been a union member for more than twenty years.

> **Until** Jared walked on a picket line, he didn't fully understand what it meant to be a union member.

14b–3 **Subordinate one part of a sentence to another to emphasize the most important idea.** Usually this means you should make the main independent clause carry the main point of the sentence and have a subordinate clause or clauses carry less important information. Otherwise you're likely to mislead your readers. For example:

Misleading subordination	Constantly cultivating his image as a man who enjoyed such "manly" pursuits as drinking, brawling, and big-game hunting, Ernest Hemingway was obsessed with virility. The important point about Hemingway gets lost here.
Revised for better emphasis	Obsessed with virility, Ernest Hemingway constantly cultivated his image as a man who enjoyed such "manly" pursuits as drinking, brawling, and big-game hunting.

Here's another example.

Misleading subordination	Although the first printing of *Sister Carrie* in 1900 sold only five hundred copies before being withdrawn from publication on moral grounds, today it is widely admired as the first modern American novel. The important information gets lost.
Revised for better emphasis	Although today *Sister Carrie* is widely admired as the first modern American novel, its first printing in 1900 sold only five hundred copies before being withdrawn from publication on moral grounds.

14b–4 **Use subordinate clauses to create sentences with more information.** Notice that a subordinate sentence can be both complex and efficient in the way it arranges ideas.

Original	Myra was always an attractive woman. When she was in graduate school, however, she tried to play down her good looks. She feared people would assume she wasn't intelligent or interested in scholarship.
Revision	Although Myra was always an attractive woman, in graduate school she tried to play down her good looks, fearing that people would assume she wasn't intelligent or interested in scholarship.

14b
subord

You will find more on this strategy in the next section on sentence combining.

14b-5 Avoid stringing several subordinate clauses together. You can overdo subordination in a sentence and wind up with a sentence that incorporates so many ideas that the reader gets lost, as in the following example.

Too many clauses   Hector began to realize that people **who** made a big deal about not caring about clothes were often those who couldn't afford many clothes and who preferred to cultivate an image that they were indifferent to fashion, not poor.

Revised   Hector began to realize that often people who couldn't afford many clothes preferred to cultivate an image that they were indifferent to fashion, not poor.

14b
subord

■ **Exercise 14.2** Join the following pairs of sentences, making one of them a subordinate clause.

1. The original books of Babylonia and Assyria were collections of inscribed clay tablets stored in labeled containers too heavy for one person to move. We think of books as portable, bound volumes.

2. Clay had many drawbacks. It remained the most convenient medium for recording information until the Egyptians developed papyrus, around 3000 B.C.

3. Egyptian books were lighter but still awkward to carry or read. A single book comprised several very large and unwieldy scrolls.

4. The Greeks learned about papyrus from the Egyptians. They developed papyrus leaflets, which they folded and bound to produce the first modern-looking book.

5. The book was the Greek Bible. It takes its name from Byblos, the Phoenician city that supplied Greece with papyrus.

■ **Exercise 14.3** Working with other students in a group, read the following sentences and decide which sentences have too many subordinate clauses strung together or in which sentences the subordination seems to emphasize the most important idea. As a group, rewrite those sentences for better organization or better emphasis. Some may work well as they are.

1. Although chances are good that their first names, Ben and Jerry, make you think of dessert, their last names, Cohen and Greenfield, may make you think of a law firm.

2. Ben and Jerry have become two men who are practically folk heroes since they started producing ice cream, which was in 1978 in a building that is in Vermont and that was formerly a gas station.
3. Their greatest creation may be their publicity, which manages to link the decadent pleasures of ice cream with social and environmental concerns that are politically correct, although the fact is that Ben and Jerry's product is excellent.
4. While they readily admit that the company does indeed buy nuts from natives of the Amazon rain forest and blueberries from Indians in Maine, that it supports Vermont's family farms by paying bonuses for milk, and that it donates 7.5 percent of its profits to a foundation that supports community groups, local Vermonters regard Ben and Jerry's claims to environmental consciousness with skepticism.
5. In spite of that skepticism, which after all reflects an honored Vermont tradition that everyone boasts of, the locals love Ben and Jerry because their profits keep property taxes down.

14c comb

14c CAN YOU REVISE TO COMBINE SOME SENTENCES?

Troubleshooting

When you review sentences in your draft, you may notice that the information in some of them overlaps. Or perhaps several short sentences in a row give a simplistic "Dick and Jane" effect. Your instructor may also suggest that you would have more graceful sentences if you combined some of them to get more information into fewer words. You can combine sentences in several ways.

To combine sentences effectively . . .

14c–1 Use introductory phrases or clauses to put the information from two sentences into one sentence. Sometimes your sentences will be more economical if you find places where you can condense one sentence and use it as the beginning of the next one. For instance:

Original	You may see a rather large dog on your walk about the grounds. You will find it worth your while to try to get on his good side.
Combined	If you see a rather large dog on your walk about the grounds, you will find it worth your while to try to get on his good side.

Original	Every once in a while we hear a muffled explosion. The sound tells us that the honors chemistry students are hard at work.
Combined	The occasional muffled explosion tells us that the honors chemistry students are hard at work.

14c–2 Use coordination or subordination to combine simple sentences in which the information overlaps.

Original	A visit to Antietam is a moving experience. It is especially affecting because the natural beauty of the site contrasts painfully with the knowledge that thousands of men were killed there. The Battle of Antietam proved to be the single bloodiest day of the Civil War.
Combined	A visit to Antietam is especially moving because the natural beauty of the site contrasts painfully with the knowledge that thousands of men were killed there in what proved to be the single bloodiest day of the Civil War.
Original	At big urban universities, the mixture of clothing styles can be striking. One can see Indian women in flowing saris and Sikhs in turbans. One can also see Africans in colorful robes stand out against the predominant blue jeans and khakis.
Combined	One can see a striking mixture of clothing styles at a big urban university where Indian women in flowing saris, Sikhs in turbans, and Africans in colorful robes stand out against the predominant blue jeans and khakis.

14c–3 Look for sentences that can be moved into other sentences as modifiers.

Original	Seasoned shoppers don't let so-called fashion experts dictate their choices. Those experts merely want people to spend money on trendy clothes. Such clothes are poor investments.
Combined	Seasoned shoppers don't let so-called fashion experts persuade them to spend money on trendy clothes that are poor investments.
Original	Today's career women have minds of their own about fashion. They don't depend on dress-for-success books.

**14c
comb**

They want good-looking and high-quality clothes. But they also want them to reflect their own tastes.

Combined   Today's career women, who have minds of their own about fashion and don't depend on dress-for-success books, want good-looking, high-quality clothes that reflect their own tastes.

● **Tip**

Although sentence combining can be useful for smoothing out choppy writing and getting more information into your sentences, don't overdo it. If you try to condense too much material into one sentence, you can wind up with overstuffed sentences like the ones we've used as examples of wordiness (see Chapter 12). You can also lose track of your main point if you try to put too many sentences together. ●

■ **Exercise 14.4** Combine into one or two sentences the separate elements listed after each number. Remember that you can combine the elements of the sentences in several different ways. There is no one best solution to any example.

1. Elizabeth Cruz is a bright young woman. She is planning ahead for her interview with New Horizons Enterprises. It is a young company. It has the reputation of being aggressive and willing to take risks. She might well be interested in working for the company if its prospects look promising.

2. The president of the company is a Cornell graduate. He is only thirty-six years old. He is already frequently mentioned in business journals. Some call him the Wizard Boy of Wall Street. They predict a brilliant future.

3. Elizabeth began by going to the library. She checked the business indexes to see what the company's standing was. She checked its financial standing in *Dun & Bradstreet*. She checked the papers to see how much its stock was worth. She looked back to find out about its enterprises over the last year.

4. She wrote down her findings. She used the techniques she had learned in class to analyze them. She began to have doubts about the company. Its financial standing looked inflated. Its stock fluctuated too much for her taste. New Horizons Enterprises was involved in some deals that looked pretty shaky to Elizabeth. She was not impressed.

5. At the end of her stint in the library, she made up her mind. She canceled the interview. She wanted nothing to do with Wizard's com-

pany. She predicted that his future holds more indictments than glory.

14d CAN YOU REVISE TO CORRECT FAULTY SENTENCE PREDICATION?

Troubleshooting

If the people reading your drafts tell you that your subjects can't do what the verbs say they're doing, they're probably talking about *faulty predication*. Such mismatched constructions are not always easy for writers themselves to see, but once identified, they're fairly easy to fix. When your readers call your attention to sentences that don't work, you can use the following guidelines to help yourself identify the problems and correct them.

To identify and repair faulty predication . . .

14d-1 Look first for an impersonal or abstract subject used with an active verb. Check the culprit sentence to see if you've paired an active verb with a subject that couldn't possibly do what the verb says it is doing. For instance:

Faulty   Ellen Gold's pleasure in gardening yearned for a bigger yard.

> The sentence is faulty because *pleasure* is impersonal and abstract; it can't *yearn*.

Acceptable   Ellen Gold's pleasure in gardening made her yearn for a bigger yard.

Faulty   The windows of the electronics store concentrate their attention on audiophiles.

> The sentence is faulty because *windows* are inanimate and can't *concentrate* on anything.

Acceptable   The windows full of electronic components are meant to draw audiophiles into the store.

14d-2 Look for a sentence that has a subject and a linking verb but ends with a complement that can't complete the linking verb. A linking verb gives the reader an equation sign: it says $A = B$. Thus the complement (completing word or phrase) on the right side of the equation has to match logically with the word on the left side of the equation. For example:

Faulty	Patriotism is an act most people admire.
	The construction is faulty because *patriotism* is an abstraction, not an act.
Acceptable	Patriotism is a quality most people admire.
Faulty	The kinds of trips we love to take are hunting and fishing.
	The construction is faulty because *kinds of trips* on one side of the linking verb *are* can't be equated with *hunting and fishing* on the other side.
Acceptable	We love to take hunting and fishing trips.

**14d
pred**

● **Tip**

You are less likely to get into faulty predication tangles if you remember to start your sentences with concrete or personal subjects. ●

14d-3 **Look for a subject plus transitive verb construction paired with an object that can't fit with the verb.** **Transitive verbs** (verbs that take an object) have to fit logically with the objects that come after them in a sentence. If they don't, they can confuse the reader, as in the following example.

Faulty	These negative attitudes intimidate the enthusiasm of volunteers.
	The sentence is faulty because *intimidate* can't take *enthusiasm* as its object.
Acceptable	These negative attitudes undermine the enthusiasm of volunteers.

● **Tip**

When you use the phrase "(Something) is when . . . ," you're making a predication error. For example:

Bad taste **is when** you hurt someone's feelings.
Joint custody **is when** both parents have equal responsibility.

These sentences should read as follows.

Bad taste is hurting someone's feelings.
Joint custody means that both parents have equal responsibility.

Although your readers are likely to understand what you mean, the construction is still nonstandard. To avoid the problem, don't use the phrase "is when" when you write a definition. ●

■ **Exercise 14.5** Work with a group to rewrite the following sentences and untangle the faulty predication. You may find more than one way to revise any sentence.

1. Darren's college clothes feel no suitability for business.
2. However, new clothes are a difficult decision for him.
3. Inflexible is not Darren's problem; in fact, his new attitude agrees to wear a suit.
4. His first necessity, though, is in the form of a loan.
5. The thought of Darren in a suit amazed his parents' picture of him.

14d
pred

CHAPTER

15

Can You Revise
for More Polished Sentences?

A Revising for More Varied Sentences
B Revising to Add Detail
C Revising for More Stylish Sentences

The most important job any sentence has is to communicate an idea clearly, and that should be your first priority when you're writing. But just as there is more to cooking than preparing wholesome and nutritious food, there's more to writing than crafting clear, straightforward sentences. You can also revise your sentences to make them a pleasure to read because they are varied, skillfully arranged, and rich with detail. If you enjoy working with your sentences at that level, we offer some suggestions in this chapter.

15a CAN YOU REVISE FOR MORE VARIED SENTENCES?

Troubleshooting

To avoid getting caught in tangles, writers sometimes fall back on familiar patterns for most of their sentences. The most reliable formulas are the old standbys, S-V-O (subject-verb-object) and S-V-C (subject-verb-complement).

subj.   verb   obj.
S-V-O: Nancy booted up the computer.

subj. verb   comp.
S-V-C: Nancy is a doctoral student.

These patterns are basic in English, and they work well. But you need to vary them occasionally to keep your writing from becoming monotonous. It's useful, then, to become aware of some other patterns to experiment with when you revise.

To achieve more variety in your sentence patterns . . .

15a–1 **Change the usual sentence patterns by inverting the typical order and moving information.** See if you can reorganize S-V-O or S-V-C patterns by putting the verb or complement at the beginning of a sentence or even by turning a sentence into a question. You can also move information around within your sentences. For example, here is a paragraph that is solid and clear but rather monotonous because most of the sentences have the same subject-verb pattern.

15a
varied

Original

The boots a person wears are too often considered a social symbol. People believe the more expensive the boots, the better the cowboy. Most often urban cowboys will sport the most expensive boots. They wear these to social events, on dates, and to dances, never setting foot on the ranch or farm. The true cowboy can be seen in old, dirty, well-worn boots most of the time. The true cowboy buys boots for durability.

Now let's change some of the sentence openings and invert a few patterns.

Revised for sentence variety

Too often, the boots a person wears become a social symbol. The more expensive the boots, the better the cowboy, some people seem to believe. But who really wears the most expensive boots? Often it's urban cowboys, who wear them to social events, on dates, and to dances, but never set foot on the ranch or farm. On the other hand, most of the time the true cowboy can be seen in old, dirty, well-worn boots bought for durability.

You could find other equally good ways to change sentence patterns to improve the paragraph.

Let's look at ways patterns for individual sentences can be turned around. The originals are from student papers.

Original

Many sociologists concerned with the fairness of standardized tests have determined that the type of questions, if not their very wording, is biased in favor of higher-income groups.

Variation 1	Are standardized tests fair? Many sociologists concerned with such tests believe that the questions, and perhaps even their wording, are biased in favor of higher-income groups.
Variation 2	In judging the fairness of standardized tests, many experts say that the test questions, and perhaps even their wording, are biased in favor of higher-income groups.
Original	The rock-and-roll protest songs of the 1960s were the musicians' way of expressing their opinions and criticisms of political and social events.
Variation 1	To express their opinions and criticisms of political and social events, rock-and-roll musicians of the 1960s wrote protest songs.
Variation 2	In the 1960s, rock-and-roll musicians wrote protest songs as a way of expressing their opinions and criticisms of political and social events.

In the left margin: **15a varied**

In neither of these examples are the variations necessarily *better* than the original. They're just different, and they show some of the many options for crafting sentences.

TRICKY

15a-2 Vary sentence length. One way to add variety to your sentences is to use sentences of different lengths in one paragraph. To some extent, of course, you'll consider who your readers are and what kind of writing you're doing when deciding how long your sentences should be. If you're explaining a process to an uninformed audience or writing for very young readers, you'll want to use relatively short sentences most of the time. If you're writing a long article on a complex topic for a well-informed audience, your sentences will probably be longer.

Regardless of the kind of writing you're doing, however, it's always smart to check sentence length. If you've produced a cluster of short sentences, your writing may seem choppy. On the other hand, if your sentences are somewhat longer but all about the same length, your writing may seem monotonous. You'll achieve a more graceful style by breaking up some of those long sentences.

Here is an example of a paragraph that is monotonous because all of the sentences are too nearly the same length.

Original

Our impressions of people are in large part based on our interpretation of their body language. We notice whether or not someone meets our gaze, fidgets constantly, or gestures when speaking. We use our observations to deduce personality traits such as arrogance, submissiveness, or trustworthiness. Most of us are very confident in our ability to judge personality by reading body language. We reason that these skills must be highly developed since we rely on them all the time. Recent research shows that most people can read emotion and gauge social skills from nonverbal signals. They consistently miss or misunderstand cues to more subtle personality traits, however.

15a
varied

Revised for variety

Our impressions of people are in large part based on our interpretation of their body language. Does someone meet our gaze or look away? Does he fidget? Does she gesture? From nonverbal cues such as these we draw our conclusions: this person is arrogant, that one is trustworthy. Most of us are quite confident in our ability to judge personality from nonverbal cues—after all, we've been doing it all our lives. But how accurate are we really? Not very, it turns out. Recent research reveals that while most people can read emotion and gauge social skills correctly, they consistently miss or misunderstand nonverbal cues to more subtle personality traits.

15a-3 **Remember the power of short sentences.** Vary the rhythms of your writing by occasionally using short, direct sentences. They're good for catching your readers' attention at the beginnings of paragraphs or for highlighting important points. Mixed with longer sentences, they can mark the confident writer, someone who wants to say what he or she means boldly, without embroidery. Notice their effect in the following example.

It [the earthquake] began with a vague rolling sensation, accompanied by the tinkling of glass. Small household items fell and shattered. Then a sudden lurch moved homes, unearthed ancient trees and toppled bridges. Within 15 seconds the seizure stopped.
—"When the Earth Rumbles," *U.S. News & World Report.*

■ **Exercise 15.1** Work out at least two ways to revise each of these sentences by changing the pattern. For at least one revision, try making a person the subject of the sentence.

1. The habit of looking other people straight in the eye seems like a sign of confidence and power to many, but researchers say that interpretation isn't necessarily accurate.

2. It is more likely that a person who doesn't fiddle with things during a conversation is someone apt to have a strong, dominant personality.

3. Nonverbal cues frequently help personnel managers to assess the personalities of prospective employees.

4. Some studies have shown, however, that personnel managers are not necessarily better than anyone else at reading body language.

5. One reason it is difficult to tell when someone is telling the truth is that the fear of being disbelieved looks the same as the fear of being caught in a lie.

15b CAN YOU REVISE TO ADD MORE DETAIL TO YOUR SENTENCES?

Troubleshooting

CAUTION You may be writing papers that are clear and well focused, but your readers are asking for more details. They think your papers could be much richer and more vivid. One way to make sentences interesting is to expand them with additional information.

To enrich your papers . . .

15b-1 Add details by embedding. One way to enliven a sentence is to embed information or concrete details at the beginning, in the middle, or at the end.

You can embed additional information at the beginning of a sentence by putting details in an introductory clause or phrase. For example:

Original sentence
The humanist scholar Erasmus took up the study of Greek in 1499 at the age of thirty-four.

Expanded through embedding an introductory phrase
Convinced that he could not understand the classical world with only Latin at his command, the humanist scholar Erasmus took up the study of Greek in 1499 at the age of thirty-four.

You can embed additional information in the middle of a sentence by inserting an appositive clause or phrase that gives more details about somebody or something in the sentence. For example:

Original sentence

Li Po drowned when he fell out of a boat while trying to kiss the re-flection of the moon in the water.

Expanded through embedding an appositive

Li Po, one of the greatest of all Chinese poets, drowned when he fell out of a boat while trying to kiss the reflection of the moon in the water.

You can expand a sentence by giving additional details in a final modifier added at the end, usually after a comma. For example:

15b
detail

Original sentence

Sixteenth-century Aztec youths played a complex game called *ollamalitzli.*

Expanded through embedding a final modifier

Sixteenth-century Aztec youths played a complex game called *ollamalitzli,* which some authorities believe to have been a fore-runner of the modern game of basketball.

15b–2 **Add details by downshifting.** Remember that downshifting involves writing paragraphs that go from a sentence making a general statement to sentences that give additional concrete details. We have discussed this strategy for making your writing more specific in Section 7a–3. You can also use it effectively by adding clauses to a sentence.

Original

Toi Soldier was a magnificent black Arabian stallion.

Revision by downshifting

Toi Soldier was a magnificent black Arabian stallion, **with a fine head held high on an arched neck and large, beautiful eyes.**

Original

He was a formidable competitor in any Arabian horse show.

Revision by downshifting

He was a formidable competitor in any Arabian horse show, **equally skilled in equitation classes, under harness, or in park horse classes**.

● **Tip**

When you add details to sentences, you may not be sure whether you are embedding an appositive, adding a final modifier, or downshift-ing. It really doesn't matter whether you can label what you're doing. The point is, you're making your sentences richer and more interesting with additional information. ●

15b
detail

WINDOW ON WRITING: Enriching a Sentence with Details

Notice how Cindy Noland enriches a sentence in a paper she wrote about the movie *Body Heat*. Her original sentence was this.

```
Femme fatale Kathleen Turner keeps half-witted

lawyer William Hurt biting the apple until the

very last.
```

In her revision, that sentence became this.

```
In a labyrinth of suspense and eroticism, Kathleen

Turner keeps half-witted lawyer William Hurt biting

the apple until the very last, when he can't even be

sure if she is dead or alive.
```

■ **Exercise 15.2** Expand these sentences by adding an introductory phrase or clause. For example:

Original   Marion Keillor willed her luxurious co-op apartment to her two Burmese cats.

Expanded   Much to the dismay of her four venal children, Marion Keillor willed her luxurious co-op apartment to her two Burmese cats.

1. Mrs. Keillor enjoyed creating trouble when she was alive and was pleased to have found a way to continue doing so after she died.
2. Her own lawyer referred to her as a cantankerous crackpot.
3. The two cats continue to live in the apartment, scratching the antique furniture and biting the hands that feed them.
4. Mrs. Keillor's children often try to visit, but they never seem to find the cats at home.
5. The children don't realize that the cats have simply bribed the doorman not to let them in.

■ **Exercise 15.3** Working with others in a group, explore ways to expand these sentences by inserting an appositive with additional information somewhere in the body of the sentence. For example:

Original   Electric cars may finally have come of age.

Expanded   Electric cars, the perennial hope of the environmentally concerned, may finally have come of age.

1. An electric car will soon be available commercially in the United States.
2. With a range of sixty miles per battery charge, it is intended for short trips rather than longer journeys.
3. Because most people are wary of electric cars, the sedan will also have an internal combustion engine as a backup.
4. Perhaps the surest sign that electric cars are here to stay is that the major American automobile manufacturers all have electric cars in development.
5. Los Angeles plans to be the first "electric-vehicle-ready" city in the United States.

15c style

■ **Exercise 15.4** Working with other students in a group, explore ways to expand the following sentences by adding a final modifier at the end. For example:

Original   In the fashionable world of tennis, fans increasingly show up for a game all dressed to play.

Expanded   In the fashionable world of tennis, fans increasingly show up for a game all dressed to play, particularly at major tournaments.

1. Tennis fans well past their athletic prime clothe themselves from head to foot in designer tennis togs.
2. Many even carry rackets.
3. No one regards the phenomenon with a more jaded eye than the young attendants at these tournaments.
4. Beverages, too, are important status indicators.
5. Perhaps the most important status symbol, however, is seat location.

15c   CAN YOU REVISE FOR MORE STYLISH SENTENCES?

Troubleshooting

Perhaps your instructor or fellow students have few specific suggestions for improving your drafts, but they're saying, "See if you can make your sentences a little more polished and stylish" or "This is good, but you could fine-tune it a little." Such comments don't help much in telling you what to do; you just have to tinker around, adding, pruning, rearranging, and editing. But that toying with your sentences can be fun, and you can get some gratifying results.

To polish your sentences . . .

15c–1 **Highlight points with balanced sentences.** Try reorganizing some of your sentences into the dramatic patterns of the balanced sentence. Notice how much more forceful and rhythmic the following sentences are when they are recast into balanced patterns.

15c
style

Original	Nearly everyone in our culture takes computers for granted these days, but that doesn't mean they really understand what computers do.
Revised	Most people in our culture take computers for granted; few understand what they do.
Original	Although the general public seems to believe computers are magic machines that can work miracles, those who really understand computers know they are limited machines.
Revised	Those who are awed by computers think they can work miracles, but those who understand them know how limited they are.

15c–2 **Use parallel patterns to highlight ideas.** Although they resemble balanced sentences, sentences with a parallel structure are more flexible. They can go beyond showing contrast to building emphasis for an idea and setting up a rhythm in your writing. For even stronger emphasis, you can write a series of sentences that follow the same pattern. Here are examples of both strategies.

Original
The advertising agency hoped to change its image from a firm that seemed amateurish, dated, and set in its ways to one that seemed professional, forward-looking, flexible, and open to new ideas.

Possible revision
The advertising agency hoped to change its image to a firm that seemed **not amateurish but professional, not dated but forward-looking, not set in its ways but flexible and open to new ideas.**

Original
The young entrepreneurs decided to go to a national small business conference and buy space for a booth in order to publicize their

product and attract investors. The expense was considerable, but they had confidence in themselves and in their product. They also had confidence that the market was there and they could beat the competition.

Possible revision

The young entrepreneurs decided to go to a national small business conference and buy space for a booth in order to publicize their product and attract investors. It was an expensive move, **but they had confidence in themselves. They had confidence in their product. They had confidence that the market was there. And they had confidence that they could beat the competition.**

**15c
style**

■ **Exercise 15.5** Working in a group, explore ways you could rewrite the following sentences as balanced sentences. Here is an example.

> **Original** While many people dream about the United States, the difficulty of starting a new life here is something that few people realize.
>
> **Balanced** Many people dream about the United States; few realize how difficult starting a new life here will be.

1. In southern California, a vigorous Vietnamese community has grown up in towns such as Westminster, where the Asian Garden Mall, a shopping center, is the site of a flourishing Vietnamese culture.
2. In most American malls, stores with names such as Athlete's Foot and Harriet's Health Food preside over a constant din of English, but Sai-Gon Color Lab and Van Hoi Xuan Chinese Herbs hum with Vietnamese conversation in the Asian Garden Mall.
3. For the older refugees, who struggled through the tortured years of their country's bid for independence, the California mall is a gleaming re-creation of Saigon as they wish it could have been; yet the mall is just one facet of their children's broader American lives, since the young know Vietnam only from photographs and reminiscences.
4. Every new group of immigrants experiences this growing generation gap, and the pain it causes parents and children is part of each new addition to America's ethnic mosaic.
5. Those who remember feel the tug of the past, while the future calls to those not burdened with memories.

■ **Exercise 15.6** Working with other students in a group, try to rewrite the following sentences so each will be a parallel sentence with a repeated pattern. You can break some sentences into two or three sentences if you like. Here is an example.

Original Driving straight through the night, the four first-year students got home in just under thirty hours, with everyone exhausted but eager to see old friends and feeling both nervous and excited about the reunion.

Revision Driving straight through the night, the four first-year students got home in just under thirty hours, **exhausted but eager to see old friends, nervous but excited about the reunion.**

15c
style

1. The whole affair had been Jason's idea, and it was he who had drawn up the guest list and mailed the invitations as well as hiring the band and arranging for the food.
2. Arriving at the reunion, they found the party in full swing, which is when it hit them: they had never liked their classmates or their high school, nor had they ever even entertained much affection for Jason.
3. Looking around the room, they felt as though they were regressing: Frank was still a dweeb and *pretentious* was still the word that best described Virginia; Harriet was wearing a ridiculous outfit and still couldn't dance to save her life, while George, trying to look cool in sunglasses, was about to trip over the guitar cables.
4. The four wondered whether these people would ever change or whether the lights would never go on; would they ever grow or improve, was maturation possible and could progress ever be made?
5. While driving back the next day they had a good laugh over the way the class couple, who had grown to loathe each other, had smiled lovingly for the camera; the reunion cake bursting into flames also gave them a laugh, and how handy it was that there had been a fire extinguisher.

III

Grammar and Usage

Grammar and usage are the rules of the language game. Like the length of a football field or the number of outs in an inning of baseball, some rules and usages of grammar are relatively stable. Other grammatical conventions change more often, like the size and weight of a baseball or the rules for tackling a quarterback.

What follows is not a comprehensive description of English grammar, but a sort of "playbook" describing problems you are most likely to encounter when writing—and ways to deal with them.

Problems with Subject-Verb Agreement?

A Subject Singular or Plural
B Subject an Indefinite Pronoun
C Subject a Collective Noun
D Subject Separated from Verb
E Subject Hard to Identify

16a AGREEMENT: IS THE SUBJECT SINGULAR OR PLURAL?

Troubleshooting

A *verb* describes the action of a sentence or expresses a state of being.

verb
The wind **increases.**

verb
Predicting violent weather **is** difficult.

A *subject* names what or whom a sentence is about. The subject ordinarily performs the action described by the verb in a sentence.

subj.
A *squall line* approaches.

subj.
Much turbulent weather threatens the high plains every year.

A verb may change its form, depending upon whether its subject is singular or plural. The verb is then said to *agree in number* with its subject. With verbs in the present tense, agreement in number is relatively simple: most subjects take the base form of the verb. The base form is the word produced when *to* is placed before the verb: to *wait*; to *go*.

First person, singular, present tense: I wait.
Second person, singular, present tense: You wait.
First person, plural, present tense: We wait.
Second person, plural, present tense: You go.
Third person, plural, present tense: They go.

The single notable exception to this pattern occurs with third person singular subjects (for example, *he, she, it, Irene*). A regular verb in the present tense needs an *-s* or *-es* ending.

Third person, singular, present tense: Irene wait**s**.
                                       He wait**s**.
                                       She go**es**.

So to choose a correct verb form in the third person you must know whether the subject of a sentence is singular or plural. Sometimes it isn't easy to tell, especially with constructions that seem to form compound subjects—which usually *are* plural.

An editor will usually indicate a problem with agreement by placing the abbreviation *agr* near a faulty verb.

Hail and a rotating wall cloud(**indicates**) the possibility of a tornado. *agr*

16a
s-v ag

To be sure subjects and verbs agree in number . . .

16a-1 Pay attention only to the subject itself when a subject is linked to another noun by expressions such as *along with, as well as,* or *together with.*   The verb agrees with the subject, not with the second noun. In the following sentence, for example, a singular subject, *The National Weather Service*, is tied to another possible subject, *police officers*, by the expression *as well as*. Despite the nearness of the plural noun *officers*, the subject remains singular.

         sing. subj.   plural noun   verb
The National Weather Service, as well as many *police officers*, **wishes** amateurs wouldn't chase severe storms in their cars.

The same principle holds when a plural subject (*amateurs*) is linked to a singular noun (*press*).

         plural subj.   sing. noun   verb
Many *amateurs*, along with the *press*, **chase** storms in the American heartland.

16a-2 **In most cases, treat subjects joined by _and_ as plural.** Joining two subjects this way creates a _compound subject._

> 1st subj. + 2nd subj.   verb
> _Storm chasers and newspeople_ alike **want** great pictures of tornadoes.

> subj. + subj.   verb
> _The press and storm chasers_ alike **risk** their lives in the hazardous weather.

> subj. + subj.   verb
> _Meteorologists and the police_ **believe** the storm chasers often don't appreciate the magnitude of the great storms.

However, a few subjects joined by _and_ do describe a single thing or idea. Treat such expressions as singular.

> subj.   verb
> _Peace and quiet_ **is** rare on the plains in spring.

> subj.   verb
> _Rock and roll_ **is** as noisy as a thunderclap.

Similarly, when a compound subject linked by _and_ is modified by _every_ or _each_, the verb takes a singular form.

> subj. + subj.   verb
> _Every wall cloud and supercell_ **holds** the potential for a tornado.

> subj. + subj.   verb
> _Each spring and each fall_ **brings** the danger of more storms.

However, when _each_ follows a compound subject, usage varies.

> The meteorologist and the storm chaser each **have** their reasons for studying the weather.

> The meteorologist and the storm chaser each **has** his or her story to tell.

16a-3 **When subjects are joined by _or_, _neither . . . nor_, or _either . . . or_, be sure the verb (or its auxiliary) agrees with the subject closer to it.** Study these examples to understand how this guideline works. The arrows point to the subjects nearer the verbs.

> plural   sing.
> _Neither police officers nor the National Weather Service_ **is** able to prevent people from tracking dangerous storms.

> sing.   plural
> _Either severe lightning or powerful bouts of hail_ **are** apt to accompany the development of a supercell.

16a
s-v ag

sing.   plural

Does *the danger or the thrills of storm chasing* attract people to the "sport"?

plural   sing.

Do *the thrills of storm chasing or the danger* attract people to the "sport"?

plural   plural

Heavy rains or strong winds **cause** much damage.

sing.   sing.

Heavy rain or baseball-size hail **causes** the most damage.

The rule holds when one or both of the subjects joined by *or, either . . . or,* or *neither . . . nor* are pronouns: the verb agrees with the nearer subject.

> Neither *she* nor *we* **admit** to an opinion about the weather.
>
> Neither *we* nor *she* **admits** to an opinion about the weather.
>
> Neither *Jimail* nor *I* **have** any weather predictions today.
>
> Neither *I* nor *Jimail* **has** any weather predictions today.

Notice that when both subjects are singular, the verb may change to reflect a shift from a first person subject (*I*) to a third person subject (*Jimail*).

If a construction seems especially awkward, it can be revised—usually by making the verb plural or rewriting the sentence.

Awkward	Neither *you* nor *I* **am** bothered by thunder.
Better	Neither *I* nor *you* **are** bothered by thunder.
Better	*We* **are** not bothered by thunder.

▶ **Fine Tuning**

When subjects linked to expressions such as *as well as, along with,* or *together with* sound awkward with a singular verb, consider joining the subjects with *and* instead.

Slightly awkward	*The National Weather Service,* as well as local storm chasers, **considers** tornadoes unlikely today.
Better	*The National Weather Service and local storm chasers* **consider** tornadoes unlikely today. ◀

■ **Exercise 16.1** Decide which verb in boldface is correct.

1. Danger of all types (**continue/continues**) to attract people.

**16a
s-v ag**

2. The plains states, where dry air from the Rockies meets moisture from the Gulf of Mexico, (**has/have**) the highest incidence of tornadoes in the world.

3. A supercell and its wind currents (**undergo/undergoes**) changes as a tornado forms.

4. The storm chaser, like other thrill seekers, (**learn/learns**) to minimize the dangers of the hunt.

5. The Weather Channel on TV and the car radio (**become/becomes**) essential to the storm tracker.

6. Neither a clear sky nor the absence of wind (**mean/means**) that a storm won't develop.

7. It's unlikely that either the dangers or the boredom of storm chasing (**is/are**) going to discourage the dedicated amateur.

8. Gin and tonic (**doesn't/don't**) mix with driving in any kind of weather.

9. Every meteorologist and storm chaser (**know/knows**) that neither straight-line storms nor a tornado (**is/are**) predictable.

10. An increase in the number of serious storm watchers (**has/have**) occurred in the last decade.

16b
s-v ag

16b   AGREEMENT: IS THE SUBJECT AN INDEFINITE PRONOUN?

Troubleshooting

Indefinite pronouns are pronouns that do not refer to a particular person, thing, or group. Because it's sometimes hard to tell whether these pronouns—words like *each, none, everybody, everyone,* and *any*—are singular or plural, you may have trouble selecting a verb to agree in number with such a pronoun.

> *Each* (**has? have?**) strong ideas about building a new stadium.
>
> *None* of the development groups (**has? have?**) a lock on ideas for community development.

In both examples, **has** is the correct verb.

To be sure verbs agree with indefinite pronouns as subjects . . .

Use the following chart (or a dictionary) to determine whether a pronoun is singular, plural, or variable; then select the appropriate verb form.

> ### CHART
>
> **Indefinite Pronouns**
>
> | **Singular** | **Variable, singular or plural** | **Plural** |
> |---|---|---|
> | anybody | all | few |
> | anyone | any | many |
> | anything | either | several |
> | each | more | |
> | everybody | most | |
> | everyone | neither | |
> | everything | none | |
> | nobody | some | |
> | no one | | |
> | nothing | | |
> | somebody | | |
> | someone | | |
> | something | | |

The most troublesome indefinite pronouns are *each* and *none*. *Each* is singular in college writing; *none* varies but is usually singular. Indefinites such as *either* and *neither* are also difficult because, although singular in academic writing, they are generally plural in informal writing. The examples below show the forms to use in college.

Singular	*Each* **believes** decisive action needs to be taken.
Singular	*Nobody* **knows** what the ball club will do.
Variable	*None* of the proposals **is** easy to finance.
Variable	*None* but the stupid **favor** higher taxes.
Plural	*Many* in sports bars **hope** for a new stadium.
Plural	*Few* **intend** to pay higher ticket prices.

■ **Exercise 16.2** Decide which verb in boldface would be correct in academic writing.

1. A few of the ethnic communities in American cities (**is/are**) relative newcomers.
2. Formerly, most of the ethnic groups (**was/were**) from Europe.
3. Most of New York's immigrants (**is/are**) now non-European.

4. Everybody (**seem/seems**) to have something to contribute.
5. None of the residents (**find/finds**) the ethnic mix odd.
6. None but the least observant (**expect/expects**) ethnic influences to decrease.
7. Nobody in the city (**run/runs**) politics anymore.
8. Everybody (**expect/expects**) a piece of the pie.
9. Few (**has/have**) the wish to be silent.
10. All of the groups in the city (**want/wants**) to be heard.

16c AGREEMENT: IS THE SUBJECT A COLLECTIVE NOUN?

Troubleshooting

Collective nouns are nouns that name a group: *team*, *choir*, *band*, *orchestra*, *jury*, *committee*, *faculty*, *family*. Some collective nouns may be either singular or plural, depending on how you treat them. You often must decide, then, whether your subject will be singular or plural. Here is a sentence with the subject treated as singular.

> The *Bucci family* **believes** that *its* pizzeria business is helped by the Korean deli around the corner.

Here's the same sentence with the subject treated as plural.

> The *Bucci family* **believe** that *their* pizzeria business is helped by the Korean deli around the corner.

Both versions are acceptable.

To be sure verbs and collective nouns agree in number . . .

Decide whether a collective noun used as a subject acts as a single unit (the jury) or as separate individuals or parts (the twelve members of the jury). Then be consistent. If you decide the subject is singular, be sure its verb is singular. If the subject is plural, the verb should also be plural.

Singular	The *jury* **expects** its verdict to be controversial.
Plural	The *jury* **agree** not to discuss their verdict with the press.
Singular	The *choir* **expects** to choose a variety of hymns and chants.
Plural	The *choir* **raise** their voices in song.

Usually you'll do better to treat collective nouns as singular subjects.

16c
s-v ag

Notice how awkward the following sentences seem because the collective nouns are regarded as plural.

> The *family* **feel** that their interests aren't in jeopardy.
> The *choir* **seem** unable to make up their minds.

Revise sentences like these to make the collective subjects singular or more obviously plural.

Singular	The *family* **feels** that its interests aren't in jeopardy.
More obviously plural	The *members of the choir* **seem** unable to make up their minds.

The following chart should help you manage other collective subjects.

16c
s-v ag

C H A R T

Collective Nouns

SUBJECT	GUIDELINE	EXAMPLES
Measurements	Singular as a unit; plural as individual components.	*Five miles* is quite a long walk. *Five more miles* are ahead of us. *Six months* is the waiting period. *Six months* have passed.
Numbers	Singular in expressions of division and subtraction.	*Four* divided by *two* is two. *Four* minus *two* leaves two.
	Singular or plural in expressions of multiplication and addition.	*Two* times *two* is/are four. *Two* plus *two* is/are four.
Words ending in -ics	School subjects are usually singular.	*Physics* is a tough major. *Economics* is a useful minor. *Linguistics* is popular.
	Other -ics words vary; check a dictionary.	His *tactics* are shrewd. *Athletics* are expensive. *Ethics* is a noble study. Her *ethics* are questionable. *Politics* is fun. Francie's *politics* are radical.

SUBJECT	GUIDELINE	EXAMPLES
data	Plural in formal writing; often singular in informal writing.	The *data* are reliable. The *data* is reliable.
number	Singular if preceded by *the*; plural if preceded by *a*.	The *number* has grown. A *number* have left.
public	Singular as a unit; plural as individual people.	The *public* is satisfied. The *public* are here in great numbers.

■ **Exercise 16.3** Decide whether the collective subjects in the following sentences are being treated as singular or plural. Then select the appropriate verb form for academic writing.

16-d
s-v ag

1. Lieutenant Data **(reports/report)** to Captain Picard that the data on Klingon encroachments of the neutral zone **(is/are)** not subject to interpretation.
2. The crew of the Federation starship **(is/are)** eager to resolve the conflict.
3. Five years **(has/have)** passed since the last intergalactic crisis.
4. A number of weapons still **(needs/need)** to be brought on line, but the chief engineer reports that the actual number of inoperative systems **(is/are)** small.
5. The jury **(is/are)** still out as to whether a committee of Federation officials **(intends/intend)** to authorize action against the Klingons.

16d AGREEMENT: IS THE SUBJECT SEPARATED FROM ITS VERB?

Troubleshooting

Subject-verb agreement errors often occur when subjects are separated from their verbs by modifying words or phrases. Nouns nearer the verb can mistakenly seem like subjects.

The *killer whale*, the most widely distributed of all mammals, excepting only humans, **(demonstrates? demonstrate?)** highly complex social behavior.

Subject-verb agreement difficulties also arise when the subject of a sentence is an indefinite pronoun modified by a prepositional phrase. In cases like these, you have to pay attention both to the pronouns and the modifying phrases before choosing a verb.

Each of the whales **(makes? make?)** unique sounds.

To avoid disagreement between separated subjects and verbs . . .

16d–1 Be sure that a verb agrees in number with its real subject, not with other words that may stand between the subject and the verb. Modifying words or phrases often separate subjects and verbs, but such a separation does not change the subject-verb relationship.

> subj.   modifying phrase
> The *killer whale*, the most widely distributed of all mammals, excep-
>   verb
> ting only humans, **demonstrates** highly complex social behavior.

16-d
s-v ag

In the example above, the verb remains singular because its subject is singular. The plural nouns *mammals* and *humans* have no bearing on subject-verb agreement.

It is easy to mistake such nouns or pronouns for subjects because, standing closer to the verb than the subject does, they seem to determine its number. Remember that the phrase between the subject and verb only describes the subject; it is not the subject itself.

> subj.   modifying phrase
> *Researchers*, particularly any who have studied the killer whale on
> its own turf, not just in the limited environment of a theme park,
>   verb
> **appreciate** the intelligence of the creature.

16d–2 Remember that if a pronoun is always singular, it remains singular even if it is modified by a phrase with a plural noun in it. (See the chart on p. 282.) You are most likely to be confused when the subject of a sentence is an indefinite pronoun such as *each, everyone, all,* or *none* followed by a prepositional phrase. *Each*, for example, is usually singular in college usage, even when followed by a prepositional phrase (though this convention is often not observed in casual usage).

> subj.   verb
> *Each* of the whales **makes** unique sounds.
> *Each* of the animals **has** a personality.

When the indefinite pronoun varies in number (words such as *all, most, none, some*), the noun in the prepositional phrase determines whether the pronoun (and consequently the verb) is singular or plural.

Noun in prepositional phrase is singular
Some of the research **is** contradictory.

Noun in prepositional phrase is plural
Some of the younger whales **are** playful.

If the indefinite pronoun is more clearly plural, so is the verb.

ind. pron.   verb
A *few* in the scientific community **wonder** if the whale will survive.

ind. pron.   verb
Many very much **hope** so.

■ **Exercise 16.4** Choose the correct verb for academic writing.

16-e
s-v ag

1. Members of the mainstream scientific community, expecting strict adherence to traditional research methodology, generally (**dismisses/dismiss**) the work at Biosphere 2, an artificial ecosystem re-created in a giant greenhouse in the Arizona desert.
2. The proponents of the Biosphere 2 experiment, especially Jack Corliss, the chief scientist on the project, (**thinks/think**) important work is being done there.
3. Each of the five ecosystems re-created under the 3.2 acres of glass (**depends/depend**) on the others.
4. All the natural ecosystems in the upper level of Biosphere 2, an environment that duplicates a rain forest, a desert, and a grassland, (**is/are**) supported by machines in the basement.
5. The original Biospherians, a group of eight men and women who lived for two years sealed inside the huge greenhouse, (**is/are**) trailblazers for future space colonists.

16e   **AGREEMENT: IS THE SUBJECT HARD TO IDENTIFY?**

Troubleshooting

Occasionally you may simply lose track of a subject because the structure of a sentence is complicated or unusual. You may have trouble with clauses beginning with *here* or *there* or you may be confused by singular subjects tied to plural nouns by linking verbs. Inverted sentence structures can make agreement troublesome. And watch out for words like *series*, *portion*, and *majority* when they act as subjects. Remember the rule: Keep your eye on the subject.

To be sure subjects and verbs agree in number . . .

16e–1 **Don't lose track of your subject when a sentence or clause begins with *here* or *there*.** In such cases, the verb still agrees with the subject—which usually trails after it.

> **Singular subjects**
> Here **is** a surprising *turn* of events.
> There **is** a *reason* for the commotion.

> **Plural subjects**
> Here **are** my *tickets*.
> There **are** already *calls* for Coach Holcomb's resignation.

16e–2 **Don't be misled by linking verbs.** Common linking verbs are *to be, to seem, to appear, to feel, to taste, to look,* and *to become.* They connect subjects to words that extend or complete their meaning.

16-e
s-v ag

> Holcomb **was** head football coach.
> Many students **feel** betrayed.

A linking verb agrees with its subject even when a singular subject is linked to a plural noun.

> subj.   l.v.   plural noun
> Good *evidence* of the power of television **is** its effects on athletic careers.

> subj.   l.v. plural noun
> The *key* to a coach's success **is** victories.

The same is true when a linking verb connects a plural subject to a singular noun, but such sentences sound normal and don't ordinarily raise questions of agreement.

> plural subj. l.v.   sing. noun
> The many new *plays* **are** a tribute to Coach Holcomb's ingenuity.

16e–3 **Don't be misled by inverted sentence order.** A sentence is considered inverted when some portion of the verb precedes the subject. Inverted sentence structures occur most often in questions.

> verb   subj.
> Among those requesting Holcomb's resignation **were** many *alumni*.

> verb subj. verb
> **Does** he **intend** to switch quarterbacks for the last game?

A verb agrees with its subject, wherever the subject appears in the sentence.

verb   subj.   verb
Have their *cheerleading efforts* **inspired** the team?

verb   subj.
Also disappointed **is** the *athletic director*.

16e–4 **Don't mistake singular expressions for plural ones.** Singular terms such as *series, segment, portion, fragment,* and *part* usually remain singular even when modified by plural words.

> A *series* of questions **is** posed by a reporter.

> A substantial *portion* of many sports programs **is** devoted to prognostication.

The word *majority,* however, does not follow this guideline; it can be either singular or plural, depending on its use in a sentence. In this sentence, *majority* is treated as singular.

> The *majority* **rules.**

Yet it can also function as a plural noun.

> The *majority* of fans **want** Coach Holcomb's head on a platter.

▶ **Fine Tuning**

One of the subtlest subject-verb agreement problems occurs within clauses that include the phrase *one of those who.* In college English, the verb in such a clause is plural—even though it looks as if it should be singular.

> Holcomb is one of those coaches who never **seem** [not **seems**] dispirited.

The verb is plural because its subject is plural. To understand the situation more clearly, rearrange the sentence this way.

> Of those coaches *who* never **seem** dispirited, Holcomb is one.

Now watch what happens if you add the word *only* to the mix.

> Holcomb is the only one of the coaches who **seems** eternally optimistic.

Why is the verb singular here? The subject of the verb *seems* is still the pronoun *who,* but its antecedent is now the singular pronoun *one,* not the plural *coaches.* Again, it helps to rearrange the sentence to see who is doing what to whom.

> Of the coaches, Holcomb is the only one who **seems** eternally optimistic. ◀

16-e
s-v ag

■ **Exercise 16.5** Choose the correct verb.

1. The president of the university (**strides/stride**) to the microphone.
2. There (**is/are**) grumbles from the reporters, but the crowd (**take/takes**) their seats.
3. (**Does/Do**) the president's decision to fire Holcomb surprise anyone after a winless season?
4. The president claims that she is one of those people who (**objects/object**) most strongly to athletics taking precedence over academics.
5. But she knows she's not the only one who (**wants/want**) a nationally ranked football team.
6. (**Do/Does**) anyone object to the president's decision to fire Holcomb?
7. Apparently, few people in the auditorium (**does/do**), but this is not a situation in which the majority (**rules/rule**) anyway.

17

Problems with Verb Tense, Voice, and Mood?

A Choosing Verb Tenses
B Tense Consistency in Sentences
C Tense Consistency in Longer Passages
D Irregular Verbs
E Active and Passive Voice
F The Subjunctive

17a HOW DO YOU CHOOSE VERB TENSES?

Troubleshooting

Tense is that quality of a verb that expresses time. Tense is expressed through changes in verb forms and endings (*see, saw, seeing; work, worked*) and through the use of auxiliaries (*had seen, will have seen; had worked, had been working*).

Native speakers of English usually can find the verb tense they need when they write. Yet some writers rely on the simplest tenses only, even though more complex forms might better express the relationship between two actions.

Vague	Frank **was** reading the play for an hour when he **dozed** off.
More precise	Frank **had been reading** the play for an hour when he **dozed** off.

Writers need to have a clear sense of how to handle the various forms and tenses of English verbs.

Editors may simply write *tense* in the margin next to a sentence where some problem with tense is evident.

When she arrived, we will go. *tense?*

To manage verb tenses effectively . . .

17a–1 **Know the tenses and what they do.** Tense depends, in part, on *voice*. Verbs that take direct objects—that is, transitive verbs—can be either in **active** or in **passive voice.** They are in active voice when the subject in the sentence actually does what the verb describes.

subj.   action
Professor Belquist **invited** the press to the lecture.

They are in passive voice when the action described by the verb is done *to* the subject.

subj.   action
The press **was invited** by Professor Belquist to the lecture.

**17a
tense**

Below is a chart of English tenses—past, present, and future—in the *active voice*. (See also Section 17e on voice and the more complete Anatomy of a Verb on pp. 309–310.)

C H A R T

Verb Tenses in the Active Voice

WHAT IT IS CALLED	WHAT IT LOOKS LIKE	WHAT IT DOES
Past	I **answered** quickly.	Shows what happened at a particular time in the past.
Past progressive	I **was answering** when the alarm went off.	Shows something happening in the past at the same time something else happened in the past.
Present perfect	I **have answered** that question often.	Shows something that has happened more than once in the past.
Past perfect	I **had answered** the question twice when the alarm went off.	Shows what had already happened before another event, also in a past tense, occurred.

What it is called	**What it looks like**	**What it does**
Present	I **answer** when I must.	Shows what happens or can happen now.
Present progressive	I **am answering** now.	Shows what is happening now.
Future	I **will answer** tomorrow.	Shows what may happen in the future.
Future progressive	I **will be answering** the phones all day.	Shows something that will continue to happen in the future.
Future perfect	I **will have answered** all the charges before you see me again.	Shows what will have happened by some particular time in the future.
Future perfect progressive	I **will have been answering** the charges for three hours by the time you arrive at noon.	Shows a continuing future action that precedes some other event also in the future.

17a tense

Verbs usually look more complicated when they are in the *passive voice*, as shown in the following chart.

C H A R T

Verb Tenses in the Passive Voice

What it is called	**What it looks like**
Past	I **was invited** to her party last year.
Past progressive	I **was being invited** by Alicia when the phone went dead.
Present perfect	I **have been invited** to many of her parties.
Past perfect	I **had been invited** to this one too.
Present	I **am invited** to everyone's parties.
Present progressive	I **am being invited** now! That's Alicia calling, I'm sure.
Future	I **will be invited** tomorrow.
Future perfect	I **will have been invited** by this time tomorrow.

As you can see above, many tenses require **auxiliary verbs** such as *will*, *do*, *be*, and *have*. These auxiliary or helping verbs combine with other verbs to show relationships of tense, voice, and mood. Two important auxiliaries—*to have* and *to be*—are *irregular*. *Irregular* means that they show agreement by more than just an additional *-s* or *-es* in the third person singular. *To have* is only slightly irregular, forming its third person singular by changing *have* to *has*.

I have	we have
you have	you have
he/she/it *has*	they have

To be changes more often, in both the present and past tenses.

PRESENT	**PAST**
I am	I was
you are	you were
he/she/it is	he/she/it was
we are	we were
you are	you were
they are	they were

17a
tense

Other auxiliary verbs, such as *can, could, may, might, should, ought,* and *must,* help to indicate possibility, necessity, permission, desire, capability, and so on. These verbs are called **modal auxiliaries.** (See also Section 31b.)

Rosalind **can** write well.
Audrey **might** write well.
Joel **should** write well.

17a–2 **Use perfect tenses appropriately.** Some writers avoid the perfect tense in all its forms. The result can be imprecise sentences.

Vague	Audrey could not believe that Kyle actually **asked** her to pay for his lunch. simple past
Precise	Audrey could not believe that Kyle **had** actually **asked** her to pay for his lunch. past perfect

The perfect tenses enable a writer to show exactly how one event stands in relationship to another in time. Learn to use these forms; they make a difference. (See also Section 31a.)

Simple past	She already **quit** her job even before she knew that she failed the polygraph.
Past perfect	She **had** already **quit** her job even before she knew that she **had failed** the polygraph.

■ **Exercise 17.1** Replace the verb forms in parentheses below with more appropriate tenses. You may need to use a variety of verb forms (and auxiliaries), including passive and progressive forms. Treat all five sentences as part of a single paragraph.

1. Isambard Brunel **(design)** his ship the *Great Eastern* to be the largest vessel on the seas when it **(launch)** in 1857 in London.
2. Almost 700 feet long, the ship—originally named *Leviathan*—**(weigh)** more than 20,000 tons and **(power)** by a screw, paddle wheels, and sails.
3. Designed originally to be a luxurious passenger ship, the *Great Eastern* **(attain)** its greatest fame only after it **(refit)** to stretch the first transatlantic telegraph cable from England to Newfoundland.
4. In the summer of 1865, the *Great Eastern* **(lay)** cable for many difficult days when the thick line **(snap)** two-thirds of the way to Newfoundland. Nine days **(spend)** trying to recover the cable, but it never **(find)**.
5. Many people **(be)** skeptical that the *Great Eastern*, a jinxed ship, **(succeed)** in stretching a cable across the Atlantic, but it finally **(do)** so in 1866.

17a
tense

■ **Exercise 17.2** For each verb in parentheses, furnish the tense indicated. Use active voice unless passive is specified.

1. Frank retired to his room to read Shakespeare's *Macbeth*, the play his instructor **(assign**—perfect) earlier in class.
2. In the tragedy, three witches tell Macbeth that someday he **(rule**—future) Scotland.
3. Macbeth quickly explains to his wife, the ambitious Lady Macbeth, what the witches **(promise**—past perfect) him earlier that day, the Scottish crown.
4. Lady Macbeth, even more ambitious than her husband, immediately **(devise**—present) a plot to murder King Duncan that very night and then **(convince**—present) her husband to do the horrid deed.
5. But even though the plot succeeds, and Macbeth becomes king, the new ruler fears that he **(challenge**—future, passive voice) by other ambitious men.
6. For the witches also **(prophesy**—past perfect) that the children of Banquo **(be**—future) kings.
7. Macbeth decides that both Banquo and his son Fleance **(eliminate**—future, passive voice with modal auxiliary **must**).
8. And so one murder **(lead**—present) to another until the thanes of

Scotland, angered by Macbeth's bloody rule, (**conspire**—present) to remove the tyrant and his wife from the throne.

9. Macbeth is finally slain by Macduff, whose wife and children earlier in the play (**slaughter**—past perfect, passive voice) at Macbeth's orders.

10. "Gruesome stuff," Frank (**mutter**—past) to himself after closing his heavy edition of Shakespeare.

17b **PROBLEMS WITH TENSE CONSISTENCY IN SENTENCES?**

Troubleshooting

Verbs that go with the same subject often share the same verb tense and form. If they don't, the resulting sentences may be hard to read. The problem is often caused by *faulty parallelism*. Parallelism is an arrangement that gives related words, clauses, and phrases a similar pattern, making it easier for readers to see relationships between the parallel expressions. In the following sentence, the verbs are parallel because they all describe what the band is doing.

The college's marching band **played** out of tune, **marched** out of step, and yet **maintained** its dignity.

When parallelism is lacking, an editor will use double slashes to indicate a problem.

The lawyer **explained** the options to her client and **was recommending** a plea of guilty. //

When a single subject is followed by one or more verbs . . .

Check to be sure that verbs are alike in form. Don't shift the tenses or forms of parallel verbs needlessly. In the following example, the verbs describing the lawyer's action shift from past tense to past progressive tense without a good reason. The verbs lack parallelism.

Lack of parallelism   The *lawyer* **explained** the options to her client and **was recommending** a plea of guilty.

The sentence reads more smoothly when the verbs are parallel in form.

Revised for parallelism

subj. verb

The *lawyer* **explained** the options to her client and

verb

recommended a plea of guilty.

Of course, changes in verb tense within a sentence are appropriate when they indicate obvious shifts in time.

Currently, the lawyer **is defending** an accused murderer and soon **will be defending** a bigamist.

■ **Exercise 17.3** Correct any problems in tense consistency with the verbs in boldface.

1. In the middle of the nineteenth century, young French painters **were rejecting** the stilted traditions of academic art, **found** new methods and new subjects, and **would establish** the school of art one critic derided as "Impressionism."
2. The new artists **outraged** all the establishment critics and also **were challenging** all the expectations of Paris gallery owners.
3. Traditionalists thought that painters should **work** indoors, **depict** traditional subjects, and **be using** a balanced style that hid their brushwork.
4. But the youthful Impressionists, including artists like Monet, Degas, and Renoir, soon **were taking** their easels outdoors to the streets of Paris or to public gardens, **laying on** their colors thick and self-consciously, and **had been choosing** scenes from ordinary life to depict.
5. Now these revolutionary artists and their works **are regarded** as classics on their own and **being studied** and **are collected** by an artistic establishment they **are rocking** from its foundation a century ago.

17c
tense

17c **PROBLEMS WITH TENSE CONSISTENCY IN LONGER PASSAGES?**

Troubleshooting

Almost anything you write will involve the past, the present, and the future, and you use verb tenses to express these shifts in time. But writers are sometimes *inconsistent* about their choice of tenses; in longer passages, they may confuse their readers by pointlessly switching from tense to tense. Such shifts ought to be avoided.

To keep verb tenses consistent . . .

Establish a dominant time frame and stay with it. The following paragraph shows what can happen when verb forms shift inappropriately.

> After World War II and the dawn of the nuclear era, many horror movies **featured** monsters **spawned** by atomic explosions or bizarre scientific experiments. For two decades, audiences **flock** to movies with titles like *Godzilla, Them, Tarantula,* and *The Fly.* Theater screens **come** alive with gigantic lobsters, ants, birds, and lizards, which **spent** their time attacking London, Tokyo, and Washington while scientists **look** for ways to kill them.

The passage sounds confusing because it jumps between two possible time frames. The first is the past tense: "many horror movies *featured*." But subsequent sentences and clauses switch unexpectedly to the present tense: "audiences *flock*"; "theater screens *come* alive." Making the tenses consistent makes the passage more readable. Here it is in the past tense.

17c
tense

> After World War II and the dawn of the nuclear era, many horror movies **featured** monsters **spawned** by atomic explosions or bizarre scientific experiments. For two decades, audiences **flocked** to movies with titles like *Godzilla, Them, Tarantula,* and *The Fly.* Theater screens **came** alive with gigantic lobsters, ants, birds, and lizards, which **spent** their time attacking London, Tokyo, and Washington while scientists **looked** for ways to kill them.

It can also be revised to feature the present tense. Notice, however, that this shift does not simply put all verb forms in the present tense. One verbal (*spawned*) remains in the past tense.

> After World War II and the dawn of the nuclear era, many horror movies **feature** monsters **spawned** by atomic explosions or bizarre scientific experiments. For two decades, audiences **flock** to movies with titles like *Godzilla, Them, Tarantula,* and *The Fly.* Theater screens **come** alive with gigantic lobsters, ants, birds, and lizards, which **spend** their time attacking London, Tokyo, and Washington while scientists **look** for ways to kill them.

■ **Exercise 17.4** Revise the following paragraph to make the tenses more consistent. You may find it helpful to emphasize the present tense throughout the passage—but not every verb ought to be in the present. (Specific events in a literary work are usually described in present tense: After Macbeth *kills* King Duncan, he *seizes* the throne.) Verbs have been boldfaced for your convenience.

(1) *Macbeth*, one of Shakespeare's most popular plays, **is** also one of his shortest; almost all of Shakespeare's other tragedies **were** at least a thousand lines longer. (2) To explain this difference, some scholars **have been arguing** that the existing text of *Macbeth* **has been** a version shortened for stage production. (3) Others **are claiming** that the tragedy **was written** especially for King James I, who **preferred** short plays. (4) Whatever the explanation for its brevity, the drama undeniably **moved** breathlessly through its first three acts. (5) In a matter of moments, it **portrays** rebellion, conspiracy, and murder most foul. (6) The smoke of a battle **has** barely **cleared** when Macbeth **encountered** three witches who **promise** him the throne of Scotland. (7) Almost immediately, his wife **persuades** him—against his good conscience—to act, and he **has murdered** King Duncan while the old man **sleeps.** (8) But Macbeth **will sleep** no more; the play **gives** him little comfort until after he **murders** his friend Banquo. (9) Only in the fourth act **did** the pace slacken, but the action **rose** again in the fifth toward an intense and violent conclusion. (10) If *Macbeth* **left** audiences asking for more, it **may be** because it **offers** just a little less.

17d
irreg

17d PROBLEMS WITH IRREGULAR VERBS?

Troubleshooting

At some time or another almost everyone hesitates about verb forms: is it *drove* or *driven, swam* or *swum, hung* or *hanged*? These troublesome verbs are usually the ones described as *irregular.* Understanding irregular verbs requires a little background information.

All verb tenses are built from three basic forms, which are called the *principal parts of a verb.* The three principal parts of the verb are these.

- **Infinitive** (or **present**) This is the base form of a verb, what it looks like when preceded by the word *to: to walk; to go; to choose.*
- **Past** This is the simplest form of a verb to show action that has already occurred: *walked; went; chose.*
- **Past participle** This is the form a verb takes when it is accompanied by an **auxiliary verb** to show a more complicated past tense: *had* **walked;** *will have* **gone;** *would have* **chosen;** *was* **hanged;** *might have* **broken.**

Here are the three principal parts of several regular verbs.

PRESENT	PAST	PAST PARTICIPLE
talk	talk**ed**	talk**ed**
coincide	coincide**d**	coincide**d**
advertise	advertise**d**	advertise**d**

As you can see, **regular verbs** form their past and past participle forms simply by adding *-d* or *-ed* to the infinitive. **Irregular verbs,** however, do not form their past and past participle forms so simply. Instead, they change their forms in various ways; a few even have the same form for all three principal parts.

PRESENT	PAST	PAST PARTICIPLE
burst	burst	burst
drink	drank	drunk
arise	arose	arisen
lose	lost	lost

**17d
irreg**

The English verbs we use most often tend to be irregular, so most writers master these forms quickly. But certain verbs are persistently troublesome. With such verbs, you may need help.

To be sure the form of an irregular verb is correct . . .

 Consult a dictionary or check the following list of irregular verbs. The list below of troublesome irregular English verbs gives you three forms: (1) the present tense, (2) the simple past tense, and (3) the past participle. (The past participle is used with auxiliary verbs to form verb phrases: *I have ridden, I had ridden, I will have ridden.*)

Most problems occur in distinguishing between the past tense and the past participle (*wore, worn; lay, lain*). As you will discover from the list, sometimes these forms will be identical (*brought, brought; found, found*). And sometimes there may be more than one acceptable form (*dived, dove*). Your safest bet, when in doubt, is to check the list, because studies show that errors in verb form irritate readers a great deal.

CHART

Irregular Verbs

PRESENT	PAST	PAST PARTICIPLE
arise	arose	arisen
bear (carry)	bore	borne

PRESENT	**PAST**	**PAST PARTICIPLE**
bear (give birth)	bore	borne, born
become	became	become
begin	began	begun
bite	bit	bitten, bit
blow	blew	blown
break	broke	broken
bring	brought	brought
burst	burst	burst
buy	bought	bought
catch	caught	caught
choose	chose	chosen
cling	clung	clung
come	came	come
creep	crept	crept
dig	dug	dug
dive	dived, dove	dived
do	did	done
draw	drew	drawn
dream	dreamed, dreamt	dreamed, dreamt
drink	drank	drunk
drive	drove	driven
eat	ate	eaten
fall	fell	fallen
find	found	found
fly	flew	flown
forget	forgot	forgotten
forgive	forgave	forgiven
freeze	froze	frozen
get	got	got, gotten
give	gave	given
go	went	gone
grow	grew	grown
hang (an object)	hung	hung
hang (a person)	hanged, hung	hanged, hung
know	knew	known
lay (to place)	laid	laid
lead	led	led
leave	left	left
lend	lent	lent
lie (to recline)	lay	lain
light	lighted, lit	lighted, lit
lose	lost	lost

17d irreg

(continued)

Irregular Verbs (*continued*)

PRESENT	PAST	PAST PARTICIPLE
pay	paid	paid
plead	pled, pleaded	pled, pleaded
prove	proved	proved, proven
ride	rode	ridden
ring	rang, rung	rung
rise	rose	risen
run	ran	run
say	said	said
see	saw	seen
set	set	set
shake	shook	shaken
shine	shone, shined	shone, shined
show	showed	showed, shown
shrink	shrank, shrunk	shrunk
sing	sang, sung	sung
sink	sank, sunk	sunk, sunken
sit	sat	sat
speak	spoke	spoken
spring	sprang, sprung	sprung
stand	stood	stood
steal	stole	stolen
sting	stung	stung
swear	swore	sworn
swim	swam, swum	swum
swing	swung	swung
take	took	taken
tear	tore	torn
throw	threw	thrown
wake	waked, woke	waked, woken
wear	wore	worn
wring	wrung	wrung
write	wrote	written

17d irreg

The glossary at the end of this handbook treats various troublesome verbs in greater detail, including some listed above. Check the entries for *can/may*, *get/got/gotten*, *lie/lay*, *set/sit*, and so on.

■ **Exercise 17.5** Choose the correct verb form from the choices in parentheses. In some cases, you may want to consult the glossary for assistance.

1. Buck wondered whether the director had (**spoke/spoken**) too soon in welcoming anyone to audition for a part in *Macbeth*.
2. Buck, an all-star linebacker, had not (**shown/shone**) any interest in acting prior to this audition.
3. In fact, Buck had once claimed that he'd sooner be (**hanged/hung**) than appear on stage in tights.
4. In his office, the director had asked Buck to (**set/sit**) down before he broke something.
5. A thick volume of Shakespeare was (**laying/lying**) open on the director's desk.
6. Buck pulled a résumé out of his pocket and (**sat/set**) it before the director.
7. Buck claimed that he had (**got/gotten**) plenty of acting experience in summer stock.
8. The director thought that the company must have (**fell/fallen**) on hard times to recruit Buck.
9. Buck claimed that he had been (**chose/chosen**) over a dozen other actors for the part of Orlando—the wrestler in *As You Like It*—the year before.
10. The director wondered whether any stage had ever before (**bore/borne**) a three-hundred-pound Macbeth.

17e voice

17e DO YOU UNDERSTAND ACTIVE AND PASSIVE VOICE?

Troubleshooting

Voice is an aspect of verbs easier to illustrate than define. Verbs that take objects (called transitive verbs) can be either in **active** or in **passive voice.** They are in active voice when the subject in the sentence actually does what the verb describes.

> subj.   action
> *Kyle* **managed** the advertising.

They are in passive voice when the action described by the verb is done *to* the subject.

> subj.   action
> The *advertising* **was managed** by Kyle.

Although writing in the passive voice is often necessary and appropriate, many writers use passive verbs too often. By eliminating passive constructions, you can often turn vague sentences into stronger, more lively ones. That's because the action in an active sentence moves more directly from subject through verb to object. To revise effectively, you need to recognize passive voice and know how to make passive verbs active when appropriate.

To change a passive verb to an active one . . .

`17e–1` **Identify the passive verb.** In a sentence with a passive verb, the subject doesn't perform the action. Instead, the action is *done* to the subject; in effect, the object switches to the subject position.

> subj.   action
> *Jenny* **was selected** by Representative Barton for an appointment to the Air Force Academy.

> subj.   action
> *She* **had been nominated** for the honor by her teachers.

Passive verbs are always formed with some form of *be* plus the past participle.

> be   + past participle
> The van **had been wrecked** by Tracy.

> be + past participle
> The accident **was caused** by faulty brakes.

Of course, not every sentence with a form of the verb *to be* is passive, especially when *be* is used as a linking verb.

> She **was** unhappy that the damage to the van **had been** so great.

Nor is every sentence passive that contains a past participle. Perfect tenses, for example, also use the past participle. Here's an active verb in the past perfect tense.

> Tracy **had driven** for ten years without an accident.

To identify a passive verb form, look for *both* the past participle *and* a form of *be*.

> The van **had been loaded** with Waterford crystal when it **was sideswiped.**

`17e–2` **When you have identified a passive form, locate the word in the sentence that actually performs the action.** Make it the subject. When you revise the sentence in this way, the original subject usually becomes the object.

> subj.
> **Original** *Jenny* **was selected** by Representative Barton for an
> **passive** appointment to the Air Force Academy.

17e voice

	obj.
Revised	*Representative Barton* **selected** Jenny for an appointment
active	to the Air Force Academy.

Notice that the revised version is shorter than the original.

Not every passive verb can or should be made active. Sometimes you simply don't know who or what performs an action.

> Hazardous road conditions **had been predicted** the morning Tracy ventured out. To make things worse, oil **had been spilled** at the intersection where her accident occurred.
>
> She **had been assured,** however, that it was safe to drive.
>
> The van **had been loaded** with Waterford crystal before it **was destroyed.**

In this last example, you might revise the second verb, but leave the first alone.

> The van **had been loaded** with Waterford crystal before Tracy **destroyed** it.

Passive verbs are useful constructions when *who* did an action may be less important than *to whom it was done.* A passive verb puts the *victim* (so to speak) right up front in the sentence where it gets attention.

> *Tracy* **was featured** on the TV nightly news.
> *Tracy* **was interviewed** by several reporters.

The passive is also customary in many expressions where a writer or speaker chooses to be vague about assigning responsibility.

> Flight 107 **has been canceled.**
> The check **was lost** in the mail.

When you need passives, use them. But most of the time, you can improve a sentence by changing a passive construction to an active one.

**17e
voice**

■ **Exercise 17.6** Underline all the passive verbs in the following sentences; then revise those passive verbs that might be better stated in the active voice. Some sentences may require no revision.

1. Even opponents of chemical pesticides sometimes turn to poisons after they have been bitten by fire ants, aggressive and vicious insects spreading throughout the southern United States.
2. It is bad enough that these tiny creatures have been given by nature a fierce sting.
3. But they also are inclined to attack *en masse*.

4. Gardeners are hampered in their work by the mounds erected by the ants.

5. The mounds are often hidden by grasses or bushes.

6. By the time a careless gardener discovers a mound, a hand or foot has likely been bitten by numerous ants.

7. The injured appendage feels as if it has been attacked by a swarm of bees.

8. Scientists are aware that fire ants kill other insects, including roaches and other varieties of ants.

9. Even small animals, birds, and children have been hurt or killed by the vicious ants.

10. Researchers are hoping that biological techniques may eventually halt the spread of this menace.

■ **Exercise 17.7** Select a paragraph you have written and underline all the passive verbs. Then rewrite the paragraph, making passive verbs active whenever such a revision makes a sentence livelier and more economical.

**17f
mood**

17f   WHAT IS THE SUBJUNCTIVE MOOD AND HOW DO YOU USE IT?

Troubleshooting

Mood is a term used to describe how a writer intends a statement to be taken: either as a fact (the **indicative** mood), as a command (the **imperative** mood), or as a wish, desire, supposition, or improbability (the **subjunctive** mood). Mood is indicated by a change in verb form.

Indicative:	The driver **was** careful.
Imperative:	**Be** careful!
Subjunctive:	If the driver **were** more careful . . .

The only mood liable to cause you problems is the subjunctive. The subjunctive is used to express ideas that aren't factual or certain, or to state wishes or desires. The subjunctive also appears in clauses following statements of request, demand, suggestion, or recommendation. In the abstract, you may find these occasions hard to identify; in practice, they are easy enough to spot.

But even if you don't now know what the subjunctive is, you are probably using it correctly at least half the time. You employ the subjunctive mood whenever you say "God *bless* [instead of *blesses*] you" or use the expressions "If I *were* [not *was*] you . . ." or "As it *were*" [not *was*]. In English, subjunctive verb forms survive mainly in habitual expressions like these. However, when writers have to make a deliberate choice about using the subjunctive, many of them use the more familiar indicative forms. Still, using the subjunctive correctly when it's called for is not especially difficult; it's a fine point appreciated by readers attuned to language.

To use the subjunctive . . .

17f-1 Identify situations where the subjunctive might be used. The subjunctive is often used in statements that express wishes.

> I wish it **were** [not **was**] bedtime.
> Would he **were** [not **was**] here!

Or the subjunctive appears in *if* clauses describing situations that are contrary to fact, hypothetical, or improbable.

> *If* I **were** [not **was**] a wealthy banker, I'd drive a Cadillac Seville.
>
> *If* Bertha **were** [not **was**] to call, Benjamin would pretend not to hear the phone.
>
> *If* it **were** [not **was**] to rain, the protestors would move their meeting indoors.

The subjunctive is employed in *that* clauses following verbs that make demands, requests, recommendations, or motions. These sentences will often seem formal or legalistic.

> General Campo asked that his troops **be** silent.
> "I ask only that all soldiers **give** their best," he said.
> "It is necessary that you all **be** in peak condition."
> As the general left, a lieutenant asked that the soldiers **show** their spirit.

Finally, there are some common expressions that require the subjunctive.

Be that as it may . . .	**Come** what may . . .
As it **were** . . .	Peace **be** with you.

17f-2 Select the subjunctive form of the verb. As the examples above suggest, forms of the subjunctive are relatively simple. For all verbs, the present subjunctive is simply the base form of the verb—that is, the present infinitive form without *to*.

17f
mood

VERB	PRESENT SUBJUNCTIVE
to be	be
to give	give
to send	send
to bless	bless

The base form is used even in the third person singular, where you might ordinarily expect a verb to take another form.

> It is essential that *Buck* **have** [not **has**] his lines memorized by tomorrow.

> Carrie insisted that *Travis* **be** [not **is**] on time for their dinner at her mother's.

For all verbs except *be*, the past subjunctive is the same as the simple past tense.

VERB	PAST SUBJUNCTIVE
to give	gave
to send	sent
to bless	blessed

For *be*, the past subjunctive is always *were*. This is true even in the first and third person singular, where you might expect the form to be *was*.

First person	I wish *I* **were** [not **was**] the director.
Second person	Suppose *you* **were** the director.
Third person	I wish *she* **were** [not **was**] the director.

■ **Exercise 17.8** In the following sentences, underline any verbs in the subjunctive mood.

1. It is essential that you be in my office at 2:00 p.m. today.
2. If I were a betting man, I wouldn't wager on the Chicago Cubs winning a pennant again this century.
3. The officer insisted that Tracy take the ticket.
4. It is necessary that Freon be replaced soon as a refrigerant.
5. If only I were less susceptible to throat infections!
6. Far be it from me to criticize your writing!
7. Come what may, the show must go on.
8. If Avery were to arrive early, what would his children do?
9. It is essential that you take over as accountant.
10. If I were you, who would you be?

■ **Exercise 17.9** Write five sentences that include verbs in the subjunctive mood. Underline the subjunctive verbs and their subjects, and then write another sentence with the verb (and same subject) in the indicative mood. For example:

Subjunctive   I wish <u>Thalia were</u> more careful with my camera.

Indicative   Thalia was careful with my camera.

CHART

Anatomy of a Verb: *to pay*

PRINCIPAL PARTS

Infinitive:	pay
Past tense:	paid
Past participle:	paid

TENSE

Present:	I pay
Present progressive:	I am paying
Present perfect:	I have paid
Past:	I paid
Past progressive:	I was paying
Past perfect:	I had paid
Future:	I will pay
Future progressive:	I will have been paying
Future perfect:	I will have paid

PERSON/NUMBER

1st person, singular:	**I** pay
2nd person, singular:	**you** pay
3rd person, singular:	**he** pays
	she pays
	it pays
1st person, plural:	**we** pay
2nd person, plural:	**you** pay
3rd person, plural:	**they** pay

MOOD

Indicative:	I pay.
Imperative:	Pay!
Subjunctive:	I suggested that he pay me.

(continued)

17f mood

Anatomy of a Verb: *to pay* (*continued*)

VOICE

Active: I pay
you paid
he will pay

Passive: I am paid
you were paid
he will be paid

NONFINITE FORMS

Infinitives: to pay [present tense, active voice]
to be paying [progressive tense, active voice]
to have paid [past tense, active voice]
to have been paying [past progressive tense, active voice]

to be paid [present tense, passive voice]
to have been paid [past tense, passive voice]

Participles: paying [present tense, active voice]
having paid [past tense, active voice]

being paid [present tense, passive voice]
paid, having been paid [past tense, passive voice]

Gerunds: paying [present tense, active voice]
having paid [past tense, active voice]

being paid [present tense, passive voice]
having been paid [past tense, passive voice]

18

Problems with Verbals?

A   Verbals
B   Verbals and Sentence Fragments
C   Split Infinitives

18a   WHAT ARE VERBALS?

Troubleshooting

Many writers have difficulty understanding the concept of verbals. **Verbals** are simply verb forms that act like other parts of speech—nouns, adjectives, adverbs. But like verbs, verbals can express time (present, past), take objects, and form phrases. The three types of verbals are infinitives, participles, and gerunds. You need to understand each type. (See also Section 31c.)

To use verbals correctly . . .

18a-1   **Understand infinitives.** **Infinitives** can be identified by the word *to* preceding the base form of a verb: *to seek; to find.* Infinitives also take other forms to show time and voice: *to be seeking; to have found; to have been found.* Infinitives sometimes act as nouns, adjectives, and adverbs.

Infinitive as noun	**To work** in outer space is not easy. subject of the sentence
Infinitive as adjective	Astronauts have many procedures **to learn.** modifies the noun *procedures*
Infinitive as adverb	NASA compromised **to fund** the space shuttle. modifies the verb *compromised*

An infinitive can also serve as an *absolute*—that is, a phrase, standing alone, that modifies an entire sentence.

> **To make** a long story short, the current space shuttles are less advanced than they might have been.

In some sentence constructions, the characteristic marker of the infinitive, *to*, is deleted.

> Shuttle crews perform exercises to help them **[to] deal** with the consequences of weightlessness.

18a–2 Understand participles. A **participle** is a verb form used as a modifier. The present participle ends with *-ing*. For regular verbs, the past participle ends with *-ed*; for irregular verbs, the form of the past participle varies. Participles serve only as modifiers and take various forms, depending on whether the verb they are derived from is regular or irregular. Following are the participle forms of two verbs.

CHART

Forms of the Participle

perform (a regular verb)	**Participles**
Present, active:	performing
Present, passive:	being performed
Past, active:	performed
Past, passive:	having been performed
write (an irregular verb)	**Participles**
Present, active:	writing
Present, passive:	being written
Past, active:	written
Past, passive:	having been written

(For the forms of some irregular past participles, check the list of irregular verbs on pp. 300–302.)

As modifiers, participles may be single words. In the following example, the participle *waving* modifies *astronaut*.

> **Waving,** the astronaut turned a cartwheel in the space shuttle for the television camera.

But participles often take objects, complements, and modifiers to form verbal phrases. Such phrases play an important role in structuring sentences.

> **Clutching** a camera, the astronaut moved toward a galley window.
>
> The shuttle designers, **knowing** they had to work within tight budget constraints, decided to use solid rocket boosters.

Like an infinitive, a participle can also serve as an *absolute*—that is, a phrase, standing alone, that modifies an entire sentence.

> All things **considered**, the space shuttle has been a remarkable machine.

18a–3   **Understand gerunds.**   A **gerund** is a verb form used as a noun: *smiling, flying, walking.* Because most gerunds end in *-ing,* they look exactly like the present participle.

| Gerund | **Daring** is a quality moviegoers admire in heroes. |
| Participle | Most airline passengers, however, would prefer not to have a **daring** pilot. |

The important difference, of course, is that gerunds function as nouns, while participles act as modifiers. Gerunds usually appear in the present tense, but they can take other forms. In the following example, the gerund is in the past tense (and passive voice) and acts as the subject of the sentence.

> **Having been treated** inconsistently by the news media has confused the space agency.

Here the gerund is in the present tense and passive voice.

> **Being asked** to design a space station was an opportunity NASA wouldn't have missed.

Gerunds have many functions.

Gerund as subject	**Keeping** within current budget restraints poses a problem for NASA.
Gerund as object	Some NASA engineers prefer **flying** unmanned space missions.
Gerund as appositive	Others argue that NASA needs to cultivate its great talent, **executing** daring missions.
Gerunds as subject and complement	subj. comp. **Exploring** the heavens is **fulfilling** the dreams of humankind.

■ **Exercise 18.1** Identify the boldfaced words or phrases as infinitives, participles, or gerunds.

1. Perhaps **regretting** compromises in the original design, engineers refined the shuttle after the *Challenger* explosion.
2. At the time, the press questioned both NASA's **engineering** and its **handling** of the shuttle program.
3. To be fair, NASA's record in the **challenging** task of space exploration has been remarkable.
4. Costing even more than the space shuttle, NASA's proposed space station, *Freedom,* is sure **to stimulate** new controversies.
5. To make matters more interesting, NASA has recommended **exploring** the possibility of a human mission to Mars.

18b HOW DO VERBALS CAUSE SENTENCE FRAGMENTS?

Troubleshooting

CAUTION An important difference between verbs and verbals is that the verbals alone cannot make phrases into complete sentences. For that reason, verbals are sometimes described as **nonfinite** (that is, "unfinished") verbs. A complete sentence requires a **finite** verb—that is, a verb that changes form to indicate person, number, and tense.

Nonfinite verb— infinitive	**To have found** success . . .
Finite verb	I **have found** success.
Nonfinite verb— participle	The comedian **performing** the bit . . .
Finite verb	The comedian **performs** the bit.
Nonfinite verb— gerund	**Directing** a play . . .
Finite verb	She **directed** the play.

A verbal phrase standing alone is a sentence fragment.

> Harold now had an opportunity for revenge. **Having been ridiculed in the past by friends.**

Occasionally, such constructions are appropriate in informal writing. You'll often see them in magazine articles or advertising copy.

Harold loved playing comedy clubs—every bit of it. **Telling the jokes. Making rude noises.** It made life worthwhile.

But in academic writing, fragments usually need to be corrected.

To turn a verbal phrase into a complete sentence . . .

18b–1 **Attach a verbal phrase to a complete sentence to avoid a fragment.** Quite often, a comma, colon, or dash is adequate to join a verbal phrase to an appropriate sentence.

Fragment	Harold now had an opportunity for revenge. **Having been ridiculed in the past by friends.**
Revised	Harold now had an opportunity for revenge**, having been ridiculed in the past by friends.**
Fragment	**To make his audiences roar with laughter.** That was just as important as getting even.
Revised	**To make his audiences roar with laughter**—that was just as important as getting even.

18b–2 **Make the verbal phrase itself a complete sentence.**

Fragment	Harold's fraternity brothers sat in the audience nervously. **Fearing they might bear the brunt of his humor.**
Revised	Harold's fraternity brothers sat in the audience nervously. **They feared they might bear the brunt of his humor.**

■ **Exercise 18.2** In the following passages, correct any verbal phrases that are sentence fragments. Defend any fragments you think are appropriate.

1. At the comedy club, Harold preferred not to think about his nerves. Knowing that his material was good.
2. Other matters were on his mind as he waited for his time on stage. Mocking his girlfriend's diet. Exposing the bathroom habits of his roommate. Memorializing his mother's vile cooking.
3. Harold discovered that being a humorist was fun. Especially when the targets of his jokes were in the audience.
4. He had learned a lot from watching David Letterman. How to time a joke, how to capitalize on the news, how to ridicule a person's foibles without being cruel.

**18b
verbal**

5. To teach his targets to laugh at themselves. That would be Harold's goal now.

18c WHAT IS A SPLIT INFINITIVE?

Troubleshooting

Infinitives cause few difficulties. One problem, though, is quite famous: the matter of the **split infinitive.** An infinitive interrupted by an adverb is considered split.

> to **boldly** go
> to **really** try
> to **actually** see

Some writers believe that constructions such as these are incorrect. Split infinitives are, however, such common expressions in English that many writers use them without apology. Here are some guidelines to help you through this minor, but often disputed, point.

To avoid problems with split infinitives . . .

18c-1 Check that no words separate the *to* in an infinitive from its verb. If a sentence sounds awkward because a word or phrase splits an infinitive, move the interrupter.

Split infinitive	Harold's intention as a stand-up comic was **to,** as best he could, **make** people laugh at themselves.
Revised	Harold's intention as a stand-up comic was **to make** other people laugh at themselves, as best he could.

18c-2 Revise any split infinitives that cause modification problems. In the following sentence, for example, *only* seems to modify *describe* when it should refer to *the funniest aspects*.

Confusing	Harold intended **to only describe** the funniest aspects of human behavior.
Clearer	Harold intended **to describe** only the funniest aspects of human behavior.

Consider, too, whether a word dividing an infinitive is needed at all. Where the interrupting word is a weak intensifier that adds nothing to a sentence (*really, actually*), cut it.

Weak intensifier	Harold found it possible **to** really **enjoy** describing the disgusting habits that make people funny.
Intensifier cut	Harold found it possible **to enjoy** describing the disgusting habits that make people funny.

18c–3 **Consider whether a split infinitive may be acceptable.** In many situations, split infinitives are neither awkward nor confusing, so revising them won't always improve a sentence.

Split infinitive	Words fail **to** adequately **describe** the zaniness of human nature.
Revised	Words fail **to describe** adequately the zaniness of human nature.

In academic and business writing, it's probably best to keep *to* and the verb together because some readers do object strongly to violations of the convention.

**18c
sp inf**

■ **Exercise 18.3** Find the split infinitives in the following sentences and revise them. Decide which revisions are necessary, which optional. Be prepared to defend your decisions.

1. Harold decided to candidly mention his girlfriend's problem with diets in his comedy spot on the Letterman show.
2. Harold didn't want his personal life to too much inhibit his routines.
3. After all, it was a comedian's duty to always strive for laughs.
4. His problem was to really convey how funny his girlfriend's diets were without hurting her feelings.
5. To clumsily mention her chunky thighs on national television might be to quickly terminate his own social life.

Problems with Plurals, Possessives, and Articles?

19a PROBLEMS WITH PLURALS OF NOUNS?

Troubleshooting

Most plurals in English are formed by adding *-s* or *-es* to the singular forms of nouns, which are words that name persons, places, things, ideas, or qualities.

demonstration → demonstration**s**
picture → picture**s**
dish → dish**es**

Yet adding *-s* or *-es* can cause spelling complications in words ending in *-y, -o, -um, -us,* or *-f*. Notice the exceptions below. If you have any doubts about the correct plural for such words, check your dictionary.

SINGULAR	PLURAL
thief	→ thie**ves**
lady	→ lad**ies**
curriculum	→ curriculum**s**/curricul**a**
bus	→ bus**es**/bus**ses**
chief	→ chief**s**

Some English words use the same form for both singular and plural meanings; others seldom appear in singular form.

SINGULAR/PLURAL	ALMOST ALWAYS PLURAL
athletics	cattle
mathematics	trousers
spacecraft	headquarters
Sioux	scissors

A substantial number of words are simply irregular. You couldn't reliably predict what their plurals would be if you didn't know them.

IRREGULAR

man → m**e**n
ox → ox**en**
mouse → m**ic**e
goose → g**ee**se
child → child**ren**
fungus → fung**i** (or fungus**es**)

Also troublesome are the plurals of compound words and of figures. In short, plurals merit your careful attention.

An editor may indicate a faulty plural by circling the problem and writing *pl* in the margin. Or the error may be marked as a misspelling.

We rented two vide*oes.* *pl*
Two sentr*ys* stood guard. *sp*

When you are unsure about a plural . . .

19a–1 **Check the dictionary for the plural form of a noun.** Most college dictionaries provide the plurals of all troublesome words. If your dictionary does not give a plural for a particular noun, assume that it forms its plural with *-s* or *-es*.

You may eliminate some trips to the dictionary by referring to the following guidelines for forming plurals. But the list is complicated and full of exceptions, so keep that dictionary handy.

19a–2 **Add *-s* to most nouns to form the plural.**

demonstration → demonstration**s**
picture → picture**s**

19a–3 **Add *-es* when the plural adds a syllable to the pronunciation of the noun.** This is usually the case when a word ends in a soft *ch, sh, s, ss, x, or zz.* (If the noun already ends in *-e*, you add only *-s*.)

19a
plural

dish → dish**es**
glass → glass**es**
bus → bus**es** or bus**ses**
buzz → buzz**es**
choice → choice**s**

19a–4 Add *-s* to form a plural when a noun ends in *-o* and a vowel precedes the *o*; add *-es* when a noun ends in *-o* and a consonant precedes the *o*. This guideline has exceptions. A few words ending in *-o* even have two acceptable plural forms.

VOWEL BEFORE *-O* (ADD *-S*)	**CONSONANT BEFORE *-O* (ADD *-ES*)**
video → video**s**	hero → hero**es**
rodeo → rodeo**s**	tomato → tomato**es**
studio → studio**s**	veto → veto**es**

EXCEPTIONS (ADD *-S*)	**TWO ACCEPTABLE FORMS**
banjo → banjo**s**	cargo → cargo**s**/cargo**es**
nacho → nacho**s**	no → no**s**/no**es**
soprano → soprano**s**	motto → motto**s**/motto**es**
piano → piano**s**	zero → zero**s**/zero**es**

When in doubt about a word ending in *-o*, check a dictionary.

19a–5 Add *-s* to form a plural when a noun ends in *-y* and a vowel precedes the *y*. When a consonant precedes the *y*, change the *y* to an *i* and add *-es*.

VOWEL PRECEDES *-Y* (ADD *-S*)	**CONSONANT PRECEDES *-Y* (ADD *-ES*)**
attorney → attorney**s**	foundry → foundr**ies**
Monday → Monday**s**	candy → cand**ies**
boy → boy**s**	sentry → sentr**ies**

An exception to this rule occurs with proper nouns. They usually retain the y and simply add *-s*.

PROPER NAMES ENDING IN *-Y* (ADD *-S*)	**EXCEPTIONS TO THE EXCEPTION**
Gary → Gary**s**	Rocky Mountains → Rock**ies**
Nestrosky → Nestrosky**s**	Smoky Mountains → Smok**ies**
Germany → Germany**s**	

19a–6 Check the plural of nouns ending in *-f* or *-fe*. Some form plurals by adding *-s*, some change *-f* to *-ves*, and some have two acceptable plural forms.

19a plural

TRICKY

ADD -S TO FORM PLURAL	**CHANGE -F TO -VES IN PLURAL**
chief → chief**s**	leaf → lea**ves**
belief → belief**s**	wolf → wol**ves**
roof → roof**s**	knife → kni**ves**

TWO ACCEPTABLE FORMS

elf → elf**s**/el**ves**
hoof → hoof**s**/hoo**ves**
scarf → scarf**s**/scar**ves**
wharf → wharf**s**/whar**ves**
dwarf → dwarf**s**/dwar**ves**

19a-7 Check the plural of multisyllabic nouns ending in -*us* preceded by a consonant. Some form plurals by changing -*us* to -*i*. But notice that even these may have a second, regular plural.

CHANGE -US TO -I

focus → foc**i**/focus**es**
cactus → cact**i**/cactus**es**
syllabus → syllab**i**/syllabus**es**

19a
plural

19a-8 Check the plural of multisyllabic nouns ending in -*um* preceded by a consonant. Some form plurals by changing -*um* to -*a*. But notice, again, that these often have a second, regular plural.

CHANGE -UM TO -A

addendum → addend**a**
curriculum → curricul**a**/curriculum**s**
medium → medi**a**/medium**s**

19a-9 Check the plural of compound words. The last words in most compounds are pluralized.

dishcloth → dishcloth**s**
bill collector → bill collector**s**
housewife → housewi**ves**

TRICKY

However, the first word in a compound is pluralized when it is the important term. This is often the case in hyphenated expressions.

attorney general → attorney**s** general
father-in-law → father**s**-in-law
chief-of-staff → chief**s**-of-staff
woman-of-the-year → wom**en**-of-the-year
passerby → passer**s**by

Naturally, there are exceptions.

> add-on → add-on**s**
> sit-in → sit-in**s**
> thirty-year-old → thirty-year-old**s**

Words that end with *-ful* add *-s* to the end of the whole word, not to the syllable before *-ful*.

> handful**s** [not hand**s**ful]
> tablespoonful**s** [not tablespoon**s**ful]
> cupful**s** [not cup**s**ful]

19a-10 Check the plural of letters, abbreviations, acronyms, figures, and numbers. These constructions usually form their plurals by adding either *-s* or *-'s*. The *-'s* is used where adding *-s* without the apostrophe might cause a misreading.

> three **e's** and two **y's**
> several of the **I's** in the paper

An apostrophe may also be used when periods occur in an abbreviation.

> twenty V.I.P.**'s**
> two urgent S.O.S.**'s**

Quite often, though, the apostrophe is left out, especially when it might mistakenly indicate possession.

> the SAT**s**
> five CRT**s**

In many cases, either form of the plural is acceptable.

> the 1960**s**/the 1960**'s**
> 8**s**/8**'s**

◆ **Point of Difference**

Data is the plural form of *datum*. Yet you will often see *data* treated as if it were singular.

> The *data* **is** not convincing.

This is a case where popular usage differs from formal and some business writing. The style manuals of both the Government Printing Office and the American Psychological Association, for instance, insist on treating *data* as a plural noun.

> The *data* **are** not convincing. ◆

■ **Exercise 19.1** Form the plurals of the following words. Use the guidelines above or a dictionary as necessary.

basis	gas	soliloquy
duo	loaf	zero
tooth	alkali	mongoose
alumnus	datum	heir apparent
moose	Oreo	court-martial

■ **Exercise 19.2** Form the plurals of the boldfaced words in the passage below. Use the guidelines on plurals above or a dictionary as necessary.

1. The café sold typical coffeehouse beverages, including various choco-lates, **espresso,** and **mocha.**
2. On the walls of the café were **photo** of the owners in their youth, tak-ing part in protests, antiwar **symposium,** and **sit-in.**
3. The decor was a lament for the passing of the **1960.**
4. Who are the **Bob Dylan** and **Joan Baez** of the current generation?
5. Many college students today share the passionate **belief** of earlier generations; others are more concerned with earning their **A** and **B.**

19b

poss

19b PROBLEMS WITH POSSESSIVES?

Troubleshooting

A noun or pronoun takes a possessive form to show ownership or some similar relationship: *Rita's, hers, the students', the governor's approval, the pride of the nation, the day's labor, the city's destruction.*

Possessives in English aren't particularly complicated. But many writers mistakenly omit the apostrophe before or after an *s* that indicates ownership. As a result, their possessives look like plurals.

Incorrect   Ritas opinion
the students concern
the days labor

Although you may occasionally see the apostrophe omitted in signs—*mens room, Macys*—in writing it is necessary to use the apostrophe to in-dicate the possessive.

Even when you remember to mark the possessive, problems may

arise with positioning the apostrophe (Ross**'s** or Ross**'** handball?), with possessives of plurals (the hostesses**'** or the hostesse**s's**?), or with joint possession (Al**'s** and Peg**'s** shop or Al and Peg**'s** shop?). Sometimes you must choose between the two possible forms of the possessive (the book**'s** spine or the spine **of** the book?).

Forming the possessive of pronouns can cause major problems too. Unlike nouns, the possessives of personal pronouns never take an apostrophe, yet they look as if they might.

> The problem is **theirs.** not **their's**
> Be sure you know **its** measurements. not **it's**

All of these issues (and more) are addressed in detail below.

An editor might signal problems with possessives in several ways. An error in possession might be circled and *poss* written in the margin.

> Al lived a dogs⟩ life. *poss*

19b
poss

Or the editor may simply use an inverted caret to insert an apostrophe where one is required.

> The teacher listened to his students⌃opinions. ⌄

To form the possessive . . .

19b–1   Add an apostrophe + -*s* to most singular nouns and to plural nouns that do not end in -*s*.

SINGULAR NOUNS	PLURALS NOT ENDING IN -*s*
dog**'s** life	geese**'s** behavior
that man**'s** opinion	women**'s** attitude
the NCAA**'s** ruling	children**'s** imaginations

Singular nouns that end in -*s* or -*z* may take either an apostrophe +-*s* or the apostrophe alone. Use one form or the other consistently throughout a paper.

> Ross**'s** handball or Ross**'** handball
> Goetz**'s** play or Goetz**'** play

The apostrophe alone is used with singular words ending in -*s* when the possessive does not add a syllable to the pronunciation of the word.

> Texas**'** first settlement
> Jesus**'** words

19b–2   Add an apostrophe (but not an *s*) to plural nouns that end in -*s*.

hostesses**'** job	senators**'** chambers
students**'** opinion	Smiths**'** home

19b–3 Indicate possession only at the end of compound or hyphenated words.

> president-elect**'s** decision
> fathers-in-law**'s** Cadillacs
> the United States Post Office**'s** efficiency

19b–4 Indicate possession only once when two nouns share ownership.

> Peg and Al**'s** shoe store
> Vorhees and Goetz**'s** project

But when ownership is separate, each noun shows possession.

> Peg**'s** and Al**'s** educations
> Vorhees**'** and Goetz**'s** offices

19b–5 Use an apostrophe + -s to form the possessive of living things and titled works; use *of* with nonliving things. This guideline should be followed sensibly. Many common expressions violate the convention, and many writers simply ignore it.

TAKE APOSTROPHE + -S	TAKE *OF*
the dog**'s** bone	the weight **of** the bone
Professor Granchi**'s** taxes	the bite **of** taxes
*Time***'s** cover	the attractiveness **of** the cover

Use *of* whenever an apostrophe + -s might be awkward or ridiculous.

Ridiculous   The **student** sitting next to Peg**'s** opinion was radical.

Revised   The opinion **of the student** sitting next to Peg was radical.

In a few situations, English allows a double possessive, consisting of both the -'s and *of*.

> The suggestion **of** Al**'s** didn't win support, although an earlier one did.

> An opinion **of** Peg**'s** soon spurred another argument.

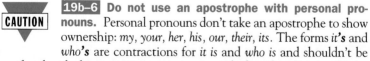

19b–6 Do not use an apostrophe with personal pronouns. Personal pronouns don't take an apostrophe to show ownership: *my, your, her, his, our, their, its.* The forms *it***'s** and *who***'s** are contractions for *it is* and *who is* and shouldn't be confused with the possessive pronouns *its* and *whose* (see Section 22g).

> **It's** an idea that has **its** opponents alarmed.
> **Who's** to say **whose** opinion is right?

19b
poss

Indefinite pronouns—such as *anybody, each one, everybody*—do form their possessives regularly: *anybody's, each one's, everybody's.* For more about possessive pronouns, see Section 22f.

■ **Exercise 19.3** Decide whether the forms boldfaced in the passage below are correct. Revise any you believe are faulty.

1. That claim **of her's** may be right.
2. **Pegs** belief was that the main concern **of most citizens'** was a thriving economy.
3. **Society's** problems today are not as great as they were in the **1890s';** each generation benefits from its **parent's** sacrifices while tackling **it's** own problems.
4. **Its** a shame that people forget how much they have benefited from **someone elses** labor.
5. Children are notorious for ignoring their **elders** generosity; ingratitude is even one of the major themes of **King Lear's** plot.

19c ARE POSSESSIVES NEEDED BEFORE GERUNDS?

Troubleshooting

Gerunds (see Section 18a–3) are verb forms that function like nouns: *eating, biking, walking.* Nouns or pronouns often precede gerunds. When they do, you must decide whether the noun or pronoun will be possessive or not.

	noun gerund
Noun without possessive	The customers pointed at the *shelf* **collapsing** in the shoe store.

	poss. noun gerund
Noun with possessive	The customers pointed at the *shelf's* **collapsing** in the shoe store.

A few guidelines may help you decide when the noun or pronoun should be possessive.

When a noun or pronoun precedes a gerund . . .

19c–1 Use the possessive form of the noun in formal or academic writing; use the common (nonpossessive) form in informal situations.

C H A R T

Possessives Before Gerunds

ACADEMIC WRITING	INFORMAL WRITING
Possessive + gerund	Regular + gerund
the *student's* **arguing**	the *student* **arguing**
the *owner's* **complaining**	the *owner* **complaining**

This first guideline does not apply to proper nouns or to pronouns.

19c–2 Use the possessive form in *both* formal and informal writing when the word preceding the gerund is a proper noun or a pronoun.

proper
noun gerund
Students had little respect for *Al's* **whining** about the sixties.

pron. gerund
They ridiculed *his* **talking** like a radical.

19c–3 Use the common form of the noun even in formal writing when the subject of the gerund is modified by other words.

Bud admitted that he enjoyed the thought of *Al,* the respectable shoe salesman, **being** arrested at Woodstock.

19c–4 Use the common form even in formal writing when the subject of the gerund is plural, collective, or abstract.

His *parents* **going** to rock festivals and love-ins was a phenomenon Bud could not imagine.

The *quartet* **playing** folk music on the mall was a quaint idea.

Al's problem with the sixties was *nostalgia* **getting** out of hand.

19c
poss

■ **Exercise 19.4** Select the appropriate form for the nouns or pronouns used before gerunds in the passage below. Gerunds are boldfaced. Assume that the passage is written for an academic audience.

1. Al's faulty recollections of Woodstock were a frequent topic at the (*coffeehouse/coffeehouse's*) **gathering** of Peg's friends.
2. (*Al/Al's*) **pretending** not to remember (*Peg/Peg's*) **bailing** him out of jail was amusing.

3. Peg knew she could always count on (*his/him*) **being** broke.

4. Al, however, did not appreciate (*Mrs. Leroy/Mrs. Leroy's*), one of his regular customers, **reminding** Peg that Al was still usually broke.

5. (*He/His*) **forgetting** to repay Peg for several years only made the situation more comic.

19d   IS IT *A* OR *AN*?

Troubleshooting

English has only one form for its definite article: *the*. So you cannot choose a wrong form: *the* argument, *the* European, *the* house, *the* historic day. But the indefinite article has two forms: *a* and *an*. Some writers think that they should simply use *a* before all words that begin with consonants and *an* before all words that begin with vowels. In fact, usage is just a bit more complicated, as a few examples show: *an* argument, *a* European, *a* house, *an* honorable person. (See also Section 31d.)

To choose between *a* and *an* . . .

Use *a* when the word following it begins with a consonant *sound;* use *an* when the word following it begins with a vowel *sound.* In most cases, it works out so that *a* actually comes before words beginning with consonants, *an* before words with vowels.

Initial consonants	Initial vowels
a **b**oat	an **aa**rdvark
a **c**lass	an **E**gyptian monument
a **d**uck	an **i**gloo
a **f**inal opinion	an **o**dd event
a **h**ouse	an **u**tter disaster

But *an* is used before words beginning with a consonant when the consonant is silent, as is sometimes the case with *h*. It is also used when a consonant itself is pronounced with an initial vowel sound (F → *ef*; N → *en*; S → *es*), as often happens in acronyms.

Silent consonant	Consonant with a vowel sound
an hour	an F in this course
an heir	an SAT score
an hors d'oeuvre	an X-ray

Similarly *a* is used before words beginning with a vowel when the vowel is pronounced like a consonant. Certain vowels, for example, sound like the consonant *y*, and in a few cases, an initial *o* sounds like the consonant *w*.

Vowel with a consonant sound

a European vacation (**eu** sounds like **y**)
a unique painting (**u** sounds like **y**)
a one-sided argument (**o** sounds like **w**)
a U-joint (**u** sounds like **y**)

■ **Exercise 19.5** Decide whether *a* or *an* ought to be used before the following words or phrases.

1. _____ L-shaped room
2. _____ hyperthyroid condition
3. _____ zygote
4. _____ X-rated movie
5. _____ Euclidean principle
6. _____ evasive answer
7. _____ jalapeño pepper
8. _____ unwritten rule
9. _____ unit of measure
10. _____ veneer of oak

19d
a(n)

Problems with Pronoun Reference?

A   Pronouns Without Antecedents
B   Ambiguous Pronoun References
C   *This, That, Which, It*

20a   PRONOUNS LACK ANTECEDENTS?

Troubleshooting

Pronouns are words that stand in for and act like nouns, but don't name a specific person, place, or thing—*I, you, he, she, it, they, whom, this, that, one,* and so on. The person, place, or thing a pronoun stands in for is called the **antecedent.** The antecedent is the word you would have to repeat in a sentence if you couldn't use a pronoun; it usually shares the number (singular or plural) and gender (masculine, feminine, or neuter) of the pronoun. This connection between a pronoun and antecedent is called *pronoun reference*.

Jill demanded that the clerk speak to **her.**

ANTECEDENT	**PRONOUN**
Jill	her
Number: singular	*Number:* singular
Gender: feminine	*Gender:* feminine

Workers denied that **they** intended to strike.

ANTECEDENT	**PRONOUN**
Workers	they
Number: plural	*Number:* plural
Gender: neuter	*Gender:* neuter

You have a problem with pronoun reference if readers can't find a specific word in your sentence that could logically serve as an antecedent, the word the pronoun replaces.

> **Vague**   We checked the box offices at a dozen theaters in London, but our budget was so tight we couldn't afford to attend **one.**

In this example, the potential antecedent for the singular pronoun *one* is either *box offices* or *theaters*, but both are plural nouns and neither makes sense when substituted for the pronoun *one*. To make the sentence clearer, you may have to replace the pronoun with a noun.

> **Revised**   We checked the box offices at a dozen theaters in London, but our budget was so tight we couldn't afford to attend a **play.**

You shouldn't leave readers guessing. Don't use pronouns without providing obvious antecedents.

An editor will usually indicate a problem with pronoun reference by circling or underlining the troublesome pronoun and writing *ref* in the margin.

**20a
prn ref**

> Passengers had been searched for weapons, but (it) *ref?*
> did not prevent the hijacking.

To be sure your sentences are clear . . .

TRICKY

Revise a sentence or passage to eliminate pronouns without clear antecedents. When you aren't sure that the pronoun has an antecedent, ask yourself whether another word in the sentence could substitute for the pronoun. If none can, replace the vague pronoun with a word or phrase that explains precisely what it is.

> **Vague**   Passengers had been searched for weapons, but **it** did not prevent the hijacking.

> **Revised**   Passengers had been searched for weapons, but **this precaution** did not prevent the hijacking.

When a word that might stand in for the pronoun is possessive, you need to look at the potential antecedent carefully. In the sentence below, *they* seems to refer to *experts*, but that word doesn't act as a noun in the sentence.

> **Vague**   As for the **experts'** opinion of the Miata, **they** either praise it or wish it had more power.

Experts' is a possessive form. But since *they* can't refer to *experts'* (or to *experts' opinion*), the sentence has to be revised.

| Revised | As for the **experts, they** either praise the Miata or wish it had more power. |

■ **Exercise 20.1** Revise or rewrite the following sentences to eliminate vague pronouns. Treat the sentences as a continuous passage.

1. Leah read avidly about gardening, although she had never planted one herself.

2. Her fondness for the convenience of apartment living left Leah without a place for one.

3. Leah found herself buying garden tools, seeds, and catalogs, but it did not make much sense.

4. Leah's friends suggested building planters on her deck or installing a garden window, but Leah doubted the landlord would permit it.

5. As for her parents' idea that she invest in a condominium, they overestimated her bank account.

20b   PRONOUN REFERENCES AMBIGUOUS?

Troubleshooting

You have a problem with pronoun reference when a pronoun could refer to more than one antecedent.

| Ambiguous | When Cher talked to Audrey that noon, **she** did not realize that **she** might be resigning before the end of the day. |
| Ambiguous | When the rain started, we pulled out an umbrella, which was under the seat, and opened it. **It** dampened our spirits for a while, but we decided to stick **it** out. |

In the first sentence, who is resigning is not clear; in the second *it* might be the umbrella or the rain. Such ambiguities must be clarified by making it possible for pronouns to refer to only one term.

To keep your pronoun references precise . . .

Revise a sentence to eliminate confusing or ambiguous antecedents. You can usually make a confusing sentence clearer by replacing the pronouns with more specific words or by rearranging the sentence. Sometimes you have to do both.

Revised   When **they** talked to each other at noon, **Audrey** did not realize that **Cher** might be resigning before the end of the day.

Revised   We pulled out and opened the **umbrella** stowed under the seat. The **rain** dampened our spirits for a while, but we decided to **stay for the entire game.**

■ **Exercise 20.2** Revise the following sentences to eliminate ambiguous pronoun references. Treat the sentences as a continuous passage. Several versions of each sentence may be possible.

1. Maria could hardly believe that Luke and Jason had decided to room together while attending San Diego State University. She doubted whether it would last since it was rare that either of them agreed about anything.
2. If you asked Luke to describe Jason, he would say that he was an ultraliberal, Volvo-driving Democrat, and then he would chuckle to himself.
3. Ask Jason about Luke, and he would say that, while he wouldn't engage in gossip, he was sure he had ties to powerful, well-funded, right-wing organizations.
4. When Luke dated Maria, Jason would usually hide the keys to his Harley-Davidson to be sure Maria was safe.
5. He didn't want her cruising with him on his motorcycle.

20c   **PROBLEMS WITH *THIS, THAT, WHICH,* AND *IT?***

Troubleshooting

Your readers may be confused if you use the pronouns *this, that, which,* or *it* to refer to ideas and situations you haven't named or explained clearly in your sentence or paragraph. You expect readers to understand what *this* is—and they often do, especially in spoken English. But in written English you should be more specific. This problem is one best explained through an example.

Many readers find constructions such as the following confusing or imprecise.

Confusing   The typical British mystery is filled with violence, brutality, and refined language. I especially like **this.**

Readers can't tell whether you like violence, brutality, or refined language—or all three. The *this* in the second sentence could refer to any one of those terms or to all of them. Vague references of this sort need to be clarified.

To avoid vague references . . .

20c–1 **Revise a sentence or passage to make it clear what *this*, *that*, *which*, or *it* means.** When a reader might mistake what a *this* or *that* means, you can usually remedy the problem by inserting an imaginary blank space after the pronoun (*this* _____? or *that* _____?) and filling it in with a word or phrase that explains what *this* or *that* is.

> **Confusing** The typical British mystery is filled with violence, brutality, and refined language. I especially like **this _____?**

Now fill in the blank.

> **Revised** The typical British mystery is filled with violence, brutality, and refined language. I especially like **this combination of toughness and grace.**

When the unclear pronoun is *which* or *it,* you ought either to revise the sentence or to supply a clear and direct antecedent. Here's an example with *it* as the vague pronoun.

> **Vague** While atomic waste products are hard to dispose of safely, **it** remains a reasonable alternative to burning fossil fuels to produce electricity.

What is the alternative to burning fossil fuels? Surely not *atomic waste products*. The *it* needs to be replaced by a more specific term.

> **Revised** While atomic waste products are hard to dispose of safely, **nuclear power** remains a reasonable alternative to burning fossil fuels to produce electricity.

Here's an example with *which* as the vague pronoun.

> **Vague** The house has a tiny kitchen and a slate roof, **which** Mario and Paula intend to remodel.

The *which* seems to refer to the roof, but it's more likely that Mario and Paula plan to remodel their tiny kitchen. Here are two possible revisions.

> **Revised** The house has a tiny **kitchen, which** Mario and Paula intend to remodel, and a slate roof.

> **Revised** The house has a slate roof and a tiny **kitchen, which** Mario and Paula intend to remodel.

20c-2 Avoid using *they* or *it* without antecedents to describe people or things in general.

Vague	In Houston, **they** drive worse than in Dallas.
Revised	In Houston, **people** drive worse than in Dallas.

20c-3 Avoid sentences in which a pronoun merely repeats the obvious subject. Such constructions are unacceptable in writing.

Incorrect	The **mayor,** a Democrat, **he** lost the election.
Revised	The **mayor,** a Democrat, lost the election.

▶ **Fine Tuning**

Don't let a nonpossessive pronoun refer to a word that is possessive.

Inaccurate	Seeing **Rita's** car, Hector waved at **her.**
Revised	Seeing **Rita** in her car, Hector waved at her. ◀

■ **Exercise 20.3** Decide whether a reader might find the pronouns in boldface unclear. Revise the sentences as necessary.

1. Traditionally rivals, José and Agnes decided to work together on a video, producing a first-class effort, **which** was unusual.
2. José was enthusiastic since he had experience as a writer, director, and actor. **It** was something that came naturally to him.
3. **It** occurred to José that **their** film project might also interest Tricia, so he decided to bring **her** in on **it.**
4. Film students like Tricia, José knew from experience, **they** like to acquire all the experience they can get.
5. Agnes suspected that José had doubts about her scriptwriting ability, although he hadn't actually said **that.**

Problems with Pronoun Agreement?

A Lost Antecedents
B Agreement Problems with *Or, Nor, Either . . . Or, Neither . . . Nor*
C Agreement Problems with Collective Nouns
D Agreement Problems with Indefinite Pronouns

21a PROBLEMS WITH LOST ANTECEDENTS?

Troubleshooting

Pronouns and nouns are either singular or plural. You would ordinarily use a singular pronoun (such as *she, it, this, that, her, him, my, his, her, its*) when referring to something singular and a plural pronoun (such as *they, these, them, their*) when referring to plural things.

You have a problem with *pronoun agreement* when you use a singular pronoun to substitute for a plural noun (or its *antecedent*) or a plural pronoun to substitute for a singular noun (or its antecedent).

In most cases, you will have no difficulties with pronoun agreement when the pronoun and its antecedent occur close together in a sentence and when the antecedent is clearly either singular or plural.

The soccer **players** gathered **their** equipment.

ANTECEDENT	**PRONOUN**
players	their
Number: plural	*Number:* plural

The **coach** searched for **her** car.

ANTECEDENT	PRONOUN
coach	her
Number: singular	*Number:* singular

But sometimes, words and phrases that come between pronouns and their antecedents cause a kind of "misdirection." A writer loses track of the real antecedent and mistakenly gives the pronoun the wrong number, as in the following example.

Agreement error   A typical **voter** today expects all sorts of government
<small>sing.</small>
services, but **they** don't want to pay for them.
<small>plural</small>

The plural pronoun *they* incorrectly refers to a singular noun, *voter*. The simplest way to be sure that pronouns and antecedents agree in this sentence is to make *voter* plural.

Revised   Typical **voters** today expect all sorts of government ser-
<small>plural</small>
vices, but **they** don't want to pay for them.
<small>plural</small>

Errors of this kind are among the most common in writing, so give subject-verb agreement careful attention when editing.

Some editors will mark an agreement error by placing *agr* in the margin next to a problem sentence.

(Everyone) believes that (they) are fair. *agr?*

**21a
prn ag**

To be certain pronouns and antecedents agree . . .

21a–1 **Be sure that singular pronouns refer to singular antecedents and plural pronouns to plural antecedents.** Here's an example.

Agreement error   An **American** always takes it for granted that
<small>sing.</small>
government agencies will help **them** when trou-
<small>plural</small>
ble strikes.

Since *American* is singular and *them* is plural, revision is necessary to make pronoun and antecedent either consistently plural or consistently singular.

Revised— first version	plural **Americans** always take it for granted that gov- plural ernment agencies will help **them** when trouble strikes.
Revised— second version	sing. An **American** always take**s** it for granted that gov- sing. ernment agencies will help **him or her** when trouble strikes.

21a–2 **Keep pronouns consistent in number throughout a passage.**
Don't switch back and forth from singular to plural forms of pronouns
and antecedents. The following paragraph—with pronouns and antecedents boldfaced—shows this common error.

> One reason some **teenagers [pl.]** quit school is to work to
> support **their [pl.]** families. If **he or she [sing.]** is the eldest child,
> the **teen [sing.]** may feel an obligation to provide for the family.
> So **they [pl.]** look for a minimum wage job. Unfortunately, the
> **student [sing.]** often must work so many hours per week that
> **they [pl.]** cannot give much attention to schoolwork. As a result,
> **he or she [sing.]** grows discouraged and drops out.

To correct such a tendency, be consistent. Treat the troublesome key
term—in the passage above it is *teenager*—as either singular or plural, but
not both. Notice that making such a change may require adjustments
throughout the passage.

> One reason some **teenagers [pl.]** quit school is to work to
> support **their [pl.]** families. If **they [pl.]** are eldest children, such
> **teens [pl.]** may feel an obligation to provide for their families. So
> **they [pl.]** look for minimum wage jobs. Unfortunately, these
> **students [pl.]** often must work so many hours per week that **they
> [pl.]** cannot give much attention to schoolwork. As a result, **they
> [pl.]** grow discouraged and drop out.

■ **Exercise 21.1** Revise the following sentences wherever pronouns
and antecedents do not agree in number. You may change either the pronouns or the antecedents.

1. Many a college class is conducted using the Socratic method, but
   they aren't always successful.

21a
prn ag

2. In the Socratic method, a teacher leads a student through a series of questions to conclusions that they believe they've reached without the instructor's prompting.

3. Yet when instructors ask leading questions, the cleverer students sometimes answer it in unexpected ways.

4. However, no instructor, except perhaps for Socrates himself, can foresee all the questions and answers eager students might have for them.

5. But an instructor should be as open as students to accepting new ideas when lively debates lead them to question their beliefs.

21b   AGREEMENT PROBLEMS WITH *OR, NOR, EITHER . . . OR, NEITHER . . . NOR?*

Troubleshooting

Quite often, writers have problems with pronoun agreement simply because they aren't sure whether the word or phrase a pronoun refers to is singular or plural—especially when a pronoun refers to more than one antecedent. When antecedents are joined by *and,* it is usually apparent that the pronoun should be plural.

>   plural   plural
> When **Lewis and Clark** explored the upper Missouri, **they** relied on their Indian guide Sacajawea.

But when the antecedents for a pronoun are nouns joined by *or, nor, either . . . or,* or *neither . . . nor,* the choice of a pronoun can become difficult.

> **Neither Brazil nor Mexico** will raise (**their? its?**) oil prices today.

> **Either poor diet or long, stress-filled hours** in the office will take (**its? their?**) toll on the business executive.

To be sure pronouns agree with antecedents . . .

21b-1   When two nouns joined by *or, nor, either . . . or,* or *neither . . . nor* are singular, be sure any pronoun referring to them is singular.

>   sing.
> **Neither Brazil nor Mexico** will raise **its** oil prices today.

21b-2   When two nouns joined by *or* are plural, be sure any pronoun referring to them is plural.

plural

Players and managers alike may file **their** grievances with the commissioner.

> **TRICKY** **21b–3** When a singular noun is joined to a plural noun by *or, nor, either . . . or,* or *neither . . . nor,* any pronoun should agree in number (and gender) with the noun nearer to it. This guideline should be modified if it produces a sentence that sounds unnatural or awkward.

sing.   plural

Either poor **diet** or long, stress-filled **hours** in the office will take

plural

their toll on the business executive.

plural   sing.

Either long, stress-filled **hours** in the office or poor **diet** will take

sing.

its toll on the business executive.

Pronouns also agree in gender with the nearer antecedent when two nouns are joined by *or.*

masc.   fem.   fem.

Either a **priest** or a **nun** will escort you to **her** office.

fem.   masc.   masc.

Either a **nun** or a **priest** will escort you to **his** office.

Here's a third example, with yet a further complication.

> Neither the **students** nor the **professor** wanted to recalculate (**her? their?**) numbers.

Students is plural; *professor,* singular. The pronoun is nearer to *professor,* and so it should be singular.

plural   sing.

Revised   Neither the **students** nor the **professor** wanted to re-

sing.

calculate **her** numbers.

Notice, however, that it would be easy to assume from this revised sentence that only the numbers of the professor were being talked about—and not those of the students as well. The sentence might need to be revised if a different meaning were intended.

sing.   plural

Revised   Neither the **professor** nor the **students** wanted to re-

plural

calculate **their** numbers.

■ **Exercise 21.2** In the sentences below, select the appropriate words in parentheses.

1. Neither the tour guide nor any of his customers had bothered to confirm (**his/their**) flight from Chicago's O'Hare Airport back to Toledo.
2. Either the ticket agents or a flight attendant working the check-in desk had misread (**their/her**) computer terminal and accidentally canceled the group's reservations.
3. Either the tourists or their guide had to make up (**their/his**) (**minds/mind**) quickly about arranging transportation back to Toledo.
4. Neither the guide nor his wife relished the thought of spending (**his/her/their**) hard-earned money on yet another expensive ticket.
5. Wandering about the vast terminal, the guide located a commuter airline willing to fly either the group or its bags to (**its/their**) destination cheaply.

21c AGREEMENT PROBLEMS WITH COLLECTIVE NOUNS?

Troubleshooting

Agreement problems occur frequently with pronouns that refer to nouns describing groups or collections of things: *class, team, band, government, jury*. These so-called **collective nouns** can be either singular or plural, depending on how they are used in a sentence.

The **chorus** sang **its** heart out.
The **chorus** arrived and took **their** seats.

The **team** looks sharp today.
The **team** lost their luggage.

A pronoun referring to a collective noun should be consistently either singular or plural.

To handle references to collective nouns . . .

Identify any collective noun in a sentence to which a pronoun refers. Decide whether to treat that noun as a single body (the *jury*) or as a group of more than one person or object (the twelve members of the *jury*). Then be consistent. If you decide to treat the word as singular, be sure pronouns referring to it are singular. If you decide it is plural, all pronoun references should be plural.

The **jury** rendered **its** decision.
The **jury** had **their** pictures taken.

In most cases, your sentences will sound more natural if you treat collective nouns as single objects. Notice how awkward the following sentence seems because the collective noun is treated as plural.

The **band** are unhappy with **their** latest recordings.

Sentences like this can be improved either by making the collective nouns more clearly plural or by making them singular.

Members of the band are unhappy with **their** latest recordings.
The **band** is unhappy with **its** latest recordings.

■ **Exercise 21.3** In the following sentences, select the appropriate words in parentheses. Be prepared to defend your answers.

**21d
prn ag**

1. The **class** entered the lecture hall and took (**its/their**) seats, eager to hear from the architect after (**its/their**) field trip to several of his buildings.
2. He belonged to a revitalized **school** of design that had enjoyed (**its/their**) best days four decades ago.
3. The aging architect was accompanied by several **members of his firm,** carrying (**its/their**) designs in huge portfolios.
4. Students hoped that the **board** of directors of the college might give (**its/their**) blessings to a commission by the architect.
5. Any **panel** of experts was likely to cast (**its/their**) vote in favor of such a project.

21d AGREEMENT PROBLEMS WITH INDEFINITE PRONOUNS?

Troubleshooting

A troublesome and common agreement problem involves references to pronouns described as **indefinite.** Common indefinite pronouns include *everyone, anybody, anyone, somebody, all, some, none, each, few,* and *most.* It is not always easy to tell whether one of these indefinite words is singular or plural.

Everyone should keep (**his? their?**) temper.
No one has a right to more than (**his or her? their?**) share.

Yet a decision usually has to be made before a pronoun can be selected.

To handle problems with indefinite pronouns . . .

21d–1 Use the chart below or a dictionary to determine whether an indefinite pronoun or noun in your sentence is singular, variable, or plural. The chart, which is not exhaustive, reflects formal and college usage.

CHART

Indefinite Pronouns

Singular	**Variable, singular or plural**	**Plural**
anybody	all	few
anyone	any	many
anything	either	several
each	more	
everybody	most	
everyone	neither	
everything	none	
nobody	some	
no one		
nothing		
somebody		
someone		
something		

21d
prn ag

21d–2 If the indefinite word is regarded as singular, make any pronouns that refer to it singular.

    sing.   sing.
Did **anybody** misplace **her** notes?

  sing.   sing.
Everyone should keep **his** temper.

   sing.   sing.
No one has a right to more than **his or her** share.

Using singular pronouns in these cases may seem odd at times because the plural forms occur so often in speech and informal writing.

Informal **Each** of the candidates has **their** own ideas.

Informal We discovered that **everyone** had kept **their** notes.

But in college and professional writing, you should still respect the principle of consistent agreement between pronouns and antecedents.

> **Revised—formal**   **Each** of the candidates has **his or her** own ideas.

> **Revised—formal**   We discovered that **everyone** had kept **her** notes.

In a few situations, however, the singular indefinite pronoun does take a plural referent, even in formal and college writing.

> sing.   plural
> Because **each** of the players arrived late, the coach gave **them** a stern lecture on punctuality.

> sing.   plural
> **Nobody** was late, were **they?**

> sing.   plural
> **Everybody** has plenty of money, and **they** are willing to spend it.

♦ **Point of Difference**

> Some grammarians now support constructions like the following.

> **Everyone** is entitled to **their** opinion.
> **Each** of the legislators had **their** say.

They point out that indefinite pronouns like *everyone* or expressions like *each of the legislators* have the effect of describing groups, not individuals. That's why most speakers of English intuitively treat them as plurals. Moreover, treating such indefinites as plurals avoids the need to use a clumsy *his or her* to avoid sexist language.

> **Everyone** is entitled to **his or her** opinion.

Still, most editors and professional writers do not approve of these usages—yet. ♦

21d-3 **If the indefinite word is usually plural, make any pronouns that refer to it plural.**

> plural   plural
> **Several** of the jet fighters had to have **their** wings stiffened.

> plural   plural
> **Few,** however, had given **their** pilots trouble.

21d-4 **If the indefinite word is variable, use your judgment to determine which pronoun suits the sentence better.** In many cases, words or phrases modifying the pronoun determine its number.

var.   plural   var.
All of the portraits had yellowed in **their** frames. **Some** will be re-
        plural
stored to **their** original condition.

var.   sing.   var.
All of the wine is still in **its** casks. **Some** of the vintage is certain
        sing.
to have **its** quality evaluated.

None is considered variable because it is often accepted as a plural form. However, in formal writing, you should usually treat *none* as singular. Think of *none* as meaning *not one*.

> **None** of the women is reluctant to speak **her** mind.
> **None** of the churches has **its** doors locked.

▶ **Fine Tuning**

Person is singular, not plural. Don't use *they* to refer to *person*.

Agreement error	If a **person** watches too much television, **they** may become a couch potato.
Revised	If a **person** watches too much television, **he or she** may become a couch potato. ◀

21d
prn ag

■ **Exercise 21.4** Select the word or phrase in parentheses that would be correct in formal and college writing.

1. Anybody can learn to drive an automobile with a manual transmission if (**they are/he or she is**) coordinated.
2. But not everyone will risk (**his or her/their**) (**life/lives**) trying.
3. Few today seem eager to take (**his or her/their**) driver's tests in a five-speed.
4. Everyone learning to drive a manual car expects (**his or her/their**) car to stall at the most inopportune moment.
5. Most of all, nobody wants to stop (**his or her/their**) manual-shift car on a steep hill.

Problems with Pronoun Case?

22a
case

22a   DO YOU UNDERSTAND CASE: SUBJECT/OBJECT/POSSESSIVE?

Troubleshooting

Some personal pronouns (and *who*) change their form according to how they are used in a sentence. These different forms are called **case.** **Subjective** (or **nominative**) **case** is the form a pronoun takes when it is the subject of a sentence or a clause: *I, you, she, he, it, we, they, who.* A pronoun is also in the subjective case when it follows a linking verb as a **predicate nominative.**

It is **I**.
It was **they** who cast the deciding votes.

Objective case is the form a pronoun takes when something is done to it: Elena broke *them;* Buck loved *her.* This is also the form a pronoun takes after a preposition: (to) *me, her, him, us, them, whom.* The subjective and objective forms of the pronouns *you* and *it* are identical.

The **possessive case** is the form a pronoun takes when it shows ownership: *my, mine, your, yours, her, hers, his, its, our, ours, their, theirs, whose.*

In most situations, writers are able to select the appropriate form (or *case*) without thinking much about their choices.

Whose book did **she** give to **him?**

They were more confident of **their** position than **we** were of **ours.**

But at other times, selecting the right case is no easy matter. The correct pronoun choice may even look or sound wrong.

An editor will ordinarily circle an error in case and write *case* in the margin next to a sentence with such a problem.

(Who) did you write to? *case*

To manage pronoun case . . .

22a–1 Use subject forms when pronouns act as subjects, object forms when pronouns act as objects (especially in prepositional phrases), and possessive forms when pronouns show ownership. Use the chart below to select the appropriate forms.

22a

case

CHART

Pronoun Case

SUBJECT FORMS	OBJECT FORMS	POSSESSIVE FORMS
I	me	my, mine
we	us	our, ours
you	you	your, yours
he	him	his
she	her	her, hers
it	it	its, of it
they	them	their, theirs
who	whom	whose

You are most likely to have a problem selecting the correct case when faced with a pair of pronouns. The second pronoun is usually the troublesome one.

You and (**I? me?**) don't have an honest relationship.

The pronouns here are both part of the subject. So you should select the subjective form of the *I/me* pair—which is *I.*

But even if you didn't recognize the need for a subject form, you could still make the right choice by imagining how the sentence would read if you dropped the first pronoun. With only one pronoun in the sentence, you can usually tell immediately what the correct form should be.

Wrong   **Me** don't have an honest relationship.

Right   **I** don't have an honest relationship.

Given this choice, most people will select the correct pronoun—*I.*

Revised   **You** and **I** don't have an honest relationship.

This simple but effective technique works with many confusing pairs of pronouns or nouns and pronouns.

22a-2   **When a pronoun is followed by an appositive, the pronoun and noun share the same case.** An appositive is a noun or noun phrase that describes or explains another noun.

Subject   **We** *lucky sailors* missed the storm.

Object   The storm missed **us** *lucky sailors*.

You may run into a problem when a pronoun in a prepositional phrase is followed by an appositive noun. The proper form for the pronoun is the objective case, even though it may sound odd to the ear.

For **us** engineers, the job market looks promising.

We engineers may sound more correct, but *we* is the subjective form and should not be used after the preposition *for*.

22b   PROBLEMS WITH PRONOUN CASE IN PREPOSITIONAL PHRASES?

Troubleshooting

Prepositions are words that link nouns or pronouns to the rest of sentences; they point out many basic relationships: *on, above, to, for, between, beyond,* and so on. Combining a preposition and a pronoun produces a *prepositional phrase: above it, to him, of whom.* Pronouns in such phrases are the objects of the prepositions and are almost always in the objective case. Difficulties with case are rare when a single pronoun closely follows its preposition.

Come *with* **me** now.
Wait *for* **us.**

You would never say *Come with I now* or *Wait for we.*

But add another pronoun or noun after the preposition, and you may suddenly have questions about the correct form.

Come *with* Travis and (**I? me?**) now.
Wait *for* (**he? him?**) and (**I? me?**).

To select the right pronoun form . . .

Use the objective case when pronouns are the objects of prepositional phrases. Difficulties are most likely to arise when a preposition takes two objects.

     prep. obj.   obj.
Come *with* **Travis** and (**I? me?**) now.

    prep.   obj.   obj.
Wait *for* (**he? him?**) and (**I? me?**) now.

    prep.   obj.   obj.
Just *between* **you** and (**I? me?**), the answer is "Yes."

A quick glance at the chart on page 347 shows that the forms needed in these sentences are the objective ones: *me* and *him*.

Come with Travis and **me** now.
Wait for **him** and **me.**
Just between you and **me,** the answer is "Yes."

In some cases, you can reach the same conclusion by deleting the object causing problems and considering the alternatives.

First version   Come *with* **I** now.

Second version Come *with* **me** now.

In this case, the deletion makes it clearer that the second version is correct, and so the full sentence can be restored.

Revised   Come *with* Travis and **me** now.

■ **Exercise 22.1** Select the correct pronoun from the choices offered in parentheses.

1. In the reporter's opinion, neither (**she/her**) nor her competitors had done a good job in covering the city's financial crisis.
2. It was likely that both political parties would now accuse (**she/her**) and (**they/them**) of media bias.
3. Knowing her colleagues at the competing TV stations, the reporter was convinced that both she and (**they/them**) had rushed their stories.
4. She had assumed that the city manager's staff had been honest about

22b
case

the financial problems, but now she wasn't sure they had been straight with (**she/her**).

5. "You and (**I/me**) will just have to accept the criticism," the reporter told a professional colleague, who just frowned at (**she/her**).

22c   PROBLEMS WITH PRONOUN CASE IN COMPARISONS?

Troubleshooting

Expect problems with pronoun case when writing a comparison that includes *than* or *as* followed by a pronoun. You'll recognize this familiar difficulty immediately.

> I am taller *than* (**him? he?**).
> Politics does not interest me as much *as* (**she? her?**).

**22c
case**

To select the right pronoun after *than* or *as* . . .

22c–1 **Expand the comparison into a complete clause.** For example, you might be puzzling over a choice like this.

> I am taller *than* (**him? he?**).

To expand the comparison—"*than* (*him? he?*)"—into a clause, you need to add a verb, in this case *is*.

> I am taller *than* (**him? he?**) *is*.

22c–2 **Now choose the appropriate form of the pronoun.** The correct pronoun form will usually be more obvious once a verb is in place.

> **Revised**   I am taller *than* **he** (is).

To work as the subject of the verb *is*, the pronoun (*him/he*) must take its subjective form (*he*). However, you don't have to write the verb *is* into the sentence; it can remain implied.

Here is another example, with *as*.

> Politics does not interest me as much *as* (**she? her?**).

Notice, however, that the comparison can be expanded in two different ways.

> Politics does not interest me as much *as* it interests (**she? her?**).
> Politics does not interest me as much *as* (**she? her?**) does.

As a result, the pronoun you select will determine what the sentence means. Select the subjective pronoun *she*, and this is the result.

Revised Politics does not interest me as much *as* **she** (does).

Choose the objective pronoun *her*, and the sentence has a different meaning.

Revised Politics does not interest me as much *as* (it interests) **her.**

For the sake of clarity, it often makes sense to write out the implied verbs in such situations.

Here's a second example.

Shawn likes Connie better *than* (**I? me?**).

First version Shawn likes Connie better *than* **I** do.

Second version Shawn likes Connie better *than* he likes **me.**

■ **Exercise 22.2** Select the correct pronoun from the choices offered in parentheses.

1. Although the Cowardly Lion needed the Wizard's help as much as Dorothy did, the King of the Jungle was less determined than **(she/her)** to hike to Oz.
2. Dorothy probably felt more confident than **(he/him)** that she could deal with the wily Wizard.
3. Perhaps Dorothy could relate more easily to **(he/him)** than a lion could.
4. Although more cautious in his appraisal of the Wizard than Dorothy, the Scarecrow was no less eager for guidance than **(she/her).**
5. Perhaps the Scarecrow even feared that Dorothy would like the Wizard more than **(he/him).**

22d | **PROBLEMS WITH PRONOUN CASE AFTER LINKING VERBS?**

Troubleshooting

Linking verbs, such as *to be, to seem, to appear, to feel,* and *to become,* connect a subject to a word or phrase that extends or completes its meaning—the **subject complement.** When complements are pronouns, they are in the subjective case.

   subj. l.v.   subj. comp.
The *culprits* are obviously **they.**

22d
case

subj.   l.v.   subj. comp.

The *commander-in-chief* will be **he.**

subj.   l.v. subj. comp.

The *one* who will prevail is **I.**

Yet complements can be puzzling. Many writers would have a tough time deciding which of the following pairs of sentences is correct.

It is **I.**	It is **me.**
That is **she.**	That is **her.**
This is **he.**	This is **him.**

In college English, the left-hand column is considered correct. The pronouns after the verb are all subject complements in the subjective case: *I, she, he.* But exceptions are allowed: *It is me* is acceptable too.

To select the right pronoun . . .

22d-1 In most instances, use the subjective case of a pronoun when it is the complement of a linking verb.

> The next CEO of the corporation will be **she.**
> The director was **he.**

It might sound more natural here to reverse the order and write "He was the director."

22d-2 If it sounds more natural, you may use the objective case of a pronoun when it is the complement of a linking verb. You'd certainly use these forms when writing dialogue, for example.

> It is **me.**
> That's **her.**

But in most college writing you'll do well to stay with the subjective form.

■ **Exercise 22.3** Review Sections 22a through 22d. Select the correct pronoun from the choices in parentheses below.

1. That is (**he/him**) in the office there.
2. The guilty party certainly was not (**she/her**).
3. Spying three men in uniform, we assumed that the pilots were (**they/them**).
4. They are (**who/whom**)?
5. We were surprised that the person who had complained was (**she/her**).

22d
case

22e   DO YOU HAVE TROUBLE CHOOSING BETWEEN *WHO* AND *WHOM?*

Troubleshooting

TRICKY   In informal spoken English, the distinction between *who* and *whom* (or *whoever/whomever*) has just about disappeared. In written English, however, many readers still expect the distinction to be observed.

To choose between *who* and *whom* . . .

22e–1 Select the subjective form (*who*) when pronouns act as subjects, the objective form (*whom*) when pronouns act as objects. The appropriate choice is especially important in prepositional phrases.

> **Subjective form**   **Who** wrote this letter?
> **Objective form**   You addressed **whom?**
> **Objective form**   To **whom** did you write?

The problem, of course, with *who/whom* is figuring out whether the word is acting as a subject or an object. Both versions of some troublesome sentences are likely to seem acceptable.

> **Who** did you address?
> **Whom** did you address?

To select the appropriate form, you need to identify the subject and the object.

> obj.   subj.
> **Appropriate**   **Whom** did you address?

If you can locate the verb, you can usually figure out who is doing what to whom.

> (**Who? Whom?**) are you taking on the tour?

The verb is *are taking*. The doer of the action is clearly *you: you are taking*. The person receiving the action, then, is the objective form of *who/whom: whom*.

> **Appropriate**   **Whom** are you taking on the tour?

Be careful with sentences containing passive verbs, where the subject remains in the subjective case (*who*) even though it does not actually perform the action described by the verb.

> **Appropriate**   **Who** was accused of cheating?

22e
who(m)

22e–2 When *who/whom* (or *whoever/whomever*) is part of a dependent clause, *who/whom* takes the form it would have in the dependent clause, not in the sentence as a whole. Constructions of this kind are quite common. The phrases underlined in the following examples are clauses within full sentences.

> The system rewards **whoever** works hard.
> The deficit will increase no matter **whom** we elect president.
> **Whomever** we nominate is likely to be elected.

● **Tip**

When you can't recall all the fine points of *who/whom* (or can't consult your handbook), play it safe by using *who* in most situations—except immediately after a preposition. After a preposition, use *whom: to whom, for whom, with whom.* Using *who* in all other circumstances will mean you are technically incorrect whenever the word is acting as an object. But *who* misused as an object usually sounds less stodgy than *whom* misused as a subject.

Who **misused as an object**	You addressed **who?**
Whom **misused as a subject**	**Whom** wrote this letter? ●

■ **Exercise 22.4** Decide which of the pronoun forms in parentheses is correct in each of the following sentences.

1. Sam Donaldson looks like a man (**whom/who**) wouldn't trust a nun with a prayer.
2. (**Whom/Who**) wouldn't like to win the state lottery?
3. To (**who/whom**) would you go for sound financial advice?
4. Are these the children (**who/whom**) you took to Santa Fe?
5. Officials couldn't determine (**who/whom**) rigged the contest.

22f **PROBLEMS WITH POSSESSIVE PRONOUNS?**

Troubleshooting

The most common way of showing ownership in English is to add an apostrophe + *-s* to a noun: Sarah's book, the dog's owner. The familiar *-'s* is not, however, used with **personal pronouns** (and *who*)—and this exception confuses some writers who are inclined to add *-'s* to personal pronouns that don't require it.

The possessive forms of *indefinite pronouns* can be troublesome as well. Some indefinite pronouns take the apostrophe + -*s* to indicate ownership, but others do not.

To be sure you are using the right possessive pronoun . . .

22f–1 **Remember that personal pronouns do not require an apostrophe to show ownership.** This is true whether the possessive pronoun comes before or after a noun.

BEFORE THE NOUN	AFTER THE NOUN
That is **my** *book*.	The *book* is **mine**.
That is **your** *book*.	The *book* is **yours**.
That is **her** *book*.	The *book* is **hers**.
That is **his** *book*.	The *book* is **his**.
That is **our** *book*.	The *book* is **ours**.
That is **their** *book*.	The *book* is **theirs**.
Whose *book* is this?	The *book* is **whose?**

22f–2 **Remember that while some indefinite pronouns can form the possessive by adding -'s, others cannot.** Among the indefinite pronouns that cannot add -'*s* to show possession are these.

22f

poss

CHART

Possessive Forms of Indefinite Pronouns

INDEFINITE PRONOUN	FORM OF THE POSSESSIVE
all	the opinion **of all**
any	the sight **of any**
each	the price **of each**
few	the judgment **of few**
most	the dream **of most**
none	the choice **of none**
some	the expectation **of some**

Indefinite pronouns ending in -*body* or -*one* can form the possessive with -'*s* or with *of*.

INDEFINITE PRONOUN	FORMS OF THE POSSESSIVE
anybody	**anybody's** opinion
	the opinion **of anybody**
someone	**someone's** hope
	the hope **of someone**

22g   SPECIAL PROBLEMS: *ITS/IT'S* AND *WHOSE/WHO'S*

Troubleshooting

CAUTION

One of the most common and *avoidable* of mechanical errors in English is mistaking the possessive pronoun *its* for the contraction *it's* (which means *it is* or *it has*). This simple error is so pervasive that we have chosen to treat it in a special section. A related error is mistaking *whose* for *who's*.

To avoid confusing possessive pronouns and contractions . . .

22g–1   Remember that *its* is a possessive form; *it's* is a contraction.

> **Wrong**   The van lost **it's** hubcaps while parked on the street.
>
> **Right**   The van lost **its** hubcaps while parked on the street.
>
> **Wrong**   **Its** a shame that thefts in the neighborhood have increased.
>
> **Right**   **It's** a shame that thefts in the neighborhood have increased.
>
> **Wrong**   **Its** unlikely that the aircraft will lose **it's** way in the dark. **Its** equipped with radar.
>
> **Right**   **It's** unlikely that the aircraft will lose **its** way in the dark. **It's** equipped with radar.

The apostrophe makes the contracted form—*it's*—look suspiciously like a possessive. And the possessive form—*its*—sounds like a contraction. But don't be fooled. The possessive forms of a personal pronoun never take an apostrophe, while contractions always require one.

> **Possessive form**   The iron left **its** grim outline on the silk shirt.
>
> **Contraction**   **It's** a stupid proposal.

If you consistently misuse *its/it's*, circle these words whenever they appear in your work and then check them. It may help if you always read *it's* as *it is*. Eventually you will eliminate this error.

22g–2   Remember that the possessive of *who* is *whose*. Don't mistake *whose*, the possessive, for *who's*, the contraction for *who is* or *who has*.

> **Possessive form**   **Whose** teammate is on first base?
>
> **Contraction**   **Who's** on first?

■ **Exercise 22.5** Circle all occurrences of *its/it's* in the following passage and correct any errors.

1. Its been decades since Americans have felt as comfortable traveling in Eastern Europe as they do now.
2. Its likely that tourism will soon become a major industry in Hungary, Poland, and the Czech Republic.
3. Each of these countries has much to attract tourists to its cities.
4. Yet its the small towns of Eastern Europe that many Americans may find most appealing.
5. In rural areas, sensitive travelers often get a better feel for a country and its people.

■ **Exercise 22.6** Review Sections 22f and 22g. Identify and correct any pronoun-related errors in the sentences below.

1. There is usually not much doubt about whose responsible for enormous environmental disasters.
2. Its not hard to spot a capsized oil tanker.
3. Yet anybodys home or yard can contribute to environmental pollution.
4. The earth is our's to protect or despoil.
5. Ecology has to be everyone's responsibility.

22g poss

Other Pronoun Problems?

23a PROBLEMS WITH REFLEXIVE AND INTENSIVE PRONOUNS?

Troubleshooting

Reflexive and **intensive pronouns** are the pronoun forms created when *-self* is added to singular personal pronouns and *-selves* to plural personal pronouns: *myself, yourself, herself, himself, itself, oneself, ourselves, yourselves, themselves.*

These words are *reflexive* in sentences like the following, where both the subject and the object of an action are the same person or thing.

>   subj.   obj.
> *They* took **themselves** too seriously.

They are *intensive* when they modify a noun or other pronoun to add emphasis.

>   noun
> *Warren* **himself** admitted he was responsible.

>   pron.
> *I* never vote **myself.**

Writers sometimes use reflexive pronouns—especially *myself*—inappropriately, believing that intensive forms are somehow more correct or formal than simple personal pronouns. Other writers use the nonstandard forms *hisself* or *theirselves*. Both issues are addressed in this section.

There are no specific proofreading symbols for problems with reflexive and intensive pronouns. An editor is likely just to circle a doubtful form and mark *pron.* in the margin.

Jack (hisself) appeared at the meeting. *pron*

To handle reflexive/intensive pronouns correctly . . .

23a–1 **Don't use a reflexive pronoun to make a sentence sound more formal.** The basic pronoun form is adequate.

| **Nonstandard** | The gift is for Matthew and **yourself.** |
| **Revised** | The gift is for Matthew and **you.** |

Use the pronoun reflexively only when the subject and object in a sentence refer to the same person or thing.

subj.   obj.
Maggie rediscovered **herself** in her painting.

subj.   obj.
Corey had only **himself** to blame.

Problems occur most often with the form *myself* when it is used in place of a more suitable *I* or *me.* In such cases, the subject and the object of the sentence are not the same. So the reflexive form (*myself*) is not needed. The simple subject form—*I* in the example below—suffices.

subj.   obj.
Nonstandard   *Kate and myself* wrote the lab **report.**
Revised   *Kate and I* wrote the lab **report.**

Compare the sentence above to a similar one using *myself* correctly as an intensive pronoun.

I wrote the lab report **myself.**

23a–2 **Use intensive pronouns where emphasis is needed.**

The gift is for *you* **yourself.**
The *residents* did all the plumbing and wiring **themselves.**

23a–3 **Never use the forms *hisself* or *theirselves*.** Although you may hear these expressions—especially *theirselves*—in speech, the correct forms in writing are always *himself* and *themselves.*

| Wrong | Lincoln wrote the letter **hisself.** |
| Correct | Lincoln wrote the letter **himself.** |

| Wrong | They saw **theirselves** on television. |
| Correct | They saw **themselves** on television. |

■ **Exercise 23.1** Correct any problems with reflexive or intensive pronouns in the sentences below.

1. "God helps them who help themselves" is an adage credited to Benjamin Franklin.
2. The delegates to the Federal Constitutional Convention in 1787 were not sure they could agree among theirselves on a new form of government.
3. George Washington hisself presided over the convention.
4. Aaron and myself wrote a paper on Madison's contribution to the Constitution.
5. You might want to read about the topic yourself.

23b **PROBLEMS WITH *THAT*, *WHICH*, AND *WHO*?**

Troubleshooting

You may recall a rule requiring the use of the pronoun *that* with essential or restrictive modifiers (clauses that determine the meaning of the word modified) and *which* with nonessential or nonrestrictive clauses (modifiers that add information but aren't essential to the meaning of a sentence).

| Essential clause | The car **that hit me** rolled into the shallow ditch. |
| Nonessential clause | My car, **which is a station wagon,** sustained little damage. |

Yet in reading you may have encountered writers who use *which* both restrictively and nonrestrictively.

| Restrictive clause | The car **which hit me** rolled into the shallow ditch. |

What is the correct form? When is *who* an appropriate alternative to *which* and *that*?

To decide among *that, which,* and *who*. . .

23b–1 **Understand that both essential (restrictive) and nonessential (nonrestrictive) clauses may begin with *which*.** A clause introduced by *that* will almost always be essential. No commas are used around such clauses.

> The concept **that** intrigued the shareholders most involved profit sharing.

> The report **that** I wrote recommended the concept.

Context and punctuation, however, determine whether a *which* clause is essential or nonessential. If the clause is essential, no commas separate it from the rest of the sentence; if nonessential, commas enclose the clause.

Essential clause	The car **which** hit me rolled into a ditch.
Nonessential clause	The car, **which** hit me, rolled into a ditch.
Essential clause	The idea **which** intrigued the shareholders most was the simplest one.
Nonessential clause	The idea, **which** intrigued the shareholders a great deal, was quite simple.

23b
pron

It makes sense to maintain the distinction between *that* and *which* if you understand it clearly. In general, you'll be right most of the time if you use *that*, unless *which* is very clearly the necessary choice.

23b–2 **Use *who* rather than *that* or *which* when modifying a human subject.**

Inappropriate	The woman **that** waved was my boss.
Better	The woman **who** waved was my boss.

■ **Exercise 23.2** Decide among *that/which/who* in the following sentences. Add commas where needed.

1. Charlie Chaplin's tramp (**that/which/who**) wore a derby, baggy trousers, and a mustache may still be the most recognized character on film.
2. The popularity (**that/which/who**) Chaplin had in the early days of film may never be equaled either.
3. His graceful gestures and matchless acrobatics (**that/which/who**) some critics likened to ballet were perfectly suited to the silent screen.
4. A flaw (**that/which/who**) weakens many of Chaplin's films is sentimentality.

5. Chaplin's tramp made a last appearance in *The Great Dictator* (1940) (**that/which/who**) satirized Hitler's regime.

23c WHEN SHOULD YOU USE *I, WE, YOU,* OR *ONE?*

Troubleshooting

Many writers are unsure when—if ever—they may use *I, we,* or *you* in professional or college writing. Some teachers and editors effectively outlaw *I* or *you* in all but personal essays. As a result, writers resort to the passive voice ("it is believed"), to awkward references to self ("this writer," "the author of this piece"), or to the pronoun *one.* All of these strategies for avoiding *I* and *you* can make college papers sound awkward or unduly formal.

Pronouns do, in fact, alter the distance between writer and reader. Choosing *I* or *we* puts you closer to readers; using *one* creates distance. You may find the following suggestions helpful.

When setting the tone for a paper . . .

23c-1 Use *I* whenever it makes sense for you or your opinions to appear in an essay. In general, avoid the first person *I* in scientific reports and expository essays where your identity or your personal opinions are likely to be unimportant to readers.

> **With *I*** **I learned** through a survey **I did** that students who drive a car on campus are more likely to have jobs than those who do not.

> **Revised** **A survey showed** that students who drive a car on campus are more likely to have jobs than those who do not.

However, when you find that avoiding *I* makes you resort to an awkward passive verb, use *I* instead.

> **Wordy** **It is believed** that the semester is too long.

> **Revised** **I believe** the semester is too long.

You can often eliminate an awkward passive without using *I.*

> **Revised without *I*** The semester is too long.

The same advice—to use *I* sensibly—applies when you find yourself cobbling clumsy phrases just to avoid the pronoun.

Wordy	**In the opinion of this writer,** federal taxes should be lowered.
Revised	**I believe** federal taxes should be lowered.
Revised without *I*	Federal taxes should be lowered.

◆ Point of Difference

Some editors and teachers simply will not allow *I* in college and scientific prose. When writing for them, respect their rules. However, most writers today recognize that using *I* is both natural and sensible even in relatively formal work. Not using *I* or *we* (when more than one author is involved) can even lead to doubts about who is taking responsibility for a statement. ◆

23c–2 **Use *we* whenever two or more writers are involved in a project or when you are writing to express the opinion of a group.**

23c
pron

When **we** compared our surveys, **we** discovered the conflicting evidence.

We believe that the city council has an obligation to reconsider its zoning action.

Or use the first person *we* to indicate a general condition when it is appropriate to comment editorially.

We need better control of our medical-care systems in the United States.

Avoid *we* or *us* as a chummy way of addressing your reader. When introducing a paper or handling a transition, don't make it sound as if you are narrating a travelogue.

Now that **we** have completed our survey of mental disorders, let **us** turn to . . .

In most college writing, *we* used this way sounds pompous.

23c–3 **Use *you* whenever it makes sense to address your readers personally or when you are giving orders or directions.** *You* sounds direct, cordial, and personal. So be sure you really want your readers included when using the second person in college writing. The following sentence, for example, may be too personal. It seems to implicate readers directly in scholastic dishonesty.

Inappropriate	A recent student government survey suggested that you will cheat in two courses during your college career.
Revised	A recent student government survey suggested that **most students** will cheat in two courses during their college careers.

Also, be sure that when you write *you*, you aren't describing an experience that would be handled better from first person (*I*) or third person (*he, she, they*) points of view.

Inappropriate	**You** are likely to be puzzled by the hero's character when **you** first read *Hamlet*.
Revised	**Some people** might be puzzled by the hero's character when **they** first read *Hamlet*.

23c–4 Use *one* when you want to express a thought that might be yours, but which should be understood more generally. *One* is often useful for conveying moral sentiments or general truths.

> Consider the anxiety of not knowing where **one's** next meal is coming from.

> **One** learns a great deal about old Russia from reading Dostoevsky.

Notice that *one* makes the sentence more formal than it would be if *one* were replaced by *I* or *you*.

Sentences with too many *ones*, however, may seem like the butlers of British comedy—sneering and superior.

Pompous	**One** can never be too careful about maintaining **one's** good reputation, can **one?**

In most cases, *you* or an appropriate noun sounds less stiff than *one*, especially when giving directions.

Wordy	If **one** is uncertain about the authority of **one's** sources, **one** should consult a librarian in the reference room.
Revised	If **you** are uncertain about the authority of **your** sources, consult a librarian in the reference room.

23c–5 Whatever pronoun forms you use, be reasonably consistent. Don't switch pronouns in the middle of a sentence or paragraph. Problems are most likely to occur with the indefinite pronoun *one*.

Nonstandard **One** cannot know what **their** future holds.

Here the pronoun shifts incorrectly from *one* to the plural form *they*. Several revisions are possible.

> **Revised** **One** cannot know what **his or her** future holds.
>
> **Revised** **People** cannot know what **their** futures hold.
>
> **Revised** **One** cannot know what the future holds.

You may shift between *one* and *he* or *she*, as the example above demonstrates.

■ **Exercise 23.3** Revise the sentences below to create a passage appropriate for a college report. Pay particular attention to the words and phrases in boldface.

1. **I was amazed to learn that** the Chinese speak a variety of dialects of a language **they** describe as Han.
2. Although there are only eight major varieties of Han, **you would find them** as different from each other as one Romance language is from another.
3. **One finds,** moreover, that each of the eight versions of Han occurs in a great many dialects, adding to **your** linguistic confusion.
4. **You will be glad to know,** however, that the Chinese use only one system of writing—a set of common ideographs—for expressing all **their** dialects.
5. As **you** might expect, there have been efforts to reform the Chinese language to make it easier **for you** to communicate between one region and another in the vast and populous country.

23d
pron

23d DO YOUR PRONOUNS TREAT BOTH SEXES FAIRLY?

Troubleshooting

What happens when you need to use a pronoun but don't know whether it should refer to a man or a woman?

Each of the editors walked to (**his? her?**) car.

Until fairly recently, you would have been expected to use a masculine pronoun (*he, him, his*) in any such situation—on the grounds that when you are talking about *man*kind you are also thinking about *woman*kind.

> **Sexist** Each of the editors walked to **his** car.

But, in fact, such male-only constructions can exclude women from more than just grammar. (See also Section 10d–1.) Notice the broader implications in these sentences.

> **Sexist**　After he wins election, a **senator** chooses **his** own staff.
>
> **Sexist**　An experienced **pilot** can sense when **his** plane has a problem.

English has a second person singular form that includes men and women alike: *you*. But, unfortunately, the third person singular forms are either male (*he, him, his*), female (*she, her, hers*), or neuter (*it, its*). And *it* just doesn't work as a substitute for a person.

Despite this limitation, in your writing you should remember that members of either sex may belong to almost every profession or group—students, athletes, coal miners, truckers, secretaries, nurses. Let your language reflect that diversity. Obviously, you should acknowledge the inevitable exceptions.

23d
pron

> Each of the nuns received an award for **her** service to the community.
>
> None of the NFL quarterbacks received a payment for **his** appearance at the benefit.

But in situations where you cannot assume that members of a group will all be male or female, be sure your language accommodates both sexes. You can do that in a variety of ways.

To avoid pronouns that exclude some people . . .

23d–1 **Use the expressions** *he or she, him or her,* **or** *his or her* **instead of the pronoun of either sex alone.**

> **Sexist**　Every secretary may invite **her husband.**
>
> **Revised**　Every secretary may invite **his or her spouse.**

Unfortunately, *he or she* expressions can be awkward and tiresome when they occur more than once in a sentence. In many cases, you'll want to try another strategy for avoiding an exclusionary usage.

23d–2 **Change a singular reference to a plural one.** Because plural pronouns do not have a specific gender in English, you can often avoid the choice between *he* or *she* simply by turning singular references into plural ones.

> **Sexist**　**Every** secretary may invite **her husband.**
>
> **Revised**　**All** secretaries may invite **their spouses.**

Here's a second example.

Tiresome	Before **he or she** leaves, **each** member of the band should be sure **he or she** has **his or her** music.
Revised	Before leaving, **all** members of the band should be sure **they** have **their** music.

Notice that this version eliminates *he or she* entirely.

23d-3 **Cut the troublesome pronoun.** The preceding example shows that in some cases you can simply cut the feminine or masculine pronoun from a sentence. Here are more examples.

Original	*Anybody* may bring **his or her** favorite record.
Revised	*Anybody* may bring **a** favorite record.
Original	*Nobody* should leave until **he or she** has signed the guest book.
Revised	*Nobody* should leave until after **signing** the guest book.
Original	*Each* should keep a record of **his or her** losses and gains in weight.
Revised	*Each* should keep a personal record of losses and gains in weight.

These options are useful, but not always available.

23d-4 **Use *he* and *she* alternatively.** You can try to balance references to males and females in a particular article. This does not mean arbitrarily shifting gender with every pronoun. In most cases, pronouns can be varied sensibly and naturally within chunks of prose—between paragraphs, for example, or between the examples in a series. Handled skillfully, the shift between masculine and feminine references need not attract a reader's attention.

> The dean of students knew that any student could purchase term papers through mail-order term paper services. If **he** could afford the scam, a student might construct **his** entire college career around papers **he** had purchased.
>
> Yet the dean also acknowledged that the typical plagiarist was rarely so grossly dishonest and calculating. **She** tended to resort to such highly unethical behavior only when **she** believed an assignment was beyond **her** capabilities or **her** workload was excessive.

Avoid varying pronoun gender within individual sentences.

23d
pron

23d-5 **Use a plural pronoun with indefinite pronouns formerly considered singular.** Although this pronoun-referent *dis*agreement—very common in speech—is gaining limited acceptance in writing, be warned that many readers still consider such forms simply wrong.

> *Every skier* took **their** turn on the ski slopes.

Technically, *every skier* is singular and thus requires a singular pronoun: *his or her.*

> *Every skier* took **his or her** turn on the ski slopes.

The problem is easy to avoid.

> *Every skier* took **a** turn on the ski slopes.

◆ Point of Difference

Most writers and editors favor handling pronouns in a way that acknowledges the role both sexes play in society. But some people object to particular pronoun constructions devised to express that diversity, expressions such as *he/she, s/he,* and *s'he.* In most situations, you are better off using the widely accepted (if sometimes clumsy) *he or she.* ◆

■ **Exercise 23.4** Revise the following sentences to make them read more easily and to eliminate pronouns that might be considered exclusionary.

1. Earlier this century, a laborer might fear that heavy equipment would mangle his limbs or that pollutants might damage his system.
2. Today, a worker has to be concerned with new threats to her health.
3. Anybody who faces a computer terminal eight hours a day must worry about his exposure to radiation and wonder whether his muscles and joints are being damaged by the repetitive limb motions required by his job.
4. Frankly, the typical worker is often so concerned with her job performance that she may not consider that her workplace poses risks.
5. Of course, every worker wants their job to be safe.

Problems with Sentence Boundaries: Fragments, Comma Splices, and Run-ons?

A Sentence Fragments
B Intentional Fragments
C Comma Splices
D Run-on Sentences

Three of the most troublesome and common sentence problems are the fragment, the comma splice, and the run-on. As you'll see, all three problems arise from confusion about what the boundaries of a sentence are. Once you get a feel for those boundaries and the signals writers use to mark them off, you are less likely to have these problems.

24a HOW CAN YOU GET RID OF SENTENCE FRAGMENTS?

Troubleshooting

You may be getting comments on your papers warning you about problems with incomplete sentences or fragments. If so, it's worth figuring out what's going wrong because **sentence fragments** can distract or confuse a reader. They can also make you look like a careless writer. This section will show you how to identify sentence fragments, how to fix them, and how to avoid writing them in the first place.

An editor or instructor will usually mark such sentences with the abbreviation for sentence fragment, *frag.*

The bill died. Because the president vetoed it. *frag*

To eliminate fragments . . .

24a–1 **Check that you have not tried to make a dependent or subordinate clause stand alone as a sentence.** Dependent clauses—clauses that start with words such as *although, because, if, since, unless, when, while, whose*—won't work as sentences by themselves even though they have a subject and a verb.

> **Fragment**   If the mail comes on time.

> **Fragment**   Because there had been no rain for three months.

These are fragments or broken sentences—that is, parts of a sentence left suspended in air and needing something else to finish them. By themselves, they leave the reader puzzled, waiting to find out what they should be attached to. Such fragments can usually be repaired by linking them to another sentence. For example, the previous fragments could be attached to independent clauses to make full sentences.

24a
frag

> **Complete sentence**
> If the mail comes on time, it will be a miracle.

> **Complete sentence**
> Because there had been no rain for three months, the town started an emergency water-rationing program.

Here are some additional examples that show the dependent clause fragments or broken sentences in boldface.

> **Fragment**
> More than 1,400 women were interviewed for the part of Scarlett O'Hara. **Before Vivien Leigh won the role in *Gone With the Wind*.**

> **Fragment eliminated**
> More than 1,400 women were interviewed for the part of Scarlett O'Hara before Vivien Leigh won the role in *Gone With the Wind.*

> **Fragment**
> Rainbows can be observed only in the morning or late afternoon. **When the sun is less than forty degrees above the horizon.**

> **Fragment eliminated**
> Rainbows can be observed only in the morning or late afternoon when the sun is less than forty degrees above the horizon.

CHECKLIST

Whenever you write a clause that begins with a subordinating word, check for a fragment. Subordinating words include the following.

after	how	sooner than	whether
although	if	that	which
as	in order that	though	while
as soon as	once	unless	who
because	rather than	until	whose
before	since	when	why
even though	so	whenever	
for	so that	where	

24a–2 **Check that you have not tried to make a relative clause or appositive stand alone as a sentence.** Words like *who, which, that,* and *where* frequently signal the beginning of a relative clause that must be connected to the main part of a sentence to make sense.

24a
frag

Fragment

She was just plain Hilda Holby. **Who had never won a thing in her life.**

Another sort of clause that often turns into a sentence fragment is the appositive, a group of words that gives more information about a noun. When such clauses are separated and made to look like sentences, you get sentence fragments. Here is an example with the fragment in bold-face.

Fragment

Hilda nearly fainted when she opened the letter from Publisher's Clearing House Sweepstakes. **The contest she'd been entering faithfully for twenty years.**

The phrase starting with *The* is punctuated as a sentence, but it doesn't express a full idea by itself.

Fragment eliminated

Hilda nearly fainted when she opened the letter from Publisher's Clearing House Sweepstakes, the contest she'd been entering faithfully for twenty years.

24a–3 **Check that you have not mistaken a verbal for the verb in a sentence.** Verbals (see Sections 18a and 18b) are tricky constructions that can easily mislead a writer into mistaking a phrase for a sentence. Verbals look like verbs, but they really act as nouns, adjectives, or adverbs. For instance, in the phrase "to look at something," *to look* is the infinitive of the verb, but it doesn't act as a verb. In the phrase "running for office," *running* is a gerund, not a verb. In the phrase "recognizing his weakness," *recognizing* acts as a noun, not a verb. To eliminate fragments caused by verbals, it helps to remember that

- An *-ing* word by itself can never act as the verb of a sentence. To qualify as a verb, it must have an auxiliary word such as *have*, *is*, or *were*.
- An infinitive, such as *to run*, *to go*, and so on, can never act as the verb of a sentence.

Here are examples of how verbals cause sentence fragments. The fragments are boldfaced.

24a
frag

Fragment

When his fifth-grade class launched a blizzard of paper airplanes, Ramon consulted his student teacher's manual. **Suspecting that somehow the situation had gotten out of control.**

The boldfaced portion is a phrase modifying *Ramon* and cannot act as a sentence.

Fragment eliminated

When his fifth-grade class launched a blizzard of paper airplanes, Ramon consulted his student teacher's manual, suspecting that somehow the situation had gotten out of control.

Fragment

To send the ringleaders to the principal's office. That was one possible response.

The entire boldfaced portion is an infinitive phrase acting as a noun and shouldn't be punctuated as a sentence.

Fragment eliminated

To send the ringleaders to the principal's office was one possible response.

● **Tip**

We know all these references to verbals, appositives, infinitives, gerunds, and so on are enough to make your eyes glaze over. Don't worry if you can't remember these terms or don't know which kind of fragment you've written. Just check your drafts to see if everything you have punctuated as a sentence actually has a subject and verb. If it doesn't, rethink it. ●

`24a-4` **Check that you have not treated a disconnected phrase as a sentence.** Sometimes—particularly in advertising copy—a phrase with no subject or verb is punctuated as a sentence.

> **The classic text. Exhaustive and definitive. Profusely illustrated. Above all, relevant.**

Such constructions are not always puzzling, but they're out of place in most serious academic or professional writing.

Turning a disconnected phrase into a full sentence usually requires adding a subject or a verb (sometimes both), depending on what has been omitted from the phrase. Here is an example of disconnected phrases that are sentence fragments. The fragments are boldfaced.

Fragment

David cleaned his glasses. **Absentmindedly. With the hem of his lamb's-wool sweater.**

The prepositional phrase—*with the hem of his lamb's-wool sweater*—can be joined to the end of the sentence. *Absentmindedly* needs to be attached to the word it modifies: *David*.

24a frag

Fragment eliminated

Absentmindedly, David cleaned his glasses with the hem of his lamb's-wool sweater.

`24a-5` **Check that you have not treated a list as an independent sentence.** Sometimes a list gets detached from the sentence that introduced or explained it. The result can be a sentence fragment that needs to be revised either by connecting it to the preceding sentence or by making it stand as a sentence on its own.

Fragment

Bucking a Hollywood trend, some stars have had marriages lasting more than fifty years. **Charlton Heston, Robert Mitchum, and Bob Hope among them.**

Fragment eliminated

Bucking a Hollywood trend, some stars have had marriages lasting more than fifty years, among them Charlton Heston, Robert Mitchum, and Bob Hope.

Fragment eliminated

Bucking a Hollywood trend, some stars have had marriages lasting more than fifty years. Charlton Heston, Robert Mitchum, and Bob Hope are among them.

Lists are often introduced by words or phrases such as *especially, for example, for instance, such as,* and *namely.* If a fragment follows such an expression, be sure to correct it—usually by attaching the fragment to the preceding sentence.

Fragment

People suffer from many peculiar phobias. **For example, ailurophobia (fear of cats), aviophobia (fear of flying), ombrophobia (fear of rain), and vestiphobia (fear of clothes).**

Fragment eliminated

People suffer from many peculiar phobias—for example, ailurophobia (fear of cats), aviophobia (fear of flying), ombrophobia (fear of rain), and vestiphobia (fear of clothes).

■ **Exercise 24.1** Write full sentences that incorporate these sentence fragments.

24a
frag

1. Learning to drive a car.
2. Who'd rather be watching football than teaching you.
3. Especially the emergency brake.
4. Because you mistook the light switch for the windshield wipers.
5. Also how to enter a freeway on-ramp safely.
6. So that you don't plow into the school bus in front of you.
7. Figuring out what a clutch is for.
8. Stalling in the middle of an intersection.
9. Mainly, about parallel parking.
10. When the officer said you'd passed your driver's test.

■ **Exercise 24.2** Rewrite the following sentences and eliminate any sentence fragments.

1. Although most movie stars are human and created by the usual birds-and-bees process. One of the most popular movie stars in recent memory, the liquid metal cyborg in *Terminator 2*, was created by a computer.
2. The technology of computer animation has developed rapidly over the past decade. Making a spectacular range of special effects possible.
3. Industrial Light and Magic was responsible for the astonishing cyborg. A special-effects company owned by director George Lucas.
4. The company was founded to create the special effects for *Star Wars*. Subsequently creating the special effects for a string of hits, including *ET: The Extra-Terrestrial* and *Who Framed Roger Rabbit?* Also the special effects for *Ghost*.
5. While the cyborg appears in *Terminator 2* for only about five minutes,

creating the footage cost millions of dollars. Keeping thirty-five computer animators busy for ten months.

24b DO YOU RECOGNIZE INTENTIONAL FRAGMENTS AND KNOW HOW TO USE THEM?

Troubleshooting

When students in writing classes become concerned about avoiding sentence fragments in their own writing, they sometimes begin to notice how often fragments appear in newspapers or certain magazines. Inevitably such students ask, "How can those writers get away with using fragments when we can't?" For example, this passage might appear in a specialized car magazine.

> Some classic car buffs are fanatics. **No moderation. No control.** When they restore a car, they'll go to any extreme to see that it's perfect. **Total authenticity.** That's their goal, whatever the cost.

It does make one wonder. Are sentence fragments considered wrong at some times but not at others? The answer is "Yes." It depends on the writer's purpose and audience.

TRICKY Certain constructions can be described as intentional fragments—that is, phrases or groups of words that don't have all the traditional components of a sentence but effectively convey a full idea. They don't leave you with the sense that something is missing. Such constructions appear frequently in informal essays, magazine pieces, and advertisements. For example:

> Do such obstacles mean that amateur auto detailers are doomed to failure? **Not necessarily. Persistence and luck.** If they have those, they can achieve their goal.

So writers can sometimes use fragments effectively when writing for certain purposes. For instance, they may want to achieve a quick pace or a staccato effect in their writing, they may want to create a series of images, or they may want to give their writing a very casual tone. One way to accomplish these goals is to use a series of fragments.

> The classic car connoisseur with a good eye can always recognize a master's work. **The gleaming, immaculate finish. The authentic hood ornament. The perfectly restored hubcaps and manufacturer's insignia.**

The problem is that intentional fragments can look just like the fragments many readers consider major errors. Thus it's a good idea to use such constructions cautiously in most writing, particularly when your audience is a college instructor.

To avoid problems with intentional fragments . . .

24b–1 **Use them sparingly.** Intentional fragments should not appear regularly in any formal or academic writing, and certainly not in a research paper, report, job application letter, or literary analysis. You might use them in narratives, journal pieces, humorous essays, or autobiographical sketches.

24b–2 **Be sure readers understand that your fragments are deliberate.** Careful readers who think that fragments are accidental may object to them, thinking the writer doesn't understand sentence structure. For readers who you know are conservative about grammar, don't use fragments. For other readers, be sure you have some special reason for using them.

> The following passage, for example, uses a series of minor sentences and effective fragments to achieve an upbeat, rapid pace.

> One would think that anyone as sharp as David Barrett wouldn't be overwhelmed by a car. **Any car. Not so.** But then a Corvette Sting Ray is not just any car. It's a cult item. **An icon. A grunting, pulsing emblem of America. Something every car nut worthy of his or her tachometer would kill for.** So no wonder David was overwhelmed.

■ **Exercise 24.3** Working with other students in a small group, bring to class advertisements that use intentional fragments. Working together, identify the fragments, then join forces to rewrite them and eliminate all incomplete sentences. Assess the difference between the original ads and the revised versions. Why do you think the copywriters of the ads used fragments?

24c **HOW CAN YOU AVOID COMMA SPLICES?**

Troubleshooting

A comma splice occurs when you try to join two independent clauses with a comma only. Because the error is so common, it is worth your time to understand what comma splices are and how to fix them. Look at this example of a comma splice.

Comma splice
Local shopkeepers were concerned about a recent outbreak of graffiti, they feared that it indicated the arrival of troublesome gangs in the neighborhood.

Notice that the groups of words on each side of the comma could stand alone as sentences. When that happens, you ordinarily have a comma splice.

An editor or instructor will usually mark a comma splice with the abbreviation *cs*.

Yellowstone is the oldest of America's national
parks, it is located in Wyoming.   *cs*

To avoid comma splices in your writing . . .

24c-1 Remember that the comma is a weak mark of punctuation. When two independent clauses are joined, they require a linkage stronger than a comma to show their relationship. In fact, using a comma where a semicolon or conjunction is needed will usually just blur the meaning of a sentence: readers may not know if a writer wants to show a connection between the clauses, a subordination of ideas, or a contrast. Consider how confusing these sentences are.

24c
cs

Comma splice
The report is highly critical of the media, it has received little press coverage.

Comma splice
Shawna is an outstanding musician, she has no formal training in music.

Although the independent clauses are obviously connected, the comma splices do not explain how. Replacing the commas with conjunctions relieves the confusion.

Comma splice eliminated
The report is highly critical of the media, **so** it has received little press coverage.

Comma splice eliminated
Shawna is an outstanding musician, **although** she has no formal training in music.

Here are more examples of typical kinds of comma splices.

Comma splice

Keiko carefully measured the chemicals for the experiment, she made sure all the beakers were clean.

Comma splice eliminated

Keiko carefully measured the chemicals for the experiment, **and** she made sure all the beakers were clean.

Comma splice

Maria was supposed to be at rehearsal in thirty minutes, nevertheless, she continued to pace nervously around her room.

This illustrates a frequent mistake: using a comma before *nevertheless* or *however* in a compound sentence. You need a semicolon.

Comma splice eliminated

Maria was supposed to be at rehearsal in thirty minutes; nevertheless, she continued to pace nervously around her room.

● **Tip**

24c
cs

Very short sentences, usually in threes, may be joined by commas.

I came, I saw, I conquered.
He ate, I paid, we left. ●

24c-2 **Substitute a semicolon for the faulty comma.**

Comma splice

As David cleaned his car, every sponge, Q-tip, toothbrush, toothpick, and pipe cleaner was laid out in one neat row, every linen towel, chamois square, cotton ball, and silk handkerchief was laid out in another row.

The separation between these two closely related independent ideas gets lost among the commas that are separating items in the series.

Comma splice eliminated

As David cleaned his car, every sponge, Q-tip, toothbrush, toothpick, and pipe cleaner was laid out in one neat row; every linen towel, chamois square, cotton ball, and silk handkerchief was laid out in another row.

24c-3 **Substitute a period for the faulty comma.**

Comma splice

Like a surgeon going to work, David began to wash one square inch of the car at a time, by the end of the morning he had finished the hood and one fender.

These two independent clauses should have a stronger separation to emphasize their difference.

Comma splice eliminated

Like a surgeon going to work, David began to wash one square inch of the car at a time. By the end of the morning, he had finished the hood and one fender.

24c–4 Keep the comma, but insert a coordinating conjunction such as *but, and, for, yet,* or *or* after it.

Comma splice

The reason his progress was so slow was that he probed each door crevice with a Q-tip, after he finished a section, he polished it to a high shine.

These two independent clauses need a strong separation to stress that they are in a sequence. The comma doesn't provide that separation.

Comma splice eliminated

The reason his progress was so slow was that he probed each door crevice with a Q-tip, **and** after he finished a section, he polished it to a high shine.

24c–5 Rewrite the sentence and make one of the independent clauses a dependent, subordinate clause. Subordinate clauses are introduced by words such as *although, because, since, when,* and so on. For a list of subordinators, see the checklist on page 371.

Comma splice

David untangled himself from a squatting position, he balanced his buckets and sponges in his hands.

The two clauses of the sentence are not equally important, so the first one should be changed to a subordinate clause and the comma retained.

Comma splice eliminated

As David untangled himself from a squatting position, he balanced his buckets and sponges in his hands.

◆ Point of Difference

Although comma splices are definitely considered nonstandard in academic writing, alert readers may well notice an occasional comma splice when they are reading fiction. In that genre, perhaps authors feel less bound by strict conventions, or they may be trying to create certain rhythms in their writing by relaxing the rules a bit. Whatever the reason, we know that you may encounter a comma splice now and then in the novels of respected writers. Here are two instances.

The first pair is from *The Desert Rose* by the Pulitzer Prize–winning novelist Larry McMurtry.

24c
cs

. . . If she needed money she could always just steal it out of Billy's billfold, she had done that a few times and he hadn't even noticed.

Bonventre didn't bother to say anything else, he knew perfectly well he'd get his way and was not interested in lengthy discussion.

The second pair is from *Monk's Hood,* a medieval mystery by the English historian Edith Pargeter, who writes mysteries under the name of Ellis Peters.

. . . There was no sign of either Aelfirc or Aldith, she had taken good care that the two of them should be able to talk in absolute privacy.

Brother Mark had done his part, the habit was there, rolled up beneath Brother Cadfael's bed.

Don't be surprised, then, if you occasionally see comma splices in fiction, but that doesn't mean they're acceptable in academic or formal writing. ◆

24c

cs

■ **Exercise 24.4** Working with a group of other students, identify which of the following sentences have comma splices and correct them.

1. At one time the walls in many Philadelphia neighborhoods were covered with graffiti, today they are covered with murals.
2. Since 1984 a city-sponsored program has been teaming young graffiti writers with professional artists, the result is the creation of over one thousand works of public art.
3. The murals are large, they are colorful, they are 99 percent graffiti-free.
4. A forty-foot-tall mural of Julius ("Dr. J.") Erving has become a local landmark, even Dr. J. himself brings friends by to see it.
5. The theory behind the program is that graffiti writers, being inherently artistic, will not deface a work of art they respect, so far the theory holds.

■ **Exercise 24.5** Working with another student, look at these sentences and decide which have comma splices; then work out some ways to correct the problem.

1. Harold Lattimore, the man in charge of the commuter railroad's Lost and Found, thought he had seen it all, nevertheless, he was taken aback when the crew of the five-o'clock local brought in a Great Dane.

2. At first he suspected it was a practical joke on the part of the crew, after three days, however, he realized that the huge dog was there to stay.
3. Commuters are creatures of habit, they are all too prone to forget anything they do not normally carry every day.
4. Briefcases, coats, umbrellas, and gifts are commonly left behind, even false teeth and television sets occasionally fall victim to forgetfulness.
5. Unusual though it was, the Great Dane was not the strangest item ever to grace Harold's department, that honor belongs to a wooden leg once left on the seven-o'clock express.

24d PROBLEMS WITH RUN-ON SENTENCES?

Troubleshooting

A *run-on* sentence occurs when no punctuation at all separates two independent clauses. The reader is left to figure out where one sentence ends and a second begins.

Run-on
We were surprised by the package quickly we tore it open.

You need to provide a boundary strong enough to separate the independent clauses clearly.

Run-on eliminated
We were surprised by the package; quickly, we tore it open.
We were surprised by the package. Quickly, we tore it open.

If your instructor has told you to be careful about run-on sentences, learn to check any long sentences in your draft. Have you run together two or more sentences that should be separated? If so, you have a punctuation problem that is easily fixed in several ways.

Run-on	Corinna hoped her movie would enjoy modest success in art theaters she never dreamed it would win an award at the Cannes festival.
Corrected	Corinna hoped her movie would enjoy modest success in art theaters. She never dreamed it would win an award at the Cannes festival.
Corrected	Though Corinna hoped her movie would enjoy modest success in art theaters, she never dreamed it would win an award at the Cannes festival.

An editor or instructor will usually write *run-on* (or *r-o*) next to a sentence with such a problem.

> The Taj Mahal is one of the world's most beautiful
> buildings it is located near Agra in India.   *run-on*

To eliminate run-on sentences . . .

24d–1 **Separate the two independent clauses with a period.**

Run-on

In the affluent 1980s, advertising for products as diverse as *Money* magazine and Grey Poupon mustard flaunted snob appeal and greed now advertising firms are scrambling to revise their clients' images for the harsher economy of the 1990s.

The sentence needs to be punctuated after *greed* so as not to confuse the readers. Adding a period makes a natural separation.

Run-on eliminated

In the affluent 1980s, advertising for products as diverse as *Money* magazine and Grey Poupon mustard flaunted snob appeal and greed. Now advertising firms are scrambling to revise their clients' images for the harsher economy of the 1990s.

24d–2 **Insert a semicolon between two independent clauses that have been run together.** A semicolon suggests that the ideas in the two sentences are closely related.

Run-on

Rosa's entire life revolved around her new baby she could think of nothing else.

The two clauses are closely related but need to be separated to show they are separate ideas. A semicolon separates the sentences but preserves a relationship between them.

Run-on eliminated

Rosa's entire life revolved around her new baby; she could think of nothing else.

For more on semicolons, see Section 27a.

24d–3 **Join the independent clauses with a comma and a coordinating conjunction.** The coordinating conjunctions are *and, or, nor, for, but, yet,* and *so.*

Run-on

Poisonous giant toads were introduced to Australia in the 1930s to control beetles they have since become an ecological menace.

Run-on eliminated

Poisonous giant toads were introduced to Australia in the 1930s to control beetles, **but** they have since become an ecological menace.

Run-on

The manager suggested a cut in our hourly wages then I walked out of the negotiations.

Run-on eliminated

The manager suggested a cut in our hourly wages, **so** then I walked out of the negotiations.

24d–4 Make one of the independent clauses subordinate to the other.

Run-on

Albert had to finish the report by himself his irresponsible co-author had lost all interest in the topic.

Run-on eliminated

Albert had to finish the report by himself **because** his irresponsible coauthor had lost all interest in the topic.

24d run-on

■ **Exercise 24.6** Working with a group, rewrite these sentences to eliminate punctuation problems that create run-on sentences.

1. Centuries of superstition and ignorance have given bats a bad reputation millions of the flying mammals are killed each year in a misguided effort to protect livestock, crops, and people.
2. Entire species of bats are being wiped out at an alarming rate for example, in the 1960s a new species of fruit-eating bat was discovered in the Philippines by the 1980s it was extinct.
3. In truth, bats are industrious and invaluable members of the natural order they spread the seeds of hundreds of species of plants.
4. Strange as it may sound, bats are essential to the economies of many countries the plants they pollinate or seed include such cash crops as bananas, figs, dates, vanilla beans, and avocados.
5. Many plants essential to such delicate ecosystems as the African savanna and the South American rain forest rely solely on bats for propagating should the bats disappear, the entire system could collapse.

Problems with Modifiers?

25a
adj

25a HOW DO YOU PLACE ADJECTIVES EFFECTIVELY?

Troubleshooting

Adjectives are words that modify nouns or pronouns, describing and limiting them by explaining how many, which color, which one, and so on. All the words in boldface function as adjectives.

A **successful** mayor is rare these days.
The **darkest** nights are **moonless.**
German beer pours slowly.
The truck, **tall** and **ungainly,** rolled on the hill.
Tall and **redheaded,** he looked **Irish.**

Most, but not all, adjectives precede the nouns or pronouns they modify: *red* Viper; *outstanding* athlete.

But you must take care to place adjectives carefully to avoid ambiguity and pileups. An adjective becomes ambiguous when readers can't tell which word it modifies. For example:

Ambiguous	Adam had his **enthusiastic parents' support.**
	Enthusiastic attaches itself to *parents* instead of to *support.*
Clarified	Adam had his **parents' enthusiastic support.**

Adjectives pile up when writers place one modifier after another until readers get confused or bored. For example:

Tedious	Our **confident, stylish,** and **experienced marching** band won a national title.
Revised	Our **confident marching** band, **stylish** and **experienced,** won a national title.

To place adjectives effectively . . .

25a–1 **Relocate adjectives that are potentially confusing or ambiguous.** You may have to read your sentences carefully to appreciate how they might be misread. Better still, ask a friend to read your paper and point out where readers might get confused.

Ambiguous	The **long-lost spy's memoirs** were revealing.
	Does *long-lost* go with *spy* or *memoirs?*
Clarified	The **spy's long-lost memoirs** were revealing.
Ambiguous	The **colorful student's clothes** created a sensation.
	Does *colorful* go with *student* or *clothes?*
Clarified	The **student's colorful clothes** created a sensation.

25a–2 **Consider placing adjectives after the words or phrases they modify.** You can avoid tedious strings of adjectives this way and make sentences more graceful.

Tedious	A **new, powerful, quick,** and **easy-to-use** database was installed today.
Revised	A new database, **powerful, quick,** and **easy-to-use,** was installed today.

25a
adj

■ **Exercise 25.1** Rearrange the adjectives in each of these sentences to make the sentences clearer or more effective. You could do that in several ways.

1. Lisa and Julia wanted to find an experienced women's group that could help them plan their lobbying strategy.
2. Intelligent child care in the workplace for working parents was one of their goals.

3. They viewed the negative board members' attitudes as a challenge to their persuasive abilities.

4. Before explaining their plan, Lisa asked for the undivided employees' attention.

5. Obtaining an enthusiastic union endorsement was essential if they were to overcome the entrenched management's resistance.

25b   HOW DO YOU HANDLE PREDICATE ADJECTIVES?

Troubleshooting

If you're sometimes unsure which modifier to select after verbs such as *seem, become, look, appear, feel,* or *smell,* you are in good company. Many people struggle to choose, for example, between "I feel bad" and "I feel badly." When you are confused, decide which word in the sentence you want to modify. If that word is the subject (a noun or pronoun), complete the sentence with an adjective—not with an adverb ending in *-ly.* An adjective that follows a linking verb and describes the subject is called a **predicate adjective.**

> I *feel* **bad.**
> You *seem* **uneasy.**
> The politician *became* **angry.**
> The perfume *smells* **vile.**
> Dick *appears* **quick** on his feet.

To handle predicate adjectives effectively . . .

25b-1 **Remember that only adjectives, not adverbs, can modify a noun.** If you want to complete the verb of a sentence with a word that gives information about the *subject* of that sentence, you need to use an adjective because you are modifying a noun. In the following examples, the first version of the sentence shows the incorrect *adverb* modifier; the second version shows the correct *adjective* form.

Incorrect   Geoff feels **enviously** of the amount of attention his younger brother gets.

> The modifier *enviously* completes the linking verb *feels* and describes *Geoff,* a noun, so it should be the adjective *envious.*

Correct   Geoff feels **envious** of the amount of attention his younger brother gets.

Correct	Geoff thinks **enviously** of the amount of attention his younger brother gets.
	Now the modifier describes *thinks*, which is not a linking verb, so the adverb form is correct.
Incorrect	Lillian feels **hopefully** about her chances for getting into the graduate program.
	The term modifies *Lillian*, a noun, so it must be an adjective.
Correct	Lillian feels **hopeful** about her chances for getting into the graduate program.

The same principle applies when you modify a noun that acts as the object in a sentence, as in the following example.

Incorrect	The tenant kept the woodwork in his apartment **flawlessly.**
	To describe the woodwork (a noun), the writer should use the adjective form (*flawless*) rather than the adverb (*flawlessly*).
Correct	The tenant kept the woodwork in his apartment **flawless.**

25b
adj

25b-2 **Learn to manage *good* and *well*.** Among the trickiest modifiers are *good* and *well*. *Good* is always an adjective; *well* is usually an adverb, but sometimes it too can be an adjective. No wonder writers sometimes get confused about which one they should use. Here are some guidelines.

- Use *good* after a linking verb when you want to give information about the subject. For example:

Jasper Hayes looks **good.**
His scholastic record is **good.**
He feels **good** about being a father.

- But when you are referring to someone's state of health, you should use *well* to finish the linking verb.

Most college students feel **well** in spite of their eating habits.

Despite undergoing five hours of heart surgery, Mr. Seltzer looks remarkably well.

Don't use *good* as an adverb. For example, don't write

No	The system doesn't run **good.**
No	Most jobs in child care don't pay **good.**

Instead write

> **Yes**   The system doesn't run **well**.
>
> **Yes**   Most jobs in child care don't pay **well**.

■ **Exercise 25.2** In these sentences, replace the boldfaced modifier with a better one.

1. Many Native Americans feel **angrily** about the hoopla surrounding the annual observance of Columbus Day.
2. They find it difficult to think **good** of a day that celebrates the invasion of their forebears' homeland.
3. A standard textbook illustration of Columbus discovering America may look **well** to European eyes, but Native Americans wonder how the continent could have been considered undiscovered if their ancestors were there to meet the boat.
4. Recently, however, some Native Americans have started to feel more **hopefully** about the public's seeing their side of the story.
5. As evidence, they point to films such as *Dances with Wolves*, which led many Americans to feel more **ambivalently** about the settling of their country.

25c PROBLEMS WITH ABSOLUTE ADJECTIVES?

Troubleshooting

An absolute adjective is a word such as *unique*, *perfect*, or *equal* that logically cannot be limited or qualified. For that reason, some readers may complain, "You can't write *most unique* or *most perfect*. That just doesn't make sense." Of course such expressions and others like them— *less perfect*, *more equal*, *more round*—do make sense; certainly, we understand what they mean. But technically, the critics are right. Careful writers avoid such illogical phrases.

To handle absolute adjectives correctly . . .

Don't add qualifiers to words that already express an *absolute*, something that cannot be compared or compromised. In conversation we use such expressions frequently, but writing demands more precision. So avoid using qualifiers (such as *less*, *more*, *most*, *least*, or *very*) with the following words: *unique*, *perfect*, *singular*, *empty*, *equal*, *full*, *definite*, *complete*, *absolute*, and, of course, *pregnant*.

For example, since *equal* means "exactly the same," logically you shouldn't write that something is *more equal* any more than you'd say it is *more empty*. Similarly, either a thing is *perfect* or it's flawed in some way. Either an object is *unique* or there are others like it. Consider these examples.

Illogical   Janice thought the software program was **very perfect.**

Revised   Janice thought the software program was **perfect.**

Illogical   Jack's story is **more unique** than Jane's.

Revised   Jack's story is **unique;** Jane's is not.

■ **Exercise 25.3** Working with other students in a group, read over these sentences and decide which ones have faulty modifiers. Confer to decide how any problems with modifiers might be solved.

1. Djahna was disappointed with the galleries she visited—she thought the work they showed should have been more unique.
2. She was looking for the most perfect present possible for her parents' anniversary.
3. Her parents had very definite opinions about art, which made her a little nervous.
4. But although her own knowledge of art was less complete than her parents', she still felt she understood their taste.
5. For example, the minute she saw the paintings of skeletons on black velvet with real moose antlers and crockery shards stuck all over she knew her parents would hate them, although they were the most singular pictures she had seen all day.

25d   **PROBLEMS WITH ADVERB FORM?**

Troubleshooting

Adverbs are words that modify verbs, adjectives, or other adverbs, explaining where, when, and how. Many adverbs end in *-ly*.

The Secretary of State spoke **angrily** to the press.
The water was **extremely** cold.
The candidate spoke **evasively.**

But some adverbs have both short and long forms.

slow/slowly	fair/fairly	rough/roughly
quick/quickly	tight/tightly	deep/deeply

EXAMPLES

The Redskins play **rough.**   She treats him **roughly.**
Connie drives **slow.**   We drive **slowly** in town.
Darwin thinks **quick.**   A dolphin thinks **quickly.**
Richard plays **fair.**   The children play **fairly.**

The problem for many writers is that the short adverb forms look suspiciously like adjectives. Is it correct then to say "drive slow" or "tie it tight" instead of "drive slowly" and "tie it tightly"? The answer is "Yes"—but you have to consider your audience.

In most cases, the short form of the adverb sounds more casual and colloquial than the long form. Consequently, in most academic and business situations, you'll do better to use the -ly form.

To choose the right verb . . .

Use the adverb form ending in -ly in most writing situations. Here are some examples that show the colloquial and formal usages.

<table>
<tr><td>**Colloquial**</td><td>Benjamin edited the report **quick.**</td></tr>
<tr><td>**Standard**</td><td>Benjamin edited the report **quickly.**</td></tr>
<tr><td>**Colloquial**</td><td>Sioban tried not to think too **deep** about her emotions.</td></tr>
<tr><td>**Standard**</td><td>Sioban tried not to think too **deeply** about her emotions.</td></tr>
<tr><td>**Colloquial**</td><td>The employees asked to be treated **fair.**</td></tr>
<tr><td>**Standard**</td><td>The employees asked to be treated **fairly.**</td></tr>
</table>

25d
adv

■ **Exercise 25.4** Working with a group of other students, discuss the following sentences and decide what the problems are. Then replace nonstandard adverb forms with appropriate ones.

1. Clara was real surprised when she got a letter back from the doughnut company.
2. The president of the company seemed to take her suggestion very serious.
3. He had written back prompt and that made her think good of him.
4. As she read the letter, however, she began to suspect that the president hadn't written it personal after all.
5. She sat down quick and started to plan her next move to improve working conditions.

25e WHERE DO YOU PLACE ADVERBS?

Troubleshooting

TRICKY

Adverbs are generally easier to work with than adjectives because they're flexible and can take several different positions in a sentence. For example:

George daydreamed **endlessly** about his vacation, **excitedly** reviewing each colorful brochure.

George daydreamed about his vacation **endlessly,** reviewing **excitedly** each colorful brochure.

Endlessly George daydreamed about his vacation, reviewing each colorful brochure **excitedly.**

But because adverbs are so flexible, it's also easy to get them in an inappropriate place, particularly if the sentence has two verbs and the adverb might modify either one of them. The result may be a confusing or ambiguous sentence.

**25e
adv**

Adverb misplaced   Analyzing an argument **effectively** improves it.

> Does *effectively* go with *analyzing* or *improves?*

To position adverbs accurately . . .

25e-1 Check that you have placed your adverbs so that your reader can't get confused about which words they modify. Sometimes you may want to ask a friend to help you double-check for misplaced modifiers. For example:

Adverb misplaced   Hearing the guard's footsteps approach **quickly** Mark emptied the safe.

> The reader doesn't know whether *quickly* goes with *footsteps* or *Mark.*

**Adverb
repositioned**   Hearing the guard's footsteps approach Mark **quickly** emptied the safe.

A comma after *approach* in both sentences would also help.

25e-2 Be sure the adverbs *almost* and *even* are next to the words they modify. These common words are adverbs that can cause confusion in a sentence. Notice the ambiguities they cause in the following sentences because they are misplaced.

Adverb misplaced	Much to his dismay, Hugo realized he had **almost** dated every woman at the party.
	Putting *almost* next to *dated* instead of *every* confuses the meaning.
Adverb better placed	Much to his dismay, Hugo realized he had dated **almost** every woman at the party.
Adverb misplaced	A true workaholic, Jen **even** thought time spent driving to the office could be used productively.
	Even could modify *thought* here, but it really goes with *time*.
Adverb better placed	A true workaholic, Jen thought **even** time spent driving to the office could be used productively.

25e-3 **Place the adverb *only* directly before the word you want it to modify in a sentence.** The word *only* has one specific meaning: "this one and no other." Unfortunately, writers tend to let *only* drift around in sentences, slipping into positions where it can be confusing. Here are some examples.

Confusing	Verna **only** knew of one person who opposed her marriage plans.
	Could be misinterpreted to mean that Verna was the only person who knew of someone opposed to her marriage.
Clearer	Verna knew of **only** one person who opposed her marriage plans.
Confusing	Her parents **only** worried about how much the elaborate affair would set them back.
	Could be misinterpreted to mean that Verna's parents never worried about anything except the cost of their daughter's wedding.
Clearer	Her parents worried **only** about how much the elaborate affair would set them back.

■ **Exercise 25.5** Rewrite the sentences to clarify them.

1. People who attend the theater regularly complain that the manners of the average audience member are in severe decline.
2. Far from listening in respectful if not attentive silence, he broadcasts a running commentary frequently modeled, no doubt, on his behavior in front of the television at home.
3. Sitting next to a woman who spends most of the evening unwrapping cellophane-covered candies slowly can provoke even the most saintly theatergoer to violence.

25e
adv

4. Cellular phones, beepers, and wristwatch alarms even go off inter-
mittently causing an evening in the theater to resemble a trip to an
electronics store.

5. For their part, actors marvel at how today's audiences only manage to
cough during the quietest moments of a play.

25f PROBLEMS WITH DOUBLE NEGATIVES?

Troubleshooting

Although sentences that say *no* in two different ways can be
emphatic, you probably already know that they're nonstandard English and will jolt your readers' sense of good usage.
Try to avoid them even when you're writing drafts, and be
very careful to get rid of them when you revise.

To avoid double negative constructions . . .

25f-1 Check to see that you don't have two *no* words in the same
sentence or independent clause. In addition to *no,* look for such words
as *not, nothing, nobody,* and *never.* If you find you've doubled them, usually you can just drop or alter a single word.

Double negative	That parrot **doesn't never** talk.
Corrected	That parrot **never** talks.
Double negative	John doesn't want **no help** tying his shoes.
Corrected	John doesn't want **any** help tying his shoes.

25f-2 Don't mix the negative adverbs *hardly, scarcely,* or *barely*
with another negative word or phrase. If you do, you will have a sentence with a double negative, not considered standard English. Here are
some examples of such faulty English usage.

Double negative	The morning was so cool and clear that the hik-ers **couldn't hardly** wait to get started.
Corrected	The morning was so cool and clear that the hik-ers **could hardly** wait to get started.
Double negative	They figured there **wouldn't be scarcely** any other groups on the trail.
Corrected	They figured there **would be scarcely** any other groups on the trail.

● **Tip**

You may use two negatives in a sentence when you want to state an idea positively but perhaps with some reservation. Consider the difference in tone between these simple statements, framed negatively and positively.

| **Negative** | Bertha was not unintelligent. |
| **Positive** | Bertha was intelligent. |

| **Negative** | Sean was hardly unattractive. |
| **Positive** | Sean was attractive. ● |

■ **Exercise 25.6** Rewrite any of the sentences that contain double negatives to eliminate the problem. Not every sentence is faulty.

1. Americans are notorious for not knowing hardly any geography.
2. On an unlabeled map they can't barely find their own state, much less the countries they read about in the news.
3. More depressing, most people don't feel no need to improve their knowledge.
4. There can hardly be two places more talked about in the United States than Bosnia and the Persian Gulf.
5. Yet the majority of Americans couldn't no more tell you where those places are than they could fly.

25g PROBLEMS WITH MISPLACED OR DANGLING MODIFIERS?

Troubleshooting

CAUTION   Words tend to attract any modifiers that come near them; they pick up meaning whether or not that is what the writer intended. If you write a sentence with a modifying adverbial or adjectival phrase that is *not* next to the word it should modify, your sentence is going to derail. Two forms of this problem are **misplaced modifying phrases** and **dangling modifiers.** Here's an example of a misplaced modifier, one attached to the wrong word in a sentence.

| **Misplaced modifying phrase** | **Short of money,** the plans for the library had to be scrapped by the university. |
| **Corrected** | **Short of money,** the university had to scrap its plans for a new library. |

A dangling modifier occurs when a writer writes a sentence with a modifying phrase but doesn't supply anything in the sentence it could sensibly modify. As a result, the modifier just hangs there. For example:

Dangling modifier	**Before sending out the invitations,** a date for their wedding has to be chosen.
	The boldfaced phrase doesn't apply to anything in the main part of the sentence. The sentence needs people to carry out the action.
Corrected	**Before sending out the invitations,** the couple will have to decide on a date for their wedding.

An editor who spots a dangling modifier in your paper will write *dm*, *dang*, or *dang mod* in the margin next to the offending phrase or clause.

Angered by the crowd's booing, the concert was canceled. *dang mod*

To eliminate misplaced or dangling modifiers . . .

25g
mm/dm

25g-1 Be sure that an introductory modifying phrase is followed by the word it modifies. Ask yourself who or what the modifying phrase refers to. (Usually the word or phrase modified will be the subject of the sentence.) Then make any necessary revisions. Sometimes you will have to supply a word that the introductory phrase can modify. In other cases, the whole sentence may have to be rearranged.

Misplaced modifier	**Never having had children,** rising college costs do not concern Mirella.
	The boldfaced phrase doesn't describe *costs*, the closest noun to it; it describes *Mirella*.
Revision	**Never having had children,** Mirella is unconcerned about rising college costs.
Misplaced modifier	**Insulting, trivial, and predictable,** fewer and fewer television viewers were attracted to the comedian's late-night monologues.
	The boldfaced phrase doesn't describe *viewers;* it describes *monologues*.
Revision	**Insulting, trivial, and predictable,** the comedian's late-night monologues attracted fewer and fewer viewers.

25g-2 Supply a word for a dangling modifier to modify. This often means rewriting the entire sentence, since you must usually add a word or phrase that the sentence alludes to but doesn't actually include. For example:

Dangling modifier	**On returning to the room,** the furniture had been rearranged.
	There is nothing in the sentence for *On returning to the room* to modify. In this case, the sentence has to be revised to include a subject.
One possible revision	**On returning to the room,** La Tisha found the furniture had been rearranged.

● **Tip**

You are less likely to get yourself in a tangle with modifiers if you write actor/action sentences. When you use people as the subject of your sentences, it's easier to keep modifiers under control (see Section 11c–1). ●

25g–3 **Distinguish between absolute modifiers and misplaced modifiers.** Some modifying phrases may look like misplaced modifiers but are actually what we call **absolute modifiers;** that is, they are complete in themselves, serving only to give additional information about the sentence of which they are a part. Writers find such absolute modifiers useful, so it's important to learn to distinguish them from faulty constructions.

absolute
Given the fiasco at dinner, nobody was surprised when Perri pushed her husband into the pool.

absolute
To be quite honest, Robert is a spoiled brat and we would prefer that you leave him at home.

To distinguish an absolute modifier that does work from a misplaced or dangling modifier that doesn't work, see if you could convert the absolute modifier into a subordinate clause. For instance, the first sentence above could be rewritten.

When they took into consideration the fiasco that had occurred at dinner, the guests were not surprised when Perri pushed her husband into the pool.

If you can do this, your absolute works. You can also ask yourself, "Is there any possible confusion here?"

■ **Exercise 25.7** Rewrite these sentences, placing modifiers in appropriate positions. You may need to add a noun for the modifier to modify. Not all of the sentences need to be revised.

1. Although they are among the most famous of reptiles, biologists have only recently begun to study rattlesnakes.

2. The deadly snakes, which take their name from the two characteristic pits on their snouts, belong to the family of pit vipers.

3. After studying the habits of pit vipers, the pits, which serve as infrared sensors and enable the snakes to see heat, evolved to detect danger rather than to hunt prey.

4. Given their lethal capabilities, it is not surprising that pit vipers are universally loathed.

5. Despite their fearful reputation, however, people are seldom bitten by the snakes unless they are provoked.

25h   PROBLEMS WITH COMPARATIVES AND SUPERLATIVES?

Troubleshooting

The comparative and superlative forms of most adjectives and a few adverbs can be expressed two ways.

25h
modif

ugly (an adjective)

comparative	uglier	more ugly
superlative	ugliest	most ugly

slowly (an adverb)

comparative	slower	more slowly
superlative	slowest	most slowly

You can usually trust your ear when selecting the forms. As a general rule, you add *-er* and *-est* endings to one-syllable adjectives and adverbs but use the terms *more* and *most* (or *less* and *least*) before words of two or more syllables.

Curtis likes **brighter** colors than Kyle.
Kyle wears **more conservative** clothes than Curtis.
Kyle's white Oxford is the **most conspicuous** shirt he owns.
Camille talk **faster** than Susi.
Susi usually speaks **more deliberately.**

Two problems typically arise with comparatives and superlatives. The first is using a superlative form when comparing only two objects.

Faulty comparison	Jason was the **tallest** of the two men.
	should be *taller*
Faulty comparison	Martina was the **most talented** of the two gymnasts.
	should be *more talented*

A less frequent error involves doubling the comparative and superlative forms, using both the ending -*er* or -*est* and *more* or *most*.

Faulty comparison   That was the **most ugliest** dog of all.
should be *most ugly* or *ugliest*

To avoid problems with comparisons . . .

`25h–1` **Be sure to use the comparative, not the superlative, form when you are comparing two items.** That means using an adverb or adjective with an -*er* ending or modified by *more* or *less*.

Faulty comparison   John was the **smartest** of the two children.
Smartest is the superlative, not the comparative, form.

Revised   John was the **smarter** of the two children.

Faulty comparison   Celeste, his twin, was the **most imaginative,** although that wasn't always good.
Most imaginative is the superlative, not the comparative, form.

Revised   Celeste, his twin, was the **more imaginative,** although that wasn't always good.

`25h–2` **Use the superlative form when comparing more than two objects or qualities.** In most cases when you compare three or more things or qualities, you need to use -*est* adjectives or adverbs or preface the modifiers with *most* or *least*. For example:

Given the choice of several toys, Celeste would choose the one that was the **most** challenging.

Of all the children in his kindergarten class, John was the **liveliest.**

`25h–3` **Avoid doubling the comparative or superlative forms.** You'll confuse your reader if you use the two comparative forms in the same phrase. For example:

Confusing   Jasper was **more stricter** as a parent than Janice was.

Clear   Jasper was **stricter** as a parent than Janice was.

Confusing   Of all the members of the archery team, Diana was the **most angriest** about the stolen targets.

Clear   Of all the members of the archery team, Diana was the **angriest** about the stolen targets.

■ **Exercise 25.8** Write sentences in which you use the appropriate forms of comparison for the situation given.

1. Julio and Corinne couldn't decide which would be the (**better/best**) family to spend Thanksgiving with, his or hers.

2. On the one hand, Julio's family had the (**larger/largest**) house and lived close by.

3. On the other, Corinne's family was (**friendlier/the most friendly**) and had the (**more eccentric/most eccentric**) bunch of relatives Julio had ever seen.

4. In the end, even though they could have traveled to Julio's family (**more cheaply/most cheaply**), they flew back East to Corinne's parents' place.

5. For years afterwards, they couldn't decide which was (**funnier/funniest**)—Aunt May's ventriloquism with the turkey, Uncle Len's psychic trance and subsequent communication with the Pilgrims, or Louise's demonstration of the principles of interpretive dance.

25h
modif

S U M M A R Y

Key Points About Modifiers

- Remember that only adjectives, not adverbs, can modify nouns.
- Learn the difference between those tricky modifiers *well* and *good.*
- Don't add modifiers to absolute terms that logically cannot be compared: *unique, complete, empty, perfect,* and so on.
- Watch for modifiers that may be confusing and relocate them if necessary.
- Be sure *almost, even,* and *only* come directly before the words they modify.
- Avoid combining *hardly, scarcely,* or *barely* with another negative term—for example, don't write "He can't hardly finish that."
- Check to see that an introductory modifying phrase is followed immediately by the word it modifies.
- Use the comparative (*better*) not the superlative (*best*) form when comparing two items.

26

Problems with Commas?

A Commas That Separate
B Commas That Enclose
C Commas That Link
D Commas That Don't Belong
E Commas with Special Uses

The central fact about commas is that they are interrupters, signals to pause. As signals, they aren't as strong as semicolons, which mark major intersections in sentences (those that warrant a traffic light). And they're certainly not as forceful as periods, which mark the ends of sentences (rather like police officers at intersections). But commas do make readers slow down and pay attention to the words and ideas they mark off. For that reason, it's just as important to omit commas where they aren't needed as it is to include them where they are.

A list of guidelines for using commas will help you get them in the right places, but the truth is that knowing every rule won't solve every comma problem. Ultimately, you have to develop a *feel* for these marks, a sense for when to interrupt the flow of your writing and when not to. That requires paying attention to the structure and meaning of your sentences, and not just inserting commas according to a formula. One way to develop a feel for these subtle marks of punctuation is to observe how good writers use them. The next time you read an article you particularly enjoy, notice how commas make that piece easier to read, clearer, or more lively, and consider why they worked well where they did.

An editor will usually indicate where a comma is needed with a comma and caret.

The garden, which had been neglected for years now ∧
flourished under the rabbi's care.

If you need to delete a comma, an editor may draw a slash through the mark and write "no comma" (*no,*) in the margin.

The car/that I sold had declined in value. *no* ⌃

26a DO YOU UNDERSTAND COMMAS THAT SEPARATE?

Troubleshooting

Commas are frequently used to keep words and phrases from running into each other and confusing readers, so use one at any juncture where your readers might get lost if a comma is left out. Often, however, you may have to depend on your judgment as well as a rule. If you use too many commas, your writing can seem fussy and old-fashioned, but if you omit one where it's needed, your readers may be puzzled. So where inserting a comma is a judgment call, try reading your draft out loud. Are there places where the reader should pause? Put in a comma if it is compatible with the guidelines in this chapter. Is a comma needed to make the sentence clearer or easier to read? If so, insert one.

26a
⌃
,

To handle commas effectively . . .

26a–1 **Use commas after introductory phrases of more than three or four words.** Pauses at these points can make a sentence easier to read.

To appreciate the pleasures of driving in snow, you have to live in Michigan or Wisconsin.

Over the loud objections of all the occupants of the Jeep, I turned off the main road.

An introductory comma isn't necessary when an introductory phrase is only three or four words long and the sentence is clear without the punctuation.

On glare ice the Jeep just spun its wheels.
On Tuesday we'll be in New Mexico.

CAUTION

26a–2 **Use commas after introductory subordinate clauses.** **Subordinate clauses** are signaled by words like *although, if, when, because, as, after, before, since, unless, while,* and so on. (See Section 9a–2.)

Although the roads were crowded, we drove on to Detroit.

While the military band played Taps, the flag was lowered.
When the police officer arrived, he found the windows broken.

When you forget a comma after an introductory clause, your readers may slide past the place where the main idea of the sentence begins. Suddenly, they find themselves confused. To make sense of the sentence, they have to reread it and insert a comma mentally. Here's an example.

> ### comma missing
>
> Although the forest fire seemed out of control after a week firefighters succeeded in taming it.

In the example above, the reader may run right through the intersection between *control* and *after*, wonder whether the phrase *after a week* goes with the part before or after it, and then have to reread the sentence. Adding a comma ends the confusion.

> ### comma added
>
> Although the forest fire seemed out of control, after a week firefighters succeeded in taming it.

26a-3 Use commas before clauses that follow a main clause when the additional thought is incidental or contrasting. Such clauses may be signaled by words like *although, though, if, when, because, as, after, before, since, unless, while, that is,* and so on.

> We do expect to attend the lecture on Germanic philology, **unless** we can find an excuse to miss it.
> The meal was excellent, **though** the prices were steep.

Commas are not used, however, when the additional clause is closely related to the main idea of the sentence.

> We drove on to Detroit **even though** the roads were crowded.
> The flag was lowered **while** the military band played Taps.
> The police officer found the windows broken **when** he arrived.

Notice, however, that if these sentences started with the subordinate clause, most writers would put a comma after it. For instance, "While the band played, the flag was lowered."

26a
^
,

◆ Point of Difference

The authors of this book don't always agree about where to put commas in sentences like those above. One of us would usually put a comma after a subordinate clause at the beginning of a sentence but leave it out when the clause signal comes in the middle. For instance:

> Although we sympathize with the cause, we aren't ready to donate.

But,

> We aren't ready to donate although we sympathize with the cause.

The other author would insert a comma before *although* in the second sentence. Neither of us is necessarily right; this is a case where informed opinions differ. ◆

TRICKY

26a–4 **Use commas after conjunctive adverbs at the beginning of sentences or clauses.** Commas are needed because words of this kind—*consequently, nevertheless, however, therefore*, and so on—are interrupters that mark a shift or contrast in a sentence. For a chart of conjunction adverbs, see page 422.

26a
^
,

> Howard failed the chemistry exam. **However,** he did not drop the course.
> He worked hard; **therefore,** he passed the class.

Putting a comma after these words sets them off and draws attention to them (see also Sections 26b–3 and 27a–2).

26a–5 **Use commas to set off absolute phrases.** Technically, absolutes are phrases made up of nouns and participles. You are most likely to recognize them through examples.

> **His head shaven,** Martin was in the Marines now.
>
> The pioneers pressed forward across the desert, **their water almost gone.**

Absolutes like these are always separated from the rest of the sentence by commas. See Section 25g–3 for more information about absolutes.

26a–6 **Use commas to mark contrasts.**

> Owning a car in most cities is a necessity, not a luxury.
> Ollie had seen many celestial events, but never an eclipse.
> Ellie's chief requirement in a house is not glamor, but economy.

26a-7 **Use commas to separate words where verbs or predicates have been deleted to avoid repetition.** Constructions of this kind are fairly common.

> Appollonia is the patron saint of toothaches; Blaise, of throat infections; Vitus, of epilepsy.

> Brad Pitt once worked as a giant chicken; Rod Stewart, as a gravedigger; Whoopi Goldberg, as a makeup artist in a mortuary.

26a-8 **Use commas to keep ideas clear and distinct.**

> The motto of some critics seems to be whatever is, is wrong.
> People who must, can operate cars with hand controls only.
> Those who can, do; those who can't, complain.

26a-9 **Use commas to separate various conversational expressions from the main body of a sentence.** Such expressions are probably more common in speech than in writing, but here's how they are punctuated.

> No, I am sure the door was locked.
> The demonstrators are full of themselves, aren't they?
> "Well, I'm not sure I recall," said the former governor.

26b
∧
,

■ **Exercise 26.1** Insert commas in these sentences where needed.

1. When Mount Saint Helens erupted in 1980 the north slope collapsed sending torrents of mud and rock down into the Toutle River valley.
2. Stripped of all vegetation for fifteen miles the valley was left virtually lifeless; whatever trees there were were dead.
3. In an effort to prevent erosion and speed the valley's recovery ecologists planted grasses and groundcovers.
4. However the species they planted were not native but alien or exotic.
5. All things considered the scientists probably should have left nature to take its own course since the alien plants are now inhibiting the regrowth of native species.

26b   **DO YOU UNDERSTAND COMMAS THAT ENCLOSE?**

Troubleshooting

If you wonder why you need to put commas around some parts of a sentence, the answer is that they can help you clarify meaning. One of the useful things commas do is to chunk information into manageable segments so readers can understand it more quickly. But it's important to place commas only around expressions that really do need to be separated from the rest of a sentence. Remember that it usually takes two commas to bracket material in the middle of a sentence; it's easy to forget that second comma. Of course, only one comma is needed before a modifier at the end of a sentence.

To set off information . . .

26b–1 **Use commas to mark nonessential (nonrestrictive) modifiers.** A **nonessential modifier** is one that adds information to a sentence but can be removed without radically altering its basic meaning. (Although many texts use only the terms *restrictive* and *nonrestrictive* modifiers, we prefer the terms *essential* and *nonessential* because they are less technical and more descriptive.) Observe what happens when nonessential modifiers are removed from some sentences.

With nonessential (nonrestrictive) modifier	The police officers**, who looked sharp in their dress uniforms,** marched in front of the mayor's car.
Modifier removed	The police officers marched in front of the mayor's car.
With nonessential modifier	The chemistry building**, which had been erected in 1928 and badly needed repairs,** was scheduled for demolition.
Modifier removed	The chemistry building was scheduled for demolition.

As you can see, some information is lost when a sentence loses a nonessential modifier, but good sense is maintained.

When you can't remove a modifying expression from a sentence without affecting its meaning, you have an *essential modifier*—which is not surrounded by commas. Watch what happens when essential modifiers are removed from sentences.

Essential modifier	Diamonds **that are synthetically produced** are more perfect than natural diamonds.
Essential modifier removed	Diamonds are more perfect than natural diamonds. The sentence now makes little sense.
Essential modifier	We missed the only presentation **that dealt with business ethics**.

Essential modifier removed	We missed the only presentation. Removing the modifier changes the sentence significantly.
Essential modifiers	The fruit basket **that we received** was not the one **we ordered**.
Essential modifiers removed	The fruit basket was not the one. The sentence makes no sense with the essential modifiers removed.

26b–2 **Use commas to enclose nonessential (nonrestrictive) appositives.** An **appositive** is a noun or noun equivalent that follows a noun and gives additional information about it. Appositives are usually nonessential modifiers.

Colleen O'Brien, **our neighborhood-watch coordinator,** was arrested last week for shoplifting.

When Rodney's father, **now a child psychiatrist,** learned of his son's latest exploit, he hired a lawyer.

George Washington, **the first president of the United States,** served two full terms.

There are, however, also essential (or restrictive) appositives that follow a noun and give information that is necessary. Such modifiers shouldn't be set off by commas.

Sue Ellen reflected that Dr. Rizzo **the psychiatrist** was quite a different person from Dr. Rizzo **the father.**

Because *the psychiatrist* and *the father* are essential to the meaning of the sentence, setting them off with commas would confuse readers.

Deciding whether modifiers are essential or nonessential can be especially tricky when the appositives involved are titles. The basic principle remains the same, though: use commas around titles when they can be deleted from a sentence, no commas when they cannot. Compare the following examples.

Essential	Shakespeare's tragedy ***Hamlet*** is one of his longest plays. Cut *Hamlet* here and the sentence is meaningless.
Nonessential	Shakespeare's longest tragedy, ***Hamlet,*** lasts more than four hours. The sentence would still make sense with *Hamlet* cut.

26b
^
,

Essential   The Beatles' song **"Yesterday"** remains one of the most popular tunes of all time.

Nonessential   The Beatles' final album, *Let It Be,* remains my favorite.

26b-3 **Use commas to enclose various interrupting words, phrases, and clauses.** It is important to use commas in pairs when the interruptions come in the middle of sentences.

The president intends, **predictably,** to veto the bill in its current form.

The senators, **it seemed,** were eager for a fight.

He could not, **in good conscience,** ignore the clamor for passage of the measure.

He could, **of course,** make a strong case in the media.

♦ **Point of Difference**

Teachers and professional editors might not agree about where to put commas in the last two examples. In many magazines and newspapers—even the august *New York Times*—often you would find no commas around "of course" if it appeared in the middle of a sentence. Many editors would also favor omitting commas around "in good conscience" in the third sentence above, arguing that the phrase doesn't need to be set off for clarity.

Increasingly, magazine and newspaper editors seem to be moving to fewer commas, partly, we think, to create a smooth-flowing, informal style. It's worth noting, however, that when editors find they can omit commas without affecting meaning, they save space, and in the publishing business, saving space eventually means saving money. It's through decisions such as these that the conventions of a language change. ♦

Be especially careful with words such as *however, nevertheless, moreover, therefore,* and *consequently*. They should usually appear between commas when they fall in the middle of a sentence because they're interrupters.

Popular opinion, **however,** began to move toward the president's position.

■ **Exercise 26.2** Working with two or three other students, discuss the following sentences to decide which modifiers are essential and which are not; then fix the sentences that need to be changed.

26b
∧
,

1. Benjamin a fourth grader with an overactive imagination was telling his friend Shawna about his adventure of that morning.
2. A large dog that he had encountered on the way to school it seems had experienced a sudden craving for paper.
3. It had eaten the history report that he had so diligently prepared the night before.
4. A second friend Ricardo who happened to overhear the tale doubted whether their teacher would believe it.
5. Ricardo was right: Ms. Freer their history teacher asked whether the story with all its bizarre plot twists and moments of pathos might not actually concern a shaggy dog rather than a large one.

26c DO YOU UNDERSTAND COMMAS THAT LINK?

26c
∧
,

Troubleshooting

Though commas often mark separations, they can also tell readers that certain ideas belong together. When commas come before linking words, they let readers know that the ideas will continue. The stop isn't as full as it would be if it were marked by a semicolon or period. Similarly, commas that mark off the items in a series help readers understand that those items belong together.

To join ideas . . .

CAUTION

26c–1 Use commas before the coordinating conjunctions *and, but, for, yet, so, or,* and *nor* when those words link independent clauses to form compound sentences.

Clauses are described as **independent** when they can stand on their own as sentences. Joining two independent clauses with a comma and a coordinating conjunction produces a compound sentence. (See Section 14a–1.)

Dogs are smarter than cats, **and** they are more sociable too.

Some people prefer cats, **but** such persons often need professional help.

Cats seem friendly at times, **yet** they cannot be trusted.

Dogs are gregarious and playful, **so** they often seem less serene than cats.

A comma is especially important when the two clauses separated by the conjunction are lengthy.

> ### missing comma
>
> Experts have tried to explain why dogs wag their tails
> but they have yet to come up with a satisfactory reason
> for this attention-grabbing behavior.

In this example a comma is missing before the conjunction *but*. A comma would emphasize the break between the two clauses and prevent any misreading. Note that the *yet* in this sentence does not function as a conjunction.

> ### comma added
>
> Experts have tried to explain why dogs wag their tails,
> but they have yet to come up with a satisfactory reason
> for this attention-grabbing behavior.

26c
∧
,

Be especially careful not to place the comma after a conjunction that joins independent clauses.

> ### comma misplaced
>
> Bart's father remembers his first car fondly so, he knows
> how Bart feels sitting behind the wheel of his Camaro Z28.

> ### comma corrected
>
> Bart's father remembers his first car fondly, so he knows
> how Bart feels sitting behind the wheel of his Camaro Z28.

STOP   **26c-2** **Don't use commas alone to link independent clauses.** Doing so produces the error called a *comma splice*.

> ### comma splice
>
> The plane was late, we missed our connecting flight to
> Indianapolis.

You produce a comma splice when you attempt to join two independent clauses in a sentence with a comma. Proper compound sentences are formed when independent clauses are linked by semicolons (see Section 27a–1), by commas *and* coordinating conjunctions (see Section 24c–4), or more rarely by colons (see Section 27b–4).

> **comma splice eliminated**
>
> The plane was late; we missed our connecting flight to Indianapolis.

26c–3 **Use commas to link more than two items in a series.** Commas are needed to mark pauses for readers and to keep the items in a series from colliding.

The mapmaker had omitted the capital cities of Idaho, New York, and Delaware!

Maggie found traces of spaghetti sauce on the floor, in the cabinets, under the rug, and on the ceiling.

The tabloid exposé failed to explain who had seen the aliens, where exactly they had landed, or why they had decided to visit New Orleans.

◆ **Point of Difference**

Most English teachers and book editors recommend that you use a comma before the conjunction (usually either *and* or *or*) that signals the end of a series.

    . . . for tax cuts, job security, and pay equity.
    . . . the Indians, White Sox, or Yankees.

But this guideline is not followed by journalists, who usually omit what they regard as an unnecessary comma.

    . . . for tax cuts, job security and pay equity.
    . . . the Indians, White Sox or Yankees.

Leaving out the final comma can occasionally cause confusion, which is why many editors think it should be used.

    . . . chicken, peas, and pork and beans.
    . . . by coach, wagon, and horse and buggy. ◆

26c–4 **Use commas to link coordinate adjectives in series.** **Coordinate adjectives** modify the noun they precede, not each other.

Arnie is an **intelligent, creative, manipulative** boss.
It was an **intriguing, careful, and lengthy** report.
Drew is a **frazzled, tired, and slightly frantic** baby-sitter.

When adjectives are coordinate, they can be switched around without affecting the sense of a phrase. The examples above could just as easily and accurately read like this.

Arnie is a **manipulative, intelligent, creative** boss.
It was a **lengthy, careful, and intriguing** report.
Drew is a **tired, slightly frantic, and frazzled** baby-sitter.

26c–5 Do not use commas to mark off noncoordinate adjectives in series. **Noncoordinate adjectives** or **adjectivals** work together to modify a noun or pronoun. As a result they cannot be switched around.

her six completed chapters
a shiny blue Mustang convertible
our natural good humor

26d
no ⌃
,

■ **Exercise 26.3** Rewrite the following sentences, adding commas if they are needed to link ideas, moving commas that may be misplaced, and correcting any comma splices. Some sentences may be correct.

1. The mower cut its final swath across the deep green grass, the long golden rays of the setting sun toyed listlessly with the dancing grasshoppers in its wake.
2. Although all of the day's daylilies had already closed up shop the night-blooming flowers were starting to offer their perfumes to the hushed expectant air.
3. An orchestra of crickets tree frogs and, whippoorwills warmed up for the evening's concert; fireflies silently urgently signaled their ardor in the undergrowth.
4. Overhead, the moon's bright silver slipper held court with an audience of stars: Orion the Pleiades Pegasus Cassiopeia.
5. Wafting romantically out of the gazebo and across the lawn, Heather slipped on a lone red roller skate and pitched headlong into the pool.

26d   DO YOU PUT COMMAS WHERE THEY AREN'T NEEDED?

Troubleshooting

If you're unsure about the guidelines for commas, you may find yourself inserting them where they *might* belong even though you're not sure why. As you have learned already, that approach doesn't usually work. A comma where none is needed disrupts the flow of meaning in a sentence. If your instructor or editors complain that you're using too many commas, train yourself to ask, "Why am I putting a comma here?" Every comma in a sentence should be placed for a reason: to mark a pause, to set off a unit, to keep words from running together. Cut commas that aren't needed for a specific reason.

To avoid problems with unnecessary commas . . .

26d–1 **Eliminate commas that interrupt the flow of a sentence.** Sentences with commas inserted where they are not needed can be more confusing to a reader than those with a few commas omitted. Sometimes a comma interrupts what otherwise would be a clear statement.

> **unnecessary comma**
>
> Five years into graduate school, Jolene found herself, without a degree or prospects for a job.

The writer doesn't mean "Jolene found herself," but "Jolene found herself without. . . ." Revision is necessary.

> **comma eliminated**
>
> Five years into graduate school, Jolene found herself without a degree or prospects for a job.

At other times, unneeded commas seem to fit a guideline, but really don't. Here, for example, the writer may recall that commas often follow introductory words, phrases, and clauses and so places a comma after what looks like an introductory word.

> **unnecessary comma**
>
> Although, Jolene is fifty-one, she has decided to pursue a new career.

In this case *although* introduces a subordinate clause: *Although Jolene is fifty-one. Although* can't be separated from the rest of the clause and still make sense. The comma must be cut.

> #### comma eliminated
>
> Although Jolene is fifty-one, she has decided to pursue a new career.

26d-2 **Don't use a comma to separate a subject from a verb.** This common error usually occurs when the full subject of a sentence is more complex than usual—perhaps a noun clause or a verb phrase.

> #### unnecessary comma
>
> What happened to the team since its last game, isn't clear.

What happened to the team is the subject of the sentence, so it shouldn't be separated from the verb *is* with a comma. The comma must be cut.

> #### comma eliminated
>
> What happened to the team since its last game isn't clear.

Here are some additional examples.

| **Wrong** | Fighting for the championship, means playing hard. |
| **Right** | Fighting for the championship means playing hard. |

| **Wrong** | To keep the team's spirit up, won't be easy. |
| **Right** | To keep the team's spirit up won't be easy. |

Of course, when modifiers separate subjects from verbs, commas are used to set off the modifying expressions. (For more details, see Section 26b.) Compare these sentences.

| **No modifier/ no commas** | Jolene is determined to complete her education. |
| **Modifiers/ commas** | Jolene, who just turned fifty-one, is determined to complete her education. |

> **TRICKY** **26d-3** Don't use commas to separate compound expressions—except when coordinating conjunctions join independent clauses to produce compound sentences.

This rule is simpler than it sounds, though it requires some attention. That's because commas do correctly appear before the coordinating conjunctions in compound sentences (see Section 26c–1).

Compound sentence   Dogs are smarter than cats, **and** they are more sociable too.

However, in other compound constructions, commas aren't needed before the conjunction.

---

unnecessary comma

Dogs are smarter, and more sociable than cats.

The comma should be cut.

---

comma eliminated

Dogs are smarter and more sociable than cats.

Here are more examples of this important point with compound subjects, predicates, and objects.

Wrong   The Mississippi,/and the Missouri are two of the United States' great rivers.

Right   The Mississippi and the Missouri are two of the United States' great rivers.

Wrong   We toured the museum,/and then explored the monument.

Right   We toured the museum and then explored the monument.

Wrong   Alexander broke his promise to his agent,/and his contract with his publisher.

Right   Alexander broke his promise to his agent and his contract with his publisher.

26d-4 Don't use commas around modifiers that are essential to the meaning of the sentence. When a modifying phrase is essential to the meaning of the sentence, it should *not* be set off with commas (see Section 26b–1). Such a modifier is called essential or restrictive.

---

unnecessary commas

Some things Jolene learned, as an unpaid wife and mother, changed her mind about getting a college degree.

Husbands, who say they don't want their wives to work, don't sound so wonderful anymore.

In both examples, the writer has put commas around parts of the sentences that are important to their meaning. Without the information in those sections, the main clauses lose their point. Thus the parts marked off by the commas are not interrupters; they're necessary and shouldn't be separated from the rest of the sentence.

---

commas eliminated

Some things Jolene learned as an unpaid wife and mother changed her mind about getting a college degree.

Husbands who say they don't want their wives to work don't sound so wonderful anymore.

26d
no ^;

■ **Exercise 26.4** Working in a group, analyze these sentences to see if all the commas are needed. Then work together to rewrite sentences to get rid of commas that cause awkward interruptions. Notice that some of the commas are necessary.

1. Psychologists, who have studied moods, say that such emotional states are contagious, and compare them to social viruses.
2. Moreover, some people are emotionally expressive, and likely to transmit moods; others, seem to be more inclined to "catch" moods.
3. Trying to pinpoint the exact means by which moods are transmitted, is difficult, since the process happens almost instantaneously.
4. One transmission mechanism is imitation: by unconsciously imitating facial expressions, people produce, in themselves a mood that goes with the expression.
5. People who get along well with others, generally, synchronize their moods, by making a series of changes in their body language.

26e   DO YOU UNDERSTAND THE SPECIAL USES OF COMMAS?

Troubleshooting

Aside from the important role commas play within sentences both in linking and separating ideas, commas have a variety of special jobs that are purely conventional. These are the types of uses you simply have to memorize to get right. You can master them with just a little practice.

To master the comma conventions . . .

26e–1 **Use commas correctly to separate units of three within numbers.** Commas are optional in four-digit numbers.

> 4,110 or 4110
> 99,890
> 1,235,470
> 10,000,000,000

Do not use commas in decimals, social security numbers, street addresses, telephone numbers, or zip codes.

26e–2 **Use commas correctly in dates.** In American usage, commas separate the day from the year. Note that a year is enclosed by commas if it appears in the middle of a sentence.

> World War II began on September 1, 1939.
>
> Germany expanded the war on June 22, 1941, when its armies invaded Russia.

Commas aren't required when only the month and year are given.

> World War II began in September 1939.

Commas are not used when dates are given in British form, with the day preceding the month.

> World War II began on 1 September 1939.

26e–3 **Use commas correctly in addresses.** Commas ordinarily separate street addresses, cities, states, and countries. When these items occur in the middle of a sentence, they are enclosed by commas.

> Miami University is in Oxford, Ohio.
>
> Though born in London, England, Denise Levertov is considered an American writer.

The prime minister lives at No. 10 Downing Street, Westminster, London, England.

Commas aren't used between states and zip codes.

Austin, Texas 78712

26e–4   Use commas correctly to separate proper names from titles and degrees that follow.

Tulla Charizo, Ph.D., has been chosen to replace Cornelius Brill, M.D.

26e–5   Use commas to follow the salutation in personal letters.

Dear Dr. Rizzo,
Dear Ms. Bowen,

26e–6   Use commas to introduce quotations or to follow them.

The lawyer insisted, "He can't be held responsible."

"Don't tell me he can't be held responsible," bellowed Judge Carver.

Ms. Rice said, "I'm not sure about the motion on the floor."

She then asked, "Would the secretary read the motion?"

However, no commas are needed when a quotation fits right into a sentence without an introductory phrase or frame. Compare the following examples.

Commas needed

"Experience," said Oscar Wilde, "is the name everyone gives to their mistakes."

Said P. G. Wodehouse, "I always advise people never to give advice."

No commas needed

Oscar Wilde defined experience as "the name everyone gives to their mistakes."

P. G. Wodehouse advised people "never to give advice."

26e
∧
,

■ **Exercise 26.5** Review the following sentences and add commas where necessary.

1. In the autumn of 1863, Abraham Lincoln president of the United States traveled to Gettysburg Pennsylvania to speak at the dedication of a cemetery there.

2. The cemetery was for the soldiers who had fallen at the Battle of Gettysburg, and Lincoln's speech—now known as the *Gettysburg Address*—opened with the famous words "Fourscore and seven years ago."

3. The Battle of Gettysburg had started on July 1 1863 and had raged for three days.

4. The Civil War would not end until April 1865.

5. The bloodiest battle of the war took place near Sharpsburg Maryland along the banks of Antietam Creek, where a single day of fighting produced over 23000 casualties.

26e
^
,

27

Problems with Semicolons and Colons?

A Semicolons
B Colons

27a DO YOU HAVE PROBLEMS WITH SEMICOLONS?

Troubleshooting

A semicolon is a stronger pause than a comma, but a weaker pause than a period. Semicolons usually separate items of equal grammatical weight: comparable clauses, phrases, or items in a complicated list.

independent clause ; independent clause
▲

Wes Craven directed A *Nightmare on Elm Street*; he later made the terrifying *The Serpent and the Rainbow*.

phrase ; phrase
▲

My course in cinema taught the basics of movie production, including how to write treatments, outlines, and scripts; how to audition and cast actors; and how to edit.

item in a list ; item in a list ; item in a list
▲   ▲

We rented cassettes of *Baby, It's You*; *Star Trek VI: The Undiscovered Country*; and *Twilight Zone—the Movie*.

Problems with semicolons are very common. Typically, writers who are uncertain about semicolons use commas where semicolons are required—or vice versa. In your papers, an editor may use a caret and a semicolon to indicate where a semicolon is needed.

Give Matthew the book⁄it belongs to him. $\hat{;}$

To handle semicolons appropriately . . .

27a–1 **Use semicolons to join independent clauses closely related in thought.** Notice that conjunctions (such as *and, but, so*) aren't needed when clauses are linked by semicolons.

> Films focus on action and movement; plays emphasize language and thought.

> The history of British cinema is uneven; the best British films come from the period just before and during World War II.

> Italian cinema blossomed after World War II; directors like de Sica, Fellini, and Antonioni won critical acclaim.

Leaving out the semicolons, however, would create run-on sentences.

If a comma alone is used to join two independent clauses (that is, clauses that could stand as complete sentences), the result is a *comma splice*.

> **comma splice**
>
> Ethel Waters was a distinguished actress, her autobiography is titled *His Eye Is on the Sparrow*.

To correct the error, replace the comma with a semicolon.

> **comma splice eliminated**
>
> Ethel Waters was a distinguished actress; her autobiography is titled *His Eye Is on the Sparrow*.

Remember that while a semicolon alone is strong enough to join two independent sentences, a comma can link them only with the help of coordinating conjunctions—*and, but, for, yet, or, nor*, and *so*.

 CAUTION

27a–2 **Use semicolons to join independent clauses connected by words such as *however, therefore, nevertheless, nonetheless, moreover*, and *consequently*.** These

27a

;

words are called *conjunctive adverbs*, but by themselves they cannot link sentences. They require a semicolon.

> Bob Hope started his career in vaudeville**; however,** he made his major mark as a film star and television comic.

> The original *Rocky* was an Oscar-winning movie**; unfortunately,** its many sequels have exhausted the original idea.

> Films about British spy 007 have been in decline for years**; nevertheless,** new James Bond films continue to appear.

In sentences like those above, using a comma instead of a semicolon before the conjunctive adverb produces a comma splice. This is a common punctuation error.

---

comma splice

Good films often spawn sequels, however, the sequels rarely equal the originals.

27a
;

To correct the error, replace the comma with a semicolon.

---

comma splice eliminated

Good films often spawn sequels; however, the sequels rarely equal the originals.

But here's an important point: when a word like *however* or *therefore* occurs in the middle of an independent clause, it *is* preceded and followed by commas. In the following pairs of sentences, note carefully where the boldfaced words appear and how the shifts in their location change the punctuation required.

> *Airplane!* was a parody of disaster movies**; however,** its chief target was probably the popular thriller *Airport*.

> *Airplane!* was a parody of disaster movies; its chief target**, however,** was probably the popular thriller *Airport*.

> Some students in the film class had never seen *Gone With the Wind***; moreover,** some had not even heard of Clark Gable.

> Some students in the film class had**, moreover,** never seen *Gone With the Wind* or heard of Clark Gable.

CHART

Frequently Used Conjunctive Adverbs

consequently	meanwhile	rather
furthermore	moreover	then
hence	nonetheless	therefore
however	otherwise	thus

27a-3 Use semicolons to join independent clauses connected by words or phrases such as *indeed, in fact, at any rate, for example, on the other hand.* These expressions, like conjunctive adverbs, ordinarily require a semicolon before them and a comma after.

Box office receipts for the sci-fi epic's opening week were spectacular**; in fact,** the film's take broke all previous records.

The film's publicity had been great**; on the other hand,** word-of-mouth pans from disappointed viewers soon killed the box office.

The studio isn't discouraged; **indeed,** a sequel is planned.

27a-4 Use semicolons to separate clauses, phrases, or series that might be confusing if commas alone were used to mark boundaries. Semicolons are especially helpful when complicated phrases or items in a list already contain commas or other punctuation.

One student listed her favorite films as *Airplane!***;** *Come Back to the 5 & Dime, Jimmy Dean, Jimmy Dean***;** *M*A*S*H***;** *Victor/Victoria***;** and *Plan 9 from Outer Space.*

The sound track for the film included the Supremes' "Stop in the Name of Love!"**;** Bob Dylan's "Rainy Day Women #12 & 35"**;** and Rodgers and Hart's "Glad to Be Unhappy."

Bob Hope's films include *Road to Morocco,* which also features Bing Crosby and Dorothy Lamour**;** *The Paleface,* a comic western with Jane Russell as Calamity Jane**;** and *The Seven Little Foys,* a biography about vaudeville performer Eddie Foy, Sr.

Notice how, in the following example, the commas fail to separate the various items in the series effectively. As a result, the sentence is difficult to read.

> ### confusing commas
>
> A $50 lab fee for the cinema course covered the rental of lights, costumes, and other equipment, film and film-processing expenses, and duplication costs for scripts and other paperwork.

Semicolons eliminate the confusion. Since semicolons mark stronger pauses than commas do, they are better able to set off the separate items.

> ### semicolons replace commas
>
> A $50 lab fee for the cinema course covered the rental of lights, costumes, and other equipment; film and film-processing expenses; and duplication costs for scripts and other paperwork.

27a
;

27a–5 **Do not use semicolons between phrases and independent clauses or dependent clauses and independent clauses.** Remember that a semicolon joins like to like.

> independent clause ; independent clause

> phrase ; phrase

> item in a list ; item in a list

▲

So a semicolon would also be incorrect between an independent clause and a prepositional phrase or between a dependent clause and an independent clause. Commas are usually the correct punctuation in such cases.

> independent clause , prepositional phrase

Wrong   Many young filmmakers regularly exceed their budgets; in the tradition of the finest Hollywood directors.

Right   Many young filmmakers regularly exceed their budgets, in the tradition of the finest Hollywood directors.

> dependent clause , independent clause

Wrong   Although director Alfred Hitchcock once said that actors should be treated like cattle; he won fine performances from many of them.

Right   Although director Alfred Hitchcock once said that actors should be treated like cattle, he won fine performances from many of them.

27a–6   Do not use semicolons to introduce quotations.

incorrect semicolon before quotation

Wasn't it Mae West who said; "When I'm good I'm very good, but when I'm bad I'm better"?

Direct quotations can be introduced by commas or colons.

replace semicolon with a comma

Wasn't it Mae West who said, "When I'm good I'm very good, but when I'm bad I'm better"?

27a–7   Do not use semicolons to introduce lists.

incorrect semicolon before a list

Paul Robeson performed in several distinguished films; *Showboat, Song of Freedom, King Solomon's Mines.*

Note that lists may be introduced by colons, commas, or—much more rarely—dashes.

semicolon replaced with a colon

Paul Robeson performed in several distinguished films: *Showboat, Song of Freedom, King Solomon's Mines.*

27a

;

Semicolons may, of course, separate items within a list (see Section 27a–4).

▶ **Fine Tuning**

1. Placing semicolons between very short independent clauses can seem like punctuation overkill.

   With semicolons   For best director, Norman picked Alfred Hitch-cock; Adele nominated François Truffaut; Cleo chose Agnes Varda.

   When such clauses are short and closely related, they can be sep-arated by commas.

   With commas   For best director, Norman picked Alfred Hitch-cock, Adele nominated François Truffaut, Cleo chose Agnes Varda.

2. Semicolons ordinarily fall outside quotation marks (see Section 28e–6).

   The first Edgar Allan Poe work filmed was "The Raven"; movies based upon the poem appeared in 1912, 1915, and 1935. ◀

27a
;

■ **Exercise 27.1** Use semicolons to arrange the following clauses, phrases, and bits of information into complete sentences. You may have to add some words and ideas.

1. The action in mad-killer movies like *Friday the 13th*. Jason pinions two teenagers making love. Jason splits the skull of a camper. Jason drags a skinny-dipper to a watery grave. Jason drills an ice pick into a camp counselor's brain.
2. Strange titles of Bob Dylan songs from the 1960s. "Subterranean Homesick Blues" "It's Alright, Ma (I'm Only Bleeding)" "Love Minus Zero/No Limit" "Don't Think Twice, It's All Right" "I Shall Be Free— No. 10."
3. Items in E. D. Hirsch's list of everything Americans should know. Carbon-14 dating. "Veni, vidi, vici." "Doctor Livingstone, I presume." "Yes, Virginia, there is a Santa Claus."
4. Exceptionally long movie titles. *Alice Doesn't Live Here Anymore. They Shoot Horses, Don't They? Jo Jo Dancer, Your Life Is Calling. Effect of Gamma Rays on Man-in-the-Moon Marigolds. Close Encounters of the Third Kind: The Special Edition.*

■ **Exercise 27.2** Revise the following sentences, adding or deleting semicolons as they are needed. Not all semicolons below are incorrect.

You may have to substitute other punctuation marks for some of the semicolons.

1. For many years, biblical spectacles were a staple of the Hollywood film industry, however, in recent years, few such films have been produced.
2. Cecil B. De Mille made the grandest epics; he is quoted as saying; "Give me any couple of pages of the Bible and I'll give you a picture."
3. He made *The Ten Commandments* twice, the 1956 version starred Charlton Heston as Moses.
4. The most famous scene in *The Ten Commandments* is the parting of the Red Sea; the waters opening to enable the Israelites to escape the pursuing army of Pharaoh.
5. De Mille made many nonbiblical movies, many of them, however, were also epic productions with casts of thousands and spectacular settings.

27b   DO YOU HAVE PROBLEMS WITH COLONS?

Troubleshooting

Colons are strong directional signals. They show movement in a sentence, pointing your reader's attention to precisely what you wish to highlight, whether it is an idea, a list, a quotation, or even another independent clause. Colons require your attention because their functions are limited and quite specific. In your papers, an editor may use a caret and a colon to indicate where a colon should be used rather than another mark of punctuation.

He spoke just one word⁁ "Rosebud." ⁝

To handle colons correctly . . .

27b-1   Use colons to direct readers to examples, explanations, or significant words and phrases.

Orson Welles' greatest problem may also have been his greatest achievement: the brilliance of his first film, *Citizen Kane*.

Citizen Kane turns on the meaning of one word uttered by a dying man: "Rosebud."

A colon that highlights an item in this way ordinarily follows a complete sentence. In fact, many readers object strongly to colons placed after linking verbs.

colon misused

America's most bankable film star is: Arnold
Schwarzenegger.

To correct this miscue, remove the colon. No additional punctuation is
needed.

unneeded colon cut

America's most bankable film star is Arnold
Schwarzenegger.

27b-2 **Use colons to direct readers to lists.**

Besides *Citizen Kane*, Welles directed, produced, or acted in
many movies: *The Magnificent Ambersons*, *Journey into Fear*,
The Lady from Shanghai, and *Macbeth*, to name a few.

Colons that introduce lists ordinarily follow complete sentences. Here is
a pair of sentences—both correct—demonstrating your options.

**Version one—
with a colon** The filmmakers the professor admired most were a
diverse group: François Truffaut, Spike Lee, Alain
Robbe-Grillet, and David Lean.

**Version two —
without a
colon** The filmmakers the professor admired most were
François Truffaut, Spike Lee, Alain Robbe-Grillet,
and David Lean.

Similarly, colons are omitted after expressions such as *like, for example,
such as,* and *that is.* In fact, colons are intended to replace these terms.

colon misused

Shoestring budgets have produced many financially
successful films, such as: *Flashdance*, *Breaking Away*,
and *Halloween*.

To correct such an error, just remove the colon. No additional punctuation is needed.

> **unneeded colon cut**
>
> Shoestring budgets have produced many financially
> successful films, such as *Flashdance, Breaking Away*, and
> *Halloween*.

Colons are used, however, after phrases that more specifically announce
a list, expressions such as *including these, as follows, such as the following*.
Compare the following sentences to understand the difference.

Version one — **with a colon**	The producer trimmed her budget by cutting out some **frills:** special lighting, rental costumes for the cast, and crew lunches.
Version two — **without a** **colon**	The producer trimmed her budget by cutting out **frills, such as** special lighting, rental costumes for the cast, and crew lunches.
Version three — **with a colon**	The producer trimmed her budget by cutting out some **frills such as these:** special lighting, rental costumes for the cast, and crew lunches.

27b–3 Use colons to direct readers to quotations or dialogue.

Orson Welles commented poignantly on his own career: "I started
at the top and worked down."

Don't introduce short quotations with colons. A comma or no punctuation mark at all will suffice. Compare the following sentences.

Dirty Harry said "Make my day!"
As Dirty Harry said, "Make my day!"
We recalled Dirty Harry's memorable phrase: "Make my day!"

In the last example, the colon *is* appropriate because it directs attention
to a particular comment.

27b–4 Use colons to join two complete sentences when the second sentence illustrates or explains the first.

Making a film is like writing a paper: it absorbs all the time you'll
give it.

27b–5 Use colons to separate titles from subtitles.

Nightmare on Elm Street 3: Dream Warriors
"Darkest Night: Conscience in *Macbeth*"

27b-6 **Use colons in conventional situations.** Colons separate numbers when indicating time or citing Bible passages.

    12:35 p.m.   Matthew 3:1

Colons traditionally follow salutations in business letters.

    Dear Ms. Kael: Dear Mr. Ebert:

Colons separate place of publication from publisher and date from page numbers in various MLA bibliography entries.

    Glenview: Scott, 1961   14 August 1991: 154–63

▶ **Fine Tuning**

1. Colons and semicolons are not interchangeable, but you can use both marks in the same sentence. A colon, for example, might introduce a list of items separated by semicolons.

   Errol Flynn played many roles: an Indian in *Kim*; a pirate in *Against All Flags*; an outlaw in *The Adventures of Robin Hood*.

2. Don't separate a preposition from its objects(s) with a colon—or any other punctuation mark.

   Wrong   Katharine Hepburn starred in: *Little Women*, *The Philadelphia Story*, and *The African Queen*.

   Right   Katharine Hepburn starred in *Little Women*, *The Philadelphia Story*, and *The African Queen*.

3. Don't use more than one colon in a sentence. A dash can usually replace one of the colons.

   Problem   Most critics agree on this point: Orson Welles made one of the greatest of films: *Citizen Kane*.

   Solution   Most critics agree on this point: Orson Welles made one of the greatest of films—*Citizen Kane*. ◀

■ **Exercise 27.3** Revise the following sentences by adding colons or making sure colons are used correctly. Don't assume that every sentence contains an error.

1. No one ever forgets the conclusion of Hitchcock's *Psycho*; the discovery of Norman's mother in the rocking chair.
2. Hitchcock liked to use memorable settings in his films, including: Mt. Rushmore in *North by Northwest*, Radio City Music Hall in *Saboteur*, and the British Museum in *Blackmail*.

27b

:

3. One actor appears in every Hitchcock film Hitchcock himself.

4. *Rear Window* is a cinematic tour de force: all the action focuses on what Jimmy Stewart sees from his window.

5. Hitchcock probably summed up his own technique best; "There is no terror in a bang, only in the anticipation of it."

Problems with Sentence Markers?

A Dashes
B Hyphens
C Parentheses
D Brackets
E Quotation marks
F Ellipses
G Italics
H Slashes

28a WHEN DO YOU USE DASHES?

Troubleshooting

Used alone, a dash attaches one idea to another more vigorously than a comma would. Used in pairs, dashes highlight words or phrases by separating them from the rest of a sentence. Too many dashes, however, can clutter a passage. It's also important to type a dash correctly: it is two hyphens, --.

Professional editors will use a caret and the symbol $\frac{1}{M}$ to indicate where a dash is needed.

> They were brave soldiers ‸ men and women the country $\frac{|}{m}$
> could cheer for.

To handle dashes correctly . . .

28a–1 **Use dashes to attach phrases to the end of sentences.** The phrase might be an example, illustration, or summary. Or it might be a surprise, an idea that contradicts or undercuts a reader's expectations.

Like colons, dashes point to ideas. But where colons provide formal introductions, dashes introduce unanticipated guests.

> Dvorak's *New World* Symphony reflects musical themes the composer heard in the United States—including Native American melodies and black spirituals.

> Beethoven's Ninth Symphony was a great accomplishment for an artist in bad health—and completely deaf.

28a–2 **Use dashes to insert a phrase or clause into the middle of a sentence.** The interruption might be an example, explanation, illustration, observation, amplification, or contradiction. In any case, the interrupting passage, surrounded by dashes, could be lifted out of the sentence without affecting its overall sense.

> The giants of nineteenth-century Italian opera—Rossini, Donizetti, Bellini, Verdi—worked for demanding and sensitive audiences.

> Many regard Verdi's *Otello*—based on Shakespeare's story of a marriage ruined by jealousy—as the greatest of Italian tragic operas.

28a–3 **Use dashes to highlight an interruption, especially in dialogue.**

> "When—perhaps I should say *if*—I ever sit through Wagner's *Ring*, I expect to be paid for it," Joshua remarked.

> Candice sputtered, "The opera lasted—I can hardly believe it—five hours!"

28a–4 **Use dashes to set off items, phrases, or credit lines.**

> Aaron Copland, George Gershwin, William Grant Still—these composers sought to create an American musical idiom.

> Members of the audience are asked
> —to withhold applause between movements
> —to stifle all coughing and sneezing
> —to refrain from popping gum.

> "Music is the universal language."
>
> —Henry Wadsworth Longfellow

CAUTION **28a–5** **Don't type a hyphen where a dash is required.** Typed dashes are made up of two unspaced hyphens: --. No space is left before or after a dash.

28a
—

hyphens used instead of dashes

```
Much of Beethoven's music-unlike that of

Mozart-uses emphatic rhythms.
```

It is easy to misread a sentence when hyphens are used instead of dashes.

dashes replace hyphens

```
Much of Beethoven's music--unlike that of

Mozart--uses emphatic rhythms.
```

28a-6 **Don't use too many dashes in a sentence or passage.**
Dashes are vigorous pieces of punctuation that should be used cautiously—one pair of dashes per sentence.

too many dashes

Mozart—recognized as a genius while still a child—produced more than 600 compositions during his life—including symphonies, operas, and concertos.

Here some of the dashes need to be replaced with commas.

some dashes replaced

Mozart, recognized as a genius while still a child, produced more than 600 compositions during his life—including symphonies, operas, and concertos.

■ **Exercise 28.1** Add and delete dashes as necessary to improve the sentences below.

1. Legend has it that Beethoven's Third Symphony was dedicated to

Napoleon Bonaparte the champion of French revolutionary ideals until he declared himself emperor.

2. Scholars believe—though they can't be sure—that the symphony was initially called *Bonaparte*—testimony to just how much the idealistic Beethoven admired the French leader.

3. The Third Symphony a revolutionary work itself is now known by the title *Eroica*.

4. The Third, the Fifth, the Sixth, the Seventh, the Ninth Symphonies, they all contain musical passages that most people recognize immediately.

5. The opening four notes of Beethoven's Fifth, da, da, da, da, may be the most famous in all of music.

28b HOW DO YOU USE HYPHENS?

Troubleshooting

Hyphens either link words or divide words between syllables. Quite often, it is a judgment call whether modifying phrases or related words require hyphens; useful guidelines are available. Dividing words at the end of lines is a simpler matter. If you divide words at all, you must divide them only at breaks between syllables.

An editor will usually place carets within the line to indicate missing hyphens.

Our editor in chief will retire in June. ‸

To use hyphens correctly . . .

TRICKY

28b-1 Use hyphens to link compound nouns and verbs. Hyphens join words in a variety of situations, but the conventions guiding their use are complicated. Sometimes you'll have to rely on instinct—as well as a dictionary or a reference tool such as the Government Printing Office's *A Manual of Style*. Here are some noun expressions that do take hyphens.

mother-in-law	son-in-law	great-grandmother
two-step	walkie-talkie	water-skier
bull's-eye	hocus-pocus	president-elect

Here are a few verbs that take hyphens.

cold-shoulder	double-up	gold-plate

Note, however, that many compound expressions don't take hyphens.

They can be either single words or separate words—and no simple rule explains the difference. You must check a dictionary or style manual.

cabdriver	horsehair	schoolchildren
cab owner	horse fence	school board

28b-2 Use hyphens to link unit modifiers. Here are some modifiers that require hyphens.

air-cooled	bare-armed	double-edged
hot-blooded	long-haired	mid-American
power-driven	steam-driven	wooden-hulled

When such modifiers work together before a noun, they are called *unit modifiers*.

> a **lump-sum** settlement
> an **up-or-down** vote
> an **English-speaking** country
> a **sharp-looking** suit
> a **stop-motion** sequence
> a **seventeenth-century** vase

How can you tell when you are dealing with a unit modifier? Try removing one of the modifiers or placing a comma between them. If the expression changes in meaning, it is probably a unit modifier that requires a hyphen (but see also Sections 28b–3 and 28b–4).

> a blood, red tie? → a **blood-red** tie
> a well, known artist? → a **well-known** artist
> a bone, chilling scream? → a **bone-chilling** scream

28b-3 Do not use hyphens to link compound modifiers that follow a noun.

> The artist was **well known.**
> The scream was **bone chilling.**

28b-4 Do not use hyphens with adverbs that end in *-ly*. Nor should you use hyphens with *very.*

a **sharply honed** knife	a **quickly written** note
a **bitterly cold** morning	a **very hot** day

28b-5 Use hyphens to link prefixes to proper nouns.

> **pre-**Columbian
> **anti-**American

28b–6 Use hyphens if you write out numbers from twenty-one to ninety-nine. Fractions also take hyphens, but use only one hyphen per fraction.

> **twenty-nine**
> **two-thirds**
> **one forty-seventh** of a mile
> **one-quarter** inch
> two hundred **forty-six**

28b–7 Use hyphens to create compound phrases.

Some classmates resented her **holier-than-thou** attitude.

28b–8 Use hyphens to prevent words from being misread.

> co-op   re-elect   co-worker

28b–9 Use hyphens in some technical expressions.

> light-year
> A-bomb
> T-square

28b–10 Use hyphens to divide words at the end of lines when you run out of space. However, both the MLA and APA style manuals now discourage breaking words at the end of lines. If you are using a computer, word wrap will eliminate most end-of-line divisions; some programs offer automatic hyphenation.

When you do need to divide a word, break it only at a syllable. If you are unsure about a syllable break, check a dictionary. Don't guess.

> fu / se / lage   vin / e / gar / y
> lo / qua / cious   cam / ou /flage

28b–11 Don't hyphenate words of one syllable. Don't let a single letter dangle at the end of one line, either. Divisions like the following would be either wrong or inappropriate.

> mo- uth   cry- pt   cough- ed
> o- boe   e- clipse   i- dea

Nor should you strand a letter or two at the beginning of a new line. Divisions like the following are inappropriate.

> Ohi- o   clump- y   flatfoot- ed
> log- ic   oversimpli- fy   yo- yo

Don't leave a syllable at the end of a line that might be read as a complete word. The following sentence might be misread at first because of faulty division.

> Nothing could deter Mary Elizabeth in her pursuit of a management degree.

28b–12 Don't hyphenate contractions, numbers, abbreviations, or initialisms at the end of lines. The following divisions are inappropriate.

would- n't	250,- 000,000	NA- TO
U.S.- M.C.	Ph.- D.	NB- C

28b–13 Divide compound expressions between words, not syllables.

> **Wrong** self-confi- dent
>
> **Right**   self- confident

Divide expressions that contain hyphens at the hyphen—but don't add a second hyphen!

> **Wrong** Last night, thieves robbed Anson's fast-/ food shop.
>
> **Right**   Last night, thieves robbed Anson's fast- food shop.

▶ **Fine Tuning**

Sometimes a word or phrase may have more than a single hyphenated modifier. These **suspended modifiers** look like the following.

> Annie planned her vacation wardrobe to accommodate **cold-, cool-,** and **wet-weather** days. ◀

28b
-

■ **Exercise 28.2** In the following sentences, indicate which form of the words in parentheses is preferable. Use a dictionary if you are not familiar with the terms.

1. Local citizens have a (**once in a life-time/once-in-a-lifetime**) opportunity to preserve an (**old-growth/oldgrowth**) forest.
2. A large, wooded parcel of land is about to be turned into a shopping mall by (**real-estate/realestate**) speculators and (**pinstripe suited/ pinstripe-suited**) investors.

3. The forest provides a haven for (**wild-life/wildlife**) of all varieties, from (**great horned owls/great-horned owls**) to (**ruby throated/ruby-throated**) hummingbirds.
4. Does any community need (**video stores/video-stores**), (**T shirt/T-shirt**) shops, and (**over priced/overpriced**) boutiques more than acres of natural habitat?
5. This (**recently-proposed/recently proposed**) development can be stopped by petitioning the (**city-council/city council**).

28c WHEN DO YOU USE PARENTHESES?

Troubleshooting

Both parentheses and brackets act as enclosures. Parentheses are used more often than brackets and more generally—usually to show when something needs to be separated from the rest of a sentence or paragraph. Parentheses lack the snap of dashes; instead, they quietly accommodate an extra bit of information, a comment, or an aside. Brackets, on the other hand, are specialty pieces of punctuation used only in a few specific situations (see Section 28d).

An editor will indicate a need for parentheses with carets and symbols in the margin.

During his first term 1968–1972 as president,   *(/)*
Richard Nixon visited both Moscow and Beijing.

To use parentheses correctly . . .

28c-1 Use parentheses to separate material from the main body of a sentence or paragraph. This material may be a word, a phrase, a list, even a complete sentence.

The flight to Colorado was quick **(only about ninety minutes)** and uneventful.

The emergency kit contained all the expected items **(jumper cables, tire inflator, roadside flares).**

The buses arrived early and by noon the stagehands were working at the stadium. **(One of the vans carried a portable stage.)** Preparations for the concert were on track.

28c-2 Use parentheses to insert examples, directions, or other details into a sentence.

The call to the police included an address **(107 West St.).**

If the children get lost, have them call the school **(346-1317)** or the church office **(471-6109).**

28c-3 Use parentheses to highlight numbers or letters used in listing items.

The labor negotiators realized they could **(1)** concede on all issues immediately, **(2)** stonewall until the public demanded a settlement, or **(3)** hammer out a compromise.

28c-4 Place parentheses properly either inside or outside end punctuation, depending on circumstances. When a complete sentence standing alone is surrounded by parentheses, its end punctuation belongs inside the parentheses.

The neighborhood was run-down and littered. (Some houses looked as if they hadn't been painted in decades**.)**

However, when a sentence concludes with a parenthesis, the end punctuation for the complete sentence falls outside the final parenthesis mark.

On the corner was a small Protestant church (actually a converted store**).**

▶ **Fine Tuning**

1. If parentheses enclose a full sentence within another sentence, the enclosed sentence ordinarily begins without capitalization and ends without punctuation.

The editor pointed out a misplaced modifier **(the writer glared at her),** crossed out three paragraphs **(the writer grumbled),** and then demanded a complete rewrite **(it would, after all, be a lead story).**

Punctuation may be used, however, if an enclosed sentence is a question or exclamation.

The coup ended **(who would have guessed it?)** almost as quickly as it began.

2. No punctuation is needed to introduce a parenthetical expression in a sentence. A comma before a parenthesis is incorrect.

Wrong Although the Crusades failed in their announced objective̷ (Jerusalem still remained in Muslim hands afterward) the expeditions changed the West dramatically.

28c
( )

However, if necessary, a parenthesis may be followed by a comma.

Right   Although the Crusades failed in their announced objective (Jerusalem still remained in Muslim hands afterward), the expeditions changed the West dramatically.

3. Parentheses are used around in-text notes with MLA or APA documentation. See Chapters 34 and 35 for details. ◀

■ **Exercise 28.3** Add parentheses as needed to the following passage.

1. Native Americans inhabited almost every region of North America, from the peoples farthest north the Inuit to those in the Southwest the Hopi, the Zuni.

2. In parts of what are now New Mexico and Colorado, during the thirteenth century, some ancient tribes moved off the mesas no one knows exactly why to live in cliff dwellings.

3. One cliff dwelling at Mesa Verde covers an area of 66 meters 216 feet by 27 meters 89 feet.

4. Spectacular as they are, the cliff dwellings served the tribes known as the Anasazi for only a short time.

5. The Anasazi left their cliff dwellings, possibly because of a prolonged drought A.D. 1276–1299 in the entire region.

28d
[ ]

28d   WHEN DO YOU USE BRACKETS?

Troubleshooting

Like parentheses, brackets are enclosures. But they have fewer and more specialized uses. Brackets and parentheses are usually *not* interchangeable. An editor will indicate a need for brackets with carets and symbols in the margin.

"She ˄Aretha Franklin˄ is almost as gifted a pianist [ ]
as she is a singer," the reviewer commented.

To use brackets correctly . . .

28d-1   **Use brackets to insert comments or explanations into direct quotations.** You cannot change the words in a direct quotation, but you can add information by using brackets.

The mayor pulled a newspaper from his jacket and said to the crowd, "This [the newspaper] proves I had nothing to do with the cable TV scandal."

"He [George Lucas] reminded me a little of Walt Disney's version of a mad scientist."   —Steven Spielberg

28d–2 Use brackets to clarify situations where parentheses fall within parentheses. When possible, avoid parentheses within parentheses. If you cannot, the inner set of parentheses should become brackets.

The house the volunteers were assigned to work on had barely escaped a condemnation order (City of Cleveland [order no. 34209]).

28d–3 Use brackets to acknowledge or highlight errors that originate in quoted materials. In such cases the Latin word *sic* ("thus") is enclosed in brackets immediately after the error. See Section 33e–6 for additional details.

28d
[ ]

The sign over the cash register read "We don't except [sic] personal checks for payment."

The menu included "potatoe [sic] salad."

28d–4 Don't use parentheses where brackets are needed even if you are using a typewriter that lacks bracket keys.

parentheses mistakenly used instead of brackets

```
"He (George Lucas) reminded me a little of

Walt Disney's version of a mad scientist."
```

When you face this problem, simply leave spaces where the brackets should appear and draw them in after you've typed your paper. But don't forget.

brackets drawn in

```
"He [George Lucas] reminded me a little of

Walt Disney's version of a mad scientist."
```

28e WHEN DO YOU USE QUOTATION MARKS?

Troubleshooting

Quotation marks—which always occur in pairs—highlight whatever appears between them. Conventionally, double marks (" ") are used around the actual words of a speaker (called **direct discourse**) and around titles. However, single marks (' ') appear with quotations or titles inside quotations.

An editor will use a quotation mark within an inverted caret to indicate that a quotation mark has been omitted.

> "She stole everything but the cameras, George Raft ˇ"
> once said of Mae West.

To use quotation marks correctly . . .

28e-1 **Use quotation marks to signal that you are quoting word-for-word from printed sources.** Notice the capitalization and punctuation before and after the quotations in the following examples.

> "Heroism," says Ralph Waldo Emerson, "feels and never reasons and therefore is always right."

> Emerson reminds us that "nothing great was ever achieved without enthusiasm."

> "Next to the originator of a good sentence is the first quoter of it," writes Emerson.

28e-2 **Use quotation marks to show dialogue.** Quotation marks enclose the exact words of various speakers. When writing extended dialogue, you ordinarily start a new paragraph each time the speaker changes.

> "It would be nobler," said politically correct Willie, "to spend spring break cleaning trash from roadsides rather than roasting ourselves on crowded beaches in Cozumel."
> "Get a life!" Angela replied.
> "That's telling him," said Travis.

However, when dialogue is provided not for its own sake, but to make some other point, the words of several speakers may appear within a single paragraph.

> Father Norman was confident that his parishioners would eventually see his point. "They'll come around," he predicted. "They always do." And Mrs. Brown, for one, was beginning to soften. "I've spent my money on many causes not half as worthy."

28e-3 Use quotation marks to cite the titles of short works. These ordinarily include titles of songs, essays, magazine and newspaper articles, TV episodes, unpublished speeches, chapters of books, and short poems. Longer works appear in *italics*. (See also Section 28g–1.)

> "Love Is Just a Four-Letter Word" song
> "Love Is a Fallacy" title of an essay
> "Byzantium" poem

28e-4 Use quotation marks to draw attention to specific words. Italics can also be used in these situations (see Section 28g–3).

> People clearly mean different things when they write about "democracy."

28e-5 Use quotation marks to signal that you are using a word ironically, sarcastically, or derisively.

> The clerk at the desk directed the tourists to their "suites"—bare rooms crowded with bunks. A bathroom down the hall would serve as the "spa."

But don't overdo it. This technique for adding emphasis loses its punch quickly.

28e
" "

TRICKY

28e-6 Place quotation marks correctly around other pieces of punctuation. Periods and commas always go *inside* closing quotation marks.

> Down a hotel corridor lined with antiwar posters, I heard someone humming "Blowin' in the Wind."
> "This must be what the sixties were like," I thought.

However, when a sentence ends with a citation in parentheses, the period follows the parenthesis.

> Hitchcock claims, "The sequence was never filmed" (21).

In American usage, colons and semicolons go *outside* closing quotation marks.

> Riley claimed to be "a human calculator"; he did quadratic equations in his head.
> The young Cassius Clay bragged about being "the greatest"; his opponents in the ring soon learned he wasn't boasting.

Question marks, exclamation points, and dashes can fall either inside or outside quotation marks, depending on the context. These punctuation marks fall inside the closing quotation when they are the correct punctuation for the phrase inside the quotes, but not for the sentence as a whole.

> When Mrs. Rattle saw her hotel room, she muttered, "Good grief!"
>
> She turned to her husband and said, "Do you really expect me to stay here?"
>
> Mr. Rattle began to answer, "I'm sure it's not so bad—" but his foot went through a floorboard before he could finish.

These punctuation marks fall outside the closing quotation mark when they are the appropriate mark for the complete sentence.

> Who was it who said, "These are the times that try men's souls"?

▶ **Fine Tuning**

Don't use quotation marks to draw attention to clichés. Highlighting a tired phrase just makes it seem more fatigued.

> Working around electrical fixtures makes me more nervous than ⁄"a cat on a hot tin roof." ◀

■ **Exercise 28.4** Rework the following passage by adding or deleting quotation marks, moving punctuation as necessary, and indenting paragraphs where you think appropriate.

> Much to the tourists' surprise, their "uproar" over conditions at their so-called "luxury resort" attracted the attention of a local television station. (In fact, Mrs. Rattle had read "the riot act" to a consumer advocate who worked for the station.) A reporter interviewed Mrs. Rattle, who claimed that she had been promised luxury accommodations. This place smells like old fish she fumed. Even the roaches look unwell. Didn't you check out the accommodations before paying? the reporter asked, turning to Mr. Rattle. He replied that unfortunately they had prepaid the entire vacation. But Mrs. Rattle interrupted. I knew we should have gone to Paris. You never said that! Mr. Rattle objected. As I was trying to say, Mrs. Rattle continued, I'd even rather be in Philadelphia.

■ **Exercise 28.5** Write a passage extending the reporter's interview in Exercise 28.4. Or create a dialogue on a subject of your own.

◆ Point of Difference

The guidelines in this section on the use of quotation marks apply in the United States. You should know, however, that the conventions for marking quotations differ significantly from language to language and country to country. French quotation marks, called guillemets, look like this: « ». Guillemets are also used as quotation marks in Spanish. In addition, dashes are used to indicate dialogue in Spanish. Even in books published in Britain, you'll find single quotation marks (' ') used where American publishers generally use double quotation marks (" "), and vice versa. These sentences illustrate the difference.

American   Carla said, "I haven't read 'The Raven.' "

British   Carla said, 'I haven't read "The Raven".'

American and British practices differ, too, on the placement of certain punctuation marks within quotation marks. In general, British usage tends to locate more punctuation marks (commas especially) outside quotation marks than does American usage.

American   To be proper, say "I *shall* go," not "*will.*"

British   To be proper, say 'I *shall* go', not '*will*'.

Don't worry about these differences between conventions: when writing in the United States you should follow standard American practice. But be aware that books you read may occasionally follow guidelines different from those you've learned. ◆

28f

...

28f WHEN DO YOU USE ELLIPSES?

Troubleshooting

The three spaced periods that form an ellipsis mark indicate a gap. Either you are leaving something out of a sentence or you want an idea to seem to trail away. Ellipses can be useful when you're quoting lengthy material in a research paper, but you must pay attention to the spacing around the marks.

To use ellipses correctly . . .

28f-1 **Place ellipses where material has been omitted from a direct quotation.** This material may be a word, a phrase, a complete sentence, or more.

Complete passage

   In *Walden* (1854), Henry David Thoreau describes his forest in spring: "Early in May, the oaks, hickories, maples, and other trees, just putting out amidst the pine woods around the pond, imparted a brightness like sunshine to the landscape, especially in cloudy days, as if the sun were breaking through the mists and shining faintly on the hill-sides here and there."

Passage with ellipses

   In *Walden* (1854), Henry David Thoreau describes his forest in spring: "Early in May, the oaks, hickories, maples, and other trees ... imparted a brightness like sunshine to the landscape . . . as if the sun were breaking through the mists and shining faintly on the hill-sides here and there."

28f–2   Use ellipses to indicate any gap or pause in a sentence, not necessarily in quoted material.

28f

. . .

   I was sure I could repair the faulty fuse box ... until it began shooting sparks.

28f–3   Use ellipses to suggest that an action is incomplete or continuing.

   At the limits of his patience, Secretary Perry began counting under his breath, "One, two, three ..."

TRICKY

28f–4   Use the correct spacing and punctuation before and after ellipsis marks.   An ellipsis is typed as three spaced periods (. . . not ...). When an ellipsis mark appears in the middle of a sentence, leave a space before the first and after the last period.

```
Most governments . . . are sometimes
```

If a punctuation mark occurs immediately before the words you are cutting, you may include it in your edited version if it makes your sentence easier to read. The punctuation mark is followed by a space, then the ellipsis mark.

```
It is excellent, . . . yet this government
```

When an ellipsis occurs at the end of a complete sentence, the end punctuation of the sentence is retained in the edited version, followed by a space, followed by the ellipsis. No gap is left between the last word in the sentence and its original end punctuation.

```
the people can act through it. . . .
```

When a parenthetical reference follows a sentence that ends with an ellipsis, leave a space between the last word in the sentence and the ellipsis. Then provide the parenthetical reference, followed by the closing punctuation mark.

```
the right to revolution . . ." (102).
```

■ **Exercise 28.6** Abridge the following passage, using at least three ellipses. Be sure the passage is still readable after you have made your cuts.

> Within a week, the neglected Victorian-style house being restored by volunteers began to look livable again, its exterior sheathed in gleaming paint, its gables restored, its gutters rehung, its roof reshingled. Even the grand staircase, rickety and worm-eaten, had been rebuilt. The amateur artisans made a number of mistakes during the project, including painting several windows shut, papering over a heating register, and hanging a door upside down, but no one doubted their commitment to restoring the grand old house. Some spent hours sanding away layers of paint and varnish accumulated over almost six decades to reveal beautiful hardwood floors. Others contributed their organizational talents—many were managers or paper-pushers in their day jobs—to keep other workers supplied with raw materials, equipment, and inspiration. The volunteers worked from seven in the morning to seven at night, occasionally pausing to talk with neighbors from the area who stopped by with snacks and lunches, but laboring like mules until there was too little light to continue. But they felt the effort was worth it every time they saw the old house standing on the corner in all its former glory.

28g
ital

28g WHEN DO YOU USE ITALICS?

Troubleshooting

Italics, like quotation marks, draw attention to a title, word, or phrase. But they are even more noticeable because italics change the way words look. In a printed text, italics are *slanted letters*. In typed or handwritten papers, italics are signaled by underlining the appropriate words. In either case, italicized words get noticed.

If you are using a computer than can print italicized words, ask your instructor if you should print actual italics in your paper. (Your instructor may prefer that you simply use an underscore.)

An editor will underline a word that needs to be italicized and mark *ital* in the margin.

I was reading Stephen King's Christine. *ital*

To use italics correctly . . .

28g–1 **Use italics to set off some titles.** Some titles and names are italicized; others appear between quotation marks. The chart below provides some guidance. Notice that the titles of longer works and names of large objects tend to be italicized while shorter works (chapters, articles) fall between quotation marks. Neither italics nor quotation marks are used for the names of *types* of trains, ships, aircraft, or spacecraft.

DC-10   Boeing 727   Trident submarine
space shuttle Atlas Agena rocket

CHART

Titles *Italicized* or "In Quotes"

TITLES *ITALICIZED*

books	*All the Pretty Horses*
magazines	*Time*
journals	*Written Communication*
newspapers	*The New York Times*
	or
	the *New York Times*
films	*Casablanca*
TV shows	*The Tonight Show*
radio shows	*All Things Considered*
plays	*Measure for Measure*
long poems	*Paradise Lost*
long musical pieces	*The Mikado*
albums	*Dookie*
paintings	the *Mona Lisa*
sculptures	Michelangelo's *Pietà*
ships	*Titanic*
	U.S.S. *Saratoga*
trains	the *Orient Express*
aircraft	*Enola Gay*
spacecraft	*Apollo 11*
software programs	*PageMaker*

TITLES "IN QUOTES"	
chapters of books	"Lessons from the Pros"
articles in magazines	"What's New in Moscow?"
articles in journals	"Vai Script and Literacy"
articles in newspapers	"Inflation Heats Up"
sections in newspapers	"Living in Style"
TV episodes	"Cold Steele"
radio episodes	"McGee Goes Crackers"
short stories	"Araby"
short poems	"The Red Wheelbarrow"
songs	"God Bless America"

Neither italics nor quotation marks are used with titles of major religious texts, books of the Bible, or classic legal documents.

the Bible	the Koran
Genesis	Exodus
1 Romans	the Declaration of Independence
the Constitution	the Magna Carta

28g
ital

28g-2 **Use italics to set off foreign words or phrases.** Foreign terms that haven't become an accepted item of English vocabulary and scientific names are given special emphasis.

Pierre often described his co-workers as *les bêtes humaines*.

Staring out the window, Jessye was convinced that she had spotted the first *Turdus migratorius* of spring.

However, the many foreign words absorbed by English over the centuries should not be italicized. To be sure, look them up in a recent dictionary.

crèche   gumbo   gestalt   arroyo

Common abbreviations from Latin also appear without italics or underscoring.

etc.   et al.   i.e.   viz.

28g-3 **Use italics (or quotation marks) to emphasize or clarify a letter, a word, or a phrase.**

When some people talk about *social commitment*, they really mean *higher taxes*.

Does that word begin with an *f* or a *ph?*

▶ **Fine Tuning**

1. You may use italics to highlight words you intend to define in a sentence.

   "A *fascist*," Allan complained, "is apparently anyone who doesn't agree with you, Lynda."

2. You may italicize words to indicate where emphasis should be placed in reading.

   "That may be how *you* define fascist," she replied. ◀

■ **Exercise 28.7** Indicate whether the following titles or names in boldface should be italicized, in quotation marks, or unmarked. If you don't recognize a name below, check an encyclopedia or other reference work.

1. launching a **Titan III** at Cape Kennedy
2. **My Fair Lady** playing at the **Paramount Theater**
3. watching **I Love Lucy**
4. sunk on the passenger ship **Andrea Doria**
5. returning **A Farewell to Arms** to the public library
6. playing **Casablanca** again on a **Panasonic** video recorder
7. discussing the colors of Picasso's **The Old Guitarist**
8. reading Jackson's **The Lottery** one more time
9. picking up a copy of **The Los Angeles Times**
10. whistling **Here Comes the Sun** from the Beatles' **Abbey Road**

28h
/

28h   WHEN DO YOU USE SLASHES?

Troubleshooting

Slashes are used to indicate divisions. They are rare pieces of punctuation with just a few specific functions. About the only problem slashes pose concerns the spacing before and after the mark. That spacing depends on how the slash is being used.

To use slashes correctly . . .

28h-1 Use slashes to divide lines of poetry quoted within sentences. You may recall that when quoting more than three lines of poetry, you simply indent the passage ten spaces.

```
. . . But as King Lear wanders the heath in the

horrible storm, he realizes for the first time how

much the poor in his kingdom must endure:

        Poor naked wretches, wheresoever you are,

        That bide the pelting of this pitiless

          storm,

        How shall your houseless heads and unfed

          sides,

        Your looped and windowed raggedness, defend

          you

        From seasons such as these?
```

But when you cite fewer than three lines, the verses are treated like regular sentences in a paragraph, with slashes dividing the individual lines of poetry. A space is left on either side of the slash.

```
Only then does Lear understand that he has been a

failure as a king: "O, I have taken / Too little care

of this!"
```

28h-2 Use slashes to separate expressions that indicate a choice. In these cases, no space is left before or after the slash.

either/or	he/she	yes/no	pass/fail
win/lose	s/he	on/off	right/wrong

Such expressions are more accepted in technical and scientific writing than they are in the humanities. Many people prefer "he or she" to "he/she" and find "s/he" unacceptable.

28h-3 Use slashes to indicate fractions when typing. Use a hyphen to attach a whole number and a fraction. Again, no spaces are left between the numbers, slashes, and hyphens.

2/3   2-2/3   5-3/8

29

How Do You Punctuate Sentence Endings?

A Periods
B Question Marks
C Exclamation Marks

29a WHEN DO YOU USE PERIODS?

Troubleshooting

Periods say "That's all there is." They terminate sentences and abbreviations. Occasionally writers will forget to put periods where they are needed, but these punctuation marks cause few problems.

An editor will use a caret and a circled period to indicate where a period has been omitted.

He told me, "Yes" But he lied. ⊘

To handle periods correctly . . .

29a–1 Use periods to end statements.

Hannibal, general of Carthage, has been called the father of military strategy.

29a–2 Use periods to end indirect questions and many commands.

Military theorists wonder whether any battle plan has been more tactically perfect than Hannibal's at Cannae (216 B.C.).
Look at the Roman and Carthaginian battle lines.

Strong commands may also be punctuated with exclamation points.

29a-3 **Use periods to punctuate abbreviations.**

abbr.   anon.   Cong.   natl.
rpt.   sing.   pl.   pp.

Not all abbreviations require periods. When in doubt, check a dictionary.

NASA   HEW   GPO   GOP

29a-4 **Use periods to indicate decimals.**

0.01 $189.00   75.4%

▶ **Fine Tuning**

1. If a statement ends with an abbreviation, the period at the end of
    the sentence is not doubled.

    We visited the Folger Library in Washington, D.C.

    However, the period at the end of the abbreviation is retained if
    the sentence is a question or exclamation.

    Have you ever been to Washington, D.C.?
    Our flight departs at 6 a.m.!

2. If an abbreviation occurs in the middle of a sentence, it retains its
    period. The period may even be followed by another punctuation
    mark.

    Though she had not yet earned her Ph.D., Jackie knew her job
    prospects were bright. ◀

29b
?

29b **WHEN DO YOU USE QUESTION MARKS?**

Troubleshooting

Question marks terminate questions or raise doubt. They pose
problems for writers chiefly in what are called *indirect questions*—which
are statements that look like questions. Question marks can also be difficult to place properly within quotations.

An editor will use a caret and a question mark (or sometimes a
question mark alone) to show where this piece of punctuation is needed.
Unnecessary question marks are noted by "no?"

To whom did you speak/ ?
I asked Sue if she were angry/ *no?*

To handle question marks correctly . . .

29b–1 Use question marks to end direct questions.

Have you ever heard of the Battle of Cannae?
Who fought in the battle?
Do you know that Hannibal defeated the Roman legions?
How?

29b–2 Use question marks to indicate uncertainty about dates, numbers, or statements.

Hannibal (247?–183 B.C.) was a Carthaginian general and military tactician.

TRICKY

29b–3 Do not use question marks to terminate indirect questions. **Indirect questions** are statements that seem to have questions within them. Compare these examples to see the difference.

Indirect question	Varro wondered whether Hannibal's strategy would succeed.
Direct question	Will Hannibal's strategy succeed?
Direct question	Varro wondered, "Will Hannibal's strategy succeed?"

Following are two sentences that have been mistakenly punctuated as questions.

---

incorrect question marks

Hannibal wondered if his troops were ready? He asked his cavalry officers whether they might need reinforcements?

Look closely and you'll discover that what look like questions really are statements: *Hannibal wondered* [what?]; *He asked* [what?]. Such statements should not be punctuated as questions.

---

periods replace question marks

Hannibal wondered if his troops were ready. He asked his cavalry officers whether they might need reinforcements.

29b
?

29b–4 Punctuate as questions any compound sentences that begin with statements but end with questions.

> The strategy looked fine on paper, but would it work on the battlefield?

Don't confuse these constructions with indirect questions.

29b–5 Place question marks after direct questions that appear in the middle of sentences—usually surrounded by parentheses, quotation marks, or dashes.

> Skeptical of their guide—"Did Hannibal really position cavalry here?"—the tourists consulted a map.

29b–6 Place question marks outside quotation marks except when they are part of the quoted material itself.

> Was it Terence who wrote "Fortune helps the brave"?
> The teacher asked, "Haven't you read any Cicero?"

For a more detailed explanation of quotation marks, see Section 28e.

29c

!

29c WHEN DO YOU USE EXCLAMATION MARKS?

Troubleshooting

Exclamations give emphasis to statements. They are vigorous punctuation marks with the subtlety of a Ferrari Testarossa. In academic writing, they should be about as rare too.

An editor will use a caret and an exclamation point (or sometimes an exclamation alone) to show where this piece of punctuation is needed or should be omitted.

> I won the $90,000,000 lottery. !
> Columbus wasn't the first European in America. no !

To handle exclamation marks correctly . . .

29c–1 Use exclamation marks to express strong reactions or commands.

> They are retreating!
> Our time has come at last!

Save exclamations for those occasions—rare in college and business writing—when your words really deserve emphasis. Too many exclamations can make a passage seem juvenile.

> #### unnecessary exclamations
>
> The Roman forces at the Battle of Cannae outnumbered Hannibal's forces roughly two to one! It is no wonder, then, that the Roman general Varro planned to overwhelm the Carthaginians by sheer force of numbers! Yet Roman casualties would be ten times higher than those suffered by Hannibal's army!

In this case, the expository passage reads better with all the exclamations removed.

> #### exclamations cut
>
> The Roman forces at the Battle of Cannae outnumbered Hannibal's forces roughly two to one. It is no wonder, then, that the Roman general Varro planned to overwhelm the Carthaginians by sheer force of numbers. Yet Roman casualties would be ten times higher than those suffered by Hannibal's army.

29c-2 Don't use commas or other punctuation marks after exclamations in the middle of sentences.

Wrong   "Please check your records again!/" the caller demanded.

Right   "Please check your records again!" the caller demanded.

29c-3 Don't use more than one exclamation point.

Wrong   Don't shout!///

Right   Don't shout!

■ **Exercise 29.1** Edit the following passage, adding, replacing, and deleting periods, question marks, exclamation points, and any other marks of punctuation that need to be changed.

1. Hannibal simply outfoxed the Roman general Varro at Cannae!!!

2. Hannibal placed his numerically smaller army where the Aufidius River would protect his flank—could the hotheaded Varro appreciate such a move—and arrayed his forces to make the Roman numbers work against themselves!

3. It must have seemed obvious to Hannibal where Varro would concentrate his forces?

4. "Advance!," Hannibal ordered!

5. Is it likely that Varro and the Romans noticed how thin the Carthaginian forces were at the center of the battle line?

6. The Romans predictably pressed their attack on the weakened Carthaginian center. But in the meantime, Hannibal's cavalry had destroyed its Roman counterpart!

7. You might be wondering, "Why didn't Hannibal use his cavalry to strengthen his weak center"?

8. It was because he wanted it behind the Roman lines to attack from the rear!

9. Hannibal expected the troops at the ends of his battle line to outflank the Romans, but would such a strategy work.

10. It did! The Romans found themselves surrounded and defeated!

29c
!

Problems with Capitalization, Apostrophes, Abbreviations, and Numbers?

A Capitalization of Sentences, Titles, and Poems
B Capitalization of Persons, Places, and Things
C Apostrophes
D Abbreviations
E Numbers

30a HOW DO YOU CAPITALIZE SENTENCES, TITLES, AND POEMS?

Troubleshooting

Capital letters can cause problems simply because you have to learn the rules for their use. Fortunately, the guidelines are quite easy because you see them operating in almost every sentence you read. In your papers, an editor may place a *cap* in the margin next to a small letter that needs to be changed to uppercase.

I wrote a letter to president Clinton. *cap*

An editor will place an *lc* (lowercase) in the margin next to a capital letter that needs to be changed to a small letter.

We spoke to the Librarian today. *lc*

To be sure your capitalization is right . . .

30a–1 Capitalize the first word in a sentence.

Naomi picked up the tourists at their hotel.
What a great city Washington is!

30a–2 Capitalize the first word in a direct quotation that is a full sentence.

> Ira asked, "**W**here's the Air and Space Museum?"
> "**G**ood idea!" Naomi agreed. "**L**et's go there."

Don't use a capital when a quotation merely continues after an interruption.

> "It's on the Mall," Naomi explained, "**n**ear the Hirschhorn Gallery."

30a–3 Capitalize the titles of papers, books, articles, poems, and so on.

> *Parliament of Whores*
> *With Fire and Sword*
> "Stopping by Woods on a Snowy Evening"

30a
cap

CHECKLIST

Capitalizing Titles

To capitalize a title, follow these three steps.

- Capitalize the first word.
- Capitalize the last word.
- Capitalize all other words *except*
  — Articles (*a, an, the*)
  — The *to* in infinitives
  — Prepositions
  — Coordinating conjunctions.

Articles and prepositions are capitalized when they follow a colon, usually as part of a subtitle.

> King Lear: **A**n *Annotated Bibliography*

30a–4 Capitalize the first word in a line of quoted poetry. Don't capitalize the first letter in a line where a poet has used a lowercase letter.

> **S**umer is ycomen in,
> **L**oude sing cuckoo!
> **G**roweth seed and bloweth
>   meed,
> **A**nd springth the wode now.
> **S**ing cuckoo!
>   —"The Cuckoo Song"

> Ida,
> **ho**, and, Oh,
> Io!
> **s**paces
> **w**ith places
> **t**ween 'em.
>   —T. Beckwith, "Travels"

▶ **Fine Tuning**

1. Don't capitalize the first word of a phrase that follows a colon unless you want to give it unusual emphasis or it is part of a title.

No caps after colon	They ignored one item while parking the car: **a** no-parking sign.
Caps for emphasis	The phrase haunted her: **Y**our license has expired!
Caps for title	*Marilyn: **T**he Untold Story*

2. Don't capitalize the first word of a phrase or sentence enclosed by dashes.

   Audrey's first screenplay—**a** thriller about industrial espionage—had been picked up by an agent.

   Her work—**s**he couldn't believe it—was now in the hands of a studio executive. ◀

■ **Exercise 30.1** Correct problems in capitalization in the following sentences.

1. The passenger next to me asked, "do you remember when air travel used to be a pleasure?"
2. I couldn't reply immediately: My tray table had just flopped open and hit me on the knees.
3. The plane we were on—A jumbo jet that seated nine or ten across—had been circling Dulles International for hours.
4. "We'll be landing momentarily," the flight attendant mumbled, "If we are lucky."
5. I had seen the film version of this flight: *airplane!*

30b WHEN DO YOU CAPITALIZE PERSONS, PLACES, AND THINGS?

Troubleshooting

The following section provides guidelines for capitalizing a variety of items. When you are not sure whether a particular word needs to be capitalized, check a dictionary. Don't guess, especially when you are dealing with proper nouns (nouns that name a particular person, place, or thing—*Geoffrey Chaucer, Ohio, Lincoln Memorial*) or proper adjectives

(adjectives formed from proper nouns—*Chaucerian*). The guidelines be-low move from persons to places to things.

To be sure your capitalization is right . . .

30b–1 Capitalize the names and initials of people and characters.

W. C. Fields	**A**nzia **Y**ezierska
Cher	**M**innie **M**ouse
I. M. Pei	**J. H**ector **St. J**ean **C**rèvecoeur

30b–2 Capitalize titles that precede names.

Commissioner Angela Brown
Vice **P**resident Al Gore
Justice Sandra Day O'Connor
Auntie Mame

30b–3 Capitalize titles after names when the title describes a specific person. But don't capitalize such a title when the title is more general. Compare:

30b
cap

Robert King, the **D**ean of Liberal Arts
Robert King, a **d**ean at the university

Don't capitalize the titles of relatives that follow names. Compare:

Anthony Pancioli, Cathy's **u**ncle
Cathy's **U**ncle **A**nthony

Exception   Capitalize academic titles that follow a name.

Iris Miller, **Ph.D.**
Enriquez Lopez, **M**aster of **A**rts

30b–4 Don't capitalize minor titles when they stand alone without names.

a **c**ommissioner in Cuyahoga County
a **l**ieutenant in the Air Force
the first **p**resident of our club

Exceptions   Prestigious titles are regularly capitalized even when they stand alone. Lesser titles may be capitalized when they clearly refer to a particular individual or when they describe a position formally.

President of the United States
the **P**resident
Secretary of **S**tate
the **C**hair of the Classics Department argued . . .

◆ Point of Difference

Style manuals don't always agree about capitalizing titles. Some recommend, for example, that you not capitalize expressions such as *the president* or *the secretary of state* unless they are followed by a name: *President Clinton, former Secretary of State Henry Kissinger.* Obviously, you should follow whatever manual of style is recommended in your course, field, or office. ◆

30b-5 Capitalize the names of national, political, or ethnic groups.

Kenyans	**A**ustralians	**A**frican **A**mericans
Chinese	**C**hicanos	**C**roatians
Libertarians	**D**emocrats	**R**epublicans

Exception Titles of racial groups, economic groups, and social classes are usually not capitalized.

blacks	whites
the proletariat	the knowledge class

30b-6 Capitalize the names of businesses, organizations, unions, clubs, and schools.

Time, **I**nc.
Oklahoma **S**tate **U**niversity
National **R**ifle **A**ssociation
Chemical **W**orkers **U**nion

30b-7 Capitalize the names of religious figures, religious groups, and sacred books.

God	the **S**avior	**B**uddha
Buddhism	**C**atholics	**J**udaism
the **B**ible	the **K**oran	**T**almudic tradition

Exceptions The terms *god* and *goddess* are not capitalized when used generally. When *God* is capitalized, pronouns referring to God are also capitalized.

The Greeks had a pantheon of **g**ods and **g**oddesses.
The **G**oddess of **L**iberty appears on our currency.
The cardinal praised **G**od and all **H**is works.

30b-8 Do not routinely capitalize academic ranks. Such ranks include terms like *freshman, sophomore, junior, senior, graduate,* and *postgrad.*

30b
cap

The college had many fifth-year **s**eniors.
The **f**reshman dormitory was a dump.
The teacher was a **g**raduate student.

Exception Capitalize academic ranks when these groups are referred to as organized bodies or institutions.

a representative of the **S**enior **C**lass
the **F**reshman **C**otillion

30b–9 Capitalize academic degrees when they are abbreviated. Abbreviated degrees include the following: Ph.D., LL.D., M.A., M.S., B.A., B.S. Do not capitalize those degrees when they are spelled out.

Maria earned her **Ph.D.** the same day Mark picked up his **LL.D.**
Leon Railsback, **M.A.**
Leon has a **m**aster of **a**rts degree.
Who conferred the **b**achelor of **s**cience degrees?

Exception Academic degrees spelled out in full are capitalized when they follow a name.

Leon Railsback, **M**aster of **A**rts
Maria Ramos, **D**octor of **P**hilosophy

30b–10 Capitalize the names of places. Also capitalize words based on place names and the names of specific geographic features such as lakes, rivers, and oceans.

Asia	**O**ld **F**aithful
Asian	the **A**mazon
the **B**ronx	the **G**ulf of **M**exico
Lake **E**rie	**D**eaf **S**mith **C**ounty
Washington	the **A**tlantic **O**cean

Exception Don't capitalize compass directions unless they name a specific place or are part of a place name.

north	**N**orth **A**merica
south	the **S**outh
eastern Ohio	the **M**iddle **E**ast

30b–11 Capitalize the names of buildings, structures, or monuments.

Yankee **S**tadium	**H**oover **D**am
the **A**lamo	the **G**olden **G**ate
Trump **T**ower	**I**ndianapolis **S**peedway

30b
cap

30b–12 **Capitalize abstractions in some situations.** Terms such as *love, truth, mercy,* and *patriotism* (which ordinarily appear in small letters) may be capitalized when you discuss them as concepts or when you wish to give them special emphasis, perhaps as the subject of a paper.

> What is this thing called **L**ove?
> The conflict was between **T**ruth and **F**alsehood.

There is no need to capitalize abstractions used without special emphasis.

> Byron had fallen in **l**ove again.
> Either tell the **t**ruth or abandon **h**ope of rescue.

30b–13 **Capitalize the names of particular objects.** This might include ships, planes, automobiles, brand-name products, events, documents, and musical groups.

S.S. Titanic	**B**oeing 747
Ford **C**ontour	**E**skimo **P**ie
Super **B**owl XXVII	the **C**onstitution
Rolling **S**tones	**F**ifth **A**mendment

HIGHLIGHT

Brand Names and Trademarks

In public and business writing, it is important not to violate the right companies have to brand names or trademarks, even familiar ones. Names such as **K**leenex, **F**rigidaire, and **X**erox should be capitalized because they refer to specific, trademark-protected products.

30b–14 **Capitalize most periods of time.** Periods of time include days, months, holidays, historical epochs, and historical events.

Monday	the **R**eformation
May	**W**orld **W**ar II
Victorian **A**ge	**B**astille **D**ay
Fourth of **J**uly	**P**ax **R**omana

Exception Seasons of the year are usually not capitalized.

winter	**s**pring	**s**ummer	**f**all

30b–15 Capitalize terms ending in *-ism* when they name specific literary, artistic, religious, or cultural movements. When in doubt, check a dictionary.

Impressionism	**V**orticism
Judaism	**C**atholicism
Buddhism	**R**omanticism

Exceptions Many terms ending in *-ism* are not capitalized.

socialism   capitalism   monetarism

30b–16 Capitalize school subjects and classes only when the subjects themselves are proper nouns.

biology	**c**hemistry
English	**R**ussian history
French	**p**hysics

Exception Titles of specific courses (such as you might find in a college catalog) are capitalized.

Biology 101   **C**hemistry **L**ab   **E**nglish 346K

30b
cap

30b–17 Capitalize all the letters in acronyms and initialisms. (See Section 30d–2 for more details.)

NATO	OPEC	SALT
DNA	GMC	MCAT

Exception Don't capitalize familiar acronyms that seem like ordinary words. When in doubt, check a dictionary.

radar   sonar   laser

● **Tip**

Many writers forget to capitalize words that identify nationalities or countries—words such as *English*, *French*, or *Mexican*.

Wrong   Kyle has three english courses.
Right   Kyle has three **E**nglish courses.

Wrong   Janet drives only american cars.
Right   Janet drives only **A**merican cars.

When proofreading, be sure to capitalize most words derived from the names of countries. ●

■ **Exercise 30.2** Capitalize the following sentences as necessary.

1. The east asian students visiting the district of columbia were mostly juniors pursuing b.a.'s while the african-american students were predominantly graduate students seeking master's degrees.

2. The constitution and the declaration of independence are on view at the national archives.

3. I heard the doorkeeper at the hilton speaking spanish to the general secretary of the united nations.

4. Visitors to washington include people from around the world: russians from moscow, egyptians from cairo, aggies from texas, buckeyes from ohio.

5. At the white house, the president will host a conference on democracy and free enterprise in the spring, probably in april.

30c WHEN DO YOU USE APOSTROPHES?

Troubleshooting

The problem with apostrophes is that writers often forget them, especially in contractions or possessives. Some expressions are written so often these days without apostrophes that they almost look right even when they are not: *mens room, ladies day, drivers license.* An editor will use an inverted caret to show where you have forgotten an apostrophe.

> Abbie couldnt be persuaded to watch. ˇ
>
> Is that Carols book or mine? ˇ

To use apostrophes correctly . . .

30c–1 Place apostrophes in contractions where letters have been omitted.

can't—can**not**	hadn't—had n**ot**	it's—it **is**
you're—you **are**	haven't—have n**ot**	who's—who **is**
o'clock—o**f the** clock never used		

Contractions are used not because they have fewer letters, but because they are spoken more quickly and sound less formal. Contractions change the tone of what you are writing from black tie to jeans.

> **Cannot** you join us?
> **Can't** you join us?

The apostrophe is not optional in a contraction. Leaving it out can alter the meaning of a word or create a misspelling.

> it's—its   won't—wont   you're—youre

The *it's/its* problem is an especially tricky one. See Section 22g–1 for more exploration of *it's/its*.

◆ Point of Difference

Some readers and editors regard contractions as too familiar for college and professional writing. For this reason, consider your audience carefully before using contractions. ◆

30c–2 Place apostrophes as needed to form the possessives of nouns and some pronouns.

> Kyle**'s** report   Travis**'** poems or Travis**'s** poems
> the Rhoades**'** daughters   everyone**'s** opinion

Personal pronouns do not require an apostrophe to show ownership.

> mine   yours   hers
> his   ours   theirs

For a thorough explanation of possessive nouns and pronouns, see Section 19b on possessive nouns and pronouns and Section 22f on possessive pronouns.

30c–3 Place apostrophes as needed to indicate the plurals of numbers, symbols, individual letters, abbreviations, words used as words, and dates.

> 2**'s** and 3**'s**   three $5**'s**
> two .45**'s** and a .22   two &**'s**
> three *the***'s** and four *an***'s**   1960**'s**

The apostrophe is often omitted, especially when the *-'s* might be mistaken as a possessive.

> 3600 rpm**s**   the ACT**s**
> 42 lb**s**   the CEO**s**

In many cases, either form of the plural is acceptable.

> the 1980**s** / the 1980**'s**
> 10**s** / 10**'s**

Whichever form you use, be consistent. For more details, see Section 19a–10.

▶ **Fine Tuning**

Apostrophes are sometimes used to replace the first two numbers in a date.

"Summer of '69"   Spirit of '76   '64 Mustang

However, in academic and professional writing, write out the complete date unless the contraction is part of a familiar expression, such as "Spirit of '76." ◀

■ **Exercise 30.3** Add or delete apostrophes and revise spelling as necessary in the following sentences.

1. It will be youre fault if we arrive after five oclock, when the stores close.
2. The blame wont be Susans or anybody elses.
3. Its been more than a decade since Ive seen you.
4. Lets find someone who remembers the '50s.
5. Mel dropped three quarter's into the soda machine, and to everyones surprise, he got a soda.

30d
abbr

30d **HOW DO YOU HANDLE ABBREVIATIONS?**

Troubleshooting

Using abbreviations, acronyms (NATO, radar), and initialisms (HBO, IRS) can make some writing simpler. Many conventional abbreviations are acceptable in all kinds of papers.

a.m.   p.m.
Mrs.   Mr.
B.C.   A.D.
Ph.D.   M.D.

Other abbreviations are appropriate on forms, reports, and statistics sheets, but not in more formal writing.

Jan.—January
ft.—foot
no.—number
mo.—month

Issues of appropriateness are discussed below, following some guidelines on punctuating and capitalizing abbreviations.

An editor will usually indicate a problem with an abbreviation by circling a word or expression and marking *abbr* in the margin.

The house has more than 2400 (sq. ft.) *abbr*

To handle abbreviations correctly . . .

30d–1 Be consistent in punctuating abbreviations, acronyms, and initialisms.

CHECKLIST

Punctuating Abbreviations

- Abbreviations of single words usually take periods: *vols.*, *Jan.*, *Mr.*
- Initialisms are usually written without periods: *HBO, IRS, AFL-CIO.* You may still use periods with these terms, but be consistent.
- Acronyms ordinarily do not require periods: *CARE, NATO, NOW.* Acronyms that have become accepted words never need periods: *sonar, radar, laser, scuba.*
- Periods are usually omitted after abbreviations in technical writing unless a measurement or other item might be misread without a period—for example, *in.*
- Consistently use three periods or none at all in terms such as the following: *m.p.g.* or *mpg*, *r.p.m.* or *rpm*, *m.p.h.* or *mph*.

30d–2 Be consistent in capitalizing abbreviations, acronyms, and initialisms.

CHECKLIST

Capitalizing Abbreviations

- Capitalize the abbreviations of words that are capitalized when written out in full: *General Motors*—*GM, University of Toledo*—*UT, U.S. Navy*—*USN, 98° Fahrenheit*—*98°F.*
- Don't capitalize the abbreviations of words not capitalized when written out in full: *pound*—*lb.*, *minutes*—*min.*
- Capitalize most initialisms: *IRS, CRT, UCLA, NBC.*
- Always capitalize *B.C.* and *A.D.* Printers ordinarily set them as small caps: B.C. and A.D.
- You may capitalize *A.M.* and *P.M.*, but they often appear in small letters: *a.m.* and *p.m.* Printers ordinarily set them as small caps: A.M. and P.M.
- Don't capitalize acronyms that have become accepted words: *sonar, radar, laser, scuba.*

30d
abbr

30d–3 **Use the appropriate abbreviations for titles, degrees, and names.** The following titles and degrees are ordinarily abbreviated.

Mr.	Mrs., Ms.	Jr.	M.D.
Dr.	Ph.D.	D.D.S.	
LL.D.	M.A., M.S.	C.P.A.	

Give credit for degrees either before or after a name—not in both places. Don't, for example, use both *Dr.* and *Ph.D.* in the same name.

> **Wrong** **Dr.** Katherine Martinich, **Ph.D.**
>
> **Right** **Dr.** Katherine Martinich
> Katherine Martinich, **Ph.D.**

Abbreviations for academic titles often stand by themselves, without names attached.

> Professor Martinich received her **Ph.D.** from Illinois, her **M.S.** from UCLA, and her **B.S.** from St. Vincent College.

Other titles are normally written out in full; they may be abbreviated only when they precede a first name or initial—and then chiefly in informal writing. In most cases, use the full, unabbreviated title.

President	President Clinton	Pres. Bill Clinton
Senator	Senator Gramm	Sen. Phil Gramm
Secretary	Secretary Reno	Sec. Janet Reno
Professor	Professor Upton	Prof. Doris Upton
Reverend	Reverend Call	Rev. Ann Call
	the Reverend Dr. Call	Rev. Dr. Call

Never let abbreviated titles of this kind appear in a sentence.

> **Wrong** The **gov.** agreed to debate the **amb.** at the invitation of the **prof.**
>
> **Right** The **governor** agreed to debate the **ambassador** at the invitation of **Professor Howell.**

Notice that titles attached to proper names are ordinarily capitalized.

30d–4 **Use the appropriate abbreviations for technical terms.** Abbreviations are often used in professional, governmental, scientific, military, and technical writing.

DNA	UHF	EKG	START
SALT	GNP	LEM	kW

When you are writing to a nontechnical audience, write out any unfamiliar term in full the first time you use it. Then in parentheses give the abbreviation you will use in the rest of the paper.

30d abbr

Al Gore and Ross Perot debated the effects the **North American Free Trade Agreement (NAFTA)** would have on the **gross national product (GNP).**

30d–5 Use the appropriate abbreviations for agencies and organizations. In some cases, the abbreviation or acronym regularly replaces the full name of a company, agency, or organization.

FBI	IBM	MCI	AT&T
AFL-CIO	GOP	PPG	MGM
A&P	BBC	NCAA	MTV

30d–6 Use the appropriate abbreviations for dates. Dates are not abbreviated in most writing. Write out in full the days of the week and months of the year.

Wrong   They arrived in Washington on a **Wed.** in **Apr.**

Right   They arrived in Washington on a **Wednesday** in **April.**

30d
abbr

Abbreviations of months and days are used primarily in notes, lists, forms, and reference works.

30d–7 Use the appropriate abbreviations for time and temperatures. Abbreviations that accompany time and temperatures are acceptable in all kinds of writing.

43 B.C.	A.D. 144	1:00 a.m.	4:36 p.m.
13°C.	98°F.	143 B.C.E.	

Notice that the abbreviation B.C. appears after a date, but A.D. usually before one. Both expressions are always capitalized.

30d–8 Use the appropriate abbreviations for weights, measures, and times. Technical terms or measurements are commonly abbreviated when used with numbers, but written out in full when they stand alone in sentences. Even when accompanied by numbers, the terms usually look better in sentences when spelled out completely.

28 m.p.g.	3 tsps.	40 km.	450 lbs.
50 min.	30 lbs.	2 hrs.	

Mariah didn't care how many **miles per hour** her Audi could travel on the autobahn. She just wished it hadn't been towed so many **kilometers** from her hotel.

The abbreviation for number—*No.* or *no.*—is appropriate in technical writing, but only when immediately followed by a number.

Not   The **no.** on the contaminated dish was **073.**

But   The contaminated dish was **no. 073.**

No. also appears in footnotes, endnotes, and citations.

30d–9 **Use the appropriate abbreviations for places.** In most writing, place names are not abbreviated except in addresses and in reference tools and lists. However, certain abbreviations are accepted in academic and business writing.

USA   USSR   UK   Washington, D.C.

In addresses (but not in written text), use the standard postal abbreviations, without periods, for the states.

Alabama	AL	Montana	MT
Alaska	AK	Nebraska	NE
Arizona	AZ	Nevada	NV
Arkansas	AR	New Hampshire	NH
California	CA	New Jersey	NJ
Colorado	CO	New Mexico	NM
Connecticut	CT	New York	NY
Delaware	DE	North Carolina	NC
Florida	FL	North Dakota	ND
Georgia	GA	Ohio	OH
Hawaii	HI	Oklahoma	OK
Idaho	ID	Oregon	OR
Illinois	IL	Pennsylvania	PA
Indiana	IN	Rhode Island	RI
Iowa	IA	South Carolina	SC
Kansas	KS	South Dakota	SD
Kentucky	KY	Tennessee	TN
Louisiana	LA	Texas	TX
Maine	ME	Utah	UT
Maryland	MD	Vermont	VT
Massachusetts	MA	Virginia	VA
Michigan	MI	Washington	WA
Minnesota	MN	West Virginia	WV
Mississippi	MS	Wisconsin	WI
Missouri	MO	Wyoming	WY

All the various terms for *street* are written out in full, except in addresses.

boulevard	road	avenue	parkway
highway	alley	place	circle

But *Mt.* (for *mount*) and *St.* (for *saint*) are acceptable abbreviations in place names when they precede a proper name.

    Mt. Vesuvius   **St.** Charles Street

30d-10 Use the correct abbreviations for certain expressions preserved from Latin.

    i.e. (*id est*—that is)
    e.g. (*exempli gratia*—for example)
    et al. (*et alii*—and others)
    etc. (*et cetera*—and so on)

In most writing, it is better to use English versions of these and other Latin abbreviations. Avoid using the abbreviation *etc.* in formal or academic writing.

30d-11 Use the appropriate abbreviations for divisions of books. The many abbreviations for books and manuscripts (*p., pp., vols., ch., chpts., bk., sect.*) are fine in footnotes or parenthetical citations, but don't use them alone in sentences.

Wrong   Richard stuck the **bk.** in his pocket after reading **ch.** five.

Right   Richard stuck the **book** in his pocket after reading **chapter** five.

**30d
abbr**

▶ **Fine Tuning**

1. The *ampersand* (&) is an abbreviation for *and*. Do not use it in formal writing except when it appears in a title or name: *Road & Track.*

2. You may use symbols in technical and scientific writing—%, +, =, ≠, <, >—but in other academic papers, spell out such terms. Most likely to cause a problem is %—*percent*.

Acceptable   Mariah was shocked to learn that **80%** of the cars towed belong to tourists.

Preferred   Mariah was shocked to learn that **80 percent** of the cars towed belong to tourists.

3. You can use a dollar sign—$—in any writing as long as it is followed by an amount. Don't use both the dollar sign and the word *dollar*.

Wrong   The fine for parking in a towing zone is **$125 dollars.**

Right   The fine for parking in a towing zone is **$125.**

Right   The fine for parking in a towing zone is **125 dollars.** ◀

■ **Exercise 30.4** Correct the sentences below, abbreviating where appropriate or expanding abbreviations that would be incorrect in college or professional writing. Check the punctuation for accuracy and consistency. If you insist on periods with acronyms and initialisms, use them throughout the passage.

1. We hailed a cab cruising slowly down the ave.
2. It's nearly 6:00 Pm.
3. The meeting was held at the Vfw Hall in Alexandria, VA.
4. There's a better than 70% chance of rain today.
5. We took Constitution Ave. down past the F.b.i. Building, eased onto the 12th Street Expressway, cruised by the Dept. of Agri., and followed I–395 till we got to the George Washington Mem. Pky.
6. The city guide was published in two vols. and a dozen different languages.
7. Irene sent angry ltrs. to a dozen networks, including NBC, A.B.C., ESPN, and CNN.
8. The Emperor Claudius was born in 10 b.c. and died in 54 A.D.
9. Dr. Kovatch, M.D., works for the Federal Department of Agriculture (FDA).
10. I owe the company only $175 dollars, & expect to pay the full amount before the end of the mo.

30e
num

30e **HOW DO YOU HANDLE NUMBERS?**

Troubleshooting

Numbers can be expressed either through numerals or through words.

1	one
25	twenty five
100	one hundred
1/4	one fourth
0.05%	five hundredths of a percent

Deciding which to use depends on the kind of writing you are doing. Technical, scientific, and business writing tends to employ numerals. Other kinds of writing rely more on words. The following guidelines will help you figure out which form to use.

To be sure your numbers are right . . .

30e-1 Write out numbers from one to nine. Use numerals for numbers above nine.

one	three	nine
10	15	39
101	115	220
1001	1021	59,000
101,000	10,000,101	50,306,673,432

◆ **Point of Difference**

This guideline has variations and exceptions. The MLA style manual, for example, allows you to spell out any number that can be expressed in two words when relatively few numbers appear in the paper you are writing.

thirteen   twenty-one   three hundred

The APA style manual suggests using figures for most numbers above ten unless they appear at the beginning of a sentence.

Thirty-three workers were rescued from an oil platform.

Be sure to check any style manual in your discipline to confirm how numbers ought to be used. ◆

30e-2 Don't begin sentences with numerals. Either spell out the number or rephrase the sentence so that the numeral is not the first word.

Wrong **32** people were standing in line at the parking violation center.

Right **Thirty-two** people were standing in line at the parking violation center.

Sentences may, however, begin with dates.

1989 was the year Marla graduated from high school.

30e-3 Combine words and figures when you need to express large round numbers.

100 billion   432 million   103 trillion

But avoid shifting between words and figures within a sequence of numbers. If you need numerals to express one of several numbers in a series, express all the other numbers in numerals as well—even if they might ordinarily be set down in words.

> There were over **125,000** people at the protest and **950** police officers, but only **9** arrests.

30e–4 Alternate words and figures when one number follows another.

> 33 fifth graders   12 first-term representatives
> two 4-WD vehicles   five 5-gallon buckets

30e–5 Use numerals when comparing numbers or suggesting a range.

> A blackboard at the traffic office listed a **$50** fine for jaywalking, **$100** for speeding, and **$125** for parking in a towing zone.
>
> The students' in-pocket cash reserves ranged from a high of **$76** to a low of **$1.43** and some bubble gum.

**30e
num**

30e–6 Use numerals for dates, street numbers, page numbers, sums of money, and various ID and call numbers.

> July 4, 1776   1860–1864
> 6708 Beauford Dr.   1900 East Blvd.
> p. 352   pp. 23–24
> $2749.00   43¢
> Channel 8   103.5 FM
> PR 105.5 R8   SSN 111-00-1111

Don't use an ordinal form in dates.

> **Wrong**   May 2**nd,** 1991
> **Right**   May **2,** 1991   or   **2** May 1991

30e–7 Use numerals for time with *a.m.* and *p.m.*; use words with *o'clock.*

> **2:15** p.m.   **6:00** a.m.   **six** o'clock

30e–8 Use numerals for measurements, percentages, statistics, and scores.

> **35** mph   **13**°C.   **5′10″**
> **75** percent   **0.2** liters   **5.5** pupils per teacher
> **2½** miles   **15**%   Browns **42**—Bears **7**

▶ **Fine Tuning**

1. In large figures, commas separate thousands, millions, billions, and so on. Commas are omitted, however, in dates, after street numbers, and sometimes in four-digit numbers.

   $1,700,000   **1988**
   4,453,500,000 protons   **7865** Hershey's Kisses
   4,342 parking spaces   **1205** Sophia Gate

2. Form the plural of numbers by adding *-s* or *-'s.*

   five 6**s** in a row   five 98**'s**

   See Section 19a–10 for more on plurals.

3. In most cases, ordinal numbers (that is, numbers that express a sequence) are spelled out: *first, second, third, fourth,* and so on. ◀

■ **Exercise 30.5** Decide whether numbers used in the following selection are handled appropriately. Where necessary, change numerals to words, words to numerals. Some expressions may not need revision.

1. 4 people will be honored at the ceremony beginning at nine p.m.
2. The culture contained more than 500,000,000,000 cells.
3. We forgot who won the Nobel Peace Prize in nineteen ninety-one.
4. The examination will include a question about the 1st, the 4th, or the Tenth Amendment.
5. We paid $79.80 for the hotel room and twenty dollars for admission to the park.

**30e
num**

Are You an ESL Writer?

JOCELYN STEER, *ESL SPECIALIST*

If English is not your first language, then you probably have some questions about grammar, usage, and punctuation that have not been answered in the other chapters of this handbook. This chapter is intended especially for the ESL (English as a second language) writer. In it we have tried to include rules, explanations, exercises, and charts that will help you write more accurately and clearly, focusing on the areas in which ESL writers have the most problems—verbs, modal auxiliaries, gerunds and infinitives, and articles.

Of course, no one chapter could possibly cover all the ESL information you need. We suggest, therefore, that you refer regularly to ESL reference books for help with grammar and usage. ESL grammar textbooks can give you more detailed grammatical explanations. Some ESL dictionaries provide useful spelling and usage information. (A list of ESL reference books can be found on p. 512.)

We have also included a section in this chapter that lists some persistent ESL errors you need to be aware of as you proofread your own writing. As a final word of advice, we would like to encourage you to check your work several times before you hand it in. Many of the errors that instructors mark on your final drafts could probably have been corrected by more thorough checking.

31a DO YOU HAVE PROBLEMS WITH VERBS?

Troubleshooting

Do you often find yourself wondering which verb tense to choose? Native speakers of English can ordinarily use verbs intuitively, but if you are a nonnative speaker, you probably still have questions, even after many years of studying English. For example, do you have difficulty deciding between the past and present perfect? Are you still confused about transitive and intransitive verbs? Do you often use the wrong preposition after a two-word verb? This section will answer some of your verb questions.

To use verbs correctly . . .

31a–1 Choose the most appropriate verb tense. The chart on pages 479 through 482 shows the twelve verb tenses, along with a list of some common adverbs and expressions that accompany each tense. These words and phrases are important because they are the signposts that will help you choose the best verb tense. (Refer to Chapter 17 for more information on verbs.) A diagram illustrates the time line for each tense. In the diagram, an X indicates an action and a curved line indicates an action in progress.

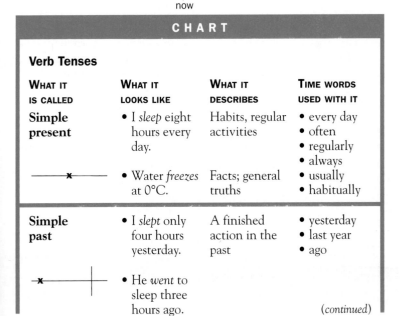

past ———— | ———— future
now

CHART

Verb Tenses

What it is called	What it looks like	What it describes	Time words used with it
Simple present	• I *sleep* eight hours every day.	Habits, regular activities	• every day • often • regularly • always
	• Water *freezes* at 0°C.	Facts; general truths	• usually • habitually
Simple past	• I *slept* only four hours yesterday.	A finished action in the past	• yesterday • last year • ago
	• He *went* to sleep three hours ago.		

(continued)

31a
ESL

Verb Tenses *(continued)*

What it is called	What it looks like	What it describes	Time words used with it
Simple future	• I *will try* to sleep more. *or* • I *am going to sleep* early tonight.	A single action in the future A planned action in the future (use *be going to*)	• tomorrow • in *x* days • next year
Present perfect	• I *have* already *written* my paper. • I *have lived* here for three months.	A past action that occurred at an unspecified time in the past An action that started in the past and continues to the present	• already • yet • before • recently • so far • for + time period • since + date
Past perfect	• She *had* already *slept* three hours when the burglar broke into the house.	One action in the past that occurs before another action in the past	• when • after • before • by the time
Future perfect	• I *will have finished* the paper when you stop by tonight.	One action in the future that will be completed before another action in the future	• by the time • when
Present progressive	• He *is sleeping* now.	A continuous activity in progress now	• right now • at this time • this week/year

31a ESL

WHAT IT IS CALLED	**WHAT IT LOOKS LIKE**	**WHAT IT DESCRIBES**	**TIME WORDS USED WITH IT**
Past progressive 	• While he *was sleeping*, the telephone rang. • He *was sleeping* at 10 a.m.	A continuous activity in progress in the past; often interrupted by another time or action	• while • during that time • between *x* and *y*
Future progressive 	• He *will be sleeping* when his wife comes home. • He *will be sleeping* at eight tonight.	A continuous activity in the future; in progress at a specific time in the future	• at *x* time • tonight, tomorrow • between *x* and *y*
Present perfect progressive 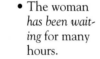	• The woman *has been waiting* for many hours. • He *has been sleeping* since eight o'clock.	A continuous activity that began in the past and continues to the present; emphasis is on the duration	• for + time period • since + exact date
Past perfect progressive 	• She *had been waiting* for three hours before he arrived. • He *had been sleeping* an hour when the train crashed.	A continuous activity in the past that is finished before another action in the past	• for • since

31a
ESL

(continued)

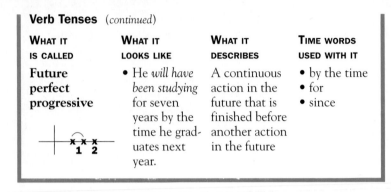

Verb Tenses *(continued)*

WHAT IT IS CALLED	WHAT IT LOOKS LIKE	WHAT IT DESCRIBES	TIME WORDS USED WITH IT
Future perfect progressive	• He *will have been studying* for seven years by the time he graduates next year.	A continuous action in the future that is finished before another action in the future	• by the time • for • since

31a–2   **Learn the difference between the simple present and present progressive tenses.**   You may be confused because the **simple present tense** doesn't really refer to an action going on in the present; rather, it is used to talk about repeated and habitual actions. You should use the simple present tense when you want to talk about *regular, repeated activity*.

Simple present   The mail carrier usually **arrives** at 10 a.m.
This is an activity that is repeated daily.

Present progressive   Look! She **is putting** the mail in the box now.
This is an activity occurring at the moment of speaking—now.

Present progressive   She **is delivering** mail for John this month.
This is an activity that is in progress over a period of time. Use the progressive tense with the expression *this + time period*.

CAUTION   **31a–3**   **Learn which verbs are nonaction verbs.**   Some verbs in English can't be used in a progressive form because they express a state and not an activity. If you want to use one of these **nonaction verbs,** you must use a simple form of the verb even though the time intended is *now*.

Incorrect   I can't study because I **am hearing** my roommate's singing.

Correct   I can't study because I **hear** my roommate's singing.

Incorrect   Maria **is preferring** Carlos' apartment to her own.

Correct   Maria **prefers** Carlos' apartment to her own.

Nonaction verbs include verbs of existence, of thought, of emotions, and of sense perceptions. The chart on page 483 lists some of these verbs.

C H A R T

Nonaction Verbs*

appear	forget	owe	seem
be	hate	own	smell
belong	have	possess	sound
consist	hear	prefer	surprise
contain	know	recognize	taste
deserve	like	remember	think
desire	love	require	understand
dislike	mean	resemble	want
feel	need	see	wish

*There are some exceptions to the nonaction rule (e.g., "I **am thinking** about getting a job"; "He **is seeing** a doctor about his insomnia"). These exceptions can usually be paraphrased using other verbs (e.g., "He **is seeing** a doctor about his insomnia" means "He **is consulting** a doctor about his insomnia"). You will need to keep a list of these exceptions as you come across them.

**31a
ESL**

31a-4 **Learn the difference between the simple past and present perfect tenses.** If an action happened in the past and is finished, you can always use the simple past tense to describe it. (See Chapter 17 for information on how to form the past tense and a list of irregular verbs.) Often, you will also use a time word like *ago* or *yesterday* to show the specific time of the past action.

Simple past   My brother **saw** that movie three days ago.

> We know exactly when the brother saw the movie—three days ago. You *must* use the simple past in this sentence.

Use the **past tense** to show that something is completed, and use the **present perfect tense** to indicate that the action may continue, or that it still has the possibility of occurring in the future. Compare these sentences to see how the two tenses express two different ideas.

Simple past   My grandmother never **used** a computer.

> This implies that the grandmother may no longer be alive.

Present perfect   My mother **has** never **used** a computer.

> This sentence indicates the mother is still alive and may use a computer in the future.

If you don't know or you don't want to state the exact time or date of a past action, use the present perfect tense.

Present perfect   Sarah **has seen** that movie before.

> We don't know when Sarah saw the movie; she saw it at an unspecified time in the past.

You must use the present perfect for an action that begins in the past and continues up to the present moment, especially when you use the time words *for* and *since*.

Present perfect   This theater **has shown** the same film for three months! I hope they change it soon.

> This action started in the past—three months ago—and continues to the present. The film is still playing.

31a–5 **Learn the difference between the present perfect and present perfect progressive tenses.** You can use a **present perfect progressive tense** to show that an action is still in progress.

Present perfect progressive   Catherine **has been writing** that letter since this morning.

> She hasn't finished; she's still writing.

In general, if the statement emphasizes *duration* (length of time), then you need to use a present perfect progressive tense.

Present perfect progressive   My best friend **has been writing** her novel for five years.

> This tells you how long the friend has been writing; the emphasis is on duration, or length of time.

However, if the statement emphasizes *quantity* (how much), then you will use a **present perfect tense.**

Present perfect   James Michener **has written** over twenty novels.

> This tells you how many books; it talks about quantity.

31a–6 **Learn the difference between intransitive and transitive verbs.** Why is the sentence "She raised her children" correct but the sentence "She grew up her children" incorrect? The answer to this question has to do with the difference between transitive and intransitive verbs. (See Section 17a–1 and Section 17e for more information.)

The verb *grow up* is an **intransitive verb** because it is complete without a direct object. In fact, you cannot put a direct object after an intransitive verb, and that is why the sentence "She grew up her children" is incorrect.

Incorrect   She grew up **her children.**

> *Her children* cannot come after the verb *grew up* because *her children* is an object; objects cannot come after intransitive verbs.

31a
ESL

However, other words can come after intransitive verbs, as shown in the sentences below.

Correct She grew up **quickly.**

> *Quickly* is an adverb. You can put an adverb after this verb. This sentence means that she herself matured at a very fast rate.

Correct She grew up **on a farm.**

> *On a farm* is a prepositional phrase, not a direct object.

There are two kinds of intransitive verbs—linking verbs and action verbs. (See the chart on p. 486 for a list of these verbs.)

                        subj.   l.v.   comp.
Linking verbs   This book **seems** very old. (l.v. = linking verb)

                        subj.   l.v.   comp.
                    Your professor **is** an expert in law.

                        subj.   a.v.
Action verbs   Jacqueline **complained.** (a.v. = action verb)

                        subj.   a.v.   prep. phrase
                    Jacqueline **complained** to me before breakfast.

A **transitive verb** is a verb that has a direct object. This means that the verb has an effect on, or does something to, that object. The verb *raise* in the sentence "She raised her children" is transitive because the subject of the sentence (*she*) is acting on someone else (*her children*). Without the direct object (*her children*), this sentence would be incomplete; it would not make sense.

Incorrect She raised.

> This thought is incomplete; you need to know *what* she raised.

Correct She raised **her children** on a farm.

There are two types of transitive verbs. (See the chart on page 486 for a list of these.) One type—verb + direct object—*must* be followed directly by a noun or pronoun.

Verb + direct object (trans. v. = transitive verb)

                    subj.   trans. v.   noun
                    This university **needs** more parking lots.

                    subj.   trans. v.   pron.
                    The trustees **discussed** it at the last meeting.

The other type—verb + (indirect object) + direct object—*can* be followed by an indirect object (a person receiving the action) before the direct object. If you use *to* or *for* in front of the indirect object, the position changes, as you can see in the following examples.

**31a
ESL**

Verb + (indirect object) + direct object

direct obj.
Ron bought **a rose.**

indirect obj. direct obj.
Ron bought *his wife* **a rose.**

or

direct obj. + (for/to + indirect obj.)
Ron bought **a rose** *for his wife.*

C H A R T

Intrinsic and Transitive Verbs

Intransitive and Transitive Verbs

INTRANSITIVE VERBS

- **Linking verbs:** appear, be, become, seem, look
- **Action verbs*:** arrive, come, get dressed, go, grow up, laugh, lie, listen, live, rise, run, sit, sleep, walk, work

TRANSITIVE VERBS

- **Verb + direct object*:** attend, bring up, choose, do, have, hit, hold, keep, lay, need, raise, say, spend, use, want, watch, wear
- **Verb + (indirect object) + direct object*:** bring, buy, get, give, make, pay, send, take, tell

*These lists are not complete. You can always consult your dictionary to find out if a verb is transitive or intransitive.

31a-7 **Learn how to use two- and three-word verbs.** Some verbs in English consist of two or three words. These verbs, sometimes called "phrasal verbs," usually have a main verb and a "particle," also called a preposition. These verbs are idioms, because you can't understand the meaning of the verb simply by knowing the separate meaning of each of the two or three words. For example, the verb *put* has a completely different meaning from the verb *put off* (to postpone), and the verb *put up with* (to tolerate) has yet another distinct meaning. There are many, many two- and three-word verbs in English. Since it would be very difficult to memorize all of them, it's best for you to learn them as you hear them and to keep a list of these verbs for reference. The chart on page 487 lists common two- and three-word verbs.

Two-word verbs that are transitive, which means they can have a direct object, are divided into two groups: **separable** and **inseparable.** (See Section 31a–b for an explanation of transitive verbs.)

C H A R T

Common Two- and Three-Word Verbs

Here are some common two- and three-word verbs. Such verbs have two parts: the main verb and one (or more) prepositions. This list is not complete; there are many more such verbs in addition to these.

break down*	stop running
bring on	cause something to happen
call off	cancel
catch up with*	attain the same position, place
check into*	explore, investigate
come across*	encounter unintentionally
cut down on*	reduce the amount of
do over	repeat
figure out	solve a problem, dilemma
find out	discover
get along with*	have harmonious relations
get in*	enter a car
get off*	exit from (a bus, a train, a plane)
get on*	enter (a bus, a train, a plane)
get over*	recover from (a sickness, a relationship)
give up	stop trying
go over*	review
grow up*	mature, become an adult
keep up with*	maintain the same level
look after*	take care of
look into*	explore, investigate
make up	invent
pass away*	die
pick out	make a selection
put off	postpone
put up with*	tolerate
run into*	meet by chance
show up*	appear, arrive
stand up for*	defend, support
sum up	summarize, conclude
take after*	resemble, look like
touch on*	discuss briefly

31a
ESL

*These are *inseparable* verbs. This means that the verb and preposition cannot be separated by an object.

1. Separable verbs. The object can come *before* or *after* the preposition, as in the examples below.

Correct Lee checked **the book** *out* from the library.
> The object (**the book**) is placed *before* the preposition (*out*).

Correct Lee checked *out* **the book** from the library.
> The object comes *after* the preposition.

However, whenever the object is a *pronoun* (such as *it* in the following example), the pronoun *must* come *before* the preposition.

Incorrect Gary checked out **it** from the library.

Correct Gary checked **it** out from the library.

2. Inseparable verbs. You cannot separate the verb and the preposition for inseparable verbs, as in the examples below.

Incorrect My sister **majored** history **in.**

Correct My sister **majored in** history.

Incorrect The frantic student **stayed** all night **up** to study.

Correct The frantic student **stayed up** all night to study.

Incorrect Please **after** your brother **look.**

Correct Please **look after** your brother.

Incorrect The detective **looked** the case **into.**

Correct The detective **looked into** the case.

■ **Exercise 31.1** Review Sections 31a–2 and 31a–3. Circle the correct tense—simple present or present progressive. (For answers, see p. 513)

1. Many people have very bizarre dreams, but I usually (**dream/am dreaming**) about something that (**happens/is happening**) during the day.
2. I often (**remember/am remembering**) my dreams right after I (**wake/am waking**) up.
3. Sometimes if I (**hear/am hearing**) a noise while I (**dream/am dreaming**), I will incorporate that into my dream.
4. I (**know/am knowing**) a lot about dreams because I (**write/am writing**) a paper about them this semester.
5. To prepare for the paper, I (**research/am researching**) many psychological explanations for various dream symbols, such as snakes, bodies of water, and people.
6. I'm not sure if I (**believe/am believing**) those explanations, but they are very interesting.

31a
ESL

■ **Exercise 31.2** Review Section 31a–4. Circle the best verb tense—simple past or present perfect. Use the present perfect whenever possible. (For answers, see p. 513.)

1. Recently, the newspapers (**had/have had**) many articles about a phenomenon called "the glass ceiling."
2. This refers to an unofficial limitation on promotion for women who (**worked/have worked**) in a corporation for several years and who cannot advance beyond middle management.
3. Last year, my mother (**applied/has applied**) for the position of vice president of her company, but they (**did not promote/have not promoted**) her.
4. She (**had/has had**) the most experience of all the candidates for the job, but a man was chosen instead.
5. She (**was/has been**) with that company for ten years. Now she doesn't know how much longer she will stay there.

■ **Exercise 31.3** Review Sections 31a–1 to 31a–5. Fill in the blanks with the most precise and appropriate tense of the verb *talk*. Pay special attention to time words. Incorporate the adverbs in parentheses into your answers. (For answers, see p. 513.)

1. They _____ about the issue since yesterday.
2. Some employees _____ about it when we arrived at work.
3. They _____ (**probably**) about the issue when they leave work.
4. We _____ about it many times in the past.
5. I never _____ about this topic last week.
6. We _____ about this problem for two hours by the time the president visited our office.
7. Workers _____ about this issue quite often these days.
8. They _____ about the subject right now.
9. After they _____ about it for many weeks, they reached a consensus.
10. They _____ (**never**) about this issue again.

■ **Exercise 31.4** Review all of Section 31a. Each of the following sentences contains errors related to verb tense, transitive/intransitive verbs, and two-word verbs. Identify the errors and correct them. (For answers, see pp. 513–514.)

1. Before I study psychology, I thought it was an easy subject.
2. Now I am knowing that it isn't easy.
3. It has had a lot of statistics.
4. I am studying psychology since April, and I only begin to learn some of the concepts.

31a
ESL

5. I have been tried to learn more of the concepts every day.
6. Last night, I have studied from 9:00 to midnight.
7. I went my adviser last Monday.
8. She told to me to see her after class.
9. But when I went to see her after class, she already left.
10. It's January. By the middle of June, I have studied psychology for six months.

31b   WHICH MODAL SHOULD YOU USE?

Troubleshooting

You already know that a verb's tense expresses time. A *modal*, which is an auxiliary or helping verb, expresses an attitude about a situation. For example, if you want to be polite, you can say, "Open the door, please." If you want to be even more polite, you can also add a modal auxiliary verb: "*Would* you open the door, please?" Modals are used for many purposes; some of these are to express necessity, obligation, regret, and formality. Modals can be used to express ideas about the past, present, or future.

Past	I **could** speak Japanese as a child.
Present	My brother **can** speak Japanese now.
Future	I **might** learn another language next semester.

You probably already know the common modals, such as *should*, *must*, and *have to*. However, you may still have questions about others, such as *had better*, or perhaps you are still not sure about the difference between, for example, *have to* and *ought to*. In this section, we've listed the modals by their uses or functions. You will also find a list of common modal errors to avoid.

To use modal auxiliaries correctly . . .

31b–1 **Choose the modal that best expresses your idea.** The chart on pages 492–493 summarizes the functions of modals. It also lists the past form of the modals. Modals in the present are followed by the base form of the verb (subject + modal + base form of the verb). The form of modals in the past varies. (See Section 31b–3 for more details.)

31b–2 **Be sure to use the correct form of the modal auxiliary and the main verb that follows it.** Modals that express present and future time have this form:

subj.   +   modal   +   base form of verb
Clarissa **had better** register for classes soon.

Here are some specific tips to help you with modal formation.

1. Don't use *to* after the modal.

Incorrect	Jacquie **can** ~~to~~ play the guitar very well.
Correct	Jacquie **can** play the guitar very well.
Incorrect	**Must** I ~~to~~ hand in this paper tomorrow?
Correct	**Must** I hand in this paper tomorrow?
Except	We **have to** write a ten-page paper.

2. There is no *-s* on the third person singular of a modal.

Incorrect	Kwang **might**~~s~~ go to graduate school.
Correct	Kwang **might** go to graduate school.

3. You cannot use two modals together.

Incorrect	They **might** ~~could~~ drive all night.
Correct	They **might** drive all night.

4. *Do, does,* and *did* are not used in questions with modals, except for the modal *have to.*

Incorrect	**Do** I **must** answer all the questions?
Correct	**Must** I answer all the questions?
Except	**Do** I **have to** answer all the questions?

5. *Do, does,* and *did* are not used in negative statements with modals; use *not* instead, placed after the modal.

Incorrect	They **do not** can enter the test room.
Correct	They can**not** enter the test room.
Incorrect	Jorge **did not** could have worked any harder.
Correct	Jorge could **not** have worked any harder.

CAUTION

31b-3 **Use the perfect form to express past time.** As you can see from the chart of modals on pages 492–493, many modals have a past form. The past of modals that give advice or express possibility, expectation, and conclusion have a *perfect* verb form (modal + *have* + past participle), as you can see in the following examples.

Advice	Gail **should have taken** that marketing job last year. Gail didn't take the job.
Possibility	Although he chose not to, Bob **could have gone** to Mexico over spring break. Bob didn't go to Mexico.

31b
ESL

CHART

Modals

What it means	Present or future form	Past form
Permission *(Informal → Formal)*		
can	**Can** I be excused?	He **could have**
could	**Could** I be excused?	**been** excused, but
may	**May** I be excused?	he didn't ask.
would you mind*	**Would you mind if** I *brought* my dog?	**Would you have minded if** I *had brought* my dog?
Ability		
can	Joe **can** drive a car.	He **couldn't** drive a car last year.
be able to	Carl **is able to** study and listen to music at the same time.	Celia **was never able to** play the Mozart concertos.
Advice		
should	You **should** quit.	He **should have**
ought to	You **ought to** quit.	quit last year.
had better	You **had better** quit.	(He didn't quit; this sentence shows regret.)
Necessity		
have to	He **has to** pay a fine.	He **had to** pay a fine
must	She **must** pay her taxes.	last week. (No past form; use **had to**.)
Lack of necessity		
not have to	You **don't have to** attend school in summer.	He **didn't have to** take the final exam last year.
not need to	You **don't need to** pay in advance.	You **didn't need to** pay in advance.

*Would you mind is followed by if + the past tense of the verb.

31b
ESL

WHAT IT MEANS	PRESENT OR FUTURE FORM	PAST FORM
Possibility *(More sure → Less sure)*		
can	It **can** get cold in May.	No past form.
may	It **may** get cold in June this year.	I'm not sure, but it **may have** just happened.
could	It **could** get cold in July this year.	It **could have** just happened.
might	It **might** get cold in July this year.	It **might have** just happened.

Expectation **should/ ought to**	Your keys **should be** on the desk where I left them. (I expect them to be there.)	John **should have been** elected. (He didn't get elected, but I expected him to.)

31b
ESL

Conclusion **must**	Your eyes are all red; you **must have** allergies. (I'm almost certain that this is true.)	You got an A on your test. You **must have studied** hard! (I'm certain that you did this in the past.)

Polite requests *(Informal → Formal)*		
can	**Can** you give me a hand?	No past forms.
will	**Will** you give me a hand?	
could	**Could** you give me a hand?	
would you mind + present participle	**Would you mind giving** me a hand?	

Expectation	Where is Sue? She **should have been** here by now. Sue hasn't arrived yet.
Conclusion	Ted finished his paper; he **must have worked** all night.

■ **Exercise 31.5** Review Section 31b–1. Fill in the blanks with an appropriate modal from the list below. More than one answer is possible for each blank. Try not to use each modal more than once. (For answers, see p. 514.)

| would | must | have to | ought to | should have |
| should | can | might | had better | must have |

1. Can you believe the line waiting to see the movie *Apollo 13*? That _____ be a good movie!
2. Where is my purse, Mom? It _____ be on the table where you put it last night.
3. I'm sorry, Professor Jones, but I _____ not take the test tomorrow because I _____ go to Immigration about my visa.
4. Jason, you _____ eat your vegetables or you won't get any dessert.

■ **Exercise 31.6** Review Sections 31b–1 and 31b–2. Each of the following sentences contains errors related to modal auxiliaries. Identify the errors and correct them. (For answers, see p. 514.)

1. Carol's boss told her, "You had better to improve your attitude, or we will have to take disciplinary action."
2. Carol was very distressed by this news; she did not could understand the basis for her boss's complaints.
3. She tried to think of things that she had done wrong. She knew that she should had been more enthusiastic at the last meeting, but she felt she couldn't be hypocritical. She simply didn't agree with her boss.
4. Carol was really worried. Her boss mights send her a "pink slip," which would mean that she had been fired.

31c
ESL

31c DO YOU HAVE PROBLEMS WITH GERUNDS AND INFINITIVES?

Troubleshooting

The many different functions of gerunds and infinitives in English may be confusing to you. (See Section 18a for a definition of *gerund* and *infinitive*.) An **infinitive,** for example, can be the subject of a sentence, and also the object of a verb.

> subj.
> **To find** a parking space here is impossible!

> obj.
> My sister hopes **to be** a marine biologist.

Gerunds also have several functions: subject, object, complement, and object of a preposition. (See Sections 14d–2 and 22b for an explanation of *complement* and *object of a preposition*.)

> subj.
> **Finding** a parking space is impossible here!

> obj.
> George enjoys **reading** for half an hour before bed.

> comp.
> His favorite hobby is **cooking.**

> obj. prep.
> She is afraid of **flying.**

ESL writers often have difficulty with gerunds and infinitives when they function as objects in a sentence, so this section will focus on this problem.

31c
ESL

To use gerunds and infinitives correctly . . .

31c–1 **Learn which form—gerund or infinitive—to use.** You probably already know that some verbs in English are followed by gerunds and other verbs are followed by infinitives. Here are two common examples.

> **Infinitive (*to* + base form of verb)**
> I want **to go** with you.

> **Gerund (base form of verb + *-ing*)**
> He enjoys **jogging** in the park.

There are other verbs, however, that can have *either* a gerund or an infinitive after them without a difference in meaning.

> **Gerund or infinitive (no change in meaning)**
> gerund
> The dog began **barking** at midnight.
> infinitive
> The dog began **to bark** at midnight.
> These two sentences have exactly the same meaning.

Finally, some verbs in English (e.g., *forget, regret, remember, stop, try*) can be followed by *either* a gerund or an infinitive, but with a change in meaning.

Gerund or infinitive (change in meaning)

Paul stopped **working** in the cafeteria.

This sentence means that Paul *no longer* works in the cafeteria.

Paul stopped his tennis game early **to work** on his homework.

This sentence means that Paul stopped his game *in order to* work on his homework.

Paul forgot **to visit** his cousin while he was in Mexico.

This sentence means he did *not* visit his cousin.

Paul will never forget **visiting** Mexico.

This sentence means that Paul visited Mexico and he will always remember the trip.

Native speakers know intuitively whether to use a gerund or an infinitive after a verb, but this is not usually true for ESL students.

The charts on pages 496 and 497 can help you; be sure to keep these charts handy for reference when you are writing.

**31c
ESL**

CHART

Verbs Followed by Gerunds or Infinitives

VERB + INFINITIVE

These verbs must be followed by **infinitives.**

afford	decide	manage	refuse
agree	deserve	mean	seem
appear	expect	need	swear
arrange	fail	offer	threaten
ask	hesitate	plan	wait
beg	hope	prepare	wish
claim	intend	pretend	
consent	learn	promise	

VERB + GERUND

These verbs must be followed by **gerunds.**

admitt	discuss	mind	resent
anticipate	dislike	miss	resist
appreciate	enjoy	postpone	risk
avoid	escape	practice	suggest
complete	finish	quit	tolerate
consider	can't help	recall	understand
delay	keep	recollect	
deny	mention	recommend	

VERB + GERUND OR INFINITIVE

These verbs can be followed by either a **gerund** or an **infinitive**, with no change in meaning.

begin	continue	love
can't bear	hate	prefer
can't stand	like	start

C H A R T

Verbs Followed by Gerunds or Infinitives with a Change in Meaning

VERB + GERUND OR INFINITIVE

These verbs can be followed by either a **gerund** or an **infinitive**, but the meaning of the sentence will change depending on which one you use.

31c
ESL

try (to be)	make an attempt to be
try (being)	do an experiment
regret (to be)	feel sorry about
regret (being)	feel sorry about *past* action
remember (to be)	not forget
remember (being)	recall, bring to mind
forget (to be)	not remember
(never) forget (being)	always remember
stop (to be)	stop in order to be
stop (being)	interrupt an action

31c-2 Learn when a verb must be followed by a noun or pronoun.
As we've seen, some verbs in English (called *transitive verbs*) need to have a noun or pronoun after them. For example, when you use *tell* in a sentence, you need a direct object (*what did you tell*) or an indirect object (*whom did you tell*) to complete the sentence.

Incorrect   I told to write me a letter.
> The object is missing; the sentence is incomplete.

Correct   I told **my son** to write me a letter.
> *My son* is the indirect object; this sentence is complete.

Remember that an *infinitive* verb comes after transitive verb + noun or pronoun constructions. The chart below lists the verbs that follow this pattern.

CHART

Verbs Followed by Nouns, Pronouns, or Infinitives

VERB + (NOUN OR PRONOUN) + INFINITIVE

These verbs must be followed by a **noun or pronoun** + **infinitive.**

advise	encourage	order	tell
allow	force	persuade	urge
cause	hire	remind	warn
challenge	instruct	require	
convince	invite		

31c–3 **Use a gerund after a preposition.** Many verbs are followed by prepositions. Sometimes adjectives are also followed by prepositions. Always remember to use a gerund, not an infinitive, after prepositions. Here are two common sentence patterns with prepositions, followed by gerunds.

>   verb   adj.   prep. gerund
> Carla has been very worried **about passing** her statistics class.

>   verb   prep. gerund
> Mrs. Short apologized **for interrupting** our conversation.

The chart on page 499 lists some common preposition combinations with verbs and adjectives.

31c–4 **Use the base form of the verb after** *have, let,* **and** *make.* These verbs, called "causative verbs," are exceptions to the rule explained in Section 31c–2. Instead of being followed by an infinitive, these verbs are followed by a noun or pronoun and the **base form** of the verb. This means that you omit the *to* before the verb.

have   I **had** my mother *cut* my hair.
            Here *had* means to cause someone to do something.

make   The teacher **made** him *leave* the class.
            Here *made* means to force someone to do something; it is stronger than *had.*

let   Professor Betts **let** the class *leave* early.
            Here *let* means to allow someone to do something.

CHART

Common Verb (+ Adjective) + Preposition Constructions

Here is a list of many common verb (+ adjective) + preposition constructions.

be accustomed to	be faithful to	pray for
be afraid of	be familiar with	prevent from
approve of	be fond of	prohibit from
be aware of	be good at	protect from
believe in	be grateful to	be proud of
be capable of	be guilty of	rely on
be committed to	hope for	be responsible for
complain about	insist on	be satisfied with
be composed of	be interested in	be scared of
consist of	be jealous of	stop from
depend on	look forward to	succeed in
be disappointed in	be made of	take advantage of
be divorced from	be married to	take care of
dream of/about	object to	be tired of
be envious of	be opposed to	be worried about
be excited about	be patient with	

31c
ESL

■ **Exercise 31.7** Fill in the blanks with the infinitive, gerund, or base form of the verb in parentheses. (For answers, see p. 514.)

1. Women who have not wanted (**work**) _____ because of health threats can now relax.
2. A 1992 study completed in Rancho Bernardo, California, shows that women who work outside the home seem (**have**) _____ fewer health problems than those who work inside the home.
3. Another federal study reports that women employed outside the home do not risk (**have**) _____ more "stress-induced" heart attacks than women working inside the home.
4. In fact, this study appears (**support**) _____ the benefits of working outside the home for women.
5. In general, working women are found (**be**) _____ both physically and mentally healthier than women who stay at home.
6. Many working women will appreciate (**hear**) _____ that their chances for depression actually increase if they decide (**drop**) _____ out of the work force.

7. These studies do not pretend (**decide**) _____ for women what is best for them.

8. However, the studies might help some women (**make**) _____ a decision about (**go**) _____ back to work outside the home or about (**quit**) _____ their jobs because they have children at home.

31d **DO YOU HAVE PROBLEMS WITH ARTICLES AND NUMBER AGREEMENT?**

Troubleshooting

Are you sometimes confused about which article to use—*a, an,* or *the?* Do you know when no article should be used? Are you still uncertain about whether to use *a few* or *a little* before some nouns? If so, you are certainly not alone. Many ESL students ask these questions. We will deal with questions about articles and expressions of quantity in this section.

31d
ESL

To choose the best article—*a/an/the* or *no article* . . .

31d–1 **Decide if the noun is count or noncount.** Before you can know which article to use, you will need to determine whether the noun in question is *count* or *noncount.* Perhaps you already know, or can guess from the word itself, that a **count noun** refers to something that you can count or that you can divide easily.

> **Count nouns**   There are sixty **seconds** in one **minute.**
> Joan bought **six books** for her class.

In the above sentences, you can see that when there is more than one of the noun (e.g., *seconds*), then the count noun must be plural. (See Section 19a for a discussion of plural nouns.) If there is only one (e.g., *one minute*), the count noun is singular.

On the other hand, a **noncount noun** usually refers to something that cannot be counted or divided. Noncount nouns often include **mass** nouns such as materials (*wood, plastic, wool*), food items (*cheese, rice, meat*) and liquids (*water, milk*), or **abstract nouns** (*beauty, knowledge, glory*).

> **Noncount nouns**   Joe drank a lot of **milk** as a teenager.
> "Give me **liberty** or give me **death!**"

Some nouns that are noncount in English seem like things that you can count. A good example is the noncount noun *money.* Unfortunately, there are many noncount nouns in English that confuse ESL students. Some examples are *furniture, hair, traffic, information,* and *advice.*

It is always a good idea, therefore, to consult your ESL dictionary when you are unsure if a noun is count or noncount.

As you can see from the sample sentences above, unlike count nouns, which can be singular or plural, noncount nouns have only one form, the singular form. In addition, since you can't count these nouns, you can't use numbers with them or other expressions that express number (e.g., *several, many*). You will use other types of expressions to indicate quantity for noncount nouns. These expressions, called *quantifiers*, will be discussed in Section 31d–5.

Generally speaking, most nouns are either count or noncount. However, some noncount nouns can change to have a count meaning. Using a noncount noun as a count noun usually limits the noncount noun in some way. For example, imagine you are ordering your dinner at a restaurant, and your friend says to the waiter, "Can we have three waters, please?" You are confused because you learned that *water* is a noncount noun, but your English-speaking friend has used it in the plural form, with a number. In this case, *three waters* means *three glasses of water*, and it is acceptable to say that. Other instances in which a noncount noun changes to a count noun include when you mean *an instance of, a serving of,* or *a type of* the noncount noun.

31d
ESL

count noun
His grandmother started **a business.** One instance of business

count noun
I'd like two **coffees** to go, please. Two servings of coffee

count noun
There are three new **wines** on the menu. Three types of wine

31d–2 Decide if the count noun requires a definite (*the*) or an indefinite (*a/an*) article. If the count noun is singular, you'll need an article, either *a/an* or *the*, in front of it. But how do you know which article to use? Basically, when you introduce the noun for the first time, without having referred to it before, then you will use the *indefinite* articles, *a* or *an*. (See Section 19d for the difference between *a* and *an*.)

Indefinite meaning
Bob: I just signed up for **a** literature class.
Ted: Oh, really? I didn't know you were interested in that.
This is the first time Bob has mentioned the class to Ted.

After that, when both of them know what is being discussed, Bob will use the *definite* article, *the*.

Definite meaning
Bob: Can you believe **the** class meets on Friday evenings?
Both Bob and Ted now share the same information, so Bob uses the definite article, *the*.

Note how the same guidelines apply to written English in the following sentences on homelessness.

> There are several reasons why ⓐ person may end up homeless. Perhaps ⟨the⟩ person lost his or her job and could not pay for ⟨an⟩ apartment. Or perhaps ⟨the⟩ apartment was sold to ⓐ new owner, who raised the rent. ⟨The⟩ new owner may not realize how expensive the rent is for that person.

There are also other situations that require the definite article, *the*.

1. When there is only one of the noun.

> **The** earth is round.
> There is only one earth.

2. When the noun is superlative.

> This is **the best** brand you can buy.
> There can only be one brand that is the best.

3. When the noun is limited. You will usually use *the* before a noun that has been limited in some way to show that you are referring to a *specific* example of the noun.

> **The** book **that I read** is informative.
> *That I read* limits the book to a specific one.

> **The** book **on Robert Kennedy** is out.
> *On Robert Kennedy* limits the book.

If you are making a *generalization*, however, *the* is not always used. (See Section 31d–3 for details on this.)

> **A** book **on plants** can make a nice gift.
> *On plants* limits the noun, but the sentence does not refer to a specific book on plants—the sentence refers to *any or all books on plants*. A definite article is not correct here.

 TRICKY

31d–3 Choose articles before general nouns carefully. When you want to make generalizations, choosing the correct article can be very tricky. As a rule, you can use *a/an* or *the* with most *singular count nouns* to make generalizations. Here are some examples.

> **A** dog can be good company for **a** lonely person.
> You can use *a/an* to mean any dog, one of many dogs.

> **The** computer has changed the banking industry dramatically.
> Use *the* to mean the computer *in general*.

The spotted owl is an endangered species.
The capitalist believes in free enterprise.

The is used to make general statements about specific species of animals (e.g., the spotted owl) or groups of people (e.g., capitalists).

You can also use a *plural count noun* to make general statements, but without *the*.

Capitalists believe in free enterprise.
Computers have changed the banking industry dramatically.

Finally, *noncount nouns* in general statements do not have an article in front of them.

Sugar is a major cause of tooth decay.

Many educators question whether **intelligence** can be measured.

Consumed in moderate amounts, red **wine** is thought by some researchers to reduce chances of heart disease.

The above points are only general guidelines to help you in your choice of articles. There are many finer points about article use that are not covered here. We suggest, therefore, that when you have questions, you consult one of the ESL grammar reference books listed on page 512 at the end of this chapter.

31d-4 **Be aware of possible article problems with noncount nouns.** You may want to be especially careful of the following points regarding noncount nouns. First of all, make sure that you don't use *a/an* with noncount nouns.

Incorrect I need a̶ work.

Correct I need work.

In addition, you should keep in mind that a noncount noun can never be plural:

Incorrect Joe needs some **information**s̶ about the class.

Correct Joe needs some **information** about the class.

(Sometimes noncount nouns can change to have a count meaning—see 31d–1.)

31d-5 **Pay careful attention to quantifiers.** The words that come before nouns and tell you *how much* or *how many* are called **quantifiers.** Quantifiers are not always the same for both count and noncount nouns. See the following chart for a list of these.

31d
ESL

C H A R T

Quantifiers

USE THESE WITH COUNT AND NONCOUNT NOUNS	USE THESE WITH COUNT NOUNS ONLY	USE THESE WITH NONCOUNT NOUNS ONLY
some books/money	**several** books	**a good deal of** money
a lot of books/money	**many** books	**a great deal of** money
plenty of books/money	**a couple of** books	**(not) much** money*
a lack of books/money	**a few** books	**a little** money
most of the books/money	**few** books	**little** money

Much is ordinarily only used in questions and in negative statements: "Do you have *much* milk left? No, there isn't *much* milk."

31d
ESL

31d–6 **Learn the difference between *a few/a little* and *few/little*.** It may not seem like a big difference, but the article *a* in front of the quantifiers *few* and *little* changes the meaning. A *few* or *a little* means "not a lot, but enough of the item," as in the following examples.

> There are **a few books** in the library on capital punishment.
> Use *a few* with count nouns.

> There is **a little information** in the library on capital punishment.
> Use *a little* with noncount nouns.

Few or *little* (without *a*) means that there is *not enough* of something. These quantifiers have a negative meaning, as in these examples.

> There are **few** female leaders in the world. Not enough of them
> My mother has **little** hope that this will change. Not much hope

31d–7 **Learn how to use *most* and *most of*.** Using *most of* can be tricky. You can use *most of* before either a count or a noncount noun, but if you do, don't forget to put *the* before the noun. Here are some examples that will help you use this quantifier correctly.

Most of **+** ***the*** **+ specific plural noun**

Most of the *women* in the class were married.

Not: **most of** *women*

Most of **+** ***the*** **+ specific noncount noun**

Most of the *jewelry* in the house was stolen.

Not: **most of** *jewelry*

Most **+ general plural noun**

Most *cars* have seat belts.

Not: **most of** *cars*

31d–8 **Learn the difference between** *another* **and** *the other.* Use *another* to talk about an additional person or thing. Use *the other* to talk about the last item in a pair or a series of things or people. Compare these sentences.

> I have three sisters. One sister lives in Virginia.
> **Another** sister lives in Florida. An additional one
> **The other** sister lives in New York. The last one

31d

ESL

■ **Exercise 31.8** Below is a list of nouns. Write C after the count nouns and NC after the noncount nouns. If you are not sure, consult an ESL dictionary. Then make a note of the nouns you had to check. (For answers, see p. 514.)

1. furniture _____
2. work _____
3. dollar _____
4. job _____
5. advice _____

6. people _____
7. equipment _____
8. money _____
9. newspaper _____
10. traffic _____

■ **Exercise 31.9** Review all of Section 31d. Each of the following sentences has at least one error in the use of articles or quantifiers. Circle the error and correct it. (For answers, see p. 514.)

1. Much people have visited the new restaurant downtown, called Rock-and-Roll Hamburger Haven.

2. Most of customers are young people because music in restaurant is very loud.

3. The restaurant serves the usual food—hamburgers, pizza, and pasta. It is not expensive; in fact, most expensive item on the menu is only $8.

4. Food is not very good, but the atmosphere is very appealing to these young men and women.

5. There are much posters on the walls of famous rock star. There is even authentic motorcycle of one star on a platform.

6. Some of regular customers say they have seen some stars eating there.
7. These "regulars" give these advices to anyone who wants to spot a star there—look for dark glasses and a leather coat.

■ **Exercise 31.10** Write a paragraph describing your favorite restaurant. Refer to the chart on page 504, which lists quantifiers used with count and noncount nouns, and use at least four words from this list in your paragraph. Underline all the nouns in your paragraph and write C (for count nouns) and NC (for noncount nouns) above them. Then check your use of articles. (For help, you may refer to Sections 31d–2, 31d–3, and 31d–4.) Make sure your subject-verb agreement is correct.

31e WHAT SHOULD YOU LOOK FOR WHEN YOU PROOFREAD YOUR PAPERS?

31e
ESL

Troubleshooting

It is always a good idea to proofread your papers for grammar and punctuation errors before handing in the final copy to the teacher. (See Section 4c.) You'll find that the mistakes you notice when you are proofreading are usually mistakes you know how to correct. In this section you'll find a series of common ESL proofreading problems and their solutions. Why not make a list of your own common mistakes?

To proofread your paper . . .

31e–1 **Be sure each clause has a subject.** Every clause in English must have a subject, except for imperative sentences (e.g., "Sit down").

Incorrect	I'm going swimming because am hot.
Correct	I'm going swimming because **I** am hot.
	You must repeat *I* after *because*.

Incorrect	Is difficult to write in English.
Correct	**It** is difficult to write in English.
	You must have *it* before the verb *is*.

31e–2 **Be sure a main or an auxiliary verb isn't missing from your sentence.** If your teacher writes "verb missing" on your papers, then you probably are making one of the following errors.

THE MAIN VERB IS MISSING

Incorrect	The teacher extremely helpful. *verb missing*
Correct	The teacher **is** extremely helpful.

THE AUXILIARY VERB IS MISSING

Incorrect   Hurry! The plane leaving right now. *verb missing*

Correct   Hurry! The plane **is** leaving right now.

31e-3 **Don't forget the -s on verbs used with third person singular nouns and pronouns (*he, she, it*).** It is easy to forget the -s on present tense verbs used with the third person singular. If this is a problem for you, it is a good practice to check all the present tense verbs in a paper to make sure you haven't forgotten an -s.

Incorrect   The library close at 5:00 today. 3rd person sing. -s

Correct   The library close**s** at 5:00 today.

When you have the auxiliary *do* or *does* in a sentence, add the -s to the auxiliary, and not to the main verb.

Incorrect   He don't know the answer to the question.
          3rd person sing. -s

Correct   He **doesn't** know the answer to the question.

31e
ESL

31e-4 **Don't confuse adjective pairs like *bored* and *boring*.** The following sentences are very different in meaning although they look similar.

John is **bored.**
This means that John is bored by *something*—maybe his class or his homework; it is a feeling he has as a result of something.

John is **boring.**
This means that John has a personality that is not interesting; he is a boring person.

The ending of the adjective—*-ed* or *-ing*—is what creates a difference in meaning. Adjectives ending in *-ed* have a passive meaning. Adjectives ending in *-ing* have an active meaning. (See Section 17e for an explanation of passive voice.)

The English spelling system often confuses Jorge.

-ed **ending**   Jorge is **confused** by the English spelling system.
          Passive

          The **confused** student looked up words in his spelling dictionary. Passive

-ing **ending**   English spelling is **confusing.** Active
          It is a **confusing** system. Active

Joan's work satisfies her.

-ed ending   She is **satisfied** by her work. Passive
She is a **satisfied** employee. Passive

-ing ending   Her work is **satisfying.** Active
Joan does **satisfying** work. Active

Here are some common pairs of adjectives that confuse students, along with the preposition that is used after the -ed adjectives.

C H A R T

Adjective Pairs

amusing	amused by	embarrassing	embarrassed by
annoying	annoyed by	exciting	excited by/about
boring	bored by	frightening	frightened by
confusing	confused by	interesting	interested in
disappointing	disappointed	irritating	irritated by
	in someone/	satisfying	satisfied with
	by something	surprising	surprised by/at

31e–5 **Don't forget the -ed endings on past participles.** Check your papers to be sure that you use the past participle (-ed ending) for verbs in the following cases. (See Section 17d for a list of the three parts of a verb.)

IN PASSIVE VOICE (see Section 17a)

Incorrect   The amenities were **provide** by the hotel.

Correct   The amenities were **provided** by the hotel.

Incorrect   The documents were **alter** by the thief.

Correct   The documents were **altered** by the thief.

IN THE PAST PERFECT TENSE (see Section 31a)

Incorrect   Juan had **finish** the race before Fred came.

Correct   Juan had **finished** the race before Fred came.

IN PARTICIPLE ADJECTIVES (see Section 31e–4)

Incorrect   She was **frighten** by the dark.

Correct   She was **frightened** by the dark.

You also want to be sure that you *don't* add -*ed* endings to infinitives.

Incorrect	George started to **prepared** dinner.
Correct	George started to **prepare** dinner.

31e–6 Avoid repetition of sentence elements. You may find that you often repeat unnecessary words in your sentences. You'll want to be on your guard for the three types of repetition in the examples below.

IN ADJECTIVE CLAUSES

The store that I told you about **it** closed down.
It is not necessary because *that* replaces *it*.

The man whom I met **him** yesterday was kind.
Whom replaces *him*.

The school where I go **there** is very expensive.
Where replaces *there*.

IN THE SUBJECT OF THE SENTENCE

My brother **he** is the director of the hospital.
Because *my brother* and *he* refer to the same person, the *he* is unnecessary repetition.

MULTIPLE CONNECTORS

Although the employee was diligent, **but** she was fired.
In this sentence, *although* and *but* both express contrast. You don't need two connectors in one sentence with the same meaning. You must take out one of them.

Because she fell asleep after eating a big lunch, **so** she missed her class.

31e–7 Place adverbs correctly in the sentence. Adverbs can appear in many different places in a sentence—at the beginning, in the middle, at the end. However, there are a few positions where adverbs *can't* be placed. Here are some guidelines.

DON'T PUT AN ADVERB BETWEEN THE VERB AND ITS OBJECT

	verb / adverb / obj.
Incorrect	She answered **slowly** the question.

	verb / obj. / adverb
Correct	She answered the question **slowly.**

DON'T PLACE ADVERBS OF FREQUENCY BEFORE THE VERB *BE*

Incorrect	Louise **regularly** is late for class.
Correct	Louise is **regularly** late for class.

C H A R T

Order of Adjectives

1. Amount	2. Descriptive Adjective	3. Size	4. Shape, Length	5. Age
a/an	expensive	large	oblong	new
a few	pretty	small	round	old

Don't place adverbs of frequency after other verbs

Incorrect	Juan arrives **often** late to class.
Correct	Juan **often** arrives late to class.

31e
ESL

31e-8 **Learn which adjective comes first.** An adjective is a word that modifies a noun. (See Chapter 25 for more information on modifiers.) In English, most adjectives come before the noun they modify. In addition, it is often possible to have more than one adjective modifying a noun. In such cases, there is a specific order in which adjectives appear, and the chart above lists that order. Of course, there are exceptions to this sequence, but you will have to make note of those as you come across them. Here are some examples of sentences with multiple adjectives.

> size   origin   qualifier
> The **small Japanese sports** car has gained popularity here.

> descriptive
> adj.   age   material
> The **beautiful old wooden** table was tucked away in a barn.

■ **Exercise 31.11** Review Section 31e–4. Circle the correct form of the adjective. (For answers, see p. 514.)

1. My mother was (**encouraging/encouraged**) to me when she told me that I could do anything I wanted in my life.
2. A man approached an old lady on the street and tried to steal her purse. The (**horrifying/horrified**) victim screamed for help.
3. There is really nothing as (**exhilarating/exhilarated**) as an early morning swim in the ocean.
4. The tired businesswoman took a two-week vacation in Hawaii. When she returned to work, she was a (**rejuvenating/rejuvenated**) person.
5. I heard some very (**discouraging/discouraged**) news yesterday—my brother lost the election.

6. COLOR	7. ORIGIN	8. MATERIAL	9. QUALIFIER	10. NOUN
black	American	enamel	writing	table
blue	Chinese	porcelain	soup	bowls

■ **Exercise 31.12** Review Section 31e; then read the following paragraph and proofread it for the mistakes described in that section. In some cases you will need to add something and in others you will delete an element. (There are seven errors. For answers, see p. 514.)

31e
ESL

```
    There are long lines at the cashier's office

because students signing up for financial aid. Is

extremely frustrating to spend the entire day in

line. Because some students they have other jobs

and classes, so they can't wait very long. Then

you very tired when you finally arrive at the

desk where you can talk to the clerk there. The

clerk usually give you a form to fill out, and

then you have to wait in another line!
```

■ **Exercise 31.13** Review Sections 31e–7 and 31e–8; then insert the adjective or adverb in parentheses in the most appropriate position in the sentence. (For answers, see p. 514.)

1. The singer had thick red hair. (**long**)
2. I bought a large wooden table for my dining room. (**Chinese**)
3. The professor is running behind schedule. (**always**)
4. The answer to such questions can be found in an almanac. (**often**)
5. The clerk handed him the ice cream cone. (**quickly**)

31f OTHER ESL PROBLEMS?

You probably have plenty of other questions about grammar or punctuation that we haven't covered in this chapter. There is a good chance that native speakers of English have many of these questions too. In the chart on pages 512–513 you will find a list of possible problems, each with a cross-reference to a chapter or section in the handbook that deals with that point.

31f
ESL

H I G H L I G H T

Reference Books for ESL Students

The following reference books are especially useful for ESL students. We suggest these books for questions about grammar and usage.

- Irwin Feigenbaum. *The Grammar Handbook.* Oxford: Oxford UP, 1985.
- Jocelyn Steer and Karen Carlisi. *The Advanced Grammar Book.* New York: Newbury, 1991.

We also recommend the following dictionary written for the ESL student.

- *The Longman Dictionary of Contemporary English.* NY: Longman, 1979.

C H A R T

Where to Find Help for Other ESL Problems

IF YOU HAVE A QUESTION ABOUT . . .	EXAMPLES	GO TO THIS CHAPTER/SECTION IN THE HANDBOOK:
Abbreviations	Dr., APA, Ms.	30d
Adjective clauses	clauses beginning with *who, which, that*	12b, 23b, 26b
Capitalization	English, Japanese	30a, 30b
Comparatives/ superlatives	more interesting/ the most interesting	22c, 25h
Dangling modifiers	Reading the paper, the phone rang.	25g
Irregular verbs	sit, sat, sat	17d

IF YOU HAVE A QUESTION ABOUT . . .	EXAMPLES	GO TO THIS CHAPTER/SECTION IN THE HANDBOOK:
Parallelism	I like swimming and fishing.	7c, 13d
Passive voice	I was hit by a car.	17e
Plural nouns	child–children	19a
Possessives	the teacher's book	19b, 19c
Pronouns	his gain; their loss	20–23
Punctuation	commas, periods	26–29
Sentence problems:		
run-ons	I am a student I come from Mexico.	24c, 24d
fragments	Because it is my house.	24a
Spelling		37a, 38b
Subject-verb agreement		16a–16e, 21b
Transition words	however, thus	9a, 9b

31 ESL

Answer Key

Exercise 31.1
1. dream; happens
2. remember; wake
3. hear; am dreaming
4. know; am writing
5. am researching
6. believe

Exercise 31.2
1. have had
2. have worked
3. applied; did not promote
4. had
5. has been

Exercise 31.3
1. have been talking
2. were talking
3. will probably be talking
4. have talked
5. talked
6. had been talking
7. are talking (*or* talk)

8. are talking
9. had talked
10. will never talk

Exercise 31.4
1. Before I **studied** psychology, I **(had) thought** it was an easy subject.
2. Now I **know** that it isn't easy.
3. It **has** a lot of statistics.
4. I **have been studying** psychology since April, and I **have only begun** to learn some of the concepts.
5. I **have been trying** to learn more of the concepts every day.
6. Last night, I **was studying** from 9:00 to midnight.
   or
   Last night, I **studied** from 9:00 to midnight.
7. I went **to** my adviser last Monday.
8. She told ʇo me to see her after class.
9. But when I went to see her after class, she **had** already **left**.

10. It's January. By the middle of June, I **will have studied** psychology for six months.

Exercise 31.5
1. must; should
2. should; ought to; must; had better
3. cannot/might have to; might/should
4. had better; must; should; ought to

Exercise 31.6
1. Carol's boss told her, "You had better to improve your attitude, or we will have to take disciplinary action."
2. Carol was very distressed by this news; she **could not** (or **did not**) understand the basis for her boss's complaints.
3. She tried to think of things that she had done wrong. She knew that she **should have been** more enthusiastic at the last meeting, but she felt she couldn't be hypocritical. She simply didn't agree with her boss.
4. Carol was really worried. Her boss might send her a "pink slip," which would mean that she had been fired.

Exercise 31.7
1. to work
2. to have
3. having
4. to support
5. to be
6. hearing; to drop
7. to decide
8. to make; going; quitting

Exercise 31.8
1. NC	6. C
2. NC	7. NC
3. C	8. NC
4. C	9. C
5. NC	10. NC

Exercise 31.9
1. **Many** people have visited the new restaurant downtown, called Rock-and-Roll Hamburger Haven.
2. Most of **the** customers are young people because **the** music in **the** restaurant is very loud.
3. The restaurant serves the usual food —hamburgers, pizza, and pasta. It is not expensive; in fact, **the** most expensive item on the menu is only $8.
4. **The** food is not very good, but the atmosphere is very appealing to these young men and women.
5. There are **many** posters on the walls of famous rock star**s**. There is even **an** authentic motorcycle of one star on a platform.
6. Some of **the** regular customers say they have seen some stars eating there.
7. These "regulars" give **this advice** to anyone who wants to spot a star there—look for dark glasses and a leather coat.

Exercise 31.10
Answers will vary.

Exercise 31.11
1. encouraging
2. horrified
3. exhilarating
4. rejuvenated
5. discouraging

Exercise 31.12
There are long lines at the cashier's office because students **are** signing up for financial aid. **It** is extremely frustrating to spend the entire day in line. Because some students they have other jobs and classes, so they can't wait very long. Then you **are** very tired when you finally arrive at the desk where you can talk to the clerk there. The clerk usually give**s** you a form to fill out, and then you have to wait in another line!

Exercise 31.13
1. The singer had **long,** thick red hair.
2. I bought a large wooden **Chinese** table for my dining room.
3. The professor is **always** running behind schedule.
4. The answer to such questions can **often** be found in an almanac.
5. The clerk handed him the ice cream cone **quickly.**
   or
   The clerk **quickly** handed him the ice cream cone.

This section explains how to write a variety of assignments that require either research or specialized approaches to information, organization, and style. Chapters 32 and 33 provide a general introduction to research, with the emphasis on a type of library paper still common in introductory college writing courses. Chapter 34 explains the conventions of MLA documentation for papers in the humanities—disciplines such as English, history, philosophy, and foreign languages; it also discusses two kinds of writing frequently required in humanities courses: the essay examination and the literary analysis. Chapter 35 presents APA and CBE documentation for papers written in social and natural science courses—psychology, anthropology, political science, economics, sociology, biology, chemistry—and includes a section on writing an abstract. Chapter 36 briefly surveys the conventions for two kinds of business writing important to college writers: the résumé and the business letter.

32

How Do You Begin a Research Paper?

Only a few years ago, students doing research typically spent most of their time locating sources of information in traditional card catalogs, printed indexes, and bibliographies. Using these tools, a novice researcher could sometimes have a chore in turning up a dozen leads, and the most current of these sources might be a year old. Today with computerized library catalogs, electronic indexes, databases and CD-ROM networks, and on-line information services more widely available, a writer can identify dozens—even hundreds—of potential sources with only a few keystrokes. Indexes that formerly supplied only title, date, and page now may provide complete articles on screen, ready for downloading to your computer. And new technologies for finding and sharing information appear almost daily—so fast that no book like this can keep up with them. Research at the college level isn't what it used to be.

What are the consequences for you? They are mostly positive. If you are a student at a college with reasonably up-to-date facilities (or if you have a computer, a modem, and access to information services on your own), you can locate more information faster today than even the most skilled and dedicated researchers could a decade ago. That information will be current, accessible, and available in a variety of formats, from traditional books and articles to hypertextual, multimedia presentations. You may even be able to join on-line discussion groups and Listservs, putting your thoughts on the information highway, collaborating on projects not only with people from your own class and campus but with researchers from across the country and around the world. The new technology makes it more obvious than ever that doing research is a dynamic process that doesn't always follow the sturdy design or predictable steps of a traditional research paper.

The downside to all this new technology is that you may be overwhelmed by the sheer variety of research options available and by the number of leads your searches generate. Many people find on-line library catalogs and computerized indexes so intimidating that they shy away from them entirely. Or they try to cling to a single technology that they've managed to master, even after it becomes obsolete. Such fears are natural, and you shouldn't be embarrassed if you find yourself overwhelmed at first by electronic technology. Many people are.

Nor should you be frustrated when the technologies don't work exactly as promised. Just logging onto crowded networks can be frustrating at peak hours of usage. Then you may have to follow directions closely at first to navigate new research tools (see Section 32c). But in most cases you'll find that electronic technologies make it possible to do things with information that were simply impossible when libraries and scholars relied solely on cards and paper. Your efforts to master computer terminals, CD-ROMs, Internet search engines, and other devices will pay off handsomely, and your world will grow larger and more interesting.

True, you can be buried under all this information. For example, your subject search using an electronic index may turn up hundreds of articles on a topic published in just the last five years. What do you do then? More than ever, you need ways of defining your research topics, narrowing your options, and assessing the nature and quality of your sources. Obviously, you can afford to choose just the best authorities when you have so many choices—but you also need to know how to identify those sources. We'll offer some suggestions in Section 32d.

Because so many new electronic sources function like ongoing conversations among numerous participants, you'll also need to think more about who owns information, how information is shared, how reliable information is, and how borrowings from these new kinds of resources can be acknowledged in papers you write. We suspect that before too many years, college research papers will look very different from the sample papers in this edition. They may be cooperative efforts by students on different campuses in different states working on common problems, their conversations connected in hypertextual documents, their ideas illustrated with animation or sounds imported from yet other collections, their product emended constantly by updated information from scholars listening in around the world. A few students are working this way already.

For now, though, the traditional research papers still required in

32
resrch

many college courses merit your respect and attention: whatever technologies you use to gather and assemble information, you still need to know where to look for information, how to focus your research, how to interpret that information responsibly, how to write it up, how to document it, and how to present it in suitable form. We can't anticipate all the kinds of work you'll do in college, but we can suggest some general (and reliable) methods for doing research. That's what this and subsequent chapters are about. Adapt what we recommend here to your assignments and your interests. Above all, don't allow our advice—particularly about sources and research techniques—to restrict your creativity. After all, the point of research is not to limit horizons, but to expand them.

32a HOW DO YOU SELECT A TOPIC?

Troubleshooting

For many writers, the most difficult part of doing a research paper can be choosing a subject. Yet the importance of a good topic can be overestimated: in and of themselves, topics aren't simply good or bad. What makes the difference is treatment—that is, how well you shape any topic idea to your assignment, your readers, and your abilities. Finding a good subject for research is not a matter of chance or luck. It involves, instead, deciding what you want to achieve and then carving out a path to that goal.

32a
resrch

A first step is determining the nature of the research you are doing. Many kinds of research are required in college, some explanatory, some exploratory. Research tends to be *explanatory* when it focuses on facts which a writer needs to report clearly. You rely on explanatory materials every day: the newspaper, the encyclopedia, the directions in a computer manual, the brochure describing something you intend to buy. Whenever you consult such information, you are counting on someone else having done a professional job of research. Your obligation with explanatory assignments is to do the same—and it is a responsibility to be taken as an intellectual challenge.

Other types of research are more clearly exploratory; such writing and research is idea centered and speculative, reflecting upon concepts and experiences. Exploratory work goes beyond the material facts (*who? what? where? when?*) to examine abstract and puzzling questions (*how? why?*). It creates or discovers new knowledge. But such inquiry differs enormously from field to field. Exploration can involve performing a controlled scientific experiment, or theorizing about the nature of human behavior, or examining the social implications of a literary work. Any time you bring data, information, and sources into creative *conversation*, you are performing a type of exploratory research.

A second step in identifying a subject is determining what is manageable. Assigned, for example, to write a 1,500-word essay on a subject in contemporary history, you may be so worried about meeting the required length that you gravitate toward subjects as massive as the Holocaust, the U.S. space program, the American auto industry, or modern literary discoveries. But topics like these have hundreds of aspects that can be explored in thousands of ways. You need to narrow your focus to something suitable to a 1,500-word attempt.

To narrow a subject, you may want to look for an angle or a hook—an idea that grabs and holds an audience. The point seems elementary: a research paper should convey information that surprises readers. Finding an angle on a subject can transform a research paper from an *assignment* to what it should be—an *investigation* interesting for both the writer and the reader. Your initially vague interest in the space program might become a more focused *explanatory* study of the *Voyager* mission to Neptune, leading to a report on the bizarre terrain of Neptune's moon Triton. Or speculation about the deeper implications of space exploration may initiate an *exploratory* paper that attempts to defend the expenditure of billions of tax dollars on interplanetary adventures.

Put simply, when you have the opportunity to choose the subject of your research paper, follow your inclinations, interests, and instincts. You will write a better paper if you have a stake in it.

32a
resrch

To select a topic for a research paper . . .

32a–1 **Size up the assignment carefully.** Be sure you understand what you are being told to do. Pay attention to key words in the assignment. Are you being asked to analyze, examine, classify, define, discuss, evaluate, explain, compare, contrast, prove, disprove, persuade? Each of these words means something different. Each suggests how to approach your subject and how to organize it.

SUMMARY

Key Terms in a Research Assignment

- **Analyze. Examine.** Break your subject into its parts or components. Discuss their relationship or function.
- **Classify. Define.** Place your subject into larger categories. Distinguish it from other objects in those categories. What are its significant features? What is unique? Recognizable?
- **Discuss.** Talk about the problems or issues your subject raises.

Which issues are the most significant? What actions might be taken? Look at the subject from several points of view.

- **Evaluate.** Think about the subject critically. What criteria would you use to judge it? How well does it meet those standards? How does it compare to other similar subjects?
- **Explain.** Show what your subject does or how it operates. Provide background information on it. Put your subject in its context so that readers will understand it better.
- **Compare.** Show how your subject resembles other things or ideas.
- **Contrast.** Show how your subject differs from other things or ideas.
- **Prove.** Provide evidence in support of an idea or assertion.
- **Disprove.** Provide evidence to contradict or undermine an idea or assertion.
- **Persuade.** Come to a conclusion about your subject and explain why you believe what you do. Use evidence to persuade others to agree. Or provide good reasons for someone to think or act in a particular way.

Once you know what your assignment requires, appraise the length of the paper you are expected to produce. Be realistic about how much you can accomplish in five typed pages (roughly 1,200 words), eight typed pages (2,000 words), ten pages (2,500 words), and so on. Your worry shouldn't be finding enough to write, but determining what you can cover within a given length. In general, the shorter the assignment, the narrower the scope of the essay. But even longer papers—say, twenty pages—require well-focused subjects.

32a
resrch

32a–2 **Explore several topic areas for your paper.** Like signs in grocery store aisles, topic areas direct you to plausible locations, but leave you with plenty of searching to do. Here are some examples of broad topic areas.

affirmative action	the Holocaust
the U.S. auto industry	sexual harassment
the federal deficit	science fiction
rain forest destruction	political correctness
the aging U.S. population	computer viruses
African-American poetry	artificial intelligence
the alternative media	the information superhighway

You can begin with such topic areas when no specific subject is assigned. Select areas that intrigue you—not topics you vaguely suspect your teacher prefers. Treat yourself to an idea you will enjoy exploring for several weeks.

Not all subjects will work equally well. Avoid stale topics—don't be one of a half a dozen students submitting essays on gun control, capital punishment, or legalization of marijuana. Be careful too with topics drawn from today's newspapers or magazines (unless you are specifically directed to explore recent events or controversies). Such subjects may be fresh and exciting, but you'll exhaust your research leads quickly if you rely only on current magazines, newspapers, and electronic news groups. Finally, don't try to resuscitate an old paper—something you wrote in high school or in a previous college class. Your previous paper may have had a different purpose and audience. Don't adapt a paper written for another class unless you are so eager to know more about its subject that you will, in effect, produce a new essay.

32a-3 **Read in that topic area.** Select the topic area you find most promising and do some selective background reading.

CHECKLIST

Your Background Reading Should . . .

- Confirm whether you are, in fact, interested in your topic.
- Survey the main points of your subject so you can begin narrowing it.
- Determine whether the resources of your library or community will support the topic you want to explore in the time available.

Background reading will also help you decide whether to approach your paper from an explanatory or exploratory perspective. Will your paper on the U.S. automobile industry provide an explanatory comparison of the differences in design philosophy between General Motors and the Ford Motor Company—an interesting subject that you could explore by gathering data, reading interviews, and surveying some historical accounts of the companies? Or do you wonder what role the U.S. auto companies play in shaping American popular culture—a more ambiguous and open-ended exploratory subject that might lead you to explore topics as different as music, architecture, city planning, and color palettes? Your preliminary reading will help you decide.

The most efficient sources for *preliminary* reading are encyclopedias, beginning with any that deal specifically with your subject. The more specialized the encyclopedia, the more authoritative its coverage of a subject area is likely to be. If you check the reference room of your library, you will find specialized encyclopedias covering all the major disciplines and majors. Here are just a few.

CHECKLIST

Specialized Encyclopedias

DOING A PAPER ON . . . ?   **BEGIN BY CHECKING . . .**

American history	*Encyclopedia of American History*
Anthropology, economics, sociology	*International Encyclopedia of the Social Sciences*
Art	*Encyclopedia of World Art*
Astronomy	*Encyclopedia of Astronomy*
Communication, mass media	*International Encyclopedia of Communication*
Computers	*Encyclopedia of Computer Science*
Crime	*Encyclopedia of Crime and Justice*
Economics	*Encyclopedia of American Economic History*
Ethical issues in life sciences	*Encyclopedia of Bioethics*
Film	*International Encyclopedia of Film*
Health/medicine	*Health and Medical Horizons*
History	*Dictionary of American History; Guide to Historical Literature*
Law	*The Guide to American Law*
Literature	*Cassell's Encyclopedia of World Literature*
Music	*The New Grove Dictionary of American Music*
Philosophy	*Dictionary of the History of Ideas; Encyclopedia of Philosophy*
Political science	*Encyclopedia of American Political History*
Psychology, psychiatry	*International Encyclopedia of Psychiatry, Psychology, Psychoanalysis and Neurology; Encyclopedia of Psychology*
Religion	*The Encyclopedia of Religion; Encyclopedia Judaica; New Catholic Encyclopedia*
Science	*McGraw-Hill Encyclopedia of Science and Technology*
Social sciences	*International Encyclopedia of the Social Sciences*
Sociology	*Encyclopedia of Sociology*

32a
resrch

If no such specialized encyclopedia is available or if the specialized volume proves too technical for your level of knowledge, move to one of the more familiar general encyclopedias.

BOUND	**ELECTRONIC**
The Encyclopaedia Britannica	*Encarta*
Collier's Encyclopedia	*Grolier's*
Encyclopedia Americana	*Comptons*

Reading about the general topic should provide you with enough perspective to select a narrower subject. If you discover that a topic won't work, choose another and examine it the same way. When you've found an area worth exploring, start narrowing your topic.

32a–4 Explore what others are saying about your subject. You might do this right in the classroom, working with your colleagues in small writing groups or via an electronic network. Introduce your general topic to them and see what they have to offer; you may discover points of view you might never have considered. If you have access to on-line discussion groups via the Internet, search for a group exploring your subject and join the discussion there.

32a–5 Narrow the topic to a preliminary thesis or hypothesis. Find a question to answer. You can't stay with a general subject for too long without wasting time. Even a relatively focused general subject—say, recreational biking—would be too large to explore randomly. You need to identify a single aspect of the subject worth extended study. For example, an explanatory paper on the subject might describe the history of mountain biking as a sport in the United States. An exploratory essay might explore a specific controversy having to do with the bikes: Should mountain bikes be permitted on hiking trails in state and national parks? Narrowing the subject this way can make your search of card catalogs, tables of contents, indexes, and databases easier by focusing on just one aspect of a subject.

Any subject you choose at this stage is going to be preliminary: it will be shaped and reshaped by what you learn from your reading and research. What you may have initially is no more than a question or issue to guide your work.

> Why are mountain bikes banned in many parks?
> How were the Nazis able to conceal the Holocaust?
> What makes people abuse children?
> How do scientists explain acupuncture?

32a
resrch

How likely is Earth to be struck by an asteroid or comet?
How much will health-care reform really cost?

● **Tip**

Focusing your topic will make you more confident about writing a successful paper and save hours of research. It is an essential step for most writers. Don't go on to the next step—*finding sources*—until you have a tentative thesis or a question to answer. ●

32b WHERE DO YOU GO FOR INFORMATION?

Troubleshooting

Many would-be researchers simply ramble to library terminals these days, punch in the first subject that comes to mind, print out a list of items, and then go off to the stacks, hoping that the books or articles they've identified will get them started. This method seems easy at first, even natural. But, in the long run, it wastes time because it ignores quicker, more intelligent ways of finding information. What follows is a "no excuses" approach to finding sources, a method that is systematic, strategic, comprehensive, and repeatable: it produces results every time you use it.

As you begin a research paper or project, your goal is to prepare a working bibliography, a preliminary list of books, articles, magazine pieces, newspaper stories, interviews, book reviews, videotapes, Web sites, and so on, that are germane to your research topic. Library catalogs and electronic indexes now routinely allow you to print out any relevant sources you locate. You can use index cards to keep track of other sources (3-by-5-inch cards are ideal); cards are efficient because you can add, delete, alphabetize, and annotate your entries quickly.

**32b
info**

To find information on your subject . . .

32b–1 **Use the library catalog efficiently.** Begin researching your subject by examining the library's basic holdings in your subject area. Most libraries now give you access to their resources through computer terminals, although some facilities may still rely on card files to keep track of all or part of their collections. Since computerized catalogs are easy to update, they reflect the current state of a library collection—even indicating which books are checked out, lost, or recalled. It is important to spend a few minutes learning to use your library catalog—particularly its commands and search techniques. Some catalogs now permit searches of periodical indexes and encyclopedias, for example. Almost all catalogs allow you to search by author, title, subject, and keywords.

Here, for example, is the search menu screen for the library catalog at the University of Texas at Austin. Notice that the screen allows you to begin many different searches simply by typing an appropriate command. Note, too, the combinations of keyword searches that this system offers.

UTCAT -- SEARCH CHOICES MENU
===

BROWSE	Author	**a** hemingway ernest
SEARCHES	Title	**t** sun also rises
	Subject...........................	**s** mexican american authors
	Call number..................	**c** ps 153 m4 c48 1989
KEYWORD	Author Keyword............	**ak** appropriations committee
SEARCHES	Title Keyword	**tk** texas education
	Subject Keyword	**sk** computer security
	Mixed Keyword.............	**mk** hemingway sun rises
MORE SEARCH CHOICES........................		press ENTER
RESERVE	INstructor......................	**in** clarke, s
LISTS	COurse Number	**co** his 389

SERVICES RENew books, request items (EXP, ILS, DOX, PUR) ... **ser**
===
Type your search (example: tk texas education), then press ENTER,
OR for more examples, type only the search command, then press ENTER

-> _____
? = other commands   STOp = main menu

32b
info

Librarians find that most people search on-line catalogs by using *keyword* searches. Keywords are simply terms that name or identify your subject in some way; a keyword search identifies all the titles in a catalog containing the keyword(s) you have selected. For example, if you are exploring the ecological controversy over whether mountain bikes should be permitted on park trails, you might begin with these keyword searches.

bicycle
bike
mountain bike
trail bike
biking
trail biking

off-road biking
recreational biking

Any of these words might appear in the title of a potentially useful book or article (if the catalog you are using searches periodical indexes). Each search will probably generate a different number of items. In a sample search, for example, one library catalog listed 211 items for *bicycle*, 51 items for *bike*, and 7 items for *mountain bike*, but no items for the less familiar term *trail bike*. As you can see, the keywords you choose are important in determining the scope of your search. In this case, you might want to begin with the seven items specifically on mountain bikes and then expand your search if necessary to include the material on bicycles.

An on-line catalog will provide you with a great deal of information on any given book. You'll usually be presented first with a short entry—typically the author, title, publication information, and call number of a work—and then have the option to see a fuller entry. Here, for example, is the full entry for a book on mountain bikes in an on-line catalog.

UTCAT LIBRARY CATALOG -- FULL DISPLAY

===

AUTHOR:	Van der Plas, Rob, 1938-
TITLE:	The mountain bike book : choosing, riding, and maintaining the off-road bicycle / Rob van der Plas ; illustrated by the author.
EDITION:	2nd ed., 3rd printing rev. and updated.
PUBLISHED:	San Francisco, CA : Bicycle Books, 1989, c1988.
DESCRIPTION:	207 p. : ill. ; 23 cm.
NOTES:	Includes index.
BIBLIOGRAPHY:	p. (199)-200.
SUBJECTS:	Bicycles Cycling Mountains--Recreational use
ISBN:	0933201184 (pbk.)
OCLC NUMBER:	20157068

===

FOR CALL NUMBER / LOCATION / STATUS, PRESS ENTER TO RETURN TO BRIEF DISPLAY.

32b
info

As you can see, the full display provides you information useful in evaluating the source: the book is 207 pages long; it is illustrated; it is in a second edition. Notice in particular the subject listings.

Bicycles
Cycling
Mountains—Recreational use

Your original list of keywords didn't consider two of those terms. Now you can do a subject search with them and find even more items to review.

CHECKLIST

For a book, on-line catalogs usually list . . .

- The call number and library location
- The author, title, publisher, and date of publication
- The number of pages and its physical size
- Whether the source is illustrated
- Whether it contains a bibliography and index
- What subject headings it is cataloged under
- Whether the source is on the shelf, charged out, on order, or being held at the reserve desk

---

32b–2 **Locate suitable bibliographies.** You will save time if you can locate an existing bibliography—preferably an annotated one—on your subject. Bibliographies list books, articles, and other materials that deal with particular subjects or subject areas.

S U M M A R Y

Types of Bibliographies

- **Complete bibliographies** attempt to list all the major works in a given field or subject.
- **Selective bibliographies** usually list the best-known or most respected books in a subject area.
- **Annotated bibliographies** briefly describe the works they list and may evaluate them.
- **Annual bibliographies** catalog the works produced within a field or discipline in a given year.

An up-to-date bibliography on your subject will furnish you with a far more thorough list of sources, both books and articles, than a run through the library catalog alone can. To determine whether a bibliography has been compiled on your subject, first check the *Bibliography Index* in the reference room of your library. Chances are, however, that you won't find a bibliography precisely on your subject area; instead, you may have to use one of the more general bibliographies available for almost every field. The professor of your course or the reference librarian should be able to suggest an appropriate volume or computerized index. Only a few of the many bibliographies in specific disciplines are listed below.

CHECKLIST

Bibliographies

DOING A PAPER ON . . . ? CHECK THIS BIBLIOGRAPHY . . .

American history	*Bibliographies in American History*
Anthropology	*Anthropological Bibliographies: A Selected Guide*
Art	*Guide to the Literature of Art History*
Astronomy	*A Guide to the Literature of Astronomy; Astronomy and Astrophysics: A Bibliographic Guide*
Classics	*Greek and Roman Authors: A Checklist of Criticism*
Communications	*Communication: A Guide to Information Sources*
Engineering	*Science and Engineering Literature*
Literature	*MLA International Bibliography*
Mathematics	*Using the Mathematical Literature*
Music	*Music Reference and Research Materials*
Philosophy	*A Bibliography of Philosophical Bibliographies*
Physics	*Use of Physics Literature*
Psychology	*Harvard List of Books in Psychology*
Social work	*Social Work Education: A Bibliography*

**32b
info**

32b-3 **Locate suitable periodical indexes.** You shouldn't undertake any college-level research paper without searching the periodical literature on your topic.

Fortunately, you can track articles on a subject by using periodical indexes, some general and wide-ranging, others more specialized and sophisticated. For most college research projects you will need to use specialized indexes to find journals in your discipline. These indexes—which are usually located in the library's reference room—indicate which periodicals contain articles about a given subject during a given period of time. To use these powerful tools properly, you should read the front matter of printed indexes and the on-line help screens and handouts of computerized indexes. Check for the following general and multidisciplinary indexes in your library.

> *Academic Abstracts*
> *Academic Index*
> *Expanded Academic Index*

Magazine Index
Periodicals Abstracts
Readers' Guide to Periodical Literature

There are guides to periodical literature in every major academic field, most of them computerized. Because new indexes may be added to a library's collection at any time, check with your reference librarian about sources in any given subject area.

CHECKLIST

Computerized and Printed Indexes

DOING A PAPER ON . . . ?	CHECK THIS INDEX . . .
Anthropology	*Anthropological Literature: An Index to Periodical Articles and Essays*
Art	*Art Index*
Astronomy	*INSPEC*
Biography	*Biography Index*
Business	*Business Periodicals Index; ABI/INFORM: Business and Company Profile; Investext; Corporate Profile*
Computer science	*Computer Literature Index*
Contemporary events	*NewsBank*
Economics	*PAIS (Public Affairs Information Service)*
Education	*Education Index; ERIC*
Film	*Film Literature Index; Art Index*
General information	*Academic Abstracts; Magazine Index; Proquest*
Humanities	*Social Science & Humanities Index; Humanities Index; InfoTrac*
Literature	*Essay and General Literature Index; MLA Bibliography*
Mathematics	*MATHFILE*
Music	*Music Index*
Philosophy	*The Philosopher's Index*
Psychology	*Psychological Abstracts; Psyc Lit*
Public affairs	*PAIS (Public Affairs Information Service)*
Science	*General Science Index*
Social sciences	*Social Science & Humanities Index; Social Sciences Index; InfoTrac*
Technology	*Applied Science and Technology Index*

32b
info

Electronic indexes, like on-line catalogs, allow you to do many kinds of valuable searches, again by author, title, subject, and keywords. In some cases, the indexes will provide you not only with the titles of useful sources, but with the articles themselves. Here, for example, is an item listed on an on-line periodical index that can be called up on screen should the user require it.

> 18 Pedal power. (popularity of bicycling; includes related article on mountain biking). / Chisholm, Patricia / Maclean's : July 26 1993, v106, n30, p48 / 4 page(s)
> *** TEXT AVAILABLE ONLINE – TYPE 18 AND PRESS ENTER ***

To conduct a keyword search of electronic indexes, define your topic as clearly as possible. Focus your topic by combining keywords with *and*, allow for various synonyms by combining words with *or*, and disallow subjects or sources by prefacing words with *not* or *no*.

AND	video games AND gender
OR	juvenile OR youth
NOT	united states AND civil war NOT book review

The specific index you are using may require you to use one or more of these limiting terms, or permit *and* and *or* but not *not*.

32b-4 **Consult dictionaries of biography.** Quite often in preparing a research project, you'll need information about famous people, living and dead. There are dozens of sources to help you in the reference room. Good places to start are the *Biography Index: A Cumulative Index to Biographic Material in Books and Magazines, Bio-Base, Current Biography,* and *The McGraw-Hill Encyclopedia of World Biography.* There are also various *Who's Who* volumes, covering living British, American, and world notables. Deceased figures may appear in *Who Was Who.* Probably the two most famous dictionaries of biography are the *Dictionary of National Biography* (British) and the *Dictionary of American Biography.*

**32b
info**

CHECKLIST

Biographical Information

YOUR SUBJECT IS IN . . . ?   CHECK THIS SOURCE . . .

Art	*Index to Artistic Biography*
Education	*Biographical Dictionary of American Educators*
Music	*The New Grove Dictionary of Music and Musicians*

(continued)

Biographical Information (*continued*)

YOUR SUBJECT IS IN . . . ?   **CHECK THIS SOURCE . . .**

Politics   *Politics in America*
Psychology   *Biographical Dictionary of Psychology*
Religion   *Dictionary of American Religious Biography*
Science   *Dictionary of Scientific Biography*

YOUR SUBJECT IS . . . ?   **CHECK THIS SOURCE . . .**

African   *Dictionary of African Biography*
African American   *Dictionary of American Negro Biography*
Asian   *Encyclopedia of Asian History*
Australian   *Australian Dictionary of Biography*
Canadian   *Dictionary of Canadian Biography*
Female   *Index to Women; Notable American
                    Women*
Hispanic   *Chicano Scholars and Writers: A
                    Bibliographic Directory*

32b–5 **Check guides to reference books.** The reference room in most libraries is filled with helpful materials. But how do you know what the best books are for your needs? Ask your reference librarian if guides to the literature for your topic are available, or check the reference section using the call number area that you used to locate circulating books.

Also useful in some situations are printed or CD-ROM indexes that list all books currently available (that is, books that are in print), their publishers, and their prices. Updated frequently, such indexes include

Books in Print
Paperbound Books in Print

32b–6 **Locate statistics.** Your library has many volumes of statistics. Be sure to find up-to-date and reliable figures.

CHECKLIST

Statistics

TO FIND . . .   **CHECK THIS SOURCE . . .**

General statistics   *World Almanac*
Statistics about the   *Historical Statistics of the United States;*
   United States   *Statistical Abstract of the United States*

To find . . .	Check this source . . .
World information	*The Statesman's Yearbook; National Intelligence Factbook; UN Demographic Yearbook; UNESCO Statistical Yearbook*
Business facts	*Handbook of Basic Economic Statistics; Survey of Current Business; Dow Jones Irwin Business Almanac*
Public opinion polls	*Gallup Poll*

Additional electronic or computerized statistical sources may be available, so be sure to consult your reference librarian.

32b-7   Check news sources. Sometimes you'll need information from newspapers. If you know the date of a particular event, you can usually locate the information you want. If your subject isn't an event, you may have to trace it through an index. Only a few papers are fully indexed. The one newspaper you are most likely to encounter in most American libraries is *The New York Times*, usually available on microfilm. *The New York Times Index* provides chronological summaries of articles on a given subject. Since the printed version of the *Times* index takes several months to arrive in a library, you may need to use a computerized tool such as the *Academic Index* for more recent events. Many computerized periodical indexes keep several months of the *Times* on file. A second American paper with an index is *The Wall Street Journal*.

Another useful reference tool for current events—available since 1982 in computer format—is *NewsBank,* an index of more than 400 newspapers from across the country keyed to a microfiche collection. You can use *NewsBank* to locate a sampling of journalistic coverage and opinion on major issues and notable people. *Facts on File* summarizes national and international news weekly; *CQ Researcher* gives background information on major problems and controversies. To report on what editors are thinking, examine *Editorials on File,* a sampling of world and national opinion.

Be sure to check with your reference librarian about news sources. What is available, particularly on CD-ROM databases, is changing quickly. You may also wish to examine on-line news services such as ClariNet.

32b
info

32b-8   Check book reviews. To locate reviews of books, check out *Book Review Digest* (1905), *Book Review Index* (1965), or *Current Book Review Citations* (1976). *Book Review Digest* does not list as many reviews as the other two collections, but it summarizes those it does include—a useful feature. Reviews of current books are included in most electronic periodical indexes.

32b–9 **Consult experts.** Sometimes people are the best sources of up-to-date and authoritative information. If you can discuss your subject with an expert (without being a nuisance), you'll add credibility, authenticity, and immediacy to a research report. If you are writing a paper about an aspect of medical care, talk to a medical professional. If exploring the financial dilemmas of community theaters, try to interview a local producer or theater manager. If writing about problems in the building industry, find a builder or banker with thirty minutes to spare.

CHECKLIST

Conducting an Interview

- Write or telephone your subject for an appointment and make it clear why you want the interview.
- Be on time for your appointment.
- Be prepared: have a list of questions and possible follow-ups ready.
- Take careful notes, especially if you intend to quote your source.
- Double-check direct quotations, and be sure your source is willing to be cited "on the record."
- If you plan to tape the interview, get your subject's approval before turning the machine on.
- Promise to send the authority you interview a copy of your completed paper.
- Send a thank-you note to an expert who has been especially helpful.

32b–10 **Write to professional organizations.** Almost every subject, cause, concept, or idea is represented by a professional organization, society, bureau, office, or lobby. If you have time (you'll need lots of it), write to an appropriate organization for information on your topic; ask for pamphlets, leaflets, reports, and so on. The *Encyclopedia of Associations*, published by Gale Research, can be your source for addresses. Also remember that the U.S. government publishes huge amounts of information on just about every subject of public interest. Check the *Index to U.S. Government Periodicals* or the *Monthly Catalog of United States Government Publications* for listings.

32b–11 **Check on-line sources.** A great deal of information will be available to you if you have access to the Internet, World Wide Web, or other electronic services. Such information may sometimes be the most current and lively information you can gather on a subject. You can also use these electronic networks to work collaboratively on projects, to participate in discussions, and to get and give feedback on ideas. For more information on navigating such sources, see Section 32c.

32c HOW DO YOU NAVIGATE ELECTRONIC SOURCES?

Troubleshooting

Electronic research tools serve a full range of expertise levels, from the world-class expert to the computer novice writing a letter to the editor. But both expert and novice must make basic decisions about how to use these tools. One key decision is what format is appropriate for the work they are doing. Some electronic tools are based on well-established printed titles. Others are unique tools that have never existed in print.

Researchers need to know how to use both types of tools appropriately, understanding their strengths and limitations. You also need to be a little adventurous. It's easy to be intimidated by the complexity of some computer tools and frustrated by the various irritations that plague electronic searches—difficulty logging on, systems going down, machines that lack adequate memory to handle information overloads. The fact is, however, that a researcher on a computer can accomplish in a few minutes what it used to take a print-bound colleague days—if he or she could do it at all. Be grateful!

**32c
on-line**

To use electronic sources effectively . . .

32c–1 **Decide whether an electronic source will serve you better than a printed one.** Much research information available on the computer—especially periodical indexes—has been adapted from more traditional printed formats. For example, an on-line catalog may replace a card catalog, the familiar *Readers' Guide to Periodical Literature* may be on a CD-ROM as well as in a printed volume, or the same *Time* magazine article may scroll across a computer screen and appear on the corner newsstand. Be careful to document electronic versions of printed material accurately. If you print out an article that originally appeared in a magazine, for example, page numbers may not match the original or may be missing altogether.

Still, there are some real advantages to choosing electronic sources over their printed counterparts. In an on-line catalog or periodical index, for example, you are not limited to one or two or three ways of searching your subject, such as by author, title, or subject. Such print-oriented searches require that you know some specific fact before you begin your inquiry—whether it's the name of an author, the title of a book, or a specific subject descriptor assigned to the work by an indexer. In electronic formats, you have many other choices and more inventive ways of approaching data.

For example, a keyword search is a common electronic option that allows you to select a variety of words to describe your subject, not just ones chosen by the person who created the research tool. You can direct the computer to explore different combinations of terms until you find the material you want—or until you discover a subject heading you may not have anticipated (see Section 32b–1). Such searching can be addictive once you've mastered the simple commands that control most catalogs and indexes. And one thing is certain: more and more electronic search options will be available in the near future.

A totally different kind of exploration is possible with the on-line resources you find on the Internet or the World Wide Web (WWW), many of which have no print equivalents. The Internet is an expanding worldwide network of more than 3.5 million computers and supercomputers that share information in a variety of ways. Some of the information on the Net is fairly traditional: news stories, press releases, books, articles, research reports, and software. But the Internet also supports electronic conversations on a global bulletin board called *Usenet;* more restricted conversations called *Listservs;* virtual reality environments of all sorts (some quite serious and academic) with acronyms such as *Mud, Mush,* and *Moo;* and, of course, *e-mail.*

32c
on-line

The World Wide Web is a hypertextual pathway into the Internet that presents information via "pages" that can contain text, graphics, and sound (see the WWW page in the document design, p. 97). Because of its format, the Web can share just about any information that fits onto a screen, including photo archives, artwork, maps, movie clips, charts, and magazines. Even better, Web users can move through different "sites" by clicking on words or graphics that link to other related resources.

If keyword searches of electronic indexes and databases encourage you to explore topics systematically, Internet and Web investigations may send you down unique and unpredictable research paths, one site on the Net leading to a dozen other links, and then to a dozen more.

However, some tools have been developed for exploring the Internet and the Web systematically—or at least as systematically as is possible in a rapidly changing and expanding environment. Of course, you can always ask librarians or computer-savvy friends to suggest Internet sources or Web sites appropriate to your research interests. But you can gain access to this information on your own by learning a few basic tools.

One Internet search tool is called *Gopher*. Developed at the University of Minnesota, Gopher presents menus of items you can open more and more deeply until you find a particular Internet resource or site suited to your work. Gopher can direct you to databases worldwide, nationally, or locally and permits you to do various searches of these resources by using one of its several search engines: *Veronica*, *Jughead*, *Archie*, and *WAIS*. *Veronica* acts as a catalog and index for Gopher when you need to search by keywords. *Veronica* will try to locate the keyword you specify in the titles of items in Gopher menus around the world (some fifteen to twenty million items), listing all the matches it finds. *Jughead* operates like *Veronica*, but searches only local Gopher menus. *Archie* is different in that it searches Internet sites either for files or for software you wish to download to your computer. Millions of these file locations (called FTP sites) can be searched by *Archie*, giving access to books, journals, photographs, artwork, hypercard stacks, sound files, and more. *WAIS* (*Wide Area Information Server*) enables you to search for particular words *within* specific files accessed through Gopher. Thus *WAIS* works like an index. For example, course catalogs at the University of Texas at Austin can be searched using *WAIS*. To find out what courses a professor is teaching, all you have to do is type his or her name into a *WAIS* catalog search. The student newspaper is similarly searchable via *WAIS*.

Fortunately, Gopher sites themselves include rather detailed explanations and advice for using the search engines, so don't be intimidated. Just look for items titled "About *WAIS*" or "About *Veronica*" and click for more information.

The World Wide Web has its search engines too. A favorite is *Yahoo*, which provides a hierarchically arranged outline of important Web sites. When you move to the Yahoo page on the Web, you'll first see a list of general topics. Click on any of these and subtopics appear. You then select the subtopic you wish to follow and keep narrowing the search until you locate the Web sites you want to use. For example, if you were researching a paper on mountain biking, you would follow a path like this one.

**32c
on-line**

Entertainment
   → *Sports*
      → *Cycling*
        → *Mountain Biking*

Under Mountain Biking, you'd find a dozen or so links to Web pages about the specific subject, including sites from cycle clubs in the United Kingdom and New Zealand.

A similar Web search engine is *EINet Galaxy*. Like Yahoo, Galaxy presents a hierarchical list of search categories, beginning with such general categories as Arts and Humanities, Business and Commerce, Community, and Engineering and Technology. Like Yahoo, Galaxy also allows you to do a keyword search of the Web (limiting that search in various ways) and to suggest modifications of the research tool itself, identifying new sites or correcting any problems you discover. Both Yahoo and Galaxy are frequently modified; you should look for new WWW research tools, too, as they are developed.

Fortunately, the software tools you'll use for browsing the Web (*Mosaic, Netscape*) also permit you to keep track of Web sites you've visited by marking them with "bookmarks." Use this feature when you do research because you may have to document Web pages as sources. Web sites and addresses change too frequently to list definitively, but you might ask your librarian or computer specialists how to find these valuable or interesting tools or sites.

- *Yahoo*—a search engine for WWW
- *EINet Galaxy*—a search engine for WWW
- *Thomas: Legislative Information on the Internet*—access to congressional information and the Library of Congress
- *The Electronic Text Center at the University of Virginia*—access to a wide variety of literary works
- *American Universities*—access to the Web sites of American colleges and universities
- *The Central Intelligence Agency Home Page*—access to the *World Factbook*, a useful compendium of information
- *The Progressive Directory*—political information from the political left
- *The Right Side of the Web*—political information from the political right

**32c
on-line**

32c–2 **Evaluate your electronic search.** In electronic formats like *Proquest* or *Lexis/Nexis*, you can retrieve results quickly and determine whether (or how) new material illuminates your chosen subject: Did you get the results you expected, or something quite different? But don't be satisfied with your initial searches, even when they supply ample information. Another combination of keywords or a different search path might provide still better material. Because computer searches can furnish lists of potential sources quickly, it's tempting for a novice to terminate exploration too soon.

Each time you search and get an unexpected response, ask why. Ideas may be hidden under synonyms of the word you searched. If the first try doesn't work, look for clues in the results you receive (or don't receive). Check spellings and try synonyms.

Be sure to evaluate the materials you do find, especially when searching on-line catalogs and periodical indexes (see Section 32d). What words worked best? Are there other combinations to try? What kinds of sources are you finding? Each time you refine your vocabulary and think about the results, you learn more about your topic—how it is described in publications, what aspects of your topic are discussed most often, what's available in a particular set of resources. Be aware of this additional information and consider ways to use it.

One caution: Don't assume all computer services are alike just because they look alike. Read the descriptions of each service to find out what it is and how to use it. Expect similar patterns, but be aware of variations too.

CHECKLIST

Evaluating an Electronic Search

- **Know which database you are logged onto.** One computer may have several different databases or indexes. Make sure that you are searching the appropriate database for your subject.

- **Read the description of the service to find out how to access information.** Each database may have a slightly different structure.

- **Check to see if a list of subject headings is available.** If a list of subject headings or a thesaurus is available, you can check your search terms against the list and revise them before you start your search, thus saving valuable time.

- **Find synonyms for search terms.** If your subject or keyword search is not leading you to the information you need, try using synonyms for your terms.

- **When using keywords, use AND to limit your search and OR to search for synonyms.** You can avoid spending hours scrolling through hundreds of entries by properly limiting your search.

- **Check spellings.** A spelling error in a search term can prevent you from finding information.

**32c
on-line**

32c–3 **Explore various electronic indexes.** Don't think you have exhausted the possibilities when you've examined one electronic index or searched just your library's on-line catalog. Different sources provide different kinds of electronic information. What differences, for example, do you find when you use an on-line index to popular periodicals and one that focuses on sociological issues or legal aspects? Many of these resources feature abstracts or even the full text of the items indexed.

Trace the people too. Because scholarly work is peer reviewed, experts create and codify knowledge by working together in an orderly system to arrive at a consensus. Naturally, these scholars and researchers are identified with their ideas, and you can track issues by tracing the names often linked to them.

But don't assume that quantity of information outweighs quality. *More* information does not automatically produce *better* arguments or *better* papers. It is valuable only when it adds evidence to your arguments and meaning to your analysis.

32c–4 **Enter electronic conversations.** Some on-line resources have no print antecedents and have a different connection to the research and publication cycle: they represent *work in progress*. These are the resources that you will find on the Internet's Usenet newsgroups and Listserv discussion groups. On the Internet, you can sometimes watch or participate in conversations between researchers occurring *before they publish* their findings in journals and magazines.

Usenet and Listserv resources can be tricky to use, but they may provide you with up-to-the-second information, multiple points of view on a topic, and the opportunity to question people actively doing the research or living the experience you are writing about. These electronic dialogues may introduce you to experts on your subject from all over the world.

32c on-line

In writing a paper, treat Internet resources as the close-up view of a bigger picture. Whenever you notice gaps in your thinking derived from Internet material, or when your critics point out aspects of your argument you've overlooked, go back to more traditional resources that provide overviews or summaries. The background you find in textbooks, encyclopedias, and other comprehensive sources should bring the big picture back into focus.

Internet sources (and other on-line presentations like them) require that you pay attention, because they have not passed through the stages that an article in a serious journal would before being printed. On-line information hasn't been selected for publication in a magazine with a limited number of pages, checked for accuracy (or grammar or spelling, for that matter), edited, polished, and presented in an authoritative setting. Anyone can join the conversation: schoolchildren publish their essays on some of these electronic sources, and college students sometimes post their term papers—even the ones that got *D*'s. Also, ask your instructor whether you may cite electronic conversations in your research paper; some instructors will permit you to cite only electronic information that has been published in print form.

The Internet is too extensive to ignore, but still too volatile to chart. Without question, e-mail and Internet discussion groups have had a powerful impact on contemporary conversations in the academy, in the military, in government, and elsewhere. Every topic seems more immediate on the Internet, more crucial, more relevant. But are these conversations really so different from ideas you might encounter in carefully edited journal or magazine articles or at a campus roundtable? You are the one who must decide.

CHECKLIST

Internet Resources

There are different layers to Internet resources, but here are some that can enliven and enhance your thinking and writing.

GOPHER

A client/server program that uses menus in a hierarchical fashion. A top menu can be divided into submenus, those submenus into sub-submenus, and so forth.

Major characteristics: Allows users to move forward and backward quickly through a large amount of textual information.

Use for: Structured navigation through Internet resources. The menus help you develop a mental map of the Internet. May provide subject access to electronic journals, documents, and indexes.

Searching: Keyword searches are supported when appropriate. A *bookmark* feature enables you to keep a record of key addresses and to facilitate subsequent searches.

WORLD WIDE WEB (WWW)

A type of client/server program (examples are *Mosaic, Netscape, Cello, Lynx*) that supports hypertext. Users may effortlessly follow connections or "links" from document to document by simply clicking or choosing the connection.

Major characteristics: Weaves together Internet functions to form a smooth work surface for users, who can concentrate on subject matter instead of computer commands. Formats can be images, sounds, video, or text.

Use for: Easiest interface with information in cyberspace.

Searching: A variety of search methods are available now and others are being developed. Results will vary, so try different search starting points, or search engines. Save locations of sources to a *hot list* so you can return to them later. *(continued)*

**32c
on-line**

Internet Resources *(continued)*

LISTSERV

A type of mail program that maintains lists of subscribers interested in discussing a specific topic. Users must subscribe in order to read or post messages.

Major characteristics: Lists are run on large computers; subscribers tend to be active experts working in fields related to the list topic. Lists are often moderated, thereby screening out nonrelevant material or 'noise.' Old text may be archived.

Use for: Excellent window on current issues. Good for listening in on the practitioners' conversations, discovering opinions, noting solutions to common problems.

Searching: When you subscribe, check the welcome message for instructions for searching the archives.

USENET NEWS GROUPS

Interest groups publicly accessible in a conference format.

Major characteristics: Thousands of groups focus on topics ranging from A to Z. Wide variation in expertise of contributors. Anyone may read or post messages. Just browsing the list of Usenet groups can suggest topic ideas.

Use for: Conversations about popular topics and about little-known, obscure subjects. Almost every political group, social interest, religion, activity, hobby, and fantasy has a Usenet group.

Searching: Check the welcome messages and the FAQs (frequently asked questions) for information on how to search. Many lists have archives of older discussions.

**32d
sources**

32d HOW DO YOU SELECT REPUTABLE SOURCES?

Troubleshooting

Writers have always had to be selective about their sources of information to be sure that they were relying on accurate, comprehensive, and up-to-date data. But thanks to electronic search techniques of library catalogs and periodical indexes, it is possible to generate more potential sources than most researchers have time to review. When you find yourself with such an embarrassment of riches, you should first try to narrow the scope of your search (see Section 32a–5). Don't, for instance, use *television* in a keyword search; use *television* and *children*, or better yet *television* and *children* and *violence*.

Even after you've narrowed your search, you may still find yourself with a list of fifty books and a hundred periodical citations. What do you do then? As always, consider your audience and purpose first, and then carefully examine the items you have turned up. You probably know more about your sources than you realize, even at this preliminary stage. And don't forget to ask for advice.

To determine what sources to examine . . .

32d–1 **Consider titles.** You can of course eliminate many books and articles from your preliminary bibliography just by scanning titles. But don't jump to conclusions, especially about citations from popular magazines. Would you guess that a piece in *Rolling Stone* titled "Birth of the Gearhead Nation" was about conflicts between mountain bikers and environmentalists? Probably not. However, you might draw exactly such a conclusion about a piece titled "Trouble on the Mountain" appearing in *Bicycling.* Sometimes you have to read titles in context, being sensitive to allusions and popular idioms.

32d–2 **Look for an abstract or summary.** Many on-line catalogs and electronic indexes allow you to get more information about the items they list; often you need to do nothing more than punch an additional key. Even a brief abstract or summary may tell you, for example, whether an article with the title "The New MBA: Is It Finally in the Driver's Seat?" contains the specific information you need about environmental issues and trail riding.

If you cannot locate the actual article summarized in an abstract, some instructors will allow you to cite the abstract itself in your paper. Be precise so your readers will be able to find your source—for example, "Abstract from Info-Search."

32d–3 **Consider the intended audience of the source.** Obviously, books and periodicals written by experts for experts on a given subject will differ from those written by general writers for casual readers. In researching a subject, the best book or article for you is likely to be one just a step or two above your current level of knowledge—you want to push yourself to learn more without exceeding your depth.

With books, you can sometimes be guided by the identity of a publisher. A work published by a university press (Harvard UP; Oxford UP) is likely to be more technical and scholarly than one published by a commercial publisher (Random House; Little, Brown). That doesn't mean that a university press book will be a better source than a trade

32d
sources

publisher's book. Look at these two types of books as offering different kinds of sources and serving different audiences. In many cases, a university press book will be more carefully documented than a comparable trade book. But at the start of a project, you may prefer a book from a reputable popular publisher because it may be closer to your level of expertise.

Books and periodicals are sometimes divided into roughly three categories, from the most technical to the least.

- *Scholarly journals and books.* These are written for serious readers assumed to already possess technical expertise in a field. They will make claims intended to advance what is known in a discipline, and those claims will be carefully and fully documented. You may find these materials highly technical and difficult to read, yet as you learn more about a subject, such sources will become essential. Scholarly journals have titles such as *Journal of Counseling Psychology, Memory and Cognition, Critical Inquiry.*

- *Serious periodicals and books.* These are written for well-educated but nonexpert readers, people who wish to acquire more than general knowledge about a subject. Serious periodicals and books will often report information derived from scholarly works and explore its implications. Claims will be made carefully with evidence specified, but such books and essays may not be fully documented. Serious works may require careful reading, but they try to avoid the technical language of scholarly pieces and may often be stylish and personal. Works in this category are excellent sources for much college writing, particularly for papers written outside your own field of expertise. Serious periodicals include *Scientific American, New York Review of Books, The New Republic, National Review, New Yorker, Atlantic,* and *Humanist.*

- *Popular magazines and books.* Works of this kind do not assume that readers know a great deal about the subjects of their articles. As a result, such works tend to be less demanding and somewhat shorter than serious or scholarly materials. Quite often, popular books and magazines base their claims on other, more technical sources, but these sources may not be specifically named. Sometimes, however, popular magazines are designed expressly for people with narrow and specific interests, everything from skiing Colorado to repairing old furniture. In these areas, they may claim a kind of expertise unavailable in other sources. Popular sources may also report events, trends, and political currents more quickly than other materials. So you can base a college paper on popular sources when your subject is derived from current events or popular culture. Some familiar

32d
sources

popular magazines include *Time, Psychology Today, Natural History*, and *Smithsonian*.

Be aware that these categories are not hard and fast, nor are they judgments on the quality of a source. You have to find the item best suited to your subject. But you also need to know that there are important differences among the sources you are liable to face on a printout from a catalog or periodical index. Choose wisely.

32d-4 **Consider the thoroughness of the source.** Scholarly sources are likely to be far more thorough in reporting their facts and information than popular sources. Yet it is also possible to be overwhelmed by sources if you are new to the material. So you may want to start with less intimidating materials. Once again, check your bibliography entries. Both online catalogs and periodical indexes may tell you how long a source is.

32d-5 **Consider the credentials of the author.** This advice might not seem too useful at first when you are exploring a new subject. But you'll quickly pick up names as you read about any subject—people mentioned frequently as experts or authorities. (You may even hear your instructors mention writers who deal with your topic.) When scanning a lengthy printout of potential sources, look for these familiar names. But don't be drawn in by fame alone—particularly when the names of famous persons are attached to subjects about which they may have no special expertise.

32d-6 **Consider the biases of the source.** You'll especially need to consider political, social, and religious leanings when you are dealing with controversial subjects. In deciding which items on a lengthy list to read, it may help to select opinions from across the spectrum. Otherwise you may write a whole paper unaware that some important perspectives are being ignored.

It is important to realize that almost all published sources have biases and points of view that shape the information they contain (and determine what they exclude). Sometimes those biases will be readily apparent. You do not have to read much to realize, for example, that the editorial page of *The New York Times* tends to be liberal in its politics and that of *The Wall Street Journal* conservative. It may be harder to detect similar biases in scholarly journals or popular magazines, but be assured that they are there. If you are in doubt about the representativeness of the sources you have selected, consult with instructors or librarians—aware that they, too, have points of view and may try to influence your selection.

Consider too that, even granting the biases of sources, there are degrees of objectivity and subjectivity in sources that will affect your credibility with readers. For example, the newsletters of the Democratic or Republican parties are likely to be less objective in their political judgments and materials than even partisan sources such as *The New Republic* and *National Review*, which in turn are likely to be less objective in their political reporting than *Time* or *Newsweek*. That doesn't mean that *Time* and *Newsweek* are always fairer or more accurate sources than other journals. Far from it. But a general audience is likely to perceive them as less partisan—and that perception may be important to you as a writer. As you see, choosing a balanced selection of sources can be tricky.

32d–7   **Consider the timeliness of the source.** For many subjects, you'll want sources as up-to-date as possible, and new electronic search tools make it easy to find those current pieces. You can scan the dates of your sources, looking for the most recent information in the best sources. But sometimes you'll also want older pieces that may give you perspective on a subject—showing, for instance, how opinions have changed over time on an issue. In such cases, you'll want your reading to cover a range of dates. Remember that *primary* sources record events at the time they occur; *secondary* sources comment on those same events from a distance, analyzing and commenting on them. An effective paper may require both primary and secondary sources.

32d–8   **Consider the features of the source.** Take advantage of any information that an on-line library catalog or periodical index gives you. For example, sources with indexes and bibliographies are likely to prove more useful than those without. For some subjects, you'll want sources with illustrations and graphs; for others, an illustrated article may be one you'll want to avoid as juvenile.

32d–9   **Follow a chain of references.** Quite often papers evolve from one or two articles that grab a researcher's interest. When you have found a credible and authoritative source, mine it for all the possible references it may contain. You've struck gold if the essay concludes with a bibliography or notes. Follow up on the sources your author used. Sometimes the sources may be imbedded in the article itself in names or allusions to particular institutions or subjects. Use the on-line catalog or periodical indexes to search these references for additional subjects. Be creative. Treat each source as a potential link to other useful materials.

32d–10   **Consult librarians and instructors.** Remember that these people are resources too. They often have the expertise to cut right through a lengthy list of sources to suggest the three or four you should not miss. Those leads are often enough to give you the knowledge to make subsequent judgments on your own.

32d
sources

HIGHLIGHT

Primary and Secondary Sources

Do you recall the difference between *primary* and *secondary* sources? *Primary sources* are the materials on a topic upon which subsequent interpretations or studies are based, anything from firsthand documents such as poems, diaries, court records, and interviews to research results generated by experiments, surveys, ethnographies, and so on. When using a primary source in a research paper, you look at the subject in its raw shape, before others have commented on it or influenced you. Materials that provide interpretation and commentary are called *secondary sources*. Such works would include most encyclopedias and reference volumes, as well as books and articles that expand upon primary records. In the humanities, a novel would be a primary source and the book interpreting it a secondary source. In the sciences, an article reporting the results of original experiments on IQ might be a primary source, while a book using that information to draw conclusions about college entrance policies would be a secondary source. Research papers should draw upon primary materials as much as possible, looking either at raw data or the results of original research. However, secondary sources are not necessarily less "good" than primary works; for many topics, the only sources available will be those that interpret existing data.

**32e
resrch**

32e HOW DO YOU KEEP TRACK OF INFORMATION?

Troubleshooting

After you have located all your printed sources, you have to read and evaluate them. And somehow, you have to keep track of *what* you have read and *where* so that you can locate and use the information when you actually write your paper.

For many writers, keeping tabs on information may be more difficult than finding it. Initially, at least, it seems easier to rely on luck and memory than system and strategy to get the right information in the right slots.

But that's a false impression. The reward for careful planning and systematic note taking comes near the conclusion of a research project when you discover that you have comprehensive information, accurate Works Cited entries, and all the page numbers you need for accurate documentation.

To keep track of research data efficiently . . .

32e-1 **Keep track of your computer printouts.** For decades, writers preparing research papers were expected to prepare bibliography cards to keep track of sources (see Section 32e–2). Today, with on-line catalogs and periodical indexes providing printouts of sources, many writers ignore that advice. They simply consult these paper lists. Yet such printouts can get misplaced in the stack of materials research generates, and the items on the separate lists can't be readily combined, alphabetized, or discarded. So if you do rely on printouts when preparing either a preliminary or final bibliography, be sure to keep the various lists in one place and keep track of the information they furnish. Most on-line catalogs do provide most of the data you'll need in preparing a Works Cited or References list: title of work, author, edition, publication information, date, and page numbers for periodicals (consult the following checklist for bibliographic information). But always examine printouts while you're still at the terminals. You don't want to discover at the last minute that your entries omit some necessary details.

CHECKLIST

Necessary Bibliographic Information

BOOK
- Call number and location in the library
- Name of author(s), last name first, followed by a period
- Title of work, underlined, followed by a period
- Place of publication, followed by a colon
- Publisher, followed by a comma
- Date of publication, followed by a period

ARTICLE IN A SCHOLARLY JOURNAL
- Call number and location
- Name of author(s), last name first, followed by a period
- Title of work, followed by a period and between quotation marks
- Name of the periodical, underlined
- Volume number, followed by the date (usually just the year) in parentheses and a colon
- Page or location, followed by a period

ARTICLE IN A POPULAR MAGAZINE OR NEWSPAPER
- Call number and location
- Name of author(s), last name first, followed by a period
- Title of work, followed by a period and between quotation marks
- Name of the periodical, underlined

- Date, month, and year of publication, followed by a colon
- Page or location, followed by a period

ITEM FROM AN ON-LINE SOURCE

- Name of the author if available, last name first, followed by a period
- Title of the source, document, file, or page, followed by a period and between quotation marks
- Date of the material if available, followed by a period
- Name of the database or on-line source, underlined, followed by a period
- Description of medium, followed by a period—for example, Online.
- Name of computer service, followed by a period—for example, Prodigy.
- Date the source was accessed, followed by a period
- Electronic address (optional), followed by a period—for example, Available: http://www.utexas.edu:80/ftp/student/cr/. (The period following this item is *not* a part of the electronic address.)

32e–2 **Prepare an accurate set of bibliography cards.** It still makes sense—especially on longer projects—to prepare 3-by-5-inch bibliography cards for all the sources you examine, one source per index card.

Each bibliography card should contain all the information you will need to record one source in the Works Cited or References list at the end of the paper. Be sure to include a library call number or location (current periodicals may not have call numbers) in case you have to look up the source a second time. A typical bibliography card might look like this.

**32e
resrch**

```
TL
410
V36
1989
PCL Stacks


van der Plas, Rob. The Mountain Bike Book: Choosing,

        Riding, and Maintaining the Off-road Bicycle.

        3rd ed. San Francisco: Bicycle, 1993.
```

For the exact Works Cited or References form of any bibliography card entry, check the MLA or APA Form Directory (pp. 601 and 685). If you cannot record the source precisely according to form (you may not have your handbook with you), at least copy all the information needed to transform the card into a correct Works Cited or References entry when the time comes. If your bibliography cards *are* accurate, compiling these lists will require that you do no more than stack the bibliography cards in alphabetical order and type them up.

32e–3 **Photocopy or print out passages you know you will quote from directly and extensively.** While a strong case can be made for taking notes on cards, the fact is most researchers—faculty and students—now routinely photocopy their major sources or print them out if they are online. Or they work with sources such as *Proquest* that furnish complete articles. Be sure, though, that your copies are complete and legible (especially the page numbers). Record any and all bibliographical information directly onto the sheets so you don't forget where a photocopied or downloaded article came from. Highlight passages you expect to refer to or quote later, and keep your copies in a folder.

Then be very careful how you use the sources. You might annotate the margins to highlight points you disagree with or comment on paragraphs essential to your research. Or you might try writing a summary of an entire piece or a paraphrase of some key idea in a chapter or article, putting key concepts into your own words. Working with photocopied and printed sources helps to ensure the accuracy of your research, but it does not relieve you of the responsibility of reading and synthesizing what you have read. Those remain major challenges to any researcher (see Section 32f).

32e–4 **Keep a set of note cards.** If you are conscientious and well organized, you'll probably want to record some information on index cards. Like bibliography cards, note cards have some distinct advantages: they can be neatly stacked, they are easy to organize and carry, and they compel you to think about your sources as you read them. While 3-by-5-inch cards are fine for bibliography entries, larger index cards may be more practical for notes.

When you begin taking notes from a source, be sure that each note card includes the author's last name and (if necessary) a short title so that you can easily connect your notes with an appropriate bibliography card or printout. For example, a note card using information from Rob van der Plas's *The Mountain Bike Book* might be headed simply "van der Plas, *Mountain*."

Try to record only one major point per card. Don't crowd too much information onto a single slip. Later when you use the cards to help organize your paper, you'll find it much easier if you can move ideas, arguments, statistics, and quotations independently—even if they come from the same source. If you crowd three or four ideas onto a single card, they are locked together, unless you later waste time recopying them.

For the same reasons, write on only one side of a note card. Information on the flip side of a card is easily overlooked. Moreover, you won't be able to lay out your cards in a tentative outline—as sort of a flow chart—if you use two-sided cards. Writing on both sides is a false economy.

C H E C K L I S T

Information for Note Cards

- Author's last name and a shortened version of the source's title (for accurate reference to the bibliography card)
- A heading to identify the kind of information on the card
- The actual information itself
- Page numbers accurately locating the information in the source

---

32e-5 **Record page numbers for all material.** Whether you use note cards or photocopies for your sources, you will eventually have to cite page numbers for all ideas and quotations you find in your sources. So, to save yourself trips back to the library, be sure you have page numbers on your cards or photocopies. Similarly, your instructor may ask you to record where any electronic information you used is available. Be sure, then, to record Internet or WWW addresses.

> etext.virginia.edu
> gopher://marvel.loc.gov/
> http://WWW.teleport.com/~pcllgn/cgx.html

32f
notes

32f **HOW DO YOU SUMMARIZE AND PARAPHRASE YOUR SOURCES?**

Troubleshooting

Many writers have a hard time understanding how to take notes. Even if you are photocopying source materials, you will still have either to summarize or to paraphrase much of the material in them when you write a paper. A *summary*

captures the gist of a source or some portion of it, boiling it down to a few words or sentences. Summaries tend to be short and do not attempt to outline an entire source. A *paraphrase* will usually run longer than a summary because it is more faithful to the structure of a source, listing major and relevant minor points in their original order.

To report on sources accurately . . .

32f-1 **Decide whether a given source should be summarized or paraphrased.** Summarize those materials that support your thesis but do not provide new information. Paraphrase any materials that will play a significant part in your paper, either for the facts they provide or the ideas they present. Practically speaking, any distinction between summaries and paraphrases is less important than simply taking helpful notes that record all the information you'll need when writing a paper. In taking notes, you'll usually find yourself switching between summary and paraphrase, depending on what you are reading. Some of the information may even be so important you will want to copy it word for word from the source, marking it clearly with quotation marks as *direct quotation*.

To illuminate these points, let's look at an article you might turn up in writing a paper about mountain biking in local and national parks. It's a very short piece from *Texas Monthly* announcing the closing of horse stables in Big Bend National Park because horses—like bikes—may damage park trails. Your bibliography card for the source might look something like this.

**32f
notes**

```
Reading Room
Level 3



O'Keefe, Eric. "Destabilized: Big Bend's Remuda

     Stable Bites the Dust." Texas Monthly: Sept.

     1994: 82.
```

Here's the entire article as it appears in *Texas Monthly*.

DESTABILIZED

Big Bend's remuda stable bites the dust

HOLD YOUR HORSES—at least if you're planning a trail ride in Big Bend National Park any time soon. For 45 years, tourists have enjoyed guided horseback trips from the Chisos Remuda stables in the basin to the two most scenic points in the park: the Window and the South Rim. But this summer the operators of the remuda, Lynn and Cathey Carter, chose not to renew their lease with the National Park Service and bought a ranch just north of the park. The Carters' decision was influenced by the Park Service's ongoing review of allowing horses in national parks. The NPS worries that horses are damaging trails and the immediate terrain around them. In the case of Big Bend, the NPS also believes that there isn't enough room for horses and hikers in the Chisos basin.

Though you can't saddle up in the park anymore, there are several options outside Big Bend's boundaries: Turquose Trailrides (915-371-2212) in Study Butte, by the park's west entrance; the Lajitas Stables (424-3238), 25 miles farther west on FM 170 in Lajitas; and the Carters' new remuda at Spring Creek Ranch (376-2260), on U.S. 385 46 miles north of Panther Junction and 23 miles south of Marathon.   ERIC O'KEEFE

**32f
notes**

Even a source this brief can be either summarized or paraphrased depending on the use you see for it. If the only point relevant to your paper is the fact that horses, like mountain bikes, damage park trails, a summary would suffice. But if you intend to do more with this information, you'd need a paraphrase.

32f-2 **When summarizing a source, identify the key ideas in it and put them in your own words.** When an article is quite long, you might summarize it by looking for a topic idea in each paragraph or cluster of related paragraphs. If you have a photocopy of the piece, you might underscore or highlight any sentences that state or emphasize the key themes of the article. Then assemble these ideas in a coherent statement, keeping the summary as brief as possible. An article as brief as "Destabilized" might be summarized in a sentence and in several different ways, depending upon what you intend to emphasize.

Version 1: Eric O'Keefe reports that at Big Bend National Park, stable operators have decided to close their operations because of qualms about horses on park trails.

Version 2: According to Eric O'Keefe, worries about the damage horses do to park trails means visitors to Big Bend National Park will no longer be able to trail ride to scenic points.

Version 3: Horses too, says Eric O'Keefe, have become a target of the National Park Service, worried about damage to trails and surrounding terrain in Texas' Big Bend National Park.

**32f
notes**

Note that each of these summaries—which might be directly incorporated into a paper—provides the gist of the short article without borrowing the author's language directly.

Also note that because the article "Destabilized" is only one page long and the author's name is given in the summaries, no in-text parenthetical note would be necessary to document the source. A reader would be able to find O'Keefe on the Works Cited page and any quotation would have to be from page 82.

32f-3 **When paraphrasing, put an article in your own words to gain a sense of its overall argument.** Since you alone will use the paraphrase initially, it should be arranged to suit your interests and habits, but it should be adaptable for use in your paper. In preparing a paraphrase, you should be sure that

- The material is entirely in your own words—except for clearly marked quotations.
- The material is arranged to highlight important information.
- Each important fact is accompanied by a specific page number from the source.

- The material you record is relevant to your theme. Don't waste time paraphrasing those parts of the source of no use to your paper.

Here's a paraphrase of "Destabilized" as it might appear on a note card. Notice that the paraphrase includes all page numbers you would need if this material were to appear in your paper. Notice, too, that none of the information in the final paragraph of the article is paraphrased, because it is irrelevant to a paper on mountain biking.

```
O'Keefe, "Destabilized"

p. 82.

Horses on National Park Trails

For forty-five years, visitors at Big Bend National
Park have been able to ride horses to sites. Now
stable operators Lynn and Cathey Carter are shutting
down their operation because of pressure from the
National Park Service. The park service "worries that
horses are damaging trails and the immediate terrain
around them" (82). Horses also get in the way of
hikers.
```

Longer articles would, of course, require much lengthier paraphrases.

**32g
plag**

32g HOW DO YOU HANDLE SOURCES RESPONSIBLY?

Troubleshooting

You should summarize, paraphrase, quote, and document research materials carefully not because you want to avoid charges of plagiarism, but because you have a professional responsibility to represent the ideas of other writers accurately, back up your own claims, and assist readers in checking your research. We're not just being pious in championing scholastic honesty. Readers and writers alike depend on the integrity of their sources. And these days, as collaborative and electronic projects make authorship more complex (who is the "author" in an on-line discussion group?), we need to depend more than ever on the good faith of researchers and writers. As questions about intellectual property rights buzz across the Internet, you still need to be responsible in documenting your sources.

Most students understand, of course, that it is wrong to buy a paper, to let someone heavily edit a paper, or to submit someone else's work as their own. This kind of activity is simply dishonest, and most institutions have procedures for handling such scholastic dishonesty when it occurs.

But many students do not realize that taking notes carelessly or documenting sources inadequately may also raise doubts about the integrity of a paper. Representing the words or ideas you found in a source as your own constitutes *plagiarism*. Instructors take this seriously and assume their legitimate right to reprimand students who do not. Plagiarism is easily avoided if you take good notes (see Sections 32e and 32f) and follow the guidelines discussed in this section. In fact, you will find that time spent carefully thinking about the ideas in your sources and then putting them in your own words pays off later when you sit down to write a draft. When you can explain complex material on your own, you gain authority over a subject that enlivens every paragraph.

To treat sources and authorship responsibly . . .

32g-1 **Understand the special nature of collaborative projects.** Whether working with writers in your own classroom or with students in other locations across a network, you'll find that in truly collaborative projects, it can be tough to remember who wrote what. And that's good. So long as everyone understands the ground rules an instructor sets for a project, joint authorship ought not to be a problem. But legitimate questions do arise.

32g
plag

- Must we write the whole project together?
- Can we break the project into separately authored sections?
- Can one person research a section, another write it, a third edit and proofread?
- What do we do if someone's not pulling her weight?
- Do we all get the same grade?

The time to ask such questions is at the beginning of a collaborative effort. First, determine what your instructor's guidelines are. Then sit down with the members of your group and hammer out the rules.

32g-2 **Appreciate the unique features of some electronic discourse.** The authorship and source problems of collaborative projects done on paper pale when compared with the intellectual property rights issues raised by electronic documents. To create a hypertext or World Wide Web site, for example, a writer might link words and images from dozens of authors and artists and various sources and media. Every part of the resulting collage might be borrowed, but the arrangement of the hypertext itself will be unique. Who then deserves credit as the *author* of the hypertext? Similar problems can arise with Listserv and Usenet conversations. Such sources cannot be documented in conventional ways.

Over the next decade as hypertexts and online materials become more common, standards for documenting electronic sources will evolve. For ways to cite WWW pages, e-mail, MUDs, MOOs, and other electronic forms, consult Section 34g, How Do You Use ACW Documentation? Or for more technical advice, see *Electronic Style: A Guide to Citing Electronic Information* by Xia Li and Nancy B. Crane.

32g-3 **For conventional sources, acknowledge all direct or indirect uses of anyone else's work.** Suppose, for example, that in preparing a research paper on mountain biking, you come across the following passage from *The Mountain Bike Book* by Rob van der Plas.

106

. . . In fact, access and right-of-way are the two intangibles in trail cycling these days. The sport is getting too popular too fast, and in defense, or out of fear, authorities have banned cyclists from many potentially suitable areas.

You will probably use forest service or fire roads and trails intended for hikers most of the time. Don't stray off these trails, since this may cause damage, both to the environment and to our reputation. As long as you stay on the trails and do it with a modicum of consideration for others, you have nothing to fear and should not risk being banned from them by public agencies.

In many areas a distinction is made between single-track trails and wider ones. Single tracks are often considered off-limits to mountain bikers, although in most cases they are perfectly suitable and there are not enough hikers and other trail users to worry about potential conflicts. In fact, single trails naturally limit the biker's speed to an acceptable level.

**32g
plag**

If you decide to quote all or part of the selection above in your essay, you must use quotation marks (or indention) to indicate that you are borrowing the writer's exact words. You must also identify the author, work, publisher, date, and location of the passage through documentation. If you are using MLA documentation (see Chapter 34), the parenthetical note and corresponding Works Cited entry would look like this.

> As Rob van der Plas reminds bikers, they need
> only use common sense in riding public trails: "As
> long as you stay on the trails and do it with a
> modicum of consideration for others, you have nothing
> to fear and should not risk being banned from them by
> public agencies" (106).

Works Cited

van der Plas, Rob. The Mountain Bike Book. 3rd ed.

San Francisco: Bicycle, 1993.

You must use *both* quotation marks and the parenthetical note when you quote directly. Quotation marks alone would not tell your readers what your source was. A note alone would acknowledge that you are using a source, but it would not explain that the words in a given portion of your paper are not entirely your own. (By the way, the author in this case spells his last name exactly as shown, so *van der* is not capitalized in the Works Cited entry—though most last names, of course, would be capitalized.)

32g
plag
You may need to use the selection above in indirect ways, borrowing the information in van der Plas's paragraphs, but not his words or arrangement of ideas. Here are two acceptable summaries (see Section 32f) of the passage on mountain biking that report its facts appropriately and originally. Notice that both versions include a parenthetical note acknowledging van der Plas's *The Mountain Bike Book* as the source of information.

> Rob van der Plas asserts that mountain bikers
> need not fear limitations on their right-of-ways if
> they ride trails responsibly (106).

> Though using so-called "single-track" trails
> might put mountain bikers in conflict with the
> hikers, such tracks are often empty and under-
> utilized (van der Plas 106).

Without documentation, both versions above might be considered plagiarized even though only van der Plas's ideas—and not his actual words—are borrowed. You must acknowledge ideas and information you take from your sources unless you are dealing with *common knowledge* (see Section 33c–2).

32g–4 **Summarize and paraphrase carefully.** A proper summary or paraphrase of a source should be entirely in your own words (as in the examples on p. 558). Some writers mistakenly believe that they can avoid a charge of plagiarism by rearranging or changing a few words in a selection; they are wrong. The following passage would be considered plagiarism—with or without a parenthetical note—because it simply takes the source's basic words and ideas and varies them slightly.

Plagiarized

> . . . In trail cycling today, access and right-of-way are the two intangibles. The sport of mountain biking is getting too popular too quickly, so defensive authorities have banned cyclists from many potentially suitable areas out of fear.
>
> Mountain bikers typically use forest service or fire roads and trails intended for hikers most of the time. They shouldn't stray off these trails, since this may cause damage, both to the environment and to the reputation of cyclists. As long as mountain bikers remain on the trails and do it with a modicum of consideration for others, they need not fear and should not risk being restricted from them by public agencies.
>
> In many areas, mountain bikers make a distinction between single-track trails and wider ones. Single tracks are often considered off limits to mountain bikers, although in most cases they are

quite suitable and there are not enough hikers and other trail users to worry about possible conflicts. In fact, single trails naturally lower the mountain biker's speed to a more acceptable level.

32g
Plag

How Do You Write a Research Paper?

33a HOW DO YOU REFINE YOUR THESIS?

Troubleshooting

As the previous chapter suggests, finding material on almost any research topic is manageable. But what do you do with that information once you have it? For many writers, developing a significant thesis—an idea that brings all that information to a point—is more difficult. Especially in explanatory essays that report facts, it is easy to rely on thesis statements that simply break a sprawling research topic into parts.

Child abuse is a serious problem with three major aspects: cause, detection, and prevention.

The most prevalent types of white collar criminals are people who work in business, in the military, or in the government.

The environmental crisis involves pollution of the water, the earth, and the air.

These are shopping lists more than thesis statements.

Writers of such theses have good rhetorical intentions: they divide their research papers into simple parts to assure comprehensiveness and clarity. But this simplistic approach deadens almost any subject by preventing readers (and, in most cases, writers) from appreciating how the various aspects of a topic might be related—how a particular cause of child abuse, for example, might suggest a method of prevention or why white collar crime in the government poses a threat to the work ethic. When issues are simply strung out, one after another, no serious questions are likely to be raised.

To be sure your thesis is effective . . .

33a–1 **Make sure you have a point to make.** Don't be surprised if you have doubts about your topic early in the writing process. All the while you are reading and taking notes, you should be testing your preliminary thesis.

CHECKLIST

Testing Your Research Thesis

- Is it a substantial issue?
- Is it a debatable issue?
- Will the issue affect or interest my readers?
- Will my readers understand how the issue affects them?
- How might I stimulate interest in my subject?

33a–2 **Focus on problems and conflicts.** In your reading and research, challenge yourself to develop a point that might be surprising or unconventional.

Tentative thesis	Students who read extensively may perform no better on achievement tests than those who read hardly at all.

You may eventually find that the point you are developing cannot be sustained by the evidence. If that's the case, you have learned something important about your thesis and can explain your discovery to readers in an intriguing way.

Final thesis	If you think you can do well on achievement tests without cracking a book, you're simply wrong.

33a-3 **Ask basic questions about your topic, particularly *how* and *why*.** Get to the heart of a matter in defining a topic. Examine issues that matter.

Lifeless	Child abuse is a serious problem with three major aspects: cause, detection, and prevention.
Challenging	The charge of child abuse sometimes serves the interest of political groups eager to have the government define the relationship between parents and children.
Lifeless	The most prevalent types of white collar criminals are people who work in business, in the military, or in the government.
Challenging	White collar crime is rarely punished severely because—down deep—many people admire the perpetrators.
Lifeless	The environmental crisis involves pollution of the water, the earth, and the air.
Challenging	To save the global environment, citizens and nations may ultimately have to make sacrifices greater than those experienced during war.

33a-4 **Refine your thesis in light of your reading.** Your thesis statements are likely to seem like shopping lists if you commit yourself too quickly to topics—without allowing reading and writing to shape and reshape the focus of a paper. You *do* want to narrow the scope of your research, but be prepared to refine and reshape a thesis idea until it says something interesting and important. Such reshaping is almost essential in exploratory papers, but also common in explanatory essays.

33a
resrch

33a-5 **Finally, make a commitment.** Sooner or later you have to commit to a topic idea. Even if it isn't perfect, you still have time to work it into shape. Don't be shy about asking your instructor and classmates what they think of your idea. Get second and third opinions. An outsider may see a side to your subject you have missed.

So you needn't rush into a topic, but don't expect a great notion to drop from the sky either. As you approach the first draft, you should have a reasonable idea of what you want to write about. You may end up arguing something different from your initial idea, but you need to start somewhere.

33b   HOW DO YOU ORGANIZE A RESEARCH PAPER?

Troubleshooting

The basic principles of organization explained in Section 2e apply to research papers. But because of their greater length, research papers may require more careful planning than shorter essays. Keep your readers in mind as you arrange information; they'll appreciate your efforts to shape and connect ideas. You may even need to use divisions, headings, and subheadings when a paper extends beyond eight or ten pages.

To organize a research paper . . .

33b-1   Make scratch outlines for the whole essay and for smaller parts of it.   Working from a plan, even a rough one, is usually easier than writing without any direction at all, especially with explanatory papers. Begin by making a scratch outline for the whole essay—nothing elaborate, just your thesis, followed by the four or five major subpoints.

Then check carefully to see whether each of your subpoints helps to explain that thesis—which is your commitment to readers. Consider the order of your ideas too. Would a reader understand why your first point comes before your second one, and the second before the third, and so on? If not, do you *have* a rationale for the order you selected? If so, what can you do to help readers appreciate your strategy?

It may help if you ask yourself what your readers need to know about your subject *first*. Where does this background information lead? What ideas do you want your readers to be thinking about at the end of the essay? How can you get them there?

33b-2   Be flexible.   Don't shackle yourself to your original plan. Ideas have a way of following their own paths once they start moving. So don't hesitate to modify your original scratch outline while drafting an essay. And as you develop that draft, keep sketching tentative outlines for various sections. These interim outlines needn't be complicated or neat. Think of them as the scaffolding that surrounds an essay while it is under construction. Draw up several at a time to test your options; don't feel you are committed to any of them. And toss these scratch outlines out as soon as you invent something better.

33b-3   Be consistent with headings.   A short essay (five to six pages) ordinarily needs only a first-level head—that is, a title. With longer papers, however, readers will appreciate subheadings that introduce the content of major sections. All such heads should be brief, parallel in phrasing, and consistent in format like the items in a formal outline (see

Section 2f–3). For most academic papers, you probably won't use more than two levels of headings: a title and one set of subheads.

MLA style (described in more detail in Chapter 34) provides fairly loose standards for headings and subheadings. Titles of MLA papers are ordinarily centered on the first page of an essay while headings and subheadings appear flush with the left-hand margin. If you descend to a third level, you'll have to distinguish between second- and third-level heads by numbering or lettering them or by separating them typographically (usually by variations in capitalization or underlining). MLA style leaves you to decide how you will handle such choices, but in all cases, you must keep the headings clean and unobtrusive. Here are two ways of handling three levels of headings as they might appear in a moderately long MLA-style paper on mountain biking.

Mountain Biking and the Environment	1st level
The Mountain Bike	2nd level
History of Mountain Biking	2nd level
Mountain Bikes and the Environment	2nd level
<u>Trail Damage</u>	3rd level
<u>Conflicts with Hikers</u>	3rd level
Mountain Bikes and Responsible Riding	2nd level

33b
resrch

Mountain Biking and the Environment	1st level
1. The Mountain Bike	2nd level
2. History of Mountain Biking	2nd level
3. Mountain Bikes and the Environment	2nd level
3.1. Trail Damage	3rd level
3.2. Conflicts with Hikers	3rd level
4. Mountain Bikes and Responsible Riding	2nd level

APA style (described in more detail in Chapter 35) defines five levels of headings for professional articles—more than you'll likely ever use in a college paper. Here's how to handle three or fewer levels of headings.

- Titles (first-level heads) are centered, using both uppercase and lowercase letters as shown below.
- Second-level heads are capitalized like titles, but also underlined and placed flush with the left-hand margin.
- Third-level heads are underlined, indented, and run as paragraph headings with only their first letters capitalized. Third-level heads conclude with a period.

Here's how those APA guidelines look in operation.

Mountain Biking and the Environment	1st level
<u>The Mountain Bike</u>	2nd level
<u>History of Mountain Biking</u>	2nd level
<u>Mountain Bikes and the Environment</u>	2nd level
<u>Trail damage.</u>	3rd level
<u>Conflicts with hikers.</u>	3rd level
<u>Mountain Bikes and Responsible Riding</u>	2nd level

33c HOW DO YOU DOCUMENT A RESEARCH PAPER?

Troubleshooting

Documentation is the evidence you provide to support the ideas you present in a research paper. You give credit to your sources in a research paper so that readers can judge the quality, credibility, and originality of your work. Your citations let them know how thorough and up-to-date your investigation of a topic is and what they should read for more information.

Documentation usually directs readers to printed sources of information: books, articles, tables of statistics, and so on. But it may also cite interviews, software, films, television programs, databases, on-line services, and electronic sources. Various systems for handling documentation have been devised. Presented in this handbook are systems used by the Modern Language Association (MLA), the American Psychological Association (APA), the Council of Biology Editors (CBE), and the Alliance for Computers and Writing (ACW). Most examples in this handbook follow MLA form.

But writers often find it difficult to decide what exactly has to be supported by documentation. Do you credit every fact, figure, and idea that appears in a paper? If a subject is new to you, doesn't that mean that virtually every sentence will have to include a citation? When does documentation become excessive?

Sometimes you need to provide readers with information that is, strictly speaking, not a part of your essay or argument. How do you do that without distracting the reader from the main body of your report? Is it scholarly to have lengthy explanatory footnotes in an undergraduate research paper—or just fussy?

To document a paper adequately . . .

33c–1 **Provide a source for every direct quotation.** A direct quotation is any material repeated word for word from a source. Most direct quotations in a college research paper require some form of parenthetical documentation—that is, a citation of author and page number (MLA) or author, date, and page number (APA).

> **MLA** It is possible to define literature as simply
>
> "that text which the community insists on
>
> having repeated from time to time intact"
>
> (Joos 51-52).

> **APA** One researcher questions the value of
>
> attention-getting essay openings that
>
> "presuppose passive, uninterested (probably
>
> uninteresting) readers" (Hashimoto, 1986,
>
> p. 126).

You should also give credit for any diagrams, statistics, charts, or pictures in your paper that you reproduce from a source.

You need not document famous sayings, proverbs, or biblical citations ("A bird in the hand is worth two in the bush"; "The truth shall make you free"), but you should identify the author of any quotable phrases you include in your paper. A simple credit line is often enough for quotations used at the beginning of a paper or at chapter divisions.

> I remember your name perfectly, but I just can't think of your face.
> —William Archibald Spooner

TRICKY

33c–2 **Document all ideas, opinions, facts, and information in your paper that you acquire from sources and that cannot be considered common knowledge.** Many writers aren't sure what they must document in a research paper and what information they can assume is *common knowledge*—that which does not require a note. The difficulty increases when writing on an unfamiliar subject. In such a case, everything in a paper is borrowed, in one way or another, from a book, article, encyclopedia, or other source. Is it necessary to document every fact, concept, and idea since they are—indeed—someone else's material?

To answer this question, begin with the concept of common knowledge: facts, dates, events, information, and concepts that belong generally to an educated public. No individual owns the facts about history, physics, social behavior, geography, current events, popular culture, and so on. You may need to check an encyclopedia to find out that the Battle of Waterloo was fought on June 18, 1815, but that fact belongs to common knowledge. You don't have to cite a source to assert that Neil Armstrong was the first person to walk on the moon, that Bette Davis was a film star, or that the Protestant Reformation was both a religious and a political movement.

But if our culture shares a body of common knowledge, so does each discipline. And in writing a paper on a particular subject, you may also make some assumptions about *common knowledge within a field.* When you find that a given piece of information or an idea is shared among several of the sources you are using, you need not document it. If, for example, you were writing a paper on anorexia nervosa and discovered that most of your authors define the condition in approximately the same way and describe the same five or six symptoms, you could talk about these basic facts without providing a credit for every one. (You might, however, want to quote a particular definition of the condition from one of your sources.) Experts on anorexia nervosa know what the condition is and does. What the experts know collectively constitutes the common knowledge within the field about the subject; what they assert individually—their opinions, studies, theories, research projects, and hypotheses—is the material you *must* document in a paper.

33c–3 **Document all ideas, opinions, facts, and information in your paper that your readers might want to know more about or might question.** The discussion in Section 33c–2 suggests that you do not have to document every fact and idea in a research paper just because it is new to you or your readers. Your strict responsibility is to credit material that is not—so far as you can tell—common knowledge in your topic area.

But you should ordinarily go somewhat beyond your strict responsibilities, anticipating where readers might ask the question "Is this true?" or "Who says so?" The more controversial your subject, the more you may want to provide documentation even for material that might be considered common knowledge within a discipline. Suppose, for example, you are writing a paper about witchcraft and make a historical assertion well known by scholars within the field, but liable to be surprising or suspect to nonspecialists—for example, that the witches of western Europe were *not* the followers of ancient pagan religions. If you are writing to the audience of nonspecialists, you should certainly provide documentation for the historical assertion. If you are writing to experts on witchcraft, however, you do not have to cite sources for what they would consider basic information.

33c–4 **Provide content notes as needed, but sparingly.** Both major systems of documentation—MLA and APA—have done away with footnotes and endnotes for routine citations of sources. MLA, however, preserves *content notes* in a list at the end of a paper (immediately after the body of the essay and before the Works Cited page). They are identified in the paper itself by superscript numbers at the end of a sentence.

> . . . the matter remains undecided.[3]

Content notes might be used to discuss a point made in the text; to supply a definition; to provide an explanation for a statistic or calculation; to expand upon what is said in the body of the essay; or to acknowledge assistance, grants, and support.

In most cases, however, if a discussion is important enough to merit a lengthy note, it probably belongs in the body of the essay itself. Even short content notes can be distracting, especially if they are numerous. Rely on content notes only when you absolutely need them—that is, when the information is interesting and relevant to understanding your paper, yet would interrupt the flow of the essay if inserted within the text itself.

MLA also permits *bibliographical notes*. Like content notes, bibliographical notes are identified by raised superscript numbers and are gathered in a list at the end of a paper. (An essay that contains both content and bibliographical notes would combine them in a single list and number them, consecutively, from the beginning of the essay.) Bibliographical notes are used to evaluate sources, to direct readers to other sources, to list multiple sources when necessary, or to name a work or an edition that will appear many times in parenthetical citations. Sources (books, articles, newspapers) mentioned in a content or bibliographical note are also listed on the Works Cited or References page. Here are notes from an MLA-style research paper. The first is both a content and biblio-graphical note, the second a content note only.

> [1]The first contemporary mountain bikes appeared in the mid-1970s in Marin County, California. See Schwartz 77; van der Plas 16.
>
> [2]Drake explains the feelings of some bikers: "I find myself a renegade--an expatriate in the woods I love" (106).

● **Tip**

Content and bibliographical notes are relatively rare in under-graduate essays. Use them whenever your paper needs the extra expla-nations they provide. But don't get carried away. Notes can distract readers from the body of your essay. ●

33c–5 **Provide dates, identifications, and other information to as-sist the reader.** When writing a research paper, you will do readers a service if you date important events, major figures, and works of literature and art. Also be careful to identify any individuals readers might not rec-ognize.

33c
resrch

> After the great fire of London (1666), the city was . . .
>
> Henry Highland Garnet (1815-82), American abolitionist and radical, . . .
>
> <u>Pearl</u> (c. 1400), an elegy about . . .

In the last example, the *c.* before the date stands for *circa*—which means "about"; see page 628 for a list of other abbreviations common in docu-mentation.

When quoting from literary works, provide information readers would need to locate any lines you are citing. For novels, you should sup-ply page numbers; for plays, give act/scene/line information; for long po-ems, provide line numbers, and when appropriate, division numbers (book, canto, or other division). Examples of literary citations are given in the checklist on page 665.

33d HOW DO YOU SELECT QUOTATIONS?

Troubleshooting

Some writers want to treat direct quotations like electronic modules: plug them in at the appropriate spots in the circuit board and the device should operate. Unfortunately, quotations don't work that way. You have to select them purposefully. Every direct quotation in a paper should be there because it contributes something to the piece that your own words could not. In this section, we list some of the circumstances that warrant direct quotations.

You may notice, however, that not all of the passages in this section include full documentation—that is, either in-text notes or footnotes. That's because not all of the selections come from academic sources. Full documentation is more likely to appear in scholarly works than in newspapers such as *The New York Times* or in magazines such as *Newsweek*.

To handle sources well . . .

33d-1 Use a direct quotation as the focal point for a piece. Here Christina Hoff Sommers, in her book *Who Stole Feminism: How Women Have Betrayed Women*, uses several citations to open an inquiry into the way some writers use figures and statistics.

In *Revolution from Within*, Gloria Steinem informs her readers that "in this country alone . . . about 150,000 females die of anorexia each year."[1] That is more than three times the annual number of fatalities from car accidents for the entire population. Steinem refers readers to another feminist best-seller, Naomi Wolf's *The Beauty Myth*. And in Ms. Wolf's book one again finds the statistic, along with the author's outrage. "How," she asks, "would America react to mass self-immolation by hunger of its favorite sons?"[2] Although "nothing justifies comparison with the Holocaust," she cannot refrain from making one anyway. "When confronted with a vast number of emaciated bodies starved not by nature but by men, one must notice a certain resemblance."[3]

Where did Ms. Wolf get her figures? Her source is *Fasting Girls: The Emergence of Anorexia Nervosa as a Modern Disease*[4] by Joan Brumberg, a historian and former director of women's studies at Cornell University. Brumberg, too, is fully aware of the political significance of the startling statistic. She points out that the women who study eating problems "seek to demonstrate that these disorders are an inevitable consequence of a misogynistic society that demeans women . . . by objectifying their bodies."[5] Professor

33d
resrch

Brumberg, in turn, attributes the figure to the American Anorexia and Bulimia Association.

I called the American Anorexia and Bulimia Association and spoke to Dr. Diane Mickley, its president. "We were mis-quoted," she said. In a 1985 newsletter the association had referred to 150,000 to 200,000 *sufferers* (not *fatalities*) of anorexia nervosa.

Note that Sommers is using a citation style in which superscript (raised) numbers are keyed to a bibliography rather than a parenthetical citation style recommended by the MLA and APA. (See Sections 34a and 35a.)

33d-2   **Use a direct quotation as an assertion of facts.** Here in a research paper on the safety of nuclear plants, Emma Renault uses a quotation to report a surprising claim.

Despite the accident at the Chernobyl power
station, many people still believe that nuclear power
plants are inherently less life threatening than
fossil fuel plants. Roger Starr, for example, makes
this point about the dangers of nuclear radiation:

> . . . in one year, someone living next to a
> nuclear station would be exposed to no more
> extra radiation than on a single flight
> from New York to California and back, at
> altitudes partly above the atmosphere that
> filters out cosmic radiation. (373)

33d-3   **Use a direct quotation as a representative statement of an opinion or idea.**

The elderly woman just shakes her head as three teenage boys roll noisily past on skateboards, hooting and hollering, nearly running her off the sidewalk before dashing into a crowded street. Horns blow and brakes squeal. **"Kids,"** the dignified lady sighs. **"They think they'll live forever."** She's right. Most young people take terrible and unnecessary risks with their lives and abuse their health wantonly, thinking that the shadow of human frailty will never fall on them.

33d–4 **Use a direct quotation as a voice that adds authority or color to an assertion you have made.** Geoff Henley, for example, calls upon the eminent British political theorist Edmund Burke to second a point he wishes to make about some critics of contemporary society.

> One sometimes gets the impression that certain self-proclaimed political leaders on campus spend much of their time looking for grievances to exploit or reasons to be offended, either in current events or in past history. Yet such tendencies are nothing new. Edmund Burke (1729-97), the great British legal scholar and parliamentarian, made the same charge against the political extremists of his day. In Reflections on the Revolution in France, Burke complains that such people--in this case, "atheistic libelers" of the Church--
>
>> find themselves obliged to rake into the histories of former ages . . . for every instance of oppression and persecution which has been made by that body or in its favor, in order to justify . . . their own persecutions and their own cruelties.
>>
>> (169)

33d
resrch

33d–5 **Use a direct quotation to show a diversity of opinion.** Here physicist Freeman Dyson, author of *Infinite in All Directions*, quotes another scientist in order to disagree with him on the relationship of knowledge and values.

> But as soon as we mention the words "value" and "purpose," we run into one of the most firmly entrenched taboos of twentieth century science. Hear the voice of Jacques Monod, high priest of scientific rationality, in his book *Chance and Necessity*: **"Any mingling of knowledge with values is unlawful, forbidden."**

Monod was one of the seminal minds in the flowering of molecular biology in this century. It takes some courage to defy his anathema. But I will defy him and encourage others to do so.

33d–6 **Use a direct quotation to clarify a point.** Author Tom Callahan, writing about the U.S. Army's remarkably successful recruiting slogan, uses the words of Craig Reiss, an advertising expert, in examining the campaign.

Be All You Can Be started in 1981 when studies showed that young people were most interested in learning technical skills and being personally challenged. Explains Craig Reiss of *Advertising Age* magazine:

The army's approach to advertising changed with the end of the [Vietnam] war and the decline of the effectiveness of the bachelor's degree to get you job skills and an entry-level position. They began to use technology in their ads to position themselves as a big high-tech training school. That proved to be very effective because what else can you do in a peacetime army? You really can't use the emotional argument that you have to join to defend the country.

33d–7 **Use a direct quotation to demonstrate the complexity of an issue.** In an article titled "Getting Warmer?" Jane S. Shaw and Richard L. Stroup quote statistician Andrew R. Solow on the issue of global warming to explain a technical point. Note that the direct quotation in boldface is followed immediately by an indirect quotation from the same source.

Assuming, however, that the global warming trend is real, could CO_2 be the cause? If so, says Solow, we should be seeing much warmer temperatures than we have seen so far. **"For example, for the planet to warm by 2°C. in the next hundred years, the average rate of warming would have to be four times greater than that in the historic record."** Greenhouse warming is expected to be greatest at high latitudes and more rapid in the north than in the south, but this pattern hasn't appeared either, he says.

33d–8 **Use a direct quotation to emphasize a point or make it memorable.** Here Paul Johnson in his book *Intellectuals* quotes Karl Marx to suggest that the political philosopher's physical ailments may have contributed to his jaundiced view of European culture.

He rarely took baths or washed much at all. This, plus his unsuitable diet, may explain the veritable plague of boils from which he suffered for a quarter of a century. They increased his natural irritability and seem to have been at their worst while he was writing *Capital*. **"Whatever happens,"** he wrote grimly to Engels, **"I hope the bourgeoisie as long as they exist will have cause to remember my carbuncles."**[45] The boils varied in numbers, size, and intensity, but at one time or another they appeared on all parts of his body.

33e HOW DO YOU HANDLE QUOTATIONS?

Troubleshooting

The last thing a research paper should be is a patchwork of quotations. Not only do quotations need to be selected carefully, but they need to fit seamlessly into your text. That means that you have to introduce direct quotations intelligently and tailor them to fit your language. No stylistic touch makes a research paper read so well as quotations deftly handled.

To use direct quotations well . . .

33e-1 Never use a quotation as a way to avoid writing. Quotations should not be devices for padding your paper. Nor should you rely on them to say something you could have said competently in your own words. Respect your sources. Don't turn them into the equivalent of an academic cafeteria, where you pick up every quotation you have written down just to expand your paper to the required length.

33e-2 Introduce all direct and indirect borrowings in some way. Short introductions, attributions, or commentaries are needed to introduce readers to materials you've gathered from sources. To be sure readers pay attention, give all borrowed words and ideas a context or *frame*. Such frames can be relatively simple; they can *precede*, *follow*, or *interrupt* the borrowed words or ideas. The frame need not even be in the same sentence as the quotation; it may be part of the *surrounding* paragraph. Here are some ways that material can be introduced.

- *Frame precedes borrowed material*:
  In 1896, Woodrow Wilson, who would become Princeton's president in 1902, declared, "It is not learning but the spirit of service that will give a college a place in the public annals of the nation."
  —Ernest L. Boyer

- *Frame follows borrowed material:*
  "One reason you may have more colds if you hold back tears is that, when you're under stress, your body puts out steroids which affect your immune system and reduce your resistance to disease," **Dr. Broomfield comments.** —Barbara Lang Stern

- *Frame interrupts borrowed material:*
  "Whatever happens," **he wrote grimly to Engels,** "I hope the bourgeoisie as long as they exist will have cause to remember my carbuncles." —Paul Johnson

- *Surrounding sentences frame borrowed material:*
  In the meantime, [Luis] Jimenez was experimenting with three-dimensional form. "Perhaps because of the experience of working in the sign shop, I realized early on that I wanted to do it all—paint, draw, work with wood, metal, clay." **His images were those of 1960s pop culture, chosen for their familiarity and shock value.** —Chiori Santiago

- *Borrowed material integrated with passage:*
  The study concludes that a faulty work ethic is not responsible for the decline in our productivity; quite the contrary, the study identifies "a widespread commitment among U.S. workers to improve productivity" **and suggests that** "there are large reservoirs of potential upon which management can draw to improve performance and increase productivity."
  —Daniel Yankelovich

33e
resrch

Most borrowings in your research paper should be attributed in similar fashion. Either name (directly or indirectly) the author, the speaker, or the work the passage is from, or explain why the words you are quoting are significant. Many phrases of introduction or attribution are available. Here are just a few examples.

CHART

Verbs of Attribution

accept	allege	deny	mention	say
add	argue	disagree	posit	state
admit	believe	emphasize	propose	think
affirm	confirm	insist	reveal	verify

President Clinton **claimed** that ". . .
One expert **reported** that ". . .
The members of the board **declared** that ". . .

Representatives of the airline industry **contend** that ". . .

Marva Collins **asserts** that ". . .

Senator Hutchison **was quoted** as saying that ". . .

"The figures," **according to** the GAO, "are . . .

CAUTION **33e–3** Tailor your language so that direct quotations fit into the grammar of your sentences. You may have to tinker with the introduction to the quotation or modify the quotation itself by careful selections, ellipses (see Section 33e–4), or bracketed additions (see Section 33e–5).

Clumsy The chemical capsaicin that makes chili hot:
"it is so hot it is used to make antidog and
antimugger sprays" (Bork 184).

Revised Capsaicin, the chemical that makes chili hot,
is so strong "it is used to make antidog and
antimugger sprays" (Bork 184).

Clumsy Computers have not succeeded as translators
of languages because, says Douglas
Hofstadter, "nor is the difficulty caused by
a lack of knowledge of idiomatic phrases.
The fact is that translation involves having
a mental model of the world being discussed,
and manipulating symbols in the model" (603).

Revised "A lack of knowledge of idiomatic phrases" is
not the reason computers have failed as
translators of languages. "The fact is," says
Douglas Hofstadter, "that translation
involves having a mental model of the world
being discussed, and manipulating symbols in
the model" (603).

33e
resrch

33e-4 Use ellipses (three *spaced* periods . . .) to indicate where you have cut material from direct quotations. For example, ellipses might be used to trim the lengthy passage below so that it focuses more on the oldest portions of the biblical text. The ellipses tell readers where words, phrases, and even whole sentences have been cut.

Original passage

The text of the Old Testament is in places the stuff of scholarly nightmares. Whereas the entire New Testament was written within fifty to a hundred years, the books of the Old Testament were composed and edited over a period of about a thousand. The youngest book is Daniel, from the second century B.C. The oldest portions of the Old Testament (if we limit ourselves to the present form of the literature and exclude from consideration the streams of oral tradition that fed it) are probably a group of poems that appear, on the basis of linguistic features and historical allusions contained in them, to date from roughly the twelfth and eleventh centuries B.C. . . .   —Barry Hoberman, "Translating the Bible."

Passage as cut for use in an essay

Although working with any part of an original
scripture text is difficult, Hoberman describes the
text of the Old Testament as "the stuff of scholarly
nightmares." He explains in "Translating the Bible"
that while "the entire New Testament was written
within fifty to a hundred years, the books of the Old
Testament were composed and edited over a period of
about a thousand. . . . The oldest portions of the
Old Testament . . . are probably a group of poems
that appear . . . to date from roughly the twelfth
and eleventh centuries B.C. . . ."

When ellipses occur in the middle of a sentence, leave a space before the first period and after the third one. (Remember that the periods themselves are spaced.)

"We the people of the United States . . . do ordain
and establish this Constitution for the United States
of America."

When they occur at the end of a sentence or passage, place the first period immediately after the last word, and add a fourth period to mark the end of the sentence.

```
"These are the times that try men's souls.

The summer soldier and the sunshine patriot will,

in this crisis, shrink from the service of his

country. . . ."                        --Thomas Paine
```

The same form (four periods) is employed when entire sentences or paragraphs are omitted.

Occasionally ellipses appear at the beginning of quoted sentences to indicate that an opening clause or phrase has been omitted. Three spaced periods precede the sentence, with a space left between the third period and the first letter of the sentence. Any punctuation occurring at the end of the clause or sentence preceding the quotation is retained.

```
"The text of the Old Testament is in places the stuff

of scholarly nightmares. . . . [T]he books of the Old

Testament were composed and edited over a period of

about a thousand [years]."

        --Barry Hoberman, "Translating the Bible."
```

33e
resrch

TRICKY You needn't use ellipses, however, every time you break into a sentence. The quotation in the following passage, for example, reads better without the ellipses.

```
In fact, according to Richard Bernstein, ". . .

American life [has] produced the highest degree of

prosperity in the conditions of the greatest freedom

ever known on the Planet Earth" (11).

In fact, according to Richard Bernstein, "American

life [has] produced the highest degree of prosperity

in the conditions of the greatest freedom ever known

on the Planet Earth" (11).
```

Whenever you use ellipses, be sure your shortened quotation still accurately reflects the meaning of the uncut passage.

33e-5 **Use square brackets [ ] to add necessary information to a quotation.** Sometimes, for example, you may want to explain who or what a pronoun refers to, or you may have to provide a short explanation, furnish a date, and explain or translate a puzzling word.

> Some critics clearly prefer Wagner's <u>Tannhäuser</u> to
>
> <u>Lohengrin</u>: "The well-written choruses [of Tannhäuser]
>
> are combined with solo singing and orchestral
>
> background into long, unified musical scenes"
>
> (Grout 629).

But don't overdo it. Readers will resent the explanation of obvious details.

33e-6 **Use [sic] to indicate an obvious error copied faithfully from a quotation.** Quotations must be copied accurately, word by word, from your source—errors and all. To show that you have copied a passage faithfully, place the expression *sic* (the Latin word for *thus* or *so*) in brackets one space after any mistake.

> Mr. Vincent's letter went on: "I would have preferred
>
> a younger bride, but I decided to marry the old
>
> window [sic] anyway."

If *sic* can be placed outside the quotation itself, it appears between parentheses, not brackets.

> Molly's paper was titled "Understanding King Leer"
>
> (sic).

33e-7 **Place prose quotations shorter than four typed lines (MLA) or forty words (APA) between quotation marks.**

> In <u>Utilitarianism</u> (1863), John Stuart Mill declares,
>
> "It is better to be Socrates dissatisfied than a pig
>
> satisfied."

33e–8 **Indent more than three lines of poetry (MLA).** Up to three lines of poetry may be handled just like a prose passage, with slashes marking the separate lines. Quotation marks are used.

> As death approaches, Cleopatra grows in grandeur and
>
> dignity: "Husband, I come! / Now to that name my
>
> courage prove my title! / I am fire and air"
>
> (V.ii.287-89).

More than three lines of poetry are indented ten spaces and quotation marks are not used. (If the lines of poetry are unusually long, you may indent fewer than ten spaces.) Be sure to copy the poetry accurately, right down to the punctuation.

> Among the most famous lines in English literature are
>
> those that open William Blake's "The Tyger":
>
> > Tyger tyger, burning bright,
> >
> > In the forests of the night;
> >
> > What immortal hand or eye,
> >
> > Could frame thy fearful symmetry? (1-4)

33e–9 **Indent any prose quotations longer than four typed lines (MLA) or forty words (APA).** MLA form recommends an indention of one inch, or ten spaces if you are using a typewriter; APA form requires five spaces. Quotation marks are *not* used around the indented material. If the quotation extends beyond a single paragraph, the first lines of subsequent paragraphs are indented an additional quarter inch, or three typed spaces (MLA) or five spaces (APA). In typed papers, the indented material—like the rest of the essay—is double spaced.

You may indent passages of fewer than four lines when you want them to have special emphasis. But don't do this with every short quotation or your paper will look choppy.

33e–10 **Refer to events in works of fiction, poems, plays, movies, and television shows in the present tense.** When quoting passages from novels, scenes from a movie, or events in a play, think about the actions as performances that occur over and over again.

> In his last speech, Othello orders those around him
>
> to "Speak of me as I am. Nothing extenuate, / Nor set

down aught in malice" (V.ii.338-39). Then he `stabs`
himself and `dies`, falling on the bed of the innocent
wife he has murdered only moments before: "I kissed
thee ere I killed thee. No way but this, / Killing
myself, to die upon a kiss" (354-55).

33f HOW DO YOU COMBINE INFORMATION FROM SOURCES?

Troubleshooting

Don't rely on a single source for any large portion of your essay. Among the least successful research papers—explanatory or exploratory—are those that simply lump the opinions of five or six authors together like a five-course meal, one author per paragraph. For a successful essay, you have to do more than report the gist of several books and articles. You must consider how the sources work in relation to one another. Do they agree? Disagree? Offer different points of view? Support each other? Suggest new issues?

To use your sources effectively . . .

Draw the major ideas in your paper from several sources.
Your job as a writer is to establish a relationship between the authors you have read and to add your own ideas. Odds are good that the sources you've selected for your research project have never been examined in precisely the way you've read them. Your perspective on the subject can be unique, but only if you take the time to think seriously about your materials, your topic, your readers, and yourself. Don't allow a few sources to dictate the contents, point of view, and organization of your research essay.

33g
resrch

33g WHEN DO YOU WRITE THE FIRST DRAFT?

Troubleshooting

All the preparatory work that goes into a research paper can make writing the first draft a bit intimidating. You've got so much capital invested that you are suddenly afraid to take a risk. Yet all that work makes sense only when you begin writing.

To ensure a successful paper . . .

33g-1 **Write a first draft early.** Think of the first draft as the testing ground for your thesis. Many months before new automobiles are introduced to the public, hand-built prototypes are run thousands of miles on test tracks that simulate road conditions. In a similar way, your draft tests your thesis under difficult situations: Will it stand up to demands for facts, evidence, proof? Will it sustain itself against possible counterarguments? Will it be interesting and surprising enough to keep readers involved?

You really won't know until you try your ideas out. So get them down on paper early—perhaps even before you have completed all your research. Remember that you don't have to write any essay—especially a long one—straight through from beginning to end. While doing your research, compose any portion of the essay that seems ready. But as your research draws to a preliminary conclusion, commit yourself to writing a full draft. Plan on finishing this draft about halfway through the time allotted for the essay. If, for example, you have a month for the paper, resolve to have a draft in hand in two weeks.

Why so early? Because you'll want time to fill in gaps and solidify your positions. You may have to return to the library to read more and gather additional facts. You may need to revise your stance entirely or restructure your essay. You will also want to polish your style. Early versions can afford to be ragged and cluttered; a final draft cannot. The more time you allow yourself between a first attempt—even a very rough draft—and the version you turn in, the better your research paper is likely to be.

33g-2 **Anticipate complications.** Remember that the final stages of producing a research paper may involve steps not required in other essays: doing an outline, verifying the documentation, preparing a Works Cited page, arranging for typing, and so on. You have to allocate time for these extras as you bring the paper to market. So get the prototype—your first draft—on the test track as early as possible.

33h
resrch

33h HOW DO YOU REVISE AND EDIT A RESEARCH PAPER?

Troubleshooting

Because of the length and complexity of most research papers, you'll benefit from the perspective offered by friendly but critical readers—classmates, writing lab personnel, and instructors. So get feedback from readers who will approach the paper without preconceptions and without the background information you now have on the subject. Trust them to tell you where more information is needed—and where you provided too much. Ask them about focus, clarity, and style.

Then give your essay one final reading, checking matters as broad as organization and as specific as spelling.

To complete your draft . . .

33h–1 **Test your organization.** Organizing a long paper is rarely an easy job, so don't be surprised if readers or colleagues offer some suggestions for improving the structure of your draft. You can anticipate their objections by reading your own essay critically.

CHECKLIST

To Test the Organization of Your Paper . . .

- **Underline the topic idea or thesis in your draft.** It should be clearly stated somewhere in the first few paragraphs.
- **Underline just the first sentence in each subsequent paragraph.** If the first sentence is unusually short or the second is directly related to the first, underline the first two sentences.
- **Read the underlined sentences straight through as if they formed an essay themselves.** Ask yourself how each sentence advances or develops the main point or thesis statement. If the sentences, read together, sound reasonably coherent, chances are good that the paper is effectively organized.
- **If the underlined sentences don't make sense, reexamine those paragraphs not clearly related to the topic idea.** If the ideas really are not related, cut the whole paragraph. If the ideas *are* related, consider how to revise the paragraph to highlight that relationship. Often, a new lead sentence for the paragraph will solve the problem. Give more attention to transitions.

Don't be reluctant to make large-scale changes in organization. A first draft often serves only to identify the subject you really wanted to discuss. Even if you end up discarding or substantially rearranging most of what you have written, the effort won't have been wasted if the result is a clearer, more convincing piece of research.

33h–2 **Test your conclusion against your introduction and make any needed modifications.** Sometimes the ends of essays do not agree with their openings. What's happened is that the original ideas have matured and developed: the researchers have learned something.

Yet a surprising number of writers don't bother to readjust their opening paragraphs to reflect their new conclusions. They aren't necessarily lazy; they just don't realize how much they have learned since they wrote their introductions—hours or, more likely, days earlier. When you've completed a draft, put it aside for a day or two and then reread the entire piece. Does it all hang together? If not, revise.

33h–3 Edit the body of your research essay carefully.

CHECKLIST

To Edit a Research Paper . . .

- Check spelling. Look for transposed letters, slips of the pen, illegible words, and omitted endings, especially *-ed* and *-s*.
- Check possessive forms. Don't forget the apostrophe (') before or after the *-s*: boy**'s,** boy**s'.** Don't confuse *its* (possessive form) with *it's* (contraction for *it is*).
- Check that titles of books, plays, and other long or major works are underlined: The Hunt for Red October.
- Check that titles of articles, songs, and short poems are set between quotation marks: "Straight from the Heart."
- Check for words or phrases that have been omitted from your text, or words that have been inadvertently repeated.
- Check for errors that crop up habitually in your writing.

33i
resrch

33i WHAT'S THE RIGHT FORM FOR A RESEARCH PAPER?

Troubleshooting

You can recognize a research paper almost as much by appearance as by what it says. Because these essays represent a first level of serious academic and professional research, most teachers expect research papers to have features not found in ordinary essays. These requirements vary from discipline to discipline and from teacher to teacher. Some instructors are flexible about their standards, provided that your handling of textual matters (margins, headings, documentation) is reasonably consistent throughout your essay. Other instructors allow little deviation from prescribed standards. To play it safe, be consistent and careful when writing a research paper.

Many writers, however, worry too much about format requirements, forgetting that the most important feature of a research paper is its content—what it has to offer. A beautiful text is worthless if it presents no new ideas. Yet neither is it good strategy to do fine research and then make yourself look incompetent—especially when the format requirements of a research paper are relatively easy to manage.

To be sure your research paper looks right . . .

33i–1 **Type your paper.** If you type only one paper during a term, this should be it. If you aren't a good typist, you may want to take this essay to a typing service. A research paper shouldn't look like an amateur effort, full of strikeovers, whiteouts, and wandering margins. Also, be sure the keys in your typewriter are clean and the ribbon has some ink in it. Don't experiment with colors. Use good-quality paper, type only on one side, and double-space the body of your essay and the notes. Avoid onionskin paper—the kind that is so thin it's almost transparent.

If you write your research paper by hand, try to approximate a typed text: neat margins, clean surface, legible sentences. Use dark ink (blue or black), double-space (unless your instructor says otherwise), and write on only one side of the paper.

If you use a word processor, be sure your printer produces copy your instructor finds acceptable. Buy good-quality computer paper, separate the pages, and pull off the tractor tabs before handing in an essay. Make certain the ribbon in your printer is fresh. Some computers can vary type fonts and produce boldface and italics. Keep the fonts simple and use boldface strategically to highlight important headings. Never print an entire paper in boldface. You may use italics for titles you would have underlined on a typewriter, but be consistent. Don't underline some titles and italicize others. (See pp. 89–104 on document design.)

Whatever scheme or format you decide upon for your research essay, stick with it throughout the paper. Keep your margins even, all around the page: a one-inch margin works well, top, bottom, left, and right. Don't change typewriters or paper. Don't vary the way you handle titles or headings.

33i–2 **Include all the parts your assignment requires.** Before you turn a paper in, reread the assignment sheet to review your instructor's requirements for the essay. In some cases, the assignment will require you to follow a documentation scheme or style sheet different from the MLA, APA, CBE, or ACW forms described in this text. Be sure to do so.

Check to see what leeway (if any) you have in handling title pages or other features. The sample research essay on pages 630–652 presents a model paper in MLA style, and the essay on pages 696–710 presents a paper in APA style.

33i-3 **Arrange the parts of your research essay in the proper order.**
For a more complex paper such as a master's thesis or dissertation, follow
the order recommended either by an instructor or a volume such as *The
MLA Style Manual* (MLA); *Publication Manual of the American Psychological Association* (APA); or *Scientific Style and Format: The CBE Manual
for Authors, Editors, and Publishers* (CBE).

CHECKLIST

Order of a Research Paper

- **Title page** (not recommended in MLA; required in APA)
- **Outline** (optional; begins on its own page; requires separate title page)
- **Abstract** (optional, but common in APA and CBE; usually on its own page)
- **Body of the essay** (Arabic pagination begins with body of the essay in MLA; APA Arabic pagination begins with title page)
- **Content or bibliographic notes**
- **Works Cited/References** (begins on its own page separate from the body of the essay or any content or bibliographical notes)

33i-4 **Follow the rules for documentation right down
to the punctuation and spacing.** Accurate documentation
is part of professional research. Instructors and editors notice
even minor variances in documentation form. Perhaps the
two most common errors in handling the MLA format, for example, are
forgetting to put a period at the end of entries in the Works Cited list
and placing a comma where none is needed in parenthetical documentation.

Wrong   Pluto, Terry. <u>The Curse of Rocky Colavito</u>. New

York: Simon, 1994

Right   Pluto, Terry. <u>The Curse of Rocky Colavito</u>. New

York: Simon, 1994.

Wrong   (Pluto, 132-33)

Right   (Pluto 132-33)

You will survive both errors, but they are easy to avoid. Chapters 34 and 35 more fully cover MLA, ACW, APA, and CBE documentation.

33i-5 **Check special research paper requirements.** As you finish up, run through this roster of questions.

C H E C K L I S T

Research Paper Requirements

_____ Name, date, course on first or title page?

_____ Title centered? Only major words capitalized? (Your title should *not* be underlined.)

_____ Did you number the pages? Are they in the right order?

_____ Have you used quotation marks and parentheses correctly and *in pairs*? Closing quotation marks and parentheses are often forgotten.

_____ Have you placed quotation marks (" ") around all direct quotations shorter than four lines?

_____ Have you indented all direct quotations over four typed lines long (MLA) or forty words (APA)? (Remember that indented quotations are not placed in quotation marks.)

_____ Did you introduce all direct quotations with some identification of their author, source, or significance?

_____ Did you use the correct form for parenthetical notes?

_____ Did you include a list of Works Cited or a References list? Is your list of Works Cited alphabetically arranged? Did you indent the entries correctly?

33i-6 **Bind your paper sensibly.** Be proud of your research paper, but don't treat it like a Gutenberg Bible. Bind it together modestly with a paper clip. Nothing more elaborate is needed—unless your teacher also asks you to hand in all the materials used in preparing the essay. If that is the case, place the essay (still clipped) and related materials in a sturdy envelope or in a folder with pockets.

Check with your instructor before stapling a research paper; some teachers like to read essays with the outline or Works Cited list placed alongside the body of the paper. Don't even consider handing in an essay that is not clipped together.

33i-7 **Examine a sample research paper.** Check your paper against the sample essays provided in Chapter 34 or Chapter 35.

SUMMARY

Research Paper Calendar

- **Find a Topic**
  _____ Explore several potential topic areas.
  _____ Do exploratory reading.
  _____ Choose a preliminary topic/thesis.   By _____

- **Look for Information**
  _____ Check the library catalog.
  _____ Locate suitable bibliographies.
  _____ Check indexes and databases.
  _____ Check other sources, including the Internet and WWW.
  _____ Prepare a working bibliography.   By _____

- **Write a Draft**
  _____ Formulate a clear thesis or assertion.
  _____ Organize the information.
  _____ Write a first draft.   By _____

- **Revise**
  _____ Review the original assignment.
  _____ Get feedback on the first draft and revise.
  _____ Review documentation.
  _____ Review format requirements.
  _____ Edit for mechanical problems.   By _____

34

How Do You Write in the Humanities?

Courses in the humanities—that is, in philosophy, history, literature, rhetoric and communication, and the fine arts—concern themselves with the history, development, and impact of human ideas and works. Research methods within the humanities differ greatly. Scholars of literature, history, or philosophy work both to preserve human artifacts (literary works, historical records, ideas) and to interpret them. One scholar may spend an entire career searching for shards in a desert to understand an ancient culture; another may study newspapers and journals in a library to refine a theory about contemporary political discourse.

In the classroom, courses in the humanities usually focus on ideas and language. Papers written for such classes tend to be analytical: they take concepts apart, compare them, debate them, or demonstrate where they fit in relation to other ideas. While research in the humanities can involve experimentation, classroom work usually means studying and interpreting texts and artifacts—books, works of literature, films, essays.

This chapter explains how to prepare documentation in humanities courses and how to handle several assignments common in these disciplines.

◆ Point of Difference

Conventions of research, style, and documentation differ significantly. If you need to know what's appropriate in a particular field, discipline, or English-speaking country, consult a book such as John Bruce Howell's *Style Manuals of the English-Speaking World*. Look for this annotated bibliography in the reference section of your library. ◆

34a   HOW DO YOU USE MLA DOCUMENTATION?

Troubleshooting

In most college English and humanities courses, you will be expected to follow the conventions of documentation and format recommended by the Modern Language Association (MLA). The basic procedures for MLA documentation are spelled out in the following section.

If you encounter documentation problems not discussed below or go on to do advanced work in a discipline that follows MLA guidelines, you may want to refer to the *MLA Handbook for Writers of Research Papers* or *The MLA Style Manual*, both edited by Joseph Gibaldi. These books are available in most college libraries.

For common sources (books, newspapers, articles by single authors), systems of documentation are almost always more difficult to explain than to use. Once you get the hang of MLA style, you'll find it easy and efficient. But it is important to follow the rules carefully. Seemingly small matters, such as spacing and punctuation, *do* count when you are preparing notes and bibliographies. And be prepared to consult this handbook when you encounter an unfamiliar source: a computer program, a film, a government document, an interview, a musical composition, an Internet reference.

The best advice for efficient documentation is this: Know the basic procedure and verify the details. The two basic steps are outlined below, followed by an extended Fine Tuning section. The MLA Form Directory on pages 601 through 627 lists the correct forms for many kinds of parenthetical notes and for their corresponding Works Cited entries.

34a
MLA

To use MLA documentation . . .

34a-1 (Step 1) In the text of your paper, place a note in parentheses to identify the source of every passage or idea you must document. For example, here is a sentence that includes a direct quote from page 435 of *Ralph Bunche: An American Life* by Brian Urquhart.

```
Ralph Bunche never wavered in his belief that the

races in America had to learn to live together: "In
```

```
all of his experience of racial discrimination

Bunche never allowed himself to become bitter or to

feel racial hatred" (Urquhart 435).
```

As you can see, the basic MLA note consists of the author's last name and a page number within parentheses. The author's name and the page on which the quoation is located are separated by a single typed space. Page numbers are *not* preceded by *p.* or *pp.* or by a comma.

```
(Urquhart 435)

(Bly 253-54)
```

You can shorten a note by naming the author of the source in the body of the essay; then the note consists only of a page number. This is a common and readable form, one you should use regularly.

```
Brian Urquhart, a biographer of Ralph Bunche,

asserts that "[i]n all of his experience of racial

discrimination Bunche never allowed himself to

become bitter or to feel racial hatred" (435).
```

As a general rule, make all parenthetical notes as brief and inconspicuous as possible.

The parenthetical note is usually placed right after a passage needing documentation, typically at the end of a sentence and within the final punctuation mark. However, with a quotation long enough (four typed lines or more) to require indention, the parenthetical note falls outside the final punctuation mark. Compare the following examples.

SHORT QUOTATION

The quote is not indented.

```
Ralph Bunche never wavered in his belief that the

races in America had to learn to live together: "In

all of his experience of racial discrimination Bunche

never allowed himself to become bitter or to feel

racial hatred" (Urquhart 435). He continued to

work . . .        The note is placed inside the final punctuation mark.
```

LONG QUOTATION

The quote is indented one inch or ten spaces.

```
Winner of the Nobel Peace Prize in 1950, Ralph

Bunche, who died in 1971, left an enduring legacy:

          His memory lives on, especially in the long

          struggle for human dignity and against

          racial discrimination and bigotry, and in

          the growing effectiveness of the United

          Nations in resolving conflicts and keeping

          the peace.  (Urquhart 458)
```

The note is placed outside the final punctuation mark.

34a–2 **(Step 2) On a separate page at the end of your paper, list every source cited in a parenthetical note.** This alphabetical list of sources is labeled Works Cited. The Works Cited entry for Brian Urquhart's biography of Bunche discussed in 34a–1 would look like this.

```
Urquhart, Brian. Ralph Bunche: An American Life. New

     York: Norton, 1993.
```

34a
MLA

The first few entries on a full Works Cited page might look like this.

Subsequent lines indented one-half inch or five spaces   "Works Cited" centered   All Items double spaced

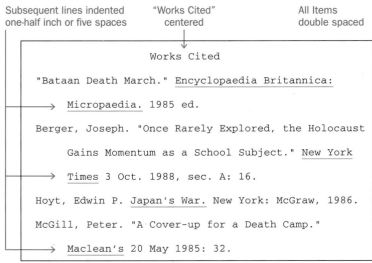

```
                    Works Cited

"Bataan Death March." Encyclopaedia Britannica:

     Micropaedia. 1985 ed.

Berger, Joseph. "Once Rarely Explored, the Holocaust

     Gains Momentum as a School Subject." New York

     Times 3 Oct. 1988, sec. A: 16.

Hoyt, Edwin P. Japan's War. New York: McGraw, 1986.

McGill, Peter. "A Cover-up for a Death Camp."

     Maclean's 20 May 1985: 32.
```

A typical **MLA Works Cited entry for a book** includes the following basic information.

- Author, last name first, followed by a period and a space.
- Title of work, underlined, followed by a period and a space.
- Place of publication, followed by a colon.
- Publisher, followed by a comma.
- Date of publication, followed by a period.

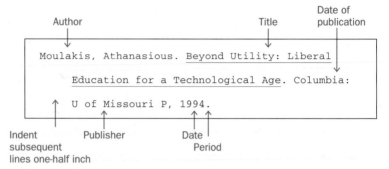

A typical **MLA Works Cited entry for an article in a scholarly journal** (where the pagination is continuous throughout a year) includes the following basic information.

- Author, last name first, followed by a period and a space.
- Title of work, followed by a period and between quotation marks.
- Name of the periodical, underlined, followed by a space.
- Volume number, followed by the date in parentheses, and a colon. For the date, you usually need to give only the year; however, if necessary to avoid confusion, you may add the season or month of the issue: 33 (Fall 1994) or 27 (May 1962).
- Page, followed by a period. Page numbers should be inclusive, from the first page of the article to the last, including notes and bibliography.

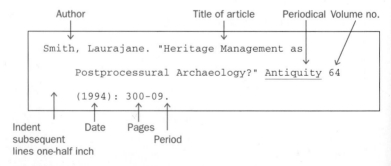

34a
MLA

A typical **MLA Works Cited entry for an article in a popular magazine or newspaper** includes the following basic information.

- Author, last name first, followed by a period and a space.
- Title of work, followed by a period and between quotation marks.
- Name of the periodical or newspaper, underlined.
- Date of publication, followed by a colon. Abbreviate all months except May, June, and July.
- Page and/or location (section number for newspapers), followed by a period. Pages should be inclusive.

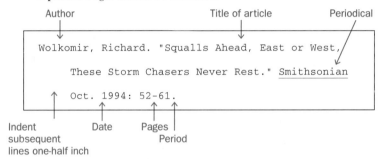

Author   Title of article   Periodical

```
Wolkomir, Richard. "Squalls Ahead, East or West,
      These Storm Chasers Never Rest." Smithsonian
      Oct. 1994: 52-61.
```

Indent   Date   Pages
subsequent   Period
lines one-half inch

A typical **MLA Works Cited entry for an electronic source** includes the following basic information.

- Author, last name first, followed by a period and a space.
- Title of work, followed by a period. Underline book titles; place article titles between quotation marks. A single space follows.
- Publication information, followed by a period and a space.
- Publication medium, followed by a period and a space.
- Name of the computer service or network, followed by a period and a space.
- The date you accessed the information.
- (Optional) The electronic address, preceded by the word *Available*, followed by a period. The period is not part of the electronic address.

34a
MLA

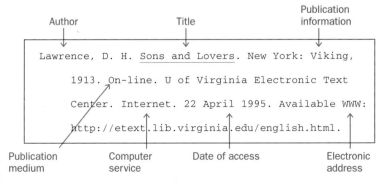

                                                       Publication
Author   Title   information

```
Lawrence, D. H. Sons and Lovers. New York: Viking,
      1913. On-line. U of Virginia Electronic Text
      Center. Internet. 22 April 1995. Available WWW:
      http://etext.lib.virginia.edu/english.html.
```

Publication   Computer   Date of access   Electronic
medium   service   address

There are so many variations to these general entries, however, that you will want to check the MLA Form Directory on pages 601 through 627 for the correct format of any unusual entry.

The Works Cited page itself follows the body of the essay (and an endnote page—if there is one). It lists bibliographical information on all the materials you used in composing the essay. You do not, however, include sources you examined but did not cite in the body of the paper itself. When an author has more than one work on the list, those works are listed alphabetically under the author's name, using this form.

```
Altick, Richard D. The Shows of London. Cambridge:

    Belknap-Harvard, 1978.

---. Victorian People and Ideas. New York: Norton,

    1973.

---. Victorian Studies in Scarlet. New York: Norton,

    1977.
```

Works published since 1900 include a publisher's name. Publishers' names should be shortened whenever possible. Drop words such as *Company, Inc., Ltd., Bro., Books*, and so on. Abbreviate *University* to *U* and *University Press* to *UP*. When possible, shorten a publisher's name to one word. Here are some suggested abbreviations.

34a
MLA

Allyn and Bacon	Allyn
Barnes and Noble Books	Barnes
Doubleday and Co., Inc.	Doubleday
Gale Research Co.	Gale
HarperCollins Publishers	Harper
Harvard University Press	Harvard UP
D. C. Heath and Co.	Heath
Rand McNally and Co.	Rand
University of Chicago Press	U of Chicago P
The Viking Press, Inc.	Viking

CHECKLIST

To set up a Works Cited page . . .

- Center the title "Works Cited" at the top of the page.
- Arrange the items in the Works Cited list alphabetically by the last name of the author. If no author is given for a work, list it according to its title, excluding articles (*The, A, An*).

- Be sure the first line of each entry touches the left-hand margin. Subsequent lines are indented one-half inch or five spaces.
- Double-space the entire list. Do not quadruple-space between entries unless that is the form your teacher prefers.
- Punctuate items in the list carefully. Don't forget the period at the end of each entry.

▶ **Fine Tuning**

1. **When two or more sources are cited within a single sentence,** the parenthetical notes appear conveniently after the statements they support.

   While the ecology of the aquifer might be hardier than originally suspected (Porter 42-48), there is no reason to believe that "the best interests of all the people of the county" (Dixon 62) would be served by the creation of a mall and shopping district in a vicinity described as "one of the last outposts of undisturbed nature in the state" (Martinez 28).

   Notice that a parenthetical note is placed outside any quotation marks, but before the period that ends the sentence.

2. **When you mention an author's name while introducing quoted or borrowed material,** you don't have to repeat the name in the parenthetical note.

   While Commissioner Porter argues in her report that the ecology of the aquifer might be hardier than originally suspected (42-48), there is no reason to build a mall and shopping district in a vicinity described by naturalist Joe Martinez as "one of the last outposts of undisturbed nature in the state" (28).

Similarly, you don't have to repeat a name in subsequent references provided that no other sources are mentioned between these references. After the first reference, page numbers are sufficient until another citation intervenes.

```
. . . the creation of a mall and shopping district

in a vicinity described by naturalist Joe Martinez

as "one of the last outposts of undisturbed nature

in the state" (28). The aquifer area provides a

unique environment for several valuable species of

birds and plant life (31). The birds, especially

the endangered vireo, require breeding areas free

from the encroaching signs of development: roads,

lights, and human presence (Harrison and Cafiero

189). The plant life is similarly susceptible to

soil erosion that has followed land development in

other areas of the county (Martinez 41).
```

34a
MLA

3. **When a work has two or three authors,** put the names of all the authors in the note: (Brooks and Heilman 24). On the Works Cited page, list the second authors in the usual order.

```
                    Works Cited

Brooks, Cleanth, and R. J. Heilman, eds.

        Understanding Drama: Twelve Plays. New York:

        Holt, 1945.
```

4. **When a work has four or more authors,** you can put either the names of all the authors in the note or just the name of the first author followed by the expression *et al.* (the Latin abbreviation for "and others"). The form you use should match your entry on the Works Cited page.

- **Note with all authors named:** (Curtin, Feierman, Thompson, and Vansina 77)

Works Cited

Curtin, Philip, Steven Feierman, Leonard Thompson,

and Jan Vansina, eds. <u>African History</u>. Boston:

Little, 1978.

- **Note with et al.:** (Curtin et al. 77)

Works Cited

Curtin, Philip, et al., eds. <u>African History</u>. Boston:

Little, 1978.

5. **When you cite more than one work by a single author** in a paper, a parenthetical note that gives only the author's last name could refer to more than one item on the Works Cited page by that person. To avoid any mix-up, place a comma after the author's name and identify the work being cited. Use a shortened version of the title. For example, a Works Cited page might list the following works by Richard D. Altick.

Works Cited

Altick, Richard D. <u>The Art of Literary Research</u>.

New York: Norton, 1963.

---. <u>The Shows of London</u>. Cambridge: Belknap-Harvard,

1978.

---. <u>Victorian People and Ideas</u>. New York: Norton,

1973.

---. <u>Victorian Studies in Scarlet</u>. New York: Norton,

1977.

**34a
MLA**

The first time—and every time—you refer to anything by Richard Altick, you'd need briefly to identify the work by name in the parenthetical note.

(Altick, <u>Art</u> 34)

(Altick, <u>Shows</u> 345)

(Altick, <u>Victorian People</u> 190-202)

(Altick, <u>Victorian Studies</u> 59)

6. **When you want to refer to an entire work,** not just to certain pages, omit page references from the parenthetical note. Let's say that you use the following article in preparing a paper on *Hamlet*.

```
                Works Cited

Wentersdorf, Karl P. "Hamlet's Encounter with the

     Pirates." Shakespeare Quarterly 34 (1983):

     434-40.
```

To cite the complete essay in your paper (not any particular pages), give only the author's name in parentheses.

```
Entire articles have been written about Hamlet's

encounter with the pirates in Act IV (Wentersdorf).
```

This is, however, an awkward type of citation. It would be better simply to name the author of the article in the body of your paper.

```
Wentersdorf has written an entire article about

Hamlet's encounter with the pirates in Act IV.
```

7. **When you need to document a work without an author**—an article in a magazine, for example, or a newspaper story—simply list the title, shortened if necessary, and the page number.

**34a
MLA**

```
("In the Thicket" 18)

("Students Rally" 11)

                Works Cited

"In the Thicket of Things." Texas Monthly Apr. 1994:

     18.

"Students Rally for Academic Freedom." The Chronicle

     of Higher Education 28 Sept. 1994: A6.
```

8. **When you want to cite more than a single work in a note,** separate the citations with a semicolon.

```
     (Polukord 13-16; Ryan and Weber 126)
```

But if a parenthetical citation contains so many sources that it interrupts the smooth reading of a sentence, a *bibliographical note* (see p. 569) may be a reasonable alternative. In a bibliographical note, you may list as many sources as you need and comment on them.

³On this matter see Polukord 13-16; Granchi and

Guillen 126; Valusek and Syrek 188-94; and Shortell

23-64. Holding the opposite view are Lyon 120-55 and

Greely 148-201. Elton is widely regarded as

unreliable. ◀

34b MLA FORM DIRECTORY

Below, you will find the MLA Works Cited and parenthetical note forms for more than sixty kinds of sources. Simply find the type of work you need to cite in either the Format Index or the Alphabetical Index and then locate that work by number in the list that follows.

MLA Format Index

Books/Dissertations

1. Book, one author
2. Book, two or three authors
3. Book, four or more authors
4. Book, revised by a second author
5. Book, edited—focus on the editor
6. Book, edited—focus on the editor, more than one editor
7. Book, edited—focus on the original author
8. Book, authored by a group
9. Book with no author
10. Book, focus on a foreword, introduction, preface, or afterword
11. Work, multivolume
12. Book, translation—focus on the original author
13. Book, translation—focus on the translator
14. Book, in a foreign language
15. Book, republished
16. Book, part of a series
17. Book, a collection or anthology
18. Book, a second, third, or later edition
19. Book, a chapter in
20. Book, published before 1900
21. Book, issued by a division of a publisher—a special imprint
22. Book, title includes the title of another work normally between quotation marks

23. Book, title includes the title of another work normally underlined
24. Dissertation or thesis—published
25. Dissertation or thesis—unpublished
26. Proceedings of a conference or meeting

Articles and Magazine Pieces

27. Article in a scholarly journal
28. Article in a popular magazine
29. Article in a weekly or biweekly magazine
30. Article in a monthly magazine—author named
31. Article in a monthly magazine—author not named
32. Article or selection reprinted in a reader or anthology

Newspapers

33. Article in a newspaper—author named
34. Article in a newspaper—author not named
35. Editorial in a newspaper
36. Letter to the editor
37. Cartoon

Reference Works/Computers

38. Reference work or encyclopedia, entry in a familiar
39. Reference work, entry in a less familiar
40. Bulletin or pamphlet
41. Government document
42. Map
43. Computer software
44. On-line database, journal, or conference

45. CD-ROM/diskette database or publication
46. Microfilm or microfiche

Miscellaneous Entries

47. Biblical citation
48. Videotape
49. Movie
50. Television program
51. Radio program
52. Interview, personal
53. Musical composition
54. Recording
55. Speech—no printed text
56. Speech—printed text
57. Lecture
58. Letter—published
59. Letter or e-mail—unpublished
60. Artwork
61. Book review—titled or untitled
62. Drama or play

MLA Alphabetical Index

**34b
MLA**

1. Book, One Author—MLA

Works Cited

Weinberg, Steven. <u>Dreams of a Final Theory</u>. New York:

Pantheon, 1992.

Parenthetical note: (Weinberg 38)

2. Book, Two or Three Authors or Editors—MLA

Invert the name of only the first author for purposes of alphabetization—in this case, Matalin, Mary. List additional authors and editors in their usual order—James Carville. In the example below, a third author is identified on the title page as assisting on the project.

Works Cited

Matalin, Mary, and James Carville. <u>All's Fair: Love,</u>

   <u>War, and Running for President</u>. With Peter

   Knobler. New York: Random, 1994.

Parenthetical note: (Matalin and Carville 346-50)

3. **Book, Four or More Authors or Editors—MLA** Either name all authors or name the first author listed on the title page and use the Latin abbreviation *et al.*, which means "and others." Although a Latin abbreviation, *et al.* is neither italicized nor underlined. Commas are needed around *et al.* only when it is followed by a specification such as *eds.* (editors) or *trans.* (translators).

Works Cited

Abrams, M. H., et al., eds. <u>The Norton Anthology of</u>

   <u>English Literature: The Major Authors</u>. 5th ed.

   New York: Norton, 1987.

Parenthetical note: (Abrams et al. 19-21)

4. **Book Revised by a Second Author—MLA** Sometimes you may need to cite a book by its original author, even when it has been revised. In such a case, place the editor's name after the title of the book.

**34b
MLA**

Works Cited

Guerber, Hélène Adeline. <u>The Myths of Greece and</u>

   <u>Rome</u>. Ed. Dorothy Margaret Stuart. 3rd ed.

   London: Harrap, 1965.

Parenthetical note: (Guerber 20)

5. **Book, Edited—Focus on the Editor—MLA** If you cite an edited work by the editor's name, identify the original author after the title of the work.

Works Cited

Noyes, George R., ed. <u>The Poetical Works of John</u>

   <u>Dryden</u>. By John Dryden. Boston: Houghton, 1950.

Parenthetical note: (Noyes v-vi)

6. **Book, Edited—Focus on the Editor, More Than One Editor—MLA** Treat multiple editors just like multiple authors, but place the abbreviation for editors (eds.) after their names.

Works Cited

Detweiler, Robert, John N. Sutherland, and Michael S.

    Werthman, eds. Environmental Decay in Its

    Historical Context. Glenview: Scott, 1973.

Parenthetical note: (Detweiler et al. 3)

7. **Book, Edited—Focus on the Original Author—MLA** Notice that because the sample Works Cited entry is an edition of Shakespeare, the parenthetical note furnishes act/scene/line numbers for a particular play—not author and page numbers one might expect with another kind of book.

Works Cited

Shakespeare, William. The Complete Works of

    Shakespeare. Ed. David Bevington. 4th ed. New

    York: Harper, 1992.

Parenthetical note: (Ham. 4.5.179-85)

34b
MLA

8. **Book Written by a Group—MLA** In the Works Cited entry, treat the group—whether a committee, commission, board, publisher, or other entity—as the author. But to avoid a confusing parenthetical note, identify the group in the body of your paper and place only the relevant page numbers in parentheses. For example, you might write a sentence like this: "The Reader's Digest *Fix-It-Yourself Manual* lists the basic tools you need for furniture repair (54–55)."

Works Cited

Reader's Digest. Fix-It-Yourself Manual.

    Pleasantville, NY: Reader's Digest, 1977.

Parenthetical note: (Reader's Digest 54-55)

9. **Book with No Author—MLA** List any items without authors by their titles, alphabetizing them by the first major word (excluding *The*, *A*, or *An*). For the parenthetical note, use a short title, but be sure it begins with the same word by which the full title will be alphabetized on the Works Cited page. In the following example, it would be wrong to shorten the title to *Atlas*; readers would find no such entry on the Works Cited page.

Works Cited

<u>Illustrated Atlas of the World</u>. Chicago: Rand, 1985.

Parenthetical note: (<u>Illustrated Atlas</u> 88-89)

10. **Book, Focus on a Foreword, Introduction, Preface, or Afterword—MLA** The note below refers to information in Tanner's introduction, not to the text of Jane Austen's novel.

Works Cited

Tanner, Tony. Introduction. <u>Mansfield Park</u>. By Jane

    Austen. Harmondsworth, Eng.: Penguin, 1966.

    7-36.

Parenthetical note: (Tanner 9-10)

11. **Work of More Than One Volume—MLA** When you use only one volume of a multivolume set, identify in your Works Cited entry both the volume you have actually used and the total number of volumes in the set. But in your parenthetical note, do *not* give a volume number since the Works Cited entry already specifies the volume you have used. Notice how to abbreviate and capitalize *volume(s)* in such an entry.

Works Cited

Spindler, Karlheinz. <u>Abstract Algebra with</u>

    <u>Applications</u>. Vol. 1. New York: Dekker, 1994.

    2 vols.

Parenthetical note: (Spindler 17-18)

If, however, you use more than one volume of a multivolume set, in the Works Cited entry list only the total number of volumes in

34b
MLA

that set. Then, in your parenthetical notes, identify the specific volumes as you used them.

Works Cited

Spindler, Karlheinz. <u>Abstract Algebra with</u>

<u>Applications</u>. 2 vols. New York: Dekker, 1994.

Parenthetical notes: (Spindler 1: 17-18); (Spindler

2: 369)

12. Book, Translation—Focus on the Original Author—MLA

Works Cited

Freire, Paulo. <u>Learning to Question: A Pedagogy of</u>

<u>Liberation</u>. Trans. Tony Coates. New York:

Continuum, 1989.

Parenthetical note: (Freire 137-38)

13. Book, Translation—Focus on the Translator—MLA

Works Cited

Swanton, Michael, trans. <u>Beowulf</u>. New York: Barnes,

1978.

Parenthetical note: (Swanton 17-18)

14. Book in a Foreign Language—MLA Copy the title of the foreign work exactly as it appears on the title page, paying special attention to both accent marks and capitalization, which may differ from English conventions.

Works Cited

Bablet, Denis, and Jean Jacquot. <u>Les Voies de la</u>

<u>création théâtrale</u>. Paris: Editions du Centre

National de la Recherche Scientifique, 1977.

Parenthetical note: (Bablet and Jacquot 59)

15. **Book, Republished—MLA** When it's important that readers know when a book was first published, give the original publication date immediately after the title. Supply original publication dates with works of fiction that have been through many editions and reprints.

Works Cited

Herbert, Frank. <u>Dune</u>. 1965. New York: Berkeley, 1977.

Parenthetical note: (Herbert 146)

16. **Book, Part of a Series—MLA** Give the series name just before the publishing information. Do not underline or italicize a series name.

Works Cited

Kirk, Grayson, and Nils H. Wessell, eds. <u>The Soviet</u>

<u>Threat: Myths and Realities</u>. Proceedings of the

Academy of Political Science 33. New York:

Academy of Political Science, 1978.

Parenthetical note: (Kirk and Wessell 62)

17. **Book, a Collection or Anthology—MLA** Notice that when you quote from the preface or introduction to the collection, the page numbers you provide in a parenthetical note may sometimes be Roman numerals. (To cite a selection within an anthology, see model 32.)

Works Cited

Lunsford, Andrea, and John Ruszkiewicz, eds. <u>The</u>

<u>Presence of Others</u>. New York: St. Martin's,

1994.

Parenthetical note: (Lunsford and Ruszkiewicz xiii-xv)

18. **Book, a Second, Third, or Later Edition—MLA** Identify the edition of a book immediately after its title: 2nd ed., 3rd ed., 4th ed., and so on. You do not provide this information for a first edition.

34b
MLA

Works Cited

Rombauer, Marjorie Dick. <u>Legal Problem Solving:</u>

<u>Analysis, Research, and Writing</u>. 5th ed. St.

Paul: West, 1991.

Parenthetical note: (Rombauer 480-81)

19. **Chapter in a Book—MLA**

Works Cited

Owens, Delia, and Mark Owens. "Home to the Dunes."

<u>The Eye of the Elephant: An Epic Adventure in</u>

<u>the African Wilderness</u>. Boston: Houghton, 1992:

11-27.

Parenthetical note: (Owens 24-27)

20. **Book Published Before 1900—MLA** In most cases, omit the name of the publisher in citations to works published prior to 1900.

Works Cited

Bowdler, Thomas, ed. <u>The Family Shakespeare</u>. 10 vols.

London, 1818.

Parenthetical note: (Bowdler 2: 47)

21. **Book Issued by a Division of a Publisher—a Special Imprint—MLA** Attach the special imprint (Vintage in this case) to the publisher's name with a hyphen.

Works Cited

Hofstadter, Douglas. <u>Gödel, Escher, Bach: An</u>

<u>Eternal Golden Braid</u>. New York: Vintage-Random,

1980.

Parenthetical note: (Hofstadter 192-93)

22. **Book Whose Title Includes the Title of Another Work Normally Between Quotation Marks—MLA**

Works Cited

Crossley-Holland, Kevin, and Bruce Mitchell, eds.

"The Battle of Maldon" and Other Old English

Poems. London: Macmillan, 1965.

Parenthetical note: (Crossley-Holland and Mitchell 29)

23. **Book Whose Title Includes the Title of Another Work Normally Underlined—MLA** Examine the sample entry carefully. *Hamlet,* the title of a play, would ordinarily be underlined if it stood alone. But as a part of a title, it is not underscored. If you use a computer capable of setting italics, the title would look like this: *The Question of* Hamlet.

Works Cited

Levin, Harry. The Question of Hamlet. London: Oxford

UP, 1959.

Parenthetical note: (Levin 10)

24. **Dissertation or Thesis—Published (Including Publication by UMI)—MLA** Many dissertations are made available through University Microfilms International (UMI). If the dissertation you are citing is published by UMI, be sure to provide the order number, the last item in the sample Works Cited entry. The abbreviation *diss.* indicates that the source is a dissertation.

**34b
MLA**

Works Cited

Rifkin, Myra Lee. Burial, Funeral and Mourning

Customs in England, 1558-1662. Diss. Bryn Mawr,

1977. Ann Arbor: UMI, 1977. DDJ78-01385.

Parenthetical note: (Rifkin 234)

25. **Dissertation or Thesis—Unpublished—MLA** Note that the titles of unpublished dissertations appear between quotation marks.

Works Cited

```
Altman, Jack, Jr. "The Politics of Health Planning

    and Regulation." Diss. Massachusetts Institute

    of Technology, 1983.
```

Parenthetical note: (Altman 150)

26. Proceedings of a Conference or Meeting—MLA

Works Cited

```
Odom, Keith C. 1983 Proceedings of the Conference of

    College Teachers of English. 3-5 Mar. 1983. Fort

    Worth: Dept. of English, Texas Christian U,

    1983.
```

Parenthetical note: (Odom 126-28)

27. Article in a Scholarly Journal—MLA Scholarly journals that
publish original academic and professional research are usually
identified by volume number or season (rather than day, week, or
month of publication). Such journals are often paginated year by
year, with a full year's work gathered together and treated as a volume. That means that page numbers for scholarly journals don't
restart with each new issue but continue throughout a year. Cite
articles from such scholarly journals by providing author, title of article, journal, volume, date, and page numbers. It is helpful, though
not required, to provide a season or month before the year of publication: (Fall 1994); (Oct. 1991).

Works Cited

```
Wentersdorf, Karl P. "Hamlet's Encounter with the

    Pirates." Shakespeare Quarterly 34 (1983):

    434-40.
```

Parenthetical note: (Wentersdorf 434)

If a scholarly journal is paginated issue by issue, place a period and
an issue number after the volume number. That is the only difference in form. For example, if the sample entry above were paginated issue by issue and the cited article were on pages 70–79 in

the third issue of the 1983 volume, the citation would end this
way: 34.3 (1983): 70–79.

28. **Article in a Popular Magazine—MLA** Magazines paginated issue by issue and identified by monthly or weekly dates of publication (instead of by volume number) are cited differently from
scholarly journals. To cite a popular magazine, give the author's
name, title of the article, name of the magazine, date, and page
numbers. If the article does not appear on consecutive pages in the
magazine, give the first page on which it appears followed by a plus
sign: 64+.

Works Cited

Sabbag, Robert. "Fear & Reloading in Gun Valley."

    Men's Journal Oct. 1994: 64+.

Parenthetical note: (Sabbag 64)

29. **Article in a Weekly or Biweekly Magazine—MLA** Give the
date of publication as listed on the issue.

Works Cited

Gray, Paul. "Hurrah for Dead White Males." Time 10

    Oct. 1994: 62-63.

Parenthetical note: (Gray 62)

30. **Article in a Monthly Magazine—Author Named—MLA**

Works Cited

Hudson, Elizabeth. "Hanging Out with the Bats." Texas

    Highways Aug. 1994: 14-19.

Parenthetical note: (Hudson 15)

31. **Article in a Monthly Magazine—Author Not Named—MLA**

Works Cited

"Shelby Charms Another Snake." Car and Driver July

    1994: 33.

Parenthetical note: ("Shelby" 33)

32. An Article or Selection from a Reader or Anthology—MLA
List the item on the Works Cited page by the author of the piece you are actually citing, not the editor(s) of the collection. Then provide the title of the particular selection, the title of the overall collection, the editor(s) of the collection, and publication information. Conclude the entry with the page numbers of the selection within the reader or anthology.

Works Cited

Paglia, Camille. "Madonna--Finally, a Real Feminist."

    The Presence of Others. Ed. Andrea Lunsford and

    John Ruszkiewicz. New York: St. Martin's, 1994.

    486-89.

Parenthetical note: (Paglia 486)

When the selection you are citing is a poem or play, the parenthetical note will ordinarily require an act, scene, or line number rather than a page number.

Works Cited

Randall, Dudley. "Old Witherington." Literature: An

    Introduction to Fiction, Poetry, and Drama. Ed.

    X. J. Kennedy. New York: Harper, 1991. 862.

Parenthetical note: (Randall 4-13)

When you must cite two or more selections from a reader or anthology in a paper, simplify the Works Cited references by first listing the reader fully on the Works Cited page.

Lunsford, Andrea, and John Ruszkiewicz, eds. The

    Presence of Others. New York: St. Martin's,

    1994.

Then list the authors and titles of any articles you are using from that collection, followed by the name of the editors and page numbers of those selections in the collection. Here's what the Works Cited entries might look like for two articles from *The Presence of Others*.

```
Dyson, Freeman. "Engineer's Dreams." Lunsford and

    Ruszkiewicz 222-31.

Paglia, Camille. "Madonna--Finally, a Real Feminist."

    Lunsford and Ruszkiewicz 486-89.
```

Sometimes you may be expected to tell readers where an article or piece was published originally, even though you read the piece in a collection. When that's the case, provide the original publication information first, then give the facts about the collection itself.

Works Cited

```
Hartman, Geoffrey. "Milton's Counterplot." ELH 25

    (1958): 1-12. Rpt. in Milton: A Collection of

    Critical Essays. Ed. Louis L. Martz. Twentieth

    Century Views. Englewood Cliffs: Spectrum-

    Prentice, 1966. 100-08.
```

Parenthetical note: (Hartman 101)

33. Article in a Newspaper—Author Named—MLA While the basic form for a newspaper citation is easy, how you designate a page number for a newspaper can get complicated. If the paper is divided into sections and the page numbers themselves include the section markers (A4, B12, C2), then the page numbers are handled as in the sample item. If, as in the Sunday *New York Times*, the paper is divided into numbered sections but those sections are not a part of the actual page number, then a form like the following is used: sec. 3: 7+. If the paper is numbered consistently from first to last page, just the page number is given. A plus sign following the page number (7+) indicates that the article continues beyond the designated page, but not necessarily on consecutive pages.

**34b
MLA**

Works Cited

```
Peterson, Karen S. "Turns Out We Are 'Sexually

    Conventional.'" USA Today 7 Oct. 1994, 1A+.
```

Parenthetical note: (Peterson 2A)

34. Article in a Newspaper—Author Not Named—MLA

Works Cited

"Nervous Robber Accidently Shoots Himself in the
    Mouth." Houston Chronicle 15 Jan. 1986, state
    final ed., sec. 1: 17.

Parenthetical note: ("Nervous Robber" 17)

35. Editorial in a Newspaper—MLA

Works Cited

"Negro College Fund: Mission Is Still Important on
    50th Anniversary." Editorial. Dallas Morning
    News 8 Oct. 1994, sec. A: 28.

Parenthetical note: ("Negro College" 28)

36. Letter to the Editor—MLA

Works Cited

Cantu, Tony. Letter. San Antonio Light 14 Jan. 1986,
    southwest ed., sec. C: 4.

Parenthetical note: (Cantu 4)

37. Cartoon—MLA To avoid a potentially confusing parenthetical note, describe any cartoon in the text of your essay: "In 'Squib' by Miles Mathis. . . ."

Works Cited

Mathis, Miles. "Squib." Cartoon. Daily Texan 15 Jan.
    1986: 19.

Parenthetical note: (Mathis 19)

38. Reference Work or Encyclopedia (Familiar)—MLA With familiar reference works, especially those revised regularly, you need only identify the edition you are using by its date. You may omit the names of editors and most publishing information. The authors of entries in the *Britannica* and other reference works are some-

times identified by initials. To find the full names of authors, you will need to check an index or, in the case of *Britannica*, the *Guide to the* Britannica included with the set. No page number is given in the parenthetical note when a work is arranged alphabetically.

Works Cited

Benedict, Roger William. "Northwest Passage."

    Encyclopaedia Britannica: Macropaedia. 1974 ed.

Parenthetical note: (Benedict)

39. Reference Work (Less Familiar, see model 38 for comparison) **—MLA** Notice that with less familiar reference tools a full entry is required, including the names of editors and publishing information.

Works Cited

Kovesi, Julius. "Hungarian Philosophy." The

    Encyclopedia of Philosophy. Ed. Paul Edwards.

    8 vols. New York: Macmillan, 1967.

Parenthetical note: (Kovesi)

40. Bulletin or Pamphlet—MLA Treat pamphlets as if they were books: underline titles and provide publishing information.

**34b
MLA**

Works Cited

Computer Services for Students. The University of

    Texas at Austin. Austin: Computation Center,

    1994.

Parenthetical note: (Computer Services 8-9)

41. Government Document—MLA For the Works Cited entry, give the name of the government (national, state, local) and agency issuing the report; the title of the document; and publishing information. If it is a congressional document other than the *Congressional Record*, identify the Congress and, when important, the session (99th Cong., 1st sess.) after the title of the document. You can avoid a lengthy parenthetical note by naming the document in the body of your essay and placing only the relevant page numbers between parentheses, as in this sentence: "This information is from the *1985–86 Official Congressional Directory* (182–84)."

Works Cited

```
United States. Cong. Joint Committee on Printing.

    1985-86 Official Congressional Directory. 99th

    Cong., 1st sess. Washington: GPO, 1985.
```

Parenthetical note: (United States. Cong. Joint Committee

on Printing 182-84)

To cite the *Congressional Record*, give only the date and page number.

```
Cong. Rec. 8 Feb. 1974: 3942-43.
```

42. **Map—MLA** For the Works Cited entry, name the map, identify it as a map, and give available publication information, including a date when available. Avoid parenthetical references by referring to the map directly in the body of your essay, not in a parenthetical note: "The *Arkansas State Highway Map* indicates that the highest elevation in the state is 2,753 feet. . . ."

Works Cited

```
Arkansas State Highway Map. Map. Little Rock:

    Arkansas State Highway and Transportation

    Department, 1992.
```

43. **Computer Software—MLA** If the author of the software is known, his or her name precedes the name of the product. If the software has a volume number, it follows the name of the software: *Microsoft Word.* Vers. 3.0. In most cases, you'll want to avoid parenthetical notes in dealing with software: "Software, such as Microsoft's *FoxPro*. . . ."

Works Cited

```
FoxPro. Vers. 2.5. Diskette. Redmond: Microsoft,

    1993.
```

Parenthetical note: (FoxPro)

44. On-line Database, Journal, or Conference—MLA On-line sources come to you via an electronic hookup—a modem, for example, or a direct link to the Internet. Because of this electronic connection, on-line information can grow and change rapidly, complicating the task of documentation. To cite a book, poem, article, Web page, or other source located on-line, begin with the elements used to document conventional printed sources: author, title, publication information, date of publication or posting, and page numbers. Then provide the following additional information: the publication medium (*Online*); the name of the computer service or computer network that provides the source (for example, *Dialog, CompuServe, Internet*); and the date you accessed the material. An optional but useful addition is the electronic address of the source, beginning with the word *Available*. (*Note carefully*: the period that ends the citation is not a part of this electronic address.)

Works Cited

Austin, Mary. "The Little Coyote." Atlantic

    Monthly 89 (1902): 249-54. Online.

    U of Virginia Electronic Text Center.

    Internet. 3 May 1995. Available WWW:

    http://etext.lib.virginia.edu/english.html.

Parenthetical note: (Austin 250)

34b
MLA

Cite an article from an on-line electronic journal or magazine (that is, one not available in a printed version) by giving the conventional information for a printed source—author, name of journal, publication information. Also give the number of pages or paragraphs if available, or use *n. pag.* to indicate *no pagination*. Then identify the publication medium (*Online*); the name of the computer service or computer network that provided the source; and the date you accessed the material. If page numbers aren't available for an electronic text, avoid in-text parenthetical citations by naming the author(s) in your paper: "Nachman and Jenkins suggest that. . . ."

Works Cited

Nachman, Tony, and Kevin Jenkins. "What's Wrong

    with Education in America?" Trincoll

    Journal 1 Dec. 1994: n. pag. Online.

```
Internet. 22 Apr. 1995. Available WWW:

http://www.trincoll.edu/tj/trincolljournal.

html.
```

If an electronic source you cite also has a printed version, begin the citation with information about that printed source, including the author's name, title, and date of publication. Provide page numbers if they are available through the on-line source—they may not be. Then give all the information required of an electronic source: title of the database underlined; publication medium (*Online*); computer service or network; and date you accessed the material. If you have no page numbers, cite the article in your paper by naming the author: "Kim describes. . . ."

Works Cited

```
Kim, Albert. "Frisco Tech." Entertainment Weekly 14

    Apr. 1995. Pathfinder. Online. Internet. 10 May

    1995. Available WWW: http://www.pathfinder.

    com.
```

When citing material from on-line electronic conferences such as Listservs, user groups, or Usenet newsgroups, identify the author of the document or posting, the title of the document or posting, the name of the conference or group, and the date the item was originally posted. Also give the medium (*Online posting*), the network name, and the date of your access.

Because there is no page number to cite, you would do well to avoid an in-text parenthetical citation by naming the author in the text of your paper: "P. J. Remner argues in favor of clipless pedals. . . ."

Works Cited

```
Remner, P. J. "Re: Toe Clips v. Clipless Pedals."

    21 Apr. 1995. Online posting. Newsgroup

    rec.bicycles.off-road. Usenet. 24 Apr. 1995.
```

**34b
MLA**

45. **CD-ROM/Diskette Database or Publication—MLA** Many electronic sources are accessed through CD-ROM disks (or other electronic media such as diskettes or magnetic tape) rather than through on-line connections. To cite a CD-ROM or similar elec-

tronic database, provide basic information about the source itself: author, title, and publication information. Identify the publication medium (whether *CD-ROM*, *diskette*, *magnetic tape*) and the name of the vendor if available. (The vendor is the company publishing or distributing the database.) Conclude with the date of electronic publication.

Works Cited

```
Bevington, David. "Castles in the Air: The Morality

    Plays." The Theater of Medieval Europe: New

    Research in Early Drama. Ed. Simon Eckchard.

    Cambridge: Cambridge UP, 1993. MLA Bibliography.

    CD-ROM. SilverPlatter. Feb. 1995.
```

Parenthetical note: (Bevington 98)

For a CD-ROM database that is often updated—Proquest, for example—you must provide publication dates for the item you are examining and for the data disk itself.

Works Cited

```
Alva, Sylvia Alatore. "Differential Patterns of

    Achievement Among Asian-American Adolescents."

    Journal of Youth & Adolescence 22 (1993):

    407-23. Proquest General Periodicals. CD-ROM.

    UMI-Proquest. June 1994.
```

Parenthetical note: (Alva 407-10)

Cite a book, encyclopedia, play, or other item published on CD-ROM or diskette just as if it were a printed source, adding the medium of publication (*diskette*, *CD-ROM*).

When page numbers aren't available, use the author's name in the text of the paper rather than a parenthetical citation: "Bolter demonstrates. . . ."

Works Cited

```
Bolter, Jay David. Writing Space: A Hypertext.

    Diskette. Erlbaum, 1990.
```

46. **Microfilm or Microfiche—MLA** Treat material on microfilm exactly as if you had seen it in its original hard-copy version. You need not mention that you used microfilm or microfiche unless the source you are using was originally printed on microfilm or microfiche.

Works Cited

"How Long Will the Chemise Last?" Consumer Reports.

    Aug. 1958: 434-37.

Parenthetical note: ("How Long?" 434)

47. **Biblical Citation—MLA** Note that in MLA style the titles of sacred works, including all versions of the Bible, are not underlined.

Works Cited

The Jerusalem Bible. Ed. Alexander Jones. Garden

    City: Doubleday, 1966.

Parenthetical note: (John 18:37-38)

48. **Videotape—MLA** A video entry is ordinarily listed by its title. Provide the information your readers need about the producer, designer, performers, and so on. The Works Cited entry for a videotape also includes information about distribution and date. Try to avoid parenthetical references to items on videocassette. Simply name the work in the body of your essay: "In Sandy Oliveri's video *Dream Cars of the 50s & 60s . . . .*"

Works Cited

Dream Cars of the 50s & 60s. Videocassette. Compiled

    by Sandy Oliveri. Goodtimes Home Video, 1986.

Parenthetical note: (Dream Cars)

49. **Movie—MLA** In most cases, list a movie by its title on the Works Cited page. But if your focus is on the director, producer, or screenwriter, the entry can be modified, like this.

Lucas, George, dir. American Graffiti. Prod. by

    Francis Ford Coppola. . . .

You can provide information about actors, producers, cinematographers, set designers, and so on, to suit your readers. Be sure to identify the company that produced or distributed the film and supply a production date. Try to avoid in-text parenthetical references to films. Simply name the works in the body of your essay: "In George Lucas's classic film *American Graffiti* . . . ."

Works Cited

American Graffiti. Dir. George Lucas. Perf. Richard

     Dreyfus and Ronny Howard. Universal, 1973.

Parenthetical note: (American Graffiti)

50. Television Program—MLA List the TV program by the episode or name of the program. Note that the name of an episode appears between quotation marks; the name of the program is underlined. Information about narrator, producer, and director follows the episode name but precedes the name of the program. If no episode name is given, the production information follows the program name.

Works Cited

"Mood Music." Prod. Peter Schindler. Dir. Matthew

     Diamond. Perf. Jamie Lee Curtis and Richard

     Lewis. Anything But Love. ABC. KVUE, Austin. 25

     Oct. 1989.

Parenthetical note: ("Mood Music")

51. Radio Program—MLA List the radio program by the episode or name of the program. Note that the name of an episode appears between quotation marks; the name of the program is underlined. Information about narrator, producer, and director follows the episode name but precedes the name of the program. If no episode name is given, the production information follows the program name.

Works Cited

Death Valley Days. Created by Ruth Cornwall Woodman.

     NBC Radio. WNBC, New York. 30 Sept. 1930.

Parenthetical note: (Death Valley Days)

52. **Interview, Personal—MLA** Refer to the interview in the body of your essay rather than in a parenthetical note: "In an interview, James Michener explained. . . ." If the person you are interviewing is not widely known, explain his or her credentials in your essay.

Works Cited

Richards, Ann. Personal interview. 4 Oct. 1993.

53. **Musical Composition—MLA** List the work on the Works Cited page by the name of the composer. If you have sheet music or a score, you can furnish complete publication information. Naming the musical work in the essay itself will usually be preferable to a parenthetical reference.

Works Cited

Joplin, Scott. "The Strenuous Life: A Ragtime Two

    Step." St. Louis: Stark Sheet Music, 1902.

Parenthetical note: (Joplin)

If you don't have a score or sheet music to refer to, provide a simpler entry.

Works Cited

Porter, Cole. "Too Darn Hot." 1949.

54. **Recording—MLA** The "publishing" information for a recording is the record label. Naming the recording in the essay itself will usually be preferable to a parenthetical reference.

Works Cited

Pavarotti, Luciano. <u>Pavarotti's Greatest Hits</u>.

    London, 1980.

Parenthetical note: (Pavarotti)

55. **Speech—No Printed Text—MLA** List the speech on the Works Cited page by the name of the speaker. Give the title of the talk, the sponsoring organization (when known), the location, and the date. If you do not have a copy of the speech, avoid the need for a parenthetical note by referring to the address by name or by speaker in your essay itself: "When President Reagan delivered his Geneva Summit address to Congress in 1985. . . ."

Works Cited

Reagan, Ronald. "The Geneva Summit Meeting: A Measure

of Progress." U.S. Congress. Washington, D.C.,

21 Nov. 1985.

56. Speech—Printed Text—MLA

Works Cited

O'Rourke, P. J. "Brickbats and Broomsticks." Capital

Hilton. Washington, D.C., 2 Dec. 1992. Rpt.

American Spectator. Feb. 1993: 20-21.

Parenthetical note: (O'Rourke 20)

57. Lecture—MLA

Works Cited

Cook, William W. "Writing in the Spaces Left."

Chair's Address. Conf. on College Composition

and Communication Annual Meeting. Cincinnati, 19

Mar. 1992.

Parenthetical note: (Cook)

**34b
MLA**

58. Letter—Published—MLA

Works Cited

Eliot, George. "To Thomas Clifford Allbutt." 1 Nov.

1873. In Selections from George Eliot's Letters.

Ed. Gordon S. Haight. New Haven: Yale UP, 1985.

427.

Parenthetical note: (Eliot 427)

59. Letter or E-mail—Unpublished—MLA Refer to the letter in
the body of the essay: "In a letter to Agnes Weinstein, dated 23
May 1917, Albert Newton blames . . . ."

Works Cited

Newton, Albert. Letter to Agnes Weinstein. 23 May

1917. Albert Newton Papers. Woodhill Lib.,

Cleveland.

Pacheco, Miguel. E-mail to the author. 14 Apr. 1995.

60. **Artwork—MLA** Refer to the work in the body of your essay rather than in a parenthetical note: "Fuseli's *Ariel* depicts . . . ."

Works Cited

Fuseli, Henri. <u>Ariel</u>. The Folger Shakespeare Lib.,

Washington, D.C.

61. **Book Review—Titled or Untitled—MLA** Not all book reviews have titles, so the Works Cited form of a book review can vary slightly.

Works Cited

Keen, Maurice. "The Knight of Knights." Rev. of

<u>William Marshall: The Flower of Chivalry</u>, by

Georges Duby. <u>New York Review of Books</u> 16 Jan.

1986: 39-40.

Parenthetical note: (Keen 39)

Works Cited

Baym, Nina. Rev. of Uncle Tom's Cabin <u>and American</u>

<u>Culture</u>, by Thomas F. Gossett. <u>Journal of</u>

<u>American History</u> 72 (1985): 691-92.

Parenthetical note: (Baym 691-92)

62. **Drama or Play—MLA** Citing a printed text of a play, whether individual or collected, differs from citing an actual performance.

For printed texts, provide the usual Works Cited information—taking special care when citing a collection in which various editors handle different plays. For parenthetical notes, give act, scene, and line numbers when the work is so divided, page numbers if it is not.

Works Cited

Stoppard, Tom. <u>Rosencrantz & Guildenstern Are Dead</u>.

New York: Grove, 1967.

Parenthetical note: (Stoppard 11-15)

Works Cited

Shakespeare, William. <u>The Tragedy of Hamlet, Prince</u>

<u>of Denmark</u>. Ed. Frank Kermode. <u>The Riverside</u>

<u>Shakespeare</u>. Ed. G. Blakemore Evans. Boston:

Houghton, 1974. 1135-97.

Parenthetical note: (<u>Ham</u>. 5.2.219-24)

For actual performances of plays, give the title of the work, the author, and then any specific information that seems relevant—director, performers, producers, set designer, theater company, and so on. Conclude the entry with a theater, location, and date. Refer to the production directly in the body of your essay; avoid parenthetical references.

**34b
MLA**

Works Cited

<u>Timon of Athens</u>. By William Shakespeare. Dir. Michael

Benthall. Perf. Ralph Richardson, Paul Curran,

and Margaret Whiting. Old Vic, London. 5 Sept.

1956.

CHART

Abbreviations

The following abbreviations are often used in notes or on a Works Cited page. Limit these abbreviations to such uses; spell the terms out fully whenever they occur in the body of your paper—except in parenthetical notes or explanations. Don't use abbreviations that might confuse your readers.

assn.	association	ms., mss.	manuscript,
bibliog.	bibliography		manuscripts
biog.	biography	narr.	narrator,
©	copyright (usually		narrated by
	followed by a date)	n.d.	no date
c.	"about" (usually	n. pag.	not paginated
	followed by a date)	ns	new series
ch.	chapter	obs.	obsolete
col.	column	OED	*Oxford English*
coll.	college		*Dictionary*
Cong.	Congress	orig.	original
DAB	*Dictionary of*	par.,	paragraph,
	American Biography	pars.	paragraphs
dir.	director,	p., pp.	page, pages
	directed by	pref.	preface
diss.	dissertation	proc.	proceedings
DNB	*Dictionary of*	PS	postscript
	National Biography	pseud.	pseudonym
ed(s).	editor(s)	rev.	review,
e.g.	for example		reviewed by
et al.	and others	rpt.	reprint,
etc.	and so forth		reprinted by
ex.	example	ser.	series
fig.	figure	sic	thus
fwd.	forward	soc.	society
govt.	government	supp.	supplement
GPO	Government	trans.	translator,
	Printing Office		translated by
i.e.	that is	U	University
jour.	journal	UP	University Press
mag.	magazine	vol.,	volume,
misc.	miscellaneous	vols.	volumes

34c   WINDOW ON WRITING: A Sample MLA Paper

The sample paper that follows is accompanied by checklists designed to help you set up a research paper correctly in MLA style. When your research paper meets the specifications described on the checklists, your essay should be in proper form. For another example of MLA style, see the Window on Writing in Section 34f.

Author's Note

I wrote "Mountain Bikes on Public Lands: Happy Trails?" (under an alias) to test how well various on-line sources would support an undergraduate research topic. Electronic indexes proved particularly helpful in locating up-to-date magazine articles while the Internet and WWW furnished three interesting references—and could have supplied many more. Unfortunately, the topic did not lend itself to articles in scholarly journals, so only one such source is included.

I was able to download several of the magazine articles used in the paper directly from the library's on-line catalog, which provides complete texts of recent articles from major publications. But there was a catch. Although it was possible to download and print the text of these articles in my office, they arrived without page numbers. To cite these materials accurately, I still had to hotfoot it to the library to find the original articles. Like any new technology, on-line research still has its frustrations.

JR

34c
MLA

Mountain Bikes on Public Lands: Happy Trails?

by

Curt Bessemer

English 306

Professor John Ruszkiewicz

4 May 1995

CHECKLIST

Title Page for a Paper—MLA

If your instructor asks for a separate title page, follow the form on the facing page. MLA style does not require such a separate cover sheet; many instructors, however, will expect one. If your instructor does *not* want a separate title page, turn to page 636.

✔ Arrange and center the title of your paper, your name, the course title (and section number if required), your instructor's name, and the date of submission.

✔ Use the correct form for your title. Capitalize the first word and the last word. Capitalize all other words in the title *except* articles (*a*, *an*, *the*), prepositions, the *to* in infinitives, and coordinating conjunctions—unless they are the first or last words.

Right: Mountain Bikes on Public Lands: Happy Trails?

Do not underline a title, capitalize every letter in it, place it between quotation marks, or terminate it with a period.

Wrong: Mountain Bikes on Public Lands: Happy Trails?

Wrong: MOUNTAIN BIKES ON PUBLIC LANDS: HAPPY TRAILS?

Wrong: "Mountain Bikes on Public Lands: Happy

              Trails?"

Wrong: Mountain Bikes on Public Lands: Happy Trails.

Titles may, however, include words or phrases that appear between quotation marks or are underlined. They may also end with question marks, as the sample title does.

Right: Marriage in Shakespeare's As You Like It

Right: Dylan's "Like a Rolling Stone" Reconsidered

Right: Mountain Bikes on Public Lands: Happy Trails?

✔ Identify your instructor by an appropriate title. When uncertain about academic rank, use *Mr.* or *Ms.*

Dr. Joseph Kelly   Professor Eberly
Mr. David Lapides   Ms. Virginia Anderson

34c
MLA

Outline

<u>Thesis</u>: If mountain bikers wish to use trails in
public lands and wilderness, they must behave
responsibly in environmentally sensitive areas and
organize politically to defend their rights.

I. Conflicts about mountain bikes in park areas

   A. Keeping trails in a natural state

   B. Opening trails to responsible use

II. The popularity of mountain biking

   A. Creating the mountain bike

   B. Developing mountain biking

   C. Finding routes for trail biking

III. The dangers mountain biking poses to parks and
trails

   A. Degrading the natural environment

   B. Threatening riders and hikers

IV. Responses to ecologists and environmentalists

   A. Examining causes of trail damage

   B. Cleaning up the mountain bike's image

   C. Negotiating with environmental groups

34c
MLA

CHECKLIST

Outline for a Paper—MLA

If your instructor requires an outline, place it immediately after the title page. Whether you use a sentence or phrase outline, be sure to observe correct form. (If your instructor does not require such an outline, go to p. 636.)

✔ Begin the outline with the thesis statement of the paper.
✔ Double-space the entire outline and align headings and sub-headings carefully. Both sentence and phrase outlines should be double spaced and consistently aligned, following this pattern.

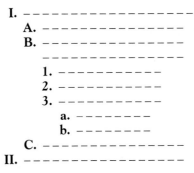

An outline preceding a short paper will probably not need to go beyond the second or third level. If a line runs beyond the right-hand margin, it carries over to the left and picks up at a point directly below where it started (see line B. above). No number or letter at any level of a formal outline stands alone: if you have a point A., there must be a point B.; a point 1. requires a corresponding point 2.

✔ Do not paginate an outline that runs only a single page. One that requires more pages is numbered—along with all other items in the front matter—in small Roman numerals (i, ii, iii, iv).

34c
MLA

Bessemer 1

Mountain Bikes on Public Lands: Happy Trails?

¶1   Imagine that you have driven hundreds of miles
to enjoy the natural splendor and serenity of one of
America's national parks. Without a care in the
world, you and your friends are hiking a breathtaking
trail up a scenic hillside or through a tranquil
canyon. Suddenly from around a bend comes a whooping
gang of men and women mounted on thick-framed,
knobby-tired bicycles rushing toward you on the trail
in a flurry of dust and noise, climbing over logs,
leaping across boulders, scattering birds and
wildlife in every direction, pushing you into the
underbrush to save your life. They clatter past in
gaudy shirts and spandex shorts, gouging ruts in the
pathway, laughing and screaming obscenities. Welcome
to the sport of mountain biking--at least the way
angry hikers and environmentalists sometimes portray
it (Coello 148).

¶2   Imagine, now, that you are a rider on a
lightweight, sturdy machine designed to take you
safely and comfortably across isolated roads and
trails miles from automobile traffic and madding
crowds, fat tires and maybe even shock absorbers

CHECKLIST

First Page of the Text of an Essay with a Separate Title Page—MLA

If your paper has a separate title page, the first page of the body of your paper will look like the facing page. Be sure to check all the items in the list.

✔ Repeat the title of your paper, exactly as it appears on the title page, on the first page of the body of the paper about two inches from the top of the sheet.
✔ Center the title and capitalize it properly.
✔ Begin the body of the essay two lines (a double space) below the title.
✔ Double-space the entire body of the essay, including all quotations.
✔ Use one-inch margins at the sides and bottom of this page; use one-inch margins all around (including at the top) on all subsequent pages.
✔ Indent the first lines of paragraphs one-half inch, or five spaces if you use a typewriter.
✔ Indent long quotations (more than four typed lines) one inch, or ten spaces if you use a typewriter.
✔ Number this first page in the upper right-hand corner, one-half inch from the top, one inch from the right margin. Precede the page number with your last name.

Now go on to page 638.

34c
MLA

Curt Bessemer

Professor Ruszkiewicz

English 306

4 May 1995

Mountain Bikes on Public Land: Happy Trails?

¶1   Imagine that you have driven hundreds of miles to enjoy the natural splendor and serenity of one of America's national parks. Without a care in the world, you and your friends are hiking a breathtaking trail up a scenic hillside or through a tranquil canyon. Suddenly from around a bend comes a whooping gang of men and women mounted on thick-framed, knobby-tired bicycles rushing toward you on the trail in a flurry of dust and noise, climbing over logs, leaping across boulders, scattering birds and wildlife in every direction, pushing you into the underbrush to save your life. They clatter past in gaudy shirts and spandex shorts, gouging ruts in the pathway, laughing and screaming obscenities. Welcome to the sport of mountain biking--at least the way angry hikers and environmentalists sometimes portray it (Coello 148).

¶2   Imagine, now, that you are a rider on a lightweight, sturdy machine designed to take you safely and comfortably across isolated roads and trails miles from automobile traffic and madding crowds, fat tires and maybe even shock absorbers

34c
MLA

CHECKLIST

No Separate Title Page—MLA

If your instructor does not require a separate title page, the first page of your paper should look like the facing page.

✔ Place your name, instructor's name, course title, and the date in the upper left-hand corner, beginning one inch from the top of the paper. The items are double spaced.

✔ Identify your instructor by an appropriate title. When uncertain about academic rank, use Mr. or Ms.

Dr. James Duban   Professor Ferreira-Buckley
Mr. Chidsey Dixon   Ms. Christy Friend

✔ Center the title a double space under the date. Use the correct form for the title. (See p. 631 for complete guidelines.)

✔ Begin the body of the essay two lines (a double space) below the title. Double-space the entire body of the essay, including quotations.

✔ Use one-inch margins at the sides and bottom of this page.

✔ Number this first page in the upper right-hand corner, one-half inch from the top, one inch from the right margin. Precede the page number with your last name.

34c
MLA

Bessemer 2

softening the trail over which you travel at a sober speed, savoring the scenery, expending no energy but your own to enjoy the wilderness your tax dollars support. You come upon a group of hikers or riders and courteously indicate that you are passing on the left. But the hikers reply to your politeness with anger, curses, and maybe even a slap on the back, or a board with nails (Drake 106). This too is mountain biking from the point of view of its enthusiasts, who feel victimized by well-connected groups eager to claim public lands for themselves.

¶3   Somewhere between these two portraits lies the truth about the conflict currently raging between mountain bikers and trail hikers (with equestrians caught somewhere in between) when it comes to access to public land. Conservation groups, ecologists, hikers, and equestrians would just as soon lump bikers with the drivers of motorized vehicles already banned from many off-road areas, especially park trails. These groups want to keep parks and wilderness areas in as natural a state as possible and don't regard mechanical vehicles of any kind as compatible with their goal. On the other hand, mountain bikers consider these lands--especially the narrow hiking trails--as their natural environment. While admitting that some bikers have been irresponsible, they also believe that problems with

34c
MLA

CHECKLIST

Body of the Essay—MLA

The body of an MLA research paper continues uninterrupted until the separate Notes page (if any) and the Works Cited page. Be sure to type or print out the essay on good-quality paper.

✔ Use margins of at least one inch all around. Try to keep the right-hand margin reasonably straight. But avoid hyphenating words whenever possible. If you must divide longer words, be sure to break them at syllable divisions (see Section 28b).

✔ Place page numbers in the upper right-hand corner, one inch from the right edge of the page and one-half inch from the top. Precede the page number with your last name.

✔ Indent the first line of each paragraph one-half inch, or five spaces if you use a typewriter.

✔ Indent long quotations one inch, or ten spaces if you use a typewriter. In MLA documentation, long quotations are any that would exceed four typed lines in the body of your essay. Double-space these indented quotations.

34c
MLA

mountain biking have been greatly exaggerated. The
Mountain Bike Book author Rob van der Plas, for
example, claims to have witnessed public officials
and hikers "manipulating or circumventing facts to
find justification for attempts to deny cyclists
access" to trails (107). When all is said and done,
if mountain bikers wish to use trails in public lands
and wilderness, they must behave responsibly in
environmentally sensitive areas and organize
politically to defend their rights.

¶4   What some have characterized as a war between
bikers and environmental groups is due in part to the
explosive popularity of mountain bikes (see fig. 1).
More comfortable and sturdy than the drop-handled 10-
speed racing bikes dominant just a generation ago,
mountain bikes now represent half the sales in what's
become a 3.5-billion-dollar industry in the United
States, with 25 million Americans riding their bikes
at least once a week (Castro 43). As the name
suggests, mountain bikes were invented in
California's Marin County in the mid-1970s for the
purpose of going "down steep, unpaved hillsides at a
murderous pace" (van der Plas 104). It occurred to
pioneer mountain bikers such as Gary Fisher and
Charlie Kelly to adapt sturdy old Schwinn bikes from
the 1930s with their heavy frames and thick tires to
the hazards of trail riding, and soon hundreds of

34c
MLA

Bessemer 4

bike bums in California, Colorado, and other places
were pounding local hills and inventing mountain bike
racing (Schwartz 77). These first mountain bikes were
custom jobs, but in 1981 a Californian named Michael
Sinyard produced the first commercial mountain bike,
the Stumpjumper, a copy of which is now in the
Smithsonian museum (Castro 42). It quickly sold out
and spawned a vigorous new industry--served eagerly
now by manufacturers in Taiwan, Japan, Italy, and the
United States. By 1993, 30 million mountain bikes had
been manufactured (Schwartz 80).

¶5   What distinguishes mountain bikes from touring
or racing bikes are flat handlebars for upright

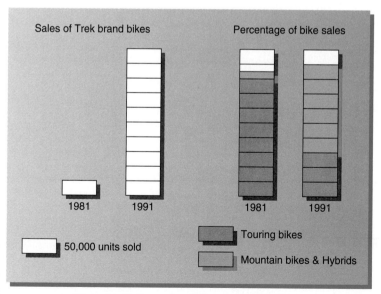

**34c
MLA**

Fig. 1. U.S. sales of mountain bikes

posture, high chainstays for greater road clearance, wide balloon tires for durability, and stout frames for overall performance (see fig. 2). These features contribute to the ruggedness of the vehicles as well as to rider comfort. The large tires in particular absorb the bumps of back roads and gravel trails, and many mountain bikes are even available with front and rear suspensions to further lessen the impact of trail riding. Mountain bikes usually come with 21- or 24-speed gearsets, enabling cyclists to pump their way comfortably up rocky trails or steep hills. Exotic materials in frames, including aluminum and titanium, further reduce weight, making the bikes even more fun to ride on any kind of terrain.

¶6   The sturdy structures and bulging tires that give trail bikes their off-road capacity also make them comfortable on-road vehicles. This versatility probably accounts for the mountain bike's current domination of the market. As Rob van der Plas puts it, ". . . it is the universal machine. It does anything my other bikes can do, most things almost as well, some better and some that the other bikes can't do at all" (104). For if early mountain bikers developed the sport for the thrill of ripping downhill as fast as possible, most bikers today take their rides for the same reason that hikers hoist a

34c
MLA

Fig. 2. Mountain bike

backpack and head for the hills--to enjoy the great
outdoors. Again, Rob van der Plas explains it well:

> What's nice about riding off road is not
> a function of the roughness, the dirt, or
> any of the other characteristics of the
> terrain. Instead what you'll relish most
> is the remoteness, the solitude, the
> experience of nature and the lack of
> traffic. (104)

In effect, the mountain bike has become the all-
terrain, off-road, and trail bike too, the most
civilized, economical, and inexpensive machine for
getting away from it all. Like sport utility trucks
that spend most of their time on pavement, many
mountain bikes may never see a slick rock trail or

downhill race. But they are always ready when their owners decide to go exploring, even if it's only a flat fire road across a Midwestern plain.

¶7   But how to get away from it all has now become the problem, especially in National Wilderness and Wilderness Study Areas, where the government controls access to thousands of potential recreational acres and where the 1964 Wilderness Act forbids "motor vehicles and other forms of mechanical transport" (van der Plas 108). In most other natural areas, service and fire roads provide the perfect routes for biking, though an important distinction is made between double-track and single-track trails. Double-track trails--which are usually just unpaved roads--are ordinarily open to bikers because they are wide and comfortably shared with other users. Single-track trails--the much narrower, more challenging, and more diverse paths through wilderness areas--are both more preferred by experienced trail bikers and more likely to be closed to them. It is on these trails that bikers compete with pedestrian and equestrian traffic and where the bulk of conflicts occur.

¶8   Mountain bikes have been accused of damaging trails and causing soil erosion, their thick and knobby tires eating away at the terrain, especially after rains (Schwartz 75). Officials in natural

areas have shown increasing concern over such damage,
going so far as to consider banning even horses on
park trails, let alone bikes (O'Keefe 82). Yet horses
at least remain on trails and move slowly while
aggressive bikers often do not. (Coello 148). The
editors of Bicycling magazine acknowledge a problem:
"We're tempted to take shortcuts, arrogantly crushing
vegetation. A second of convenience wipes out years
of growth" (36). Some critics have suggested that
erosion caused by mountain biking may even have
contributed to recent mudslides in California (van
der Plas 105). So traditional environmental
coalitions have been eager to lobby against
permitting bikers on trails, and such groups have
had considerable success in California, where the
mountain biking craze originated.

¶9   It isn't just environmental dangers which have
made some people angry at the bikers; it is their
"alien" presence and sometimes outrageous behavior. As
David Schwartz puts it: "To traditional trail users,
the new breed of bicycle was alien and dangerous,
esthetically offensive and physically menacing" (75).
Rob Buchanan describes the situation in Marin County:

>   At first Marin's old guard, the equestrians
>   and Sierra clubbers who'd always had the
>   place to themselves, grudgingly put up
>   with the new fad. Then the whole thing got

34c
MLA

> out of hand. Weekends the hills were
> overrun with "wheeled locusts," as the
> San Francisco Chronicle put it, "driven
> by speed-crazed yuppies in Day-Glo
> Lycra." (80)

It probably doesn't help that, as Richard Bails reports, many of the mountain bikers are younger men and women, Generation Xers who seem to have rejected the frail and sophisticated racing bikes of their predecessors. The new bikers seem to come from a generation that environmentalists from the sixties and earlier don't understand or like. But that impression isn't always true, as mountain biking activist and writer Geoff Drake explains, complaining about attacks on him for defending biking:

> You can't imagine how strange this is.
> A lifelong hiker and environmentalist, I
> find myself a renegade--an expatriate in
> the woods I love. What about my years of
> membership in Greenpeace and the Nature
> Conservancy? . . . Now, incredibly, I'm
> receiving the ire of environmentalists
> everywhere. (106)

¶10 Bicyclists have begun to respond to the threat the more politically experienced environmentalists pose to their sport and recreation. They point to the politically correct character of the mountain bike as

**34c
MLA**

"an ideal vehicle for global ecological change" (Buchanan 82). They challenge unproven conclusions about trail erosion in the absence of hard evidence that bikes have actually caused it. In fact, they argue that the erosion of trails may be caused largely by runoff from rain and snow (van der Plas 108).

¶11   Just as important, bikers have begun to clean up their image and to organize in order to claim their rights to responsible use of the country's natural resources. Van der Plas, for example, suggests that bikers need to present themselves as "responsible, mature adults who eat lots of apple pie and watch fireworks" (108). An associate editor of <u>Mountain Biking Magazine</u> warns that "land access and liability problems . . . could ensue if the majority of the population thinks mountain biking as a whole is a gonzo activity for those with more muscle fibers than brain cells" (Fragnoli 13). To change that perception, groups like the National Off-Road Bicycle Association (NORBA) have written codes to encourage members to behave responsibly, while the Women's Mountain Bike and Tea Society (WOMBATS) have, as Sara Corbett reports, moved aggressively to prove bikers can share trails with hikers. Biking groups and magazines have also been leaders in urging everyone to wear helmets while riding to prevent some of the

34c
MLA

almost 200,000 bike-related head injuries that occur

each year (Goldsmith 308).

¶12   Trail riders, appreciating that all politics

is local, have begun to take their civic

responsibilities seriously. For example, in Austin,

Texas, an off-road bicycle group called the Ridge

Riders made allies in the local environmental

community by helping to build trails in a state park

and to clean and maintain trails in other local

recreational areas (Skinner 8). Similar strategies

are being pursued in Colorado where the Boulder Off-

road Alliance was established to lobby for enhanced

trail access by offering various park agencies--

including the U.S. Forest Service and Boulder County

Parks--assistance with the construction and

maintenance of trails. As a founder of the group

put it,

> We understood the concept of sweat equity
>
> very early on. . . . It's my hope that
>
> someday the land use agencies in our area
>
> will have to compete for our resources.
>
> When we have reached this level, the sweat
>
> equity we have invested in will give
>
> mountain biking in Boulder County the
>
> political clout to affect [sic] real
>
> change. (Grubin)

**34c
MLA**

¶13   As a result of such political action, biking groups that have demonstrated their willingness to protect the natural environment are beginning to have success in negotiating with environmental groups. In spring 1994, the International Mountain Bicycling Association (IMBA) and the powerful Sierra Club jointly endorsed the principle that "[m]ountain biking is a legitimate form of recreation and transportation on trails, including singletrack, when and where it is practiced in an environmentally sound and socially responsible manner" (Stein 86). Several months later, the IMBA persuaded the United States Forest Service to acknowledge that bicycles, unlike motorized vehicles, have a legitimate place on trails, their agreement potentially opening up more tracks for mountain riders in the 191 million acres of land controlled by the Forest Service ("IMBA Breaks" 16). The agreements signed at Park City, Utah, and West Dover, Vermont, represent the kinds of compromises that we are likely to see more of in the future between people who wish to use our natural resources and those sworn to protect them. When such groups begin to realize their common interests and when groups like mountain bikers earn their political clout through community action, we'll probably find that there's room on the trail for everyone.

34c
MLA

Bessemer 13

Works Cited

Bails, Richard James, Jr. "Survey Results." 20 Aug.
    1994. Online posting. Newsgroup
    rec.bicycles.tech. Usenet. 3 Nov. 1994.

Bicycling Magazine, Editors of. Bicycling Magazine's
    Mountain Biking Skills. Emmaus: Rodale, 1990.

Buchanan, Rob. "Birth of the Gearhead Nation."
    Rolling Stone 9 July-23 Aug. 1992: 80+.

Castro, Janice. "Rock and Roll." Time 19 Aug. 1991:
    42+.

Coello, Dennis. Touring on Two Wheels: The Bicycle
    Traveler's Handbook. New York: Lyons, 1988.

Corbett, Sara. "Ride with Pride." Outside Magazine.
    Mar. 1995. Online. Internet. 1 May 1995.
    Available WWW:http://web2starwave.com.

Drake, Geoff. "Trouble on the Mountain." Bicycling
    Aug. 1992: 106.

Fragnoli, Delaine. "Are We Extreme?" Mountain Biking
    Magazine Sept. 1994: 13.

Goldsmith, Marsha F. "Campaigns Focus on Helmets as
    Safety Experts Warn Bicycle Riders to Use--and
    Preserve--Heads." JAMA 15 July 1992: 308.

Grubin, Rick. "Mountain Biking Advocacy Group:
    Boulder Off-road Alliance (BOA)." 19 Aug. 1994.
    Online posting. Newsgroup rec.bicycle soc.
    Usenet. 4 Nov. 1994.

CHECKLIST

The Works Cited Page—MLA

The Works Cited list contains full bibliographical information on all the books, articles, and other resources used in composing the paper. For more information about the purpose and form of this list, see pages 593 through 597.

✔ Center the title "Works Cited" at the top of the page.
✔ Include in the Works Cited list all the sources actually mentioned in the paper. Do not include materials you examined but did not cite in the body of the paper itself.
✔ Arrange the items in the Works Cited list alphabetically by the last name of the author. If no author is given for a work, list it according to its title, excluding articles (*The, A, An*).
✔ Be sure the first line of each entry touches the left-hand margin. Subsequent lines are indented one-half inch or five spaces.
✔ Double-space the entire list. Do not quadruple-space between entries unless that is the form your teacher prefers.
✔ Punctuate items in the list carefully. Don't forget the period at the end of each entry.
✔ Follow this form if you have two or more entries by the same author.

van der Plas, Rob. <u>The Mountain Bike Book:</u>

<u>Choosing, Riding and Maintaining the Off-Road</u>

<u>Bicycle</u>. 3rd ed. San Francisco: Bicycle, 1993.

---. <u>Mountain Bike Magic</u>. Mill Valley: Bicycle,

1991.

34c
MLA

"IMBA Breaks Through--Twice!" <u>Mountain Bike</u> Oct.

   1994: 16.

O'Keefe, Eric. "Destabilized." <u>Texas Monthly</u> Sept.

   1994: 82.

Schwartz, David M. "Toward Happy Trails: Bikers,

   Hikers and Olympians." <u>Smithsonian</u> June 1994:

   74-87.

Skinner, Dawn. <u>Austin Cycling Notes</u> Aug. 1994: 8.

Stein, Theo. "The New MBA: Is It Finally in the

   Driver's Seat?" <u>MTB</u> Oct. 1994: 85-89.

van der Plas, Rob. <u>The Mountain Bike Book: Choosing,

   Riding and Maintaining the Off-Road Bicycle</u>.

   3rd ed. San Francisco: Bicycle, 1993.

**34c
MLA**

34d HOW DO YOU WRITE AN ESSAY EXAMINATION?

Troubleshooting

Occasionally you may be asked to compose essays under the pressure of a time limit either to demonstrate a general ability to write or to test your command of a subject you've studied. The first type of essay may be part of a competency examination required by your school, community, or state—a test you must pass to move on to more advanced work. The second type is the familiar essay examination, common in college humanities courses and other classes. Both types of impromptu writing typically require that you respond to questions by making claims you can support with evidence, authorities, and examples. Because both competency and essay exams are written and read under pressure, it makes sense to compose them in a way that makes the writing efficient, the reading easy, and a satisfactory grade likely. Of course, such examinations can be nerve-racking, but you can master them if you employ a few basic strategies.

To write a successful impromptu essay . . .

34d-1 Read the questions carefully and plan ahead. Answer the questions actually posed, not the ones you were hoping for. And be sure to read the entire question before you start writing. Underline key verbs that tell you what to do with the topic: *describe, analyze, classify, discuss, evaluate, summarize, compare, contrast, compare and contrast.* Each of these instructions means something a little different. Underline other key terms—those that *identify* or *limit* the subject. If you don't understand a question, ask your instructor or the proctor if a clarification is possible under the ground rules of the examination.

Note carefully whether the question specifies an audience for the essay you are composing (see Section 1e). It can make a great deal of difference, for example, if you are asked to analyze contemporary music for your campus newspaper or for a senior citizens group. When no audience is specified, assume that your audience is your instructor or a generally educated reader—the kind of person likely to read a major newspaper or newsmagazine.

Once you have read the examination, estimate the time you can give to each question (if there is more than one), quickly outline your responses, work through the questions with an eye on the clock, and stick to your schedule. Answer every required question—even minimally if you have to. You may receive a few points for a tentative answer but no points at all for a blank space.

34d
exam

34d–2 **Use invention strategies to develop your topic.** This is a particularly important step on competency examinations where you may be expected to generate your own material for an essay, often based on personal experience or common knowledge. Imagine, for example, that you have sixty minutes to write an essay on the following general topic.

> Describe the best course you have taken in school and explain why it was successful.

The question obviously has two related parts, each of which must be developed.

1. Describe the best course you have taken in school.
2. Explain why it was successful.

First you'll have to identify a course you recall well enough to analyze and give readers the basic facts about it: name and subject of the course, level of instruction, methods of instruction, and so on. Some of the journalist's questions (see p. 34) may help you anticipate queries readers will have about the course: *Who? What? Where? When?*

The second part of the essay is likely to be tougher: explaining *why* the course you've identified and briefly described was successful. You must explain what exactly made the class work so well—avoiding bare-bones generalizations that won't mean much to readers, such as "It was good" or "I really learned a lot." Your job is to define what would make any such course successful and then to measure your particular class against the standards you have set, providing plenty of evidence and examples to convince readers. As you go through this thinking process—it might last ten minutes or more—you should be writing everything down and making lists to jog your memory further. Indeed, a sound inventive process for any question you face is to break it into parts and make lists of ideas and evidence.

Here's a second example of a question for an impromptu essay.

> Identify an important movie you believe everyone should see, and explain why you find it interesting or challenging.

Once again, the essay presents you with two separate but related tasks: you must identify an *important* movie and then explain why it is *interesting* or *challenging*. Here you might begin by listing movies you think are important in one column, then in a second column listing the qualities that make each of them interesting and challenging. As you go through this process, you'll find that one set of ideas will stimulate the other: when you've finally settled on one movie to write about, you'll have an entire slate of criteria by which to defend it as interesting or challenging.

34d-3 **Prepare a scratch outline.** For most impromptu essays, you won't have much time for planning, but it usually takes only a moment to organize the key ideas, points, examples, and counterexamples that come to mind as you explore a question. When you are stumped, just writing down the key words in a question might get ideas flowing. Once you have listed key points, try arranging them logically or grouping them into related clusters. Even a rudimentary scratch outline will help keep your answer on track. Then formulate a thesis—a statement you can prove or disprove with the evidence you have gathered.

Consider using a commitment and response pattern (see p. 38) to outline your intended essay in the first paragraph. In this opening paragraph, state your major point, making certain to repeat key words in the question. Indicate as clearly and briefly as you can what line of development your essay will follow. Then, if you don't complete the essay, the opening paragraph will help a reader imagine what your finished essay might have looked like if you'd had the time to write it.

34d-4 **Treat one major idea per paragraph and develop it with evidence.** State the main point of each paragraph in the first sentence—a topic sentence. (Consider the possibility that an instructor may skim your essay and read only these topic sentences.) Then, because time is limited, choose your facts and illustrations carefully. For a competency examination, select examples that are vivid and specific, the kind that will make readers believe that you have thought about the subject. For an essay test, choose evidence that suggests you know more than you can write about in the time you have to complete the essay. In particular, use names, facts, and vocabulary you have heard in lectures or have come across in your reading—and be sure you know how to spell key terms.

Be sure to use transitions, numbers, and lists. They help organize information and lead readers to important points: *first, second, third; consequently; as a result; by contrast;* and so on. But don't pad your answers, and don't wander from your subject. Readers will recognize a snow job.

34d-5 **Write clearly or print; take time to edit.** Illegible handwriting can hurt you almost as much as weak content. But don't hesitate to revise, cross out, and rearrange the elements of your impromptu essay. Such changes show you are thinking. If necessary, use arrows or balloons to insert or relocate whole sentences or paragraphs, but be as neat as possible. Be sure, too, to allow time to edit and proofread your answer. Readers will appreciate the concern you show for correct spelling, punctuation, and grammar.

34d
exam

34e   HOW DO YOU WRITE A LITERARY ANALYSIS?

Troubleshooting

Writing a literary analysis is a common assignment in most English courses, even in composition classes. But requirements and approaches vary from teacher to teacher and course to course. Clearly, instructors think about literature in different ways, depending on their background, training, inclinations, and familiarity with literary theory. How you write about works of literature may depend as much on how you are taught as what you are taught. Critical approaches to literature today can range from close readings of individual texts to wide-ranging confrontations with issues of politics and culture.

What, then, is the point of a literary analysis? It can be to heighten your appreciation for works of literature, to demonstrate your ability to support a thesis about a literary work, to give you skill at close reading and interpretation, to expand your appreciation for a particular culture, to explore what it means to read, to understand how readers respond to texts, or to heighten your sensitivity to other cultures, races, and peoples.

Obviously, in a few pages, we can't give you advice for dealing with all these possibilities. What we can do is give you a little practical advice for finding a subject and working with literary materials. Whatever your teachers' predilections, we hope that reading literature makes you wiser and gives you pleasure. Those two aims of literature have stood the test of time.

34e
lit

To write a successful literary analysis . . .

34e-1   Begin by reading carefully. The evidence you'll need to write a thoughtful, well-organized analysis may come from within the literary work itself and from outside readings and secondary sources. Your initial goal is to find a point worth making, an assertion you can prove with convincing evidence.

To find a point, you must obviously begin by reading the work (or works) carefully and recording—at first—your general reactions or major questions. Don't interrupt your reading to take detailed notes yet. Instead, enjoy the literary experience.

Then think about what you have just read. What issues interest you immediately? What questions does the piece raise that you'd like to explore in greater detail? Examine your preliminary list of issues and questions. If you had been reading *Macbeth*, here are the kinds of jottings you might produce.

- Is ambition the cause of Macbeth's defeat?

- What is the nature of the relationship between Lady Macbeth and her husband?
- Does the age of the Macbeths matter?
- Is the story of the Macbeths true?
- Why do some lines in this tragedy seem funny?
- Can Macbeth blame the witches for his tragedy?
- What is tragedy?

To stimulate more questions, you may want to compare and contrast the work(s) you have read with other similar works.

- What makes both *Macbeth* and *Romeo and Juliet* tragic plays?
- Is Macbeth as ambitious as King Claudius in *Hamlet*?
- Is Lady Macbeth a more influential character in *Macbeth* than Queen Gertrude is in *Hamlet*?
- Why does Shakespeare use comedy in *Hamlet*, *Romeo and Juliet*, and *Macbeth*?

At this point, you might stimulate your thinking either by considering various ways of approaching a literary text (see the next section) or by using one of the techniques described earlier in this handbook for finding and focusing ideas, particularly freewriting and brainstorming (see Sections 2a and 2b).

34e-2 **Understand the various approaches you can take to a literary analysis.** A few basic types of literary analysis are outlined below. When you write a literary paper, you will ordinarily limit yourself to one or two of these types in making your point.

34e
lit

- **Close reading of a text.** When doing a "close reading," you carefully explain the meaning and possible interpretations of a literary passage, sometimes line by line. You look carefully at how the language of the work makes a reader experience or think about certain images. You might do a close reading of a short poem, a speech from a play, or a passage from a longer work.
- **Analysis of theme.** You may examine the ideas or messages a literary work conveys to readers. A literary work may explore any number of themes (some general ones might be *anger*, *jealousy*, *ambition*, *hypocrisy*, or *greed*), but most poems, plays, and novels sound one or two consistent notes.
- **Analysis of plot or structure.** You may study the way a work of literature is put together and why a writer chooses a particular arrangement of ideas or plot elements to say what he or she wants.

You may look for evidence of these patterns in works of literature from different cultures, checking for common structures and themes.

- **Analysis of character.** You may study the behavior of characters in a novel, poem, play, or short story to understand their motivations and the ways characters can relate to one another. Or you explore how a writer creates a character through description, action, reaction, and dialogue.

- **Analysis of setting.** You study a writer's creation of a setting to figure out how the environment of a literary work (where things happen in a novel, short story, or play) affects what happens in the plot or to the characters. Settings can also be analyzed as the exterior representations of characters' inner beings.

- **Archetypal criticism.** When generalized themes, plots, characters, and settings are seen to represent the characteristic myths of entire cultures—the quest, the sacrificial lamb, the harrowing of hell—they are called *literary archetypes*. You can explore literary texts to reveal the cultural patterns they embody and the archetypes they incorporate, modify, or parody.

- **Analysis of literary type or genre.** You study a particular literary work by evaluating its form, as a tragedy, comic novel, sonnet, detective story, epic, and so on. You compare the work to other similar literary pieces, looking for similarities and differences and perhaps comparing the relative quality of the achievement.

- **Historical analysis.** You study a literary work as it reflects the society that produced it or as it was accepted or rejected by that society when it was published. Or you study the way historical information makes a literary work from an earlier time clearer to a reader today.

- **Cultural analysis.** You explore how a work of art embodies the culture that produced it—that is, what assumptions about the beliefs and values of a society can be traced in the literary work. Such analysis may reveal how certain groups gained or maintained power through the manipulation of literary myths or symbols. It may show how certain groups operated within supportive or repressive cultures—how, for example, African Americans or women are represented in nineteenth-century American literature or the Irish in English novels.

- **Political analysis.** You may want to read literary works for what they reveal about the economic and political relationships between classes and groups of people. Some works of art represent the ideals of dominant groups in society while other works expose the need for alternative arrangements of wealth and power.

- **Feminist analysis.** You examine how a literary work portrays women or defines their roles in society. Feminist analyses vary as much as any other kind of criticism, but many feminist critics explore the way literary works embody the relationships of power between men and women. Much feminist criticism is political in nature in that it seeks to use literary analyses to change the status of women.

- **Biographical study.** You study how a writer's life is expressed in or through a literary work. Obviously, such analyses may be related to cultural and political studies, but they may also focus on the individual psychology of a writer.

- **Study of the creative process.** You make a detailed study of how a work was composed. Such a paper might examine the sources, notes, influences, manuscripts, and revised texts of a literary work.

34e-3 **Consult secondary sources.** If reading the work itself hasn't stimulated enough questions about the literary piece or if you now do have some issues you are eager to explore, consult secondary sources. There are many in the field of literary study.

To locate secondary sources on literary topics, begin with the following indexes and bibliographies available in a library reference room.

Essay and General Literature Index
MLA International Bibliography
New Cambridge Bibliography of English Literature
Year's Work in English Studies

Many other useful reference works are available.

34e
lit

CHECKLIST

Reference Works for Literary Analyses

Beacham, Walton, ed. *Research Guide to Biography and Criticism.* Washington, DC: Research Publ., 1990.

Drabble, Margaret, ed. *The Oxford Companion to English Literature.* 5th ed. Oxford: Oxford UP, 1985.

Encyclopedia of World Literature in the Twentieth Century. New York: Ungar, 1981. 4 vols.

Evans, Gareth L., and Barbara Evans. *The Shakespeare Companion.* New York: Scribner's, 1978.

(continued)

Reference Works for Literary Analyses (*continued*)

Harner, James L. *Literary Research Guide: A Guide to Reference Sources for the Study of Literature in English and Related Topics.* New York: MLA, 1989.

Hart, James D., ed. *The Oxford Companion to American Literature.* 5th ed. New York: Oxford UP, 1983.

Holman, C. Hugh. *A Handbook to Literature.* 6th ed. New York: Bobbs, 1992.

Howatson, M. C. *The Oxford Companion to Classical Literature.* 2nd ed. Oxford: Clarendon, 1989.

Inge, M. Thomas, et al. *Black American Writers: Bibliographical Essays.* New York: St. Martin's, 1978.

Magill, Frank Northern. *Magill's Bibliography of Literary Criticism.* Englewood Cliffs, NJ: Salem, 1979.

Mainero, Lina, ed. *American Women Writers: A Critical Reference Guide from Colonial Times to the Present.* New York: Ungar, 1979–82.

Marcuse, Michael J. *A References Guide for English Studies.* Berkeley: U of California P, 1990.

Modern British Literature. New York: Ungar, 1966. Supplement, 1976.

Patterson, Margaret C. *Literary Research Guide.* 2nd ed. New York: MLA, 1983.

Rogal, Samuel. *Calendar of Literary Facts.* Detroit: Gale, 1991.

Sampson, George. *The Concise Cambridge History of English Literature.* Cambridge: Cambridge UP, 1970.

Woodress, James, et al. *Eight American Authors. A Review of Research and Criticism.* New York: Norton, 1971.

34e
lit

34e–4 **Carefully develop a thesis about the literary work(s) you are studying.** You might begin with questions you are eager to explore in greater depth, a question generated perhaps by your reading of secondary sources or by your discussions with classmates or other readers.

- Are some scenes missing from *Macbeth?*
- What limits on the power that women had in Elizabethan England might explain the behavior of Lady Macbeth?
- Did the term *equivocation* have particular political significance to the original audience of *Macbeth?*
- Did Shakespeare tailor *Macbeth* to please England's Scottish monarch, King James?

When you've put your question into words, test its energy. Is the answer to your inquiry so obvious that it isn't likely to interest or surprise anyone?

- Is Shakespeare's *Macbeth* a great play?

If so, discard the issue. Try another. Look for a surprising, even startling question whose answer you don't already know. Test your question on a friend or instructor.

- Could Shakespeare's *Macbeth* actually be a comedy?
- What role do the lower classes play in a dynastic struggle such as the one depicted in *Macbeth?*

Then turn your question into an assertion—your preliminary thesis statement.

- Shakespeare's *Macbeth* is really a comedy.
- The welfare of the lower classes seems to have been ignored in dynastic struggles such as those depicted in *Macbeth*.

Is this an assertion you are interested in proving? Is it a statement other readers might challenge? If so, write it on a note card and go on. If not, modify it or explore another issue.

34e-5 Read the work(s) a second time with your thesis firmly in mind. Read more slowly and analytically this time. Look for characters, incidents, descriptions, speeches, and dialogue that support or refute your thesis. Take careful notes. If you are using your own text, highlight significant passages in the work.

34e
lit

When you are done, evaluate the evidence you have gathered from a close reading of the piece. Modify your thesis to reflect what you have learned or discovered. In most cases, your thesis will be more specific and limited after you have gathered and assessed evidence.

- The many unexpected comic moments in *Macbeth* emphasize how disordered the world becomes for murderers like the Thane of Cawdor and his wife.

If necessary, return to secondary sources or other literary works to supplement and extend your close reading. (For many kinds of analysis, much of your reading will be in secondary sources and journals of literary criticism.) Play with ideas, relationships, implications, and possibilities. Don't hesitate to question conventional views of a work or to bring your own cultural experiences to bear upon the act of reading and interpreting literature. Jot down random thoughts or freewrite.

If you use secondary sources, take careful notes. Be sure to prepare accurate bibliography cards for your Works Cited page. (See Section 32e for advice on note taking.)

34e–6 **When you are ready to write a full draft, try out a few scratch outlines for the paper.** Choose the one you find most solid or most challenging.

> *Thesis:* **Comic moments in *Macbeth* emphasize how strange the world has become for the Macbeths.**
>
> I.   Comic moments after the murder of King Duncan
> II. Comedy at the feast for Banquo
> III. Comedy in the sleepwalking scene
> IV. Conclusion

Now write the draft. Stay open to new ideas and refinements of your original thesis, but try not to wander off into a biography of the author or a discussion of the historical period unless such material relates directly to what you are trying to prove. If you do wander, consider whether the digression in your draft might be the topic you *really* want to write about.

CAUTION

34e–7 **Avoid the paper that simply paraphrases the plot of a literary work.** Equally ineffective is the essay that merely praises its author for a job well done. Avoid extremely impressionistic judgments: "I feel that Hemingway must have been a good American. . . ." Don't expect to find a moral in every literary work either. And don't think a literary analysis requires you to search for "hidden meanings." Respond honestly to what you are reading—not the way you think your teacher expects you to. (To see how the paper on *Macbeth* sketched above might develop, see the sample literary paper on pp. 664–670.)

34e
lit

34e–8 **Introduce most direct quotations.** Do not insert a quotation from a literary work or a critic into your paper without identifying it in some way. And be sure quotations fit into the grammar of your sentences.

> **When an audience hears Macbeth call his cowering servant a** "cream-fac'd loon," it begins to understand why Macbeth's men hate and distrust him.

> **The doctor in *Macbeth* warns the gentlewoman:** "you have known what you should not" (V.i.46–47).

> **Commenting on the play, Frank Kermode observes that**

"*Macbeth* has extraordinary energy; it represents a fierce engagement between the mind and its guilt" (1311).

34e-9 Follow the conventions of literary analysis. A literary analysis may take many forms, but academic essays generally follow the conventions of the MLA research paper, including careful documentation (see especially pp. 575–582).

Cunningham 1

Arnie Cunningham

Professor Christine Mopar

English 321 Shakespeare

10 November 1990

The Comedy of Macbeth

Unlike Greek or French tragedians, Shakespeare seems more than willing to include a lively comic scene in even his most serious plays. Everyone instantly recognizes the humor of the gravedigger in Hamlet, the fool in King Lear, the porter in Macbeth. Yet Macbeth (1606?) also contains other moments that seem funny, but perhaps shouldn't be--so audiences aren't sure whether to laugh. Bolder actors might be tempted to play these troublesome lines comically, but do so at the risk of offending critics who expect Macbeth to be serious. In my view, Shakespeare creates these uneasy comic situations in Macbeth deliberately, to emphasize the absurdity of the world created by the Macbeths after they decide to murder King Duncan.

The first few such comic lines come early in the drama and could pass unnoticed if actors play them with straight faces. Yet it is hard not to smile when Lady Macbeth boldly claims victory after drugging the grooms who guard Duncan's bedchamber, discovering, "That which hath made them drunk hath made me bold"

CHECKLIST

Conventions in a Literary Paper

- Use the present tense to refer to events occurring in a literary work.

  Hester Prynne *wears* a scarlet letter.
  Hamlet *kills* Polonius.

  Think of a literary work as an ongoing performance.

- Identify passages from short poems by using line numbers.

  "Journey of the Magi," lines 21–31.

  Do not, however, use the abbreviations *l.* or *ll.* for *line* or *lines*—they are sometimes confused with Roman numerals; spell out *line* or *lines* completely.

- Provide act and scene divisions (and line numbers as necessary) for passages from plays. Act and scene numbers are now usually given in Arabic numbers, although Roman numbers are still common and acceptable.

  Ham. 4.5.179–85 or *Ham.* IV.v.179–85.

  The titles of Shakespeare's works are commonly abbreviated in citations:

  Mac. I.ii; *Oth.* 2.2.

  Check to see which form your teacher prefers.

- Provide a date of publication in parentheses after your first mention of a literary work.

  Before publishing *Beloved* (1987), Toni Morrison had written . . .

- Use technical terms accurately. Spell the names of characters correctly. Take special care with matters of grammar and documentation.

**34f
lit**

(<u>Mac</u>. II.ii.1). Then, just the way a slightly drunken person would, she goes on to apologize gruesomely for not killing Duncan herself, almost surprised by her reluctance to murder: "Had he [King Duncan] not resembled / My father as he slept, I had done't" (12-13).

   Macbeth has the next comic line, this one his reaction to Lennox's description of the horrible storm that blows while Macbeth is murdering Duncan. Deadpans Macbeth, "'Twas a rough night" (II.iii.61). The audience laughs sympathetically, knowing much better than Lennox how rough it has been for the new Thane of Cawdor. Then, when a horrified Macduff discovers that Duncan has been murdered, Lady Macbeth screams, "Woe, alas! / What, in our house?" (II.iii.87-88). Any audience that hears those lines wants to laugh at Lady Macbeth's self-centeredness. Even Banquo notices her inappropriate concern for her household's reputation when he replies "Too cruel any where" (88). The remainder of the scene has a comic edge to it, as Duncan's sleepy sons rouse themselves to learn that their father has been assassinated--"O, by whom?" (100). Then Macbeth almost gives away the whole plot by trying to explain why he killed the grooms, the only possible witnesses to the murder. Lady Macbeth understands the problem, so she faints to draw attention away from her

Cunningham 3

babbling husband. The entire ghastly episode teeters
on the brink of explosive laughter.

For several scenes afterward, though, the action
turns serious enough to make an audience almost
forget the moments of comedy in the play, as Macbeth
consolidates his power and hires men to kill his
friend Banquo. But then, at the feast visited by
Banquo's ghost (III.iv), the comedy revives as a
desperate Lady Macbeth tries to convince the
assembled thanes that her husband's odd behavior when
seeing Banquo is not unusual: "My lord is often thus,
/ And hath been from his youth" (52-53), little
comfort for men now serving a king who talks to
chairs. Lady Macbeth admits as much when she
criticizes her husband, asking "Why do you make such
faces? When all's done, / You look but on a stool"
(66-67). Macbeth's major complaint is that the
murdered Banquo isn't playing fair. Macbeth longs for
the good old days:

> . . . the time has been,
> That when the brains were out, the man
>   would die,
> And there an end; but now they rise again
> With twenty mortal murthers on their
>   crowns,
> And push us from our stools. (77-81)

**34f
lit**

Cunningham 4

If Macbeth sounds comic in these passages, Lady Macbeth echoes his absurdity in her famous sleepwalking scene (V.i), most of which is pathetic and serious. But in recalling the sight of murdered Duncan, whose blood she earlier smeared on the grooms, she speaks one comic line: "Yet who would have thought the old man to have had so much blood in him?" (39-40). "Old man" seems to mean about the same thing here as "old geezer." The remark suggests that all the blood on Duncan surprises Lady Macbeth, in much the same way that the ghost of Banquo--also bloody--surprises Macbeth.

Is it possible to tie all these comic instances together? One last example hints at the connection. The line occurs very near the end of the play when Macbeth realizes exactly how the witches have lied to him (V.viii). Thinking he can't be killed by a man born of woman, Macbeth fears no one during the battle with the rebels who have come to dethrone him. But then Macbeth's sworn enemy Macduff reveals that he was "untimely ripped" (14) from his mother's womb, making it possible for him to slay the tyrant. Macbeth curses the witches for deceiving his hopes, and then, like an angry little boy quitting a game and carrying his football home, he tells Macduff, "I'll not fight with thee" (22). The remark sounds

34f
lit

as absurd as all the others cited in this paper, because Macbeth here feels the same emotions he and his wife have been experiencing at intervals throughout the play--surprise, outrage, and insult. Time and again, the Macbeths become comically absurd in the tragedy because they don't realize that their crimes have changed their world. After they seize the throne of Scotland, they expect everything to stay as it was before they killed Duncan, but they soon discover that the old game is being played according to rules they haven't learned yet. Repeatedly they must respond to situations they haven't anticipated:

> Had he not resembled my father . . .
> 'Twas a rough night.
> What, in our house?
> Why do you make such faces . . . ?
> Now they rise again . . . and push us . . .
> Who would have thought . . . ?

34f
lit

Macbeth's comically pathetic "I'll not fight with thee" is a logical but futile attempt to escape a game the Macbeths themselves have invented, one so horrible that, time and again, it frightens them out of their wits. Spectators feel the horror, but they also detect the humor in the Macbeths' confusion. That's why audiences want to laugh but usually don't.

Cunningham 6

Work Cited

The Riverside Shakespeare. Ed. G. Blakemore Evans.

Boston: Houghton, 1974.

34f
lit

34g HOW DO YOU USE ACW DOCUMENTATION?

Troubleshooting

In doing a research project, you may find yourself exploring a wide variety of unconventional electronic sources and services—Web sites, MOOs, MUDs, Listservs, and Gophers. When the time comes to document these items, however, conventional citation systems may prove inadequate. Either they don't mention the types of sources you are using, or the guidelines for documenting them prove cumbersome and intricate, especially when it comes to providing electronic addresses. For this reason, the Alliance for Computers and Writing (ACW) has endorsed a style sheet developed by Janice R. Walker that covers unconventional electronic sources and provides simple guidelines for electronic addresses and search paths.

This new ACW system is designed to complement the current MLA forms (see Sections 34a–c), and so it follows MLA conventions in matters of capitalization, underlining, and most punctuation. It also treats authors' names and the titles of works exactly as MLA does. ACW differs significantly, however, in its presentation of electronic information. Instructors familiar with electronic formats may suggest that you follow ACW guidelines when documenting electronic sources. For non-electronic sources in the same paper, use conventional MLA formats.

But do check before using ACW documentation on your own; some instructors may prefer that you stick with conventional MLA forms throughout a paper, adapting them as best you can to any MUDs or MOOs you have to cite. Don't mix APA and ACW citations.

**34g
ACW**

To use ACW documentation . . .

34g–1 (Step 1) In the text of your paper, place a note in parentheses to identify the source of every passage or idea you must document. Conventional in-text notes usually consist of authors' last names and page numbers.

```
(Goodfeld 210)

(Brooks and Heilman 24-26)
```

But electronic sources may not have conventional authors or page numbers. You may have to adapt the parenthetical note to fit the new type of source, sometimes naming the site and date, for example, or the author and date.

```
(WorldMOO 5 Dec. 1994)

(Walker 1 May 1995)
```

These conventions are likely to evolve over the next few years.

34g-2 **(Step 2) On a separate page at the end of your paper, list every source cited in a parenthetical note.** The alphabetical list of sources is labeled Works Cited. For the general arrangement of a Works Cited page, see Section 34a–2. For individual ACW Works Cited entries, use the following formula.

```
Author's Last Name, First Name. "Title of Work."

   Title of Complete Work. [protocol and address]

   [path] [date of access, visit, or message].
```

The formula varies slightly, depending on the type of electronic source you need to document: FTP (File Transfer Protocol) sites; WWW (World Wide Web) sites; Telnet sites; synchronous communications (MUDs, MOOs, IRC); Gopher sites; Listserv and Newslist items; and e-mail.

A typical **ACW Works Cited entry for an FTP site** (where files can be downloaded) includes the following basic information.

- Name of author(s), if known, last name first, followed by a period and a space.
- Title of work, followed by a period and between quotation marks.
- Address of the FTP site and the full path needed to access the information. This address is followed by a space but no period.
- Date of access in parentheses, followed by a period.

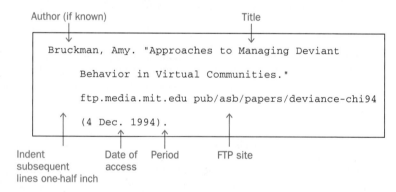

A typical **ACW Works Cited entry for a WWW site** includes the following basic information.

- Name of author(s), if known, last name first, followed by a period and a space.

- Title of work, followed by a period and between quotation marks. This might be an individual Web page within a larger Web site.
- Title of the full work (if applicable), underlined or in italics.
- Full HTTP address. This address is followed by a space but no period.
- Date of access in parentheses, followed by a period.

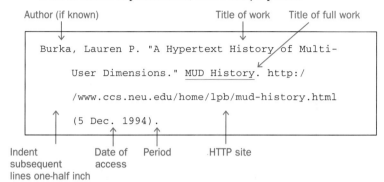

A typical **ACW Works Cited entry for a Telnet site** includes the following basic information.

- Name of author(s), if known, last name first, followed by a period and a space.
- Title of work, followed by a period and between quotation marks.
- Title of the full work (if applicable), underlined or in italics.
- Complete Telnet address, as well as any directions for accessing the source. This address is followed by a space but no period.
- Date of access in parentheses, followed by a period.

34g ACW

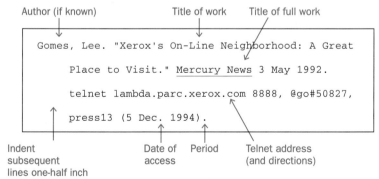

A typical **ACW Works Cited entry for Synchronous Communications (MOOs, MUDs, IRC)** includes the following basic information.

- Name of the speaker(s), followed by a period and a space.
- Type of communications—for example, a personal interview.
- Electronic address, if applicable. This address is followed by a space but no period.
- Date in parentheses, followed by a period.

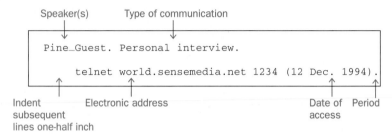

A typical **ACW Works Cited entry for a Gopher site** includes the following basic information.

- Name of author(s), if known, last name first, followed by a period and a space.
- Title of work, followed by a period and between quotation marks.
- Any print or publication information.
- The Gopher search path. This path is followed by a space but no period.
- Date of access in parentheses, followed by a period.

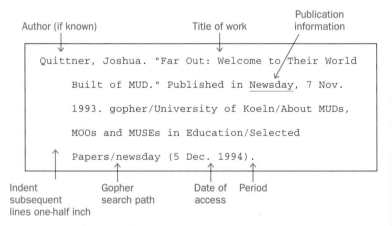

A typical **ACW Works Cited entry for Listserv and Newslist citations** includes the following basic information.

- Name of author(s), if known, last name first, followed by a period and a space.
- Subject line of the posting, followed by a period and between quotation marks.
- Address of the Listserv or Newslist.
- Date of access in parentheses, followed by a period.

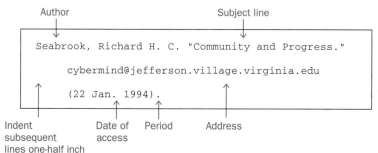

A typical **ACW Works Cited entry for e-mail** includes the following basic formation.

- Name of author(s), if known, last name first, followed by a period and a space.
- Subject line of the posting, followed by a period and between quotation marks.
- Address. This is optional. Note that the item is personal e-mail.
- Date of communication in parentheses, followed by a period.

**34g
ACW**

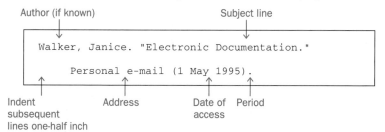

How Do You Write in the Sciences?

A APA Documentation

B APA Form Directory

C Sample APA Paper

D CBE Documentation

E How Do You Write an Abstract?

35a HOW DO YOU USE APA DOCUMENTATION?

As a group, the disciplines that apply scientific method to the exploration of the human condition are known as the social sciences—psychology, anthropology, sociology, political science, education, management. Methods of research vary widely from field to field within the social sciences, but usually involve assembling data to explore a hypothesis. Such data may be acquired through carefully designed experiments in which one variable is manipulated to determine causation. Or the research may involve the detailed observations of subjects over long periods of time—that is, case studies and ethnographies. Or it may involve surveys, polls, or some other means of sampling public opinion or behavior.

The results of experiments in the social sciences are usually reported in articles published in professional journals. These reports tend to be more formal in organization than papers in the humanities, with a structure designed to connect any new finding to older research. You can examine social science research articles in professional journals.

In many social science and related courses (anthropology, education, home economics, linguistics, political science, psychology, sociology), you may be expected to follow the conventions of documentation recommended by the American Psychological Association. An undergraduate essay in APA form appears in Section 35c. A full explanation of APA procedures is provided by the *Publication Manual of the American Psychological Association*, 4th edition (1994), available in most college libraries. The basic procedures for APA are summarized in this section. The exact forms for many kinds of parenthetical notes (books, articles, movies, collections, and so on) and their accompanying References entries are given in the APA Form Directory on pages 685 through 695.

CHECKLIST

The Components of a Social Science Report

- **An abstract**—A concise summary of the research article.
- **A review of literature**—A survey of published research that has a bearing on the hypothesis advanced in the research report. The review establishes the context for the research essay.
- **A hypothesis**—An introduction to the paper that identifies the assumption to be tested and provides a rationale for studying it.
- **An explanation of method**—A detailed description of the procedures used in the research. Since the validity of the research depends on how the data were gathered, this is a critical section for readers assessing the report.
- **Results**—A section reporting the data, often given through figures, charts, graphs, and so on. The reliability of the data is explained here, but little comment is made on its implications.
- **Discussion/conclusions**—A section in which the research results are interpreted and analyzed.
- **References**—An alphabetical list of research materials and articles cited in the report.
- **Appendixes**—A section of materials germane to the report, but too lengthy to include in the body of the paper.

35a
APA

To use APA documentation . . .

35a-1 **(Step 1) In the text of your paper, place a note in parentheses to identify the source of every passage or idea you must document.** For example, here is a sentence derived from information in an article by E. Tebeaux titled "Ramus, Visual Rhetoric, and the Emergence of Page Design in Medical Writing of the English Renaissance."

```
Technical writing developed in important ways during

the English Renaissance (Tebeaux, 1991).
```

As you can see, the basic form of the APA parenthetical note consists of an author's last name and a date. A comma follows the author's name.

```
(Tebeaux, 1991)
```

Quite often in APA notes, a research article is identified by the author's last name mentioned in the body of the essay, followed immediately by the year of publication in parentheses.

```
According to Grunman (1984), children fed a diet free

of the chemical additive had fewer behavioral

problems than those who ingested it regularly.
```

Such a note is perhaps the most common form of APA citation.

A page number may be given for indirect citations and *must* be given for direct quotations. A comma follows the date if page numbers are given. Page numbers are preceded by *p.* or *pp.*

```
During the English Renaissance, writers began to

employ "various page design strategies to enhance

visual access" (Tebeaux, 1991, p. 413).
```

When appropriate, the documentation may be distributed throughout a passage.

35a
APA

```
Tebeaux (1991) observes that for writers in the late

sixteenth century, the philosophical ideas of Peter

Ramus "provided a significant impetus to major

changes in page design" (p. 413).
```

When a single source provides a series of references, you need not repeat the name of the author until other sources interrupt the series. After the first reference, page numbers are sufficient until another citation intervenes. Even then, you need repeat only the author's last name, not a date, when the reference occurs within a single paragraph.

```
. . . The council vetoed zoning approval for a mall

in an area described by Martinez (1982) as the last

outpost of undisturbed nature in the state. The area
```

```
provides a "unique environment for several endangered

species of birds and plant life" (p. 31). The birds,

especially the endangered vireo, require breeding

spaces free from encroaching development (Harrison &

Cafiero, 1979). Rare plant life is similarly

endangered (Martinez).
```

APA parenthetical notes should be as brief and inconspicuous as possible.

35a-2 **(Step 2) On a separate page at the end of your paper, list every source cited in a parenthetical note.** This alphabetical list of sources is labeled "References." A References page entry for an article on medical writing in the Renaissance by E. Tebeaux would look like the following if it were in a *professional* paper submitted for publication in an APA journal.

```
        Tebeaux, E. (1991). Ramus, visual rhetoric, and

the emergence of page design in medical writing of

the English Renaissance. Written Communication, 8,

411-445.
```

This form, indented like a paragraph, makes typesetting a professional article easier.

However, most college papers won't be typeset; in fact, APA style describes them as "final copy." For this reason, References list items in student papers ought to look the way such entries appear in APA journal articles themselves—with hanging indents of five spaces rather than paragraph indents. Here, then, is how Tebeaux's article would appear in the References list of a *college paper* in APA style:

```
Tebeaux, E. (1991). Ramus, visual rhetoric, and the

        emergence of page design in medical writing of

        the English Renaissance. Written Communication,

        8, 411-445.
```

We use this form throughout the handbook for APA References entries.

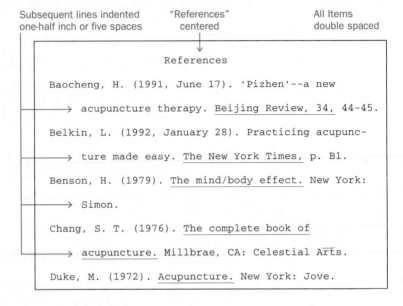

Subsequent lines indented   "References"   All Items
one-half inch or five spaces   centered   double spaced

References

Baocheng, H. (1991, June 17). 'Pizhen'--a new

→ acupuncture therapy. Beijing Review, 34, 44-45.

Belkin, L. (1992, January 28). Practicing acupunc-

→ ture made easy. The New York Times, p. B1.

Benson, H. (1979). The mind/body effect. New York:

→ Simon.

Chang, S. T. (1976). The complete book of

→ acupuncture. Millbrae, CA: Celestial Arts.

Duke, M. (1972). Acupuncture. New York: Jove.

A typical **APA References entry for a book** includes the following basic information.

35a
APA

- Name of author(s), last name first, followed by a period. Initials are used instead of first names unless two authors mentioned in the paper have identical last names and first initials.
- Date in parentheses, followed by a period.
- Title of work, underlined, followed by a period, also underlined (unless some other information separates the name of the title from the period). Only the first word of the title, the first word of the subtitle, and proper nouns are capitalized.
- Place of publication, followed by a colon.
- Publisher, followed by a period.

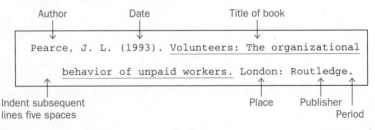

Author   Date   Title of book

Pearce, J. L. (1993). Volunteers: The organizational

behavior of unpaid workers. London: Routledge.

Indent subsequent   Place   Publisher
lines five spaces   Period

A typical **APA References entry for an article in a scholarly journal or magazine** includes the following basic information.

- Name of author(s), last name first, followed by a period. Initials are used instead of first names unless two authors mentioned in the paper have identical last names and first initials.
- Date in parentheses, followed by a period.
- Title of article, followed by a period. Only the first word of the title, the first word of the subtitle, and proper nouns are capitalized. The title does not appear between quotation marks.
- Name of the periodical, underlined, followed by a comma. All major words are capitalized.
- Volume number, underlined, followed by a comma, page numbers, and a period. Notice that the underlining of the periodical continues without interruption right up to and including the comma after the volume number.

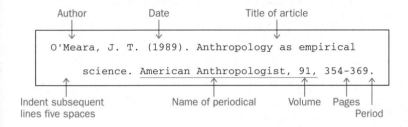

Author	Date	Title of article

O'Meara, J. T. (1989). Anthropology as empirical

    science. American Anthropologist, 91, 354-369.

Indent subsequent lines five spaces   Name of periodical   Volume   Pages   Period

**35a
APA**

A typical **APA References entry for an article in a popular magazine or newspaper** includes the following basic information.

- Name of author(s), last name first, followed by a period. Initials are used instead of first names unless two authors mentioned in the paper have identical last names and first initials.
- Date in parentheses, followed by a period. Give the year first, followed by the month (do not abbreviate it), followed by the day.
- Title of article, followed by a period. Only the first word and proper nouns are capitalized. The title does not appear between quotation marks.
- Name of the newspaper, underlined, followed by a comma, also underlined. All major words are capitalized.
- Page or location indicated by the abbreviation *p.* or *pp.*, followed by a period. When a news story appears on several discontinuous pages, list all pages and separate them with a comma.

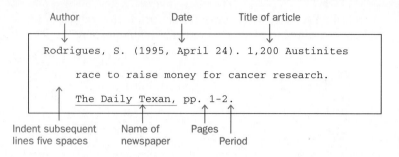

A typical **APA References entry for an on-line document** includes the following basic information.

- Name of author(s), last name first, followed by a period. Initials are used instead of first names unless two authors mentioned in the paper have identical last names and first initials.
- Date in parentheses, followed by a period. Give the year first, followed by the month (do not abbreviate it), followed by the day, if necessary.
- Title of work, followed by the publication medium—*on-line, CD-ROM, computer software*—in brackets, followed by a period.
- Path statement or electronic address, preceded by the word *Available*. Include the protocol/directory/file name or document number for retrieval. *No* period follows the path statement.

35a
APA

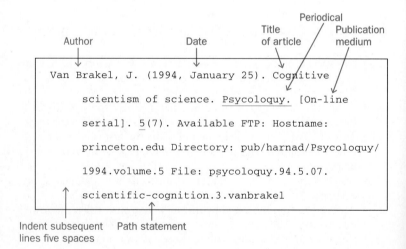

There are so many variations to these generic entries, however, that you will probably want to check the *Publication Manual of the American Psychological Association* (1994) when you do a major APA-style paper. You may especially want to read pages 331 to 340 on writing student papers.

The References page itself appears on its own page following the body of the essay (and a Notes page—if there is one). It lists bibliographical information on all the materials you used in composing the essay. Here's a checklist for a References page.

CHECKLIST

To set up a References page . . .

- Center the title "References" at the top of the page.
- Arrange the items in the References list alphabetically by the last name of the author. Give initials only for first names. If no author is given for a work, list and alphabetize it by the first word in the title, excluding articles (*A, An,* and *The*).
- The first line of each entry is flush with the left-hand margin. Subsequent lines are indented one-half inch or five spaces.
- The list is ordinarily double spaced. In student papers, APA style does permit single spacing of individual entries; double spacing is preserved between the single-spaced references.
- Conclude each entry on the list with a period.
- In the References list, capitalize only the first word and any proper names in the title of a book or article. Within a title, capitalize the first word after a colon.

35a
APA

▶ **Fine Tuning**

1. **When two or more sources are used in a single sentence,** the notes are inserted as needed conveniently after the statements they support.

   While Porter (1981) suggests that the ecology of the aquifer might be hardier than originally suspected, "given the size of the drainage area and the nature of the subsurface rock" (p. 62), there is no reason to believe that the best interests of the county

```
would be served by the creation of a mall and

shopping district in a vicinity described as "one of

the last outposts of undisturbed nature in the state"

(Martinez, 1982, p. 28).
```

Notice that a parenthetical note is placed outside of quotation marks but before a period ending a sentence.

2. **When a work has two authors,** both names are given in all references.

```
Harrison and Cafiero (1979) argue . . .

(Harrison & Cafiero, 1979)
```

Notice that an ampersand (*&*) is used between the authors' names rather than the *and* used in MLA.

3. **When a work has three to five authors,** all of them are named in the first reference or parenthetical note.

```
Harrison, Cafiero, and Dixon (1979) argue . . .

(Harrison, Cafiero, & Dixon, 1979)
```

All subsequent notes then use *et al.* (Latin abbreviation for "and others").

```
Harrison et al. (1979) argue . . .

(Harrison et al., 1979)
```

4. **When a work has six or more authors,** use the first author's name followed by *et al.* for all references, including the first.

```
Barge et al. (1988) relate . . .

(Barge et al., 1988)
```

In the References list, provide the names of all authors.

5. **When you cite more than one work written by an author in a single year,** assign a small letter after the date to distinguish between the author's works from the same year.

```
(Rosner, 1991a)

(Rosner, 1991b)
```

```
The charge is raised by Rosner (1991a), quickly

answered by Anderson (1991), and then raised again by

Rosner (1991b).
```

6. **When you must document a work without an author,** list the title, shortened if necessary, and the date.

```
("Aid to education," 1985)

the booklet Guide to Computer Resources (1995) ◀
```

35b **APA FORM DIRECTORY**

Below, you will find the APA References page and parenthetical note forms for a variety of sources. Simply find the type of work you need to cite in either the Format Index or the Alphabetical Index and then locate that work by number in the list that follows the indexes.

63. Book, One Author—APA

References

Pearson, G. (1949). <u>Emotional disorders of children.</u>

Annapolis, MD: Naval Institute Press.

Parenthetical notes:

Pearson (1949) found . . .

(Pearson, 1949)

(Pearson, 1949, p. 49)

64. Book, Two Authors—APA

References

Lasswell, H. D., & Kaplan, A. (1950). <u>Power and</u>
<u>society: A framework for political inquiry.</u> New
York: Yale University Press.

Parenthetical notes:

Lasswell and Kaplan (1950) found . . .

(Lasswell & Kaplan, 1950)

(Lasswell & Kaplan, 1950, pp. 210-213)

65. Book, Three to Five Authors—APA

References

Rosenberg, B., Gerver, I., & Howton, F. W. (1971).
<u>Mass society in crisis: Social problems and</u>
<u>social pathology</u> (2nd ed.). New York: Macmillan.

Parenthetical notes:

First note. Rosenberg, Gerver, and Howton (1971)
found . . .

Subsequent notes. Rosenberg et al. (1971) found . . .

First note. (Rosenberg, Gerver, & Howton, 1971)

Subsequent notes. (Rosenberg et al., 1971)

66. Book, Revised—APA

References

Edelmann, A. T. (1969). <u>Latin American government and</u>
<u>politics</u> (Rev. ed.). Homewood, IL: Dorsey.

Parenthetical notes:

Edelmann (1969) found . . .

(Edelmann, 1969)

(Edelmann, 1969, p. 62)

35b
APA

67. Book, Edited—APA

References

Journet, D., & Kling, J. (Eds.). (1984). <u>Readings for
technical writers.</u> Glenview, IL: Scott,
Foresman.

Parenthetical notes:

Journet and Kling (1984) observe . . .

(Journet & Kling, 1984)

68. Book with No Author—APA

References

<u>Illustrated atlas of the world.</u> (1985). Chicago: Rand
McNally.

Parenthetical notes:

in <u>Illustrated Atlas</u> (1985) . . .

(<u>Illustrated Atlas,</u> 1985, pp. 88-89)

69. Book, a Collection or Anthology—APA

References

Feinstein. C. H. (Ed.) (1967). <u>Socialism, capitalism,
and economic growth.</u> Cambridge, England:
Cambridge University Press.

Parenthetical notes:

Feinstein (1967) found . . .

(Feinstein, 1967)

70. Work Within a Collection, Anthology, or Reader—APA On
the References page, list the item by the author of the piece you are
actually citing, not by the editor(s) of the collection. Then provide
the title of the particular selection, its date, the editors of the collection, the title of the collection, pages on which the selection appears, and publication information.

References

Patel, S. (1967). World economy in transition (1850-

2060). In C. H. Feinstein (Ed.), <u>Socialism,</u>

<u>capitalism, and economic growth</u> (pp. 255-270).

Cambridge, England: Cambridge University Press.

Parenthetical notes:

Patel (1967) found . . .

(Patel, 1967)

71. Chapter Within a Book

References

Clark, K. (1969). Heroic materialism. In <u>Civilisation</u>

(pp. 321-347). New York: HarperCollins.

Parenthetical notes:

Clark (1969) observes . . .

(Clark, 1969)

72. Article in a Scholarly Journal—APA Scholarly journals that publish original academic and professional research are usually identified by volume number or season (rather than day, week, or month of publication). Such journals are often paginated year by year, with a full year's work gathered together and treated as a volume. That means that page numbers for scholarly journals don't restart with each new issue, but continue throughout a year. Cite articles from such scholarly journals by providing author, date, title of article, journal, volume, and page numbers.

References

Tebeaux, E. (1991). Ramus, visual rhetoric, and the

emergence of page design in medical writing of

the English Renaissance. <u>Written Communication,</u>

<u>8,</u> 411-445.

Parenthetical notes:

```
Tebeaux (1991) observes . . .

(Tebeaux, 1991, p. 411)
```

73. **Article in a Monthly Periodical Paginated Issue by Issue—APA** To cite a magazine published monthly, give the author's name, date (including month), title of the article, name of the magazine and volume number if available (underlined), and page numbers.

References

```
Bass, R. (1995, May/June). The perfect day. Sierra,

    80, 68-78.
```

Parenthetical notes:

```
Bass (1995) notes . . .

(Bass, 1995)
```

74. **An Article in a Weekly or Biweekly Periodical—APA** To cite a weekly or biweekly periodical or magazine, give the author's name, date (including month and day), title of the article, name of the magazine and volume number if available (underlined), and page numbers.

**35b
APA**

References

```
Moody, J. (1993, December 20). A vision of judgment.

    Time, 142, 58-61.
```

Parenthetical notes:

```
Moody (1993) observes . . .

(Moody, 1993)

(Moody, 1993, p. 60)
```

75. **Article in a Newsletter—APA** To cite a newsletter, give the author's name, date, title of the article, name of the newsletter and volume number if available (underlined), and page numbers. If no volume number is given, give as full a date as possible.

References

Busiel, C. (1995, Spring). Shakespeare and hypertext.

Virtu(re)al.news@cwr1, 7.

Parenthetical notes:

Busiel (1995) explains . . .

(Busiel, 1995)

76. **Article in a Periodical—Author Not Named—APA** Note that quotation marks are used around shortened titles in the parenthetical notes.

References

Aladdin releases desktop tools. (1993, October).

Macworld, 10, 35.

Parenthetical notes:

in "Aladdin releases" (1993) . . .

("Aladdin releases," 1993)

77. **Newspaper Article—Author Named—APA** If the newspaper article does not appear on consecutive pages in the magazine, give all the page numbers, separated by a comma. Note that abbreviations for page (p.) and pages (pp.) are used with newspaper entries.

References

Bragg, R. (1994, October 15). Weather gurus going

high-tech. San Antonio Express-News, pp. 1A, 7A.

Parenthetical notes:

Bragg (1994) reports . . .

(Bragg, 1994, p. 7A)

78. **Newspaper Article—Author Not Named—APA**

References

Scientists find new dinosaur species in Africa.

(1994, October 14). The Daily Texan, p. 3.

35b
APA

Parenthetical notes:

```
in the article "Scientists find" (1994) . . .

("Scientists find," 1994)
```

79. Computer Software—Author Named—APA

References

```
Crawford, C. (1985). Balance of power [Computer

    software]. Northbrook, IL: Mindscape, SFN.
```

Parenthetical notes:

```
Crawford (1985) includes . . .

(Crawford, 1985)
```

80. Computer Software—Author Not Named—APA

References

```
FoxPro [Computer software]. (1993). Redmond, WA:

    Microsoft.
```

Parenthetical notes:

```
using FoxPro (1993) to organize . . .

(FoxPro, 1985)
```

81. **Electronic Sources—APA** APA standards for documenting electronic materials (on-line books and articles/CD-ROM indexes) are still evolving. In most cases, begin an entry with the conventional APA form for that item, whether a book, article, or abstract. Then identify the item as an electronic source ([*On-line*]; [*CD-ROM*]), and provide a path or electronic address for the source so that a researcher can locate it. Path statements will vary, but they typically consist of the protocol (Telnet, FTP, Internet), directory, and file name of the item. Do not put periods at the end of protocols, directories, and file names.

In a citation for an *on-line book*, include the year of on-line publication and the original date of publication, both of which also appear in the parenthetical note.

References

Carroll, L. (1994). <u>Alice's adventures in wonderland</u>

    (Orig. pub. 1865). [On-line]. Available FTP:

    ftp.Germany. EU.net Directory: pub/books/carroll

    File: alice-2.2-US.dvi.gz

Parenthetical notes:

In Carroll (1865/1994), readers encounter . . .

(Carroll, 1865/1994)

In a citation for an *on-line article*, give the most recent date for the piece (electronic documents are often revised), note that the journal is an electronic publication [*On-line serial*], and record the length of the item, either in pages, paragraphs, or other forms. The item below, for example, is divided into numbered sections.

References

DeWitt, R. (1993, July). Vagueness, semantics, and

    the language of thought [8 sections]. <u>PSYCHE</u>

    [On-line serial], <u>1,</u> (1). Available FTP:

    ftp.lib.ncsu.edu Directory: pub/stacks/psyche/

    File:psyche-v1n01-dewitt-vagueness

Parenthetical notes:

DeWitt (1993) reports . . .

(DeWitt, 1993)

In a citation for an *on-line abstract*, first identify the article itself (author, date, and title), indicate that the abstract is [*On-line*], and provide an electronic path to the source of the abstract.

References

Taylor, B. A., & Harris, S. L. (1995). Teaching

    children with autism to seek information:

    Acquisition of novel information and

    generalization of responding. [On-line]. <u>Journal</u>

**35b
APA**

```
of Applied Behavior Analysis, 28, 3-14. Abstract

from WWW: http://www.envmed.rochester.edu/

wwwrap/behavior/jaba_htm/28/_28-003.htm
```

Parenthetical notes:

```
Taylor & Harris (1995) report . . .

(Taylor & Harris, 1995)
```

If the abstract is on a CD-ROM, substitute [*CD-ROM*] for [*On-line*] and give the source [*SilverPlatter, Proquest*] and retrieval number after "Abstract from."

References

```
Stewart, D. (1980). The legacy of Quintilian. [CD-

ROM]. English Education, 11, 103-117. Abstract

from: SilverPlatter File: ERIC Item: EJ 217 526
```

Parenthetical notes:

```
Stewart (1980) mentions . . .

(Stewart, 1980)
```

**35b
APA**

If a work you consult on CD-ROM or other electronic format also exists in a printed version (for example, a magazine article on Proquest), APA currently prefers that you cite it in its printed form. However, this standard may change as more works become available electronically.

82. **Electronic Correspondence, E-mail, Bulletin Boards—APA** APA style treats such information as personal communication. Because personal communications are not available to other researchers, no mention is made of them in the References list. Electronic communications like e-mail or bulletin boards that are not stored or archived have limited reference use, too, for researchers. You must use your judgment about listing them as References. Personal communications should, however, be acknowledged in the body of the essay in parenthetical notes.

Parenthetical note:

```
William Rice (personal communication, October 14,

1994) . . .
```

83. **Movie/Videotape—APA** This is also the basic form for films, audiotapes, slides, charts, and other nonprint sources. The specific type of media is described between brackets, as shown below for a film. In most cases, APA references will be listed by identifying the writer, though that will vary, as the example shows.

References

Zeffirelli, F. (Director). (1968). <u>Romeo and Juliet</u>

[Film]. Hollywood, CA: Paramount.

Parenthetical notes:

Zeffirelli (1968) features . . .

(Zeffirelli, 1968)

84. **Musical Recording—APA** Ordinarily music is listed by the writer.

References

Dylan, B. (1989). What was it you wanted? [Recorded

by Willie Nelson]. On <u>Across the borderline</u>

[CD]. New York: Columbia.

Parenthetical note:

In the song "What Was It You Wanted?" (Dylan, 1989,

track 10). . . .

85. **Book Review—APA** Notice that brackets surround the description of the article, which in this case has no title. If the review had a title, that title would precede the bracketed description—which would still be included in the entry.

References

Farquhar, J. (1987). [Review of the book <u>Medical</u>

<u>power and social knowledge</u>]. <u>American Journal of</u>

<u>Psychology, 94,</u> 256.

Parenthetical notes:

Farquhar (1987) observes . . .

(Farquhar, 1987)

Acupuncture: Energy or Nerves?

Lori S. McWilliams

The University of Texas at Austin

35c **WINDOW ON WRITING: A Sample APA Paper**

This final version of an essay by Lori S. McWilliams has been re-vised to enhance its usefulness as a model. Some material was dropped and a few paragraphs were reshaped. The language has been sharpened and mechanical errors have been edited. Yet the bulk of the essay re-mains just as Lori McWilliams wrote it in her first year of college.

CHECKLIST

Title Page for a Paper—APA

APA style requires a separate title page; use the facing page as a model and review the following checklist.

✔ Type your paper on white bond paper. Preferred typefaces (when you have a choice) include Times Roman, American Typewriter, and Courier.

✔ Arrange and center the title of your paper, your name, and your school.

✔ Use the correct form for the title, capitalizing all important words and all words of four letters or more. Articles, conjunc-tions, and prepositions are not capitalized unless they are four letters or more. Do not underline the title or use all capitals.

✔ Give your first name, middle initial, and last name.

✔ Number the cover sheet and all subsequent pages in the upper right-hand corner. Place a short title for the paper on the same line as the page number as shown; the short title consists of the first two or three words of the title.

35c
APA

Abstract

Western science has long had doubts about
acupuncture, an oriental technique for relieving
pain. But both eastern and western traditions offer
useful perspectives on how acupuncture works.
According to Chinese tradition, acupuncture works by
directing the flow of energy through the body, which
flows along channels called meridians. Western
scientists think that acupuncture works either by
interrupting pain messages conveyed by the nervous
system or by stimulating the production of natural
painkilling substances in the body called endorphins.
These explanations are not necessarily incompatible
with the explanations of Chinese tradition.

35c
APA

CHECKLIST

Abstract for a Paper—APA

Abstracts are common in papers using APA style. For information on preparing an abstract, see Section 35e. (If your instructor does not require an abstract, go to p. 700.)

✔ Place the abstract on a separate page, after the cover sheet.
✔ Center the word "Abstract" at the top of the page.
✔ Include the short title of the essay and the page number (2) in the upper right-hand corner.
✔ Double-space the abstract.
✔ Do not indent the first line of the abstract. Type it in block form. Strict APA form limits abstracts to 960 characters or fewer.

35c
APA

Acupuncture: Energy or Nerves?

¶1   Pain plagues many people. A person who experiences chronic pain experiences an invasive problem: the pain becomes part of every aspect of life. All too often, a victim tries to find relief through over-the-counter or prescription drugs. But the pain persists. Western science has continually manipulated chemistry to produce analgesics; science has also tried to relieve pain through surgery. Despite advances in treatment, Holzman (1986) notes that "there is still no satisfactory set of treatments to consistently and permanently alleviate all sources of pain" (p. 2). One technique that is effective in up to 65% of all cases of chronic pain is the ancient Chinese technique of acupuncture (Langone, 1984). Physicians and scientists in the United States, however, have long been suspicious of acupuncture, in part because of doubts about how it works. Eastern practitioners believe acupuncture relieves pain by adjusting the innate energy within the body; western scientists believe that acupuncture must work through the nervous system. In fact, both of these views--eastern and western--can contribute to an understanding of how acupuncture works.

¶2   According to Langone, the process of acupuncture involves "the insertion of hair-thin needles, singly

**35c
APA**

CHECKLIST

The Body of a Research Paper—APA

The body of the APA paper runs uninterrupted until the separate References page. Be sure to type the essay on good-quality bond paper. The first page of an APA paper will look like the facing page.

✔ Repeat the title of your paper, exactly as it appears on the title page, on the first page of the research essay itself.
✔ Be sure the title is centered and properly capitalized.
✔ Begin the body of the essay two lines (a double space) below the title.
✔ Double-space the body of the essay.
✔ Use at least one-inch margins at the sides, top, and bottom of this and all subsequent pages.
✔ Indent the first lines of paragraphs five to seven spaces.
✔ Indent long quotations (more than forty words) in a block five to seven spaces from the left margin. In student papers, APA permits long quotations to be single spaced.
✔ Include the short title of the essay and the page number (3) in the upper right-hand corner. Number all subsequent pages the same way.
✔ Do not hyphenate words at the right-hand margin. Do not justify the right-hand margin.

35c
APA

or in combination, into the strategic points on the
body to ease pain and treat a myriad of ailments" (p.
70). Needles used for insertion vary in length,
anywhere from 1/2 inch to 3 inches. In the past,
acupuncture needles have been made of gold, silver,
copper, brass, bone, flint, and stone (Duke, 1972).
Rose-Neil (1979) notes that the earliest acupuncture
needles were made of stone and called "stone piercers"
or "stone borers" (p. 65). The material used for the
presterilized and disposable needles today is 26- to
32-gauge stainless steel (Komarow, 1995).

¶3   Acupuncture needles are inserted into the body at
approximately 360 different locations from head to toe.
Since the points or acupoints to be needled depend

35c
APA

upon a patient's ailment, an acupuncturist must assess
a patient's condition and needs. After a diagnosis,
the acupuncturist inserts the needles and manipulates
them either by manual or electrical rotation. As the
points are stimulated, pain relief follows.

¶4   In China, time and tradition have proved the
effectiveness of acupuncture. Chang (1976) traces the
origins of acupuncture back 6000 years, but Langone
(1984) believes that the Chinese have been using
acupuncture medicinally for only about 2000 years.
Rose-Neil (1979) gives this account of acupuncture's
development in China:

It was noted that soldiers wounded by arrows
sometimes recovered from illnesses which had
afflicted them for many years. The idea evolved
that, by penetrating the skin at certain points,
diseases were, apparently, cured. It was observed
that the size of the wound did not matter, but
only its location and depth. The Chinese began to
copy the effects of the arrow, puncturing the
skin with needles. (p. 65)

Though the East believes in acupuncture, western
doctors tended to dismiss acupuncture as almost
whimsical. McGarey (1974) attributes this attitude to
a western focus on the process of disease rather than
on the body itself. Not until Richard Nixon's historic
trip to China in 1970, however, did the West take a
serious interest in the mechanisms of acupuncture, and
the road to acceptance has been slow (Belkin, 1992).
It was obvious that acupuncture worked, but the two
cultures did not agree on how.

¶5   To the Chinese, health is maintained by the flow
of energy in the body. Chang (1976) cites this passage
from the Nei Ching, an ancient collection of writings
on acupuncture, to illustrate the principle:

The root of the way of life, of birth and change
is Qi (energy); the myriad things of heaven and
earth all obey this law. Thus Qi in the periphery

**35c
APA**

envelopes heaven and earth, Qi in the interior
activates them. The source wherefrom the sun,
moon, and stars derive their light, the thunder,
rain, wind, and cloud their being, the four
seasons and the myriad things their birth,
growth, gathering and storing: all this is
brought about by Qi. Man's possession of life is
completely dependent upon this Qi. (p. 17)

As the passage suggests, the energy flowing within a
body governs its existence. Stiefvater (1971) observes
that "the Chinese viewed man as being ruled by the
'two great forces' which govern also our earth and our
heaven" (p. 14). The two forces are the Yin and the
Yang. Since Yin and Yang compose the energy that
governs man and woman, when Yin and Yang are in
balance, health results. If the equilibrium created by
the forces is disturbed, the result is discomfort or
disease.

¶6   To maintain health, the energy must be
transported through the body by means of lines called
meridians that conduct energy. Twelve acupuncture
meridians exist in the body. Six of the meridians
represent the six bowels: the gall bladder, the small
and large intestines, the stomach, the bladder, and
the triple heater. Kruger (1974) explains that the
triple heater is an "imaginary organ . . . that

controls [the flow of energy] Ch'i" (p. 46). Five other

meridians represent the five major organs--the lungs,

the heart, the spleen-pancreas (together forming one

meridian), the liver, and the kidneys. The remaining

meridian represents the pericardium. These meridians

join the 360 acupuncture points, each corresponding to

its organ. Thus, needling a specific point will affect

a corresponding organ.

¶7   Meridians must constantly conduct energy

throughout the body. Each meridian has a point of entry

and a point of exit. The energy enters the meridian,

flows through its entire length, then exits. Upon exit,

the energy promptly enters another meridian and repeats

its course (Chang, 1976). If the continuous flow is

disrupted, pain and disease will occur. Since the body

expends much of its energy coping with the pain of an

ailment, acupuncture intervenes by restoring energy so

that the body may heal.

¶8   Western scientists, dismissing this concept of

energy, prefer to explain acupuncture by reference to

the nervous system. One early explanation--called the

gate theory--suggested that pain is controlled by gates

located in the brain and the spinal cord. Needles

stimulating the body produce large impulses that flood

the gates, thus preventing them from transmitting

additional impulses and blocking pain. This theory was

35c
APA

gradually refined. Benson (1979) suggests, for example, that acupuncture relieves pain by "either altering the capacity of the nerves which carry impulses . . . or by changing the programming of the central nervous system itself" (p. 128). Stimulating a nerve close to an acupoint inhibits pain impulses to the brain. As Frank Warren puts it, "It's as if a fat man and a thin man want to go through a doorway, and the fat man blocks the way" (Kruger, 1974, p. 66).

¶9   More recently, western scientists have proposed that the pain relief achieved by acupuncture may be caused by endorphins. Endorphins are naturally occurring, painkilling substances produced by the body. Endorphins kill pain as effectively as morphine; hence the name endorphin, which means "the morphine within" (Olshan, 1980, p. 6). Bruce Pomeranz of the University of Toronto has conducted experiments based on endorphins and their relationship to acupuncture. Using anesthetized animals, Pomerantz "located cells that fire rapidly [within the brain] when the animal's toe was pricked with a pin. Acupuncture slowed down those cells' firing, and within about 90 minutes after acupuncture they recovered their normal response to pain" ("Neural," p. 324). Pomerantz discovered that acupuncture no longer worked when the pituitary glands of his experimental animals were removed. This suggested that the pituitary, not the brain, is the source of endorphins. Further studies on animals and humans have produced evidence that some of the main acupuncture points are near nerves. Tests also verified that the amount of endorphins in the cerebrospinal fluid and the blood increased after an acupuncture treatment (Langone, 1984). Thus, needling the skin stimulates nerve endings and releases endorphins. Once within the blood, the endorphins bind with receptors in the brain to block the transmission of pain signals. Interestingly, the Chinese have long known that the closer an acupuncture point is to a nerve, the greater the pain relief achieved by acupuncture (Chan, 1973).

¶10   The East believes that acupuncture relieves pain and sickness by restoring an energy balance in the body and continues to develop new medical techniques (Baocheng, 1991). The West attributes accupuncture's effects to the normal workings of the nervous system. But both explanations have merit. In trying to understand the medicine of the East, western scientists have come to understand a pain-suppression mechanism not previously understood. Langone (1984) quotes a New York doctor who now asserts that "for pain, [acupuncture] is probably the safest treatment, with the fewest side effects and the greatest benefit. It should be the first line of defense, not the last" (p. 72).

35c
APA

Acupuncture 10

References

Baocheng, H. (1991, June 17). Pizhen--a new

   acupuncture therapy. Beijing Review, 34, 44-45.

Belkin, L. (1992, January 28). Practicing acupuncture

   made easy. The New York Times, p. B1.

Benson, H. (1979). The mind/body effect. New York:

   Simon & Shuster.

Chan, P. (1973). Wonders of Chinese acupuncture.

   Alhambra, CA: Borden.

Chang, S. T. (1976). The complete book of

   acupuncture. Millbrae, CA: Celestial Arts.

Duke, M. (1972). Acupuncture. New York: Jove.

Holzman, A. D. (1986). Pain management: A handbook of

   psychological treatment approaches. New York:

   Pergamon Press.

Komarow, E. W. (1995). Traditional acupuncture

   [On-line web site]. Available WWW:

   http://www.dbls.inssys.com/hom/elaine/index.html

Kruger, H. (1974). Other healers, other cures: A

   guide to alternative medicine. Indianapolis:

   Bobbs-Merrill.

Langone, J. (1984, August). Acupuncture: A new

   respect for an ancient remedy. Discover, 5,

   70-73.

CHECKLIST

References Page—APA

Sources contributing directly to the paper are listed alphabetically on a separate sheet immediately after the body of the essay. For more information about the purpose and form of this list, see pages 679 through 683.

✔ Center the title "References" at the top of the page.

✔ All sources mentioned in the text of the paper must appear in the References list, including personal communications; similarly, every source listed in the References list must be mentioned in the paper.

✔ Arrange the items in the References list alphabetically by the last name of the author. Give initials only for first names. If no author is given for a work, list and alphabetize it by the first word in the title, excluding articles (*A, An,* and *The*).

✔ The first line of each entry is flush with the left-hand margin. Subsequent lines in an entry are indented five spaces.

✔ The list is ordinarily double spaced. In student papers, APA style does permit single spacing of individual entries; double spacing is preserved between the single-spaced items.

✔ Punctuate items in the list carefully. Do not forget the period at the end of each entry.

✔ In the References list, capitalize only the first word and any proper names in the title of a book or article. Within a title, capitalize the first word after a colon.

✔ If you have two or more entries by the same author, list them by year of publication, from earliest to latest. If an author publishes two works in the same year, list them alphabetically by title.

35c
APA

McGarey, W. A. (1974). Acupuncture and body energies.
Phoenix: Gabriel Press.

A neural mechanism for acupuncture. (1976, November
20). Science News, 110, 324.

Olshan, N. H. (1980). Power over your pain without
drugs. New York: Rawson, Wade.

Rose-Neil, S. (1979) Acupuncture. In Ann Hill (Ed.),
A visual encyclopedia of unconventional medicine
(pp. 64-65). New York: Crown.

Stiefvater, E. H. W. (1971). What is acupuncture? How
does it work? Bradford: Health Science Press.

35d HOW DO YOU USE CBE DOCUMENTATION?

Troubleshooting

Disciplines that study the physical world—physics, chemistry, biology—are called the natural sciences; disciplines that examine (and produce) technologies are described as the applied sciences. Writing in these fields is specialized, and no survey of all forms of documentation can be provided here. For more information about writing in the following fields, consult one of these style manuals.

- **Chemistry:** *The ACS Style Guide for Authors and Editors* (1985)— American Chemical Society
- **Geology:** *Suggestions to Authors of Reports of the United States Geological Survey* (1990)—U.S. Geological Survey
- **Mathematics:** *A Manual for Authors of Mathematical Papers* (1990)—American Mathematical Society
- **Medicine:** *American Medical Association Manual of Style* (1989)
- **Physics:** *AIP Style Manual* (1990)—American Institute of Physics

A highly influential manual for scientific writing is *Scientific Style and Format: The CBE Manual for Authors, Editors, and Publishers* by the Council of Biology Editors (6th edition, 1994). In this latest edition of *The CBE Manual*, the editors advocate a common style for international science, but they also recognize important differences between disciplines and even countries.

CBE style itself includes the choice of two major methods of documenting sources used in research: a *name-year* system that resembles APA style and a *citation-sequence* system that lists sources in the order of their use. In this section, we briefly describe this second system.

**35d
CBE**

To use CBE citation-sequence documentation . . .

35d-1 (Step 1) Where a citation is needed in the text of a paper, insert either a raised number (the preferred form) or a number in parentheses. Citations should appear immediately after the word or phrase to which they are related, and they are numbered in the order you use them.

```
Oncologists[1] are aware of trends in cancer

mortality[2].


Oncologists (1) are aware of trends in cancer

mortality (2).
```

Source 1 thus becomes the first item listed on the References page, source 2 the second item, and so on.

```
1. Devesa SS, Silverman DT. Cancer incidence and
   mortality trends in the United States: 1935-74.
   J Natl Cancer Inst 1978; 60:545-571.
2. Goodfield J. The siege of cancer. New York: Dell;
   1978. 240 p.
```

You can refer to more than one source in a single note, with the numbers separated by a dash if they are in sequence and by commas if out of sequence.

In sequence

```
Cancer treatment[2-3] has changed over the decades. But
Rettig[4] shows that the politics of cancer research
remains constant.
```

Out of sequence

```
Cancer treatment[2,5] has changed over the decades. But
Rettig[4] shows that the politics of cancer research
remains constant.
```

If you cite a source again later in the paper, you refer to it by its original number.

```
Great strides have occurred in epidemiological
methods[5] despite the political problems described in
maintaining research support and funding by Rettig[4].
```

35d-2 (Step 2) On a separate page at the end of the text of your paper, list the sources you used in the order they occurred. These sources are numbered: source 1 in the paper would be the first source listed on the References page, source 2 the second item, and so on. Notice, then, that this References list is *not* alphabetical. The first few entries on a CBE References list might look like this.

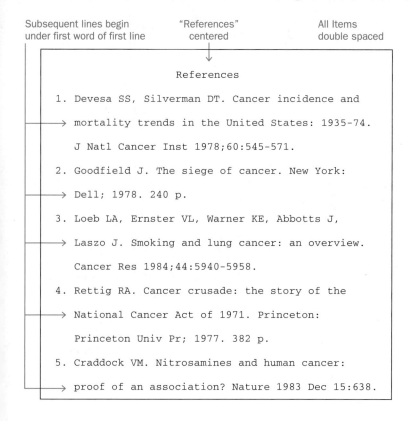

Subsequent lines begin under first word of first line · "References" centered · All Items double spaced

References

1. Devesa SS, Silverman DT. Cancer incidence and mortality trends in the United States: 1935-74. J Natl Cancer Inst 1978;60:545-571.

2. Goodfield J. The siege of cancer. New York: Dell; 1978. 240 p.

3. Loeb LA, Ernster VL, Warner KE, Abbotts J, Laszo J. Smoking and lung cancer: an overview. Cancer Res 1984;44:5940-5958.

4. Rettig RA. Cancer crusade: the story of the National Cancer Act of 1971. Princeton: Princeton Univ Pr; 1977. 382 p.

5. Craddock VM. Nitrosamines and human cancer: proof of an association? Nature 1983 Dec 15:638.

35d
CBE

A typical **CBE citation-sequence–style References entry for a book** includes the following basic information.

- Number assigned to the source.
- Name of author(s), last name first, followed by a period. Initials are used in place of full first or middle names. Commas ordinarily separate the names of multiple authors.
- Title of work, followed by a period. Only the first word and any proper nouns in a title are capitalized. The title is not underlined.
- Place of publication, followed by a colon.
- Publisher, followed by a semicolon. Titles of presses can be abbreviated.
- Date, followed by a period.
- Number of pages, followed by a period.

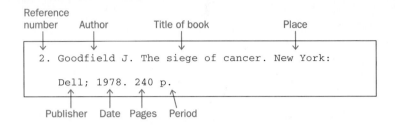

A typical **CBE citation-sequence–style References entry for an article in a scholarly journal** (where the pagination is continuous through a year) includes the following basic information.

- Number assigned to the source.
- Name of author(s), last name first, followed by a period. Initials are used in place of full first or middle names. Commas ordinarily separate the names of multiple authors.
- Title of article, followed by a period. Only the first word and any proper nouns in a title are capitalized. The title does not appear between quotation marks.
- Name of the journal. All major words are capitalized, but the journal title is not underlined. A space (but no punctuation) separates the journal title from the date. Journal titles of more than one word can be abbreviated following the recommendations in *American National Standard Z39.5-1985: Abbreviations of Titles of Publications*.
- Year (and month for journals not continuously paginated; date for weekly journals), followed immediately by a semicolon.
- Volume number, followed by a colon, and the page numbers of the article. No spaces separate these items. A period follows the page numbers.

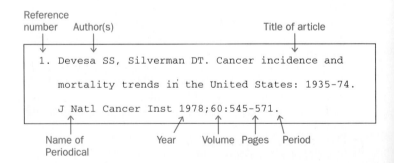

A typical **CBE citation-sequence–style References entry for an article in a popular magazine** includes the following basic information.

- Number assigned to the source.
- Name of author(s), last name first, followed by a period. Initials are substituted for first names unless two authors mentioned in the paper have identical last names and first initials.
- Title of article, followed by a period. Only the first word and any proper nouns in a title are capitalized. The title does not appear between quotation marks. (Where quotations are needed, CBE recommends British style. See *CBE Manual*, pp. 180–81.)
- Name of the magazine, abbreviated. All major words are capitalized, but the journal title is not underlined. A space (but no punctuation) separates the magazine title from the year and month.
- Year, month (abbreviated), and day (for a weekly magazine). The year is separated from the month by a space. A colon follows immediately after the date, followed by page number(s). The entry ends with a period.

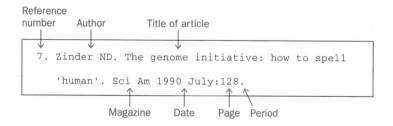

Reference number Author Title of article

7. Zinder ND. The genome initiative: how to spell 'human'. Sci Am 1990 July:128.

Magazine Date Page Period

35d
CBE

A typical **CBE citation-sequence–style References entry for an electronic item** includes the basic information provided for a print document (author, title, publication information, page numbers) with the following additions.

- Electronic medium, identified between brackets. For books and monographs, this information comes after the title [*monograph online*]; for periodicals, it follows the name of the journal [*serial online*].
- Availability statement, following the publication information or page numbers.
- Date of access, if helpful in identifying what version of an electronic text was consulted.

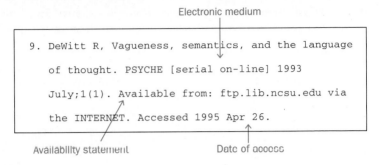

Electronic medium

```
9. DeWitt R, Vagueness, semantics, and the language

   of thought. PSYCHE [serial on-line] 1993

   July;1(1). Available from: ftp.lib.ncsu.edu via

   the INTERNET. Accessed 1995 Apr 26.
```

Availability statement   Date of access

There are so many variations to these basic entries, however, that you will certainly want to check the *CBE Manual* when you do a major CBE-style paper.

C H E C K L I S T

CBE Style

- CBE style normally requires a separate title page. The title of the essay can be centered about a third of the way from the top of the page, followed by "by" on a separate line, and the writer's name, also on a separate line. Other information such as professor's name, course title, and date can be included on the bottom third of the page.
- CBE style normally requires an abstract of about 250 words on a separate sheet immediately following the title page. The word "Abstract" is centered on the page.
- Double-space the entire manuscript of a CBE paper. Avoid hyphenating words at the end of a line.
- Number pages consecutively in the upper right-hand corner, counting the title page as the first page.
- Take special care with figures and tables. They should be numbered in separate sequences. The *CBE Manual* includes an entire chapter on handling illustrative material.
- The References page follows the text of the CBE essay on a new page. Remember that the items on this page are *not* listed alphabetically. References pages can also be titled "Literature Cited" or "References Cited."
- All works listed on the References page should be cited at least once in the body of your paper.

35e   HOW DO YOU WRITE AN ABSTRACT?

Troubleshooting

Most APA and CBE papers include an abstract, but abstracts are common across the disciplines—and for good reason. They save time by summarizing the contents of journal articles or other materials; after reading an abstract, a researcher can decide whether a piece needs to be read in its entirety. An abstract also can act as an outline, helping readers follow the argument of a complicated essay by highlighting its premises, main ideas, and conclusions.

The qualities of a good abstract aren't difficult to enumerate. First, it outlines the major ideas in the abstracted material and provides a sense of how they are related. Second, it accurately represents the contents and organization of the abstracted piece. Third, it is written in a clear style that reflects the wording of the original piece. And lastly, it is concise, falling within any word limit (100 words? 200 words?) imposed on it.

To write an effective abstract . . .

35e-1 **Respect any requirements placed upon the abstract.** The correct form of an abstract is usually determined by where it will appear. A professional journal, for example, may have detailed requirements for abstracts, especially concerning length.

An abstract included in an undergraduate essay is typed on a separate page immediately before the body of the essay. The word "Abstract" appears as the title, centered on the page, a double space before the body of the abstract. The abstract page is ordinarily numbered in APA and CBE form, unnumbered in MLA form. The APA abstract itself should be a single block paragraph (no indention), double spaced, of no more than 960 characters; CBE recommends an abstract of about 250 words for professional articles.

Abstracts separated from their original articles are often identified by the word "Abstract" followed by the title of the original piece (also see abstract 2 on p. 719).

```
Abstract: Characteristics of Rejection Letters and

        Their Effects on Job Applicants
```

35e-2 **Construct the abstract systematically.** First, read through the article carefully, underlining or listing its main points and major supporting evidence. For a longer article, extract the gist of each section or cluster of related paragraphs, giving special attention to introductory and concluding paragraphs.

Shape your abstract from the points you have underlined or the summaries you have made of each major part of the article, linking your points with helpful transitions. (Don't use direct quotations from the article in the abstract.) Finally, test the abstract against the article, evaluating how well it reflects what the original piece argues or presents.

In the abstract, try to follow the pattern of organization used in the original article. Don't try to rethink or restructure the piece, even if you discover a more economical way of arranging its argument or evidence. However, you need not summarize every topic discussed in an essay: you may, for example, explain how one type of analysis is applied to a variety of subjects rather than describe all the subjects individually (see abstract 2 on p. 719).

35e-3 **Be sure your abstract is easy to read.** Keep the piece short, but don't compress your style so much that the abstract reads like a telegram. Avoid sentence fragments and unnecessary abbreviations.

WINDOW ON WRITING: Sample Abstracts

1 ABSTRACT FROM AN UNDERGRADUATE RESEARCH PAPER

35e
abstr

                              Abstract

While conservation groups, ecologists, hikers, and

equestrians want to keep mountain bikes out of parks

and wilderness areas, mountain bikers consider these

lands--especially single-track hiking trails--their

natural environment. If mountain bikers wish to use

trails in public lands they must behave responsibly

and organize politically to defend their rights. The

war between bikers and environmental groups is due in

part to the explosive growth of mountain biking and

to the sometimes outrageous behavior of bikers in

sensitive areas. Fortunately bikers have begun to

practice more responsible trail riding. Their efforts
have won them recognition and approval from important
environmental groups and the United States Forest
Service.

2 ABSTRACT FROM A RESEARCH JOURNAL

Abstract: Expanding Roles for Summarized Information

At least seven types of summaries have emerged in common usage, especially during the past 250 years. They may be classified as either sequential summaries that retain the original order in which information was presented or synthesizing summaries that alter this sequence to achieve specific objectives. Each type of summary developed in response to challenges facing professions, government, business, and ordinary citizens—all of whom have sought to absorb increasing quantities of information being generated in a society that is becoming more complex. This taxonomy offers a definition and brief history for each of the seven techniques, describes the growth of corporations or other organizations that can be considered leading practitioners, and comments on the potential continuing role for each type of summary. The article also focuses on several contemporary issues that will affect future research, classroom writing instruction, and information management in modern computerized offices.
—Ratteray, O. M. (1985). *Written Communication, 2,* 457.

35e
abstr

How Do You Write for the Professional World?

A How Do You Write a Résumé and Job Application Letter?

B How Do You Write a Business Letter?

36a HOW DO YOU WRITE A RÉSUMÉ AND JOB APPLICATION LETTER?

Troubleshooting

Imagine for a moment that you are the personnel officer of a large firm thumbing through a stack of job applications. At this stage, the only impression you have of the people under consideration is what you gather from their résumés and accompanying job application letters. These pieces of paper will determine which candidates are examined more seriously—perhaps interviewed—and which are dropped from consideration. With so big a pile of applications, you are just looking for reasons to eliminate candidates. Under these circumstances, how would you react to a résumé that lacked basic information, was poorly arranged, or was full of spelling errors? Obviously, résumés and job letters need to be thoughtfully written, handsomely packaged, and proofread maniacally.

A résumé is a brief (usually one-page) outline of your academic and employment history, listing achievements, skills, and available references. It should give a prospective employer a sense of who you are, what you have done, and what you might be qualified to do. In preparing a résumé, you want to present an honest outline of your academic and employment record, yet one that enhances your chances of getting a job interview.

The job application letter that accompanies a résumé explains exactly how your expertise and experience make you the logical candidate for a particular job. In it, you subtly sell yourself, conveying to the employer a sense of your fitness for the position.

To write an effective résumé . . .

36a–1 **Include your name, current address, phone number(s), and** *relevant* **personal data.** You may also want to list a second, more permanent address if your current residence (an apartment, a dormitory) might change during the period of your job application. Provide only as much personal information as is essential for a particular job. Employers may, in fact, be limited in what they can expect employees to reveal about age, marital status, physical condition, and so on. Don't include a photograph with your résumé.

36a–2 **Outline your educational background.** In most cases, include the dates and institutions of your college and university degree(s) and other post–high school training, including any professional or trade school experiences. List this information either in reverse chronological order (most recent experiences first) or in order of relevance to the job you are seeking. Information about elementary and secondary school education should not be mentioned unless it is directly related to the prospective job. You may want to identify your academic major or areas of concentration, language skills, and significant academic honors, especially competitive scholarships, grants, and fellowships. A résumé you prepare immediately after graduation might list significant positions held while in college: on committees, in academic programs, and in clubs and social organizations.

36a
bus

36a–3 **Outline your work experience.** List your employment record in reverse chronological order (most recent position first) or in an order suited to the job you are seeking, most important experiences first. Be sure to state the position(s) you have held, the names of your employers, and the dates of employment. As far as possible, make sure that your résumé accounts for all recent years; don't leave gaps in your employment history that a prospective employer might worry about. Your job record should give an employer a sense of your experiences, qualifications, and reliability.

36a–4 **Let a prospective employer know how or where he or she can get more information about you.** That information may be available through people willing to serve as references, in letters of recommendation you can furnish, or in a dossier on file at a placement service.

You don't actually have to list the names of references on the résumé. A line at the bottom of the page to this effect will suffice.

```
References available upon request.
```

Before you claim to have references, be sure to talk with people willing to give you their endorsement. If you have a dossier of recommendations and credentials on file at a placement office or employment service, let a potential employer know this, again in a line such as the following.

```
Full dossier available through the Educational
Placement Service, Ohio State University, Columbus,
OH 43210.
```

36a–5 Tailor the résumé to the specific job or employer. Since a résumé should be short, include only items relevant to the type of job you are seeking. You might, for example, add or delete lines about club memberships, college committee work, church or community service, references to high school honors and achievement, and so on. In some circumstances you may want to identify your career intentions (junior accountant, medical examiner, dental hygienist); in other cases, such information might unnecessarily limit your job market potential.

For practical reasons, however, a résumé is often generic: you need one sheet suitable for many occasions. But tailoring the résumé is shrewd when you can manage it, particularly if you store your statement in a computer file and can add or delete items as needed. When you cannot modify a résumé so readily, use the job application letter to fill in details that your résumé does not cover.

**36a
bus**

36a–6 Pay attention to organization. Most résumés resemble an outline, but there is actually no standard form. So use common sense. When you need to show a steady record of employment and achievement, arrange the items on your résumé chronologically; when you want to highlight accomplishments suited to a particular job, arrange items by importance.

In either case, situate the items on your résumé so that major points stand out. Use headings to highlight major divisions and always allow for margins and white space. Don't crowd a résumé, but do try to fit everything onto a single page. A longer résumé is acceptable only if you have a lengthy employment history and significant experiences. Here's a workable order for the items on a résumé.

1. Personal information
2. Educational background
3. Job experience
4. References

A handsomely typed résumé reproduced on high-quality white paper is all an employer expects. You need not have your résumé professionally printed—though such services are widely available and relatively inexpensive. Proofread your finished résumé and job application letter several times; then get someone else to review both of these documents. Errors on them make you look careless and irresponsible. Don't let a simple mistake cost you a job interview.

36a-7 **Never send your résumé without a job application letter.** A résumé should always be accompanied by a typed cover letter explaining your interest in a position, your specific qualifications for the job, your willingness to meet for an interview, and so on. Like the résumé itself, the job application letter should ordinarily not exceed one page. (See pp. 724–726.)

Use a job application letter to draw attention to the reasons an employer should consider you for a job or interview. The letter can be more specific about these major points than the résumé; don't merely repeat information already on the résumé. Mention your notable strengths in the job application letter and make it sound tailored for the occasion—which it should be.

36a
bus

Sean M. O'Brian
2853 Sophia Gate
Latrobe, PA 15650
(412) 123-4567

OBJECTIVE   Beginning position as cinematographer,
                   film editor, writer

EDUCATION   Seminar Participant: "The American Cinema,"
                   American Film Institute, Los Angeles, CA,
                   June-July, 1995.
               Worked with Francis Ford Coppola and Sydney
                   Pollack.
               Won "Outstanding Film Student" citation.

               B.A. in Radio, Television, Film, 1994, St.
                   Vincent College, Latrobe, PA.
               Senior thesis: "The Art of Paddy Chayefsky."
               Courses in film production; screenwriting;
                   history of the film I, II, & III; editing.

               President: St. Vincent College Film Club,
                   1992-1993.
               Founded college film journal: Frame & Shoot,
                   1992.
               Coordinated Allegheny Film Festival, 1993.

               Manager: St. Vincent Photography Lab, 1992-1994.
               Managed campus photo lab. Held informal
                   classes on photography, lab work.
               Maintained and repaired cameras and equipment.

AWARDS   Best Student Film: Treed, 35 mm., 13 min.,
                   Allegheny Film Festival (1992).

               Best Animated Film: Bayou By You, 16 mm.,
                   7 min., Midwestern Film Conference (1994).

EXPERIENCE   1993-1994. Production Assistant, University
                   Films, Inc., Greensburg, PA 15640.
                   Gained experience with casting, script
                   writing and revision, crew management, film
                   stocks, development, editing.

               Summer, 1993. Intern. KYUU-TV, Cleveland, OH.
                   Worked as editor and guest coordinator.

               Summer, 1990. Gofer, Heliotrope Studios, Los
                   Angeles, CA.

               References available upon request.

36a
bus

Sean M. O'Brian
2853 Sophia Gate
Latrobe, Pennsylvania 15650
(412) 123-4567

OBJECTIVE

Beginning position as a cinematographer, film editor, or screenwriter.

SKILLS

Many courses in film studies and photography. Substantial experience in technical aspects of film production.

ACADEMIC ACHIEVEMENTS

St. Vincent College
Latrobe, Pennsylvania—May, 1994
Bachelor of Arts in Radio, Television, Film

President: St. Vincent College Film Club, 1993–1994
Creator: *Frame and Shoot*, a college film journal
Winner: Best Student Film—Allegheny Film Festival, 1992
Winner: Best Animated Film—Midwestern Film Conference, 1994

PROFESSIONAL EXPERIENCE

University Films, Inc.
Greensburg, Pennsylvania

Production Assistant
1993–1994
Gained experience with casting, script writing and rewrites, crew management, film stocks, development, editing.

KYUU-TV
Cleveland, Ohio

Intern
Summer, 1993
Worked as film editor, gofer, and guest coordinator.

St. Vincent Photography Lab
Latrobe, Pennsylvania

Manager
1992–1993
Held informal classes on photography, did lab work. Maintained and repaired cameras and other equipment.

References available upon request.

36a
bus

2853 Sophia Gate
Latrobe, PA 15650
May 23, 1994

Ms. Carina Obregon
Director of Personnel
Lamontier Films and Documentaries
5400 E. 133 St.
Garfield Heights, OH 44125

Dear Ms. Obregon:

I would like to be considered for the assistant production
supervisor position advertised by Lamontier Films in the
current issue of Film Monthly.

As my résumé demonstrates, I have a recent degree in cinema
and wide-ranging practical knowledge of film production. My
experience includes work with major movie companies and
directors in California. I have also been active in movie
productions, companies, and clubs in southwestern
Pennsylvania.

At KYUU-TV in Cleveland, I worked on several projects that
involved technicians from Lamontier who helped us develop
films about local area businesses and institutions,
including a feature on the Western Reserve Historical
Museum. Such experiences have made me particularly eager to
be involved with the kind of film production Lamontier
specializes in--locally supported, community-oriented
documentaries.

Having worked part-time with a small local film company, I
believe I have the skills required of an assistant
production supervisor--especially the ability to manage on-
the-spot assignments. I have handled more than a few crises
in the field, from revising a shooting script in order to
accommodate the sudden laryngitis of an actor to repairing
a jammed film transport on a camera forty feet off the
ground. I have also managed more routine tasks.

Since I expect to be in Cleveland early in June, an
opportunity for an interview then would be ideal. But I can
be available at any time convenient to Lamontier Films.

I look forward very much to talking with you.

Sincerely,

Sean M. O'Brian

Sean M. O'Brian

Enclosure

36a
bus

36b HOW DO YOU WRITE A BUSINESS LETTER?

Troubleshooting

Anytime you write to or for a business, institution, or office, you are expected to follow the conventions of the business letter. These conventions may seem arbitrary at first, but they make sure you provide all the essential information: dates, addresses, names and titles, routing information, and so on. Keep in mind that letters must communicate accurate information *and* furnish a record of the business transaction itself. Both of those roles are important. So don't regard business letter form as a mere formality.

To write successful business letters . . .

36b-1 Include a heading and inside address. The heading includes the address of the person sending the letter followed by the date.

```
3022 Hepshire
Missouri City, TX 77459
May 31, 1995
```

The inside address is the name and address of the person or institution to whom the letter is written. When you don't know exactly to whom you are writing, you can address the letter to an office or a position: Office of Admissions, Director of Personnel, Manager.

```
Office of Admissions
St. Vincent College
Latrobe, PA 15650
```

36b
bus

36b-2 Include a salutation. In business letters, the greeting is followed by a colon, not a comma. Most titles used in a salutation are abbreviated (Mr., Mrs., Ms., Dr.), but some are spelled out in full (Senator, President, Professor, Reverend).

```
Dear President Clinton:
Dear Senator Dole:
Dear Sister Constance:
Dear Professor Upton:
Dear Mr. Kuanahura:
Dear Mrs. Poins:
Dear Ms. Johnson:
```

Use a title when you don't have a person's name to address:

```
Dear Director of Personnel:
Dear Admissions Officer:
```

To make a general announcement, you may use the formal greeting

```
To Whom This May Concern:
```

However, this impersonal salutation seems to be losing favor; when possible, call a firm to get a name.

36b-3 **In the body of the letter, get to the point quickly.** By the end of the first paragraph, readers should understand why you are writing. Answer the *who*, *what*, *where*, *when*, and *why* questions your readers might have when they pick up your letter. Provide names, supply dates, explain circumstances. It may help if you make your basic request before you present any background information. Don't expect readers to plow through paragraphs of narrative before they get to your point.

Not

```
Dear Ms. Flowers:

    The accident occurred last week when my cat
knocked over a soft drink into the keyboard of my
computer, causing a short circuit, which then ignited
some papers on my desk, leading to a fire that
destroyed my computer, monitor, and printer.
Fortunately, I was able to put out the fire before it
spread beyond the desk. But the computer and related
equipment are, I am afraid, a total loss.
    My roommate called the local fire department,
who provided a full report on the incident
(enclosed), but by the time they arrived, there
really wasn't anything for them to do.
    Fortunately, I carry full apartment owner's
insurance with a separate rider covering my computer.
Consequently, I am asking you to explain to me how
to make a claim under that policy to replace my
computer, printer, and other properties damaged in
the fire on September 15. . . .
```

But

```
Dear Ms. Flowers:

    On September 15, my computer, printer, monitor,
and other related equipment were destroyed by a small
fire in my office. This equipment is covered by a
special rider to the apartment owner's insurance
policy I carry with your company: Policy No. 342-56-
88709-3.
    Please tell me how to make a claim against that
policy.
```

```
    The fire occurred as a result of an accidental
short circuit caused when my cat knocked a soda onto
the computer keyboard. I am enclosing a copy of the
fire department's report on the incident, which
provides full details. . . .
```

Be sure to tell readers exactly what you want from them. Don't leave them guessing.

```
Please tell me how to make a claim against my
insurance policy.
```

```
Could you send me information explaining New
Zealand's current immigration policies?
```

```
If you do not make payment by the end of this month,
we will take legal action to recover the property we
sold you.
```

36b–4 **Maintain a consistent and appropriate tone—usually formal, but cordial.** Business letters vary as much as people and institutions do. Some letters are extremely reserved, conveying information of legal weight between writers who represent the opinions of their companies, institutions, even governments. Other letters may be almost as casual as personal notes—though they still arrive in business form.

You may find it easier to decide on a tone if you put yourself in the reader's position for a moment. Ask yourself how you might feel or react if you received the letter you are sending.

If you were writing a job application letter, for example (see p. 726 for a model), you would want to assure the prospective employer that you are qualified for the position and eager to have it. But how do you show that? By taking time to find out what you can about your prospective employers and demonstrating that your strengths fill their needs. You wouldn't write the same job application letter to General Motors that you would to Joe's Auto Supply because the needs and scale of the two operations would be vastly different.

 Similarly, when writing a letter of complaint, you need to consider the point of view of the person likely to read your letter. Even if you are outraged and upset, what will you accomplish by venting your anger on that employee? You are more likely to get what you want by recognizing that your reader is—in most cases—being paid to resolve complaints like yours. A calm but firm explanation of your problem will work better than an insulting diatribe.

Remember, too, that your letter might be read by several people or become part of a permanent record. Keep these other possible readers in

**36b
bus**

mind as you decide on the tone of your communication. And, again, provide enough background information so that your letter would make sense if examined several weeks, months, or years in the future.

36b-5 **Keep the style natural, personal, and positive.** Avoid canned expressions such as

```
pursuant to
at your earliest convenience
the aforementioned document
as per your letter of . . .
enclosed please find
```

Be polite. Many business letters end with a pleasantry that affirms the goodwill or good intentions of both parties.

```
I am confident we can resolve this problem.
I look forward to seeing you in Chicago next month.
With your help, the project is sure to stay on track.
Let me know if I can be of any further assistance.
```

36b-6 **Choose an appropriate closing and sign the letter.** Like the greeting, the closing is a conventional expression. A variety of closings are available, some formal, others less so.

CHART

Closings for Business Letters

More formal	Respectfully yours,
	Yours very truly,
	Yours truly,
	Sincerely yours,
	Sincerely,
	Yours sincerely,
	Best regards,
Less formal	Best,

Only the first word in the closing is capitalized; the closing phrase is followed by a comma.

The letter is signed in ink just beneath the closing. Because some signatures are hard to read, the writer's name is typed below the signature. A title or position is often included.

Yours truly,

Velvia Johnson

Velvia Johnson
Associate Editor, <u>The Daily Texan</u>

Beneath the signature but nearer the left margin, it is common to include a pair of initials, the first identifying the person who dictated the letter, the second the secretary who typed it. The letter may also indicate whether any other materials are enclosed and to whom copies of the original have been sent.

CL/dw

Enclosures: 2

cc: Preston Partridge
    Doris Upton
    Judith Poins

36b-7 **Give your letter a consistent form and appearance.**

SUMMARY

Business Letter Forms

- **Block form**—All the components of the letter are aligned flush left and paragraphs are not indented (see page 733).
- **Modified block form**—The heading, closing, and signature are aligned at approximately the midpoint of the page, and the inside address and body paragraphs remain flush left. Body paragraphs are not indented (see page 734).
- **Indented form**—The heading, closing, and signature are aligned at approximately the midpoint of the page, and the inside address and body paragraphs remain flush left. Body paragraphs are, however, indented (see pages 735 and 736).

36b
bus

Business letters should always be typed on standard 8½-by-11-inch paper of good quality. If you are writing for a firm or institution, use its printed letterhead.

Provide wide margins (one inch or more) all around the letter to form a kind of frame. A business letter should never feel crowded. If necessary, break up long paragraphs into more readable chunks. Make the letter easy to read. Use lists when you need them.

```
I have enclosed the information you requested:

    - A copy of my birth certificate

    - Copies of my medical and dental records

    - My high school and college transcripts

    - Letters of recommendation from two previous
      employers
```

36b-8 **Address the envelope correctly.** The envelope includes the inside address found on the letter plus the writer's return address in block form. Don't forget sufficient postage.

```
Millie Connors
3022 Hepshire
Missouri City, TX 77459



              Bryce Carter, President
              Aetryn Electronics
              1241 Cannon Blvd., Suite 12
              Centralia, IL 61802
```

WINDOW ON WRITING: Sample Business Letters

Letters 1 through 4 form a sequence, dealing with the reaction to an especially harsh review of a college production of *Macbeth*. As you read, notice that each letter is written with more than one reader in mind. Check the notations at the bottom of the letters to learn who receives copies.

You might also compare the degree of formality in these letters. They are written by people who know each other well enough to sit down and talk their problem out. But once the issue is put into writing, the stakes increase. In particular, notice how carefully letter 3 is phrased. President Browning attempts to resolve the dispute firmly and judicially. She distributes praise and blame between both the parties involved, but she also acts decisively. Letter 4 indicates that a personal conversation will follow, so it is far less detailed than letter 3.

The business letters you write may not be as complicated as those presented here. But every business letter—even a simple request—takes a degree of strategy and tact.

1 Full Block Form (with letterhead)

The Rattler   **What you needed to know yesterday—today!**

102 Carlyle Hall / Viperton, IL 61802

23 April 1995

Dr. Aurelia Browning, President
Copperhead College
Mammoth Hall 101
Viperton, IL 61802

Dear President Browning:

I request that you promptly review recent actions by Professors
Judith Poins and Preston Partridge restricting freedom of the
press on this campus.

As you may know, several days ago Angus MacGivern, a reporter from
The Rattler, reviewed the current English and Drama department
production of the annual Shakespeare play. MacGivern's review of
the dress rehearsal of Macbeth sharply criticized the acting,
directing, and staging of Professors Poins and Partridge's show. A
copy of the review is enclosed.

Because of MacGivern's unfavorable review of Macbeth: The Musical,
Professor Poins has established a policy banning Rattler reporters
from all future Drama department dress rehearsals. She has also
warned students in the Drama department not to talk with reporters
and denied backstage permissions freely granted to Rattler
reporters in the past.

Professor Partridge has taken similar action in the English
department, even warning Angus MacGivern, an English major, that
his work in an English course might be subject to an evaluation as
tough as that he gave to Macbeth.

I am asking you to investigate these attempts by Professors Poins
and Partridge to limit freedom of expression at Copperhead
College. I hope specifically that you will rescind the gag orders
imposed by the Drama and English departments on The Rattler.

Respectfully yours,

Tarshia Johnson

Tarshia Johnson
Editor, The Rattler

Enclosure
cc. Preston Partridge
    Judith Poins
    Angus MacGivern
    Central Illinois ACLU

**36b
bus**

2 Modified Block Form

1425 Laudanum Dr.
Viperton, IL 61802
April 25, 1995

Dr. Aurelia Browning, President
Copperhead College
Mammoth Hall 101
Viperton, IL 61802

Dear President Browning:

I have just read--with mounting outrage--the letter Tarshia
Johnson, editor of The Rattler, sent you on April 23, demanding
that you rescind the guidelines Professor Poins and I have
promulgated to define the relationships our departments and
faculty will have with the press.

I strongly urge you to deny the petition and to consider taking
further action against The Rattler for its unprofessional and
damaging attacks upon my reputation and that of Professor Poins.
To permit the editor of The Rattler to dictate how the departments
and faculties under our authority will behave toward reporters
would set a dangerous precedent for this college.

The production of Macbeth supervised by me and directed by
Professor Poins may have had flaws. But we felt compelled to take
risks this year to be sure that the annual Spring Shakespeare
Festival--which I initiated and developed into a major campus
event--continues to attract a large audience.

I would point out that Angus MacGivern's review of Macbeth strayed
well beyond the margins of good taste and criticism. May I remind
you that he described Professor Poins's choreography of the
banquet at Macbeth's castle as "ten sweaty gymnasts tripping over
a volleyball net"? And, for agreeing to play the title role, I
have been branded as "the biggest ham since Hormel."

While I will admit that The Rattler's review has not hurt
attendance at the festival production, the students and
townspeople jamming our auditorium are attending for all the wrong
reasons. I deeply resent the cheers that my character's beheading
raises from this mob.

I hope you will act with your characteristic speed and
determination to show Ms. Johnson and Mr. MacGivern the difference
between anarchy of the press and reasonable supervision exercised
by those who know better.

Yours truly,

Preston Partridge
Chair, Department of
English

c. Judith Poins

3 Indented Form (with letterhead)

Copperhead College   **Give the People Light . . .**

Office of the President
Mammoth Hall 101

                                    April 27, 1995

Preston Partridge
Chair, Department of English
Copperhead College
12 Praline Hall
Viperton, IL 61802

Dear Preston:

    Like you, I was startled by the unusual sharpness of Angus MacGivern's review of your and Professor Poins's production of <u>Macbeth: The Musical</u>. I regret the personal tone he takes in the piece, but let us attribute that to his youth.

    It pains me to be this blunt, but the <u>Macbeth</u> I watched last week was quite the worst play I have ever seen. MacGivern's review, in most respects, accurately describes a troubled and unintentionally humorous production. Let us just say that your decision to transform <u>Macbeth</u> into a musical tragedy was not a wise one.

    Yet even if the play had been entirely successful and <u>The Rattler</u> review were as irresponsible a piece of journalism as your letter of April 25 suggests it is, I would feel obligated to rescind the restrictions you and Professor Poins have imposed upon the college paper. I understand your personal feelings in this matter and applaud your professional regard for good order within your department. But the authority of a chair--even of a university president--must always take second place to the principles of free speech and a free press.

    Consequently, I am directing you and Professor Poins to give reporters from <u>The Rattler</u> full access to your departments. I am confident that neither you nor Professor Poins will take action of any kind against Ms. Johnson and Mr. MacGivern. I will, however, talk to both students and urge greater sensitivity in reviewing nonprofessional theatrical productions in the future.

    Should you have any questions about my actions, please do not hesitate to discuss them with me.

                         Sincerely,

                         Aurelia Browning

                         Aurelia Browning
                         President, Copperhead
                              College

AB/cr
c. Judith Poins

**36b
bus**

4 Indented Form (with letterhead)

Copperhead College	**Give the People Light . . .**

Office of the President
Mammoth Hall 101

April 29, 1995

Tarshia Johnson, Editor
The Rattler
Copperhead College
102 Carlyle Hall
Viperton, IL 61802

Dear Ms. Johnson:

Responding to your letter of 25 April, I have reviewed the restrictions placed on Rattler reporters as a result of Angus MacGivern's recently published review of Macbeth: The Musical. I am directing Professors Poins and Partridge to rescind those limitations immediately. Rattler reporters are to have the same access to the Drama and English departments they have always enjoyed.

I would, however, like to discuss this entire issue with you and Angus MacGivern sometime soon. Please call my secretary to arrange a time when the three of us can talk this week.

I appreciate your action and your concern for The Rattler.

Sincerely yours,

Aurelia Browning

Aurelia Browning
President, Copperhead
   College

AB/cr

As a writer, you are rarely on your own. Instructors, editors, friends, and colleagues are often eager to help you refine a rough draft into a polished essay.

This section of the handbook is similarly intended to make writing a little easier and surer for you. It provides a chapter of advice about spelling and vocabulary, along with a guide to the one essential book for every writer—the dictionary.

A glossary of grammatical terms, rhetorical terms, and items of usage follows Part V.

37

How Good Are Your Spelling and Vocabulary?

A Spelling
B Vocabulary

37a HOW CAN YOU IMPROVE YOUR SPELLING?

Troubleshooting

Spelling errors on college papers are more likely to involve simple words rather than difficult ones. Words that look or sound alike are especially troublesome. You're far more likely to look up a challenging term such as *fluorescent* or *ubiquitous* than to check whether you've used the correct form of *it's/its, to/too/two,* or *there/their.* Even the spelling checker on your word processor will let "visual" errors slide by. It will tell you that *lisense* is a misspelling, but be silent when you've typed *where* when you meant *were* because *where* is a correctly spelled word. When it comes to spelling, habitual errors are the ones you have to work hardest to eliminate.

To be sure your spelling is right . . .

37a-1 **Proofread carefully to eliminate obvious errors.** There's no easy way around the need to proofread carefully all your academic and professional writing. This means seeing a text you've worked on for days as clearly as will a reader coming to it for the first time. Here are three proofreading techniques.

- Read your paper aloud, slowly.

- Read your paper with a pencil in hand, touching each word as you read.
- Read your paper backward to isolate individual words.

When you have found an error, check the next few words very carefully. Finding a mistake sometimes makes a writer think that another error in the immediate vicinity is unlikely. But there's no reason to make that assumption.

TRICKY

37a–2 **Pay special attention to the spelling of words that sound or look alike.** Words similar in appearance often differ widely in meaning. Unfortunately, no simple tricks prevent the misspelling (or misuse) of such terms. The best you can do is gradually accumulate a personal list of troublemakers. Here is just a sampling of the many problem clusters in English.

CHART

Homonyms

all ready [set to go]	already [by now]
altar [table]	alter [change]
bored [uninterested]	board [group/plank/climb on]
brake [stop]	break [fracture]
capital [seat of government]	capitol [government building]
cite [point out]	sight [see]; site [location]
compliment [praise]	complement [make complete]
council [group]	counsel [advice/lawyer]
dessert [treat]	desert [abandon]
gorilla [large ape]	guerrilla [soldier]
hear [perceive sound]	here [this place]
its [possessive form]	it's [contraction for *it is*]
lead [to direct/metal]	led [past tense of *to lead*]
lessen [decrease]	lesson [instruction]
past [what's occurred]	passed [go by/meet standards]
patience [tolerance]	patients [people under medical care]
peace [harmony]	piece [part or portion]
principal [head of school/ most important]	principle [standard/moral guide]
road [highway]	rode [past tense of *ride*]
stationary [not moving]	stationery [writing material]
their [possessive]	there [in that place]; they're [they are]

threw [past tense of *throw*]	through [across]
throne [royal seat]	thrown [past participle of throw]
wear [to have on]	where [place]
weather [climate]	whether [if/choice]
whose [possessive]	who's [contraction for *who is*]
your [possessive]	you're [contraction for *you are*]

CHART

Troublesome Pairs

accept [allow]	except [not including]
adverse [difficult]	averse [opposed to]
advice [noun—counsel]	advise [verb—to give counsel]
affect [to influence]	effect [consequence]
allusion [a reference]	illusion [a false impression]
are [present tense of *to be*]	our [possessive]
breath [noun—an inhalation]	breathe [verb—to inhale]
conscience [moral guide]	conscious [aware of]
elicit [to evoke]	illicit [illegal]
eminent [famous]	imminent [about to occur]
loose [not fastened]	lose [to misplace]
personal [private]	personnel [work force]
quiet [not noisy]	quite [very]
than [compared with]	then [at that time]
wear [to have on]	were [past tense of *to be*]

TRICKY

37a-3 **Eliminate errors that result from problems with pronunciation or misreading.** No one spells English right just because he or she pronounces it correctly; the language refuses to be consistent. Just consider what English does with these words spelled roughly the same: en*ough*, c*ough*, thr*ough*, th*ough*. So you shouldn't feel surprised when the English you spell looks different from the English you speak.

You may not recognize some spelling errors until an editor or reader points them out.

CHART

Common Spelling Errors

WRONG	RIGHT	WRONG	RIGHT
alot	a lot	noticable	noticeable
alright	all right	occured	occurred
arguement	argument	perscription	prescription
athelete	athlete	privlege	privilege
beleive	believe	recieve	receive
definately	definitely	reckonize	recognize
enviroment	environment	roomate	roommate
Febuary	February	seperate	separate
goverment	government	suprise	surprise
hankerchief	handkerchief	surppress	suppress
jewlery	jewelry	temperture	temperature
knowlege	knowledge	truely	truly
mispell	misspell	villian	villain
neccesary	necessary		

In fact, the only reliable way to eliminate many spelling errors is to read a lot. Spelling relies on visual memory, and reading reinforces your familiarity with spelling patterns. You are less likely to misspell a word you have seen often.

37a–4 **Identify trouble spots.** Be extra careful at those points where English spelling is most apt to go wrong.

CHECKLIST

Tricky Words in English

- Words that contain *ei* or *ie:* perceive, foreign, sieve
- Words with silent letters: *p*neumonia, de*b*t, answer
- Words that end in

    -able or *-ible:* laughable, visible
    -ance or *-ence:* guidance, obedience
    -ant or *-ent:* attendant, different
    -cede, -ceed, or *-sede:* precede, proceed, supersede

- Words with double consonants: occurrence, embarrass, exaggerate, accumulate, accommodate, recommend
- Homonyms: right, write, rite
- Contractions: who's, it's, you're, don't, won't, can't
- Possessive forms: Jones's, Boz's (see Section 19b)
- Irregular plurals: geese, media, concerti, children (see Section 19a)
- Hyphenated words: much-loved, mothers-in-law (see Section 28b)

37a-5 **Apply spelling rules—if helpful.** Spelling rules for English tend to be complicated, hard to remember, and unreliable. Still, you may want to review the basic spelling rules listed below.

- *I* comes before *e* except after *c*—except when *ei* has a long *A* sound.

  bel**ie**ve   **ei**ght
  re**cei**ve   w**ei**gh

  Significant exceptions weaken this guideline.

  counterfeit   either   seize
  weird   foreign

- When adding on to a word that ends with an *e*, keep the final *e* if the addition begins with a consonant.

  ride   ride**r**
  absolute   absolute**ly**
  retire   retire**ment**

  Drop the *e* if the addition begins with a vowel.

  ride   rid**ing**
  advise   advis**able**
  tribute   tribut**ary**

  There are significant exceptions to these guidelines, among them

  true   tru**ly** (instead of *truely*)
  argue   argu**ment** (instead of *arguement*)
  judge   judg**ment** (*judgement* is a British spelling)
  canoe   canoe**ing** (instead of *canoing*)

- When adding a suffix beginning with a vowel or *y* to a word ending with a consonant, double the consonant if the word has only

37a spell

one syllable and the final consonant is single and preceded by a single vowel.

dro**p**	dro**pp**ing
fli**p**	fli**pp**ed
sta**r**	sta**rr**y

Also, you double the consonant when the word has more than one syllable if the last syllable is accented, and if the final consonant is single and preceded by a single vowel.

rese**t'**	rese**tt**ing
unca**p'**	unca**pp**ed
omi**t'**	omi**tt**ed

In most other situations, a final consonant is not doubled.

lea**n**	lea**n**ing
offe**r**	offe**r**ing

In some cases, either the single or double consonant may be acceptable.

trave**l**	trave**l**ed	trave**ll**ed
imperi**l**	imperi**l**ed	imperi**ll**ed

- When adding to a word that ends in a y preceded by a consonant, change the y to i—except when the addition begins with an i.

cit**y**	cit**ies**	
part**y**	part**ies**	part**y**ing

Retain the y when the y is preceded by a vowel.

valle**y**	valle**ys**
sta**y**	sta**y**ing

- When faced with a decision between *-able* and *-ible* at the end of the word, it may help you to recall that *-able* tends to attach itself to words that could stand alone without it.

comfort**able**	laugh**able**	advis**able**

In contrast, many of the words that take *-ible* would be incomplete without the ending.

elig**ible**	horr**ible**	terr**ible**

As always, there are exceptions.

improb**able**	perfect**ible**	forc**ible**

- When faced with a decision between *-cede*, *-ceed*, and *-sede*, remember that *-cede* is by far the most common ending. Only three words end with *-ceed*.

pro**ceed**   suc**ceed**   ex**ceed**

Only one word ends with *-sede*.

super**sede**

All others end with *-cede*.

con**cede**   pre**cede**   se**cede**

37a–6 **When in doubt about the spelling of a word, look it up.** This will take less time than you imagine. To keep from interrupting the flow of writing, postpone trips to the dictionary until you have completed a section or need a break. But don't forget to do the checking. While composing, circle or underline questionable spellings and then return to them.

If you are an especially poor speller, you'll need to verify the correctness even of some words that look right. If they are of a type you often misspell—words that end in *-ible*, for example, or technical terms—go for the security that extra checking gives.

If you can't locate a word you are seeking in a dictionary or word list, don't assume Webster forgot it. You may have to use some ingenuity to figure out how it should be spelled. To locate an especially troublesome spelling, begin by scanning several columns in a dictionary near where you expected to find the word. It may turn up.

If you still can't find the word, consider alternatives to the way you think it is spelled. In English an *f-* sound can be spelled *ph*, a *c-* sound like an *s*, a *u* like a *y*, and on and on. Make a list of possible spellings and then check them out. Also consider alternatives to the vowel sound after an initial consonant. You are pages away if you expect to find *tyranny* spelled *tiranny*.

TRICKY

37a–7 **Use a spelling checker.** Spelling checkers help if you are writing on a word processor and have access to such a program. Because these programs compare your writing to the words stored in their internal dictionaries, they will question every word you produce that they don't recognize. All typos and errors in a paper will be found—as long as they don't form legitimate words on their own.

A spelling checker, for example, will let you know if you spell *supposed* "suposed"; but it won't tell you if you have left off the *d* at the end of the word because *suppose* is a correctly spelled word. It will let you know if you forget an *m* in *imminent*, but it probably will be silent if you mistakenly use *eminent* instead—unless it has a homonym feature that flags potential problems. Some do.

Spelling checkers will catch many errors quickly and accurately. But even after a spelling checker has read through a draft, you still need to proofread it on your own to detect the kinds of errors computers can't read. A typical spelling checker, for example, would find no mistakes in the following sentence.

> Their our to many excuses for the prejudice attitudes we sea every wear in the whirled around us.

▶ **Fine Tuning**

1. Not all words in English have a single correct spelling. Dictionaries will sometimes offer variant spellings. In most cases, you should avoid variants labeled *chiefly British* (*colour, judgement, theatre*), *archaic*, or *obsolete* unless you have a special reason for using them. You would use British spellings, for example, in quoting a London newspaper or a speech by the prime minister.

2. Avoid spellings made fashionable by advertising or the popular media: *nite, lite, thru, shur, til.* ◀

■ **Exercise 37.1** Below, three spellings are given for each word. Using memory alone, underline the spelling you think is correct. Then check the dictionary. When you are done, compute the percentage you guessed right. Can you afford to rely on memory alone for spelling?

1. parrallel	parallel	paralell
2. accommodate	acommodate	accomodate
3. unecessary	unnecessary	unneccesary
4. questionnaire	questionaire	questionnare
5. miscellaneous	miscelaneous	miscelanious
6. exxagerate	exaggerate	exagerate
7. rememberance	remembrance	remembrence
8. rhythm	rythmn	rhythmn
9. governement	governmant	government
10. ocurrence	occurence	occurrence

Percent right:
No. right × 10 = _____ %

■ **Exercise 37.2** Select five pairs of homonyms or troublesome words from the lists in Section 37a–2. Then write sentences in which both words in the pair are used correctly in a single sentence. For example:

The air conditioner was **quite quiet.**

■ **Exercise 37.3** Choose the correct words in the sentences below. Check a dictionary if necessary.

1. Because three years had (**passed/past**) since the company paid dividends to (**its/it's**) investors, stockholders began to lose (**patients/patience**) with the management team.

2. The (**plain/plane**) truth was that the (**board/bored**) of directors was (**averse/adverse**) to heeding the (**advice/advise**) of its lawyers.

3. The (**moral/morale**) of corporate (**personal/personnel**) declined.

4. Good employees began to (**dessert/desert**) what they saw as a sinking ship, taking (**there/their**) skills and talents to companies (**whose/who's**) management could make better use of them.

5. Yet no one was sure (**whether/weather**) the corporation's decline was an (**allusion/illusion**) or a fact.

37b HOW CAN YOU DEVELOP A STRONG VOCABULARY?

Troubleshooting

It's impossible to count the exact number of words available to the speaker and writer of English. But the *Oxford English Dictionary* defines more than a half-million terms. And that number does not include the many slang items, local expressions, neologisms, jargon terms, and creative variations of English we encounter almost every day.

Given this great wealth, it makes sense for writers to enjoy the resources of English. Yet many writers fear that using "big" words or an impressive vocabulary interferes with clarity; they recall the George Orwell dictum drilled into them by teachers from high school through college: "Never use a big word where a small one will do." The rule needs a corollary: "Never use a big word just to use a big word."

A strong vocabulary enhances your ability both to read and to write, so it makes sense to develop word skills. In addition, words are fun and English offers more such pleasures than just about any other language. But who's counting?

To develop a strong vocabulary . . .

37b-1 Read carefully to acquire new words. You can pick up a surprising number of vocabulary items just by paying closer attention to what you read and pausing to notice words you don't fully understand.

Textbooks, scholarly articles, even popular magazines or newspapers will often contain words you haven't encountered before.

While reading, you might not want to pause over every unknown or imprecisely understood word (we often read well enough even when a few terms are only vaguely understood), but you might circle unfamiliar items and come back to learn them later.

When you pick up a new word and learn its meaning, begin looking for it elsewhere. Once you are confident that you know what a word means—both denotatively and connotatively (see Section 10b)—begin working it into your writing and conversation.

37b-2 **Pay attention to the meaning of word roots.** You can often construct the meaning of an unfamiliar term if a portion of the word is familiar—particularly its core or root. Because so many English words are derived from Latin, Greek, and French roots, learning any one root often opens up an entire family of words. For example, the Latin word *finis*—meaning "limit, conclusion, end"—is the root of all the following English terms, which form a word family:

af**fin**ity	**fin**e
con**fine**	**fin**esse
de**fin**ite	**fin**icky
final	**fin**ish
finality	inde**fin**ite
finance	in**fin**itive
financier	re**fin**e

Clearly, knowing the meaning of basic roots (as well as some basic prefixes and suffixes—see next section) is a quick way of expanding the range of one's vocabulary.

CHART

Some Latin Roots

Root	Meaning	English terms
annus	year	biannual
aud	hear	auditorium
bene	good	benefit
cap	head	decapitate, capital
dic	speak, say	diction, dictate
duc	lead	induct, ductwork
fac	do, make	factory, manufacturer
judicium	judgment	judicial, injudicious

Root	Meaning	English terms
loqui	speak	elocution, eloquent
luc	light	lucid, translucence
med	middle	medium, intermediate
omni	all	omnidirectional
port	carry	portage, import
rog	ask	interrogatory
scrib	write	inscribe, description
secur	safe	security, insecure
spir	breathe	inspiration, expire
ter	earth	terrestrial, territory
verb	word	verbal, verbose

CHART

Some Greek Roots

Root	Meaning	English terms
aster	star	asteroid, astronomy
bio	life	biosphere
chrono	time	chronology, synchronic
geo	land, earth	geographical
graph	write	biography
logos	word, speech	monologue, dialogue
meter	measure	kilometer
pathos	feeling, suffering	empathetic, sympathy
photo	light	photograph
phys	nature	physical
psych	soul	psychiatry
pyr	fire	pyromaniac
tele	distant	telescope
thermo	heat	thermometer
xeros	dry	xerophyte

37b
vocab

37b-3 **Pay attention to prefixes and suffixes.** Root words are transformed in their meaning by the addition of prefixes and suffixes. Prefixes appear before a root or word, suffixes show up afterward. Knowing the meaning of a given prefix or suffix may help you decipher an unfamiliar term. Following is a partial list of prefixes and suffixes useful to recognize.

CHART

Prefixes

PREFIX	MEANING	EXAMPLE
a-	without	**a**symmetrical
ante-	before	**ante**chamber
anti-	against	**anti**aircraft
bi-	two	**bi**cameral
circum-	around	**circum**ference
counter-	opposite	**counter**act, **counter**feit
dec-, deca-	ten	**dec**ade, **deca**syllabic
dis-	do the opposite	**dis**enfranchise
fore-	before	**fore**see
hyper-	above, beyond	**hyper**active
hypo-	below, beneath	**hypo**dermic
in-	not	**in**hospitable
inter-	together, between	**inter**coastal
intra-	within, inside	**intra**mural
mal-	bad, unpleasant	**mal**odorous, **mal**content
mis-	incorrectly, badly	**mis**manage
per-	through, very	**per**petual
peri-	surrounding	**peri**cardium
pre-	before	**pre**menstrual
retro-	back	**retro**rocket
semi-	half	**semi**circle
super-	above, beyond	**super**sonic
trans-	across	**trans**national
tri-	three	**tri**color, **tri**motor
uni-	one	**uni**corn

37b vocab

CHART

Suffixes

SUFFIX	MEANING	EXAMPLE
-ful	full of, having	use**ful**, plenti**ful**
-hood	in the condition of	brother**hood**, state**hood**
-ish	like, the state of	boy**ish**, squeam**ish**
-ist	one who does	tour**ist**, chem**ist**

Suffix	Meaning	Example
-ize	to do, to make	lega**ize**, catego**rize**
-less	without, free of	hap**less**, law**less**
-ous	full of, state of	noxi**ous**, beaute**ous**
-ology	study of	ge**ology**, ast**rology**

37b-4 **Master words in key academic subjects, especially in your major.** You show your command of any field by how well you use its language. If you observe professionals in any field talking or writing to each other, you'll encounter many specialized words and expressions. Such professional language may be filled with technical terms and with intimidating abbreviations and acronyms.

Whatever your college major may be, it will have a vocabulary all its own, one you will acquire gradually. To speed up that process, make a conscious effort to learn technical terms that appear regularly in the headings of your textbooks, in the articles you read, or in your instructors' lectures. Don't ever be embarrassed to ask what a word means.

37b-5 **Use a thesaurus judiciously.** A thesaurus is a collection of synonyms—a book or piece of software designed to help you select the best word in a given situation. The thesaurus can also furnish choices when you wish to avoid using a particular word too often.

Be certain that any synonyms you consider match the words you intend to replace, both denotatively and connotatively. Look up the word *thin*, for example, and you will discover synonyms as different as *sheer, bony, lanky, watery, diluted, fragile,* and *feeble.* Obviously, these terms aren't interchangeable. The point is that unless you know precisely what a word you choose from a thesaurus means, you need to look it up in a dictionary before adding it to your vocabulary.

**37b
vocab**

■ **Exercise 37.4** Companies often coin names for new products by using Greek and Latin roots, prefixes, and suffixes. Discuss the meanings of the following brand and product names and the connotations that attach to the product as a result. If necessary, use a dictionary.

1. Lucite (paint)
2. Magnavox (a brand of TV, radio, stereo)
3. Xerox (a photocopier)
4. Nautica (a clothing line)
5. thermos (a container)

■ **Exercise 37.5**

1. If you have a major, make a list of key terms that might puzzle people outside your field. Then briefly define these words.
2. If you have not yet declared a major, list some puzzling terms you have encountered in various subjects. Define these terms to the best of your ability. With your classmates, discuss the definitions and see whether you can improve the less successful ones.

HIGHLIGHT

For Further Reading

If you enjoy reading about language, three valuable books are Albert C. Baugh and Thomas Cable's *A History of the English Language* (1993), David Crystal's *The Cambridge Encyclopedia of Language* (1987), and Bill Bryson's *The Mother Tongue* (1990).

How Do You Use a Dictionary?

A How Do You Select a Dictionary?
B How Do You Use a Dictionary?

38a HOW DO YOU SELECT A DICTIONARY?

Troubleshooting

Everyone needs at least one dictionary. But which of the many available volumes is right for you? Do the authority and comprehensiveness of an unabridged dictionary justify its bulk and expense? Does the portability of a pocket dictionary compensate for its limited lexicon and bare-bones definitions? Is size the only important difference between dictionaries? If not, what should you look for in making a selection?

For academic work, you should . . .

38a–1 Own a desk-size college dictionary. So-called desk or collegiate dictionaries are an almost ideal compromise between large, unabridged dictionaries and paperback "pocket" dictionaries. They usually contain between 140,000 and 200,000 entries—enough for most writing jobs. Reasonably priced and usually hardbound, they offer many helpful features, from brief histories of the English language to style manuals, lists of foreign terms, and addresses of two- and four-year colleges.

Dictionaries differ in their willingness to give you guidelines for correct usage. A few tend to be *prescriptive*, offering ample advice about how English is properly employed. Most current dictionaries, however, offer advice on usage sparingly, preferring to be *descriptive*. They explain how words *are* used, not how they *should* be used.

The most popular desk dictionaries vary in their emphases and features. But any one of these will serve you well.

- *The American Heritage Dictionary of the English Language*
- *The Random House College Dictionary*
- *Webster's Tenth New Collegiate Dictionary*
- *Webster's New World Dictionary of the American Language*
- *The Concise Oxford Dictionary of Current English*

38a–2 **Consult an unabridged dictionary when necessary.** On some occasions you may need more information about a word than your desk dictionary provides. Or the word you are looking for may be a form too rare, obscure, or old to appear in a dictionary designed for daily work. Then you need to consult one of the large *unabridged* dictionaries— works that attempt to record standard English vocabulary items as fully as practicable. Most people examine such books in the reference rooms of their libraries.

The Oxford English Dictionary is the most famous unabridged dictionary and perhaps the greatest dictionary in any language. Now in a second edition, the OED (as it is commonly known) contains over 500,000 items in its twenty volumes. Definitions are listed historically, with quotations (about 2.4 million of them) recording the earliest appearance of a word and its subsequent development across the centuries. The entries are exhaustive and perhaps more helpful to the scholar than the casual user. The second edition of the OED, which appeared in 1989, is available in both book and machine-readable (that is, computerized) form. It combines all entries from the original OED and its four supplements and adds 5,000 new words.

Webster's Third New International Dictionary of English, the best-known American dictionary, contains approximately 450,000 items in one illustrated volume. Definitions are listed historically and amply supported by quotations. *Webster's Third* is descriptive rather than prescriptive, an approach that stirred much controversy when the volume first appeared in 1961.

A third unabridged dictionary is *The Random House Dictionary of the English Language,* which contains approximately 260,000 items in one volume. Usage labels in this dictionary steer a middle course between prescriptive and descriptive. The book includes a color atlas of the world and four foreign language dictionaries. A new edition appeared in 1992.

A good companion to a college dictionary is a guide to English usage.

- Evans, Bergen, and Cornelia Evans. *A Dictionary of Contemporary American Usage.*
- Follett, Wilson. *Modern American Usage.*
- Fowler, H. W. *A Dictionary of Modern English Usage.*

38a
dict

HIGHLIGHT

What About Pocket Dictionaries?

Though no substitute for desk-size dictionaries, pocket dictionaries are certainly convenient. You can rely on them for correct spellings and basic meanings. But they do contain fewer entries, shorter definitions, and sketchier etymologies than college dictionaries. If you carry a pocket dictionary to help with spelling, you might consider using a convenient *word list*—a dictionary that lists only words, accent marks, and syllable divisions.

38b   HOW DO YOU USE A DICTIONARY?

Troubleshooting

Dictionaries are as dependable as gravity. Once you know alphabetical order, you can usually navigate one with few problems. But a great many writers, put off by all the signs and symbols that seem to clutter entries, ask no more of a dictionary than that it furnish accurate spellings and clear meanings. In fact, a dictionary can tell you a great deal more, if you know how to interpret the information it presents.

To use a dictionary well . . .

38b-1 **Consult the front matter.** Every dictionary includes a kind of owner's manual, usually a thorough explanation of how to use the information contained in its thousands of entries. You may not want to read all of this material every time you consult a new dictionary, but remember that this guide is available whenever you face an unfamiliar word, symbol, or feature. The front matter will help you understand how a dictionary handles spelling, syllabication, pronunciation, parts of speech, usage labels, definitions, and etymologies.

38b
dict

38b-2 **Understand spelling and syllabication.** Obviously, the alphabetical listing of words in a dictionary is a guide to accurate spelling. The main entry, printed in boldface type, will be separated into syllables to indicate where to divide the word at the end of a line. Spellings will also be given for various forms of the entry: verb endings, unusual or potentially troublesome plurals, suffixes.

> **com·press,** -pressed, -press·ing, -press·es
> **mouse,** *pl.* **mice**
> **lush,** -er, -est
> **trav·el,** -eled, -el·ing, -els or -elled, -el·ling, -els

Many words have alternative spellings. In most cases, choose the first spelling listed, which is usually the most common.

> **mov·a·ble,** *also* **move·a·ble**
> **me·di·e·val,** *also* **me·di·ae·val**

Avoid archaic and British spellings unless you have a special reason to use them.

> **col·or,** *also Brit.* **col·our**
> **lic·o·rice,** *also Brit.* **li·quo·rice**

38b-3 **Understand the guide to pronunciation.** Hearing a word is the best way of learning to pronounce it correctly. However, dictionaries will help you figure out the sound of an entry if you are patient enough to interpret the pronunciation key usually printed at the top or bottom of every page. The front matter will explain how the pronunciation key in any given dictionary works, but most follow the same basic principles.

Each major entry in a dictionary is followed by a pronunciation, which often looks like an odd spelling of the word decorated with accent marks, strange vowels, and unusual markings: ü, é, û. Every consonant and vowel sound in the pronunciation is keyed to familiar words in the pronunciation guide that also use those sounds.

Remember, however, that pronunciations vary from region to region. Ohioans fill their crankcases with *oy-al* while Texans pump *awl.* Dictionaries strive to provide "standard" pronunciations, but standard doesn't necessarily mean *only correct* pronunciation.

38b-4 **Understand parts of speech labels.** The meaning or pronunciation of a word may change according to the role it plays in a sentence. *Brave*, for example, can be a noun, verb, and adjective.

Noun	Kyle once dreamed of wearing the uniform of a Milwaukee **Brave.**
Verb	Instead, he **braved** the difficulties of electrical engineering and chemistry.
Adjective	It takes a **brave** student to pursue a double major.

Dictionaries, of course, must account for all these meanings in an entry. Or separate entries may be provided for words with the same spelling but different pronunciations and meanings.

38b
dict

Most dictionaries provide particularly useful information about verbs, indicating whether they are *transitive* or *intransitive* and furnishing the *principal parts* of irregular verbs.

38b–5 **Understand usage labels.** The labels used to describe words vary from dictionary to dictionary. It is common, for example, to find *field labels*, which identify words (or definitions) with special significance in specific disciplines.

Other labels describe the status of particular words in the language. The *American Heritage Dictionary*, for example, uses these labels: *nonstandard, informal, slang, vulgar, obscene, offensive, obsolete, archaic, regional,* and *chiefly British*. Each label is carefully defined in the front matter. Since people don't agree on how far a dictionary should go in saying what words are acceptable or offensive, such labels can be controversial. Yet they can also prevent blunders and embarrassing usages.

Be sure to check how any dictionary you use defines and applies its labels.

38b–6 **Understand the order of definitions.** When a word has more than one meaning, some dictionaries list the most common meaning first. Others arrange their entries historically; that is, the first meaning listed records how the word was used when it initially appeared in the language. Subsequent meanings then show how the term changed in meaning over the years. Still other dictionaries arrange their definitions according to different principles—such as "meaning clusters." A dictionary's front matter will explain what principle is used in your dictionary.

Knowing how the definitions are arranged is important in understanding the meaning of a term. The *Oxford English Dictionary*, for example, lists "Strong, powerful, mighty" as its first definition for *crafty*—not a sense we use today, but the first meaning the term had in English. If you didn't know that the *Oxford* arranged its entries historically, you might be misled in this case by what seems like a peculiar definition.

38b
dict

38b–7 **Understand etymologies.** Most dictionaries make an effort to trace the origins of words, explaining what languages they, or their roots, come from. Etymologies may not be supplied for compounds (*homework, bloodshot*), words derived from other words (*escapee*), words derived from geographical names (*New Yorker*), and so on. You can usually trace these etymologies by going back to the more basic words (*home, work, blood, shot, escape, New York*).

■ **Exercise 38.1** Browse through your dictionary to find examples of the following.

1. A word with a variant spelling.
2. A word you aren't sure how to pronounce. Use the pronunciation key to figure it out; then test your version on someone who is familiar with the word.
3. A word pronounced with a regional slant in your area. Compare your regional pronunciation with the dictionary's version.
4. Several words that can be used as more than one part of speech. Look especially for nouns that can also be used as verbs.
5. A word with a field label. You may want to begin with a technical term you sometimes use (*chip, touchdown*). Check to see whether your dictionary gives it a field label.
6. A word that might be considered slang, vulgar, offensive, archaic, or informal. See how your dictionary treats the entry.
7. A word with a simple etymology.
8. A word with a complicated etymology.

■ **Exercise 38.2** Pick a full page of your dictionary at random. Read it completely and write a short summary of what you have learned about the words on that page or about your dictionary. What is the most interesting word on that page? Which has the most impressive etymology? The most complicated definition? The most meanings? The oddest or most difficult pronunciation? Do any words on the page require labels or remarks about usage? Are the illustrations on the page (if any) useful?

38b
dict

Glossary of Terms and Usage

This glossary covers grammatical terms, rhetorical terms, and items of usage. Whether you require the definition of a key term (*verbals, proper noun*), an explanation of a rhetorical concept (*cliché, idiom*), or some advice about correct usage (What's the difference between *eminent* and *imminent?*), you'll find the information in this single, comprehensive list. For convenient review, key grammatical terms are marked by the symbol *.

a, an. Indefinite articles. **A** and **an** are **indefinite articles** because they point to objects in a general way (**a** book, **a** church), while the **definite article the** refers to specific things (**the** book, **the** church). **A** is used when the word following it begins with a consonant sound: **a** *house,* **a** *year,* **a** *boat,* **a** *unique* experience. **An** is used when the word following it begins with a vowel sound: **an** *hour,* **an** *interest,* **an** *annoyance,* **an** *illusory* image.

Notice that you choose the article by the *sound* of the word following it. Not all words that begin with vowels actually begin with vowel sounds, and not all words that begin with consonants have initial consonant sounds.

* **absolute.** A phrase that modifies an entire sentence. Absolutes are often infinitive or participial phrases. Unlike other modifying phrases, absolutes do not necessarily modify a word or phrase standing near them.

> **To put it politely,** Connie is irritating.
>
> She will publish the entire story, **space permitting.**
>
> **Scripts discarded, props disassembled, costumes locked away in trunks,** the annual Shakespeare festival concluded.

See **misplaced modifier** and **dangling modifier**.

* **absolute adjective.** A word such as *unique, dead,* or *equal* that ought not to be qualified to suggest some degree. Logically speaking, something cannot be *more* unique, *less* equal, or *very* dead.

* **abstract noun.** A noun that names ideas, concepts, and qualities without physical properties: *softness, Mother Nature, democracy,*

humanism. Abstract nouns exist in the mind as ideas. They are defined in contrast to **concrete nouns.**

accept/except. Very commonly confused. **Accept** means to take, receive, or approve of something. **Except** means to exclude, or not including.

> I **accepted** all the apologies **except** George's.

accidently/accidentally. **Accidently** is a misspelling. The correct spelling is **accidentally.**

acronym. A single term created by joining the first letters in the words that make up the full name or description. Acronyms are pronounced as single words and are ordinarily capitalized.

> **NATO**—**N**orth **A**tlantic **T**reaty **O**rganization
> **NASA**—**N**ational **A**eronautics and **S**pace **A**dministration

Some common acronyms are written as ordinary words without capitalization: *laser, radar.* See also **initialism.**

* **active verb/voice.** See **voice.**

ad/advertisement. In academic and formal writing, you should use the full word: **advertisement.**

* **adjectival.** A word, phrase, or clause that modifies a noun or pronoun.

> noun   adjectival
> the *engagement* **of Ike and Bernice**

> adjectival   noun   adjectival
> the **never-ending** *battle* **between the sexes**

> noun   adjectival
> the *ceremony* **they would have preferred**

* **adjective.** A word that modifies a noun or pronoun. Some adjectives describe the words they modify, explaining how many, which color, which one, and so on.

> an **unsuccessful** coach   a **green** motel
> the **lucky** one   a **sacred** icon

Such adjectives frequently have comparative and superlative forms.

> the **blacker** cat   the **happiest** people

Other adjectives limit or specify the words they modify.

> **this** adventure   **every** penny
> **each** participant   **neither** video

glos

Proper nouns can also serve as adjectives.

Texan wildlife   **Eisenhower** era

See also **coordinate adjective, demonstrative adjective, non-coordinate adjective,** and **predicate adjective.**

* **adjective clause.** A dependent (or subordinate) clause that functions as an adjective, modifying a noun or pronoun. See **clause** for definition of a dependent clause.

> Margery Hutton, the woman **who writes mystery stories,** lives in the mansion **that Dr. Horace Elcott built.**
>
> Her gardens were tended by Bud Smith, **who learned to garden from his father.**

* **adverb.** A word that modifies a verb, an adjective, or another adverb. Adverbs explain where, when, and how.

>   adverb   verb
> Bud **immediately** *suspected* foul play at the Hutton mansion.
>
>   adverb   adjective
> It seemed **extremely** *odd* to him that Mrs. Hutton should load a large burlap sack into the trunk of her Mercedes.
>
>   adverb   adverb
> Mrs. Hutton replied **rather** *evasively* when Bud questioned her about what she was up to.

Some adverbs modify complete sentences.

>   adverb
> **Obviously,** Mr. Hutton had been murdered!

* **adverb clause.** A subordinate clause that functions as an adverb. See also **clause.**

> **After Mrs. Hutton left,** Bud slipped into the Hutton mansion.
>
> Bud was startled **when Mr. Hutton greeted him in the living room.**

* **adverbial.** An expression that functions like an adverb, but is not actually an adverb. Adverbials can be nouns, clauses, and phrases.

> **Noun as adverbial**   They are going **home.**
>   Explains *where*
>
> **Clause as adverbial**   They go jogging **whenever they can.**
>   Explains *when*
>
> **Phrase as adverbial**   They go jogging **in the morning.**
>   Explains *when*

glos

adverse/averse. Often confused. **Adverse** describes something hostile, unfavorable, or difficult. **Averse** indicates the opposition someone has to something; it is ordinarily followed by *to.*

> Travis was **averse** to playing soccer under **adverse** field conditions.

advice/advise. These words aren't interchangeable. **Advice** is a noun meaning "an opinion" or "counsel." **Advise** is a verb meaning "to give counsel or advice."

> I'd **advise** you not to give Maggie **advice** about running her business.

affect/effect. A troublesome pair! Each word can be either a noun or a verb, although **affect** is ordinarily a verb and **effect** a noun. In its usual sense, **affect** is a verb meaning "to influence" or "to give the appearance of."

> How will the stormy weather **affect** the plans for the outdoor concert?

> The meteorologist **affected** ignorance when we asked her for a forecast.

Only rarely is **affect** a noun—as a term in psychology meaning "feeling" or "emotion." On the other hand, **effect** is usually a noun, meaning "consequence" or "result."

> The **effect** of the weather may be serious.

Effect may, however, also be a verb, meaning "to cause" or "to bring about."

> The funnel cloud **effected** a change in our plans.
> Compare with: The funnel cloud **affected** our plans.

African American. The term now preferred by many Americans of African ancestry, replacing *black* or *Negro.*

aggravate/irritate. Many people use both of these verbs to mean "to annoy" or "to make angry." But formal English preserves a fine—and useful—distinction between them. **Irritate** means "to annoy" while **aggravate** means "to make something worse."

> It **irritated** Greta when her husband **aggravated** his allergies by smoking.

* **agreement, pronoun and antecedent.** A grammatical principle which requires that singular pronouns stand in for singular nouns (*his* surfboard = *Richard's* surfboard) and plural pronouns stand in for plural nouns (*their* surfboard = *George and Martha's* surfboard; *everyone's* place = *his or her* place). When they do, the pronoun and its antecedent agree in **number;** when they don't, you have an agreement problem. See Chapter 21.

Pronouns and their antecedents also must agree in **gender.** That is, a masculine pronoun (*he, him, his*) must refer to a masculine antecedent, and a feminine pronoun (*she, her, hers*) must refer to a feminine antecedent.

Finally, pronouns and antecedents must agree in **case,** whether objective, subjective, or possessive. For example, an antecedent in the possessive case (*Lawrence's* gym) can be replaced only by a pronoun also in the possessive case (*his* gym). See Chapter 22.

* **agreement, subject and verb.** Verbs and nouns are said to agree in number. This means that with a singular subject in the third person (for example, *he, she, it*), a verb in the present tense ordinarily adds an **-s** ending to its base form. With subjects not in the third person singular, the base form of the verb is used.

Third person, singular, present tense:	Barney sit**s.**
	He sit**s.**
	She sit**s.**
First person, singular, present tense:	I sit.
Second person, singular, present tense:	You sit.
First person, plural, present tense:	We sit.
Second person, plural, present tense:	You sit.
Third person, plural, present tense:	They sit.

Most **verbs**—with the notable exception of *to be*—change their form to show agreement only in third person singular forms (*he, she, it*). See Chapter 16.

ain't. It may be in the dictionary, but **ain't** isn't acceptable in academic or professional writing. Avoid it.

all ready/already. Tricky, but not difficult. **All ready,** an adjective phrase, means "prepared and set to go."

Rita signaled that the camera was **all ready** for shooting.

Already, an adverb, means "before" or "previously."

Rita had **already** loaded the film.

all right. All right is the only acceptable spelling. **Alright** is not acceptable in standard English.

glos

allude/elude. Commonly confused. **Allude** means "to refer to." **Elude** means "to escape."

> Kyle's joke **alluded** to the fact that it was easy to **elude** the portly security guard.

allude/refer. To **allude** is to mention something indirectly; to **refer** is to mention something directly.

> Carter **alluded** to rituals the new students didn't understand.
> Carter did, however, **refer** to ancient undergraduate traditions and the honor of the college.

allusion/illusion. These terms are often misused. An **allusion** is an indirect reference to something. An **illusion** is a false impression or a misleading appearance.

> The entire class missed Professor Sweno's **allusion** to the ghost in *Hamlet.*
> Professor Sweno entertained the **illusion** that everyone read Shakespeare as often as he did.

a lot. Often misspelled as one word. It is two. Many readers consider **a lot** inappropriate in academic writing, preferring **many, much,** or some comparable expression.

already. See **all ready.**

alright. See **all right.**

American. Though often used to describe citizens of the United States of America, the term can also refer to any citizen of the Americas, North or South. Be careful how you use this term when writing to audiences that may include Americans not from the United States.

among/between. Use **between** with two objects, **among** with three or more.

> Francie had to choose **between** Richard and Kyle.
> Francie had to choose from **among** a dozen actors.

amount/number. Use **amount** for quantities that can be measured, but not counted. Use **number** for things that can be counted, not measured: the **amount** of water in the ocean; the **number** of fish in the sea. The distinction between these words is being lost, but it is worth preserving. Remember that **amount of** is followed by a singular noun, while **number of** is followed by a plural noun.

amount of money	number of dimes
amount of paint	number of colors
amount of support	number of voters

an. See **a, an.**

analogy. An extended comparison between something familiar and something less well known. The analogy helps a reader visualize what might be difficult to understand. For example:

analogy

A transitional word in a paper serves **as a road sign, giving readers directions to the next major idea.**

and etc. A redundant expression. Use **etc.** alone or **and so on.** See **etc.**

and/or. A useful form in some situations, especially in business and technical writing, but some readers regard it as clumsy. Work around it if you can, especially in academic writing. **And/or** is typed with no space before and after the slash.

Anglo. A common term in some areas of North America for designating white or nonminority people. The term is inaccurate in that many people considered white are not, in fact, *Anglo-Saxon* in origin.

angry/mad. The distinction between these words is rarely observed, but strictly speaking, one should use **angry** to describe displeasure, **mad** to describe insanity.

* **antecedent.** The person, place, or thing a pronoun replaces in a sentence. The antecedent is the word you would have to repeat if you couldn't use a pronoun. In the following sentence, *Marissa* is the antecedent of *she* and *radio* is the antecedent of *it.*

> **Marissa** turned off the **radio** because *she* was tired of listening to *it.*

See Chapter 20 for more details.

antonyms. Words with opposite meanings: *bright/dull; apex/nadir; concave/convex.*

anyone/any one. These expressions have different meanings. Notice the difference highlighted in these sentences.

> **Any one** of those problems could develop into a crisis.
> I doubt that **anyone** will be able to find a solution to **any one** of the equations.

glos

anyways. A nonstandard form. Use **anyway.**

> **Wrong**   It didn't matter **anyways.**
>
> **Right**   It didn't matter **anyway.**

* **appositive.** A word or phrase that stands next to a noun and modifies it by restating or expanding its meaning. Note that appositives ordinarily are surrounded by commas.

> Connie Lim, **editor of the paper and an arch-liberal,** was furious when President Clinton gave his only campus interview to Sue Wesley, **chair of the Young Republicans.**

* **articles.** The words **the, a,** and **an** used before a noun. **The** is called a **definite article** because it points to something specific: **the** book, **the** church, **the** criminal. **A** and **an** are **indefinite articles** because they refer more generally: **a** book, **a** church, **a** criminal. See Sections 19d and 31d.

as being. A wordy expression. You can usually cut **being.**

> In most cases, telephone solicitors are regarded **as (being)** a nuisance.

Asian American. The term now preferred by many Americans of Asian ancestry, replacing *Oriental.*

* **auxiliary verbs.** Verbs, usually some form of *be, do,* or *have,* that combine with other verbs to show various relations of tense, voice, mood, and so on. All the words in boldface are auxiliary verbs: **has** seen, **will be** talking, **would have been** going, **are** investigating, **did** mention, **should** prefer. Auxiliary verbs are also known as *helping verbs.* See Section 17a–1.

averse/adverse. See **adverse/averse.**

awful. Awful is inappropriate as a synonym for **very.**

> **Inappropriate**   The findings of the two research teams were **awful** close.
>
> **Better**   The findings of the two research teams were **very** close.

awhile/a while. The expressions are not interchangeable. **Awhile** is an adverb; **a while** is a noun phrase. After prepositions, always use **a while.**

> Bud stood **awhile** looking at the grass.
>
> Bud decided that the lawn would not have to be cut for **a while.**

bad/badly. These words are troublesome. Remember that **bad** is an adjective describing what something is like; **badly** is an adverb explaining how something is done.

> Stanley's taste in music wasn't **bad.**
> Unfortunately, he treated his musicians **badly.**

Problems usually crop up with verbs that explain how something feels, tastes, smells, or looks. In such cases, use **bad.**

> The physicists felt **bad** about the disappearance of their satellite.
> The situation looked **bad.**

because of/due to. Careful writers usually prefer **because of** to **due to** in many situations.

Considered awkward	The investigation into Bud's disappearance stalled **due to** Officer Bricker's sudden concern for correct procedure.
Revised	The investigation into Bud's disappearance stalled **because of** Officer Bricker's sudden concern for correct procedure.

However, **due to** is often the better choice when it serves as a **subject complement** after a **linking verb.** The examples illustrate the point.

<p style="text-align:center">subj.   l.v.   subj. comp.</p>

Bricker's discretion seemed **due to** <u>cowardice</u>.

<p>subj.   l.v.   subj. comp.</p>

His discretion was **due to** <u>the political and social prominence of the Huttons</u>.

being as/being that. Both of these expressions sound wordy and awkward when used in place of **because** or **since.** Use **because** and **since** in formal and academic writing.

Inappropriate	**Being that** her major was astronomy, Jenny was looking forward to the eclipse.
Better	**Since** her major was astronomy, Jenny was looking forward to the eclipse.

beside/besides. Beside is a preposition meaning "next to" or "alongside"; **besides** is a preposition meaning "in addition to" or "other than."

> **Besides** a sworn confession, the detectives also had the suspect's fingerprints on a gun found **beside** the body.

glos

Besides can also be an adverb meaning "in addition" or "moreover."

> Professor Bellona didn't mind assisting the athletic department, and **besides,** she actually liked coaching volleyball.

between. See **among/between.**

black. Falling somewhat out of favor as a term to describe people of African descent. Many American blacks now prefer the term **African American.**

British. The term refers to the people of Scotland and Wales in addition to those of England. *English* refers chiefly to those people of the British Isles who come from within the borders of England itself.

but what. In most writing, **that** alone is preferable to the colloquial **but that** or **but what.**

> | Colloquial | There was little doubt **but what** he'd learned a few things. |
> | Revised | There was little doubt **that** he'd learned a few things. |

can/may. Understand the difference between the auxiliary verbs **can** and **may.** (See also **modal auxiliary.**) Use **can** to express an ability to do something.

> Charnelle **can** work differential equations.
>
> According to the *Handbook of College Policies,* Dean Rack **can** lift the suspension.

Use **may** to express either permission or possibility.

> You **may** want to compare my solution to the problem to Charnelle's.
>
> Dean Rack **may** lift the suspension, but I wouldn't count on that happening.

cannot. **Cannot** is ordinarily written as one word, not two.

can't. Writers sometimes forget the apostrophe in this contraction and others like it: **don't, won't.**

can't hardly. A colloquial expression that is, technically, a double negative. Use **can hardly** instead when you write.

> | Double negative | I **can't hardly** see the road. |
> | Revised | I **can hardly** see the road. |

* **cardinal numbers.** Numbers that express an amount: *one, two, three.* In contrast, **ordinal numbers** show a sequence: *first, second, third.*

* **case.** The form a noun or pronoun takes to indicate its function in a sentence. Nouns have only two cases: the **possessive** form, to show ownership (*girl's, Greta's, swimmers'*), and the **common** form, to serve all other uses (*girl, Greta, swimmers*). See Section 19b.

> Pronouns have three forms: **subjective, objective,** and **possessive.** (See Chapter 22.) The **subjective** (or **nominative**) **case** is the form a pronoun takes when it is the subject of a sentence or a clause. Pronouns in this case are the doers of actions: *I, you, she, he, it, we, they, who.*

> A pronoun is in the **objective case** when something is done to it. This is also the form a pronoun has after a preposition: (*to*) *me, her, him, us, them, whom.* For the pronouns *you* and *it,* the subjective and objective forms are identical.

> A pronoun is in the **possessive case** when it shows ownership: *my, mine, your, yours, her, his, its, our, ours, their, theirs, whose.*

censor/censure. These words have different meanings. As verbs, **censor** means "to cut," "to repress," or "to remove"; **censure** means "to disapprove" and "to condemn."

> The student editorial board voted to **censor** the four-letter words from Connie Lim's editorial and to **censure** her for attempting to publish the controversial piece.

* **clause.** A group of related words that has a subject and verb. Clauses can be independent or dependent.

> Whenever it could, **the Astronomy Club scheduled meetings at an isolated hilltop observatory.**

An **independent clause** can stand alone as a complete sentence.

> The Astronomy Club scheduled meetings at an isolated hilltop observatory.

A **dependent** (or **subordinate**) **clause** is a group of words which cannot stand alone as a sentence even though it contains a subject and verb.

> **Whenever it could,** the Astronomy Club scheduled meetings at an isolated hilltop observatory.

cliché. A tired expression or conventional way of expressing something: *guilty as sin, hungry enough to eat a horse, sleep like a log, dumb as a rock.*

* **collective noun.** A noun that names a group: *team, orchestra, jury, committee.* Collective nouns can be either singular or plural, depending upon how they are used in a sentence.

* **comma splice.** The mistaken use of a comma to join two groups of words, each of which could be a sentence by itself. Also called a "comma fault." See Sections 24c and 26c–2.

> **Comma splice** David liked Corvettes, they were fast cars.
>
> **Corrected** David liked Corvettes because they were fast cars.

common knowledge. Facts, dates, events, information, and concepts which belong generally to an educated public.

* **common noun.** A noun that names some general object, not a specific person, place, or thing: *singer, continent, car.* Common nouns are not capitalized.

* **comparative and superlative.** Adjectives and adverbs can express three different levels or degrees of intensity—the positive, the comparative, and the superlative. The positive level describes a single condition; the comparative ranks two conditions; the superlative ranks three or more.

Positive	*Comparative*	*Superlative*
cold	colder	coldest
bad	worse	worst
angry	more angry	most angry
angrily	more angrily	most angrily

* **complement.** A word or phrase that completes the meaning of a verb, a subject, or an object. A **verb complement** is a **direct** or **indirect object**. A **subject complement** is a noun, pronoun, or adjective (or a comparable phrase) that follows a linking verb (a verb such as *to be, to seem, to appear, to feel,* and *to become*) and modifies or explains the subject, as in these examples.

> Eleanor is Bruce's **cat.**
> Eleanor is grossly **overweight.**
> Eleanor is the **one** on the sagging couch.

Object complements are nouns or adjectives (or comparable phrases) that follow direct objects and modify them.

> A pet food company named Eleanor **"Fat Cat of the Year."**
> Mackerel makes Eleanor **happy.**

complement, complementary/compliment, complimentary. The words are not synonyms. **Complement** and **complementary** describe things completed or compatible. **Compliment** and **complimentary** refer to things praised or given away free.

> Travis's sweater **complemented** his green eyes.
>
> The two parts of Greta's essay were **complementary,** examining the same subject from differing perspectives.
>
> Travis **complimented** Greta on her successful paper.
>
> Greta found his **compliment** sincere.
>
> She rewarded him with a **complimentary** sack of rice cakes from her health food store.

* **complex sentence.** A sentence that combines an independent clause and one or more dependent (subordinate) clauses. See also **clause.**

> **dependent clause** + *independent clause*
>
> **When Rita Ruiz first saw the announcements for the job fair,** *she began to get nervous.*

* **compound sentence.** A sentence that combines two or more independent clauses, usually joined by a coordinating conjunction (*and, or, nor, for, but, yet, so*) or a semicolon.

> *independent clause* + *independent clause*
>
> *Recruiters from industry have set up booths on campus,* and *several corporations are sending recruiters to interview students.*

* **compound-complex sentence.** A sentence that combines two or more independent clauses and at least one dependent (subordinate) clause. See also **clause.**

> **dependent clause** + *independent clause* + *independent clause*
>
> **Although business is slow,** *recruiters from industry have set up booths on campus,* and *several corporations are sending recruiters to interview students.*

* **concrete noun.** A noun that names objects or events with physical properties or existences: *butter, trees, asteroid, people.* Concrete nouns are defined in contrast to **abstract nouns.**

* **conjugation.** The forms of a given verb as it appears in all numbers, tenses, voices, and moods. See Anatomy of a Verb, page 309.

* **conjunctions, coordinating.** The words *and, or, nor, for, but, yet,* and *so* used to link words, phrases, and clauses that serve equiv-

glos

alent functions in a sentence. A coordinating conjunction is used to join two independent clauses or two dependent clauses; it would not link a subordinate clause to an independent clause. See also **conjunctions, subordinating.**

> Oscar **and** Marie directed the play.
> Oscar liked the story, **but** Marie did not.

* **conjunctions, subordinating.** Words or expressions such as *although, because, if, since, before, after, when, even though, in order that,* and *while* that relate dependent (that is, subordinate) clauses to independent ones. Subordinating conjunctions introduce subordinate clauses.

> dependent clause
> **Although** Oscar and Marie both directed parts of the show, Marie got most of the blame for its failure.

> dependent clause
> Oscar liked the story **even though** no one else did.

> dependent clause
> **When** the show opened, audiences stayed away.

* **conjunctive adverbs.** Words such as *however, therefore, nevertheless, moreover,* and so on, used to link one independent clause to another. Conjunctive adverbs are weaker links than **coordinating conjunctions** (such as *and, but, or,* and *yet*) and must be preceded by a semicolon when used to join independent clauses.

> Darwin apologized; **nevertheless,** Rita considered suing him.

See Section 27a–2.

connotation. **Connotation** is what a word suggests beyond its basic dictionary meaning—that is, the word with all its particular emotional, political, or ethical associations. While any number of words may describe a fight, for example, and so share the same **denotation** (generic meaning), such words as *scrap, brawl, battle, fisticuffs, altercation,* and *set to* differ significantly in what they imply—in their **connotations.** When using a list or collection of synonyms—such as you would find in a thesaurus—be sure you understand the connotation of any words you decide to use. See Section 10b.

conscience/conscious. Don't confuse these words. **Conscience** is a noun referring to an inner ethical sense; **conscious** is an adjective describing a state of awareness or wakefulness.

> The linebacker felt a twinge of **conscience** after knocking the quarterback **unconscious.**

consensus. This expression is redundant if followed by **of opinion; consensus** by itself implies an opinion. Use **consensus** alone.

> Redundant   The student senate reached a **consensus of opinion** on the issue of censorship.
>
> Revised   The student senate reached a **consensus** on the issue of censorship.

contact. Some people object to using **contact** as a verb meaning "to get in touch with" or "to call." The usage is common, but you might want to avoid it in formal or academic writing.

* **contraction.** A word shortened by the omission of a letter or letters. In most cases, an apostrophe is used to indicate the deleted letters or sounds: *it is* = **it's;** *you are* = **you're;** *who is* = **who's.**

* **coordinate adjective.** Coordinate adjectives are adjectives that modify the nouns they precede, not each other.

> Mali is a **bright, creative,** and **productive** artist.

See **noncoordinate adjective** and Section 26c–4.

* **coordinating conjunction.** See **conjunctions, coordinating.**

* **correlatives.** Words that work together as conjunctions: *either . . . or; neither . . . nor; whether . . . or; both . . . and; not only . . . but also.*

> **Whether** Darwin **or** Travis plays makes little difference.
>
> Brian attributed the failure of the play **not only** to a bad script **but also** to incompetent direction.

could of/would of/should of. Nonstandard forms when used instead of **could have, would have,** or **should have.**

> Wrong   Coach Rhoades imagined that his team **could of** been a contender.
>
> Right   Coach Rhoades imagined that his team **could have** been a contender.

* **count noun.** A noun that names any object that exists as an individual item: *car, child, rose, cat.*

couple of. Casual. Avoid it in formal or academic writing.

> Informal   The article accused the admissions office of a **couple of** major blunders.
>
> Revised   The article accused the admissions office of **several** major blunders.

glos

credible/credulous. Credible means "believable"; **credulous** means "willing to believe on slim evidence." See also **incredible/ incredulous.**

> Officer Bricker found Mr. Hutton's excuse for his speeding **credible.** However, Bricker was known to be a **credulous** police officer, liable to believe any story.

criteria, criterion. Criteria, the plural form, is more familiar, but the word does have a singular form—**criterion.**

> John Maynard, age sixty-four, complained that he was often judged according to a single **criterion,** age.
>
> Other **criteria** ought to matter in hiring.

curriculum, curricula. Curriculum is the singular form; **curricula** is the plural.

> Dean Perez believed that the **curriculum** in history had to be strengthened.
>
> Indeed, she believed that the **curricula** in all the liberal arts departments needed rethinking.

* **dangling modifier.** A modifying phrase that doesn't seem connected to any word or phrase in a sentence. Dangling modifiers are usually corrected by rewriting a sentence to provide a better link between the modifier and what it modifies. See Section 25g. See also **absolute.**

> **Dangling** **After finding the courage to ask Richard out,** the evening was a disaster.
>
> **Improved** After finding the courage to ask Richard out, Francie had a disastrous evening.

data/datum. Data has a singular form—**datum.** In speech and informal writing, **data** is commonly treated as both singular and plural. In academic writing, use **datum** where the singular is needed. If **datum** seems awkward, try to rewrite the sentence to avoid the singular.

> **Singular** The most intriguing **datum** in the study was the percentage of population decline.
>
> **Plural** In all the **data,** no figure was more intriguing than the percentage of population decline.

* **demonstrative adjective.** An adjective that points to a specific object: *this* house, not *that* one; *those* rowdies who disrupted *these* proceedings last month.

* **demonstrative pronoun.** A pronoun that points something out: *this, that, these, those.*

denotation. The specific meaning of a term. Sometimes called the "dictionary meaning," the denotation of a word attempts to explain what the word is or does stripped of particular emotional, political, or ethical associations. See **connotation.**

* **dependent clause.** See **clause.**

* **determiner.** A word indicating that a noun must follow. Determiners in English include articles (*a, an, the*) and certain possessive pronouns (*my, your*).

dialect. A spoken variation of a language. See Section 10c.

diction. See **word choice.**

different from/different than. In formal writing, **different from** is usually preferred to **different than.**

> **Formal**   Ike's account of his marriage proposal was **different from** Bernice's.

> **Informal**   Ike's account of his marriage proposal was **different than** Bernice's.

* **direct discourse.** The actual words of a speaker or writer. Direct discourse is enclosed within quotation marks. See **indirect discourse.**

> **Direct**   As she approached the altar, Bernice yelled, "I won't marry you!"

> **Indirect**   As she approached the altar, Bernice declared that she would not marry Ike.

discreet/discrete. **Discreet** means "tactful" or "sensitive to appearances" (*discreet* behavior); **discrete** means "individual" or "separate" (*discrete* objects).

> Joel was **discreet** about the money spent on his project.
> He had several **discrete** funds at his disposal.

disinterested/uninterested. These words don't mean the same thing. **Disinterested** means "neutral" or "uninvolved"; **uninterested** means "not interested" or "bored."

> Alyce and Richard sought a **disinterested** party to arbitrate their dispute.
> Stanley was **uninterested** in the club's management.

glos

don't. Writers sometimes forget the apostrophe in this contraction and others like it: **can't, won't.**

* **double negative.** Two negatives in a sentence that emphasize a negative idea. Such expressions are considered nonstandard in English.

> **Incorrect** **Don't never** use a double negative.
> Ike **won't** say **nothing** about his wedding plans.

To correct a double negative, eliminate one of the negatives in the sentence.

> **Correct** **Never** use a double negative.
> **Don't** use a double negative.
>
> Ike will say **nothing** about his wedding plans.
> Ike **won't** say anything about his wedding plans.

* **double possessive.** A form such as *a friend of Ruth's,* which includes two indications of possession—an *of* and an *'s.*

due to/because of. See **because of/due to.**

due to the fact that. Wordy. Replace it with **because** whenever you can.

> **Wordy** Coach Meyer was fired **due to the fact that** he won no games.
>
> **Revised** Coach Meyer was fired **because** he won no games.

effect/affect. See **affect/effect.**

elicit/illicit. These words have vastly different meanings. **Elicit** means to "draw out" or "bring forth"; **illicit** describes something illegal or prohibited.

> The detective tried to **elicit** an admission of **illicit** behavior from Bud.

* **elliptical construction.** A phrase or sentence from which words have been deleted without obscuring the meaning. Elliptical constructions are common.

> When [she is] asked about Rodney, Sue Ellen groans.
> She likes reading books better than [she likes] writing them.
> Curtis is a tough guy at heart, but [he is] a softie on the surface.
> He senses [that] he was wrong.

elude/allude. See **allude/elude.**

eminent/imminent. These words are sometimes confused. **Eminent** means "distinguished" and "prominent"; **imminent** describes something about to happen.

The arrival of the **eminent** scholar is **imminent.**

enthused. A colloquial expression that should not appear in academic or professional writing. Use **enthusiastic** instead.

> **Informal** Francie was **enthused** about U-2's latest album.
>
> **Better** Francie was **enthusiastic** about U-2's latest album.

Never use **enthused** as a verb.

equally as. Redundant. Use either **equally** or **as** to express a comparison—whichever works in a particular sentence.

> **Redundant** Sue Ellen is **equally as** concerned as Hector about bilingual education.
>
> **Revised** Sue Ellen is **as** concerned as Hector about bilingual education.
>
> **Revised** Sue Ellen and Hector are **equally** concerned about bilingual education.

Eskimo. Falling out of favor as a term to describe the native peoples of Northern Canada and Alaska. Many now prefer *Inuit.*

* **essential modifier.** See **restrictive element.**

etc. This common abbreviation for *et cetera* should be avoided in most academic and formal writing. Instead, use **and so on** or **and so forth.** Never use **and etc.**

even though. Even though is two words, not one.

everyone/every one. These similar expressions mean different things. **Everyone** describes a group collectively. **Every one** focuses on the individual elements within a group or collective term. Notice the difference highlighted in these sentences.

> **Every one** of those problems could develop into an international crisis **everyone** would regret.
>
> I doubt that **everyone** will be able to attend **every one** of the sessions.

except/accept. See **accept/except.**

* **expletive construction.** The words **there** and **it** used as sentence lead-ins.

glos

It is going to be a day to remember.

There were hundreds of spectators watching the demonstrators.

Expletive constructions often contribute to wordiness. Cut them whenever you can.

> **Revised**   Hundreds of spectators were watching the demonstrators.

fact that, the. Wordy. You can usually replace the entire expression with **that.**

> **Wordy**   Bud was aware of **the fact that** he was in a strange room.

> **Revised**   Bud was aware **that** he was in a strange room.

faith/fate. A surprising number of writers confuse these words and their variations: **faithful, fateful, faithless. Faith** is confidence trust, or a religious belief; **fate** means "destiny" or "outcome."

farther/further. Although the distinction between these words is not always observed, it is useful. Use **farther** to refer to distances that can be measured.

> It is **farther** from El Paso to Houston than from New York to Detroit.

Use **further,** meaning "more" or "additional," when physical distance or separation is not involved.

> The detective decided that the crime warranted **further** investigation.

fate/faith. See **faith/fate.**

* **faulty predication.** A term used to describe verbs that don't fit their subjects. In faulty predication, a subject could not logically perform the action specified by the verb.

> **Possible problem**   The purpose of radar detectors **is banned** in a few states.
>> What is forbidden—radar detectors or their purpose?

> **Possible revision**   Radar detectors **are banned** in a few states.

At other times a linking verb is used incorrectly to connect words that aren't really equivalent. In the following example, the noun *problem* cannot be linked to the adverb *when.*

> **Problem**   A common problem with some foreign bikes **is** *when* you have them serviced.

Revised   A common problem with foreign bikes **is** getting them serviced.

fewer than/less than. Use **fewer than** with things you can count; use **less than** with quantities that must be measured or can be considered as a whole.

The express lane was reserved for customers buying **fewer than** ten items.

Matthew had **less than** half a gallon of gasoline.

He also had **less than** ten dollars.

* **finite verb.** A verb that changes form to indicate person, number, and tense. A complete sentence requires a finite verb. Finite verbs stand in contrast to **nonfinite verb** forms such as **infinitives, participles,** and **gerunds,** which do not change form and which cannot stand as the only verb in a sentence. (See Section 18b.) Compare the following finite and nonfinite forms.

Finite verbs
He **ensures** freshness.
The baker **kneads** the dough.

Nonfinite verbs
To ensure freshness, Jean-Pierre buys eggs from local farms.
The baker **kneading** the dough sneezed.

flaunt/flout. These words are confused surprisingly often. **Flaunt** means "to show off"; **flout** means "to disregard" or "to show contempt for."

To **flaunt** his wealth, Mr. Lin bought a Van Gogh.

Flouting a gag order, the newspaper published its exposé of corruption in the city council.

* **fragment.** A group of words that does not fully express an idea even though it is punctuated as a sentence. A fragment may also be called a "broken sentence." See Section 24a.

Fragment	Despite the fact that Professor Chase had an impressive portfolio of investments.
Complete sentence	Despite the fact that Professor Chase had an impressive portfolio of investments, she was usually careful with her money.
Fragment	A safe investment most of the time.
Complete sentence	Bonds are a safe investment most of the time.

glos

fun, funner, funnest. Used as an adjective, **fun** is not appropriate in academic writing; replace it with a more formal expression.

Informal	Skiing is a very **fun** sport.
Formal	Skiing is a very **enjoyable** sport.

The comparative and superlative forms, **funner** and **funnest,** while increasingly common in spoken English, are inappropriate in writing. In writing, use **more fun** or **most fun.**

Informal	Albert found tennis **funner** than squash.
Formal	Albert found tennis **more fun** than squash.
Spoken	He thought racquetball the **funnest** of the three sports.
Written	He thought racquetball the **most fun** of the three sports.

* **fused sentence.** See **run-on sentence.**

gay. A term now widely used to mean "homosexual." Less formal than *homosexual,* **gay** is still appropriate in most writing. While **gay** is often used without regard to gender, some prefer it as a term that refers mainly to homosexual men, with **lesbian** the appropriate term for homosexual women.

* **gender.** A classification of nouns and pronouns as masculine (*actor, muscleman, he*), feminine (*actress, midwife, she*), or neuter (*tree, it*).

* **gerund.** A verb form used as a noun: *smiling, biking, walking.* (See Section 18a–3.) Most gerunds end in **-ing** and, consequently, look identical to the present participle.

Gerund	**Smiling** is good for the health.
Participle	A **smiling** critic is dangerous.

The difference is that gerunds function as nouns while participles act as modifiers. Gerunds usually appear in the present tense, but they can take other forms.

Having been criticized made Brian angry.
Gerund in past tense, passive voice, acting as subject of the sentence

Being asked to play an encore was a compliment Otto enjoyed. Gerund in present tense, passive voice, as subject of sentence

get. The principal parts of this verb are.

Present	*Past*	*Past participle*
get	got	got, gotten

Gotten usually sounds more polished than **got** as the past participle in American English, but both forms are acceptable.

> Aretha **has gotten** an A average in microbiology.
> Aretha **has got** an A average in microbiology.

Many expressions, formal and informal, rely on **get.** Use the less formal ones only with appropriate audiences.

> get it together
> get straight
> get real

good and. Informal. Avoid it in academic writing.

> **Informal**   The lake was **good and** cold when the sailors threw Sean in.
>
> **Better**   The lake was **icy** cold when the sailors threw Sean in.

good/well. These words cause many problems. (See Section 25a–2.) As a modifier, **good** is an adjective only; **well** can be either an adjective or an adverb. Consider the difference between these sentences, where each word functions as an adjective.

> Katy is **good.**
> Katy is **well.**

Good is often mistakenly used as an adverb.

> **Wrong**   Juin conducts the orchestra **good.**
>
> **Right**   Juin conducts the orchestra **well.**
>
> **Wrong**   The bureaucracy at NASA runs **good.**
>
> **Right**   The bureaucracy at NASA runs **well.**

Complications occur when writers and speakers—eager to avoid using **good** incorrectly—substitute **well** as an adjective where **good** used as an adjective may be more accurate.

> **Wrong**   After a shower, Coach Rhoades smells **well.**
>
> **Right**   After a shower, Coach Rhoades smells **good.**
>
> **Right**   I feel **good.**
>
> **Also right**   I feel **well.**

handicapped. Falling out of favor as a term to describe people with physical disabilities. However, euphemistic alternatives such as *differently abled* and *physically challenged* have been roundly criticized.

glos

hanged, hung. **Hanged** has been the past participle conventionally reserved for executions; **hung** is used on other occasions. The distinction is a nice one, probably worth observing.

> Connie was miffed when her disgruntled editorial staff decided she should be **hanged** in effigy.

> Portraits of the faculty were **hung** in the student union.

* **helping verbs.** See **auxiliary verbs.**

he/she. Using **he/she** (or *his/her* or *s/he*) is a way to avoid a sexist pronoun reference. Many readers find expressions with slashes clumsy and prefer *he or she* and *his or her.*

Hispanic. A term falling somewhat out of favor among some groups, in part because of its imprecision. Groups that have fallen under the Hispanic label now often prefer to be identified more precisely: *Chicano/Chicana, Cuban American, Latin American, Mexican American, Puerto Rican.*

hisself. A nonstandard form. Don't use it.

homonyms. Words of different meanings and spellings pronounced alike: *straight/strait, peace/piece, their/there.*

hopefully. As a sentence modifier, **hopefully** upsets some readers' sensitivities. In most situations, you will do well to avoid using **hopefully** when you mean "I hope" or "it is hoped."

> **Not** **Hopefully,** the weather will improve.
>
> **But** **I hope** the weather will improve.

Use **hopefully** only when you mean "with hope."

> Geraldo watched **hopefully** as Al Capone's safe was pried open.

idiom. A widely accepted expression that does not seem to make literal sense. Idioms often mean more than the sum of their parts.

> The aircraft **bit the big one** over Montana.
> Let's **get cracking.** We're late.
> Alyce hoped that Richard would **cough up** the money.

Idiom can also describe a vocabulary and language style shared within certain groups or professions: the *idiom* of medical personnel, the *idiom* of computer specialists, the *idiom* of literary critics.

illicit/elicit. See **elicit/illicit.**

illusion/allusion. See **allusion/illusion.**

imminent/eminent. See **eminent/imminent.**

* **imperative mood.** The form of a verb that expresses a command (see **mood**).

> **Go! Find** that missing canister of film. **Bring** it back to the lab.

imply/infer. Think of these words as opposite sides of the same coin. **Imply** means "to suggest" or "to convey an idea without stating it." **Infer** is what you might do to figure out what someone else has implied: you examine evidence and draw conclusions from it.

> By joking calmly, the pilot sought to **imply** that the aircraft was out of danger. But from the hole that had opened in the wing, the passengers **inferred** that the landing would be exciting.

incredible/incredulous. **Incredible** means "unbelievable"; **incredulous** means "unwilling to believe" and "doubting." See also **credible/credulous.**

> The press found the governor's explanation for his wealth **incredible.** You could hardly blame them for being **incredulous** when he attributed his vast holdings to coupon savings.

* **indefinite pronoun.** A pronoun that does not refer to a particular person, thing, or group: *all, any, each, everybody, everyone, one, none, somebody, someone,* and so on. See Section 21d.

* **independent clause.** See **clause.**

* **indicative mood.** The form of a verb that states facts or asks questions (see **mood**).

> Did he **find** the canister of film? It **was** in the lab yesterday.

indirect discourse. The substance of what a speaker or writer has said, but not the exact words. Indirect discourse is not surrounded by quotation marks. See **direct discourse.**

> **Direct**   At the altar Ike told Bernice, "If you don't marry me, I'll sue."
>
> **Indirect**   At the altar Ike told Bernice he would sue her if she didn't marry him.

infer/imply. See **imply/infer.**

* **infinitive.** A verbal that can usually be identified by the word **to** preceding the base form of a verb: *to strive, to seek, to find, to endure.* Infinitives do take other forms to show various tenses and voices: *to be seeking, to have found, to have been found.* Infinitives can act as nouns, adjectives, adverbs, and absolutes (see Section 18a–1).

glos

Infinitive as noun	**To capture** a market is not easy.
	Subject of the sentence
Infinitive as adjective	Greta had many posters **to redesign.**
	Modifies the noun *posters*
Infinitive as adverb	Mr. Stavros laughed **to forget** his troubles. Modifies the verb *laughed*
Infinitive as absolute	<u>To be blunt,</u> the paper is plagiarized.

⋆ **inflection.** A change a word undergoes to specify its meaning or to reflect a relationship to other words or phrases in a sentence. For instance, verbs change to reflect shifts in tense, person, and number (*walk, walks, walked*). Nouns change to indicate number and possession (*antenna, antennae; Pearl, Pearl's*). Adverbs and adjectives show degrees of comparison (*cold, colder, coldest; happily, more happily, most happily*).

initialism. A single term created by joining the first letters in the words that make up the full name or description. Unlike acronyms, however, initialisms are pronounced letter by letter.

IRS—**I**nternal **R**evenue **S**ervice
CIA—**C**entral **I**ntelligence **A**gency
HBO—**H**ome **B**ox **O**ffice

See **acronym** and Section 30d–2.

⋆ **intensifier.** A modifier that adds emphasis: *so, very, extremely, intensely, really, certainly.*

so cold   **very** bold   **extremely** complex

⋆ **intensive pronoun.** A pronoun form, created when **-self** or **-selves** is added to personal pronouns (*myself, yourself, herself, itself, oneself, ourselves, yourselves, themselves*), that modifies a noun to add emphasis. See Section 23a.

Otto **himself** admitted he was the winner.
The managers did all the printing **themselves.**

⋆ **intentional fragment.** A group of words that does not have all the usual parts of a sentence but can act as a sentence because it expresses an idea fully. See Section 24b.

Intentional fragments   So what?   Big deal!

⋆ **interjection.** A word that expresses emotion or feeling, but that is not grammatically a part of a sentence. Interjections can be punctuated as exclamations (!) or attached to a sentence with a comma. Interjections include *oh, hey, wow,* and *well.*

* **interrogative pronoun.** A pronoun used to pose a question: *who, which, what, whose.*

into. Avoid this word in its faddish sense of being "interested in" or "involved with."

Informal	The college was finally **into** computers.
More formal	The college was finally **involved with** computers.

* **intransitive verb.** A verb that does not take a direct object. This means that the action of an intransitive verb does not pass on to someone or something; the sentence is complete without an object.

Intransitive
I **slept** well.
Lawrence **wept.**

Linking verbs are intransitive.

Intransitive
I **am** happy.
You **have been** absent.

Compare intransitive verbs to **transitive** ones, which require an object to complete the action of a sentence.

Transitive
Travis accidentally **pushed** *Kyle.*
Sister Anne **bit** her *lip.*

* **inversion.** A reversal in the normal subject/verb/object order of a sentence.

Off came the wheel.
Our lives we hold less dear than our honor.

irregardless. A nonstandard form. Use **regardless** instead.

* **irregular verb.** A verb that does not form its past and past participle forms by adding *-d* or *-ed* to the infinitive (see **principal parts of a verb**). Irregular verbs are both numerous and important (see the full chart in Section 17d). They change their forms in various ways; a few even use the same form for all three principal parts.

Infinitive	Past	Past participle
burst	burst	burst
drink	drank	drunk
arise	arose	arisen
go	went	gone

glos

irritate/aggravate. See **aggravate/irritate.**

its/it's. Don't confuse these terms. **It's** is a contraction for *it is.* **Its** is a possessive pronoun meaning "belonging to it." See Section 22g for a discussion of this problem.

judgment/judgement. The British spell this word with two *e*'s. Americans spell it with just one: **judgment.**

kind of. This expression is colloquial when used to mean "rather." Avoid *kind of* in formal writing.

Colloquial	The college trustees were **kind of** upset by the bad publicity.
More formal	The college trustees were **rather** upset by the bad publicity.

less than. See **fewer than/less than.**

lie/lay. These two verbs cause much trouble and confusion. Here are their parts.

Present	*Past*	*Present participle*	*Past participle*
lie (to recline)	lay	lying	lain
lay (to place)	laid	laying	laid

Notice that the past tense of **lie** is the same as the present tense of **lay.** It may help you to remember that **to lie** (meaning "to recline") is *intransitive*—that is, it doesn't take an object. You can't lie *something.*

> Travis **lies** under the cottonwood tree.
> He **lay** there all afternoon.
> He was **lying** in the hammock yesterday.
> He had **lain** there for weeks.

To lay (meaning "to place" or "to put") is *transitive*—it takes an object.

> Jenny **lays** a *book* on Travis's desk.
>
> Yesterday, she **laid** a *memo* on his desk.
>
> Jenny was **laying** the *memo* on Travis's desk when he returned.
>
> Travis had **laid** almost three *yards* of concrete that afternoon.

like/as. Many readers object to **like** used to introduce clauses of comparison. **As, as if,** or **as though** are preferred in situations where a comparison involves a subject and verb.

> **Not** Mr. Butcher is self-disciplined, **like** you would expect a champion weightlifter to be.
>
> **But** Mr. Butcher is self-disciplined, **as** you would expect a champion weightlifter to be.
>
> **Not** It looks **like** he will win the local competition again this year.
>
> **But** It looks **as if** he will win the local competition again this year.

Like is acceptable when it introduces a prepositional phrase, not a clause.

> Yvonne looks **like** her mother.
> The sculpture on the mall looks **like** a rusted Edsel.

* **linking verb.** A verb, often a form of **to be,** that connects a subject to a word or phrase that extends or completes its meaning. Common linking verbs are *to seem, to appear, to feel,* and *to become.*

> Bob King **is** Dean of Humanities.
> She **seems** tired.

literally. When you write that something is **literally** true, you mean that it is exactly as you have stated. The following sentence means that Bernice emitted heated water vapor, an unlikely event no matter how angry she was.

> Bernice **literally** steamed when Ike ordered her to marry him.

If you want to keep the image (*steamed*), omit **literally:**

> Bernice steamed when Ike ordered her to marry him.

lose/loose. Be careful not to confuse these words. **Lose** is a verb, meaning "to misplace," "to be deprived of," or "to be defeated." **Loose** can be either an adjective or a verb. As an adjective, **loose** means "not tight"; as a verb, **loose** means "to let go" or "to untighten."

> Without Martin as quarterback, the team might **lose** its first game of the season.
> The strap on Martin's helmet had worked **loose.**
> It **loosened** so much that Martin **lost** his helmet.

mad, angry. See **angry/mad.**

glos

majority/plurality. There is a useful difference in meaning between these two words. A **majority** is more than half of a group; a **plurality** is the largest part of a group when there is *less than* a *majority.* In an election, for example, a candidate who wins 50.1 percent of the vote can claim a **majority.** One who wins a race with 40 percent of the vote may claim a **plurality,** but not a majority.

man, mankind. These terms are considered sexist by many readers since they implicitly exclude women from the human family.

> **Man** has begun to conquer space.

Look for alternatives, such as *humanity, men and women, the human race,* or *humankind.*

> **Men and women** have begun to conquer space.

many times. Wordy. Use **often** instead.

may/can. See **can/may.**

media/medium. **Medium** is the singular of **media.**

> Connie believed that the press could be as powerful a **medium** as television.
>
> The visual **media** are discussed in the textbook.

The term **media** is commonly used to refer to newspapers and magazines, as well as television and radio.

> President Xiony declined to speak to the **media** about the fiscal problems facing the college.

metaphor. A comparison that does not use the word *like* or *as.*

> All the world's a stage.
> I'm a little teacup, short and stout.

See also **mixed metaphor.**

Mexican American. A preferred term for describing Americans of Mexican ancestry.

midst/mist. Some people write **mist** when they mean **midst,** but the words are unrelated. **Midst** means "between" or "in the middle of." A **mist** is a mass of fine particles suspended in the air.

might of. A nonstandard form. Use **might have** instead.

> **Not** Ms. Rajala **might of** never admitted the truth.
> **But** Ms. Rajala **might have** never admitted the truth.

* **misplaced modifier.** A modifying word or phrase that is ambiguous because it could modify more than one thing. See Section 25g. See also **absolute.**

Misplaced modifier	Some of the actors won roles **without talent.**
Improved	Some of the actors **without talent** won roles.

mist/midst. See **midst/mist.**

mixed metaphor. A metaphor in which the terms of the comparison are inconsistent, incongruent, or unintentionally comic.

Unless we tighten our belts, we'll sink like a stone.

The fullback was a bulldozer, running up and down the field on winged feet.

* **modal auxiliary.** An auxiliary verb that indicates possibility, necessity, permission, desire, capability, and so on. Modal auxiliaries include *can, could, may, might, will, shall, should, ought,* and *must.* See Sections 17a and 31b.

Hector **can** write.
Hector **might** write.
Hector **must** write.

* **modifier.** A word, phrase, or clause that gives information about another word, phrase, or clause. Writers use modifiers, mainly adjectives, adverbs, and modifying phrases, to make important qualifications in their writing, to make it more accurate, and sometimes to give it color and depth. See Chapter 25.

* **mood.** A term used to describe how a writer regards a statement: either as a fact (the **indicative** mood), as a command (the **imperative** mood), or as a wish, desire, supposition, or improbability (the **subjunctive** mood). Verbs change their form to show mood. See Section 17f.

Indicative	The engineer **was** careful.
Imperative	**Be** careful!
Subjunctive	If the engineer **were** careful . . .

moral, morale. Don't confuse these words. As a noun, **moral** is a lesson. **Morale** is a state of mind.

The **moral** of the fable was to avoid temptation.
The **morale** of the team was destroyed by the accident.

glos

must of. Nonstandard. Use **must have** instead.

> **Not** Someone **must of** read the book.
>
> **But** Someone **must have** read the book.

Native American. The term now preferred by many people formerly described as American Indian.

nice. This adjective has little impact when used to mean "pleasant": **It was a nice day; Sally is a nice person.** In many cases, **nice** is damning with faint praise. Find a more specific word or expression. **Nice** can be used effectively to mean "precise" or "fine."

> There was a **nice** distinction between the two positions.

nohow. Nonstandard for **not at all** or **under any conditions.**

> **Colloquial** Mrs. Mahajan wouldn't talk **nohow.**
>
> **More formal** Mrs. Mahajan wouldn't talk **at all.**

* **nominal.** A word, phrase, or entire clause that acts like a noun in a sentence. **Pronouns** and **gerunds** often function as nominals.

> The wild applause only encouraged **them.**
> Pronoun *them* acts as an object
>
> **Keeping a straight face** wasn't easy.
> Gerund phrase acts as a subject

* **nominalizations.** Nouns created by adding endings to verbs and adjectives: *acceptability, demystification, prioritization,* and so on. Clumsy nominalizations of several syllables can usually be replaced by clearer terms. See Section 12c.

* **noncoordinate adjective.** Noncoordinate adjectives are adjectives or adjectivals that work together to modify a noun or pronoun. As a result they cannot be sensibly rearranged.

> **her six completed** chapters
> **a shiny blue Mustang** convertible
> **our natural good** humor

See **coordinate adjective** and Section 26c–5.

* **noncount noun.** A noun that names something that does not exist as a separable or individual unit: *blood, money, work, time.*

* **nonessential modifier.** See **nonrestrictive element.**

* **nonfinite verb.** See **finite verb** and **verbals.**

* **nonrestrictive (or nonessential) element.** A modifier, often a phrase, not essential to the meaning of a sentence. If the nonrestrictive element is removed, the basic meaning of the sentence is not altered.

> The senator, **who often voted with the other party,** had few loyal friends and a weak constituency.

> The agent, **a tall fellow from the FBI,** looked a bit self-conscious when he introduced himself.

Nonrestrictive phrases are ordinarily set off by commas. See **restrictive element** and Sections 26b–1 and 26b–2.

* **noun.** A word that names a person, place, thing, idea, or quality. In sentences, nouns can serve as subjects, objects, complements, appositives, and even modifiers. There are many classes of nouns: **common, proper, concrete, abstract, collective, noncount,** and **count.** See individual entries for details of each type.

nowheres. Nonstandard version of **nowhere** or **anywhere.**

> **Colloquial** The chemist couldn't locate the test tube **nowheres.** It was **nowheres** to be found.

> **Revised** The chemist couldn't locate the test tube **anywhere.** It was **nowhere** to be found.

* **number.** The form a word takes to indicate whether it is singular or plural. See Section 19a.

> | **Singular** | boy | his | this |
> | **Plural** | boys | their | these |

number/amount. See **amount/number.**

* **object, direct/indirect.** A word or phrase that receives the action of a verb. An object is **direct** when it states to whom or what an action was done.

> direct obj.
> Kim gave us **the signal.**

An object is **indirect** when it explains for whom or what an action is done or directed. It usually precedes the direct object.

> indirect obj.
> Kim gave **us** the signal.

* **objective case.** The form a noun or pronoun takes when it serves as a direct or an indirect object in a sentence or as the object of a preposition. See **case.**

glos

off of. A wordy expression. **Off** is enough.

Arthur drove his Jeep **off** the road.

O.K., OK, okay. Not the best choice for formal writing. But give the expression respect. It's an internationally recognized expression of approval. OK?

* **ordinal numbers.** Numbers that express a sequence: *first, second, third.* In contrast, **cardinal numbers** express an amount: *one, two, three.*

Oriental. A term falling out of favor as a description of the people or cultures of East Asia. Terms preferred are *Asian* or *East Asian.*

paragraph. A cluster of sentences working together for some purpose: to develop a single idea, to show relationships between separate ideas, to move readers from one point to another, to introduce a subject, to conclude a discussion, and so on. Paragraphs are marked by separations (indentions or open spaces). Paragraphs vary greatly in length, but may be as short as a single sentence. See Chapters 7 and 8.

The symbol ¶, meaning *paragraph,* is sometimes inserted by editors and instructors where a new paragraph is needed in a paper. *No ¶* indicates that an existing paragraph should be combined with another.

* **parallelism/parallel structure.** Ideas or items expressed in matching grammatical forms or structural patterns. Words, phrases, sentences, and even paragraphs can demonstrate parallelism.

Parallel verbs	The child was **waving, smiling, jumping, and laughing**—all at the same time.
Parallel phrases	**On the sea, in the air, on the ground,** the forces of the Axis powers were steadily driven back.
Parallel clauses	He was **the best of clowns;** he was **the worst of clowns.**
Parallel sentences	The child was **waving, smiling, and laughing**—all at the same time. Her mother was **screaming, berating, and threatening**—all **to no avail.**

* **parenthetical element.** A word or phrase that contributes to a sentence, but is not an essential part of it. Parenthetical items are usually separated from sentences by commas, dashes, or parentheses. When the element occurs in the middle of a sentence, it is set off by punctuation.

Orlando, **a wiry fellow,** climbed the sycamore tree easily.

Francie decided to climb an elm and—**still clutching her purse and camera**—soon waved from its topmost branches.

All the while, Richard (**the most vocal advocate of tree climbing**) remained on *terra firma.*

✳ **participle.** A verb form that is used as a modifier (see Section 18a–2). The present participle ends with **-ing**. For regular verbs, the past participle ends with **-ed**; for irregular verbs, the form of the past participle will vary. Participles have the following forms.

> *To perform* (a regular verb)
>
> **Present, active:**   performing
> **Present, passive:** being performed
> **Past, active:**   performed
> **Past, passive:**   having been performed

Participles can serve as simple modifiers.

> **Smiling,** Officer Bricker wrote the traffic ticket.
> Modifies *Officer Bricker*

But they often take objects, complements, and modifiers of their own to form verbal phrases, which play an important role in shaping sentences.

> **Writing** the ticket for speeding, Bricker laughed at his own cleverness in catching Arthur.
>
> **Having been ridiculed** often in the past by Arthur, Bricker now had his chance for revenge.
>
> Arthur, **knowing** what his friends were doing to Officer Bricker's car, smiled as he took the ticket.

Like an infinitive, a participle can also serve as an **absolute**—that is, a phrase that modifies an entire sentence.

> All things **considered**, the prank was worth the ticket.

✳ **parts of speech.** The eight common categories by which words in a sentence are identified according to what they do, how they are formed, where they are placed, and what they mean. Those basic categories are **nouns, pronouns, adjectives, verbs, adverbs, prepositions, conjunctions,** and **interjections.**

passed/past. Be careful not to confuse these words. **Passed** is a verb form; **past** can function as a noun, adjective, adverb, or preposition. The words are not interchangeable. Study the differences in the following sentences.

***Passed* as verb, past tense**	Tina **passed** her economics examination.
***Passed* as verb, past participle**	Earlier in the day she had **passed** an English quiz.
***Past* as noun**	In the **past,** she did well.
***Past* as adjective**	In the **past** semester, she got straight *A*'s.
***Past* as adverb**	Smiling, Tina walked **past** the teacher.
***Past* as preposition**	**Past** midnight, Tina was still celebrating.

* **passive verb/voice.** See **voice.**

persecute/prosecute. Persecute means "to oppress" or "to torment"; **prosecute** is a legal term, meaning "to bring charges or legal proceedings" against someone or something.

Connie Lim felt **persecuted** by criticisms of her political activism.

She threatened to **prosecute** anyone who interfered with her First Amendment rights.

* **person.** A way of classifying personal pronouns in sentences.

1st person:	the speaker—*I, we*
2nd person:	spoken to—*you*
3rd person:	spoken about—*he, she, it, they* + all nouns

Verbs also change to indicate a shift in person.

1st person:	I **see.**
3rd person:	She **sees.**

personal/personnel. Notice the difference between these words. **Personal** refers to what is private, belonging to an individual. **Personnel** are the people staffing an office or institution.

Drug testing all airline **personnel** would infringe upon **personal** freedom.

* **personal pronoun.** A pronoun that refers to particular individuals, things, or groups: *I, you, he, she, it, we, you, they.*

phenomena/phenomenon. You can win friends and influence people by spelling these words correctly and using **phenomenon** as the singular form.

The astral **phenomenon** of meteor showers is common in August.

Many other astral **phenomena** are linked to particular seasons.

*   **phrase.** A group of related words that does not include both a subject and a finite verb. Among the types of phrases are **noun phrases, verb phrases, verbal phrases** (infinitive, gerund, and participial), **absolute phrases,** and **prepositional phrases.**

Noun phrase	**The members of the Astronomy Club** will be going to the observatory in a van.
Verb phrase	The members of the Astronomy Club **will be going** to the observatory in a van.
Verbal phrase—infinitive	Their intention is **to observe the planet Mars.**
Verbal phrase—gerund	**Driving to the observatory** will be half the fun.
Verbal phrase—participial	The instructor **sponsoring the trip** will drive the van.
Absolute phrase	**All things considered,** the trip was time well spent.
Prepositional phrase	Whenever it could, the Astronomy Club scheduled its meetings **at the hilltop observatory.**

plurality/majority. See **majority/plurality.**

plus. Don't use **plus** as a conjunction or conjunctive adverb meaning "and," "moreover," "besides," or "in addition to."

Not   Mr. Burton admitted to cheating on his income taxes this year. **Plus** he acknowledged that he had filed false returns for the last three years.

But   Mr. Burton admitted to cheating on his income taxes this year. **Moreover,** he acknowledged that he had filed false returns for the last three years.

*   **possessive case.** The form a noun or pronoun takes to show ownership: *Barney's, Jean-Pierre's, mine, yours, hers, theirs.* See Sections 19b (nouns) and 22f (pronouns).

*   **possessive pronoun.** The form a pronoun takes when it shows

glos

ownership: *my, mine, your, yours, her, his, its, our, ours, their, whose, anyone's, somebody's.* See Section 22f.

* **predicate.** A verb and all its auxiliaries, modifiers, and complements.

> The pregnant cat, enormous and fierce, **kittened in the back seat of Officer Bricker's car, where she planned to set up housekeeping.**

* **predicate adjective.** An adjective that follows a linking verb and describes the subject.

> Coach Rhoades is **inept.**
> It was **cold.**

* **predicate nominative.** A noun or pronoun that follows a linking verb and tells what the subject is.

> Rhoades is the **coach.**
> It was **she.**

prejudice/prejudiced. Many writers and speakers use **prejudice** where they need **prejudiced. Prejudice** is a noun; **prejudiced** is a verb form.

> **Wrong**   Joe Kamakura is **prejudice** against liberals.
>
> **Right**   Joe Kamakura is **prejudiced** against liberals.
>
> **Wrong**   **Prejudice** people are found in every walk of life.
>
> **Right**   **Prejudiced** people are found in every walk of life.
>
> **Compare**   **Prejudice** is found in every walk of life.

* **preposition.** A word that links a noun or pronoun to the rest of a sentence. Prepositions point out many kinds of basic relationships: *on, above, to, for, in, out, through, by,* and so on.

* **prepositional phrase.** The combination of a preposition and a noun or pronoun. The following are prepositional phrases: *on our house, above it, to him, in love, through them, by the garden gate.*

* **principal parts of a verb.** The three basic forms of a verb from which all tenses are built. See Section 17d.

> **infinitive (present).** This is the base form of a verb, the shape it takes when preceded by **to: to walk, to go, to choose.**
>
> **past.** This is the simplest form a verb has to show action that has already occurred: **walked, went, chose.**

past participle. This is the form a verb takes when it is accompanied by an **auxiliary verb** to show a more complicated past tense: **had <u>walked</u>, might have <u>gone</u>, would have been <u>chosen</u>.**

principal/principle. Two terms commonly confused because of their multiple meanings. **Principal** means "chief" or "most important." It also names the head of an elementary or secondary school (remember the **principal** is your pal?). Finally, it can be a sum of money lent or borrowed.

> Ike intended to be the **principal** breadwinner of the household.

> Bernice accused Ike of acting like a power-mad high school **principal.**

> She argued that they would need two incomes just to meet their mortgage payments—both interest and **principal.**

A **principle,** on the other hand, is a guiding rule or fundamental truth.

> Ike declared it was against his **principles** to have his wife work.

> Bernice said he would just have to be a little less **principled** on that issue.

prioritize. Many readers object to this word, regarding it as less appropriate than its equivalents: **rank** or **list in order of priority.**

proceed to. A wordy and redundant construction when it merely delays the real action of a sentence.

> **Wordy** We **proceeded to** open the strongbox.
>
> **Tighter** We **opened** the strongbox.

* **progressive verb.** A verb form that shows continuing action. Progressive tenses are formed by the auxiliary verb *to be* + the present participle. See Sections 17a and 31a.

> *to be* + present participle
> Nelda **is conducting** her string orchestra.

> *to be* + present participle
> Nelda **had been conducting** the orchestra for many years.

> *to be* + present participle
> Nelda **will be conducting** the orchestra for many years to come.

* **pronoun.** A word that acts like a noun, but doesn't name a specific person, place, or thing—*I, you, he, she, it, they, whom, who, what, myself, oneself, this, these, that, all, both, anybody,* and so on. There are many varieties of pronouns: **personal, relative, interrogative, intensive, reflexive, demonstrative, indefinite,** and **reciprocal.** See Chapters 20 through 23 and individual entries for details about each type.

* **proper adjective.** An adjective based on the name of a person, place, or thing. Proper adjectives are capitalized.

> **British** cuisine
> **Machiavellian** politics
> **Cubist** art

* **proper noun.** A noun that names some particular person, place, or thing: *Bryan Adams, Australia, Ford.* The first letter in proper nouns is capitalized.

* **qualifier.** A modifier. Sometimes the word refers to particular classes of modifiers: **intensifiers** (*so, too, surely, certainly*), **restrictive expressions** (*many, most, both, some, almost*), or **conjunctive adverbs** (*however, nevertheless*).

* **quantifier.** A word that precedes nouns and tells *how much* or *how many:* **some, several, a little.**

quote. Some people do not accept **quote** used as a noun. To be safe, use **quotation** in formal writing.

real. Often used as a colloquial version of **very:** "I was **real** scared." This usage is inappropriate in academic writing.

really. An adverb too vague to make much of an impression in many sentences: **It was <u>really</u> hot; I am <u>really</u> sorry.** Replace **real** with a more precise expression or delete it.

reason is . . . because. The expression is redundant. Use one half of the expression or the other—not both.

> Redundant   The **reason** the cat is ferocious is **because** she is protecting her kittens.
>
> Revised   The **reason** the cat is ferocious is **that** she is protecting her kittens.
>
> Revised   The cat is ferocious **because** she is protecting her kittens.

* **reciprocal pronoun.** A compound pronoun that shows a mutual action: *one another, each other.*

> The members of the jury whispered to **one another.**

redundancy. Unnecessary repetition in writing.

refer/allude. See **allude/refer.**

* **reference.** The connection between a pronoun and the noun it stands in for (antecedent). This connection should be clear and unambiguous. When a reader can't figure out who *he* is in a sentence you have written, or what exactly *this* or *it* may mean, you have a problem with unclear reference.

> **Unclear references**
> The sun broke through the mists as Jim and Jack, fully recovered from their accident, arrived with news about the award and the ceremony. **This** pleased us because **he** hadn't mentioned anything about **it.**

> **References clarified**
> The sun broke through the mists as Jim and Jack, fully recovered from their accident, arrived with news about the award and the ceremony. **The news** pleased us because **Jim** hadn't mentioned anything about **a ceremony.**

See Chapter 20.

* **reflexive pronoun.** A pronoun form created when **-self** or **-selves** is added to personal pronouns (*myself, yourself, herself, himself, itself, oneself, ourselves, yourselves, themselves*). Use the reflexive form when both the subject and the object of an action are the same (see Section 23a).

> sub.   obj.
> **Chunyang** had only *himself* to rely on.

> subj.   obj.
> **They** took *themselves* too seriously.

* **regular verb.** A verb that forms its past and past participle forms (see **principal parts of a verb**) simply by adding **-d** or **-ed** to the infinitive. See Section 17a.

Infinitive	*Past*	*Past participle*
talk	talk**ed**	talk**ed**
coincide	coincide**d**	coincide**d**
advertise	advertise**d**	advertise**d**

relate to. A colloquial expression used vaguely and too often to mean "to identify with" or "to appreciate."

> **Vague**   Bud could **relate to** being a campus football hero.

> **Better**   Bud **liked** being a campus football hero.

glos

* **relative clause.** See **relative pronoun.**

* **relative pronoun.** A pronoun such as *that, which, whichever, who, whoever, whom, whomever, whose,* and *of which* that introduces subordinate clauses. In the following example, the relative pronoun *whichever* introduces a noun clause that forms the subject of the sentence.

> subordinate clause
> **Whichever** car you buy will cost a small fortune.

In this second example, the relative pronoun *which* introduces an adjective clause modifying *club.*

> subordinate clause
> Mr. Rao sold the club **which** he had owned for twenty years.

A clause introduced by a relative pronoun is called a **relative clause.**

* **restrictive (or essential) element.** A modifier, usually a phrase, essential to the meaning of the subject or noun it modifies. If the restrictive element is removed, the sentence no longer makes sense.

> Only the senator **who voted "nay"** remained in the chamber.
> The agent **from the CIA** was the one who called.

Restrictive phrases are *not* set off by commas. See **nonrestrictive element** and Sections 26b–1 and 26b–2.

* **run-on sentence.** A faulty sentence in which two independent clauses (groups of words which could stand alone as sentences) are joined without appropriate punctuation marks or conjunctions. It may also be called a **fused sentence.** See Section 24d.

> **Run on**   Reading *Ulysses* is one thing understanding it is another.
>
> **Corrected** Reading *Ulysses* is one thing; understanding it is another.

* **sentence.** A group of words that expresses an idea and is punctuated as an independent unit.

> Whenever it could, the Astronomy Club scheduled meetings in an isolated hilltop observatory.
> Is that true?
> Explain the situation to me.

* **sentence fragment.** See **fragment.**

* **sentence structure.** The way a sentence is put together—its orga-

glos

nization or arrangement of phrases and clauses. Sentences can be described in many ways—for example, as *simple, complex, compound,* or *compound-complex; periodic* or *cumulative;* or *direct, complicated, tangled,* and so on. See Chapters 13 through 15.

* **sequence of tenses.** The way the tense of one verb in a sentence limits or determines the tense of other verbs.

set/sit. These two verbs can cause problems. Here are their parts.

Present	Past	Present participle	Past participle
set (put down)	set	setting	set
sit (take a seat)	sat	sitting	sat

It may help you to remember that **to sit** (meaning "to take a seat") is *intransitive*—that is, it doesn't take an object. You can't sit *something.*

> Haskell **sits** under the cottonwood tree.
> He **sat** there all afternoon.
> He was **sitting** in the hammock yesterday.
> He had **sat** there for several weeks.

To set (meaning "to place" or "to put") is *transitive*—it takes an object.

> Jenny **set** a *plate* on the table.
> At Christmas, we **set** a *star* atop the tree.
> Alex was **setting** the *music* on the stand when it collapsed.
> Connie discovered that Travis **had set** a *subpoena* on her desk.

sexist language. Language that reflects prejudiced attitudes and stereotypical thinking about the sex roles and traits of both sexes. See Section 10d.

s/he. Most readers object to this construction which, like *he/she* and *she/he,* is an alternative to the nonsexist but clumsy *he or she.* Avoid **s/he.**

should of. Mistaken form of **should have.** Also incorrect are **could of** and **would of.**

simile. An explicit comparison between two things. In a simile, a word such as *like* or *as* underscores the comparison.

> Driving an RX-7 is **like** riding the surf at Waikiki.
> Graziella is **as** flaky **as** Wheaties.

glos

simple sentence. A sentence that has only one clause.

> independent clause
> **Mardi Gras is celebrated** just before Ash Wednesday.

sit/set. See **set/sit.**

slang. Casual, aggressively informal language.

> The punk wanted to bum a cigarette off us, but we told him to get lost.

Slang expressions are out of place in most academic and business writing. See Section 10a–3.

so. Vague when used as an intensifier, especially when no explanation follows **so:** "Sue Ellen was **so** sad." **So** used this way can sound trite (how sad is **so** sad?) or juvenile: "Professor Sweno's play was **so** bad." If you use **so,** complete your statement.

> Sue Ellen was **so** sad she cried for an hour.
>
> Professor Sweno's play was **so** bad that the audience cheered for the villains.

* **split infinitive.** An infinitive interrupted by an adverb: *to **boldly** go; to **really** try.* Split infinitives offend some readers and they should be avoided in formal writing, except when the revised version is more awkward than the split infinitive. To revise a split infinitive, simply place the adverb somewhere else in your sentence: *to go **boldly.*** See Section 18c–3.

stationary/stationery. **Stationary,** an adjective, means "immovable, fixed in place." **Stationery** is a noun meaning "writing material." The words are not interchangeable.

* **subject.** A word or phrase that names what a sentence is about. The **simple subject** of a sentence is a single word; the **complete subject** is the simple subject and all its modifiers.

> | | subj. | verb |
> |---|---|---|
> | **Simple subject** | The **captain** of the new team *quit.* | |
>
> | | subj. | verb |
> |---|---|---|
> | **Complete subject** | **The captain of the new team** *quit.* | |

* **subject complement.** A word or phrase that follows a linking verb, completing its meaning. Subject complements can be nouns, pronouns, or adjectives.

> subj.   l.v.   subj. comp.
> Sanjay Sacomdri is **student representative.**

> subj.   l.v. subj. comp.
> The director is **she.**

subj.   l.v.   subj. comp.

Kelly McKay seems **mysterious.**

* **subjunctive mood.** The form of a verb that expresses a wish, desire, supposition, or improbability (see **mood** and Section 17f).

> If he **were to find** the canister of film, we would be delighted.
> It is necessary that the film **be** locked in the vault.

* **subordinate clause.** See **clause.**

subordinating conjunctions. See **conjunctions, subordinating.**

* **superlative.** The highest degree in a comparison of at least three things.

> The **worst** play in thirty-seven years . . .
> The **most vicious** of three published reviews . . .

supposed to. Many writers forget the **d** at the end of **suppose** when the word is used with auxiliary verbs.

> **Incorrect**   Calina was **suppose to** check her inventory.
> **Correct**   Calina was **supposed to** check her inventory.

* **synonyms.** Words of approximately the same meaning: *street/ road, angry/mad, home/domicile.* While synonyms may share their **denotation,** or basic meaning, they often differ in **connotation—** that is, what the words imply. Both *skinny* and *svelte* denote thinness, but the terms differ significantly in how they would be used. In most situations, *skinny* sounds disparaging, while *svelte* is a positive, even glamorous description.

* **syntax.** The arrangement and relationship of clauses, phrases, and words in a sentence.

* **tense.** That quality of a verb which expresses time and existence. Tense is expressed through changes in verb forms and endings (*see, seeing, saw; work, worked*) and the use of auxiliaries (*had seen, will have seen; had worked, had been working*). Tense enables verbs to state complicated relationships between time and action—or relatively simple ones. See Sections 17a and 31a.

than/then. These words are occasionally confused. **Than** is a conjunction expressing difference or comparison; **then** is an adverb expressing time.

> If the film is playing tomorrow, Shannon would rather go **then than** today.

theirselves. A nonstandard form. Use **themselves** instead.

| Incorrect | All the strikers placed **theirselves** in jeopardy. |
| Correct | All the strikers placed **themselves** in jeopardy. |

then/than. See **than/then.**

this. As a pronoun, **this** is sometimes vague and in need of clarification (see Section 20c–1).

| Vague | We could fix the car if you had more time or I owned the proper tools. Of course, **this** is always a problem. |
| Clearer | We could fix the car if you had more time or I owned the proper tools. Of course, **my lack of proper tools** is always a problem. |

This (and **these**) may be inappropriate when used informally as demonstrative adjectives that refer to objects not previously mentioned.

| Inappropriate *this* | Jim owns **this** huge Harley motorcycle. |
| Inappropriate *these* | After she moved out, we found **these** really ugly roaches in her apartment. |

Such forms are common in speech, but should not appear in writing.

| Better | Jim owns **a** huge Harley motorcycle. |
| Better | After she moved out, we found ugly roaches in her apartment. |

throne/thrown. A surprising number of writers use **thrown** when they mean **throne.**

Charles I was **thrown** from his **throne** by an angry army of Puritans.

thusly. A fussy, nonstandard form. Don't use it. **Thus** is stuffy enough without the *-ly.*

till/until. **Until** is used more often in school and business writing, though the words are usually interchangeable. No apostrophe is used with **till.** You may occasionally see the poetic form **'til,** but don't use it in academic or business writing.

to/too. Most people know the difference between these words. But a writer in a hurry can easily put down the preposition **to** when the adverb **too** is intended. If you make this error often, check for it when you edit.

| Incorrect | Coach Rhoades was **to** surprised to speak after his team won its first game in four years. |

Revised   Coach Rhoades was **too** surprised to speak after his team won its first game in four years.

toward/towards. **Toward** is preferred, though either form is fine.

transitions. Connecting words, phrases, and other devices (repetitions, headings) that help readers move from one unit to the next in your writing. Transitions help to hold a piece of writing together, bridging gaps and linking sentences and paragraphs. **Transitional words** are individual terms used to link ideas: *therefore, moreover, nevertheless, nonetheless, consequently,* and so on. See Chapter 9.

* **transitive verb.** A verb that takes an object. The action of a transitive verb passes on to someone or something; the sentence would be incomplete without an object.

> **Transitive**
> Travis accidentally **pushed** *Kyle.* You can **push** *someone.*
> Sister Anne **wrecked** the *van.*

Transitive verbs (unlike intransitives) can usually be changed from the active to passive voice.

> **Active**   Travis accidentally **pushed** *Kyle.*
> **Passive**   *Kyle* **was** accidentally **pushed** by Travis.

Compare transitive verbs to **intransitive** ones, which do not require an object to complete the action of a sentence.

> **Intransitive**
> I **slept** well. You cannot **sleep** *something.*
> Lawrence **sat** down. You cannot **sit** *something.*

try and. An informal expression. In writing, use **try to** instead.

> **Incorrect**   After its defeat, the soccer team decided to **try and** drown its sorrows.
> **Revised**   After its defeat, the soccer team decided to **try to** drown its sorrows.

TV. This abbreviation for *television* is common, but in most writing it is still preferable to write out the entire word. The abbreviation is usually capitalized.

type. You can usually delete this word.

> **Wordy**   Hector was a polite **type** of guy.
> **Revised**   Hector was polite.

uninterested/disinterested. See **disinterested/uninterested.**

glos

unique. Something **unique** is one of a kind. It can't be compared with anything else, so expressions such as *most* unique, *more unique,* or *very* unique don't make sense. The word **unique,** when used properly, should stand alone.

Incorrect	Joe Rhoades's coaching methods were **very unique.**
Revised	Joe Rhoades's coaching methods were **unique.**

Quite often **unique** appears where another, more specific adjective is appropriate.

Incorrect	The **most unique** merchant on the block was Tong-chai.
Improved	The **most inventive** merchant on the block was Tong-chai.

until/till. See **till/until.**

used to. Many writers forget the **d** at the end of **use.**

Incorrect	Leroy was **use to** studying after soccer practice.
Correct	Leroy was **used to** studying after soccer practice.

utilize. Many readers prefer the simpler term **use.**

Inflated	Mr. Ringling **utilized** his gavel to regain the crowd's attention.
Better	Mr. Ringling **used** his gavel to regain the crowd's attention.

* **verb.** The word or phrase that establishes the action of a sentence or expresses a state of being (see Chapters 16–17).

verb
The music **played** on.

verb
Turning the volume down **proved** to be difficult.

A verb and all its auxiliaries, modifiers, and complements is called the **predicate** of a sentence.

complete subj.　　　　predicate
David's band **would have played throughout the night.**

complete subj.　　　　predicate
Turning the volume down on the band **proved to be much more difficult than the neighbors had anticipated it might be.**

* **verbals.** Verb forms that act like nouns, adjectives, or adverbs (see Chapter 18). The three kinds of verbals are **infinitives, participles,** and **gerunds.** Like verbs, verbals can take objects to form

phrases. But verbals are described as **nonfinite** (that is, "unfinished") verbs because they cannot alone make complete sentences. A complete sentence requires a **finite** verb—that is, a verb that changes form to indicate person, number, and tense.

Nonfinite verb—infinitive	**To have found** security . . .
Finite verb	I **have found** security.
Nonfinite verb—participle	The actor **performing** the scene . . .
Finite verb	The actor **performs** the scene.

very. Many teachers and editors will cut **very** almost every time it appears. Overuse has deadened the impact of the word. Whenever possible, use a more specific term or expression.

Weak	I was **very angry.**
Stronger	I was **furious.**

* **voice.** Transitive verbs can be either in the **active voice** or in the **passive voice.** They are in the **active voice** when the subject in the sentence actually performs the action described by the verb.

> subj.   action
> *Professor Chase **donated** the video camera.*

They are in the **passive voice** when the action described by the verb is done to the subject.

> subj.   action
> *The video camera **was donated** by Professor Chase.*

See Section 17e.

well/good. See **good/well.**

who/whom. Use **who** when the pronoun is a subject; use **whom** when it is an object.

> **Who** wrote the ticket?
> **To whom** was the ticket given?

See Section 22e.

-wise. Don't add **-wise** to the end of a word to mean "with respect to." Many people object to word coinages such as *sportswise, weatherwise,* and *healthwise.* However, a number of common and acceptable English expressions do end in **-wise:** *clockwise, lengthwise, otherwise.* When in doubt about an expression, check the dictionary.

with regards to. Drop the **s** in regard**s.** The correct expression is **with regard to.**

won't. Writers sometimes forget the apostrophe in this contraction and others like it: **can't, don't.**

word choice. A marginal annotation used by many instructors to suggest that the writer could find a more appropriate or effective word or phrase.

would of. Mistaken form of **would have.** Also incorrect are **could of** and **should of.**

you all. Southern expression for *you,* singular or plural. Not used in academic writing.

your/you're. Homonyms that often get switched. **You're** is the contraction for *you are;* **your** is a possessive form.

> **You're** certain Maxine has been to Java?
> **Your** certainty on this matter may be important.

Credits

LINCOLN BARNETT, *The Universe and Dr. Einstein*. William Morrow, 1968, p. 84.

HAL ZINA BENNETT, *The Doctor Within*. Clarkson Potter, 1981, p.184.

RICHARD BERNSTEIN, *Dictatorship of Virtue*. New York: Alfred A. Knopf, 1994, p. 11.

ROBERT H. BORK, "Give Me a Bowl of Texas," in *Forbes*, September 1985, p. 184.

ERNEST L. BOYER, "Creating the New American College." *The Chronicle of Higher Education*, 1994.

JANE BRODY, *Jane Brody's Nutrition Book*. W. W. Norton & Co., 1981, p. 7.

J. BRONOWSKI, *The Ascent of Man*. Little, Brown and Company, 1973, p. 83.

PAUL BURKA, from "Perils of Politics." *Texas Monthly*, July 1991, p. 120. Reprinted by permission of *Texas Monthly*.

JAMES BURKE, *Connections*. Little, Brown and Company, 1978, p. 45.

JAMES LEE BURKE, *Black Cherry Blues*. New York: Avon Books, 1989, p. 8.

TOM CALLAHAN, "Advertising the Army." *American Way*, November 26, 1985, Vol. 18, No. 24. Reprinted by permission of the author.

HÉCTOR CANALES, JR., LORIE CERECERES, MARIA C. FUENTES, DENNIS LOZANO, DAVID QUY, AND DANIEL SPRAGGINS, "Foreign Aid: Should We Keep It at Home?" Reprinted by the permission of the authors.

COUNCIL OF BIOLOGY EDITORS, from *Scientific Style and Format: The CBE Manual for Authors, Editors, and Publishers*, Sixth Edition. Copyright ©1994 by the Council of Biology Editors. Reprinted by permission.

ELLEN CHESLER, *Woman of Valor*. New York: Simon & Schuster, 1992.

MALCOLM COWLEY, *The Literary Situation*. New York: The Viking Press, 1955, p. 197.

"Crafty" from *The Compact Edition of the Oxford English Dictionary*, Vol. I, A-O, 1971, p. 1129. Copyright © 1979 Oxford University Press. Reprinted by permission.

ROBERTSON DAVIES, "A Few Kind Words for Superstition." *Newsweek*, 11/20/78. Copyright © 1978 by Robertson Davies. Reprinted by permission of the author.

CHRISTOPHER DICKEY. "Remodeling the Slopes." *Newsweek*, January 6, 1992, p. 46.

FREEMAN J. DYSON, *Infinite in All Directions*. Harper & Row, Publishers, Inc., 1988, pp. 100, 216.

DANIEL MARK EPSTEIN, "The Case of Harry Houdini," in *Star of Wonder*. Overlook Press, 1986, p. 42. Reprinted by permission.

SUSAN FALUDI, *Backlash*. New York: Crown Publishers, 1991.

LORNE K. FOSS, "Viva San Antonio." Reprinted by permission of the author.

NIKKI GIOVANNI, *Racism 101*. New York: William Morrow and Co., Inc., 1994, p. 31.

FRED HAPGOOD, "Notes From the Underground." *Atlantic Monthly*, 1994.

BARBARA GRIZZUTI HARRISON, *Harper's*, 6/92, p. 42. Copyright © 1992 by Barbara Grizzuti Harrison. Reprinted by permission of Georges Borchardt, Inc. for the author.

BARRY HOBERMAN, "Translating the Bible," as originally published in the February 1985 issue of *The Atlantic Monthly*, Vol. 255, No. 2. Copyright © 1985 Barry Hoberman. Reprinted by permission of the author.

DOUGLAS HOFSTADTER, *Gödel, Escher, Bach: An Eternal Golden Braid*. Vintage Books/Random House, 1979, p. 603.

ROBERT HUGHES, *Culture of Complaint*. New York: Oxford University Press, 1993, pp. 74–75.

WILLIAM J. JEFFREYS AND ROBERT ROBBINS, *Discovering Astronomy*. John Wiley and Sons, 1981, p. 14.

PAUL JOHNSON, *Intellectuals*. Harper & Row, Publishers, Inc., 1988, p. 73.

SARA KIESLER, LEE SPOULL, AND JACQUELYNNE S. ESSLES, "Second Class Citizens?" *Psychology Today*, March 1983, p. 47.

MARTIN LUTHER KING, JR., *I Have a Dream*. Copyright © 1963 by Martin Luther King, Jr. Copyright renewed © 1991 by Coretta Scott King. Reprinted by arrangement with The Heirs to the Estate of Martin Luther King, Jr., c/o Joan Daves as agent for the proprietor.

MICHAEL KINSLEY. "Taking Exception." *The New Republic*, January 6, 1992, p. 6.

DAVID MCCULLOUGH, *Truman*. New York: Simon & Schuster, 1992, p.324.

LARRY MCMURTRY, *The Desert Rose*. Touchstone Books. Simon and Schuster. New York: 1983.

LARRY MCMURTRY, *Lonesome Dove*. Simon and Schuster, 1985, pp. 386–387.

JOHN MCPHEE, *Coming into the Country*. New York: Farrar, Straus & Giroux, 1977.

LORI S. MCWILLIAMS, "Acupuncture: Energy or Nerves?" Copyright © 1989 by Lori S. McWilliams. Reprinted by permission of the author.

From *MLA Style Manual*. Copyright © 1995 Modern Language Association of America. Reprinted by permission.

TONI MORRISON, *The Bluest Eye*. Simon and Schuster, 1970, p. 97.

FARLEY MOWAT, *Never Cry Wolf*. Little, Brown and Company, 1963, p.80.

ERIC O'KEEFE, "Destabilized." *Texas Monthly*, 9/94, p. 82. Reprinted by permission of *Texas Monthly*.

ELLIS PETERS. *Monk's Hood*. Fawcett Crest. New York: 1980.

LETTY COTTIN POGREBIN. *Among Friends*. New York: McGraw-Hill, 1987.

OSWALD M. T. RATTERAY. From "Expanding Roles for Summarized Information." *Written Communication*, Vol. 2, No. 4, October 1985, p. 457. Reprinted by permission of Sage Publications, Inc.

RICHARD D. RILKE AND MALCOLM O. SILLARS, from *Argumentation and the Decision-making Process*, Second Edition. Copyright © 1984, 1975, by Scott, Foresman and Company.

RICHARD RODRIGUEZ, *Hunger of Memory*. David R. Godine, Publisher, Inc., 1982, p. 184.

MIKE ROSE, *Lives on the Boundary*. New York: The Free Press, 1989, pp. 21–22.

CHIORI SANTIAGO, "The Fine and Friendly Art of Luis Jimenez." *Smithsonian*, 1993.

JOHN SCHWARTZ, "Consumer Enemy No. 1." *Newsweek*, 10/28/91, p. 42. Copyright © 1991 *Newsweek*. Reprinted by permission. All rights reserved.

JANE S. SHAW AND RICHARD L. STROUP, "Getting Warmer?" *National Review*, July 14, 1989, p. 26.

CHRISTINA HOFF SOMMERS, *Who Stole Feminism?* New York: Simon & Schuster, 1994.

PETER J. STANLIS, Editor, *Edmund Burke: Selected Writings and Speeches*. Regnery-Gateway, 1963, p. 491.

SHELBY STEELE, "The New Sovereignty." *Harper's*, 1992.

BARBARA LANG STERN, "Tears Can Be Crucial to Your Physical and Emotional Health," in *Vogue*, June 1979, Condé Nast Publications.

KEVIN STREHLO, "Talk to the Animals," in *Popular Computing*, June 1982.

MIMI SWARTZ. Austin, TX: *Texas Monthly*, September 1994, p. 114.

LEWIS THOMAS, "Humanities and Science," in *Late Night Thoughts on Listening to Mahler's Ninth Symphony*. Viking Press, 1983, p. 154.

LEWIS THOMAS, "The Health Care System," in *The Medusa and the Snail*. New York: Penguin Books, 1981, p. 43.

BRIAN URQUHART, *Ralph Bunche: An American Life*. New York: W. W. Norton & Co., 1993, p. 435.

ROB VAN DER PLAS, *The Mountain Bike Book*. San Francisco: Bicycle Books, 1993, p. 106.

ALICE WALKER, "The Black Writer and the Southern Experience," *In Search of Our Mothers' Gardens*. Harcourt Brace Jovanovich Publishers, 1983, p. 21.

STEVEN WEINBERG, *The First Three Minutes*. Basic Books, Inc., Publishers, 1977, p. 9.

JONATHAN WEINER, "Glacier Bubbles Are Telling Us What Was in the Ice Age Air," *Smithsonian*, May 1989, p. 78.

JOHN WHEELER, "Black Holes and New Physics," *Discovery*. The University of Texas at Austin, Winter 1982, p. 5.

"When the Earth Rumbles." *U. S. News and World Report*, Oct. 30, 1989, p. 38.

TOM WOLFE, *The Right Stuff*. Farrar, Straus & Giroux, 1979, p. 27.

DANIEL YANKELOVITCH, "The Work Ethic Is Underemployed," in *Psychology Today*, May 1982. Ziff-Davis Publishing Co.

WILLIAM ZINSSER, *Willie and Dwike: An American Profile*. Harper & Row, Publishers, Inc., 1984, pp. 3–4.

Index

index

index

index

index